MODERN ART IN AMERICA

1908 —68

For my family, Elita, Cintra, Titus, Carolyn, Hayden,
Lilly, and Brody. In loving memory of my parents,
Elsie Burgess and William Herman Agee.

MODERN ART IN AMERICA

WILLIAM C. AGEE

1908—68

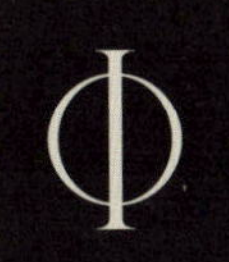

INTRODUCTION:
ON ART IN AMERICA

This book is a history – one of the many possible histories that could be written – of the years 1908 to 1968, the richest, most dynamic period of American art. It surveys the best of modern art in America made by four generations of exceptionally talented artists spanning the early years of the twentieth century to the late 1960s. Sometimes, familiar pictures will be examined in new contexts; at other times, little or virtually unknown works will be explored, all standing side by side, not always as equals, but all worthy of respect and attention.

In 1970 Barnett Newman said: 'about 25 years ago…painting was dead…I had to start from scratch as if painting didn't exist.'[1] But he was failing to acknowledge his debt to the American artists who had come before him. He was not the only one to think in this way. As art in the United States gained international attention after 1945, earlier American art was cast off by critics and curators as a kind of demented uncle, in favour of establishing a more elevated pedigree, a celebrated cast of exalted Europeans such as Pablo Picasso and Joan Miró. No doubt these Europeans were crucial, but more was owed to American art prior to 1945 than anybody understood, or cared to admit – not to mention the Mexican artists who had played such a vital role in America during the 1930s and 1940s.

This continuity has been missed, largely because historians, curators and critics have been slow to value, and to study in any depth, the history of early modernism in America.[2] They have also been reluctant to identify the best of its art; the reputations of too many secondary and tertiary artists have clung on for too long, clouding the waters. American – and all modern – art has had a difficult time determining just who its best artists are, preferring instead to affix artists to the numerous movements and the most recent spectacles. An important principle in this book is therefore to forget movements and concentrate on the artists, to look closely and carefully at their art, engaging it on its own terms, and examining the connections between them.

Study of the early modernist years languished until the 1960s, while post-1945 art attracted wide and ever-increasing attention in America. Only recently have we come to see the fullness of early modernism, or the continuity with earlier American art, so that our sense of that history has become fragmented and incomplete – and often inaccurate. Now, as a result of new and better scholarship in recent years, we know much more about earlier modernism in America, so that we counter and can tear down this wall – the strict boundary of 1945. We can and should understand American art, as diverse as it has been, as part of an ongoing and connected phenomenon with common roots, themes and styles. The primary aim in this book is to develop a sense of integration of all facets of American art, and to stress the continuities and connections within it during these years, all but overlooked until now. For the first time, essential aspects of the history of modernism in America usually treated piecemeal, and seldom if ever connected, will be thoroughly integrated.

It is often claimed that a major influence on this understanding of modernism was the negative views of pre-war American art and the promotion of Abstract Expressionism as an isolated phenomenon, by critic Clement Greenberg, and to a lesser extent the opinions of Museum of Modern Art director Alfred H. Barr, Jr., who wrote in 1933 about the 'problem' of American art.[3] Greenberg did not give earlier American modernism the sustained thought he gave to European art, thus contributing to the sense of subsequent triumph after 1945, but his admiration for the modernist painter Alfred Henry Maurer should stand as one indication that his supposed disregard of American modernism is a distortion of what he actually said and wrote. He also had high praise for John Marin, among perhaps ten Americans whose work could hold up to his severe judgements.[4] Indeed, he wrote in 1948 that if Marin were not the best painter in the country, then you had to ask who was;[5] and that same year he stated that 'since Mondrian no one has driven the easel picture quite so far away from itself… Since Marin – with whom Pollock will in time be able to compete for recognition as the greatest American painter of the twentieth century – no other American artist has presented such a case.'[6] The talents of Pollock and Marin led him to conclude that 'the main premises of western art have at last migrated to the United States.'[7]

It is certainly true, however, that as America emerged as an undisputed world power after 1945, critics, curators and artists sought a top-of-the line pedigree for the new art. The American modernists such as Marin, Georgia O'Keeffe and Arthur Dove, who had established a level of accomplishment through their practices that presaged many of the post-1945 developments, were geographically scattered – O'Keeffe in New Mexico, Dove in Long Island and Marin in Maine – with no available critical mass to assert their presence. They were mostly unassuming and following their own course. This would not do for a now triumphant art leading the world, but these artists manifested fascinating connections with the younger Americans that link the generations in important ways, rarely explored until now. It is to these artists that this book pays particular attention.

We teach modern art as a series of radical innovations introduced by ever-younger artists, but we forget that the older artists keep on working, adding immeasurably to the passing decades, often doing their best art in their old age. Think of Michelangelo, Rembrandt, Cézanne, Monet, Matisse and others; to this, in America, add Marin, Dove, Stuart Davis, Josef Albers and Hans Hofmann, all of whose late works are nothing less than glorious. Figures like Winslow Homer and others in their late years have produced some of the Western world's most deeply felt, intensely moving painting and sculpture. These artists remind us that art moves beyond any rigid chronological boundaries, as we shall see throughout this narrative, and it is essential to understand the multiple layers of significant art being made at any given time.

It was not until another generation had appeared, in the late 1950s and early 1960s, that the earlier moderns could be appreciated and acknowledged by the emerging artists, as, for example, in the case of the respect paid to Dove by Frank Stella,[8] or to Davis by Donald Judd.[9] A good part of this continuity derives from the later work done by pre-Abstract Expressionist artists such as Davis, Marin and O'Keeffe after the generational changing of the guard in 1945. They were artists of the 1950s and 1960s as much as, say, Mark Rothko, Hofmann and Stella were. Their late work was often the very best they achieved in their lives, and we cannot ignore it if we are to understand the full depth of first-rate, important post-1945 work, which extends far beyond Abstract Expressionism alone.

Earlier American art was often dismissed as provincial, since its themes were frequently American and idiosyncratic, but it is this quirky subject matter and raw power that make these compelling works of art. 'Provincial', of course, is used to suggest not of the capital, and therefore not as good. But provincial truly means having its own unique qualities, derived from a specific place and time. It is the art of the country, not of the court, and this might very well be taken as a definition of the nineteenth century and early modernism in America. Many artists early and late, such as David Smith, lauded such art, praising it for its absence of French polish,[10] its directness and authenticity, as when Stella said he 'tried to keep the paint as good as it was in the can.'[11] The nation's founding fathers, Washington, Jefferson, Madison, Franklin, Adams and all the others were provincials, but they were geniuses, and being apart from the centre enabled them to think and imagine anew, and thus to bring into being the greatest document the Western world has seen – flawed, yes, but one that gave birth to a new country of unsurpassed possibilities. So too with art: uniquely American art – such as the architecture of Thomas Jefferson at Monticello, still one of the greatest monuments in this country; the Hudson River School; the home-grown Cubism of Davis and the mesmerizing black paintings of Stella – could develop by virtue of its belief in itself, and the places from which it came. Judd proclaimed that the first struggle for any American artist was to cut himself loose from all European ties.[12] This has actually been a long-standing battle cry of the American artist, perhaps most famously found in Walt Whitman (1819– 1892) and his *Leaves of Grass*: 'Solitary, singing in the West, I strike up for a New World,'[13] adding that one 'must travel the road for yourself.'[14] But some, such as John Singleton Copley, wishing to become an artist of the English manner, lost what was best in their work, for they could neither trust themselves nor believe in America and its virtues.

In museums, pre-1945 American art is generally exhibited in a separate section, apart from modern European art. One appreciates the heightened attention to American art, the new seriousness and respect it is accorded, but the separation has had the effect of isolating it from the mainstream, as if it had never encountered or engaged with European art. As a result, we have been unable to see it side by side with contemporaneous art from Europe, to gauge how it stands up in quality, in achievement, and therefore to consider it as part of an international movement. It is as if the long-standing national inferiority complex continues to haunt American culture because it is afraid to match its best with other early modern art, to make direct and immediate comparisons. This has begun to change: in 2010 The Museum of Modern Art hung two Davis paintings and one by Gerald Murphy, all from the 1920s, in the section on French Cubism and purism of the same period. They more than held their own, even in the face of Picasso's *Three Musicians* and paintings by Fernand Léger and Amédée Ozenfant. The installation has also included works by Morgan Russell, Stanton Macdonald-Wright, Patrick Henry Bruce and others, a welcome and edifying addition, and the museum has even held exhibitions from the collection of American art. If this were to become standard practice, it would increase our understanding of both American and world art. There is no doubt that Marsden Hartley's paintings of 1912–15 would stand up well in a gallery of the best European paintings, for they represent the highest possible artistic achievement. They also rival the best of post-1945 art, but curators have seldom, if ever, dared to make these match-ups.

Another premise of this history is therefore the integration of the work of key European artists who became central to modern art in America, especially Henri Matisse and Piet Mondrian. Some, such as Mondrian and Marcel Duchamp, became American artists in all but name, and others, like Hans Hofmann and Josef Albers, became American citizens as well. Duchamp, a brilliant mind, is interjected here and there in this narrative, but plays a lesser role since so much acknowledgement has already been given to his influence. More attention is paid in these pages to European paintings that came to the United States and made a lasting impression on Americans; they are paintings that in a real sense became American, like many of the artists themselves: Mondrian's *Broadway Boogie Woogie* (1942–3, page 195), for example, might well be considered the first American post-1940 colour-field painting, while Matisse's *The Red Studio* (1911, pages 66 and 226), first introduced to America in 1913 and then again in New York in 1942 before it was acquired by MoMA in 1949, is surely the natal painting of colour field and deeply influenced American art.

WHAT IS AMERICAN MODERNISM?

To answer this question, one must firstly ask, what is America? In this book, America is considered as the United States of America, despite the understanding that 'American' is now defined in broader terms. Secondly, we must ask what we mean by modernism, in answer to which a few prefatory observations are in order.

In the latter half of the nineteenth century, the modern artist turned away from the mandatory hierarchies of the academies that had dictated a strict order of preferred modes of painting for nearly two centuries. In this hierarchy, paintings with national, historical and religious subjects were considered most important, while still life and landscape were of least significance. In France, the centre of early modernist art, Gustave Courbet and then the Impressionists expunged the obeisance to the Church and the king from their art and, by turning to nature, reversed the order of academic dictates. The elimination of hierarchies, social and personal as well as artistic, is key to the modern age, since it came in the wake of the political revolutions that upset old orders in America and France in the late eighteenth century and across Europe in 1848. The new freedom of the arts paralleled the new political and social freedom. No longer looking back to fallen man, society was enabled by democracy and its new liberties to look ahead with optimism to the future, to progress, to the triumphs of a new civilization and even to the perfectibility of men and women.

Modern Art in America

Perspective and illusionism had been the basis of Western art since the fourteenth century, creating a fictive space in which objects were placed in diminishing sizes according to hierarchies of status and importance. This was mostly eliminated in modernism, beginning with Édouard Manet. In his *Déjeuner sur l'herbe* (1863), he took on the Academy directly by compressing the pictorial space and giving all aspects – painterly and expressive – the same emphasis, thus effectively eliminating all hierarchies. Therefore the viewer has a particularly immediate and direct contact with the painting.

Indeed, immediacy and directness became paramount to the modern artist. The life of the paint, its energy and dynamism, is an important aspect. This gave the artist the means to a new individualism, based on personal choice, a freedom and expressive openness in the application of paint. Soon the paint became the form: no longer just a material means of depicting a scene, it was in itself the physical and expressive reality of the work. In turn, the artist could increasingly give vent to his inner life, to his deepest feelings, expressing not just the subject, but also his reaction to it. In the modern age, the emphasis shifted from a record of exterior objects and events to a charting of internal, emotional experience.[15] Forms are exaggerated and distorted for the purpose of heightening expression. The artist is not afraid to leave a trace of his explorations of the surface and of the materials themselves, for us to see, follow and explore. Modern art, then, becomes a process of self-discovery, both for the artist and for the viewer.

Broadly speaking, we can say that modernism turned from the known, observable world around us to a mode of exploring, in personal, expressive ways, the interior life of the artist. Thus new attitudes towards the classical norms of the figure appeared: the Cubist works of Picasso and Georges Braque featured compressed and flattened planes, while Matisse deployed strong areas of colour to indicate but not replicate three-dimensional space. 'Exactitude is not truth,' Matisse famously said.[16] Deviation from the observable world was in keeping with the new sciences developed by Sigmund Freud and Albert Einstein, who told us that reality was not what we saw, but was something so vast and distant or so deep within us that it was beyond the powers of literal description. Now the interior landscape was as immense as the exterior landscape of the physical world.

In America, the path to modernism was different from that in Europe. Its trajectory can be broken down into a number of categories and themes, which run through the narrative of this book.

Colour

The use of colour as an independent agent of formal and emotive expression provides a distinct history, never outlined before, that plays a central role, perhaps the dominant one, in this narrative, starting in 1908 with Patrick Henry Bruce and Matisse in Paris, and concluding in 1968 with the glorious Protractor colour-field paintings of Frank Stella, who vowed to make Matisse abstract:[17] 'My main interest has been to make what is popularly called decorative painting truly viable in unequivocal abstract terms. Decorative, that is, in a good sense, in the sense that it is applied to Matisse.'[18] Even Andy Warhol would say, 'I want to be Matisse.'[19]

Light

By 1830, America had developed its own type of landscape painting, known as the Hudson River School, founded by Thomas Cole. Its sources were in Romantic European art, especially John Constable and J.M.W. Turner, and also in northern painting, in particular Caspar David Friedrich. Among the special qualities of the American landscape painting, known as Luminism,[20] was the intense light, the golden tones that pervaded so many of these pictures. It was a different light from that of French art. This tradition may explain why American painting never understood the important lessons of Impressionism, its openness and direct, free application of paint to expand the vitality of the painting. American artists mostly missed the point of the movement, and did little with it, except to brighten their palette while retaining tight drawing and brushwork. It may be that Americans had less need for it: they already had their own light and openness, right there, in the grandeur of the continent itself.

This special light, and its source in the glories of the landscape, whether of Maine or New Mexico, has endured throughout American art history. It is found in abundance at the heart of work by John Marin, Arthur Dove, Georgia O'Keeffe, Charles Sheeler, Jackson Pollock, Fairfield Porter, Mark Rothko, Helen Frankenthaler, Donald Judd and countless others, often with a deeply spiritual connotation.

This tradition was severely disrupted when American artists encountered the work of Paul Cézanne. Cézanne had his own light, of course, but it was embodied in planes of colour, very different from the expansive aura of the Luminists. His painting, especially as seen through the eyes of Matisse, dramatically changed the course of modern art both in the United States and elsewhere.[21] It is now clear, however, that Symbolism, as evidenced in the work of Gustave Moreau, Odilon Redon and Pierre Puvis de Chavannes, was an equally important force, for it joined with an American tradition dating back to Washington Allston, William Rimmer, George Inness and Albert Pinkham Ryder to forge an intense spiritualism, a new emphasis on the imagination rendered through deep and brooding organic forms.

Landscape

Born of a deep love of the land, American art has gravitated to the sweep of the American continent, whether the Hudson River Valley, the Pacific Northwest, New Mexico or the vast reaches of west Texas. From the highly detailed work of Thomas Cole or John Kensett to the mysterious forces in Ryder; from the nature symbolized in the works of Hartley, Dove, Marin and O'Keeffe to the vast and sublime spaces of Rothko or Pollock, as in the latter's epic *Autumn Rhythm* (1950), or the ambitious sculpting of the very earth itself in the art of Robert Smithson and Walter De Maria in the late 1960s, the land has been an irresistible, compelling force. Even the supposedly stark geometries of Judd's late work must be understood in the context of his deep love of the soil and mountains, as well as what he understood as the mystic light of southwest Texas. In all these instances, the art is defined by a deep and strange silence, a mysterious quietude and often grandeur, as if its creators were the first to view this wondrous new world. This awe pervades American literature as well. Recall the close of *The Great Gatsby*:

Modern Art in America

I became aware of the old island here that flowered once for Dutch sailors' eyes — a fresh, green breast of the new world. Its vanished trees, the trees that had made way for Gatsby's house, had once pandered in whispers to the last and greatest of all human dreams; for a transitory enchanted moment man must have held his breath in the presence of this continent, compelled into an aesthetic contemplation he neither understood nor desired, face to face for the last time in history with something commensurate to his capacity for wonder.[22]

The theme of Modern Man versus Nature recurs throughout American art and literature, as expressed through the lonely, isolated figure. As Philip Roth's troubled Portnoy put it: 'I knew what to do! ... I ran all right, out of the hospital and up to the playground and right out to center field, the position I play...Thank God for center field! Doctor, you can't imagine how truly glorious it is out there, so alone in all that space.'[23] This is a capsule of the quest of the American artist seeking to escape daily life, to find a more bucolic existence, alone in the vast lands of the country, or alone in the city as in Edward Hopper's work. Hopper was a great admirer of John French Sloan, whose solitary figure is a trademark. That Abraham Lincoln's father moved house whenever he saw the smoke from a neighbour's cabin is a classic American myth. It is a symbol of American optimism — a rugged individual surviving by him/herself, against the odds. But this does also mean a loss of community, of interaction with friends and neighbours. It defines much of American art and artists, early and later: Hartley was a peripatetic traveller until he secluded himself on the distant coasts of Maine; Marin was also alone on the rocky Maine shores for much of his life; O'Keeffe hid herself away in distant New Mexico. Dove first lived in Westport, trying to raise chickens, then in Godforsaken Geneva, New York, with the temperature falling to minus forty at night, and lived out his days in a shack in Centerport, Long Island. We think of Davis and his love of jazz as being quintessential to New York and the urban experience, but for much of his life he spent six months of the year in Gloucester, Massachusetts, and for the last fifteen years he was alone in his New York studio, seeing almost no one. Pollock moved to Springs, New York, in 1945, when it was still a remote farming and fishing village. David Smith, as early as 1940, set up his studio-factory in upstate New York, at Bolton Landing and we picture him sitting alone with his fields of sculptures, all personage figures, silhouetted against the surrounding hills and mountains.

The isolated American was defined early on. He was the new Adam, entering the new Eden, a chosen man in a New World, made available only recently to him, a land that, as Albert Bierstadt depicted it, reached into and descended again from the cosmos itself. If in England John Donne could say 'no man is an island entire of itself', in America Herman Melville reversed that notion, suggesting in *Moby-Dick* that every man *is* an island, remote and removed unto himself, but still possessed of uncommon powers. Melville termed the crew of the *Pequod* the 'isolatoes': 'They were nearly all Islands on the *Pequod*, isolatoes, too, I call such, not acknowledging the common continent of men, but each isolato living on a separate continent of his own.'[24] Ahab, of course, was quintessentially an isolato, doomed to defeat and destruction. Before Melville, Ralph Waldo Emerson had written on solitude, calling for the poet/artist to stand alone, in order to define and capture the unique beauty of America.

Abstract vs. Figurative

For the most part, we have understood modern and avant-garde to mean abstract and non-objective art, complex and difficult to read and to understand, a kind of private language not readily accessible to most viewers. 'What does it mean?' and 'My kid could do that!' are exclamations we are still likely to hear in front of modern works. To move to the abstract has meant the advent of a higher order. To paint the figure has often *seemed* like a step back, a retreat to an art not quite as daring or as adventurous. When we consider the work of John Graham, Willem de Kooning and Arshile Gorky, however, some of whose best work was based on the figure, we see that this must be rethought.

American modern art tended towards the abstract in the sense of the word meaning distilled from natural sources for purposes of emphasis and expression through clear, bold forms. Pure abstract art, often known as non-objective art – a total invention of forms, as in the work of Piet Mondrian and the De Stijl artists – took root in the United States only during the late 1930s, and then appeared in more widespread fashion in the 1960s. Abstraction was not the final destination point of modernism, however. Figuration was a steady force in the twentieth century, existing side by side with abstraction, and enjoying equal stature after Picasso reintroduced it in summer 1914 with *Painter and his Model*. Picasso affirmed the possibilities of utilizing both figuration and abstraction in his famous statement of 1923 that different motifs called for different modes of expression, and he saw no reason to favour one over the other.[25]

Further, there is not as much difference between realism and abstraction as is commonly thought. Fairfield Porter, a fine figurative painter and articulate writer, put it well: 'The realist thinks he knows ahead of time what reality is, and the abstract artist what art is, but it is in its formality that realist art excels, and the best abstract art communicates an overwhelming sense of reality.'[26] Porter, too, felt that the American embrace of Cézanne, forsaking the natural light of the American continent, came at a great cost to its art.[27]

Realism

Virtually every modern artist, in America and in Europe, sought a new realism, and modern art might be defined at heart as a search for the Real. Think of John Singleton Copley's clear definition of shapes, the precise drawing of John James Audubon in his watercolours of North American birds, the exactitude of the landscape depiction in the work of Thomas Cole, Martin Johnson Heade and others, or the palpable verisimilitude in the *trompe-l'oeil* still lifes of William Harnett and John F. Peto. Think of Ashcan realism, the physical, relief-like surfaces of Pollock, or the emphasis on facts: John Cage could insist that in Robert Rauschenberg's work objects are facts, not symbols;[28] and Donald Judd described new art in the 1960s as 'specific objects'.[29] These are all manifestations of the 'material poetry' of the country and of American art, as described by Lawrence Gowing.[30]

The Spiritual and the Cosmos

As we have seen, the modern painting is an independent object, serving its own ends, with its own laws, and not dependent on an institutional context. Painterly elements are given freedom to act in their own right.

Artists let them dictate their course on the surface; colour, shape and line go their own way, acting solely for the good of the painting itself. Thus the painted surface becomes real, material, physical, tangible, no longer an illusion of a fictive space. Baudelaire defined modernity as the 'transient, and the fleeting'; this was one aspect.[31] Another was the eternal and the immovable, hence the emphasis in this book on the spirit and the cosmos. Indeed, Charles Baudelaire also defined modernism as Romanticism itself, with its emphasis on 'intimacy, spirituality, colour, aspiration towards the infinite, expressed by every means available to the arts'.[32]

Architecture and Photography

Some attention is also given here to architecture and photography, because it was in these arts that American modernism first appeared. By 1910, for example, Frank Lloyd Wright was influencing international practice, and as late as 1959, with the opening of the Guggenheim Museum, his genius was still flowering. So, too, Alfred Stieglitz did for photography what Picasso's *Demoiselles d'Avignon* and Matisse's *Le luxe II* or Constantin Brancusi's *Kiss* (all 1907) had done for painting and sculpture: his work offered a new structural and emotive basis for art. Stieglitz's photographs were a great influence on more than a few artists, including Marin, Dove and O'Keeffe, asking the question, in the 1920s and before, of whether photographers and painters could be seen simply as American artists. There is good evidence that Dove set out to discover if he could make a painting whose power and effect would equal those of a photograph of the same size. Photographers of the 1940s and 1950s such as Barbara Morgan and Aaron Siskind developed techniques that ran parallel with the emerging painterly abstraction of Pollock, de Kooning and Rothko. These activities presage Allan Kaprow's declaration of 1956 (published in 1958) that in the aftermath of Pollock's death, creative people would no longer be classified as painters or sculptors, but simply as 'artists', with the whole world as their field of activity.[33]

WHY 1908–68?

The span of 1908 to 1968 has been selected for good and clear reasons. In 1908, American art began to forge a specific, coherent and definable modern identity in ways it never had before, evident in the work of Hartley, Maurer, Dove, Sloan and George Bellows, among others. In fact, it can be said that American art entered into the flow of modernism precisely in 1908.

Histories of modern American art usually begin with the development of the Ashcan School, identified with Robert Henri, one of America's foremost art teachers, and the famous realist exhibition of The Eight, held at the Macbeth Galleries in 1908. But this book starts with other events, equally and in some ways more important, including exhibitions of European art in America and the travels of American artists to Europe. These will be discussed in detail in the first chapter.

The year 1908 was also the point at which the country asserted itself as a major economic, military and social force on the world stage.[34] Several significant technological events took place at this time that propelled the course of the twentieth century. Henry Ford invented the Model T and was soon mass-producing it, certainly the most transformative invention in the new century, creating a way of life based on mass mobility. Motorized transportation quickly changed America from an agricultural to an industrial, technological and urban society. Furthermore, in 1914,

Ford had granted workers a pay rate of $5 a day and thereby made his workers buyers, arguably the real beginning of American consumerism.

Meanwhile, in 1908, the aviation pioneers the Wright brothers had extended their aeroplane flights to more than two hours, promising an untold future for transportation, and shrinking the size of the country and the world.[35] America was termed the 'Great Melting Pot', acknowledging the incalculable mix of new talent, labour and ambition that defined it in this era.

On 16 December 1907, President Theodore Roosevelt, from his presidential yacht in Hampton Roads, Virginia, had officially launched the worldwide cruise of the Great White Fleet. Consisting of sixteen battleships, all painted white, plus their attending ships, the fleet announced to the world that America was a formidable military force and could reach anything, anywhere on the globe. The cruise went on throughout 1908, ending on 22 February 1909. American imperialism was here to stay. Its consequences are still with us today.

The narrative ends in 1968, the year of worldwide, profound change, much of it revolutionary, which altered the course of history in ways that make it as important as 1776, 1848 and 1917.[36] Struggle and protest, often violent, broke out throughout the country in reaction to the Vietnam War, Civil Rights and corrupt politics, by then the norm in America. The country was destabilized, old practices were challenged, any authority was deeply questioned and new ways of life were introduced. Art was not exempt from these forces, and equally saw profound change and divisions in thinking and approach. Painting as a poetic and meditative art, based on the handling of paint and materials, was widely questioned and often rejected. In its place came conceptual, video, multimedia and performance art. This was also the moment that saw the birth of postmodernism, which discredited and critiqued modernism. We have certainly seen many good artists since 1968, particularly bright moments being the emergence of Light and Land art, but I believe that 1968 saw the end of the remarkable, steady flow of high achievement in America – those four generations of deep talent, from Marin and Dove to those born in the 1930s, including Stella and Richard Serra. These artists continue to make great works of art even today. The art of younger generations that appeared after 1968, as good as some of it may be, is based on entirely new aesthetic principles that do not fit within the remit of this book and are beyond the scope of my experience and interest.

At heart, after all, this book is also *my* history, a record of my experience of looking at, thinking about and writing on art and America for sixty years and more. It is based on a roughly chronological structure, as far as is possible without fragmenting the discussion of my chosen themes, which interconnect with discussions of individual artists. Therefore, rather than aiming for encyclopaedic coverage, it focuses on fewer artists – those whom I have admired or have especially interested me and in whom I believe we can find the essential greatness of American art. Some are well known, others are not, and a few are unknown except to a handful of specialists. As Sylvan Barnet has said, we write in order to clarify, and to account for our responses to works of art that interest or excite or frustrate us.[37] I write to clarify – and reveal, if only for myself – my experience of American art.

     Modern Art in America

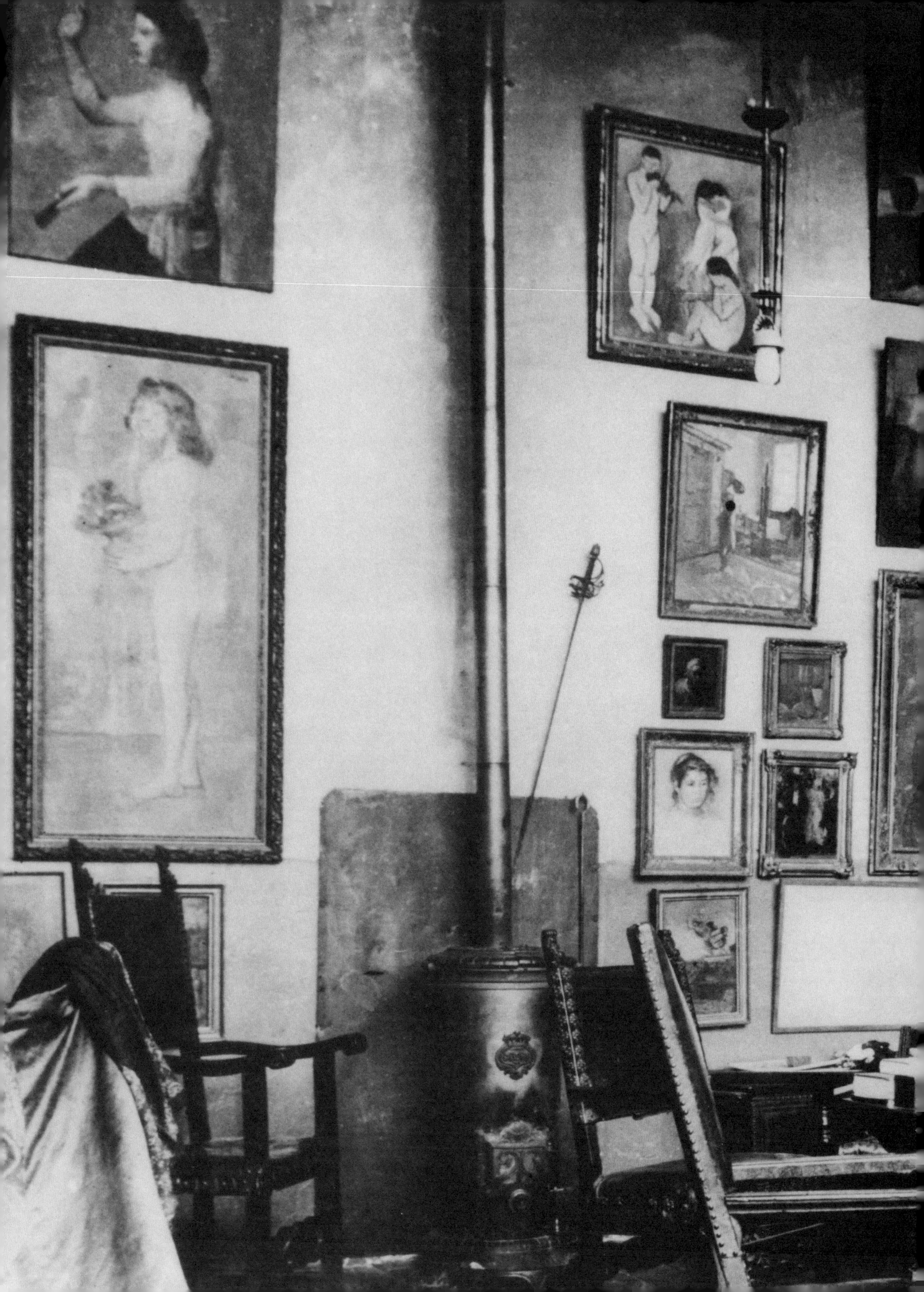

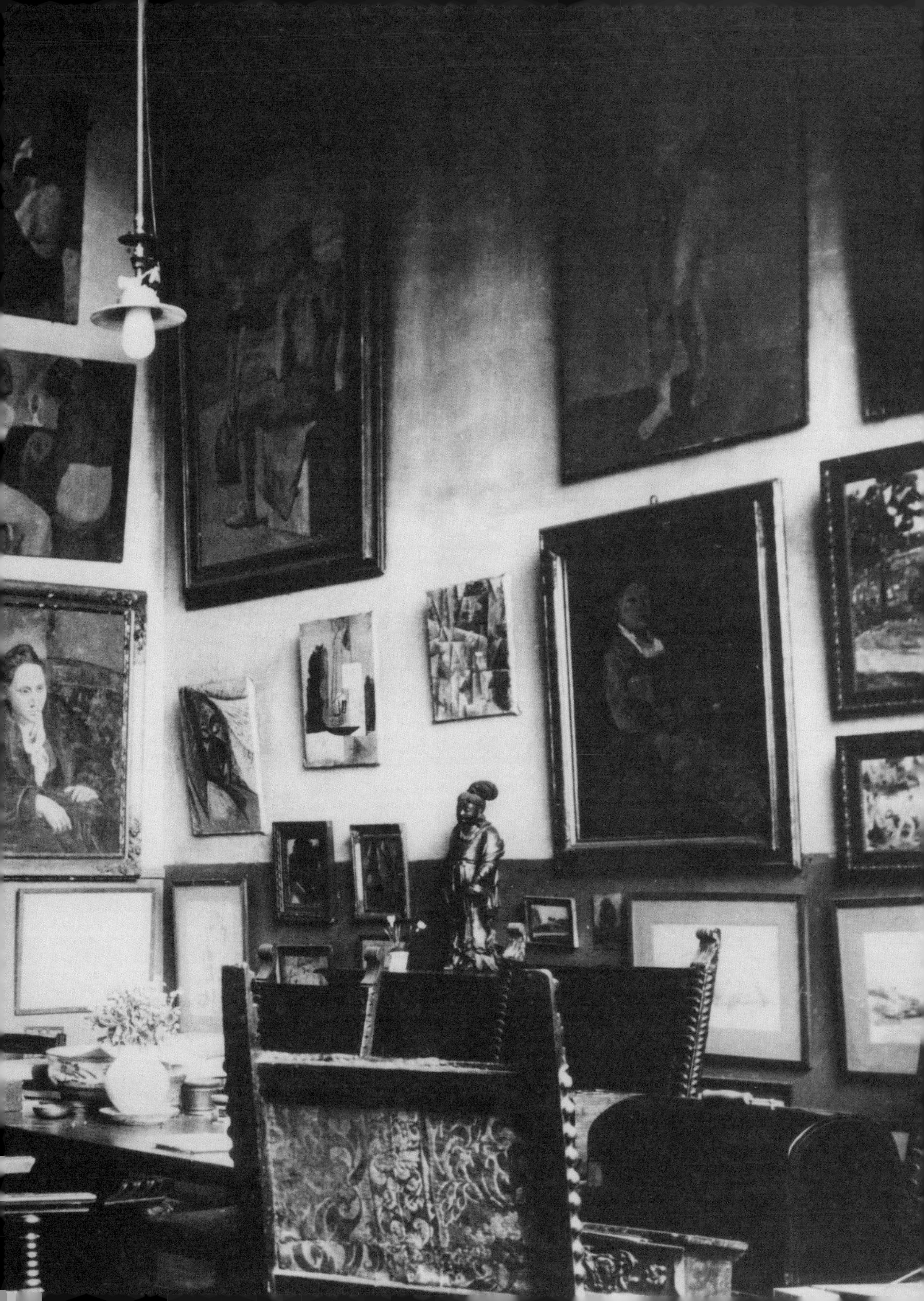

TOWARDS A NEW AND MODERN AMERICAN ART

1908 —10

THREE KEY EVENTS

A history can begin at any moment we choose, wherever we wish to make our own point of entry into the historical flow. Inevitably, even with a precisely defined starting point, the historian must look slightly further back, at what went immediately before, to identify connections and continuities and make sense of what is to follow. So while this chapter defines our story as starting in 1908 – a key year, as we shall see – it also looks back to find some of the seeds of modernism sown by artists working prior to this year.

In art, as in life, major changes are often set in motion by seemingly small events that may attract only passing interest when they occur. So it was for modernism in America, where art had been slow to mature prior to 1900. In 1908, three art-related events happened in rapid succession, almost simultaneously, that in retrospect we can say signalled a profound change in America, and in fact marked the beginnings of modern art there. None were necessarily epic in themselves, but considered together now, they were clearly key moments, turning points that brought American art abruptly into the new century. They remind us that a hallmark of the modern age has been the rapid acceleration of the pace of change.

1. The Matisse School in Paris

The first event took place in January 1908, and not in New York, but in Paris, where numerous artists, from America and elsewhere, had gone to witness and partake of the new ideas. Even today, the French capital has the allure of a magical city, sending out its irresistible call. The American artists who were travelling to Paris in unprecedented numbers by 1908 were lured by both recent and old art, by the emerging modern spirit and the glories of the City of Light that had made it the centre of the art world up to that point. The sense of new impulses and possibilities in Paris was not equalled anywhere, but there was a growing awareness

1   The Steins' art collection at
27 rue de Fleurus, Paris, 1910

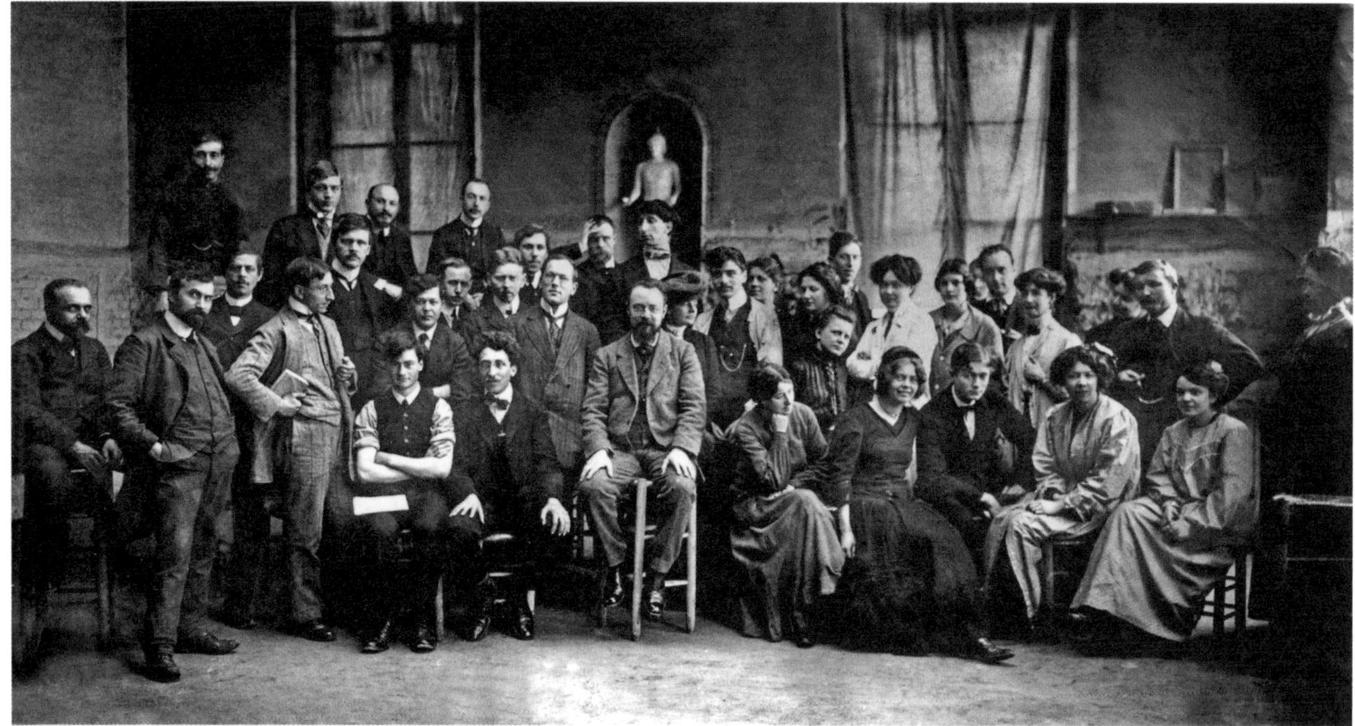

2

of America emerging in the twentieth century as a rising power, filled with promise for the future. For American artists, it meant possibilities for a modern art that would match the marvels of the twentieth century. As the achievements of Cézanne and the unlimited lessons offered by his work were being discovered in depth in the United States after his death in 1906, young and ambitious artists were compelled to go to Paris if they were to experience his legacy first hand. Of course, artists from all over the world were coming to Paris for the same reasons, so the city was a hotbed of the most progressive art, fuelled by a deep pool of young and ambitious talent.

The dawn of the new century, with changes to modern life more rapid and astounding than ever before, mixed with the new art, made the city a magnet. There were two important Cézanne exhibitions in 1907 – the first, a show of watercolours held in May at the Paris gallery Bernheim-Jeune, and the second in October, fifty-six oils in a memorial display at the Salon d'Automne. And there were the salons held by the American collectors Leo and Gertrude Stein at 27 rue de Fleurus[1], and Michael and Sarah Stein at 58 Rue Madame which became meeting places for young visitors, akin to clearing houses for modern art and ideas. Their collections formed a mini-museum of modern art, including fourteen Cézannes, several Matisses and Picassos, and their homes were places where new paintings could be seen and discussed, and where there was a chance to meet the French masters.

It is entirely possible that it was at one of the Steins' salons that Matisse was persuaded to open his school in the Couvent des Oiseaux on 6 January 1908[2], largely through the initiative of the brother and sister-in-law of Leo and Gertrude, Michael and Sarah Stein, and the US painters Patrick Henry Bruce (1881–1936) and Max Weber (1881–1961), as well as the Swiss artist Hans Purrmann (1880–1966). This demonstrates that American art was shaped both at home and abroad, and that the US was part of the international mix of forces then forging modern art. The opening of the school marked the formal beginning of a concerted

2 The Matisse School (artist in the centre, with his students) at Couvent des Oiseaux, Paris, 1909

 Modern Art in America

American engagement with Cézanne, Matisse and colour. Perhaps more than any other event, it pushed America swiftly into the twentieth century, in ways not matched by either Realism or Cubism. If you were working with Matisse in 1908, you were at the most advanced and daring edge of the modernist impulse. That same year, he published his famous *Notes of a Painter*,[1] still today an essential guide to the art of painting, and one of the seminal texts of the twentieth century, about which more will be discussed below. The primacy of colour was also asserted in 1908 in the book *Colores* by Odilon Redon, less known now, but a symptom of the new importance of colour in Western art.[2]

One young American after another went to Paris at this time, absorbing these new developments, soon to be brought back to New York and elsewhere in the country. Maurice Prendergast, in Paris by 1907, was perhaps the first modernist US painter in the sense that he was the earliest to immerse himself in Cézanne's colour. Max Weber, also in Paris, was the first to incorporate the structural principles of Cubism, even if still in nascent form. Edward Steichen, a formidable presence in the French capital, founded in 1908 the New Society of American Artists in Paris, which brought countrymen together, giving them a sense of identity as an emerging community. Steichen was the key scout for the artist and gallerist Alfred Stieglitz, identifying some of the most vital art in Paris and alerting Stieglitz to it. That leads us to the second key event.

2. Alfred Stieglitz in New York

Also in January 1908, Stieglitz, America's foremost champion of new art, and himself an artist of the highest order, opened his first exhibition of modern art in his now famous Gallery 291, named after its address on lower Fifth Avenue in New York. It was a relatively modest affair, an exhibition of drawings and watercolours by the venerable French sculptor, Auguste Rodin. Later that year, Stieglitz held an exhibition of Matisse's work, primarily of drawings but with one oil, which, as we shall discover, had wide repercussions for America. Matisse's presence – and impact – was soon evident in New York itself. In April 1908, only a few months after the founding of his Académie in Paris, Matisse had his first exhibition in America at 291.

The exhibition was mostly drawings, but important lessons were gained from them, since they revealed how Matisse constructed a painting, how he searched through his line for the right proportions and balance in his work. Also evident was the way in which he showed his process, how he left the tracings of his search, a record of his actual work, remaining for all to see. This was a far cry from the exactitude of Old Master drawing. Rather, Matisse recorded his way of working, a new and modern approach to creating a work of art. There was one small oil painting in the 291 show, a modest Fauve landscape that nevertheless offered worlds to discover for young American artists. Among those artists would have been the much older Stieglitz himself, whose influence was evident in his magazine *Camera Work*, in which he published significant new works of art, articles and interviews with leading artists. In the most recent issue at the time of the show, there appeared an interview with Matisse, conducted by Charles Caffin; it brought his ideas to an American audience for the first time.[3]

These were the first in a long line of exhibitions organized by Stieglitz that brought modernism to artists and public alike, no matter how small a group this was. They were held in the little gallery that was

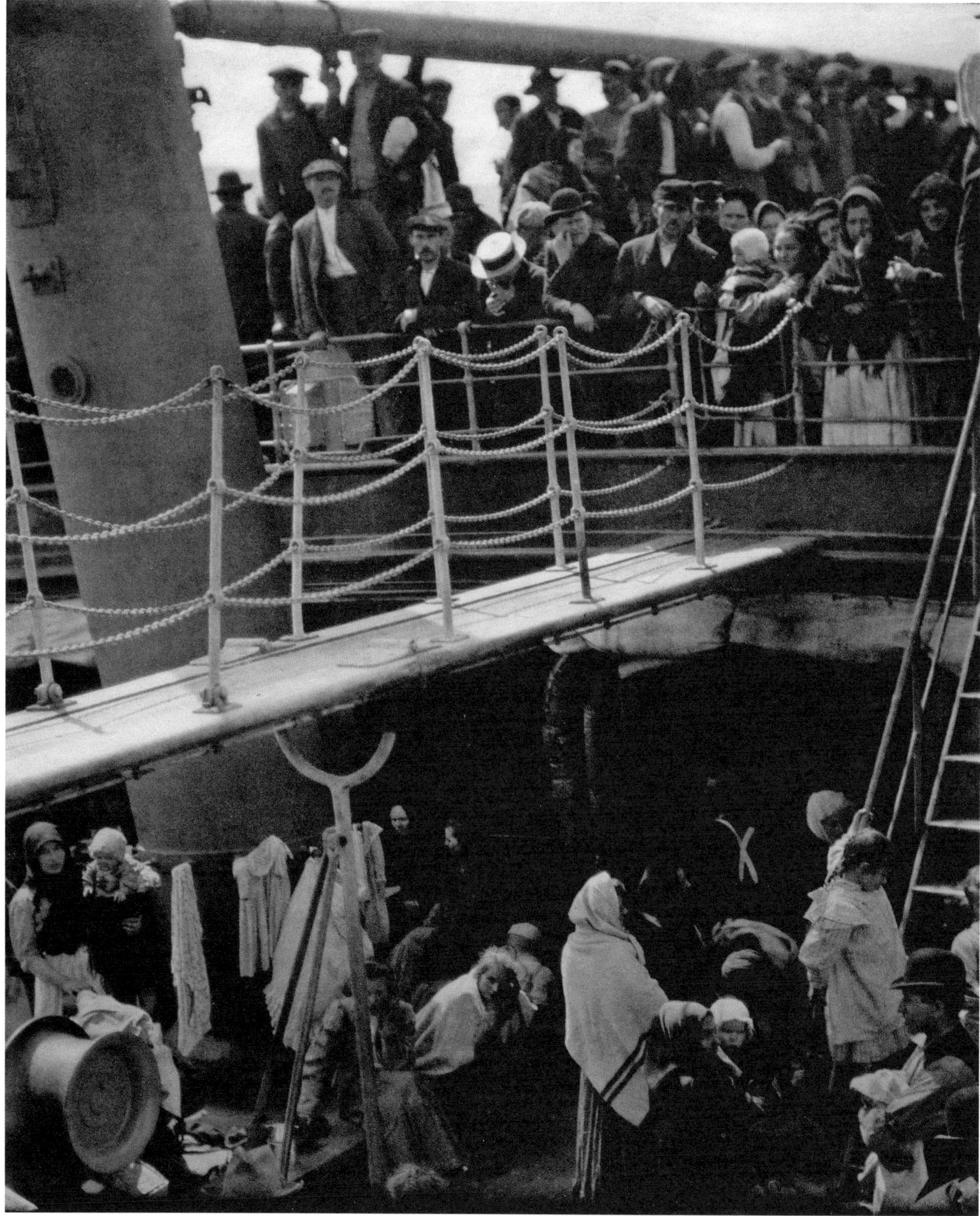

3

3   Alfred Stieglitz, *The Steerage*, 1907. Photogravure on vellum, 32.2 × 25.9 cm (12⅝ × 10³⁄₁₆ in). The Museum of Modern Art, New York

4   Edward Steichen, *The Flatiron*, 1904. Gum bichromate over platinum print, 47.8 × 38.4 cm (18¹³⁄₁₆ × 15⅛ in). The Metropolitan Museum of Art, New York

5   Robert Henri, *Street Scene with Snow (57th Street, NYC)*, 1902. Oil on canvas, 66 × 81.3 cm (26 × 32 in). Yale University Art Gallery, New Haven

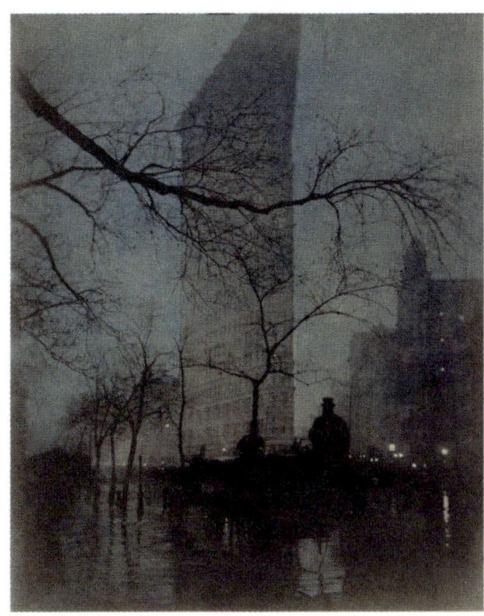

4

a place of teaching and learning, a major catalyst in transforming the course of American art, years before the crucial Armory Show of 1913,[4] which will be discussed in depth in the next chapter. Stieglitz, it must be remembered, curated exhibitions at 291 in order to teach himself and other American artists what modern art actually was. For first and foremost, above all his other roles, he was an artist. He instituted his exhibition programme after a trip to Europe the year before, in 1907, had told him that neither he nor most American artists, let alone the public, had any idea of what was truly modern.

Stieglitz had, however, made what may well be the first truly modern photograph in America, *The Steerage* (1907)[3]. Its incisive realism and formal rigour defined it as something quite different from the prevailing pictorial photography, veiled in a romantic mist, in a faraway world, well exemplified by Steichen's image *The Flatiron*[4], made just a few years earlier in 1904. This is not to say that one is better than the other; but rather that they are profoundly different. Stieglitz was surely the father of modern photography. When shown *The Steerage*, Picasso commented that the man who did it was working in the same spirit as he was.[5] In this uncompromising group portrait of the poor, Stieglitz literally faced life and reality head on. It is a memorable image, all the more so when we come to understand that it is a photograph not of reaching the promised land, but of rejection and retreat, for these passengers are returning to Europe, having been turned back at Ellis Island, or for other unknown reasons. The depiction is real and true in its sharp focus, new at the time. It also embodies an intensity of psychological and emotional realism not seen before in American art.[6] Its fusion of sharp-angle forms and round shapes gives the photo a new type of clearly defined structure. Picasso, Stieglitz and John French Sloan all came up with parallel, albeit very different, structural systems in that same year – was this a coincidence or simply the power of art?

3. The Eight and Ashcan Realism

The third and best-known event of 1908, both then and now, was the exhibition of realist painters, a group known as The Eight, at the Macbeth Gallery, New York[5]. They were led by the famous Ashcan realist Robert Henri (1865–1929), one of America's foremost art teachers, whose work and pedagogy instilled new attitudes into several generations of artists about how to approach art, and even of what art could be.[7] His insistence that art should approximate life, that it should be drawn from the world around us, the gritty urban existence of the modern city, challenged and displaced the stranglehold of the National Academy of Design on the teaching, making and exhibiting of art.

Textbooks and museums usually start with Realism as the entry to the modern age. It was important, to be sure, but even in mastering the realist approach, the American artist was some sixty years behind the times. Artists themselves would recognize this, especially after the groundbreaking Armory Show of 1913. One of Henri's most gifted students, Stuart Davis, later recalled that while his mentor's emphasis on American subject matter was important, his teaching lacked the structural, formal principles of modernism. Therefore, he declared, he 'would quite definitely have to become a "modern" artist'.[8] Further, the art of the Ashcan group was a contemporary development of a long and deep-rooted American tradition of Realism that had extended from John Singleton Copley to John F. Peto and William Harnett, and through Thomas Eakins and Winslow Homer,

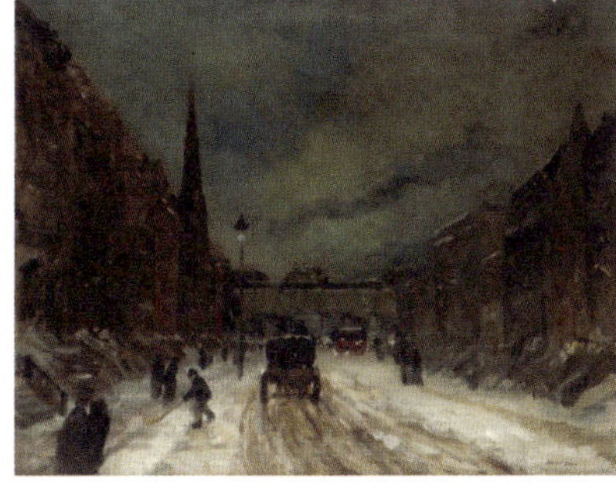

5

both of whom continued to work well into the twentieth century and therefore must be considered as part of the rich new mix of American art at the time. Of his painting *Searchlight on Harbor Entrance, Santiago de Cuba* (1901), Homer could state that he was simply 'reporting the stern facts'.[9]

THE CÉZANNE-MATISSE SYNTHESIS OF COLOUR

Notes of a Painter

When Matisse expanded on and codified his ideas of picture-making in *Notes of a Painter* in December 1908, he published one of the most important and least understood documents of modern art. 'What I am after, above all, is expression,' was his opening statement, 'an art of balance, of purity and serenity devoid of troubling or depressing subject matter, an art which might be…like an appeasing influence, like a mental soother, something like a good armchair in which to rest from physical fatigue.'[10] He proposes an art that addresses some of the highest, most noble themes of art and humanity, but it has been taken as signalling something easy, unthinking, even trifling. He recognized his error immediately and tried to compensate for it in subsequent writings, but to no avail. For Matisse, however, it meant nothing less than expressing his very 'feeling for life', a far more profound aim than simple visual satisfaction, although the two went hand in hand. A work of art must be harmonious in its entirety, with no superfluous details allowed to stand. Expression is achieved through composition, which should go beyond the momentary to find the permanent and the essential. The chief aim of colour should be to serve expression; he had no plan, but worked from intuition. 'If,' he said, 'I put down some sensations of blue, of green, of red — every new brushstroke diminishes the importance of the preceding ones. New combinations of colours follow the first one, with successive modifications, with the process repeated throughout the entire painting surface.'[11]

Thus Matisse was one of the first artists of the twentieth century to develop a key methodology of modern art, a 'working out of the materials'.[12] Here, the artist follows what the paint dictated as it was put down, as it was shifted, composed in new and ever-changing harmonies, much like creating a musical composition. The painting, and the painter, responds not to the dictates of representation, but to the needs of the painting, what it demands for its successful completion. This is a process we find repeatedly in colour painting right up until the 1960s. So, too, is the analogy of developing an art as pure and complete unto itself as music, often made by incorporating the methods of musical composition. His goal was to create harmony, order and clarity.

Painting based on colour, seen best in the works of Matisse and understood as a new, autonomous expressive and structural language, brought American art into the modern age quickly and decisively. The transformation from the strong hues of late Impressionism to a pure chromatic painting by 1912 is one of the most remarkable and important chapters in American and European art history. These few brief years might be termed the 'great leap forward', since colour instantly transformed America from an artistic backwater into one of the centres of modernism.

6   Winslow Homer, *West Point, Prout's Neck*, 1900.
Oil on canvas, 76.4 × 122.2 cm (30¹⁄₁₆ × 48¹⁄₈ in).
Sterling and Francine Clark Art Institute, Williamstown

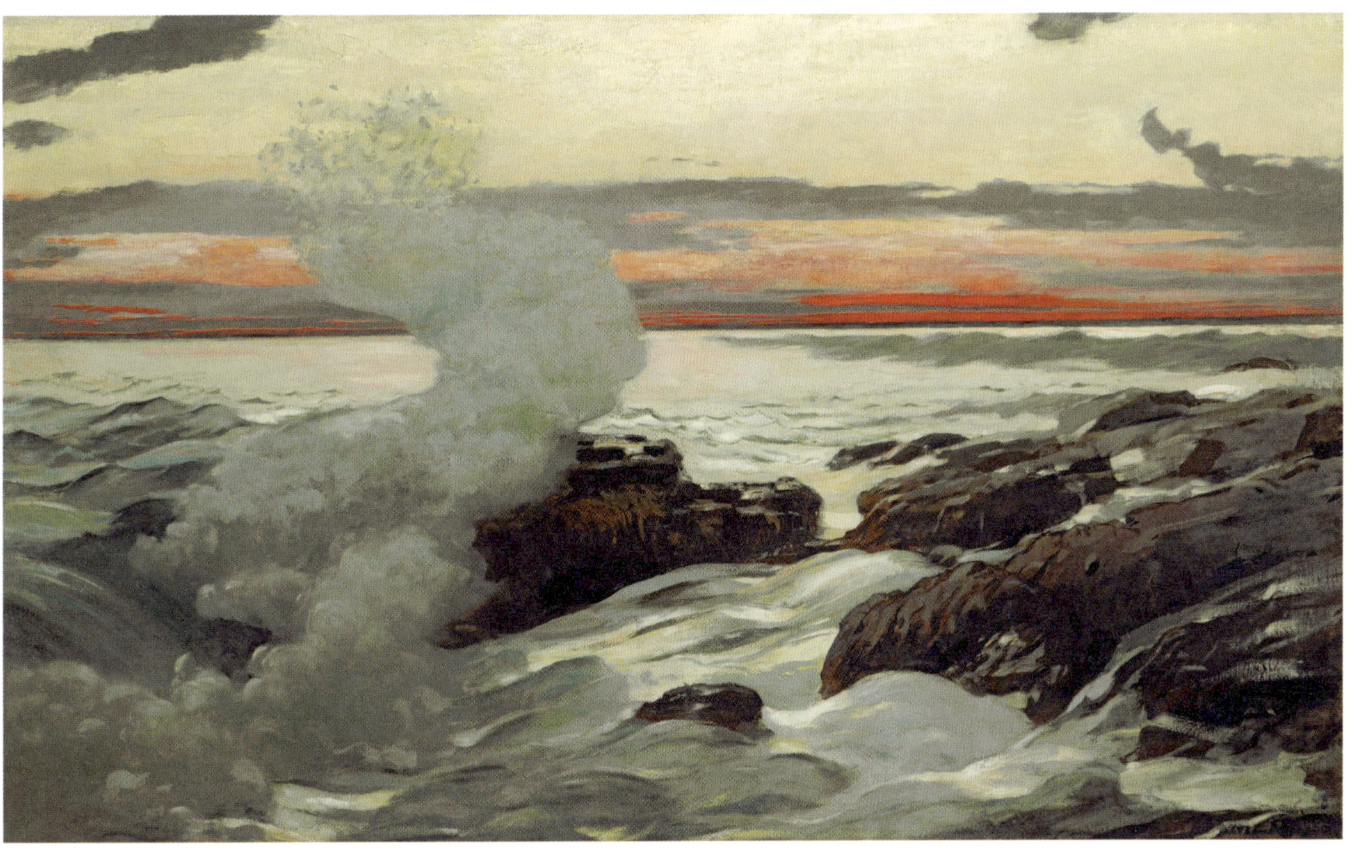

6

Winslow Homer's High-Keyed Hues

Colour, of course, was not an invention of the twentieth century. While Impressionism did not add much to American colour painting beyond brightening its palette, there were exceptions, notably the later landscapes of John Singer Sargent and, most especially, the work of Winslow Homer (1836–1910), an artist of world stature by any standard. Although well into his sixties, Homer was still America's greatest painter at the turn of the century. He became a twentieth-century painter through his new use of high-keyed hues as in *West Point, Prout's Neck* (1900)[6], in which the brilliant reds of the setting sun embodied a new awareness of the possible effects of colour expression; here, his canvases took on a proto-Fauve palette.[13] Homer had always been well aware of colour and its laws, and he owned and knew well Michel Eugène Chevreul's classic study of colour, written in 1839, *De la loi du contraste simultané des couleurs* (*On the law of simultaneous contrast of colours*). Homer's colour had after 1890 become stronger and more open, but by 1900 was essentially without precedent in his work, or in American art. This change was noted, if not always celebrated, by contemporary critics, one of whom described the colour as 'cheap'[14] because of its new intensity. Further, Homer's means of applying paint became more decidedly open, so that his broad strokes were the form itself at certain points, a wave or rock, the shapes standing alone, rather than part of a description of it, thus giving a new autonomy to the medium. We can trace this to its start, in *The West Wind* (1891)[7], where we see the sweep of wind across the dunes, made palpable and material, part of the long American search for the real. Here the brush and its marks become and are the wind, not an approximation of it. In its physicality, its sweeping strokes, the painting anticipates the broad, painterly brushstrokes we associate with Willem de Kooning, especially in his landscapes of 1959–60, and other gestural Abstract Expressionist artists of the 1950s.

Homer's command of colour was not limited to oils. His greatness also lies in his watercolour painting, done over the course of his long life. Watercolour is a difficult medium because it cannot be changed or reworked. Thus it demands a painterly confidence not given to all artists; it must be got right the first time – 'one-shot' painting, as Kenneth Noland and Morris Louis termed it in the 1950s.[15] But this very characteristic, an apparent handicap, has always seemed to bring out the best in American artists: they must work quickly, directly, with sureness and without hesitation, trusting only themselves and their best painterly instincts. We need think only of Homer, Prendergast, Morgan Russell, Charles Demuth, Charles Burchfield, Oscar Bluemner, O'Keeffe and Marin, plus the watercolour effects used so beautifully by Arshile Gorky and then Helen Frankenthaler, to understand just how deep watercolour has run through American art. Americans have worked best when they have had to be most direct, achieving a physical immediacy with the object, as was later proved by the approaches of Pollock and de Kooning, for example.

Colour in The Eight

By 1908, and the exhibition of The Eight, the advent of strong colour was readily apparent. George Bellows (1882–1925), although best known for his boxing pictures, was a far better painter than these works ever indicated. Indeed, by 1909 he had become something of a master of colour

7   Winslow Homer, *The West Wind*, 1891. Oil on canvas, 76.2 × 111.7 cm (30 × 44 in). Addison Gallery of American Art, Phillips Academy, Andover

8   George Bellows, *Blue Morning*, 1909. Oil on canvas, 86.3 × 111.7 cm (34 × 44 in). National Gallery of Art, Washington, DC

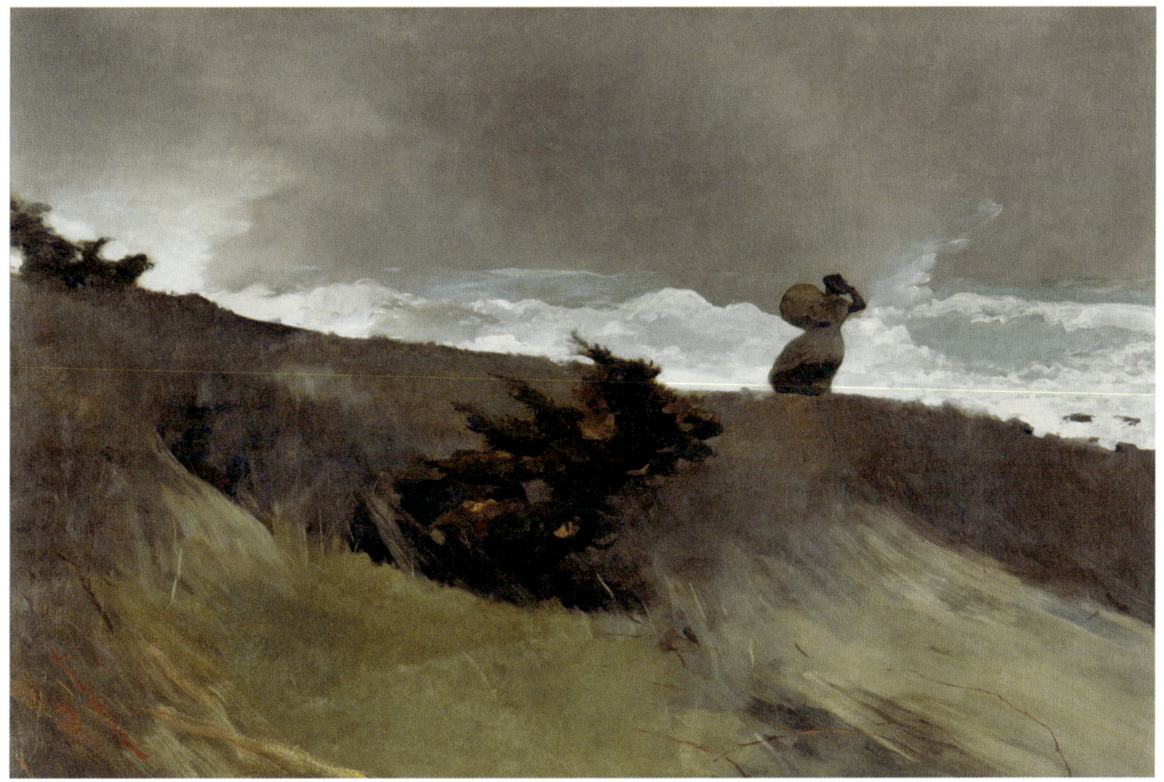

7

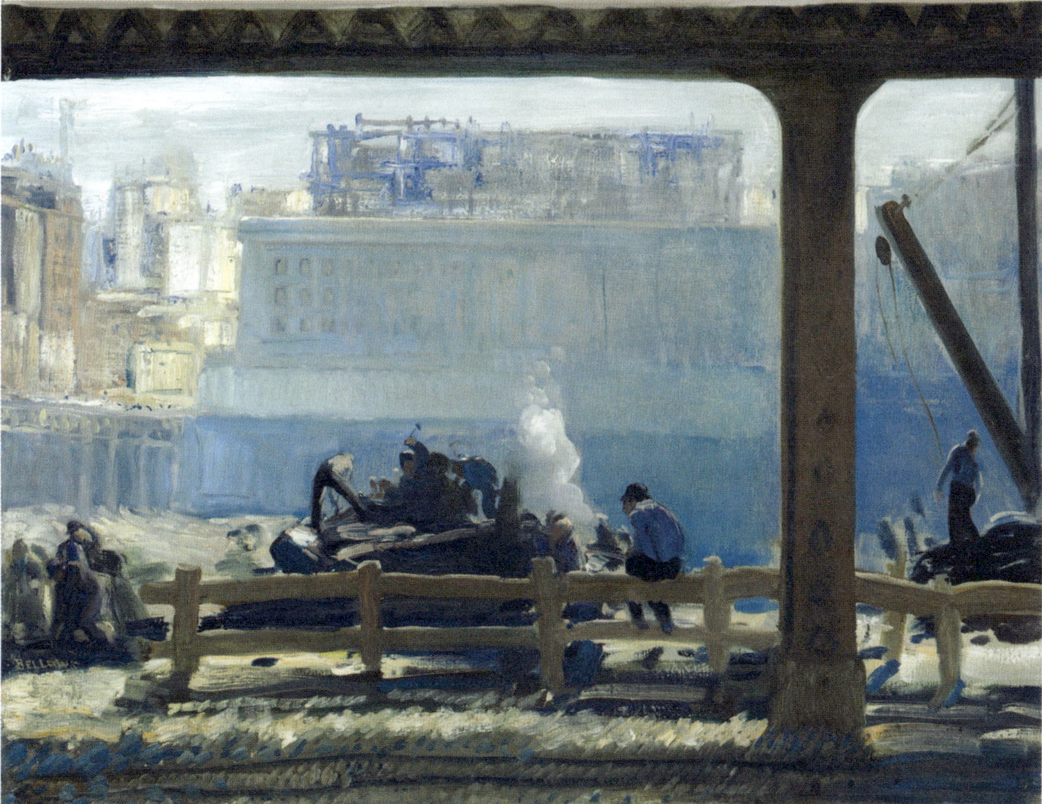

8

in paintings such as *Blue Morning* [8], in which a New York construction site is bathed in an ethereal curtain of soft blues and blue-whites hovering over the scene, as if the nascent building were covered in a protective balm of colour from a higher realm. His later paintings, too, showed a remarkable skill with colour, as in his *Portrait of Florence Pierce* (1914) [9], in which the deep blues of the sitter's dress resonate with her red hair, creating an unforgettably intense portrait. Bellows, like Henri, used the 'Maratta System' of colour, based on a systematic progression of hues on the palette and thus a controlled order of application. Just how effective this system was, or even exactly how it affected the look of the painting, is open to question. But it did mean that the artists who used it had paid careful attention to colour and its role.

America's First Real Modernist: Maurice Prendergast

The bold shades of Maurice Prendergast (1858–1924), also in The Eight, would have been in striking opposition to the muted Realist paintings, such as those of Henri. In fact, one critic described Prendergast's work as an 'explosion in a colour factory'.[16] Prendergast was a member of the older generation, an artist of already considerable achievement, who too often has been thought of as a nineteenth-century artist, when in fact his original contributions belong to the early twentieth century. In truth, he could be considered America's first real modernist. In 1908, he forged a new style of painting. Like so many aspiring artists at this time, both young and old, he had looked long and hard at the art of Cézanne. In Paris, he saw the two pivotal Cézanne exhibitions that changed the course of modern art by revealing new ways of making and thinking about art that were still resonating well into the 1960s. Prendergast, like others, found in Cézanne's layered chromatic planes a way to construct a painting from a full, solid mosaic of colour patterns without regard for what it depicted, an art that could approximate the modelling of the Old Masters. Prendergast had already made his mark in the 1890s as a first-rate artist of flat patterns of spreading colour, related to Impressionism but in his own style. He was one of the few American artists of the time who understood Impressionism as a way to open up the painting, to use colour to cover the surface in rich, interlocking patterns, to let the brush move across the canvas freely – the most valuable lesson of Impressionism.

Prendergast had also been quick to assimilate the paintings of Georges Seurat, Paul Signac, Neo-Impressionism, as well as Matisse, that were based on the primacy of colour, so that by 1910 he could be said to be America's foremost colour painter. His work had become in these years much denser, more constructed, with each touch of colour a form, a shape or a plane, lessons he had learned from Cézanne.

In the summer of 1911, Prendergast journeyed to Italy, where he discovered – or perhaps rediscovered, but now in a new light – the Old Masters of the Italian Renaissance. That 'new light' may well have been other aspects in the art of Cézanne, especially his grand bathers. By then, Cézanne's status was such that he was widely considered an Old Master, who had succeeded in his wish to make 'Impressionism solid and durable, like the art of the museums'.[17] Certainly by 1911, there was no question that Cézanne was one of the most fertile sources for new art, including Cubism and colour painting, most especially as interpreted via Matisse. Both he and Picasso called Cézanne 'the father of us all'[18] and this was no less true for Prendergast and scores of other Americans. More than

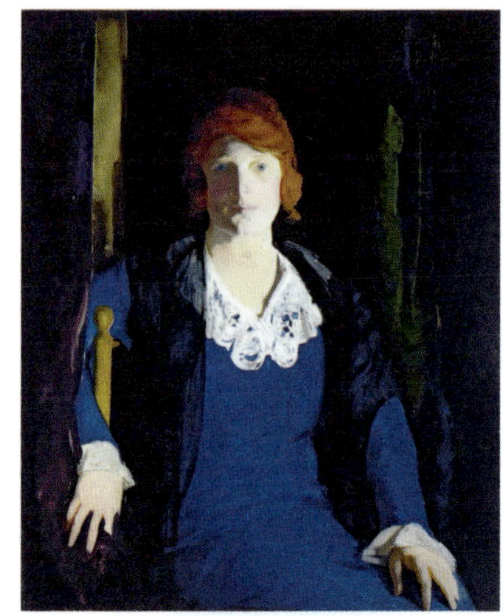

9

9 George Bellows, *Portrait of Florence Pierce*, 1914. Oil on canvas, 96.5 × 76.2 cm (38 × 30 in). The Museum of Fine Arts, Houston

10 Maurice Prendergast, *Idyl*, c. 1912–15. Oil on canvas, 61 × 81.6 cm (24 × 32⅛ in). The Barnes Foundation, Philadelphia

Modern Art in America

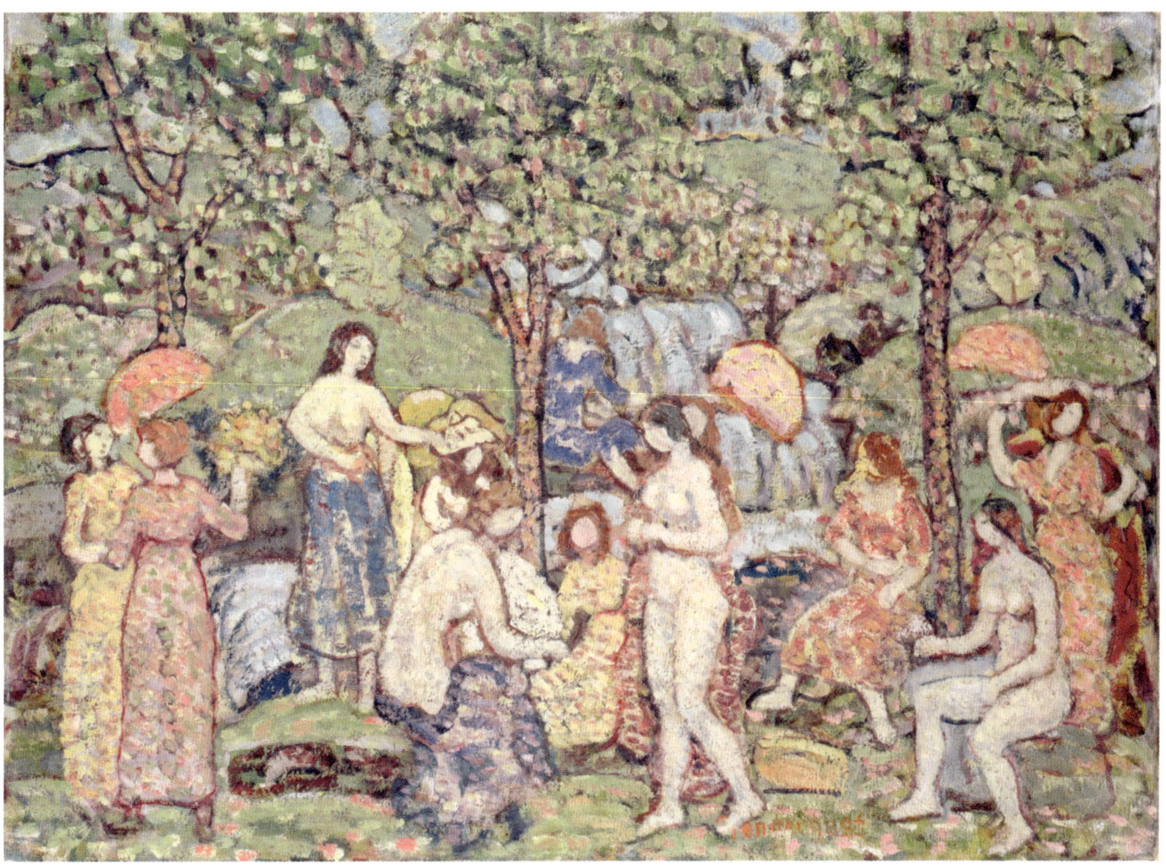

10

any artist, Cézanne forced the Americans into the new century, bringing them up to date by giving them the same multiple lessons of colour and construction as were offered to French and German artists.

Formerly based in Boston, Prendergast settled in New York in 1914, where, until his death in 1924, he worked steadily at creating a world of idylls[10], fantasies and mythological scenes, peopled by figures as solidly coloured and constructed as a Renaissance or even an Egyptian mural. These scenes had grown out of his long series of animated crowds seen in the parks of New York and Boston, depicted as if in motion, but with the permanence of a sculptural procession on a Greek temple, constructed through tightly woven bricks of colour that bind the surface tightly. This return to a classical source became a frequently recurring theme in modern art, far more common than we have understood. We often think of modern art as solely an art of revolution, of destroying the past, given to upheaval of the existing order, of rebellion against older art. This is true only in part, and at certain points, such as the programme of the Italian Futurists and the worldwide Dada movement, widely broadcast from 1910 to 1916, espousing an art that would break with the past. For many in America, Futurism and Modernism were virtually synonymous, and art of the modern age was equated with that of the Futurists' glorification of war and anarchy. This analogy has lasted longer than it should have. In fact, much of modern art sought to continue the traditions and aspirations of the Old Masters, and often made specific reference to them to do so. These painters were valued above all for their sureness, craftsmanship and high skill, and were seen as the source for all successive generations. Thus we will see how artists looked to the past for guidance, in order to make something new and personal for themselves. It is a matter of continuity, not so much of break and disavowal. But in the process, the new was created.

Maurer, Bruce, Dove and Carles:
American Modernist Pioneers

Four case studies of pioneering American modernists, Alfred Maurer, Patrick Henry Bruce, Arthur Dove and Arthur B. Carles reveal how the Cézanne-Matisse synthesis of colour helped to shape their art and American painting in the early years of the twentieth century.

Alfred Maurer (1868–1932) holds a pre-eminent place in history, fundamentally important to early modernism and indeed throughout his life. Until now, this has been largely overlooked, first because of his sad biography (a suicide in 1932 that has overshadowed his art–an all too familiar story in American art) and second because his career has often been arbitrarily split in half, first as a realist, then as a modernist, making it seem as if he came late to advanced modes, and in a lesser role. In fact, his career was of a piece, and he was a contemporary from the start, with a deep continuity underlying his art. He was the first American of the pioneering generation to settle in Paris, staying there from 1897 to 1914. At the time of his arrival, he was working in a Realist style, to be sure, but it was indebted to Manet–the starting point of modern art. Further, Realism in all its guises was an intrinsic part of early twentieth-century painting in America, and Maurer's powerful images in this vein are part of its development.

From the start, Maurer's art was marked by a love of colour, even if at first it was in the deep, rich darker end of the spectrum. His move into a higher, more intense range of hues was propelled by his encounter with Leo and Gertrude Stein, some time around 1904. Through them, he came into contact with the art of Cézanne, Picasso and Matisse, and by 1908, if not earlier, his work had taken on the strong colour of Cézanne, as filtered through Matisse.

By 1908, an awareness of Cubism had also begun to manifest itself in Maurer's paintings, as in *Head of a Woman*[11]. Cubist devices are evident in the sharp angling of the head, face and shoulders. The bulk and solidity of the figure, outlined by the firm, strong drawing, indicate a knowledge of Picasso's massive nudes of the same year. These qualities also point to Maurer's deep interest in extending the values of the Renaissance into a modern idiom. Maurer was especially drawn to Florentine drawing –*disegno*–and the art of Botticelli, which he had studied closely on a trip to Italy in 1906. These values stayed with him throughout his life. Matisse himself made the same trip the next year to ground his art in the solidity and structure of the Renaissance, paying special attention to Giotto, Piero della Francesca and Michelangelo, at a time when he feared his art was becoming too loose and unstructured. This fusion of Picasso and Matisse in Maurer's work set an important example for many artists in the next few years, Patrick Henry Bruce and Morgan Russell among them. In his day he was widely admired and respected, and was a guiding presence in Paris for newly arrived Americans, such as Arthur Dove and Marsden Hartley. Clement Greenberg, as we have seen, praised Maurer's work, as did Hans Hofmann, who said in 1950 that Maurer was a forerunner of a 'true and great tradition', then still being defined.[19] The quality of Maurer's paintings, evident as early as 1908, places him as one of the first Americans to achieve an art that could rightfully be called modern. Therefore we note that two older artists, Prendergast and Maurer, were as important to American modernism as were younger artists.

The first younger American artist (after the older Maurer) to settle in Paris in the twentieth century doubtless had little if any inkling of the work of Cézanne or Matisse when he arrived. However, these two masters soon

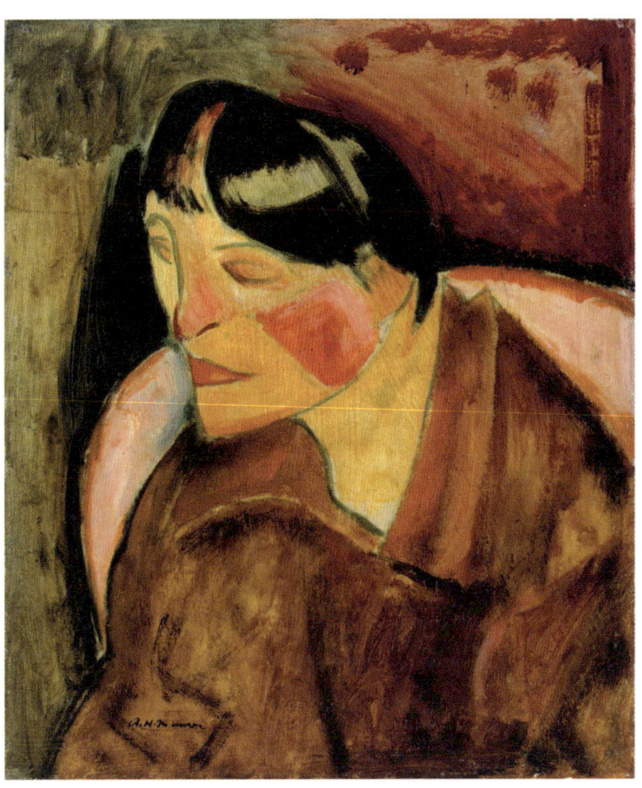

11

became the chief sources of his art throughout his life. Patrick Henry Bruce (1881–1936) was a Virginian by birth and upbringing, and that was where he first studied art. By 1902, he was in New York, one of Henri's most promising students, achieving high praise and acclaim for his portraits done in the slashing realist style taught by Henri and William Merritt Chase. However, like Thomas Jefferson, his fellow Virginian, Bruce believed that culture was French by definition, so that by early 1904 he was in Paris, where he remained for the rest of his life. For two years he continued his realist style in the manner taught by his old mentor, showing no awareness of or interest in more current art. He did, however, spend countless hours in the Louvre, as he had been encouraged to do by Henri and Chase, studying and absorbing the Old Masters, a habit that had a lasting effect on his later art. Most young artists followed a similar path, using Old Master practices, especially that of drawing, as a basis for their later art. Among them, Bruce was the most dedicated to emulating the design of older art, especially that of Andrea Mantegna, and the absolute exactitude of line in his drawing and painting. He did not know it at the time, but this study prepared him well for his immersion in modernist art. It is one of the first instances of an American modernist consciously looking to the classical past as a guiding source for his venture into the avant-garde.[20]

By mid-1906, Bruce's art reflected an awareness of Impressionism: his palette lightened and his touch became more feathery. If at first reluctant, his commitment to recent art came swiftly and decisively. By early 1907, if not late 1906, he had met the Steins and had become a regular visitor to their open houses. There he came into contact with many of the leading artists of the day, most importantly Matisse, to whom he quickly became close. Through his study of the Steins' collection, Matisse's teaching and the two great exhibitions of 1907, Bruce began to absorb the lessons of Cézanne, at first slowly then intensively. He was an original member of the Académie Matisse when it opened in January 1908, one of the four Americans—Michael and Sarah Stein, and Max Weber were

11   Alfred Maurer, *Head of a Woman*, c. 1908. Tempera on French cardboard mounted on gessoed panel. 46.3 × 38.1 cm (18¼ × 15 in). Myron Kunin Collection of American Art, Minneapolis

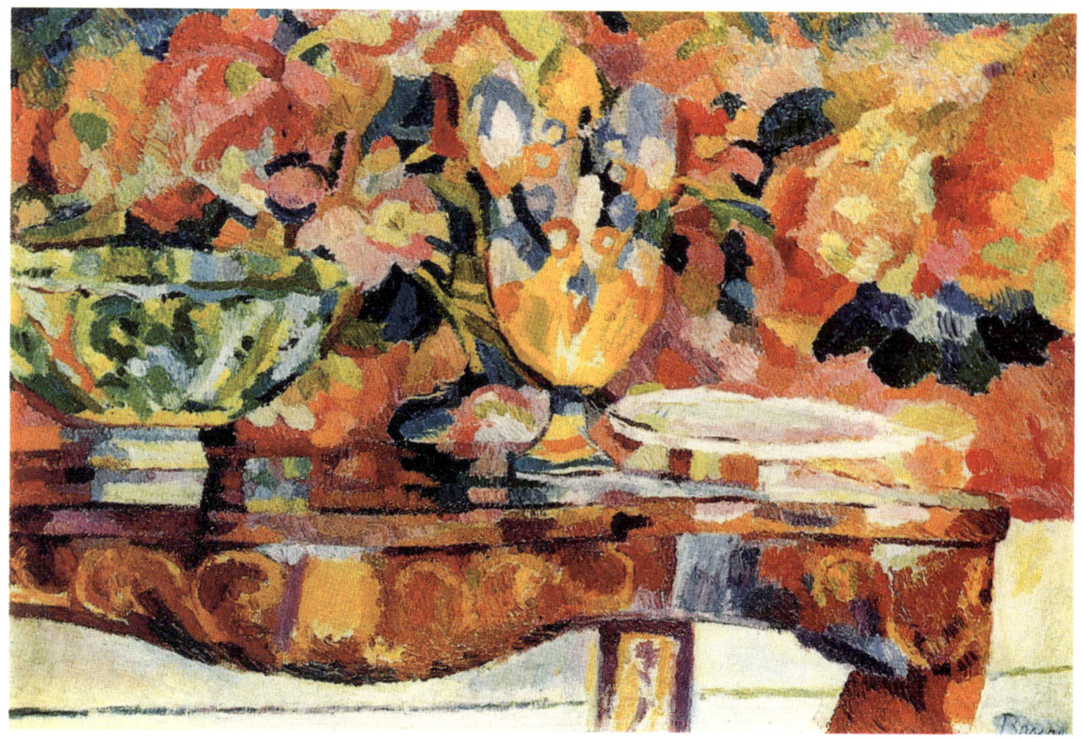

12

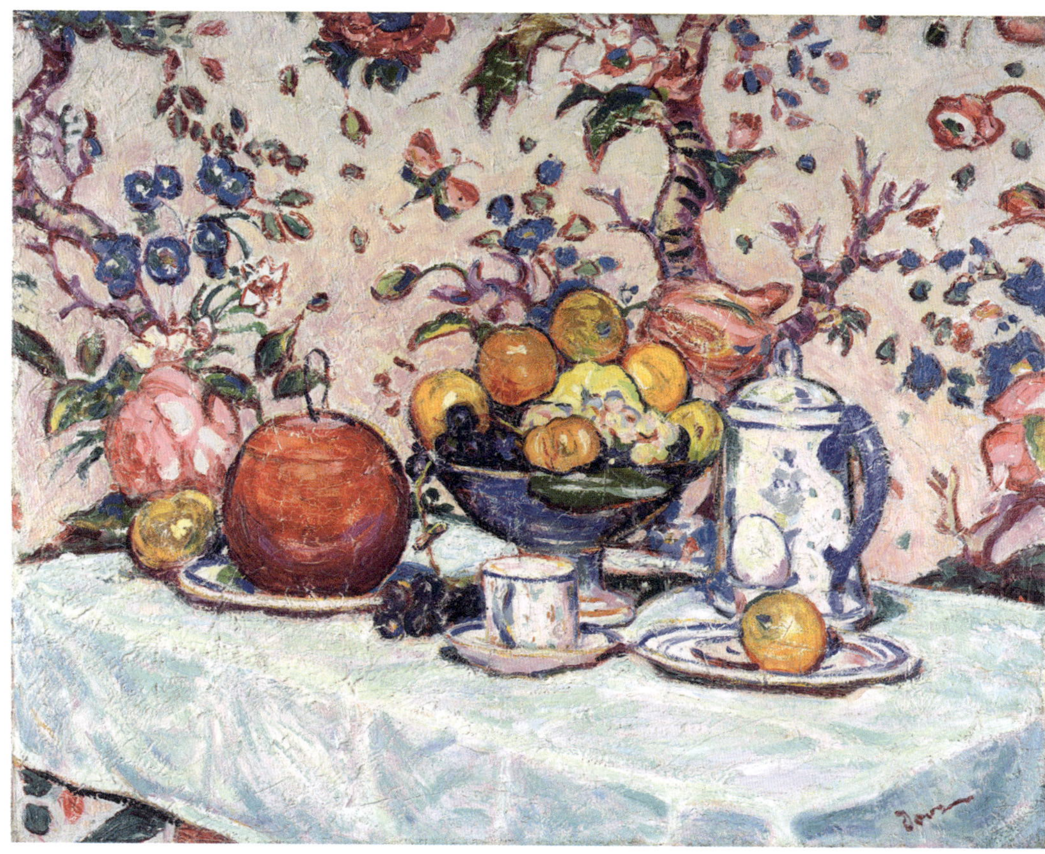

13

Modern Art in America

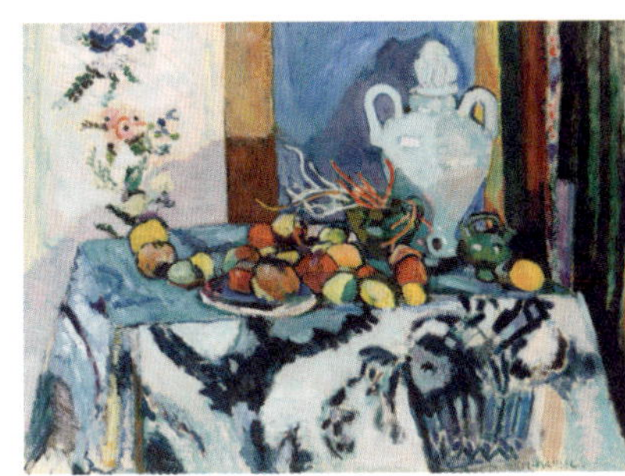

14

the others—who played an important part in its inception. The course, financed by Michael Stein, was held in the refectory of the Couvent des Oiseaux, 56 rue de Sèvres, and later that year it was moved to the Couvent du Sacré-Coeur on boulevard des Invalides, where both Matisse and Bruce and their families lived in apartments on the upper floors. While Matisse attended on Saturdays to give critiques, Bruce was in daily contact with him and witnessed many of Matisse's most important works in progress, the *Dance (I)* (1909) among them. The course lasted until early 1911 and a more valuable education in the use of colour could not be imagined; the colour principles learned there extended deeply into American art, both then and for years to come.

The students were surprised by how conservative Matisse's approach was. He scolded them for their wild, out-of-control colour effects, and made them go back to the beginning, to the study of antique casts, a practice that Henri, in New York, had dismissed out of hand. Bruce was a model student and earned Matisse's respect, since his assiduous studies in the Louvre had prepared him for this teaching, giving him the grounding on which to build the new ideas of colour as form. In his classes, Matisse spoke of drawing, painting and sculpture. In painting, he stated, 'What you are aiming for, above all, is unity. Order above all, in colour.'[21] Put three or four touches of colour that you understand on the canvas; add another if you can, he instructed. 'Construct by relations of colour; close and distant—equivalents of the relations that you see upon the model.'[22] Herein we see the very basis of much of the best colour painting in the following years. Further, Matisse insisted that the artist must render the emotions engendered by the objects before him.[23] This points to an essential fact of colour painting: that to understand it we must deal with emotions. Colour painting relates to our most profound being, our very humanity.

By 1908 (from what we know of the extant work), Bruce's art showed the impact of Cézanne's still-life and landscape motifs, as interpreted by Matisse, all composed of a brighter colour, made of constructed, stable brush marks. Within two years, his art had become far more sophisticated and showed a keen understanding of Cézanne's colour chords. Bruce, like Cézanne, often left canvases unfinished, the better to focus on and heighten the colour patches, now pure and complete in themselves. The culminating work of his early career, *Still Life with Tapestry* (1911–12)[12] and other paintings, were solid, dense, like an ancient fabric of precious threads and metals, woven into a tight, painterly mosaic of thick colour passages. Bruce was one of Matisse's most gifted students, and in turn he soon spread the colour principles developed by his teacher to young American artists in New York.

Another younger artist, Arthur Dove (1880–1946), was profoundly influenced by Cézanne, although this has only recently been noted in the literature.[24] Dove held Cézanne, as well as Stieglitz, Rembrandt and Vincent Van Gogh, among his most cherished sources of inspiration. When Dove began his career as a painter in New York, he worked in an Impressionist manner using soft, atmospheric colour and touch. In mid-1908 he went to France, where he stayed until late 1909 before returning to New York. He soon befriended Maurer, who became his mentor and lifelong friend.

Dove's stay in France coincided with the first peak of Cézanne's fame,[25] and he must have seen a considerable amount of Cézanne's art, especially under the knowledgeable guidance of Maurer. By the end of 1908, in *Still Life against Flowered Wallpaper*[13], for example, there are

12   Patrick Henry Bruce, *Still Life with Tapestry*, c.1911–12. Oil on canvas, 49.5 × 68.6 cm (19½ × 27 in). Private collection

13   Arthur Dove, *Still Life against Flowered Wallpaper*, c.1908. Oil on canvas, 63.5 × 80.6 cm (25 × 31¾ in). Myron Kunin Collection of American Art, Minneapolis

14   Henri Matisse, *Blue Still Life*, 1907. Oil on canvas, 89.5 × 116.7 cm (35⁵⁄₁₆ × 45¹⁵⁄₁₆ in). The Barnes Foundation, Philadelphia

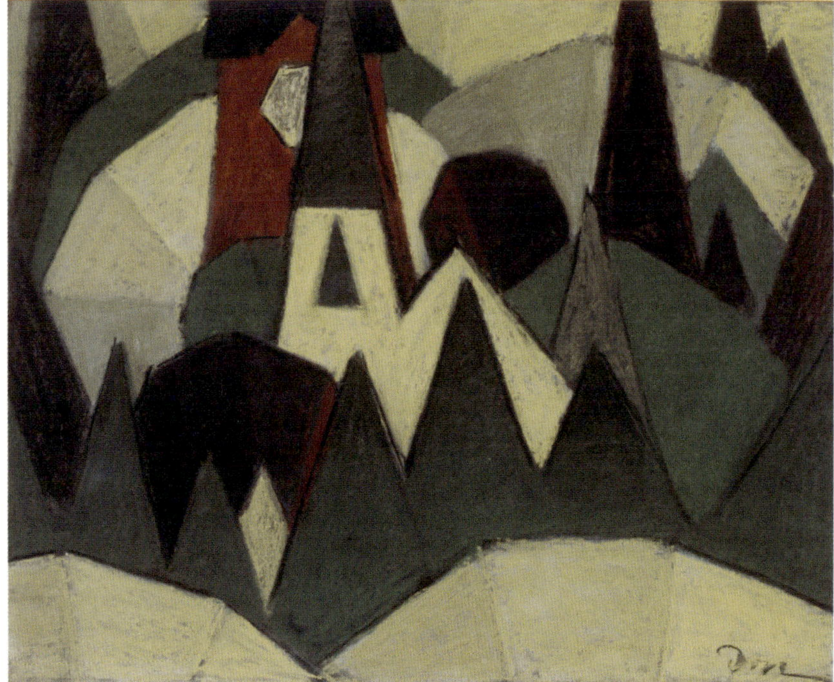

15

abundant marks of Cézanne's influence: there is a new solidity to the painting, a tactile materiality of colour and thus form. For the two are coeval throughout, and are basic tenets of Cézanne's – and Matisse's – art. The colour is brighter by far than his earlier work, indicating that Dove too, like Bruce, was looking at Cézanne, at least in part, through the eyes of Matisse. (One wonders if Dove might have at least observed Matisse's classes, even if he wasn't formally enrolled.) Indeed, this canvas has a startling similarity in composition, surface and feel to Matisse's *Blue Still Life* (1907)[14]. Dove's painting is composed part by part, each with its own order and axis, then fused into a single mosaic of colour areas in which space is compressed and the elements merge with the wall decoration, methods that were well established in Cézanne's art, and extended by Matisse. The fruits have an almost sculptural density, in keeping with the widespread reaction to the perceived lack of structure and order in Impressionism, and following Cézanne's dictum to make it 'solid'. The poetry of the repeated elliptical shapes of the fruits playing across the surface, responding only to the dictates of the picture itself and creating their own order, reminds us of Cézanne and Matisse. The painting is the first instance of Dove's lifelong search for, not Realism, but the real, something concrete, authentic and believable.

Cézanne's influence continued through much of Dove's life. His so-called abstractions of 1910 are really condensations of Cézanne's late landscapes of the rough-hewn hills and rocks of his native Provence, especially the Bibemus Quarry series. Dove's responses to these paintings are to abstract nature, to distil landscape motifs, but they are not purely invented shapes as has been claimed for so long in attempts to make him the first abstract artist. At least several of Dove's pastels of 1911–12, among them *Steeple and Trees*[15], can be traced to the broad, flattened planes of Cézanne's late architectural work, as experienced, perhaps, through the landscapes done in the same area by Picasso and Braque in 1908–9.

The group of early American modernists – Maurer, Dove, Prendergast, Hartley, Marin and others – should also include Arthur B. Carles (1882–1952), an artist of the first order who has slipped from our histories. He

15 Arthur Dove, *Nature Symbolized #3: Steeple and Trees*, 1911–12. Pastel on board mounted on wood panel, 45.7 × 54.6 cm (18 × 21½ in). Terra Foundation for American Art, Daniel J. Terra Collection, Chicago

16 Arthur B. Carles, *Nude*, 1922. Oil on linen, 71.4 × 88 cm (28⅛ × 34⅝ in). Hirshhorn Museum and Sculpture Garden, Smithsonian Institution, Washington, DC

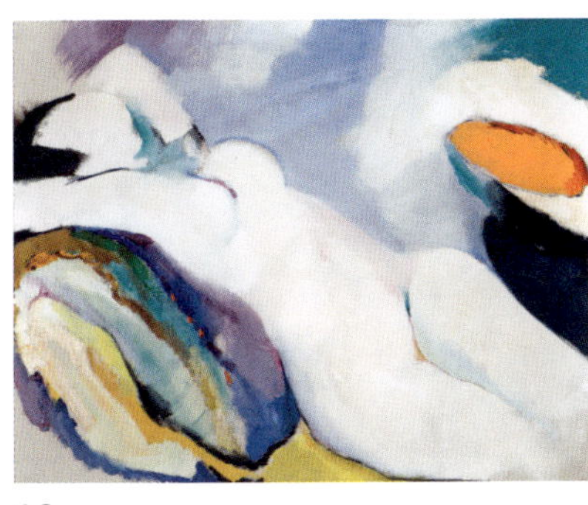

16

was in Paris by 1904 and thus is a frontline American modernist, one of the first to delve into the new worlds offered by Cézanne and colour construction. He was an uneven artist, plagued by demons, who didn't hit his peak until the 1930s, but he made more than a few paintings, such as his *Nude* (1922)[16], that for these years must be counted in the canon of American modernism. He is of special note, too, because in Paris he met Hans Hofmann, who had also arrived there in 1904 from his native Munich. Hofmann was born in 1880, the same year as Dove, and really must be counted as an artist who belonged to the pioneering generation of American modernists. This will seem odd, because we associate him primarily with Abstract Expressionism and art after 1945, but he received his training in Paris in these years, and began to develop his extensive knowledge of colour and Cubism before World War I.

LANDSCAPE

From the earliest days, American artists were hampered by a public that was struggling to survive, and that by necessity valued only the literal, the tangible and the useful. At first, there was little room to dream and to imagine. But this perhaps turned out to be a strength of American art and literature, for writers and painters set out to record the look, the feel and the experience of the country in all its facets. What else could they paint? There was no king or Church or history to record. There was only what was in front of them – the land, its flora and fauna and the few objects they used to make a life for themselves.

By the early nineteenth century a native landscape tradition had emerged. In a new country, faced with endless spaces, American artists such as Thomas Cole wished to detail the infinite bounties of what they saw as a God-given paradise.[26] A mood of wonder, even of innocence, pervaded their work, as they sought to capture the glories of the vast landscapes, far from the long European tradition of what Robert Motherwell called 'the sense of the alien past'.[27] The novelist Philip Roth summarized this attitude by saying: 'This passion for specificity, for the hypnotic materiality of the world one is in, is all but at the heart of the task in which every American novelist has been enjoined since Herman Melville and his whale and Mark Twain and his river: to discover the most arresting, evocative verbal depiction of every last thing American.'[28]

The Rapidly Changing Landscape

By the nineteenth century, this search for the real included representing a landscape that was changing rapidly. Artists and writers already understood that progress and culture would undermine the natural beauty of the continent. D.H. Lawrence commented on Crèvecœur's description in 1782 of 'cultivating the virgin soil', by lamenting the 'poor virgin, prostituted from the start'.[29] Alexis de Tocqueville, writing in 1831, believed that 'we are the last to see nature unspoiled…so great is the force that drives the white race to the complete conquest of the New World.' The awareness of forthcoming destruction, he said, gave a 'touching beauty to the solitudes of America, and we hurry to admire them, with melancholy'. Yet, at the same time, thoughts of destruction were mixed with 'splendid anticipations of the triumphant march of civilization'.[30]

The process of the country progressively and systematically destroying itself was captured in the landscapes of Hudson River School painter Sanford Gifford, showing the forests being cut down to make way for the progress of 'civilization'.

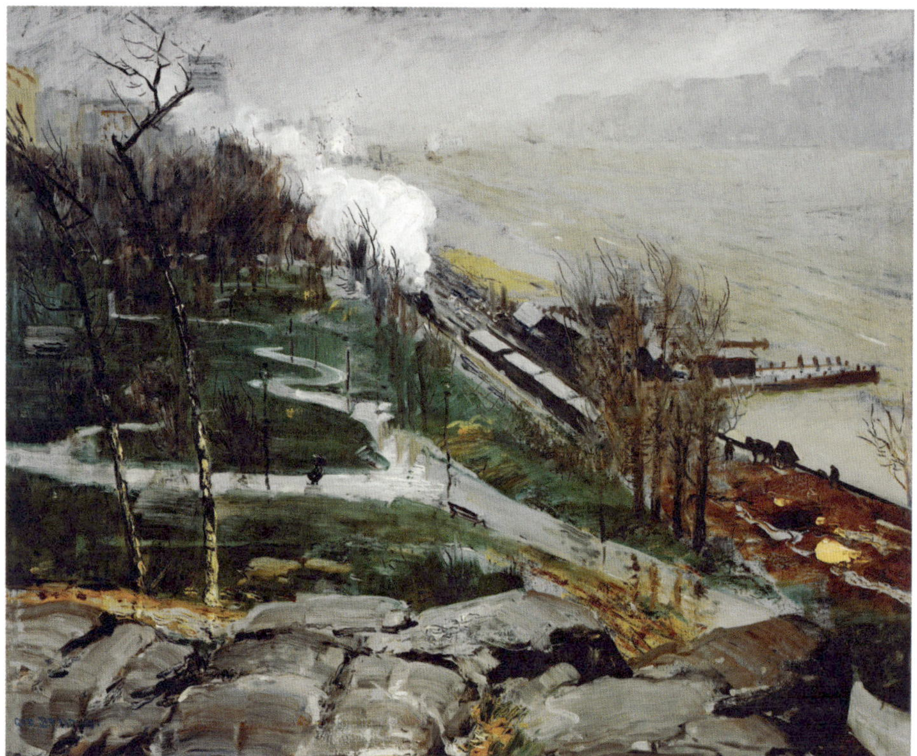

17

The materialism of America's primarily urban population has produced unbroken swathes blighted by commerce, industry and technology. The irony is, as Leo Marx discussed in *The Machine in the Garden*, that Americans have welcomed this onslaught, at every turn, with open arms.[31] The transformation is well marked in paintings by George Bellows such as *Rain on the River* (1908)[17], in which the Hudson River is portrayed not in the bucolic sunlit mode of Cole or others, but as the path for the railway, cutting through the land beside it, overtaking the boats on the river itself, spewing the coal smoke that greys the already misty air. In vigorous, ever-shifting brushstrokes, Bellows embodies the very pace of change in America. Just as prominent is the road that wends its way through the adjoining land, soon to carry the cars and trucks that transformed America, clogging its cities and polluting its skies.

It might be said that photography (via Stieglitz) achieved a true modernity, at a higher level of accomplishment, before painting in America, certainly in terms of capturing this new urban landscape. Architecture, too, was pioneering in this sense. Frank Lloyd Wright, with works such as his Unity Temple (1908), was the first American artist to gain wide attention abroad and to influence aspects of European art. In 1910, the German publisher Ernst Wasmuth produced a portfolio of 200 of Wright's drawings for buildings from 1893 to 1909.[32] The portfolio also contained a monograph by Wright and was a link between his pioneering architecture and the first generation of modernist architects in Europe. Le Corbusier had a copy and is known to have shared it; Peter Behrens, for whom Le Corbusier, Ludwig Mies van der Rohe and Walter Gropius were all working, was said to have stopped work for the day when the portfolio arrived, and Rudolph Schindler and Richard Neutra moved to America in the hope of working with Wright. Gropius claimed that the Wright portfolio was his bible. Finally, there is no doubt that Wright's work influenced the development of De Stijl in the Netherlands.

17 George Bellows, *Rain on the River*, 1908. Oil on canvas, 82.2 × 97.2 cm (32⅜ × 38¼ in). Rhode Island School of Design Museum of Art, Providence

This is not to mention the earlier worldwide attention received by the Chicago school of architecture and the development of the skyscraper there and in New York. In architecture, the spirit of Classicism remained throughout the century as a primary and rich source for buildings of high achievement. McKim, Mead & White, Mies van der Rohe, Philip Johnson, Skidmore, Owings and Merrill, Louis Kahn and Robert A.M. Stern, for example, kept the principles of Classicism alive and well, as a continuing, fertile source for buildings in the public realm. In 1908, the grand spaces of Penn Station were completed and opened, one of the most heroic parallels to Greek and Roman art. It is no coincidence that it was demolished in 1963, another disaster wrought by the calamities of that decade. But in 1908, if America was not the leading force in modern architecture, it was at least a major force in its development.

An Elemental Landscape: Marsden Hartley

By 1908, for those few who knew and were interested, a major new talent in American art had appeared. The series of powerful landscapes done by the young Marsden Hartley (1877–1943) in his native, distant Maine still astonish, so convincing are they in their depictions of that rugged state. Looking back, we can see that Hartley, often – and rightly – viewed as America's greatest early modernist, was very accomplished from the start[33] and can be ranked with Jackson Pollock in terms of sheer expressive power. With what became his lifelong intensity, Hartley – working alone – focused his vision on nature, as had so many Americans. But it was not tranquil vistas of nineteenth-century America along the Hudson River that attracted him, nor the landscape newly transformed by industry, but rather the remote and isolated forests and mountains of deepest Maine, the most elemental of settings. Hartley was a restless soul, never at peace with himself, constantly moving, with shifting modes and sites to match his ever-changing state of mind. But when he bore down and concentrated on his painting, no one else, then or later, could rival such focused, undiluted intensity.

This gift was evident as early as 1906–7, in paintings such as *Storm Clouds, Maine* [18]. Here, Hartley fused his early influences, the stitch-like strokes of the Swiss painter Giovanni Segantini and the brooding forms and emotions of Albert Pinkham Ryder, whose dark mood often appeared in Hartley's work, a sense of awe and fear and trembling in the face of nature's power. Like no other American at the time – or later – Hartley could imbue the paint with an expressive force that makes us feel as if we were there with him as he worked. The paint is palpable, the whole canvas rendered alive and real, an early manifestation of the modernist drive to make every inch as important as any other. The magic lies in the density of the clouds, or in leaves and branches, every bit as real and physical as the land itself. It is all unrelenting: there is no escaping this storm, nor is it but a passing shower. The clouds press down on us, sure to engulf us, for the eyes of the gods are staring at us from the upper left, as if it were Zeus himself. As in Ryder's work, but more so, the storm is as psychological as it is meteorological, filled with foreboding, almost a direct mirror of Hartley's ongoing anxieties. Here, and in other works of these early years, he exhibits an originality of composition and facture that no other American could yet capture.[34]

It is, we might say, an early and new form of American expressionism, related to symbolism, even Impressionism, but different from anything previously seen. It is a new strain of American modernist art, filled with

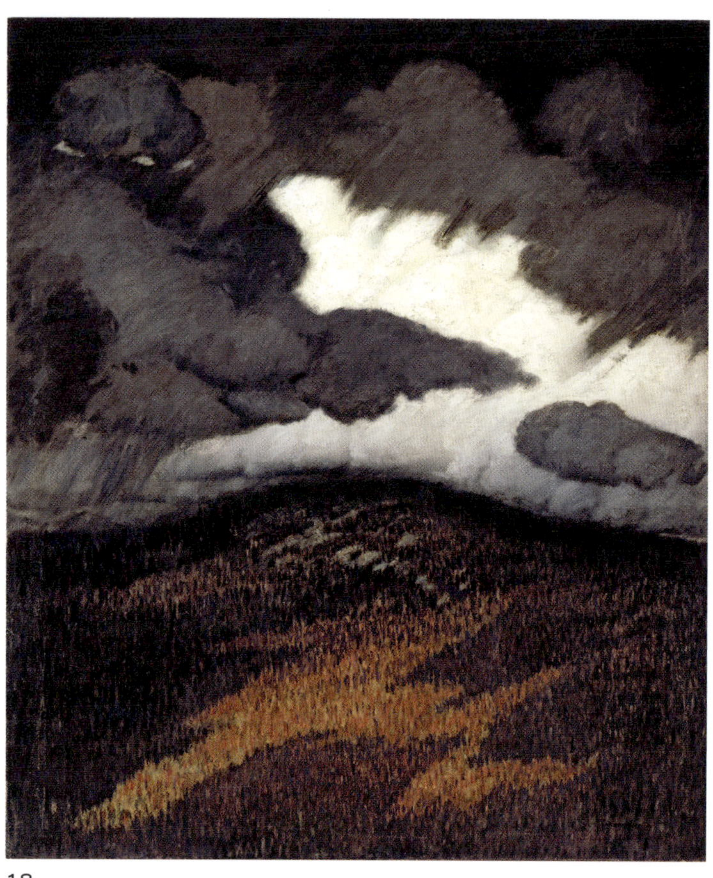

18

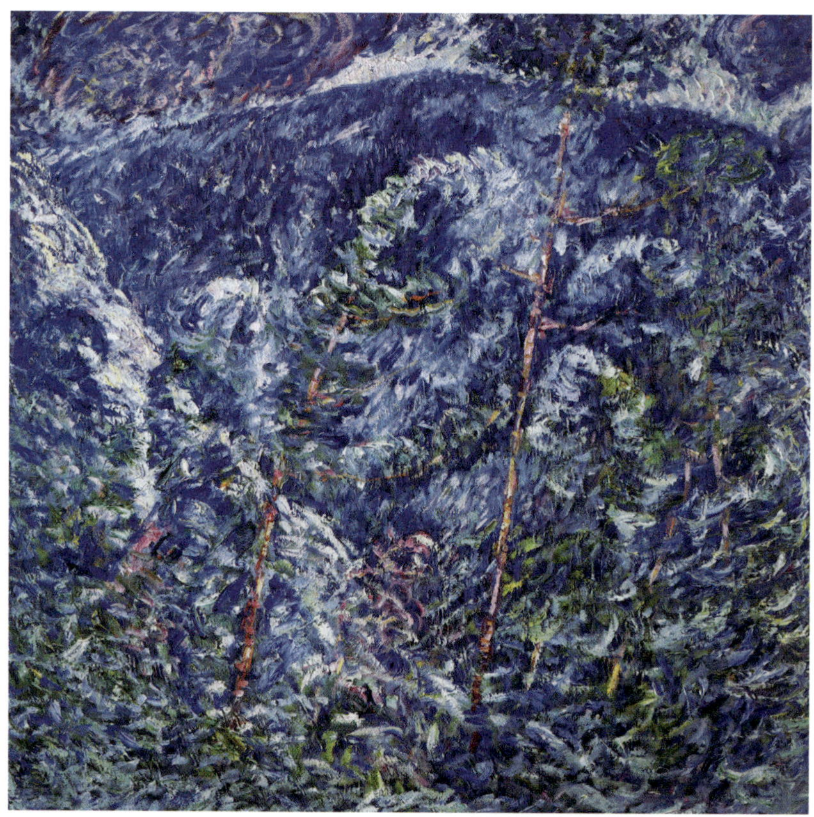

19

18 Marsden Hartley, *Storm Clouds, Maine*, 1906–7. Oil on canvas, 76.2 × 63.5 cm (30 × 25 in). Walker Art Center, Minneapolis

19 Marsden Hartley, *Winter Chaos, Blizzard*, 1909. Oil on canvas, 86.2 × 86.4 cm, (33$\frac{15}{16}$ × 34 in). The Alfred Stieglitz Collection, Philadelphia Museum of Art

20 Marsden Hartley, *The Dark Mountain, No. 2*, 1909. Oil on paper, 50.8 × 61 cm (20 × 24 in). The Alfred Stieglitz Collection, The Metropolitan Museum of Art, New York

Modern Art in America

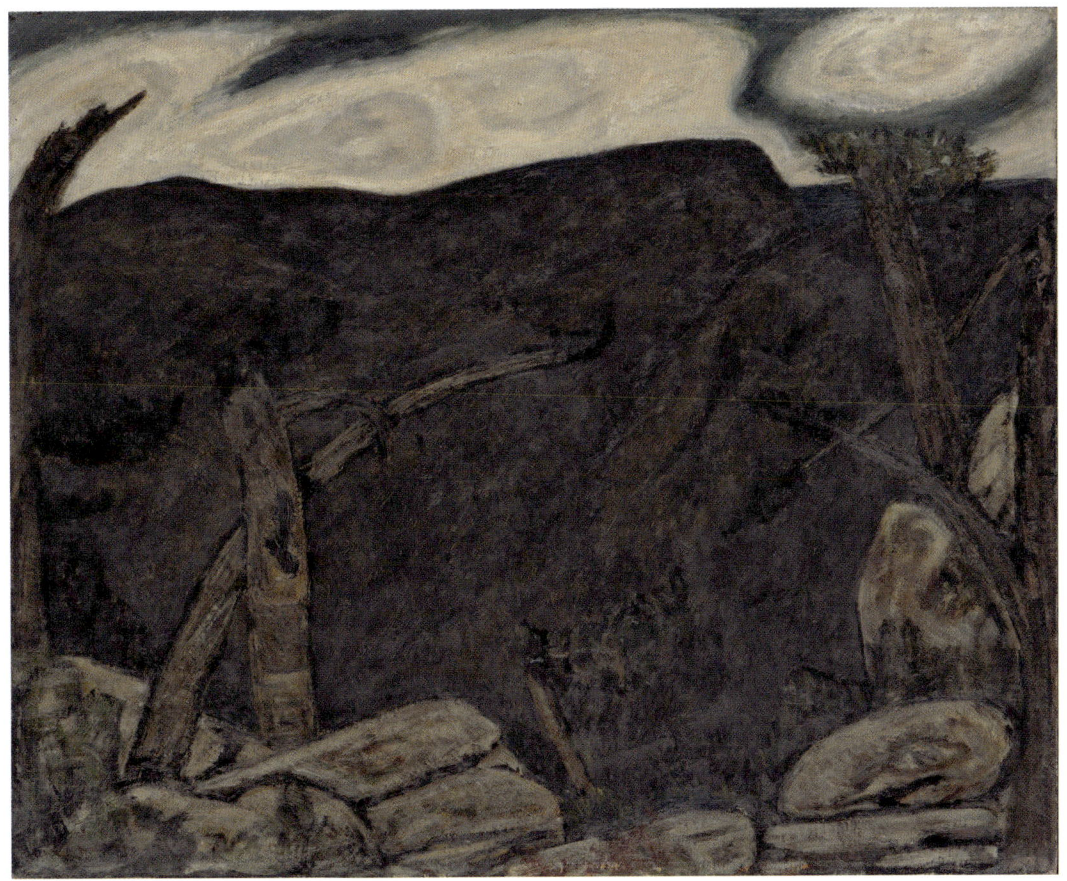

20

something large, unbridled and deeply spiritual that evokes the cosmos, as the title of Hartley's painting of 1908–9 states. He loved wild and distant places, was filled with excitement before the wonders of nature. In paintings such as the 'Song of Winter' series of 1908–9, and especially in the extraordinary *Winter Chaos, Blizzard* (1909)[19], Hartley turned his vision loose and let it go where it might. His brush was loose, too, in response to the awful weather; everything is in motion, the trees, the hills beyond, even the snow itself, a study in expanding, opening, rippling motion. It is as if the artist stands alone before God himself in the stark landscape, a solitary man caught up in the most basic and elemental struggle of life. For Hartley, art becomes a matter of felt experience, conveying a deep spirituality, the belief in and connection with an unseen animating force that lies beneath and above the landscape.

These songs of winter become a symphony of nature, and even the layers of snow ring out, like a clash of cymbals in the mountains. They are waves of sound, these strokes and ribbons of paint and colour, suggesting an early foray into synaesthesia, the embodiment of sound in paint, that Hartley and Dove, among others, later developed.

Hartley's colour was already rich and deep, but it became all the more intense and expressive in his 'Dark Mountain' series of 1910, paintings that took to new extremes the foreboding evident in Ryder's art. In *The Dark Mountain, No.2* [20], we face the void itself, the darkness of the despondent soul at the end of the road to perdition; in the memorable words of Gail Scott, it is a 'pictorial battlefield' portraying inner conflict.'[35] And in fact Hartley's mood was sometimes so black that he had apparently considered suicide, alternating between joy and depression, love of life and the pursuit of retreat. It was when he isolated himself, that old American habit, that he did his most intriguing work.

Hartley revived, though, perhaps in no small measure due to his encounter with the Matisse exhibition held at 291 in the spring of 1910. There was but one painting – the small *Nude in a Wood* (1906) [21], which sparkles with brilliant colour, now fully evident after recent conservation and cleaning. Nothing like it had ever been seen in America before. The effect was transformative on Hartley, as it was for virtually every other American who saw it.[36]

SYMBOLIST ROOTS

To be sure, Cézanne and Matisse were not the only progenitors of colour and abstract painting in the twentieth century. Less attention has been paid to the Symbolist roots of modern art, but artists such as Paul Gauguin, Pierre Puvis de Chavannes, Gustave Moreau and Odilon Redon in Europe, and Washington Allston, George Inness and Albert Pinkham Ryder in America offered another path to a modern, abstracting type of art.

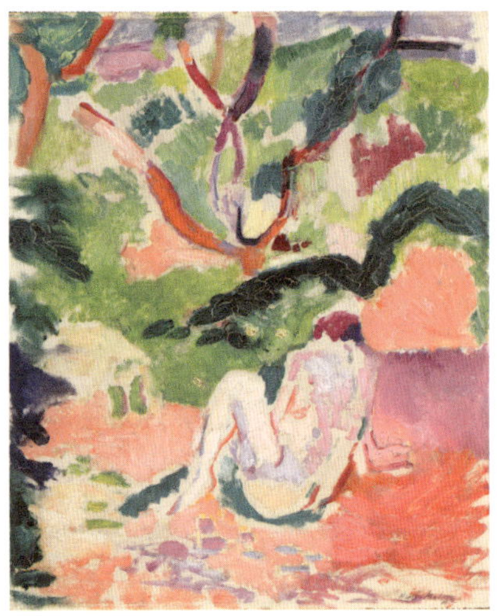

21

In its American mode, Symbolism has been traced to Washington Allston (1779–1843), whose dark, powerful and fanciful landscapes stand in opposition to those of Thomas Cole, seeking escape from the prevalent strain of American Realism. Allston sought, as did others after him, alternative modes that could capture a quiet, inner harmony, a personal vision aimed at embracing the spiritual side of man's experience. The subject was not as important as the mood of the painting. Moving from literal depiction, the artist could focus on the means of painting alone, a key element in the development of modernism.

Symbolism emphasized the idea, the mood, the sense of duration and time, through a softer, more atmospheric application of enveloping colour than the broad clear areas of Matisse or the linear scaffolding of early Cubism. We pay less attention to them now, but at the turn of the twentieth century Redon and Puvis were venerated by other artists and enjoyed wide public acclaim. (Redon was represented by seventy-seven works at the Armory Show in 1913, far more than any other artist, and many were sold.) The misty clouds of soft colour in Redon's sublime pastels, exploring the realm of what he termed the indeterminate, surely had an impact on the early work of Dove and O'Keeffe, as well as later Americans such as Theodoros Stamos and Sam Francis after 1940. Indeed, these amorphous billows of colour should be included in any list of progenitors of the colour and colour-field painting that was well under way in America by 1913. So, too, in Redon's *Silence* (c.1911) [22] we encounter a quiet plea for harmony, peace and serenity amid the clamorous modern city and shrill tones of Futurist abstraction.

When the good fathers of Boston went to select a European artist to decorate the newly constructed 1895 Public Library, they turned to the most famous muralist in France, the widely respected Puvis. His pale and chalky colours, as well as the quiet harmony of his classical themes, lived on well into the twentieth century, especially in the art of Milton Avery. Gauguin's final move to the South Pacific in 1895 had isolated him, but at his death in 1903 he was rediscovered to great acclaim and it is no accident that the memorial show given to him at the Paris Salon d'Automne gave major impetus to the emergence of Fauvism. Matisse was especially drawn to Gauguin's flat, broad areas of colour, clearly defined contours and figuration.

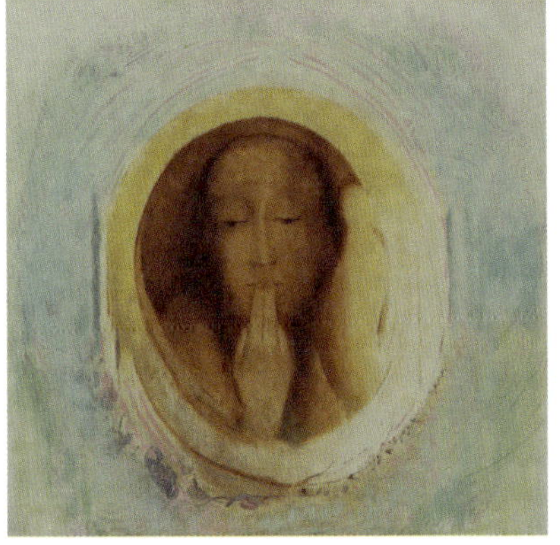

22

Modern Art in America

Oscar Bluemner: a Transitional Artist

Oscar Bluemner (1867–1938) was of German origin, and, like Stieglitz (three years his elder), was an older member of the pioneering modernists. In common with Marin and Bruce, he had first studied architecture, and he had achieved considerable success in that field before turning to painting exclusively. He toured Europe extensively in 1912, and there absorbed both the pictorial architecture of Cubism and the brilliant colour that by then had come to mark so much advanced painting. Indeed, he was one of the first modernists to combine intense colour and a full-blown Cubist vocabulary of sheer planar structure in his signature images of buildings facing us directly, almost as cut-out sheets, one overlapping the other. Bluemner is a kind of transitional figure. The first mature paintings place him, on the one hand, in the Cézannian tradition of the analysis of light and structure that defined much early modernism. On the other hand, though, his work also incorporated aspects of the Symbolist tradition. He could be wildly imaginative, giving trees, landscapes and buildings anthropomorphic qualities, turning and twisting with rapid, intense motion, as if in pain or trying to escape captivity, but adding elements of mystery and ambiguity that stem directly from Symbolism. Like Goethe, he believed that his colour carried human traits and emotions, with his singular red being a symbol of power and the life force, a far different track from the more formal direction of Cézanne.

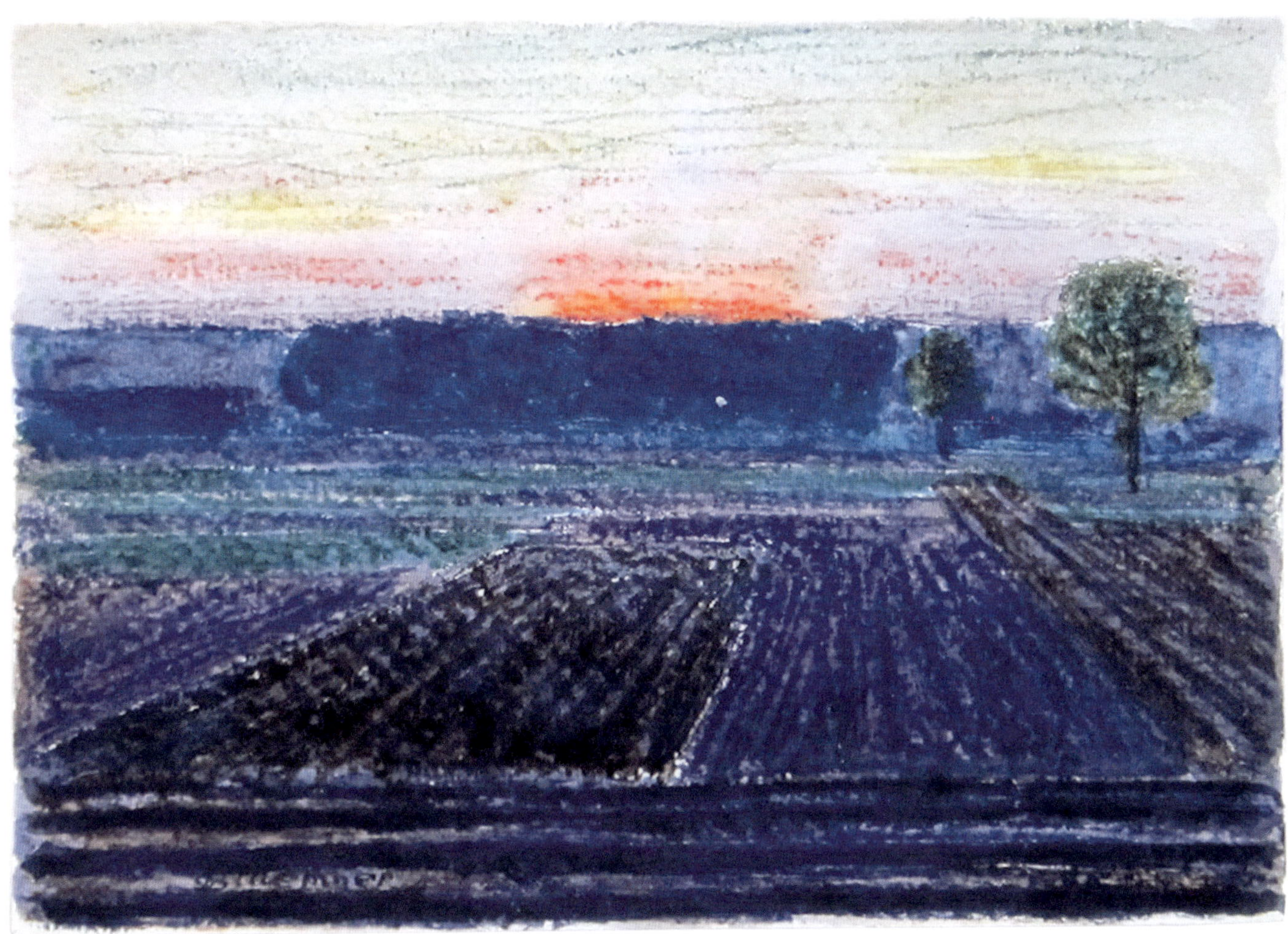

23

Bluemner's best works came later, after the death of his wife in 1926 until his own death in 1938. He turned inwards, into a more meditative and thoughtful mode, while looking to the cosmos, to develop a softer, more nuanced, finely tuned palette and structures that deviated from the strict right angle, horizontal-vertical planes of his earlier painting that seems to keep us at a distance. Not as much attention has been paid to the later work, and it is hardly ever seen – a victim of the linear interpretation of art history that champions the early art and forgets later, often richer, developments. His small, late works are subtle and sensitive, as he looks to the heavens in memorable images of the sun and moon, effecting the ecstatic transformation of matter into spirit.

These works did not appear overnight, however. Bluemner had begun as a sensitive landscape painter, with a beautiful, subtle touch, as in his watercolour *Field at Sunset* (c.1910–11) [23], which established his proclivity for the times and moods of the day. Why he deviated from this direction for several years is not clear. These early, small works placed him in the long American tradition of excellence in the watercolour medium. (It is ironic that American art became known years later for its size and scale, when a good portion of it is small and intimate.) Most of his late work is also small, even his oils, which began to loosen up from the rigid architectural framework of his earlier paintings. This seems to be a mark of humility, of not striving for too much, obeying his inner convictions, his need to connect with the larger order of the universe, which had long been vital for him.

Albert Pinkham Ryder and George Inness: Wild Nature and the Psyche

Ryder and Inness were two of the most famous artists in America, Symbolists exploring the unknown, mysterious, wild side of nature and the psyche. This art preferred the dark and uncertain terrain of the world and of the human soul. Ryder's *Jonah and the Whale* (c.1885–95) [24] recalls the 'besmoked, chaos bewitched' painting that Ismael encounters in the Spouter Inn in *Moby-Dick*:

> *what most confounded you was a long, limber, portentous, black mass of something hovering in the centre of the picture over three blue, dim, perpendicular lines floating in a nameless yeast. A boggy, soggy, squitchy picture truly, enough to drive a nervous man distracted. Yet there was a sort of indefinite, half-attained, unimaginable sublimity about it that fairly froze you to it.*[37]

This uncertainty of motif or theme set in an almost indecipherable cloud of colour or dark mass was typical of Symbolist painting, which favoured synthesis over analysis, leaving much to the spectator's imagination. It is the polar opposite of American clarity and realism.

Ryder was without doubt the most compelling and influential of the American Symbolists, universally admired and respected, a source of almost infinite inspiration for a countless array of artists. His dark and brooding clouds formed the core of Stieglitz's famous image of aviation of 1910, a single plane on high, a modern update of the old romantic theme of man versus the forces of nature. Dove made an almost literal translation of Ryder's storm-bearing skies in his work of the 1920s, a barometer of his personal and artistic uncertainties. We see Ryder's influence in Hartley's early portraits of Maine mountains and Maine

24 Albert Pinkham Ryder, *Jonah and the Whale*, c.1885–95. Oil on canvas mounted on fibreboard, 69.2 x 87.3 cm (27¼ x 34⅜ in). Smithsonian American Art Museum, Washington, DC

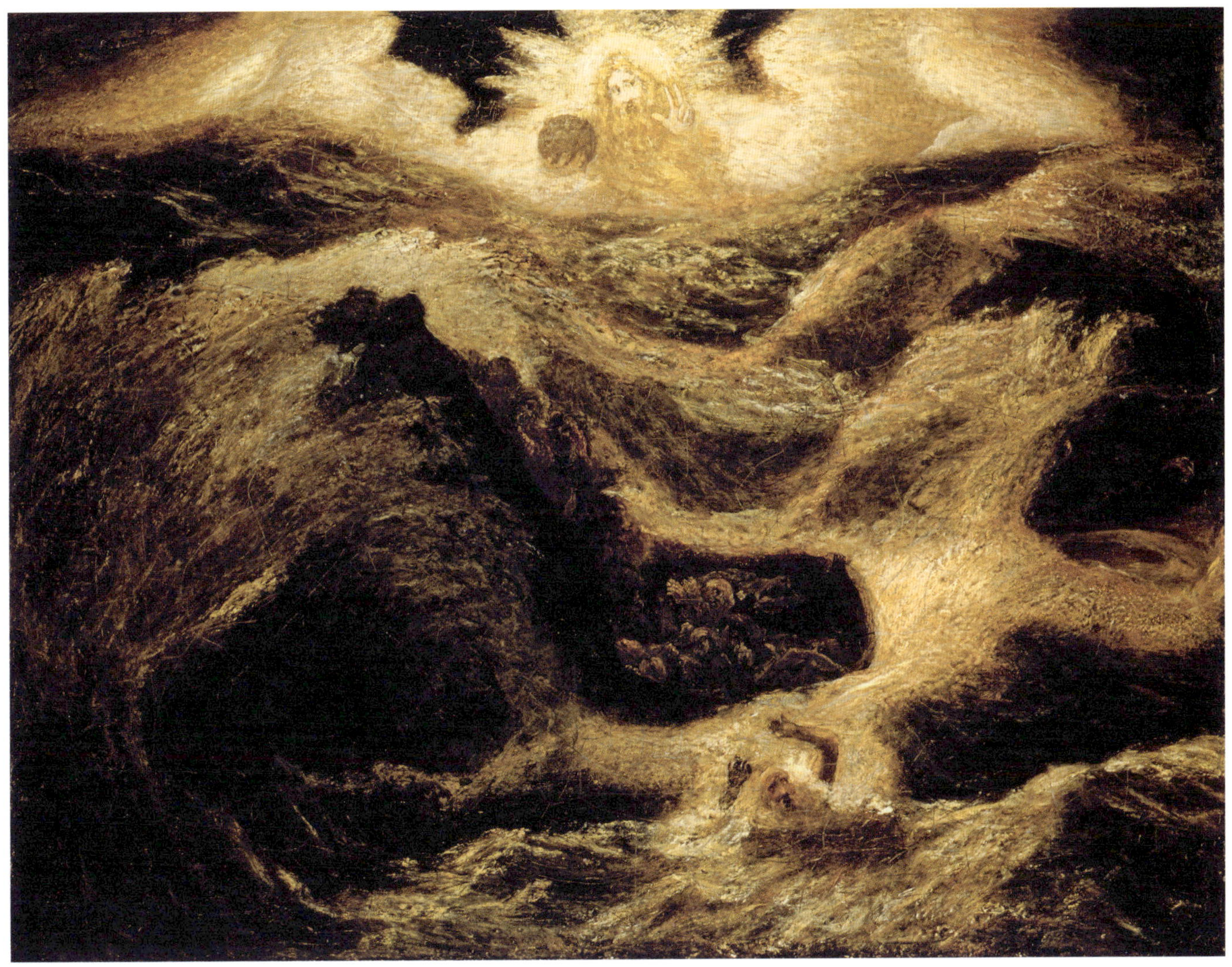

24

winter and its storms, and in his 'New Mexico Remembered' series of the 1920s, whose clouds hover over us as concrete presences. Hartley, an astute observer and perceptive writer, termed Ryder our 'finest genius'[38] and praised him especially for the mystery that shrouded his paintings. On his first day in America, in 1930, Hans Hofmann went straight to the Metropolitan Museum of Art in New York. The painting he singled out and remembered best was Ryder's *Toilers of the Sea* (1880–5), for he was particularly struck by the 'fullness of his colour'.[39] Famously, of course, Jackson Pollock remarked that the only American artist who interested him was Ryder.[40]

We can see why. The depth of the paintings, both literally in the built-up materials as well as in the psychic atmosphere, gives Ryder's work a substance of means and emotion rarely seen in any art. The works inspire and offer challenges that speak to us. Writing in 1908 Roger Fry early on understood Ryder's 'undeniable genius',[41] which lay in his almost childishly simple forms, addressing an issue of modern art, that of giving a sense of the complexity, infinity and richness of matter without involving his design with a corresponding complexity of form.[42] Could there be a better definition of modernism itself? In addition, Fry spoke of Ryder's willed awkwardness, the 'ominous splendour' of the colouring and the unending, relentless movement within, all of which added up to 'a vision that once seen, can never be forgotten'.[43] In his working and reworking of the paint and surfaces, finding in them a potent means of poetic expression, Ryder was one of the first to embody this first principle of American modernism. As early in the century as it was, America nevertheless stood ready for a major surge into the complexities of modern art.

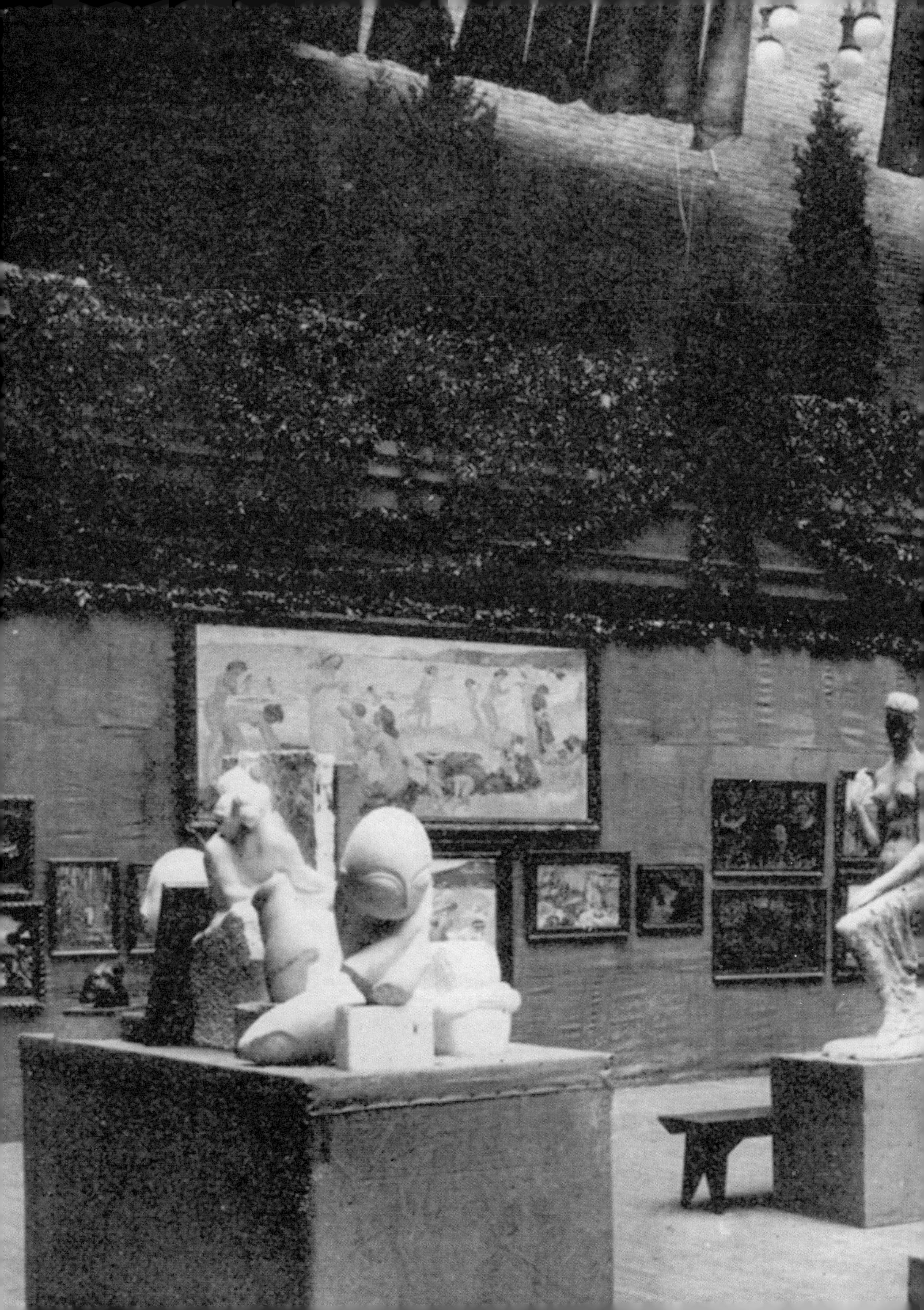

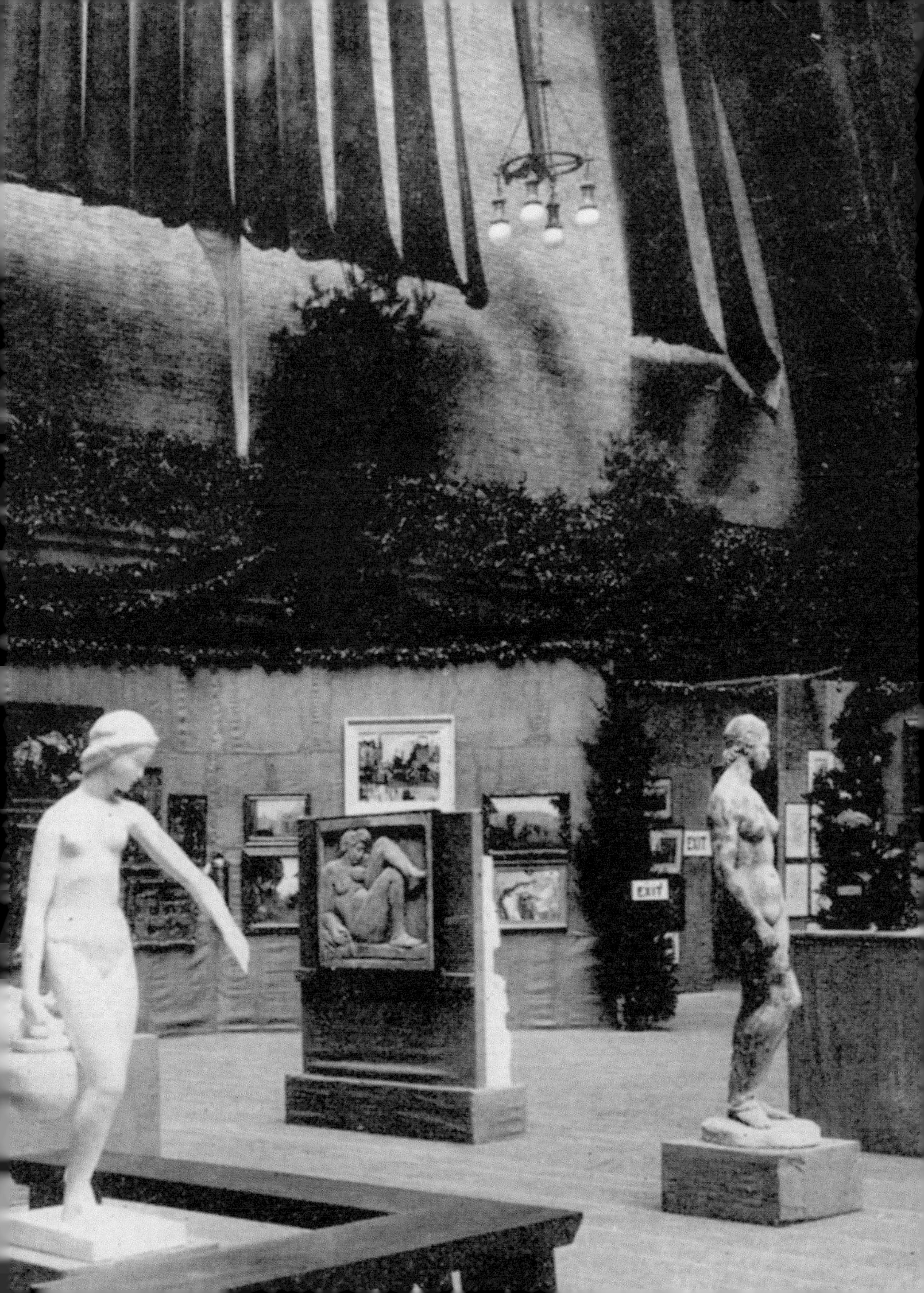
EXIT
EXIT

THE ADVANCE TO THE NEW

1910
–14

CUBISM IN AMERICA

As well as Cézanne's radical influence on colour, as discussed in the first chapter, he would be responsible for another artistic innovation that was essential to the twentieth century: Cubism. In his late landscapes of *Mont Sainte-Victoire* (c.1902–6)[26], Picasso and Braque found the inherent system of vertical and horizontal spatial delineations, coupled with the pure planes of colour, that led them to the development of the grid, a system of intersecting horizontal and vertical lines that changed the course of art. By 1910, this simple system had replaced the premise of 600 years of Western painting based on one-point perspective. The grid meant that the illusion of three-dimensional space and objects in that space could be eliminated. In its place, the essential quality of the painting, its two-dimensional surface, could now take precedence. Instead of objects being fictively modelled in space, they could now be flattened and spread across the surface, arranged and supported by the grid. Reality could be examined and experimented with from new angles. Both Einstein and Freud had clearly established that reality was something other than what the eye saw as visible. Front and back, space, void and solid could be interchanged; multiple aspects of an object could be depicted; scale and size could be inverted; marks and signs could stand for modelled objects; stencilled letters could constitute another type of reality on the surface; forms could be multifaceted, or a simple plane. The possibilities were endless. For many Americans, the Cubist grid provided the underlying structure to carry their colour sequences. The grid is still widely evident today.

Cubism was more difficult to understand and absorb outside of Paris. The first American to show an awareness of the new structure was Max Weber (1881–1961). He had come to Paris in 1905 and was a student at the Matisse School. An important pioneer of American modernism, he did some colour studies, but he never fully embraced an all-out use of colour in the way that fellow student Patrick Henry Bruce did. Rather, he was more

25 Interior view of the Armory Show exhibition, New York, 1913.

important for his early experiments with Cubism. By 1908, Weber had incorporated a rudimentary overlay of geometry into his still lifes and neo-primitive figures that show his observation of Picasso's first forays into the language of Cubism, of African sculpture and perhaps even Henri Rousseau, to whom he was close. African art was valuable to American artists for its straightforward, streamlined structure, its formal and emotive clarity, which could guide the artist into a more condensed and powerful expression. This was more easily assimilated by Americans, who by this means could emulate the new formal structures of Cubism without absorbing all the complexities of Picasso and Braque that were alien to their experience, and of another culture altogether. The American artist more often used the broad planes of Cubism arranged along the outlines of a loose grid or armature that could give him the new directness of expression he sought. Thus, in American Cubism we find the vestiges of the style's early phases, or of the open forms of Synthetic Cubism.

A full-blown Cubist idiom did not really appear in American art until 1912 or 1913, in Weber's work as well as that of Bruce and other American painters, who used Cubism as a framework to carry their colour. However, we do find a new emphasis on a clear, firm structure that would replace the Impressionist touch and surface, which was increasingly seen as too soft, lacking in real order and solid form. This drive for clarity can be traced to previous art, in particular Caravaggio, who saved painting from Mannerist corruption in the late sixteenth century. After Caravaggio and his photographic realism, we might think of Jacques-Louis David, who in turn brought new life and vitality to Western art by making painting strong and clear, after the soft, flowery pastels of the Rococo style. In 1884, first Renoir, then Seurat and Cézanne moved to make something solid of Impressionism, fearing that it had become too fussy and overworked. So, too, a need for clarity, to see what they had done and where they might take Cubism, was behind the move of Picasso and Braque in 1912 to the larger, broader forms of collage and Synthetic Cubism. Thus, Matisse had gone to Italy in the summer of 1907 to relearn painting in effect, fearing that his Fauve art had become weak and unfocused. In each movement, the drive is towards reduced formats and clearer drawing. The 'great artist is the simplifier', said Henri-Frédéric Amiel.[1]

We can find the same process in American art. From about 1860 to 1869, Martin Johnson Heade (1819–1904) did three versions of his famous haystack scenes. In each, the drawing becomes progressively sharper and clearer, the forms more reduced, the light darker and more focused. In 1916, American Cubists dramatically reduced their formats to more distilled patterns. In 1950, we can consider the intensely complex intersections of line and shape in the work of de Kooning, for example, and contrast that with the more open and simplified compositions of his *Merritt Parkway* series. Clyfford Still made a forceful statement about clarity. Kenneth Noland and Morris Louis applied the premises of colour composition in ever more discrete shapes and forms, as in Noland's circles or Louis's strip paintings of 1961–2. In similar fashion, Donald Judd and other Minimalists in the mid-1960s translated the broadness and scale of Pollock and Rothko into the clear outlines of 'specific objects'.

Robert Henri, in his famous classes at the New York School of Art, was teaching just such an emphasis on firmness and strength of form.[2] He subscribed to a fundamental modernist practice of letting materials govern the artist's reactions, so that he responds to the dictates and needs of the painting itself, as he does to the subject. This practice was crucial to Matisse, for example, as outlined in *Notes of a Painter*.[3] It relates to

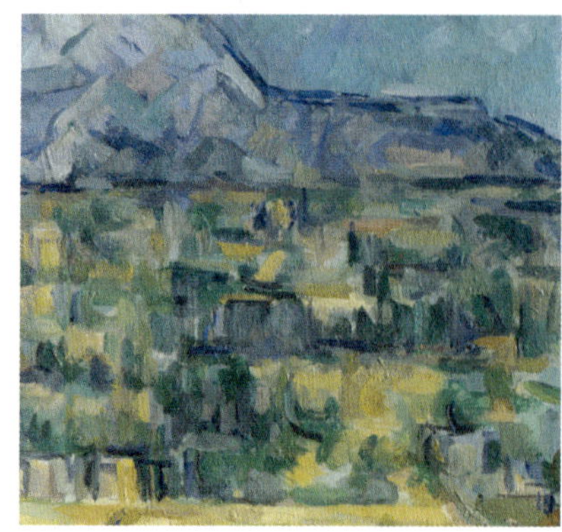

26

26 Paul Cézanne, *Mont Sainte-Victoire* (detail), *c.*1902–6. Oil on canvas, 57.2 × 97.2 cm (22½ × 38¼ in). The Metropolitan Museum of Art, New York

27 Manierre Dawson, *Meeting (The Three Graces)*, 1912. Oil on canvas, 147.6 × 121.9 cm (58⅛ × 48 in). The Metropolitan Museum of Art, New York

Wassily Kandinsky's ideas of painting from internal necessity, as detailed in his influential tract, *On the Spiritual in Art* of 1911, which points to Pollock's later gestural expressionism. The first to develop this principle was actually Alfred Stieglitz, who discussed the idea as early as 1903 and came to find his art in the materials of the film and camera, and who thus must be accorded one more claim as a leading modern artist.[4]

Only in the work of Manierre Dawson (1887–1967) do we find anything resembling the multifaceted divisions of high analytic French Cubism from 1910–11. Dawson, a Chicago artist, did a series of remarkable Cubist-based paintings before 1914 that still remain something of a mystery: he made them with no apparent exposure to Cubism, but how was this possible? Intersecting waves of flowing, broken forms executed in muted colours, as in his *Meeting (The Three Graces)* (1912)[27], a classical theme transferred to a modern setting,[5] seem to embody Henri Bergson's contemporary ideas on the passage of time not as a series of distinct moments but as a duration, with one moment eliding into the next, which in turn merges with the next. Dawson was trained as an engineer-architect, and some of his works from this period have the look and feel of mechanical drawings or engineer's diagrams transformed with soft hues and parts of a Cubist grid, embellished by free arabesques that also speak of music. Here is an American using Cubism for his own purposes, not worrying about adhering to a priori concepts of what a Cubist painting should look like. For the American artist, freedom of individual expression, based on his own experience, real and psychological, was key.

To a great extent, American artists understood Cubism well enough, but they chose to use it to incorporate aspects of an emerging America, also profoundly changing before their eyes as the new century brought one

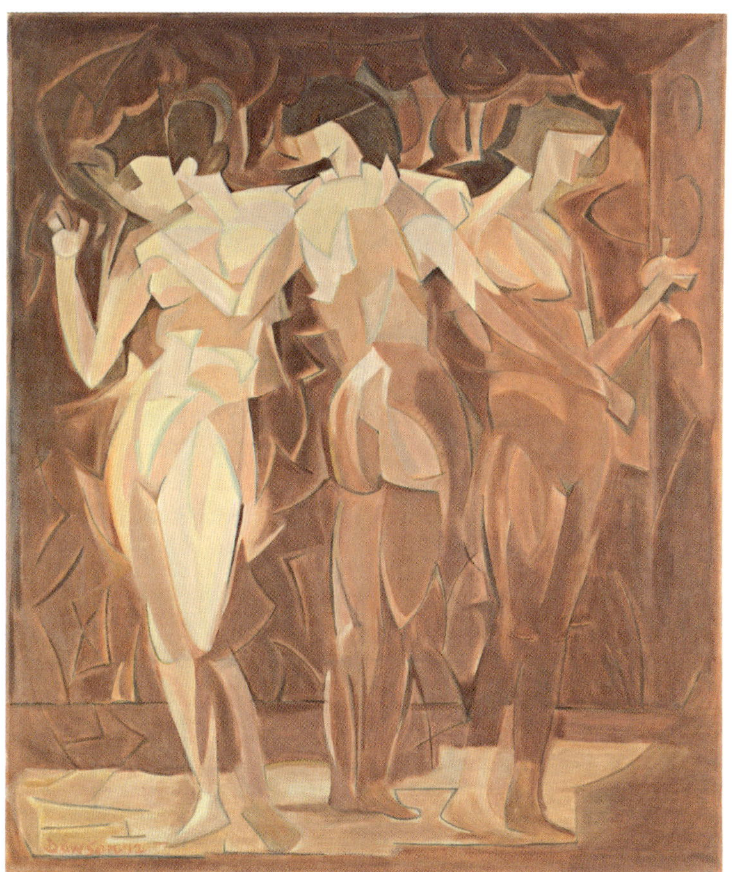

27

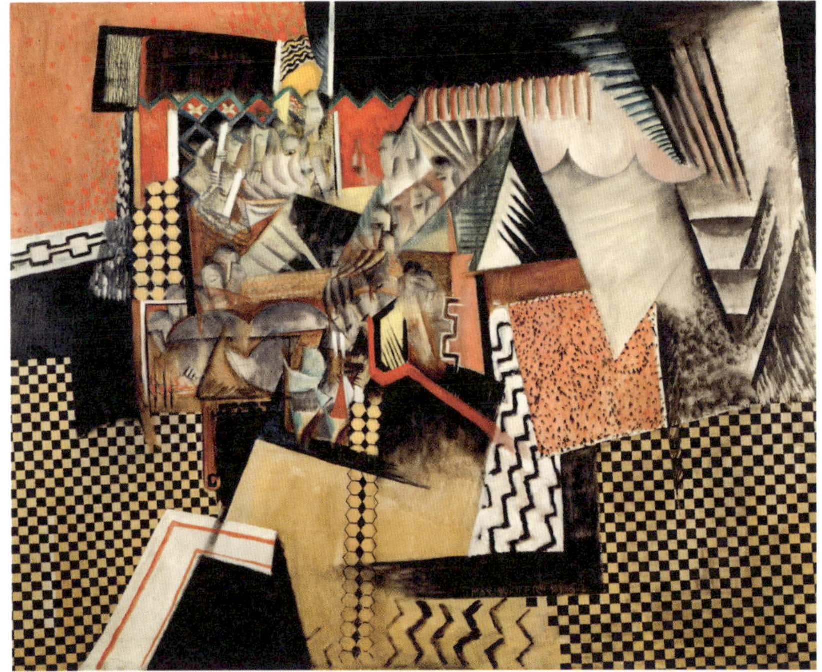

28

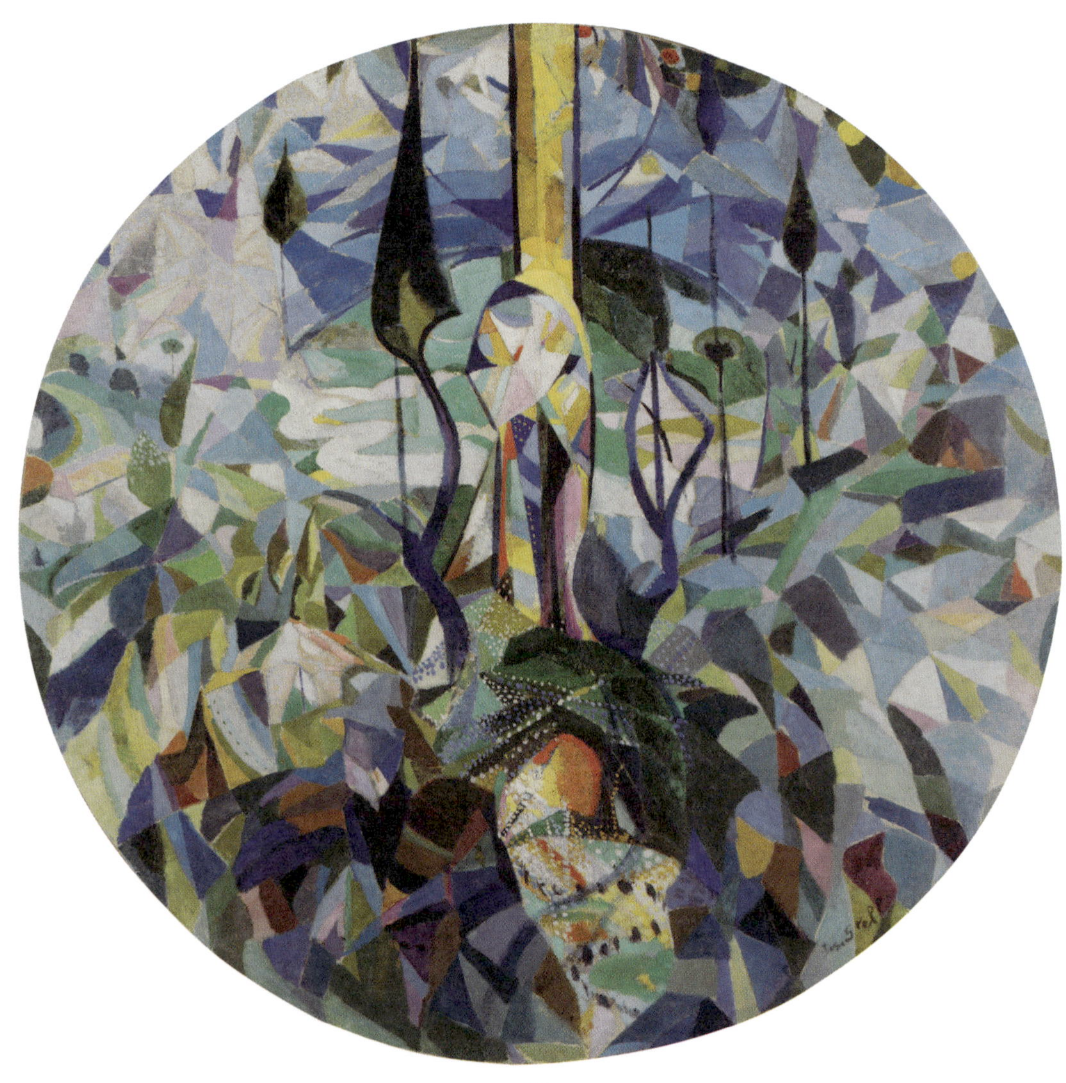

29

Modern Art in America

miracle after another. They could borrow what they needed and leave the rest, a kind of pictorial eclecticism, taken to a high level of working methodology. Speed and dynamic energy were everywhere in New York. In Weber's painting, *Chinese Restaurant* (1915)[28], the pace and constant changes of the city are fused into a brilliant tapestry of architecture, tables, the street and people, all interacting, all demarcated by brilliant colour and contrasts of black and white. In its frank incorporation of architectural elements, such as the tiled floor seen here, American art was in essence developing a new subject matter for Cubism, that of the still life within an architectural setting, virtually absent in European art.

Other American Cubists also aligned themselves in their approach to the genre with the French Cubists. In addition to Henry Fitch Taylor, Dawson and others, we can include Joseph Stella and his brilliant prismatic colour, as in the raucous *Coney Island* (1914)[29]. Here, Stella fuses his Old World experience in Italy and its strong religious life with the madcap energy of the New World, a carnival in itself. However, Cubism in America did not really become an art of high achievement until the early 1920s, when Stuart Davis began an all-out study of its possibilities. Thereafter a new Cubist vein appeared, with the work of Maurer, Bruce, Marin and John Graham, a Russian émigré who, as we shall see in Chapter V, had a deep effect on subsequent Cubist and figurative art.

Stuart Davis and Edward Hopper: Students of Henri

The influence of Henri's teachings on an entire generation – or two – before his death in 1929 was one of the most pervasive and formative factors in the development of modern art in America. Just what Henri taught and how students absorbed his lessons is worth considering. It can be best seen in the careers of Stuart Davis and Edward Hopper, two very different artists whose paths intertwined throughout their lives until their deaths in the 1960s. Hopper was eighteen when he began studying with Henri in 1900, Davis a little younger when he entered Henri's school in 1910. We do not think of Henri as avant-garde, but he was just that in terms of his approach, and his effect on both Davis and Hopper lasted their lifetimes.

Henri urged his students to get to know the properties of their materials and the laws of paint, so that they could make maximum expressive use of them, since art was a matter of invention rather than of reproduction. For Davis, this meant 'the fastest, shortest, plainst [sic] way of expressing the idea at hand', the 'spirit of clarity' that he had admired in Van Gogh, another statement of the modernist drive to eliminate the unessential, to find the most available power and immediacy in the painting.[6] It was later well expressed by Mark Rothko when he spoke of eliminating all obstacles between the artist and the painting, and then between the painting and the viewer.[7] In great part, this accounts for the strong sense of impact, of immediacy, that characterizes the entirety of Davis's art, its 'unprimed fact', 'solid certainties', with 'nothing superficial' and 'everything necessary', as Elaine de Kooning described it.[8] Davis later summed it up by saying, 'I want everything in the picture to be a single impact. That's its unity.'[9]

The same can be said of Hopper, for in his paintings everything is clear and carefully delineated, with a precise and essential place in the composition. There are no superficial or extraneous details, surely a result of his training with Henri. He had absorbed his mentor's teachings that art came from life, the very bustle and grit of the world around us, and, just back from Paris, made them evident in a painting of 1908 entitled

28 Max Weber, *Chinese Restaurant*, 1915. Oil, charcoal and collaged paper on linen, 101.6 × 122.2 cm (40 × 48⅛ in). Whitney Museum of American Art, New York

29 Joseph Stella, *Coney Island*, 1914. Oil on canvas, diameter: 106 cm (41¾ in). The Metropolitan Museum of Art, New York

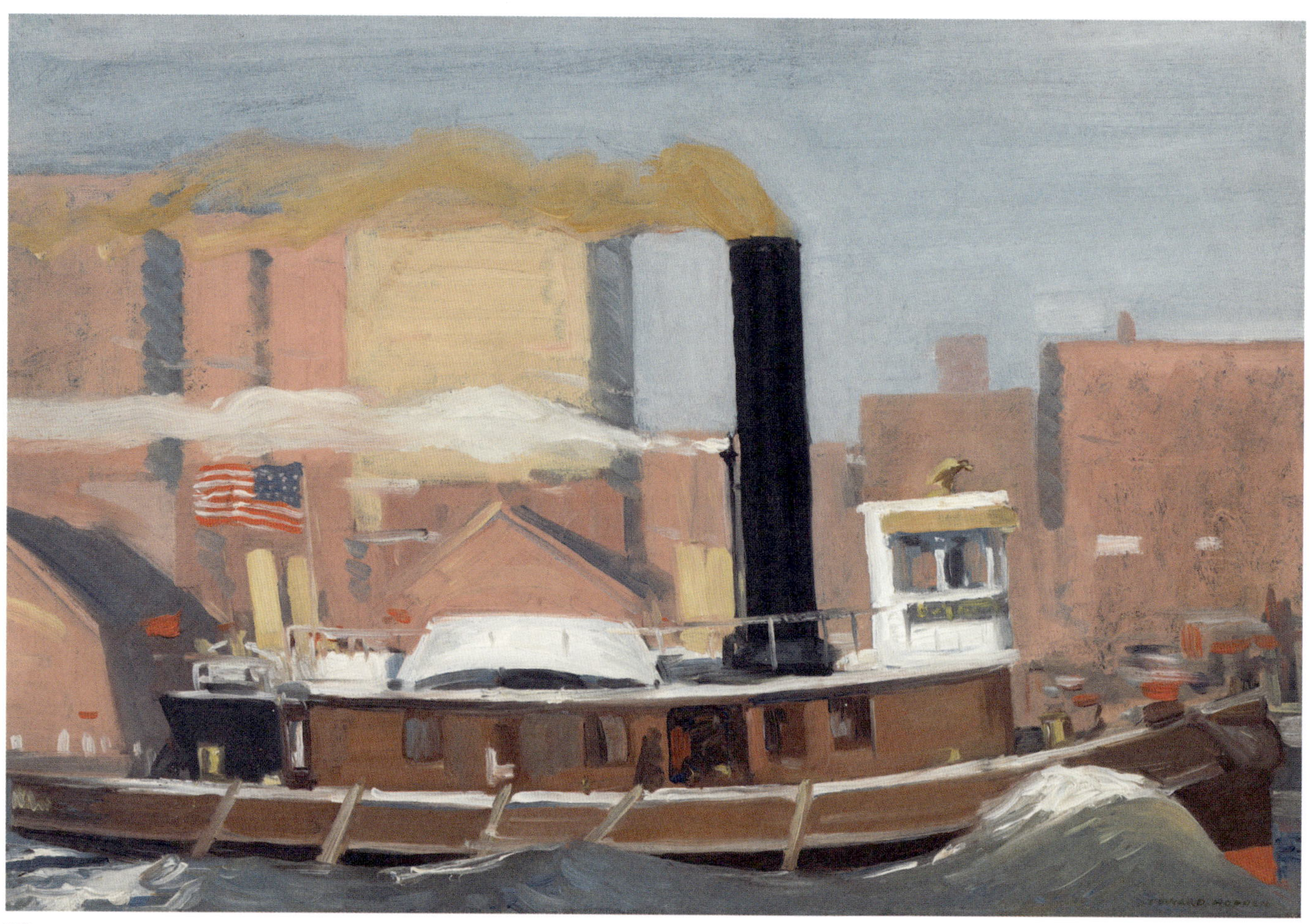

30

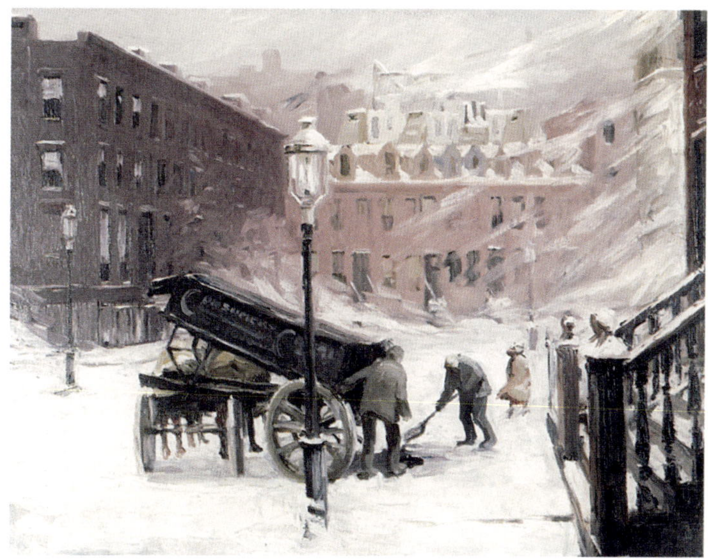

31

Tugboat With Black Smokestack [30]. Although an accurate description of a boat, its structure is based on a series of clearly delineated horizontals and verticals supporting broad planes. The painting shows that Hopper had also absorbed the architectures of Cézanne and Seurat, and the pervasive light of Impressionism, while the almost serial repetition of verticals recalls Monet's *Poplars* (1891), a series that also embodied a concern for a clearer structure. However, light was now made solid and palpable, a trait that defined Hopper's art throughout his life. This spirit of simplification, as Matisse put it to Charles Caffin in an interview of 1909,[10] was intended to make the work a single, organic whole, that could be glimpsed and seen at once, as a unity, thus taking part in the modern democratic move towards the elimination of hierarchies, as in society.

Hopper and Davis could be said to be second-generation Ashcan artists, taken with the energy and drive of the modern American city – New York – but now interested and alert to the more structural direction that contemporary art was taking. They were also more attuned to human emotion and psychology than Henri or the other earlier Ashcan artists.[11] In several of his portraits, Davis evokes concern, anxiety and even alarm, alert to the menace, real and imagined, felt by those living in a modern city. Hopper's *Tugboat* is an embodiment of the modern city and its speed, commerce and movement, and fits the Henri dictum of depicting the world around us. It is also an early, proto-Cubist painting, and forecasts the complex systems of architectural supports that Hopper used in his art throughout his life. Davis showed the same proto-Cubist proclivity in early street scenes, such as *Consumers Coal Company* (1912) [31], even though he did not formally engage Cubism until the early 1920s. For both artists, and for many others, art, as Henri stressed, was rooted in life, derived from the world. Even at his most abstract, Davis always insisted that he was a realist artist. We might say his great achievement was to fuse realism with abstraction, by making abstract art with a real content. The reverse is true of Hopper: even when his art is at its most realist, it is always verging on abstract.

Davis may have remarked later that the Armory Show of 1913 was his 'biggest single influence', but it was Henri who truly taught him how to be an artist, and how to look at art.[12] Henri alerted his students to important contemporary art and exhibitions, such as the Matisse show held at 291 in 1910, and Davis must surely have gone to see this and other significant

30   Edward Hopper, *Tugboat with Black Smokestack*, 1908. Oil on canvas, 51.8 × 74.5 cm (20⅜ × 29⁵⁄₁₆ in). Whitney Museum of American Art, New York

31   Stuart Davis, *Consumers Coal Company*, 1912. Oil on canvas, 74.9 × 95.3 cm (29½ × 37½ in). The Clay Center for the Arts & Sciences of West Virginia, Charleston

shows staged by Stieglitz. Henri encouraged his students to be open-minded, to look at avant-garde art, so that after the Armory Show, Davis could say that he responded to Gauguin, Van Gogh and Matisse because 'broad generalization of form and non-imitative use of colour were already in my own experience.'[13] The Armory Show was a bomb, but it was not a 'bomb that was unexpected', he said; not so much a challenge as 'a boost to something I already felt'.[14] He had been ready for the big event, primarily because of Henri.

Through Henri, drawing was established in Davis's practice as fundamental to the construction of a good work of art, and remained at its core throughout his life. At times, a large-scale drawing, in oil on canvas or on paper, was the complete work in itself, not a study for something else, as witnessed in his linear, open works of 1932 and the oils done solely in black and white after 1955. As late as 1954, Davis would write: 'A Drawing is the correct title for my work.'[15] Line, for Henri as well as Davis, gave sureness, solidity and clarity, making the painting an architectural construction. The belief in drawing might have been spurred in part by Picasso's masterful charcoal drawing *Standing Female Nude* (1910)[32], which Stieglitz purchased from the Armory Show and could have been seen at his various galleries until his death in 1946.

John Sloan as Teacher

Ashcan art was the first American movement to stake its roots in the principle of The Real. While Henri and Bellows are the best known of the Ashcan artists, we must also pay special attention to John Sloan (1871–1951), both as artist and teacher.[16] He was six years younger than Henri, whose tenets of an art drawn from life were also central for him. Sloan followed Henri from Philadelphia to New York, and thereafter until 1920 made compelling and powerful paintings of the latter city that are now icons of American art. In fact, he was a far better painter than Henri and at his best rivalled and even surpassed Bellows. In such well-known paintings of 1907 as *McSorley's Bar*, *The Wake of the Ferry II* and *Election Night*, Sloan truly captured the dynamism of the city through compositions that embody the movements and structures of life in New York. They are far more daring and precipitous than any that Henri or Bellows put forth. Sloan could never commit to a full-blown modernism – he was a man of the nineteenth century – but he was intrigued by it, studied it and urged others, especially younger artists, to look hard at it.

However, Sloan may have been more of a modernist than he – or his audience – knew. In *The Wake of the Ferry II*[33], a lone passenger stands under the rough rectangle formed by the steel girders of the boat's stern. The single melancholy figure points back to the work of Caspar David Friedrich, but now transferred into a modern urban setting: she is framed by the raw steel and iron, the materials of the modern age, which only partly shield her from the power of nature. It raises many questions – what are we leaving behind in our wake? Where are we going? Who are we? – that remind us of the questions posed by Gauguin in his painting *Where Do We Come From? What Are We? Where Are We Going?* (1897–8), questions central to Symbolist art. Sloan himself described the work as melancholy.[17] The woman is his wife, Dolly, on the 23rd Street ferry that she took to connect with a train in New Jersey to transport her to Philadelphia for treatment of her alcoholism. Where is Sloan himself? Standing, watching her, or imagining her from a distance while by himself? We do not know. But it is a terrifying painting, echoing and embodying

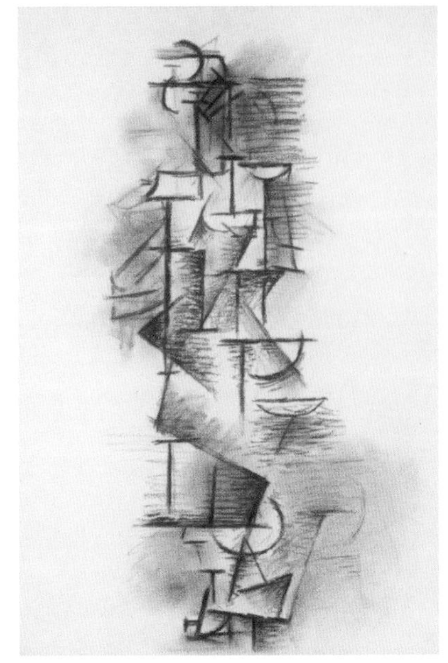

32

32 Pablo Picasso, *Standing Female Nude*, 1910. Charcoal on paper, 48.3 × 31.4 cm (19 × 12⅜ in). The Metropolitan Museum of Art, New York

33 John Sloan, *The Wake of the Ferry II*, 1907. Oil on canvas, 66 × 81.3 cm (26 × 32 in). The Phillips Collection, Washington, DC

Modern Art in America

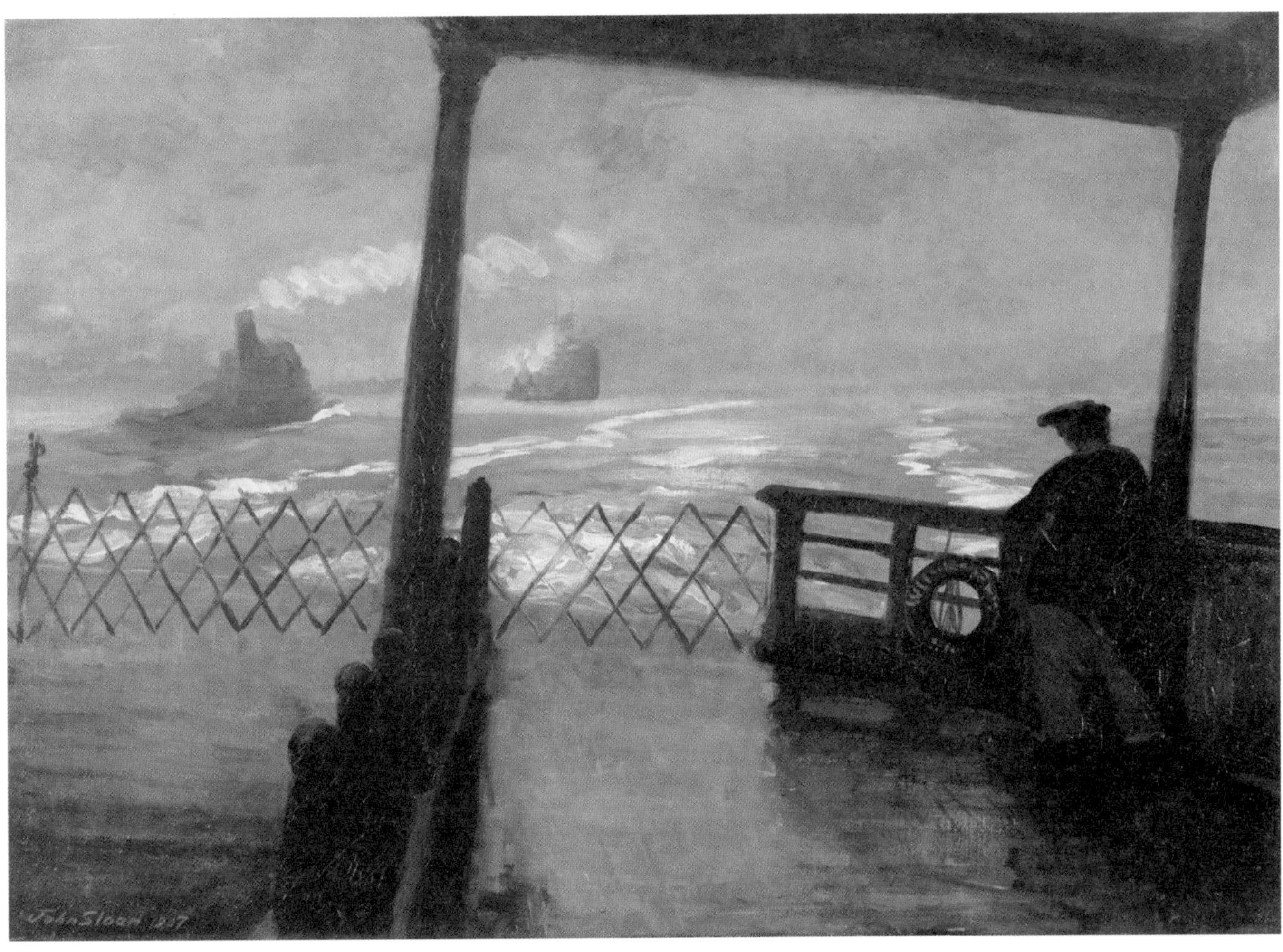

33

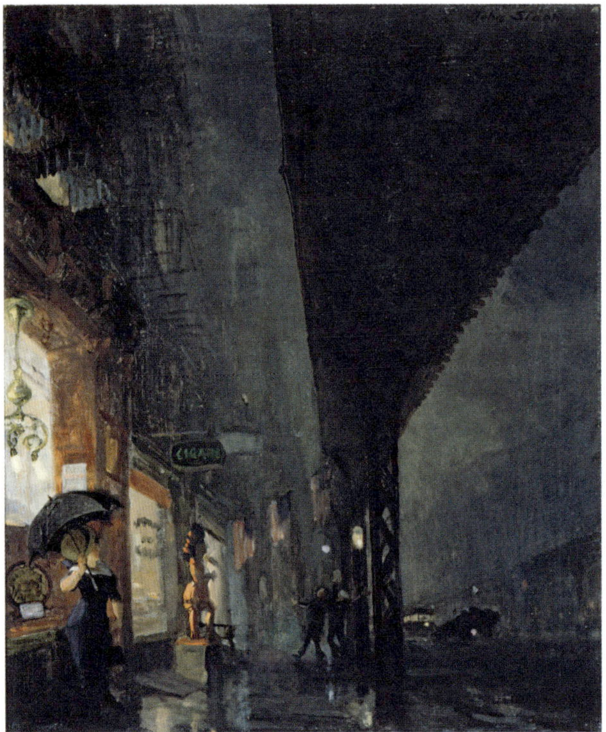

34

the powerful forces of the modern age. The uncertainty, the outright fear of alcoholism, and of the new century itself, are inherent in the grey, rainy atmosphere, the choppy waters, from which we can feel emanating a bone-chilling isolation. Sloan's melancholy mood – he was broke and mourning the recent loss of his father – is underscored by the emptiness at the centre, the place usually of prime importance to a painting. The core is absent. The overhanging frame of steel becomes the central and defining form of the painting, the new, elemental structure that, as we have seen, was making its appearance in world art. It is no coincidence that Picasso's Cubist masterpiece *Les Demoiselles d'Avignon* was also done this year, and, like Hopper's paintings of the time, Sloan's work might be termed a proto-Cubist painting in the sense of its profound shift towards a new, simplified structure, clarity and directness. With this one painting, we may well consider Sloan at the advanced edge of modern art.

The skewed tilt of the steel frame in Sloan's painting also indicates a world of speed and change, constantly being built and rebuilt, no longer given to stability and permanence. In his 1927 article on Sloan, Hopper likened this angle to those used by Edgar Degas, to destabilize the painting.[18] Similarly, we cannot help but think ahead to Franz Kline and his core construction of the rough rectangle first seen in his *Wotan*, 1950 (see page 269), particularly when we view other paintings by Sloan, such as *Wet Night on the Bowery* (1911)[34], with the overhead El tracks hurtling down the middle of the painting, a large black shape that we find so often in Kline's work. Sloan loved to depict the El, cutting across the picture plane, shooting into the night sky, and into the future, as in *Six O'Clock, Winter* (1912). Sloan's views from on high, as in *Jefferson Market* (1917 and 1922)[35] or *The City from Greenwich Village* (1922), were novel for the time and are reflected in Charles Sheeler's film *Manhatta* (1921) and his *Church Street El* (1920). These perspectives surely demonstrate an increasing sense of the world as now viewed by the aviator. Further, Sloan was one of the first, if not the first, to include scenes inside a cinema, with the

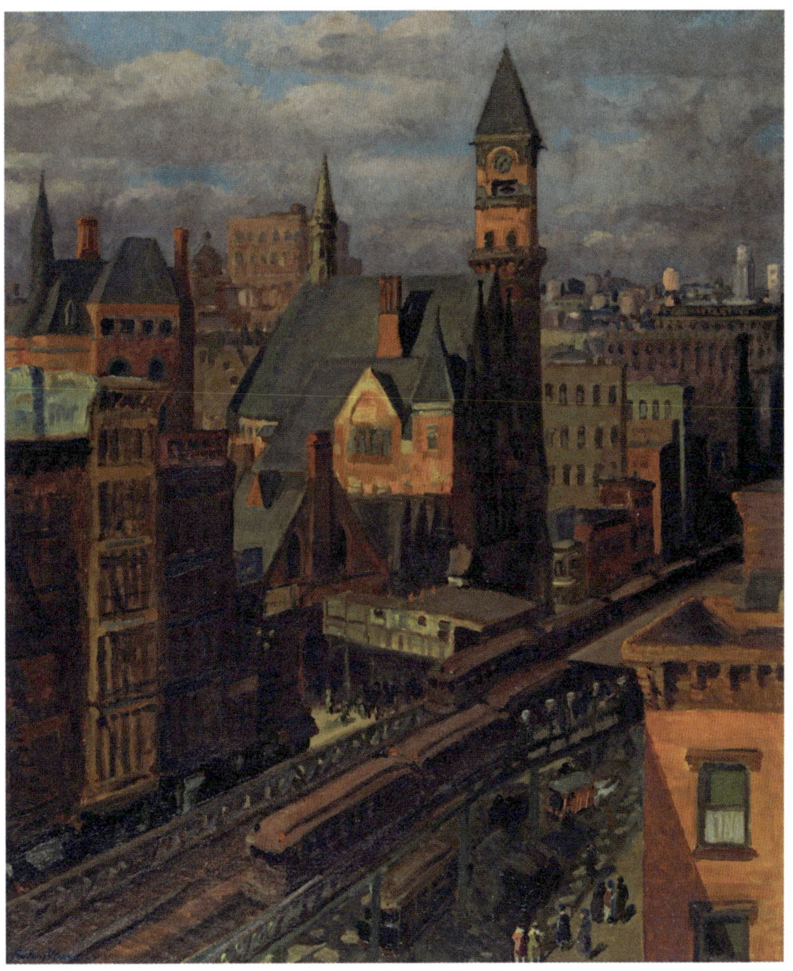

35

screen itself and the action on it dominating the painting. In *The Wake of the Ferry II*, the large rectangle resembles a cinema screen, framing the lone figure and the churning waters, so emblematic of her (and his) psychological state.

In many ways, Sloan was as great a teacher as Henri, although he has received less notice for this role. Davis, in particular, looked to his art and to his example to lead him as he began to mature as an artist and person, following Sloan's advice to go to Gloucester, Massachusetts, where he summered. It was a revelation for Davis, who subsequently visited the port every year until 1940. Davis comes out of Ashcan and New York Realism, and we think of him as a quintessential New Yorker, loving the pace and movement and the jazz of the big city. But in fact he was as much a member of the Gloucester and Cape Ann school, a marine and landscape artist responding to the beauty of the architecture, fields and sea. In Gloucester, Davis began to explore colour and expressionist brushwork that were indebted to Cézanne, Van Gogh and Matisse, much of it while working in Sloan's house there, where all manner of artists also worked and lived.

Davis looked closely at Sloan's art, too. In 1907, Sloan made his remarkable *Hairdresser's Window* [36], a kaleidoscope of urban energy, including a crowd of people and a wall of billboards and posters. It may well be the first painting that used such an array of commercial images — a distant father of the Pop sensibility first seen in the late 1950s. Further, the dyeing of the hair from blonde to red shrieks an erotic note, especially since the parting of the hair suggests a vaginal opening. Davis seems to

34   John Sloan, *Wet Night on the Bowery*, 1911. Oil on canvas, 68.6 × 55.9 cm (27 × 22 in). Delaware Art Museum, Wilmington

35   John Sloan, *Jefferson Market*, 1917, 1922. Oil on canvas, 81.3 × 66.4 cm (32 × 26⅛ in). Pennsylvania Academy of the Fine Arts, Philadelphia

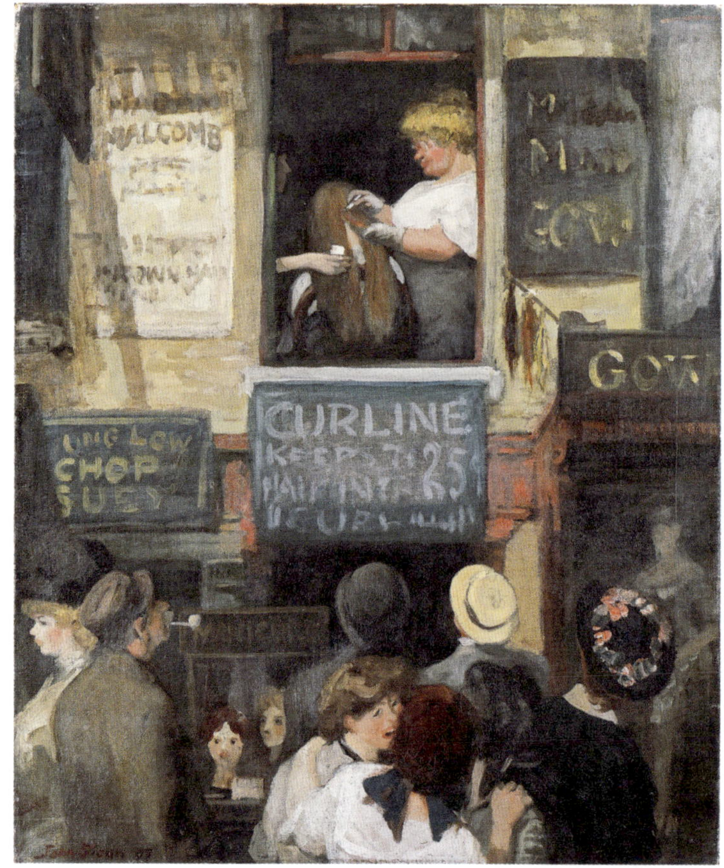

36

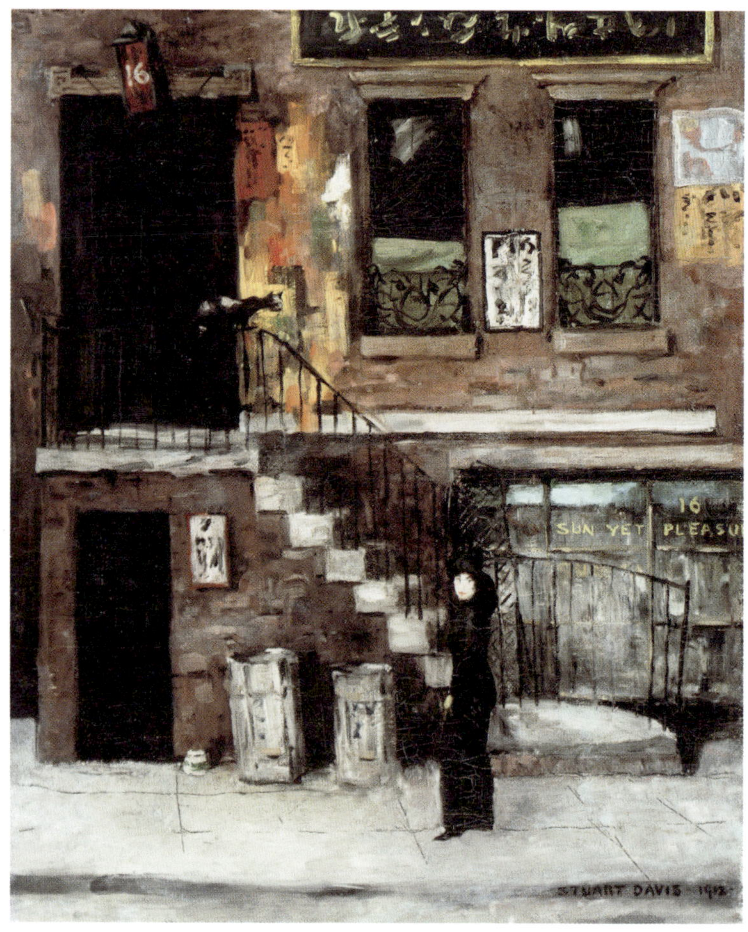

37

Modern Art in America

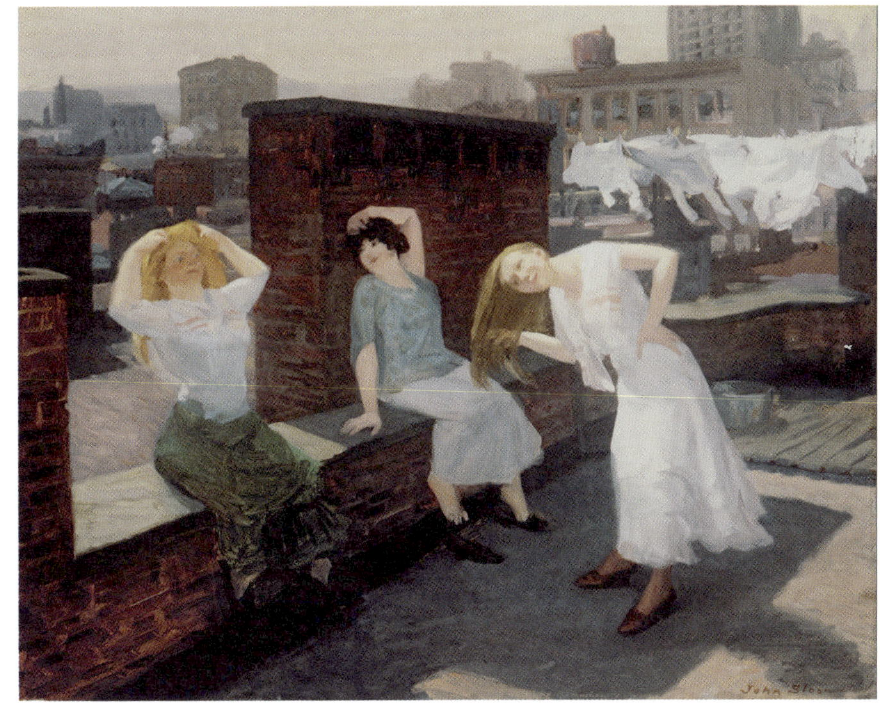

38

36 John Sloan, *Hairdresser's Window*, 1907. Oil on canvas, 81.3 × 66 cm (32 × 26 in). Wadsworth Atheneum Museum of Art, Hartford

37 Stuart Davis, *Chinatown*, 1912. Oil on canvas, 94 × 76.2 cm (37 × 30 in). Private collection

38 John Sloan, *Sunday, Women Drying their Hair*, 1912. Oil on canvas, 66.4 × 81.6 cm (26⅛ × 32⅛ in). Addison Gallery of American Art, Phillips Academy, Andover

39 Stuart Davis, *Servant Girls*, 1913. Watercolour and pencil on paper, 38.1 × 27.9 cm (15 × 11 in). Munson-Williams-Proctor Arts Institute, Utica, New York

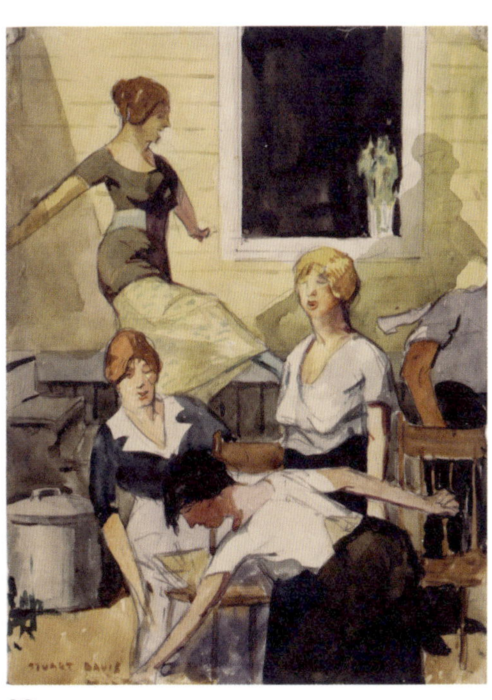

39

have used this structure as at least a partial model in his *Chinatown* (1912)[37], although he takes a more distant view, and focuses on a solitary figure, who looks at us with some curiosity and surprise. Sloan's compendium of advertisements, with their visual and audio impact, as well as an inherent order and structure, stayed with Davis, and appeared in a more abstracted version in his *Garage* (1917), as well as in his brilliant *Premiere* (1957) (see page 249), a distilled word collage of supermarket products. Sloan loved the hurly-burly low-life of New York, and often depicted women of ill repute. (In fact, he had met Dolly in a brothel in Philadelphia on a sporting night out with Davis's father.) Ladies of pleasure are surely the subjects in paintings by Sloan such as *Three AM* (1909), *Red Kimono* and *Sunday, Women Drying their Hair*[38] (both 1912). Davis was equally drawn to these illicit subjects and echoed Sloan in his versions of *Servant Girls* (1913)[39].

When Sloan began to focus on large classicizing nudes after 1920, he lost his modernist edge and his work fell off badly. But a lasting heritage came from his teaching at the Art Students League in New York. In his book *The Gist of Art* (1939), he spoke of the importance of drawing and painting figures in order to preserve and extend a long tradition. It seems certain that he passed this on in the 1920s to students such as John Graham, who deeply respected Sloan, his first teacher early in the decade. In turn, we may speculate with some confidence that Graham shared this penchant with Arshile Gorky and Willem de Kooning. Together, the three artists produced some of the best, most original figuration of the time, which was original yet carried on the grandeur of the Renaissance portrait tradition.[19] At the same time, they were all extending the second wave of Cubist abstraction in America. Their varied means can be traced to Picasso, but Sloan's teachings were certainly an important ingredient in their approaches. For de Kooning, the three ribald young women in Sloan's *Sunday, Women Drying their Hair* may well have been a prototype for his series of *Women* from the late 1930s to the late 1950s, his own take on the city girls that Sloan loved to depict.

THE ARMORY SHOW

The famous Armory Show, held in New York[25], then Boston and Chicago in 1913,[20] deservedly retains a singular place in American art, for it introduced modern art to a broad audience there for the first time and showed its true achievements with a depth and quality never seen before, either there or in Europe, for that matter. On show were paintings of intense colour that affected American art for decades to come, but they are seldom noted in our histories as conveyors of a new and heightened colour expression in modern art.

Works from Van Gogh's iconic series of paintings such as *Olive Trees* (1889) and *St Remy* (1889–90) were a major presence. If we imagine seeing them afresh, we will understand the profound effect they have had on American art. They are paintings, as was *The Starry Night* (1889)[40], that touch on every theme considered in this book. The young Davis responded to their rich hues, the deep blues and greens, the explosive brushing of the sky, in his work after 1913, especially his powerful land-scapes of 1917. When we take into consideration colour as a material, as a physical element of weight and density, both formal and expressive, we can easily project ourselves years ahead to the surfaces of Pollock and Alfred Jensen that seem to be made of nothing but dense paint, at times becoming virtual reliefs. The twisting, turning shapes, coming from

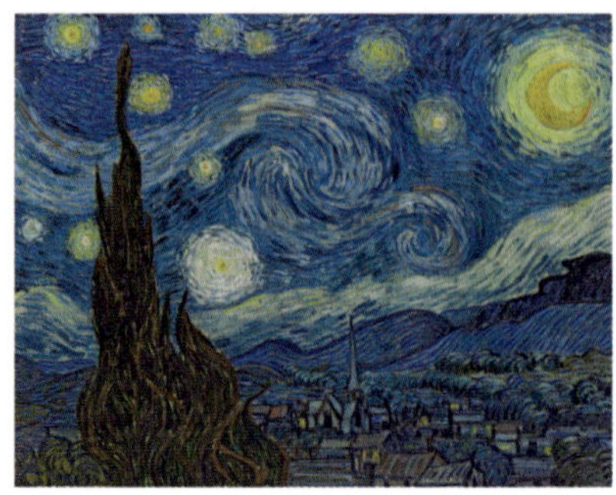

40

40   Vincent Van Gogh, *The Starry Night*, 1889. Oil on canvas, 73.7 × 92.1 cm (29 × 36¼ in). The Museum of Modern Art, New York

41   Frederic Remington, *Moonlight, Wolf*, c.1909. Oil on canvas, 50.9 × 66 cm (20¹⁄₁₆ × 26 in). Addison Gallery of American Art, Phillips Academy, Andover

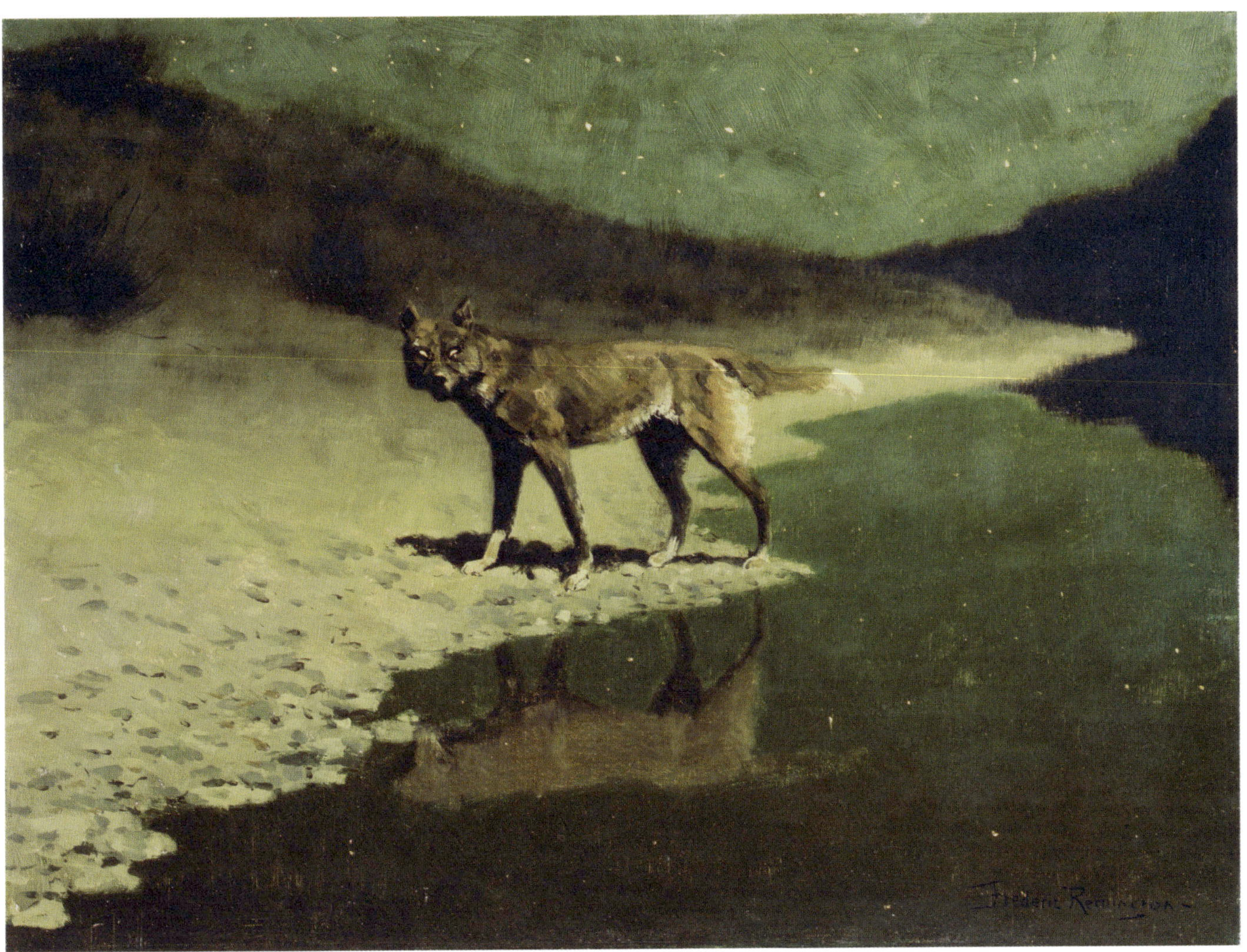

41

a painterly motor impulse, conveying energy in themselves, stand at the heart of generations of expressionist art in America. The overt sense of seeking a higher order in *Starry Night* – the tree and church spire touching the heavens – is a prime source for an ongoing American sense of spirituality, a striving for another realm beyond the material world, that was to reach deeply into American art.

A fascination with the cosmos had already appeared in the late work of Frederic Remington (1861–1909), for example, in his haunting *Moonlight Wolf* (c.1909) [41], a remarkably modern painting for its sense of the contingency of existence. Its image of a lone creature, isolated before the forces and the vastness of the cosmos, echoes the modern human condition. Its simple yet inspiring depiction of the universe, the dots of distant yellow stars reflected in the water, connecting the earth, its creatures and the heavens, suggests a New World rendition of Van Gogh. So, too, the sense of threat to the wolf seems to suggest the gradual disappearance of the western frontier. Remington's painting, filled with Symbolist mystery, may also be taken as the start of a long American interest in nocturnal scenes, as in the work of Georgia O'Keeffe and Arthur Dove in the 1920s. Its dark mood also parallels a similar mood in Hartley's haunting 'Dark Mountain' series of 1909 (see page 41).

Another artist who was shown in depth at the Armory Show, and who had a strong impact on Americans, especially Dove and O'Keeffe, was Odilon Redon. Best known for his haunting Symbolist imagery, he was at the same time a masterful colourist whose rich, velvety hues and surfaces, done in pastel, were well known and respected in the early decades of the last century. He lived until 1916, and would have been considered a living part of the older generation, including Monet, Rodin and Renoir, who continued to affect modern art well into the 1920s. The rubbed, smoothed surfaces of Dove and O'Keeffe, as well as their imagery – particularly O'Keeffe's flowers – show an awareness of Redon and the possibilities of his colour, including its hues and its diffused spread and touch.

These artists and developments form much of the backbone of modern art in America. However, they have been underplayed in considerations of the Armory Show in favour of the perceived impact of Duchamp and his single entry, the now canonical *Nude Descending a Staircase (No.2)* (1912)[42], where the movement of the subject as she descends the steps is recorded on the canvas. This perception was largely generated by two famous cartoons in the press lampooning the painting, one called 'Rude Descending a Staircase' and the other 'Here She Is: White Outline Shows "Nude Descending a Staircase".'[21] Otherwise, the effect of Duchamp at the show was nothing compared to the large walls of intense colour, unique in modern history, that culminated the progression through the installation. Indeed, it may well be that we will never see again so stunning and totally new a display. Duchamp's prominence at the Armory has also been overblown as the result of later publications, in both books and magazines, where the *Nude* became the symbol of the show – perhaps in part because its vertical format fits well into layouts on covers and interior pages.[22] Such are the ways that history can be – erroneously – written. This is not to minimize Duchamp's subsequent effect on modern art in America. It was profound and lasting, and if modern art can be said to be at heart a case of Matissean painting versus Duchampian Conceptualism, Duchamp is leading by a landslide.

The Impact of *The Red Studio*

We often forget that Matisse was also a target for the abuse of artists, critics and public at the Armory; they laughed at Duchamp and Picasso, but they were angry with Matisse. He was the one hung in effigy in Chicago when the show was there; he was the one mocked for his apparent lack of anatomical knowledge, for the four toes on one of his figures. Yet the legacy that has come down to us from his art at the Armory Show, and in particular *The Red Studio* (1911)[43], has been as important to subsequent painting as Picasso's Cubist works of the same year, a fact that has not been understood simply because the importance of colour and colour painting has not been widely enough recognized.[23]

The Red Studio galvanized countless American artists, both then and later. Davis used it rapidly and decisively as a model to define and expand his colour usage, helping him in no small measure to become, as he said, a modern artist. (It is worth restating that colour was Davis's entry point into modernism, not Cubism, which he only began to develop in the early 1920s.) Done in the summer of 1913, when he was not yet twenty-one, his painting *Ebb Tide, Provincetown*[44] speaks dramatically of its immediate impact. It was the artist's first large and important landscape painting, and represented a sharp break from urban realism. Through its flowing shapes and rich coloration, Davis introduced a broader, more open and expressive type of painting. The essence of the work, however, is a homage to the American mystic painter Albert Pinkham Ryder, whose work had been shown in depth at the Armory, and his haunting and darkened

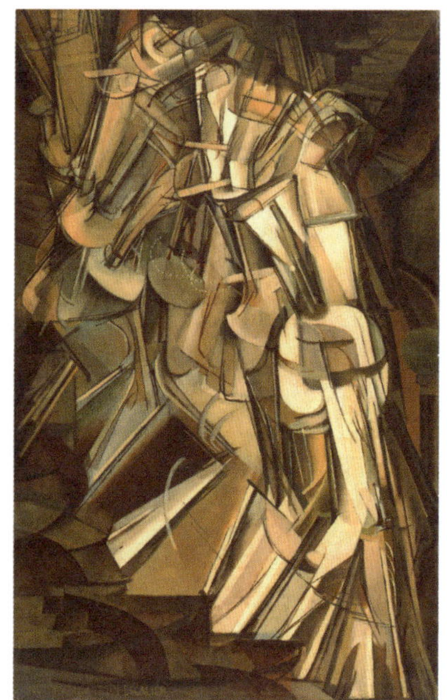

42

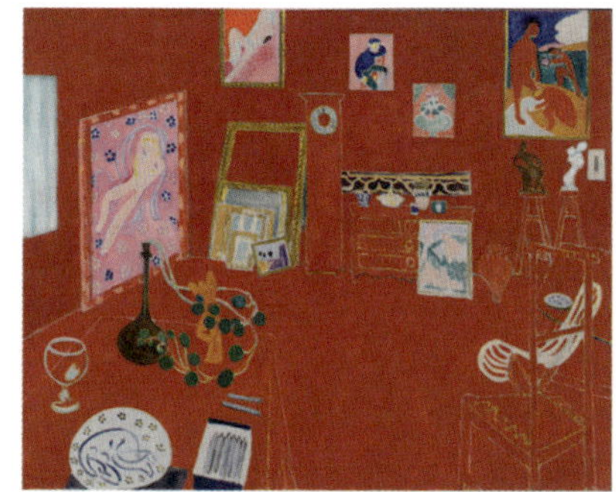

43

Modern Art in America

42 Marcel Duchamp, *Nude Descending a Staircase (No.2)*, 1912. Oil on canvas, 147 × 89.2 cm (57⅞ × 35⅛ in). Philadelphia Museum of Art

43 Henri Matisse, *The Red Studio, Issy-les-Moulineaux*, 1911. Oil on canvas, 181 × 219.1 cm (71¼ × 86¼ in). The Museum of Modern Art, New York

44 Stuart Davis, *Ebb Tide, Provincetown*, 1913. Oil on canvas, 96.5 × 76.2 cm (38 × 30 in). Curtis Galleries, Minneapolis

45 Stuart Davis, *Studio Interior*, 1917. Oil on canvas, 48.3 × 58.4 cm (19 × 23 in). The Metropolitan Museum of Art, New York

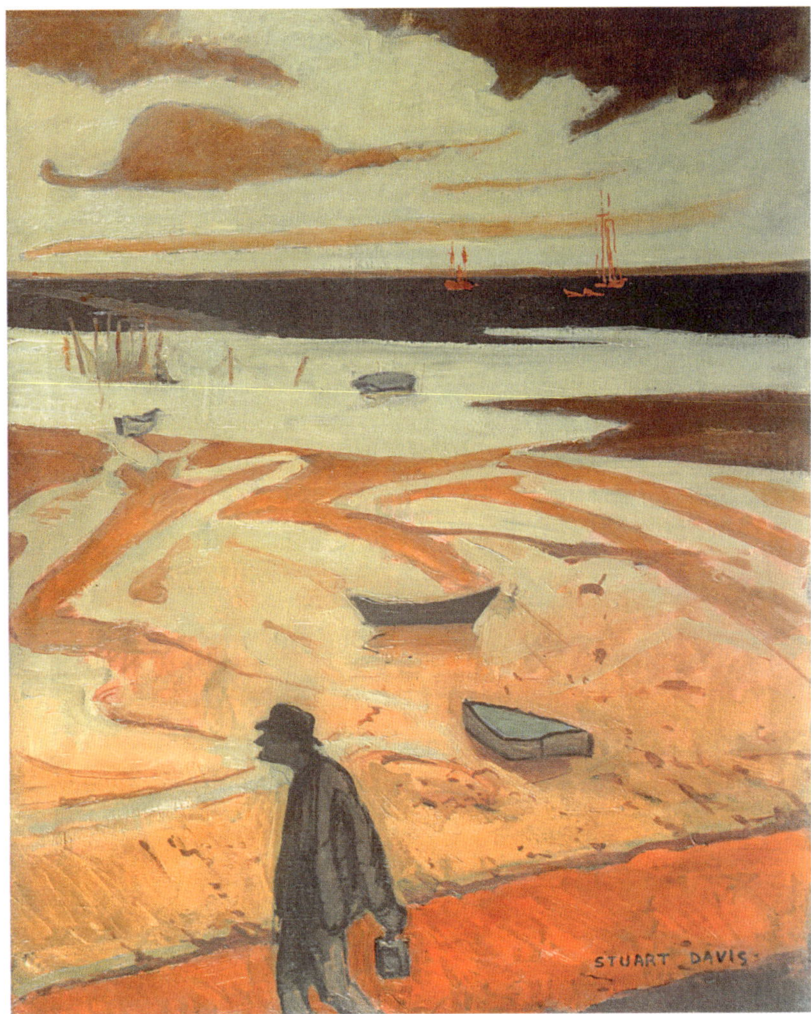

44

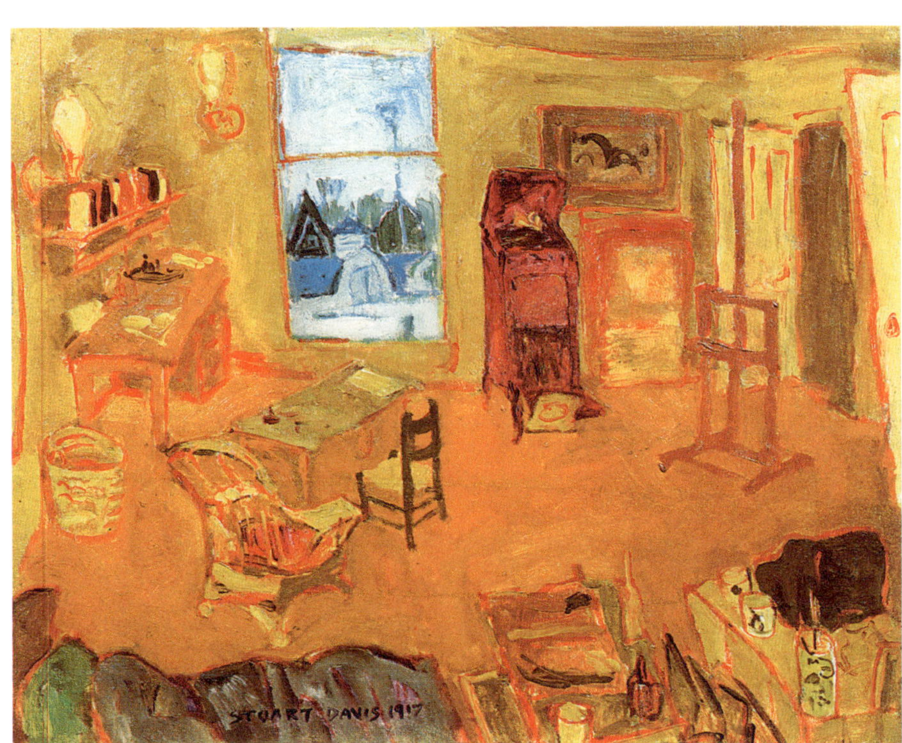

45

reveries of heavy, thick paint. After 1914, Davis's art became bright, airy and syncopated like the jazz he always loved, but here he explored the dark side of the soul, literally the ebb tide of the persona, a Symbolist venture into the very being of man.

In 1917, Davis made his own version of *The Red Studio*, called simply *Studio Interior*[45], the start of his lifelong quest to match the intensity of Matisse's colour and use it as a primary structural element to build and to carry the painting, through what he called his 'colour-space' method. Here, Davis acknowledges Matisse but offers a gentle critique, respectfully suggesting how one might really do it. Orange forms the core hue in Davis's painting, but it is only a start and the painting becomes inflected with manifold nuances of red and orange, a sharp contrast to Matisse's airtight curtain of red. Davis's studio is far from airless and hermetic: it looks out on to a snow scene with smoke curling from a nearby chimney, and is also much more homely, more personal, with such modern devices as a victrola, for he loved the most up-to-date technology and inventions.

The Red Studio's presence in the Armory Show marked a broader inroad of colour into American art. Morton Livingston Schamberg (1881–1918), an important but still lesser-known artist, owing primarily to his early death in the flu pandemic of 1918, used Matisse as his guide to take his landscapes and figures into a realm of intense colour. In his painting *Figure A* (1913)[46], Schamberg referred to two works by Matisse. One was certainly *The Red Studio*; the other was *Back I*, the first of a series of four sculptures, started in 1909, that was also shown in the Armory. Schamberg's figure is massive, even more so than Matisse's sculpture, divided into quadrants suggested by a new awareness of Cubism; however, it is the

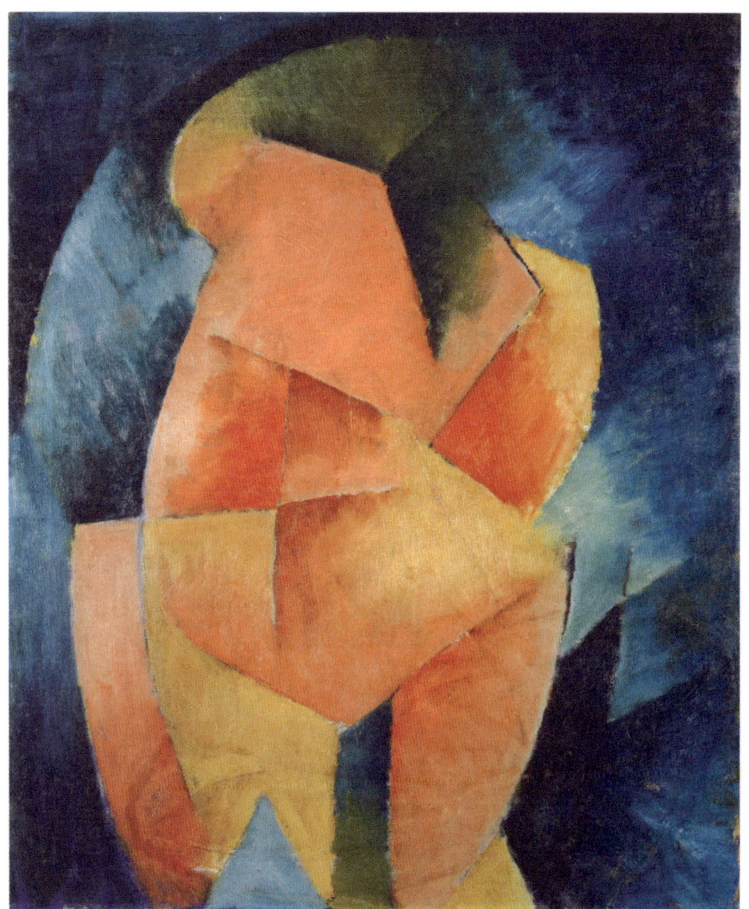

46

46　Morton Livingston Schamberg,
　　Figure A (Geometrical Patterns),
　　1913. Oil on canvas,
　　81 × 66 cm (32 × 26 in).
　　Myron Kunin Collection of
　　American Art, Minneapolis

47　Charles Sheeler, *Abstraction:*
　　Tree Form, 1914. Oil on board,
　　34.3 × 26.6 cm (13½ × 10½ in).
　　Private collection

　　　　　　　Modern Art in America

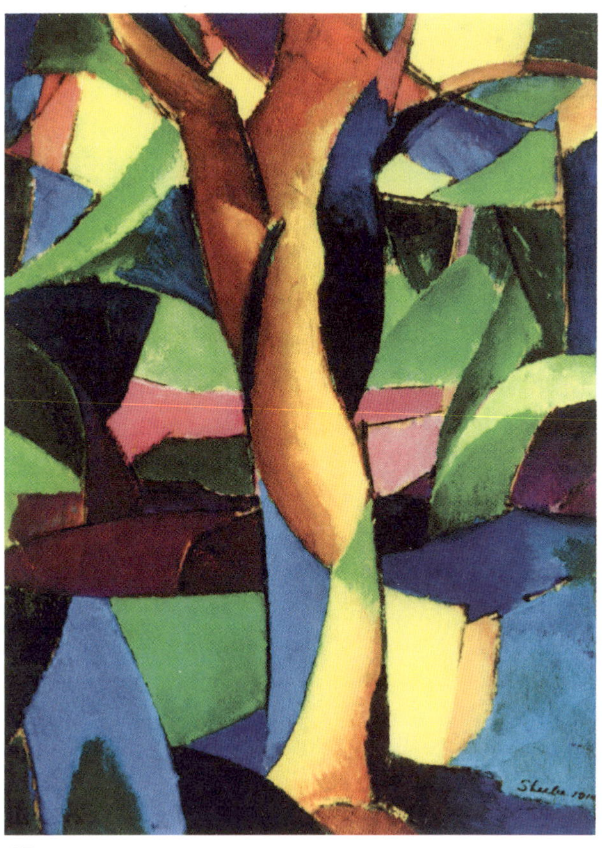

47

brilliant array of oranges and reds, bleeding together within the figure's outlines, set against a deep blue background, that defines the painting and gives it its commanding presence.

Schamberg was born and educated in Philadelphia, and trained there side by side with his dear friend Charles Sheeler. Together, they travelled to Europe in 1908, absorbing the work of the new masters of modernism, including Cézanne. But equally important to them was their close study of early Italian Renaissance art, and their goal soon became a modern, progressive art based on and embodying the sureness of Old Master drawing. By 1913, Schamberg had undertaken a series of monumental nudes recalling those of the late Cézannes, seen through the filtering eye of Matisse and his colour nuances, as was so often the case with American artists. In an article of 1913, Schamberg referred to the 'masterly production' of Cézanne, an admiration evident in his landscapes and his standing figures related to Synchromism-Orphism of 1913.[24]

Schamberg's friend, Charles Sheeler (1883–1965), also responded early on to *The Red Studio*, and in 1914 made works such as *Abstraction: Tree Form* [47], composed of chords and triads of primary and secondary hues. These paintings can properly be understood as belonging to the Synchromist-Orphist body of colour painting that was, as we shall see, such a significant part of pre-war art. Curiously enough, Sheeler stayed only briefly with colour. He was most struck by Matisse's line, and not the colour orchestrations. Even more curiously, when we look carefully at the painting, we see that the lines are not truly drawn, but are actually the interstices between the coloured areas. Strange, perhaps, but a telling indication of the kind of close attention that Matisse's art drew. In turn, the attraction to the line was in keeping with Sheeler's and Schamberg's interest in the pure drawing – the line of early Italian Renaissance art.

American Artists at the Armory

The standard narrative of the Armory Show insists that only the European artists had any real presence, with virtually no American art of note. Thanks to a historic exhibition organized by the distinguished curators and scholars Gail Stavitsky and Laurette McCarthy for the Montclair Art Museum in 2013, this view has begun to change. Established and emerging Americans of real import were exhibited, among them many of the characters already mentioned in this book – Bluemner, Bruce, Carles, Dawson, Hartley, Sloan, Henri, Marin, Schamberg, Sheeler and Prendergast – as well as Walt Kuhn and the precocious Davis and Hopper. In fact, there were numerous American artists of real talent who have virtually disappeared from our histories, but who call out for our further attention – Florence Howell Barkley (1880–1954), Leon Dabo (1864–1960), Kathleen McEnery (Cunningham) (1885–1971), Van Dearing Perrine (1867–1955), Katherine Dreier (1877–1952) and Edward Middleton Manigault (1887–1922), all of whom came to light in the Montclair exhibition. The quality and originality of their paintings startle us, all the more so for being such complete surprises. Yet in the clamour over the novelty and the sheer number of European avant-garde artists, their presence has been largely overlooked.

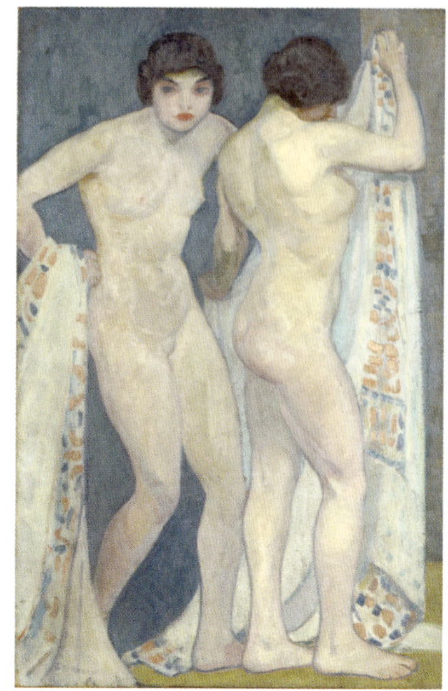

48

One example was Barkley's *Macombs Dam Bridge (Landscape over the City)* (1910–11). It depicts an ostensibly common view of New York, but its intense and rapid expressionist strokes transform the scene into a setting of cataclysmic eruptions that give us a sense of impending doom, of a world in the midst of an earthquake, about to end in violent eruptions. The brushwork is open, loose and intense, and makes us think ahead some forty years to the rise of post-1945 Expressionism. We know virtually nothing about Barkley, but she calls us into a new and unfamiliar world, perhaps a metaphor for the many sudden changes the new modern society brought on.

On the other hand, we can turn to another type of world altogether, in the soft, mysterious and calming (or disturbing) landscape rendered by Leon Dabo in *Evening North Sierra* (1910) [49]. We are enveloped in an atmosphere of infinite nuances of grey, recalling the misty greys of Whistler, through which we can hardly determine the actual substance or imagery of the scene. It too takes us away from the here and now, recalling German Romantic painting and suggesting unknown voyages yet to come.

Other Symbolist settings are found in Cunningham's startling *Going to the Bath* (c.1905–13) [48], in which two female nude figures fill the canvas. The painting is cast in an atmosphere of blues that remind us of Picasso's early work. One figure stares back at us, echoing our surprise at this new-found marvel of a painting. Only then does it become clear that the figures are the same person, caught in a turning, sequential motion that is a direct reflection of the recent studies of human and animal locomotion carried out by Eadweard Muybridge and Étienne-Jules Marey (both 1830–1904) that had captured the close attention of numerous artists, most famously Duchamp. She is a virtual prototype of a classical nineteenth-century nude, but she is now pulled, if only slowly, into the modern world in which science and art are closely intertwined. It is an extraordinary painting, yet one still labelled pale and tame by unseeing critics. In a similar vein was Arthur B. Davies's overtly Symbolist painting of the same time, *Sea Drift* (c.1912) [50], apparently a bucolic scene of graceful nudes in a sylvan setting, until we realize that it too is based on studies of sequential movement, a Symbolist parody of *Nude Descending*

48 Kathleen McEnery Cunningham, *Going to the Bath*, c.1905–13. Oil on canvas, 127.2 × 79.3 cm (50⅛ × 31¼ in). Smithsonian American Art Museum, Washington, DC

49 Leon Dabo, *Evening North Sierra*, 1910. Oil on canvas, 91.44 × 68.58 cm (36 × 27 in). Collection of Stillwell House Fine Art & Antiques, Red Bank, New Jersey

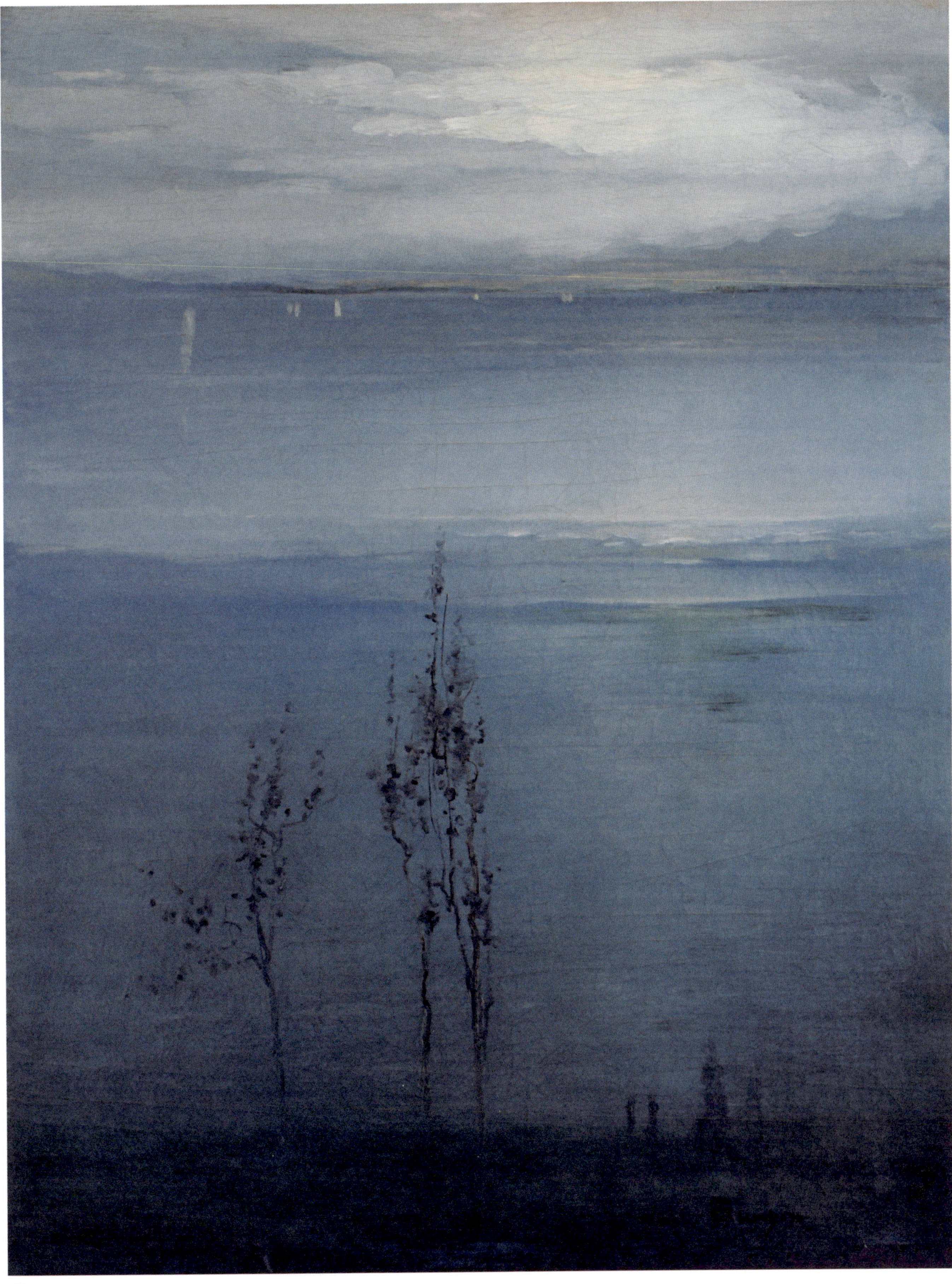

49

a Staircase. Once again, an apparently retardataire image is transformed into the most modern of images, speaking to the staying power and the continuing influence of symbolism in twentieth-century art.

The Armory's Impact on Older Artists

The transformative effects of the Armory Show on younger American artists like Stuart Davis have been well documented. Yet other, older artists especially, came to produce work of startling and unexpected originality that in some cases completely changed their lives and art, and added work of substance to American art. Although his paintings and prints were based in Realism, Sloan was deeply interested in more modern art, and in one work, *Mosaic* (1917)[51], he produced an astounding abstraction of inventive shapes that circle and intersect with one another. Intertwined with them are three messages: at lower left, 'in heaven above, or'; at centre, 'the earth beneath' and at the upper right 'or any likeness'. Despite being an etching rather than a painting, it has great impact, as well as a mysterious tone that speaks of a spiritual journey. It must surely stem, in part, from Sloan's experience of the Armory Show, and also has a distinctly Futurist overtone, although there was no true Futurism in the exhibition; this may have been more directly incited in response to the exhibition of the Italian Futurist Gino Severini held by Stieglitz at 291 in 1917. Are the messages some kind of Dada irony? It is not impossible, since the seeds of Dada were well planted by this time in America. It also begs the question – what more would Sloan have done had his roots not been so firmly planted in the nineteenth century?

A substantial and continuing body of work by Henry Fitch Taylor (1853–1926) was born directly from the Armory Show. His story is one of the most intriguing of modern art in America. He was born in Cincinnati, Ohio, and at first was involved in acting before going to Paris, where he began to study painting. In the 1880s and for some twenty years thereafter, he produced a series of good if conventional landscapes based on Impressionist and Post-Impressionist principles. By 1910 he was in New York, where he became the director of the Madison Gallery, run by Clara Davidge, whom he married in 1913. She was a patron, if still less known,

50

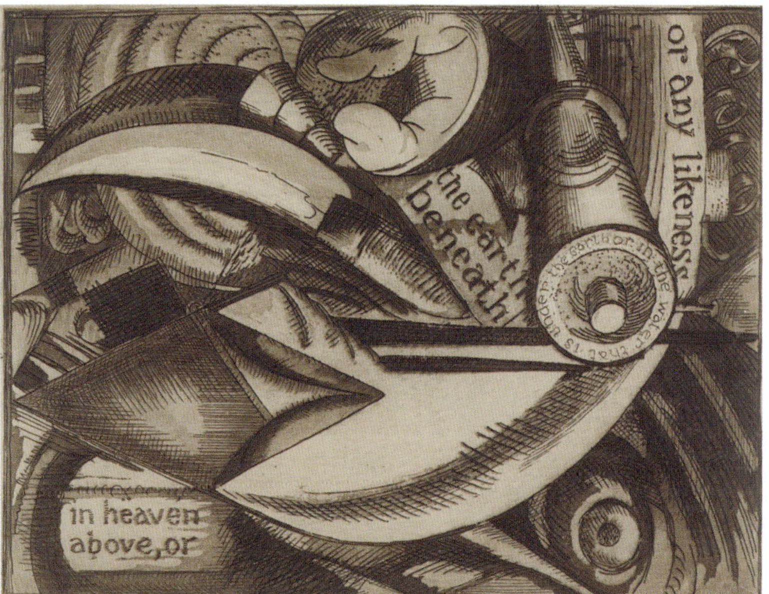

51

50 Arthur B. Davies, *Sea Drift*,
    *c.*1912. Oil on canvas,
    71.1 × 58.4 cm (28 × 23 in).
    Private collection

51 John Sloan, *Mosaic*, 1917.
    Etching and aquatint,
    19.8 × 25.1 cm (7¹³⁄₁₆ × 9⅞ in).
    The Museum of Modern Art,
    New York

52 Raymond Duchamp-Villon,
    The Horse, 1914 (cast *c.*1930–1).
    Bronze, 101.6 × 100.1 × 56.7 cm
    (40 × 39½ × 22⅜ in).
    The Museum of Modern Art,
    New York

Modern Art in America

of Advanced Art in New York, and together she and Taylor helped to organize the Armory Show. In fact, Taylor was elected the first president of the Association of American Painters and Sculptors, the founding group of the Armory Show. He gave way to Arthur B. Davies, but continued to serve as secretary and treasurer for the group.

No artist was so immediately transformed by the Armory. Within a year Taylor was making modernist paintings of remarkable skill that are an intrinsic part of the corpus of American Cubism. They began with the small, splintered parts of Synthetic Cubism, but were soon structured around the broad clear planes of Synthetic Cubism. However, his best work did not follow the path of Picasso's and Braque's Cubism. Indeed, much of American Cubism has been misinterpreted because it does not follow that direction. Rather, it is more in tune with the Cubism of the Puteaux group (named after the Paris suburb) – Duchamp, Léger, Francis Picabia, Robert and Sonia Delaunay and Albert Gleizes – and was based not on the old themes of still life, portraits and landscapes continued by Picasso and Braque but on the most dynamic and pressing themes of modern urban life, especially the changes wrought by the passage of time from the old to the new. A good example of this is Raymond Duchamp-Villon's *The Horse* (1914)[52], in which the leg changes into a piston and the neck into a missile, as it was termed by Matisse, as we walk around the sculpture, thus emulating the passage from the nineteenth-century image of horse power into a modern industrial machine.

This type of imagery was deeply influenced by the contemporary writing of Henri Bergson, France's most influential thinker and philosopher, in particular his ideas of duration and élan, of the vitality and movement of life within itself. Bergson rejected the idea of the single, independent, free-standing moment of Impressionism, and posited instead an image of change moving from one moment to another, but incorporating something of the moment just past and fusing it with something of the moment to come, so that time is a continuum, embodying past, present and future at once. Bergson's influence was enormous in France and in America and can be seen as late as the 1950s in the pools of biomorphs in the art of Sam Francis,[25] who came to maturity in Paris.

These ideas were prevalent in New York with Duchamp, Picabia and Gleizes. The latter's work was shown during the war several times in New York, for as with many French artists he stayed there in order to avoid being drafted into the French Army, and a sure and immediate death in the trenches. Gleizes, like Mondrian some twenty-five years later, was impressed by the dynamism of New York, and translated it into potent images of the city, often with overt references to the metamorphosis from old to new. In turn, his work certainly affected American art. For example, Taylor's largest and most accomplished painting was *From Generation unto Generation* (1915)[53], the very title of which embodies Bergsonian thought. At the right, a traditional figure and a still life symbolize the nineteenth century. By means of a descending triangular force, they are pulled into more abstract configurations, and thus the complexities of the twentieth century are transformed, at the left, by the brighter colours and dynamic angularities of a new pictorial language. Taylor's interest in strong colour is evident here, and was focused enough for him to go on to invent his own system of colour usage. This work perfectly represents his journey, and shows his conviction that modern art was fundamentally tied to the changing world. While his corpus of abstract paintings is not large, it is part of the evolving mosaic of American painting that we have slowly pieced together. In great part, this has been the story of the history of American art over the past half century.

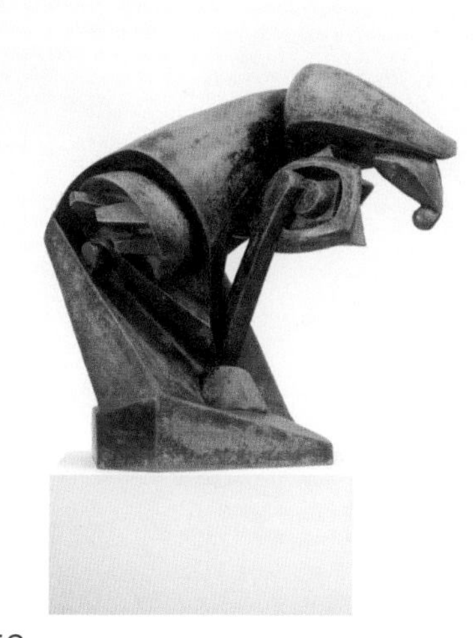

52

THE ROLE OF COLLECTORS

As mentioned in Chapter I, the salons held by Leo, Gertrude, Michael and Sarah Stein in Paris played an important role in the dissemination of modern art among Americans before World War I. The Steins were among the first of a wide array of serious American collectors who were, with the Russian collectors Sergei Shchukin (1854–1936) and Ivan Morozov (1871–1921), instrumen-tal in gathering the best of modern art in comprehensive collections. Picasso would later say, 'Without the Americans and Russians, I could not have survived.'[26]

An important upshot of the Armory Show was the emergence of a larger group of collectors whose collections would be seen by artists and later form the basis of public museums. Over the years, Stieglitz acquired for himself paintings that he considered to be of an especially high quality and importance. He had good judgement and a good eye. He kept them in his galleries, first 291, then American Place, and formed a small but choice collection, a mini and early museum of modern art that the many artists could study. To these paintings we can trace the root of many works that appeared over the years in America. One of these paintings, Kandinsky's *Improvisation 27 (Garden of Love II)* (1912)[54] was acquired from the Armory Show. In 1949, it went to the Metropolitan Museum of Art in New York, where it has been influential for numerous artists interested in both colour and drawing. Earlier, though, its soft but strong colour areas, which bleed into one another, heightened and contrasted by open areas of colour, had a definite effect on Dove and no doubt O'Keeffe and their poetic shaping and coloration, especially in the 1930s. Kandinsky's art was one key source of the organic expressionism, the flowing biomorphism of living, breathing shapes that were at the heart of much of the best American colour painting.

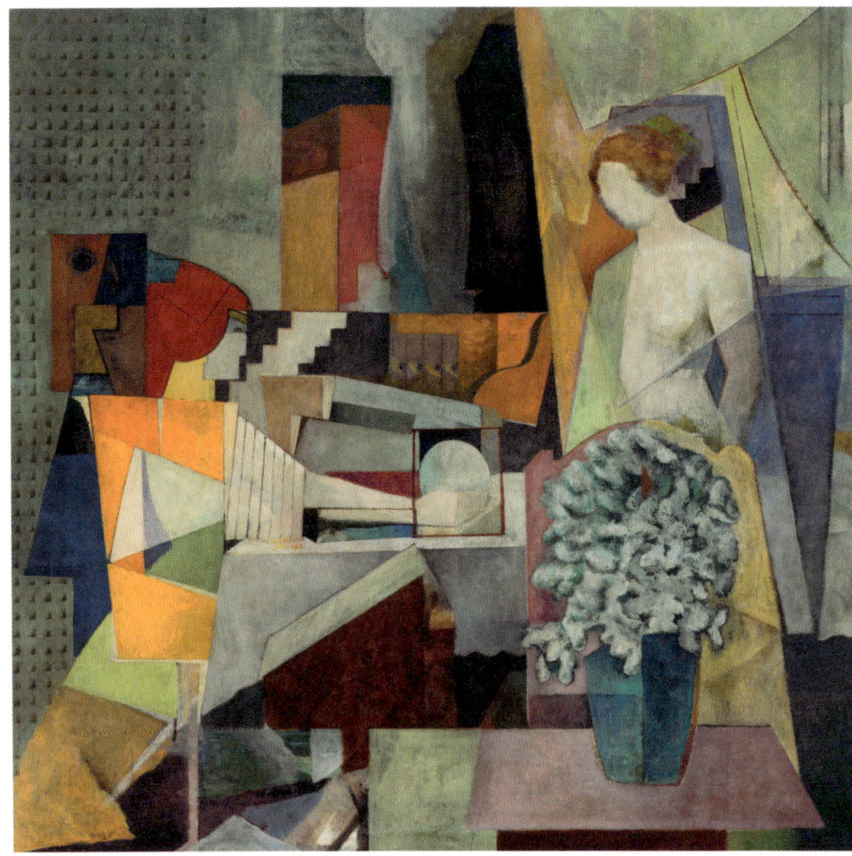

53

Modern Art in America

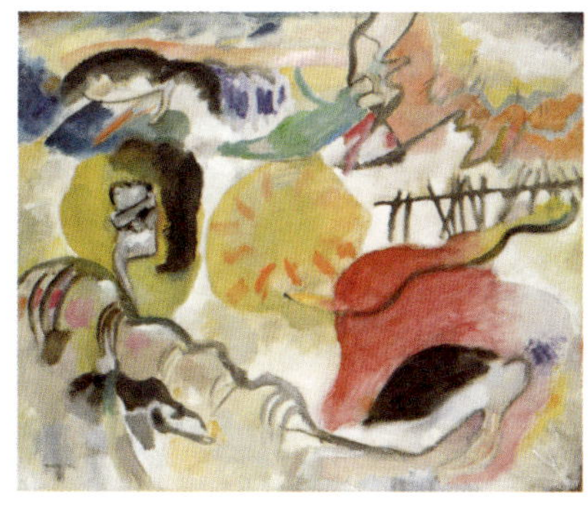

54

In addition to Stieglitz, Albert Barnes acquired one of the early and great collections of modern art, including works by Cézanne, Renoir, Seurat, Matisse and the Americans William Glackens and Charles Demuth. John Quinn was also important, as was Walter Conrad Arensberg, whose collection became a focal point of art in New York in the war years. Kandinsky's four panels, perhaps representing the Four Seasons, were commissioned by Edwin Campbell for his apartment in New York, and today are high points of MoMA's collection. Later, collectors such as Katherine Dreier and Duncan Phillips continued the modernist drive in the 1920s, continuing apace the new developments of current art.

MEANWHILE IN PARIS: RUSSELL, MACDONALD-WRIGHT, DASBURG AND SYNCHROMISM

The Armory was not the only notable exhibition of 1913, for that autumn, two young Americans, Morgan Russell (1886–1953), then twenty-seven, and Stanton Macdonald-Wright (1890–1973), only twenty-three, opened an exhibition of their colour paintings at the prestigious Bernheim-Jeune Gallery in Paris, the site of an influential Futurist exhibition the year before. They called themselves the Synchromists (from syn-chrome, meaning 'with colour'). Like the Italian Futurists, the two Americans issued a manifesto that challenged the supremacy of French art, claiming that their own art was far more advanced than any other, and proclaiming Impressionism and all other recent art movements outmoded relics of the past. One can only admire their brashness, the first frontal attack on French art in American history, and thus a milestone of sorts, but their temerity rebounded adversely both then and for years to come. Critics and scholars dismissed their exaggerated claims and ill-considered boasts for fifty years and in so doing never bothered to consider the art itself. In their manifestos and group exhibitions, Russell and Macdonald-Wright had created the first formal American art movement of the twentieth century, a significant event in itself, for it spoke of a burgeoning confidence in themselves as artists, and in the power of colour alone to make and carry a painting. Their formulation of colour principles also earned them a place in the history of colour theory dating back to the early nineteenth century, to the work of Otto Runge, Goethe and Michel Eugène Chevreul, and later Charles Blanc and Ogden Rood. By the turn of the century, these colour principles were integrated into a modern, abstracting type of painting that in great part accounted for the burst of colour art by 1913.[27]

Principles of Colour: Chevreul and Rood

A moment should be taken to summarize these old principles of colour. The best-known published source for post-1900 painting was *De la loi du contraste simultané des couleurs* (*On the law of simultaneous contrast of colours*) published in 1839 by Chevreul and further elaborated by Ogden Rood in 1879. This law, applicable to both hue and value, states that if two colours are juxtaposed, each will be influenced by the complementary of the other, and if they are of different values, the light colour will become even lighter, the dark even darker. As a corollary, Chevreul advanced the law of simultaneous contrasts, by which a new colour will be produced on the retina if the eye shifts quickly from one colour to another. Some of these laws were more fundamental to certain artists, but all used them in varying ways and extents in their art.

53 Henry Fitch Taylor, *From Generation unto Generation*, 1915. Oil on canvas, 175.3 × 175.3 cm (69 × 69 in). Cincinnati Art Museum

54 Wassily Kandinsky, *Improvisation 27 (Garden of Love II)*, 1912. Oil on canvas, 120.3 × 140.3 cm (47³⁄₈ × 55¼ in). The Metropolitan Museum of Art, New York

Chevreul advanced two other laws that were influential: the law of the harmony of analogous colours and the law of the harmony of contrasts. In the first, colours adjacent or separated by small intervals on the chromatic circle will produce harmonious combinations, as will colours of approximating values. The second proposition states that a harmony will be produced by the interaction of widely separated hues or values. Related to and actually incorporating the law of the harmony of analogy is the principle of gradation, by which colours in a given area are modulated to lighter or darker tones by small intervals, a practice that was championed by Rood, David Sutter in 1880 and even John Ruskin in his *Elements of Drawing* of 1857. These laws could produce the varied effects in the work of the American colour painters, from the sculptural density of Russell and Bruce, to the soft, open surfaces of Macdonald-Wright.

In his book *Modern Chromatics* (1879), Rood included a chapter that came to be particularly important for Macdonald-Wright and Russell. This chapter outlined the use of hues in pairs and triads, to produce harmonious and balanced colour combinations by splitting the circle into regions divided by 120 degrees. This created colour chords, composed as one would a musical composition. These combinations and then their variants could be spread throughout the painting, with the effect of major and minor scales. The analogy of painting with music was a foremost element in the work of Russell and Macdonald-Wright, and was taught to them in detail by the little-known Canadian painter and colour theoretician Ernest Percyval Tudor-Hart (1873–1954), whom they met in Paris. The analogy had a long history that can be traced to Aristotle's *Poetics*, and was developed by Isaac Newton. It came to special importance in the writings of Eugène Delacroix, who established it as an element of the *Paragone*, the comparison of the arts. By 1914, it ran through the work and words of many artists, including Gauguin, Matisse and Kandinsky, and was the basis of much advanced painting as it moved towards abstraction, for music was understood as the most abstract of all the arts.

These principles of colour theory placed the American colour painters as heirs to a long tradition of allegiance between science and art. They continued the use of the same theoretical writings made famous by Seurat, Signac and the Neo-Impressionists, and absorbed by Matisse, Delaunay, Picabia and others, all of whom went through a Neo-Impressionist phase in the years from 1904 to 1910, as did the Americans themselves. Their art therefore did not appear overnight after they had seen the Europeans, but evolved over time, at the same time as the Europeans. Thereafter, much colour theory became so technical that it was of little use to the practising artist, except for certain principles that will be discussed in the context of colour-field painting.

As important as these laws were, however, they have also had a detrimental effect on our understanding of colour art. The very words, laws and principles ('theory' is incorrect, since they all derive from actual scientific and artistic experimentation and practice) repel us, and cause us to equate them with a mechanical and unfeeling art, something applied as a robot might do. It is imperative therefore to understand that colour principles are only an initial guide to start the painting and let it evolve on its own terms, with the artist working out of the materials, namely colour and pigment itself. It is up to the talent, instinct and feel of the artist, his innate skill, to bring the picture to a successful conclusion.

Synchromist principles of colour were quickly adapted by others, forming a far wider reach than previously understood. Andrew Dasburg (1887–1979) had met Russell in New York at the Art Students League

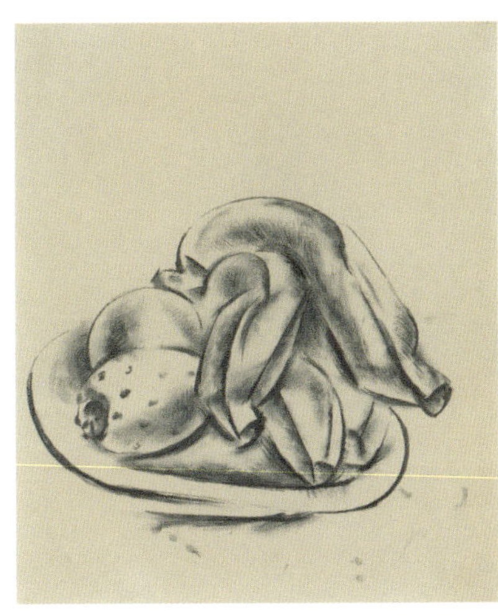

55

(a venerable and vital institution in the history of American art) in 1907. They spent that summer at the League's classes in Woodstock, then and later a locale for many American modernists, and when Dasburg went to Paris in 1909, he again joined Russell. Both worked endlessly from a small Cézanne still life of apples that Russell had borrowed from Leo Stein. Through Russell, Dasburg got to meet Matisse, and he later remembered the French artist labouring over the central figure in the majestic *Dance* (1909–10), a painting on which other American artists, such as Bruce, also saw Matisse working. Like Russell, Dasburg was profoundly influenced by Cézanne, as seen through Matisse's eyes and guidance, and incorporated vivid touches of tactile colour into his early landscapes. The Cézanne still life was probably the source or inspiration for Dasburg's finely tuned pen-and-ink still life of c.1912 [55], which although in black and white records the volumes as Cézanne did while incorporating an early Cubist format of clear and solid forms. Dasburg subsequently returned to Woodstock, but rejoined Russell in Paris in 1914.

Under Russell's stimulus, Dasburg immersed himself in colour theory and practice, with Russell's monumental *Synchromy in Orange: To Form* (1913–14) [58] as his primary guide. Its effect was decisive and helped to launch Dasburg's own original colour abstractions, which he called 'Improvisations', once again indicating their source in musical composition. In one of the few surviving 'Improvisations' (1915–16) [57], Dasburg depended on a specific key – blue-green – alternating chords in triangular and circular shapes that sweep over and through the canvas with unrelenting speed and intensity. It is like pure music, fully abstract and so well balanced that over twenty years of discussion the artist could never be certain which side should be up; the painting could be looked at either way with full and telling impact.[28]

Dasburg's *Untitled (Still Life with Artist's Portfolio and Bowl of Fruit)* [56] is a fine example of a synthetic Cubism, with planes based on a wide array of hues from greys at left to pinks and oranges at right. The date is uncertain, and I would argue for a date from 1916 to 1918 on account of its totally frontal, almost hierarchical disposition, in a kind of condensation of shapes that may parallel the tighter formats of Hartley and Bruce in 1916. On the other hand, the wide variety of texture and thickness of paint and the various types of drawing could place it closer to 1914. The colours are unique in American Cubism, except for those of Stuart Davis. The surface textures, the depth of pigment, are heavy and palpable, perhaps unique to American art, and are not seen again until the work of Davis and John Graham in the 1930s. In 1923, Dasburg wrote an article on Cubism in America, saying that most Americans did not understand it.[29] The artist sold himself and others short, but this may explain why, after moving to Taos, New Mexico, in 1918, he adopted a more condensed quasi-Cubism, applied to a figurative mode in landscapes and village scenes of his new home. They are effective and in keeping with the post-1918 shift to figuration, but one can only wish that he had found the means to continue with his abstract work. The glory of the southwestern landscape had overtaken and captivated him.

Challenging the 'Failure' of Synchromism

Russell's early abstractions, among them *Synchromy in Orange: To Form*, are early and key monuments in the history of colour abstraction, and of abstraction itself. The painting is monumental in size and scale, measuring nearly 12 × 10 feet, a *tour de force* of colour construction, an American

55 Andrew Dasburg, *Still Life – Fruit*, c. 1912. Brush pen and ink on paper, 31.4 × 25.7 cm (12⅜ × 10⅛ in). The Vilcek Foundation, New York

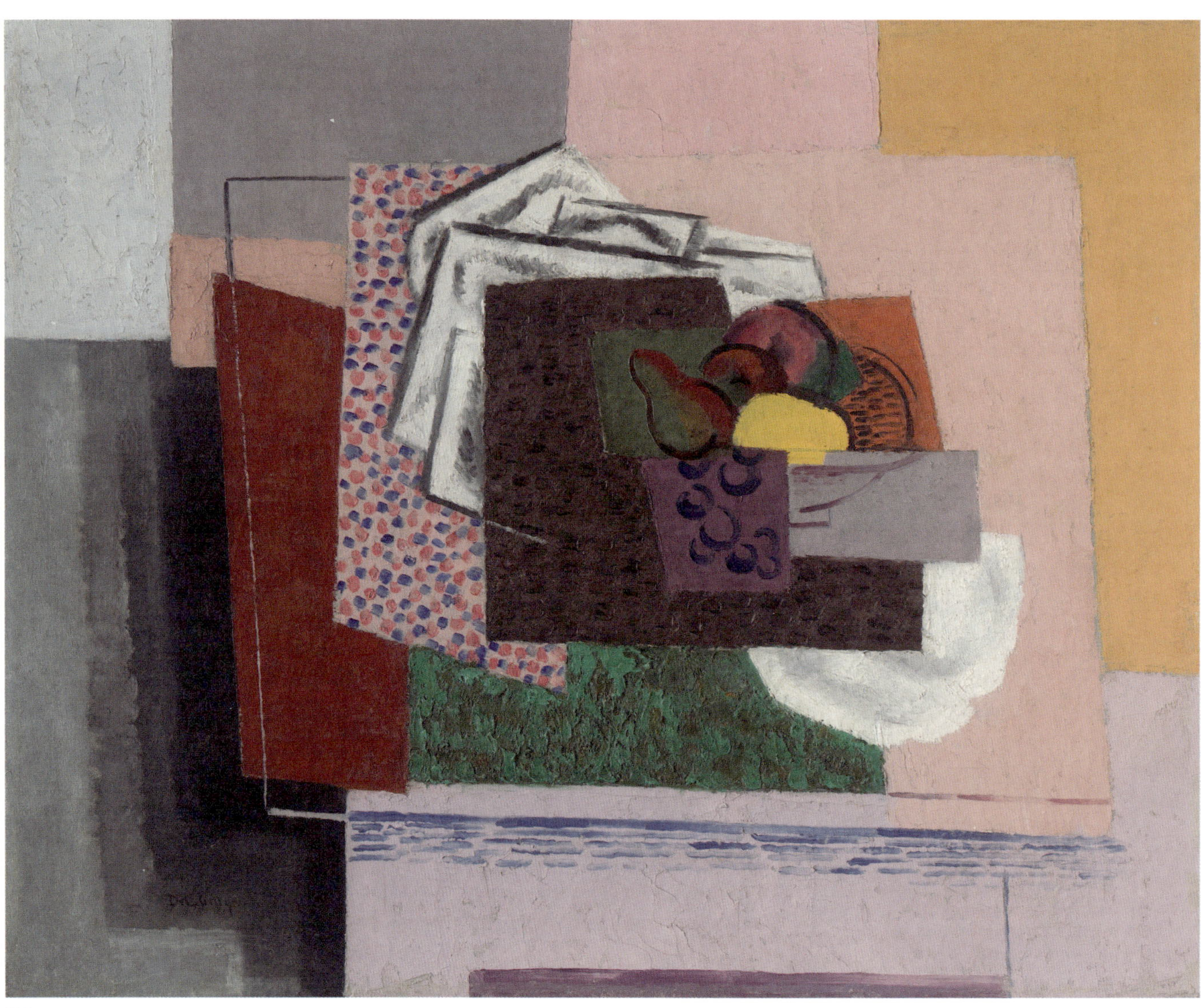

56

56 Andrew Dasburg, *Untitled
(Still Life with Artist's Portfolio
and Bowl of Fruit)*, c. 1914–18.
Oil on canvas, 50.8 × 61 cm
(20 × 24 in). The Vilcek
Foundation, New York

57 Andrew Dasburg, *Improvisation*,
1915–16. Oil on canvas,
90.2 × 74.9 cm (35½ × 29½ in).
Private collection

Modern Art in America

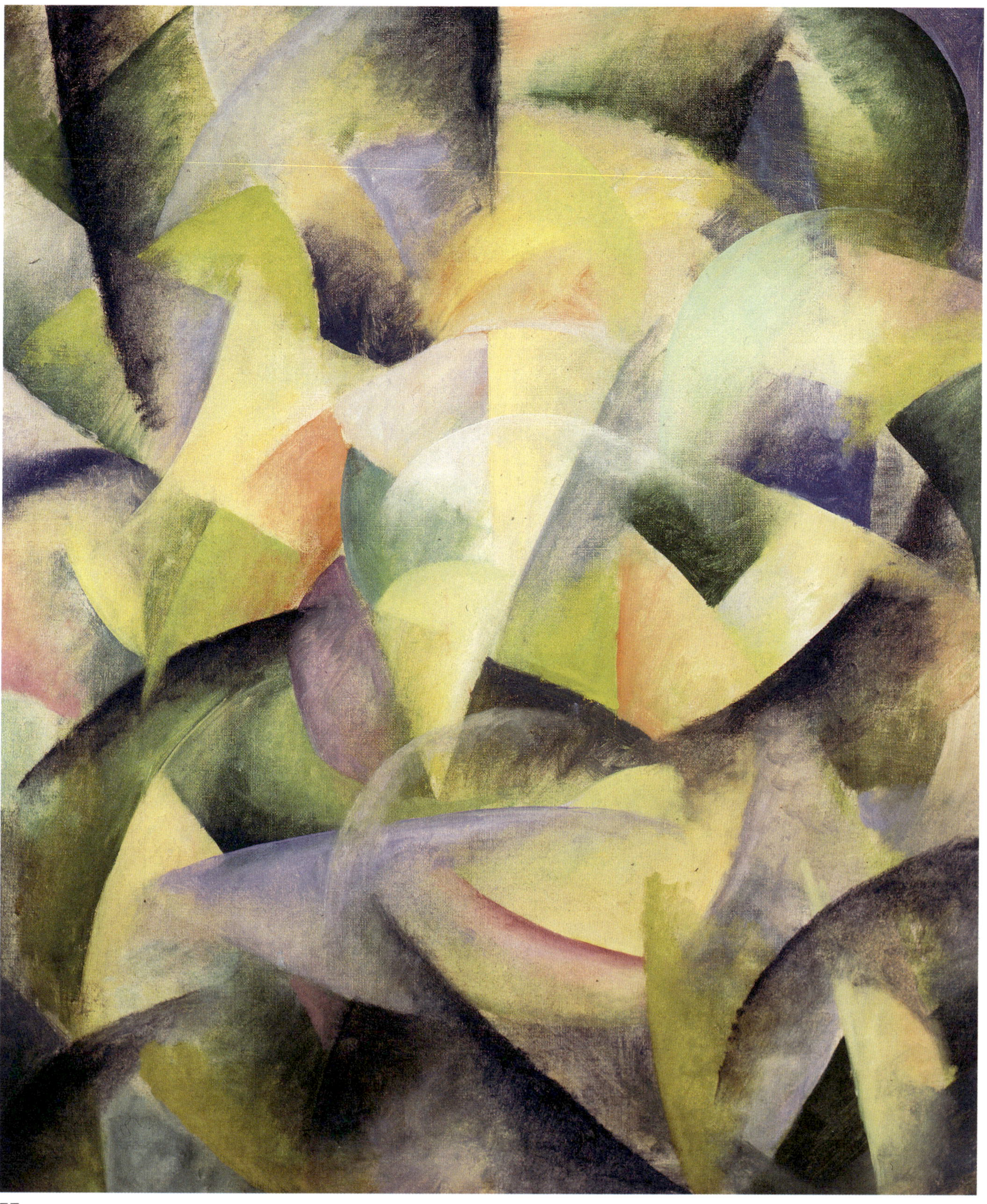

57

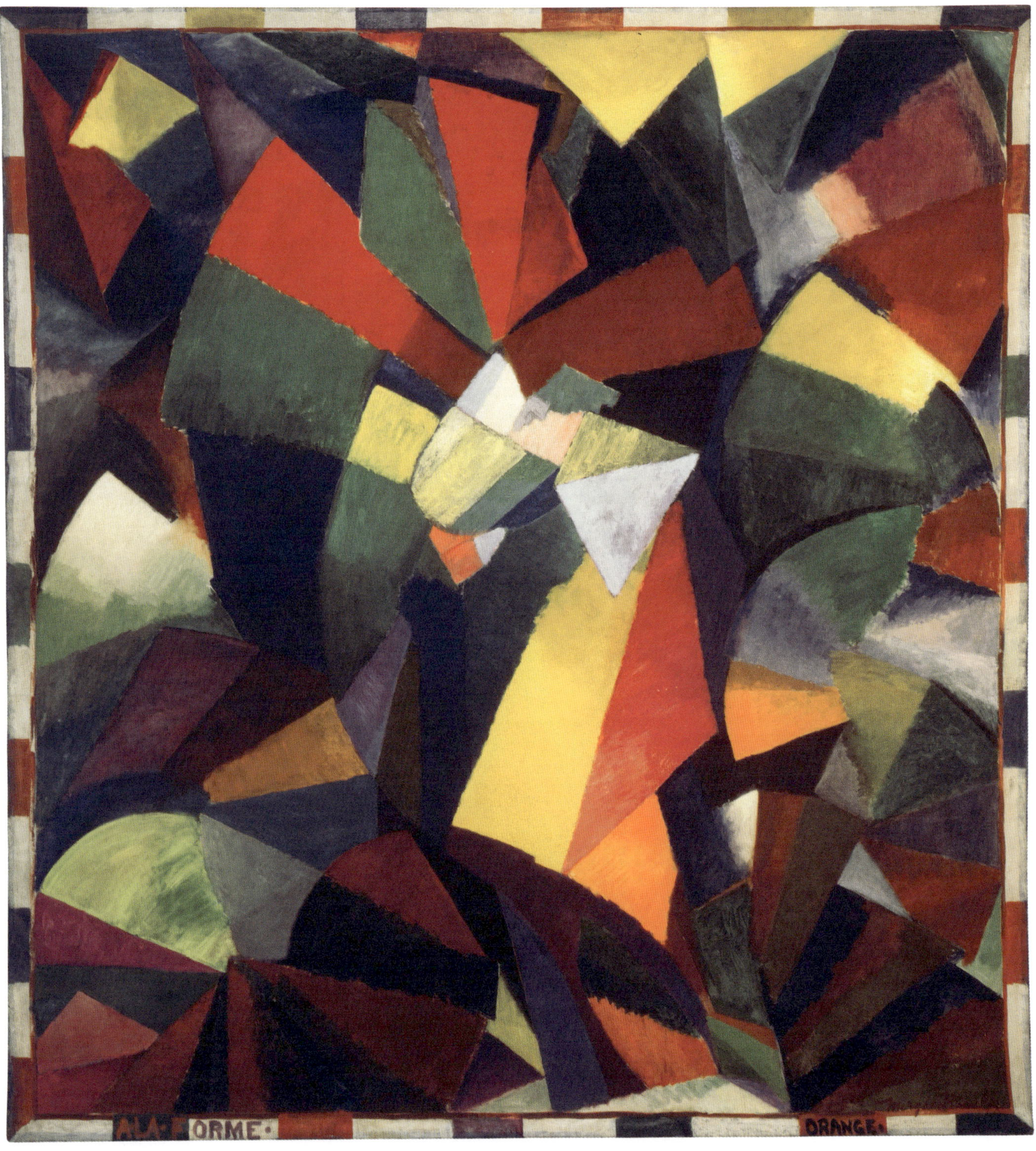

58

answer to the large Cubist canvases then being shown in the Salons in Paris. It stands in quality and impact with any of the European paintings then on view, as witnessed by its commanding presence in MoMA's exhibition of 2013 'Inventing Abstraction, 1910–1925'. Yet even in front of this overwhelming physical and pictorial presence, the author Rachael Z. DeLue of the accompanying exhibition essay could speak only of the 'failure' of Synchromism because of the artists' youthful claims (this is what happens when theory gets in the way of the art object).[30]

This negative view of Synchromism is surprising, in particular, because since the 1960s more serious attention has been paid by scholars to the Synchromists and related colour painters such as Bruce. New paintings have been uncovered and new information found, thus permitting a broader and more focused perspective on the work of Russell and Macdonald-Wright. Their corpus was found to be much larger, more diverse and more accomplished than previously thought, as they had been considered minor followers of the Delaunays, emerging only after the French artists. In fact, the new research showed that Russell and Macdonald-Wright had been in Paris since 1908, had carefully studied Cézanne and colour, and had participated in the discovery of colour and its science since their arrival in Paris, following the same course, simultaneously, as the Delaunays.[31] Finding their sources and background, and studying their work with care and respect, and in detail, yielded rich discoveries and marked the beginning of a new exploration of American modernism. Rather than followers, Russell and Macdonald-Wright can be seen best as an important part of the American participation in the Western drive to a new art based on old principles, one of the key aspects of modernism. Paris was the epicentre, no doubt, but an integrated history demands that we see it as the hub of a diverse movement that also included America, as well as Germany, England, Italy and Russia.

Orphic Cubism/Orphic Synchromism: Bruce and Hartley

Morgan Russell and Stanton Macdonald-Wright, as well as Patrick Henry Bruce (although, he was never a Synchromist himself), should be seen in the context of a growing use of pure colour in the service of a modern abstracting art that was in full evidence by 1914. They were part of a movement termed Orphic Cubism by Guillaume Apollinaire, led at first by Robert and Sonia Delaunay, and including the Duchamp brothers, Jacques, Raymond and Marcel, as well as Léger, Gleizes and Jean Metzinger. They aspired to use Cubism – and colour – to depict the marvels of the new, modern age wrought by engineering and technology, speed and dynamic movement that marked the miracles of the new century. They were intrigued, for example, by flight and the new perspectives of the world it engendered, and thus their paintings depicted the earth as seen from a higher view, as in *Homage to Blériot* (1914)[59], named after the pilot who had just flown the English Channel. Such men were seen as conquering heroes of the new age.

The Delaunays were also fascinated with the marvels of French engineering that were transforming the urban landscape of Paris. The very symbol of the new technology was of course the Eiffel Tower, which often appeared in their work.[32] It was frequently mixed with symbols of past time and culture, such as with older French buildings or with images of the Three Graces, which referred to classical art and mythology. The structure of the Eiffel Tower fused with the Three Graces, for example, represented a deliberate intersection between old and new, an image of

58 Morgan Russell, *Synchromy in Orange: To Form*, 1913–14. Oil on canvas, 347.9 × 314.9 cm (137 × 124 in). Albright-Knox Art Gallery, Buffalo, New York

the very transformation of older culture in a new century. The same is obviously at play in Duchamp's *Nude Descending a Staircase*. Here a classical nude evolves before our eyes into a clanking mechanical robot, a telling image of the coming of a new machine age that transformed even sexuality and the body. These images embodied the philosophy of Bergson.

Apollinaire's reference to Orpheus indicated an art related to music, the purest of all art forms, and colour painting certainly aspired to this state of purity. Colour, it was argued, could be composed in the manner of a musical score, and Russell and Macdonald-Wright based much of their art on chords of colour, composed in melodic sequences over the surfaces of their paintings. Seen now from a long historical perspective, this drive to colour can be called Orphic-Synchromism; it comprised a large and diverse group of artists both American and French.

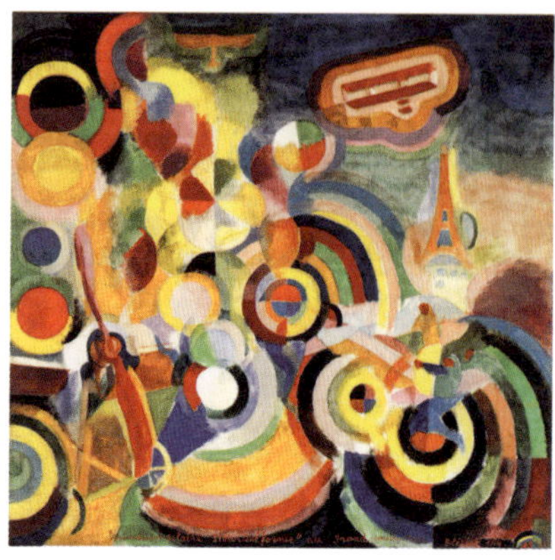
59

By 1913, Bruce's engagement with colour and its possibilities had reached new levels of intensity. He became friends with the Delaunays and began a series of his own large-scale abstract paintings that were shown in the Paris Salons, and which propelled him into the ranks of the avant-garde in Paris as a well-known and respected artist. Thus, with Russell and Macdonald-Wright and their variants of colour and colour painting, American art came to international attention at a far earlier date than many have supposed.

Such paintings as Bruce's *Mouvement, couleur, l'espace: simultané* (Movement, Colour, Space: Simultaneous), exhibited at the Indépendants in the spring of 1914 (now lost), burst open with multiple intersecting forms and colours from a jam-packed canvas that Apollinaire noted was really too full to be entirely successful. How American this seems: do it all, do it to excess, over the top, all the way! Paintings of this sort, completed in the last months before the outbreak of war, embodied perfectly the pre-war optimism of society and of art; everything and anything seemed possible with the glories of a new century to work with. Bruce had joined with the Delaunays to proclaim this new world, and had also clearly been looking at the Futurists, both for their capture of speed and movement, and for their utopian belief in the modern world. It was a world of light and colour, bright and dazzling, that the new art of colour proclaimed. Indeed, so much so that Macdonald-Wright's brother, Willard Huntington Wright, a thoughtful and articulate critic except when he went overboard in his enthusiasm for Synchromism, believed that the future of painting lay in colour, most particularly coloured light, and wrote a book by this name, *The Future of Painting*, that appeared in 1923. It did not attract much attention then, but forty years later it was seen to reflect the promise of the new age.

As a formal movement, with manifestos and group exhibitions, Synchromism itself lasted only briefly. By August 1914, it was one more casualty of World War I and the chaos that changed the course of art as well as the world. Its influence, however, had spread further and deeper than imagined, witness for example, Hartley's abstraction [60], which is a major contribution to the movement. Art history finally—and always—comes down to the individual artist; no movements, just artists, and their work. As independents, Russell and Macdonald-Wright went on to make much of their finest work, paintings that are major monuments of world art. They hold their own, but as is the case with early modern American art, their art is not as deep, as full, as European art.

We saw in the last chapter how Matisse's *Nude in a Wood* affected the work of Hartley. Overnight, his work took on strong colours, and by 1911, after seeing the Picasso show at 291 and viewing the Cézannes in

Modern Art in America

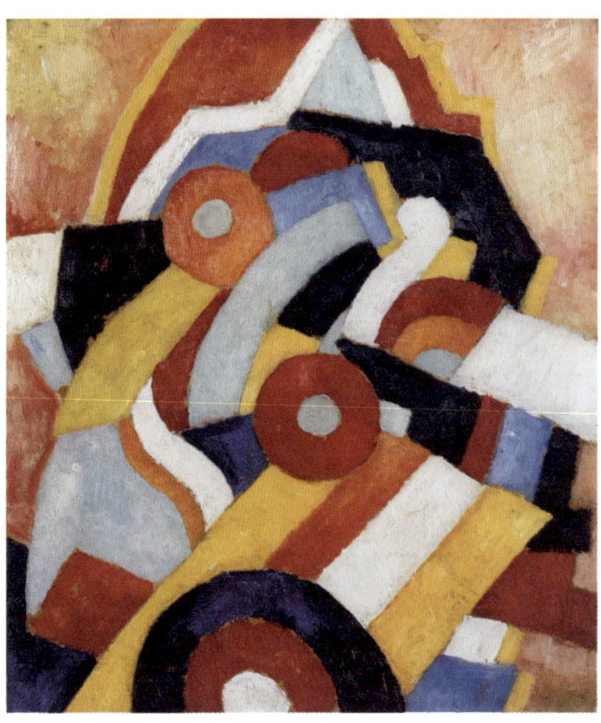

60

the Havemeyer Collection, he began a type of proto-Cubism. The die was cast by 1912 for his breakthrough into a series of paintings that rank as the best by an American in the first decades of the new century, or in the hundred years since their creation.

In the spring of that year, Hartley set sail for Paris, where he immersed himself in all the city had to offer. He discovered the work of Kandinsky and Franz Marc and read passages from Kandinsky's *On the Spiritual in Art*, published the year before, and one of the most influential treatises on modern art ever written.[33] He had also read William James's *Varieties of Religious Experience* (1902),[34] which intensified his interest in mystic experience, already evident in his work since 1907.

In one of his first masterpieces of world art, *Raptus* (c. 1913) [61], Hartley incorporated the Cubist practice of employing words: here, *raptus*, referring to James's chapter on mysticism describing the 'raptus' or ravishment experienced by Christian mystics, 'a state of ecstasy beyond intellect which imagery of verbal description cannot describe'.[35] In his early paintings, Hartley's spiritual outlook had been implied, but now he makes it visible and explicit. Indeed, he virtually shouts it out, large and bold as an American billboard in its blazing clarity (no French subtlety here). The painting captures our attention from fifty metres away, as it is installed today, across a museum courtyard, and we approach it as we would an Eastern shrine. It is a medium-sized painting, but its internal scale is exceptionally large, for it pushes out and fills the canvas to its last corner and edge. This is part of what makes Hartley, then and later, such a masterful artist, world-class from the start. But although its allure is strong, its meaning is unclear. The painting is filled with dynamic shapes working together – vertical and diagonals moving towards a higher order above the painting's edge; intersecting pulsating circles that seem to embody the world itself and its spiritual energy. Indeed, the circles may refer to Aristotle's view of the world, certainly its spheres of the universe. At the centre we find the cosmic triangle indicating the state of the world, and here it emanates beams of light uniting the painting – and the universe. We feel it is otherworldly, but also very real – the paint is in many areas

59 Robert Delaunay, *Homage to Blériot*, 1914. Oil on canvas, 250 × 250 cm (98.4 × 98.4 in). Kunstmuseum Basel

60 Marsden Hartley, *Abstraction*, c. 1914. Oil on paperboard, mounted on panel, 61.5 × 50.8 cm (24½ × 20 in). The Museum of Fine Arts, Houston

61 Marsden Hartley, *Raptus*, c. 1913. Oil on canvas, 100 × 81.3 cm (39⅜ × 32 in). Currier Museum of Art, Manchester, New Hampshire

62 Marsden Hartley, *The Aero*, 1914. Oil on canvas, 100.3 × 81.2 cm (39½ × 31¹⁵⁄₁₆ in). National Gallery of Art, Washington, DC

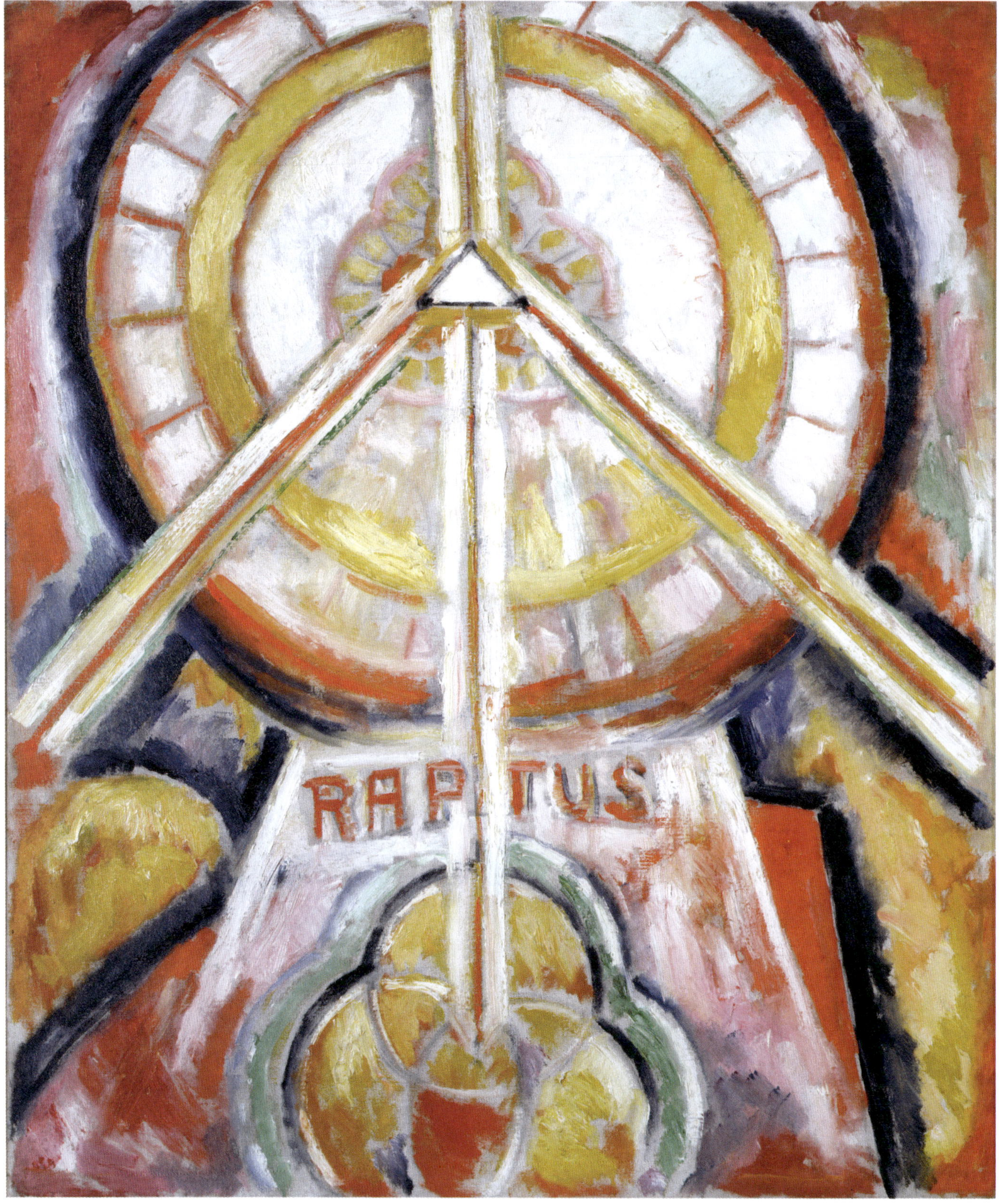

61

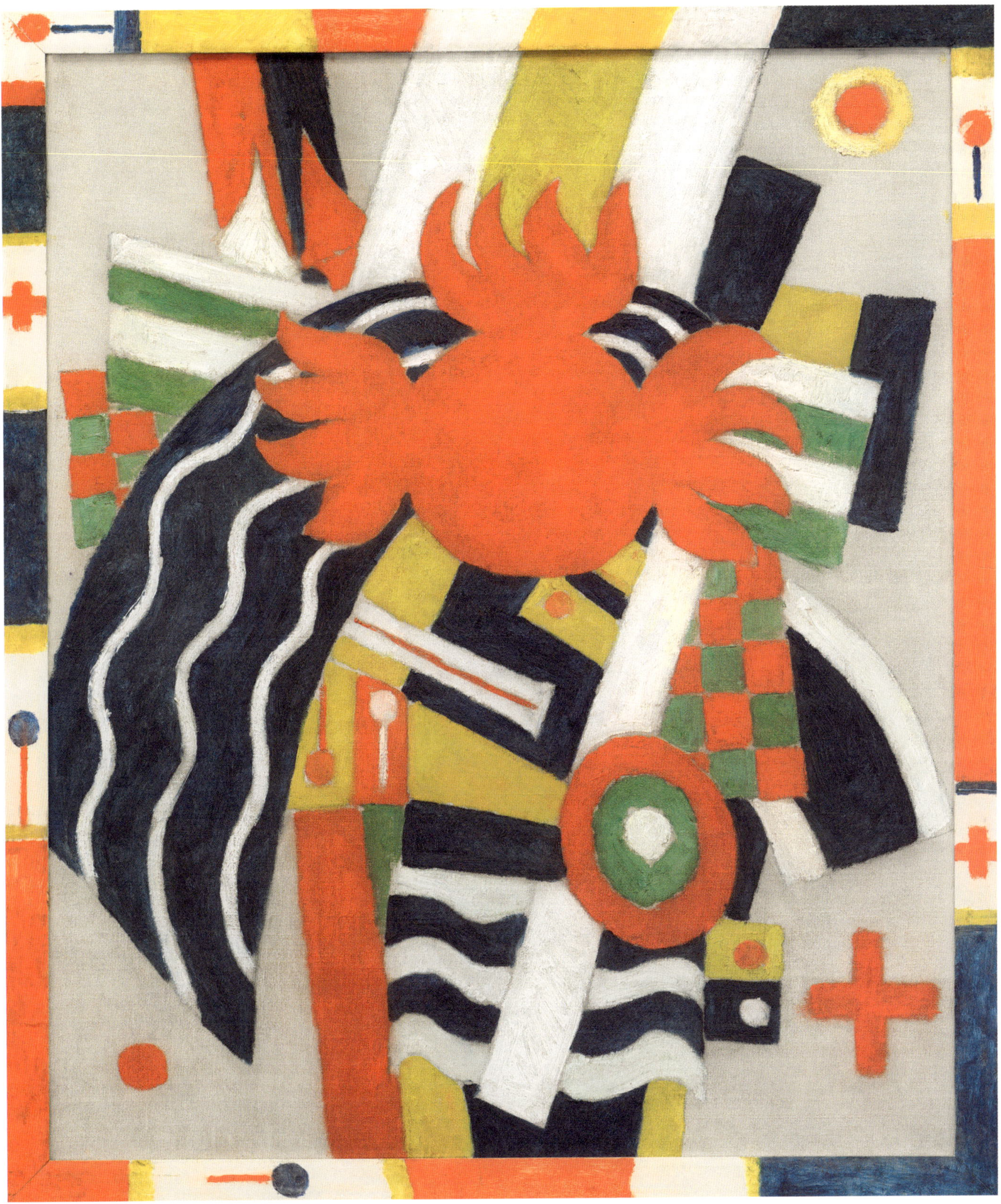

rough and textured, telling us that this is a palpable and real experience; its humanity is also clear, in that the painting, rather than being a static icon, is somewhat off balance, tilting a little to the left, as if not yet finished – the exact moment of transcendence is still a second away.

The circles themselves indicate the influence of the Delaunays, whom Hartley had visited in Paris, and, along with the high colour, place him within the Orphic-Synchromist movement, then at its peak. All this is intensified by the range of hues, themselves vibrant with textures of different sorts as his hand moves over the surface, reacting like a Geiger counter to momentary records of energy and feeling. An aura of light seems to illuminate the whole surface, rendered through a miraculous range of yellows, light reds, pinks and darker reds. These characteristics, the depth of feeling recorded in the paint itself, can be said to be at the heart of all his best work. To this end, Hartley can be at the same time a hard and linear painter, or a soft and diffuse one. Most artists are one or the other, but Hartley fuses and mixes these identities in ways rarely found. His touch is sublime, and we may have to look to Picasso of 1911, or Jasper Johns in his *Flag* of 1954–5 (page 266), for anything as subtle and masterful as the pure skill of his touch.

Hartley became increasingly intrigued by German life and culture, and thus arranged to visit Berlin, arriving in May 1913, in the midst of the marriage festivities of the Kaiser's daughter. He was fascinated by the colour and pageantry and military parades, and here he manifested the other side of his deeply spiritual art and personality, a love of sensual life. In *The Warriors* (1913), he celebrated the military procession accompanying the wedding. Soldiers on horseback march away from us in the glistening sun, conveyed by a subtle range of gradated yellows and oranges that generate this surface of light. But other overtones are present, menacing and foreboding even in their pictorial brilliance, a typical duality in Hartley. For, at the same time, the riders are German troops on the move, a grim reality despite the colour, that presages the forthcoming war, the disaster that broke out in August of the next year. Military power was also forcefully depicted in *The Aero* (1914)[62], one of the most telling uses of the theme of aviation in modern art to date. Its swooping movements high in the sky emblazoned with the strong colours of the uniforms convey a joyous sense of freedom at first, but it is a grim harbinger of the destruction to come.

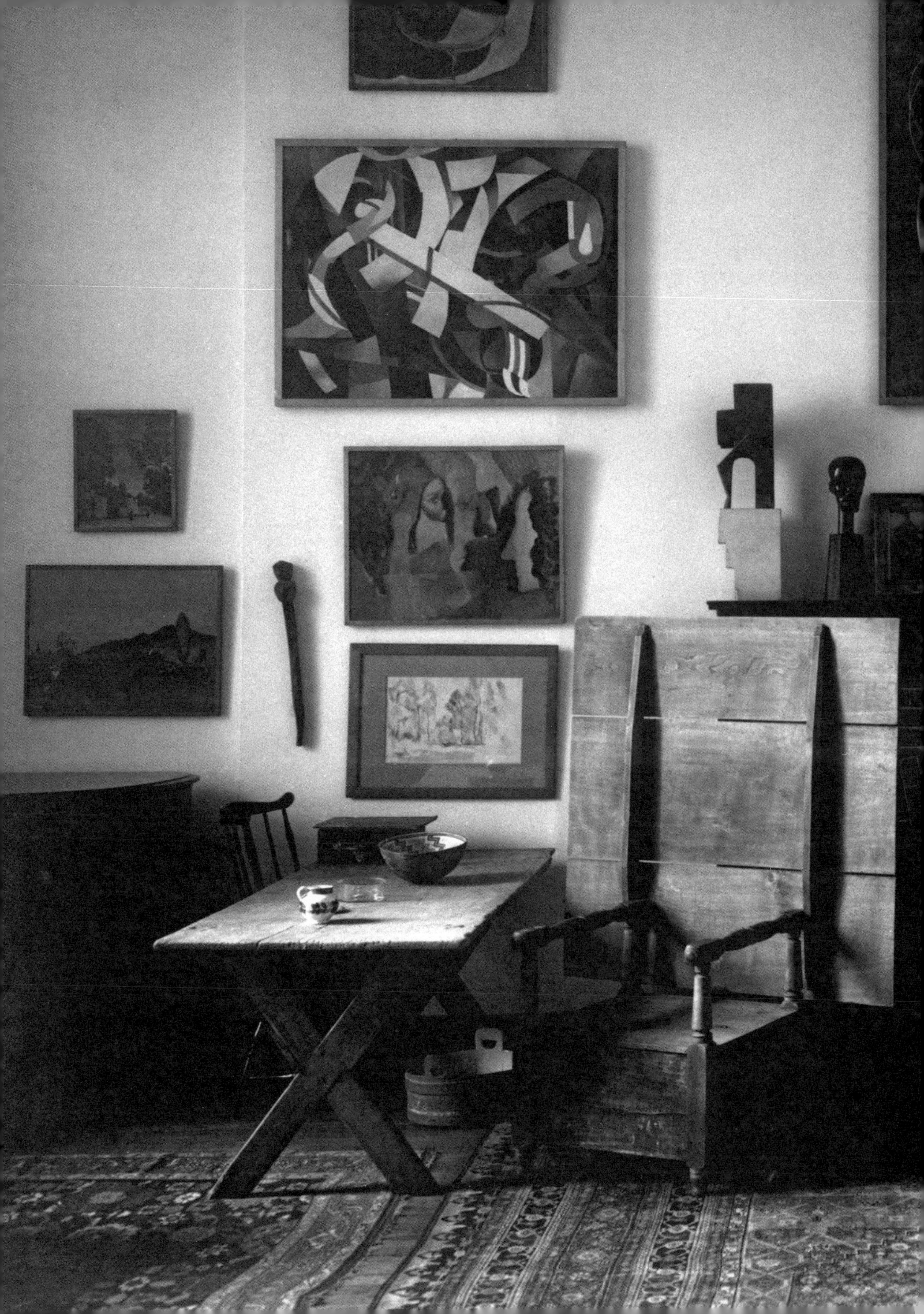

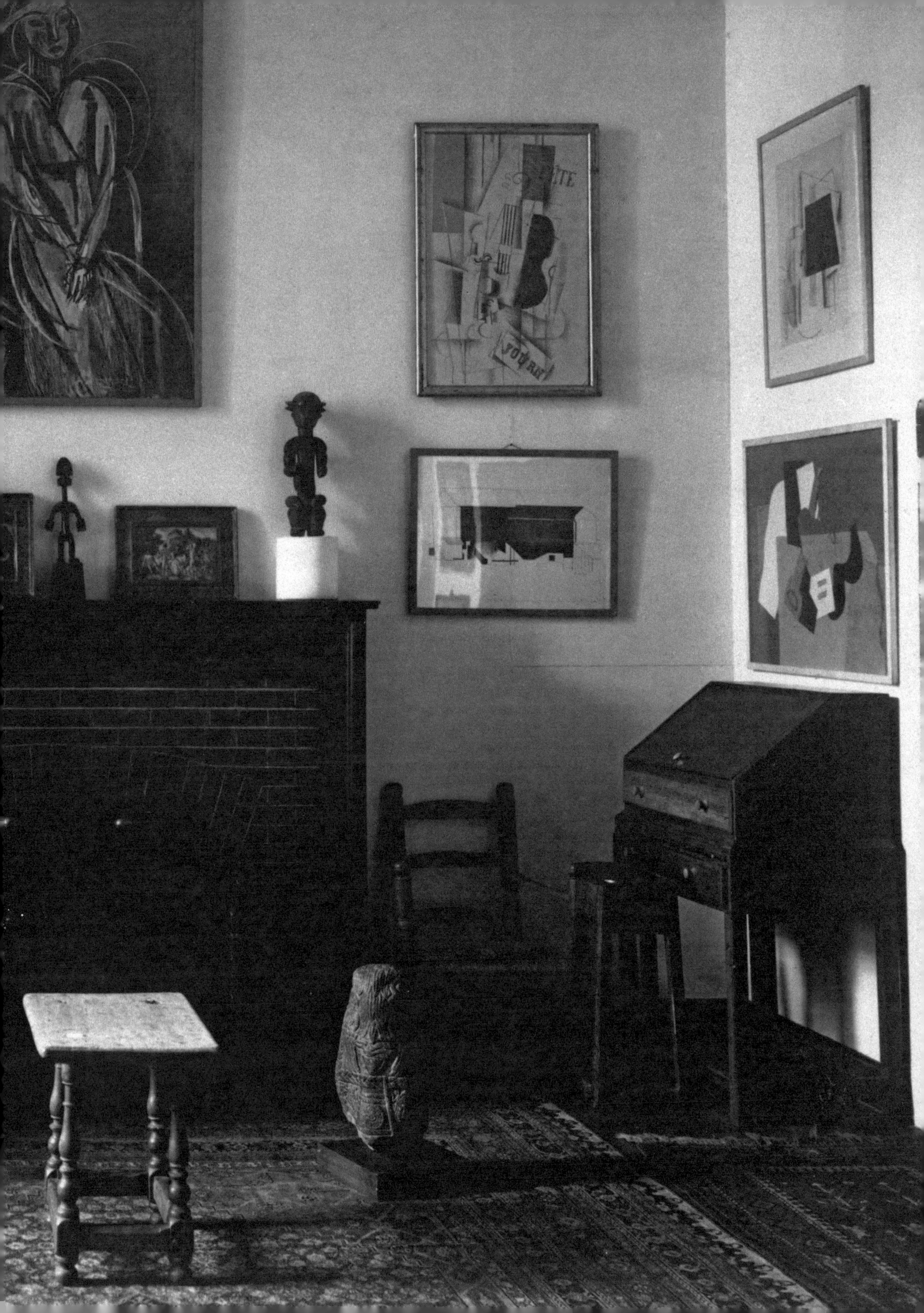

THE WORLD CHANGED FOREVER

1914
—18

The new age of art and technology had seemed to promise a world of hope and optimism, a future virtually without limits for art and society. In Europe, however, this glorious future was not to be. In early August 1914, the Great War broke out. It was a calamitous event of unprecedented destruction of human life that changed the world forever. Many thought it would be a neat and brief war, over in a matter of weeks, that would resolve tensions between the European powers so that they could get on with life and restore the world to its previous order. How wrong they were. The war slogged on, endlessly and horrendously, with generals on both sides using nineteenth-century manoeuvres in the face of modern technology and weapons. By a terrible irony, the modern machine so celebrated in pre-war art by the Futurists, who had also extolled war, now turned into instruments of death on an unknown and unimagined scale; the Futurists were mostly wiped out in the war. Hundreds of thousands of men were sent over the sides of muddy, filthy trenches to certain death in an instant in the face of withering fire. Nothing was gained. Nothing changed. Even those who survived were never the same again. Picasso recalled that he said goodbye to his colleague Georges Braque at the train station in 1914 and never saw him again – or not the man he had known.[1]

In 1916, in the Battles of Verdun and the Somme, the carnage reached new, even more horrific levels, and the war was at a stalemate, with no end in sight. The mood of the French public began to change, as did the outlook of artists. Gone was the old optimism in the face of a growing sense of a profound change in the very structure of the Western world. The old world order, it was clear, had disappeared forever. A new world would have to be made out of the utter disaster of the war. For artists, the open-ended, free-wheeling spirit of pre-war art had to be replaced by a new art, which would be simplified, focused, clarified, built on a rock-solid foundation in the way an architect would build a house. The change in mood was well documented in the small Paris magazines, among them *Sons, idées, couleurs*, published by the painter and poet Pierre Albert-Birot.[2]

63 Interior of the apartment of Louise and Walter Arensberg in New York, May 1919. Photograph by Charles Sheeler.

The simultaneist basis of pre-war abstraction that had jettisoned all semblance of order and control was now viewed as undisciplined, even decadent and self-indulgent. A new style, in fact an entirely different attitude and approach, had to be invented. It would be based on the will and spirit, discipline and order, put together and functioning with the sureness of a machine.

For some, abstract art no longer held quite the allure it once had. In the face of world crisis, it seemed self-centred and even frivolous. Old Master art, based on classicism and classical values like balance, harmony and clarity, gained a new esteem. By 1918, when the war finally ended, a call to order, to reason, was issued by Jean Cocteau for a new art, the most famous declaration of its kind that summarized the move away from pre-war abstraction.[3] This change deeply affected all aspects of modern art and will be discussed again at key points throughout this book.

1916–17: A Turning Point in American Art

In America, the spirit of optimism survived for a couple of years after 1914, but a turning point came in 1916, and by the end of the war, new developments were well under way. Once again, the art of Patrick Henry Bruce clearly embodied these changes. That year, he undertook a series of ambitious paintings based on brilliant colour chords, as his art had been for almost ten years. He was still intrigued by the spectacle of Paris, the City of Light, and its ceaseless movement, which continued even in the face of the war. He was especially taken by the merriment and excitement of the fashionable dance hall, the Bal Bullier, a popular meeting spot for artists and their friends and associates, and virtually the only place in Paris where there was still light. He set out to capture its atmosphere in a series of six 'Compositions'.

In the first, done early in 1916,[4] Bruce continued in his earlier vein of multiple, intertwining planes of colour, executed in a loose, painterly style [64]. A figure can be seen moving downwards, recalling Duchamp's *Nude Descending a Staircase*, the paradigm of continuous motion. As the series continued during the course of the year, however, the appearance, feel and structure of the paintings changed dramatically. Their colour shapes became tighter, more firmly delineated and more structural. The last two works in the series took on an almost three-dimensional cast, with the forms now seeming to invoke the architecture of the hall itself, rather than the people in it [65]. They are still marked by strong colour, but now have a mood of sobriety and seriousness, emphasized by a new use of black, which had been banished from the palette in earlier colour painting. Black gave a richness, a new depth of feeling far beyond the almost frivolous mood of the first in the series.

Bruce sent his six compositions back to the United States to his old friend and fellow colour painter Arthur B. Frost Jr. (1887–1917). Frost had not seen Bruce or his work for two years, and the recent compositions were a revelation to him. The extensive areas of black and white, a dramatic addition to Bruce's work, showed a new world of possibilities for colour abstraction. Filled with a revived energy for painting, Frost began to incorporate them into his own art. In addition, he passed on the ideas of colour and showed the Bruce paintings to his own circle of friends. They, too, were deeply impressed by the compositions and began to develop their own colour abstractions. Chief among them were James Daugherty, Jay Van Everen and Alexander Couard, who together left a body of colour painting that was not known until new research uncovered it in the 1960s.

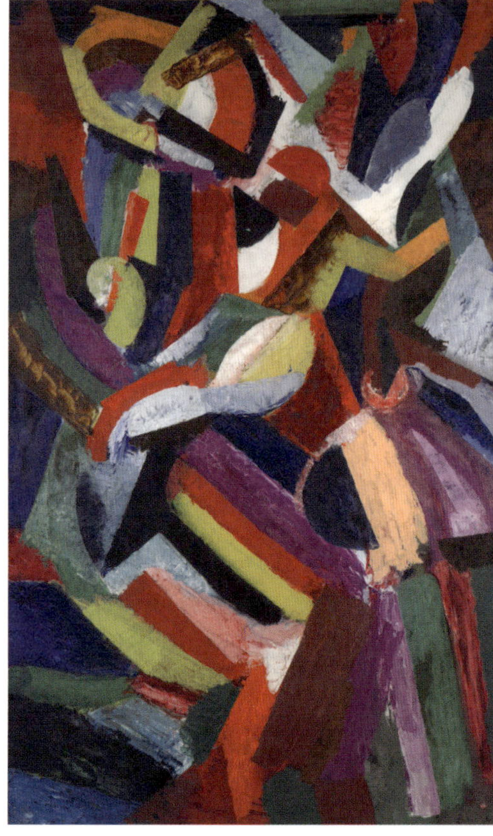

64

64 Patrick Henry Bruce,
Composition III, 1916.
Oil on canvas, 161.5 × 97 cm
(63⁹⁄₁₆ × 38³⁄₁₆ in).
Yale University Art Gallery,
New Haven

65 Patrick Henry Bruce,
Composition II, *c*.1916.
Oil on canvas, 97.4 × 130.2 cm
(38³⁄₈ × 51¼ in). Yale University
Art Gallery, New Haven

  Modern Art in America

James Daugherty (1889–1974), over the years, has emerged as a colour painter of high skill, and indeed extended the tradition well into the 1960s at an advanced age. By 1903 he was taking evening classes at the Corcoran School of Art, and in the following years he studied first with Hugh Breckenridge and then with William Merritt Chase and Henry McCarter at the Pennsylvania Academy of the Fine Arts in Philadelphia. From 1905 to 1907 he lived with his family in London, where he studied with Frank Brangwyn. He later described his time with Brangwyn as 'paralysing', but Brangwyn's long experience with mural painting surely helped to prepare Daugherty for his own career as a muralist during the 1920s and 1930s. By 1908, he had returned to the United States, settling in New York, where he did illustrations to support himself while continuing his studies at the National Academy of Design.[5]

In 1913 Daugherty's eyes were opened to a world of new possibilities by the landmark Armory Show and his discovery of a book by C. Lewis Hind, *The Post Impressionists*, which had been published in 1911. As he later described it, he 'went modern with a vengeance'.[6] Daugherty's absorption in modernism was also furthered by his friendship with his neighbour Athos Casarini (1883–1917), an Italian Futurist who was then living and working in America. In 1914, in a series of illustrations in the *New York Herald*[66], Daugherty developed a Futurist vocabulary of swirling and intersecting forms, abstracted and fragmented images of non-stop movement in popular activities such as baseball and dancing. His depiction of everyday subjects, as well as their reproduction in the daily newspapers, tells us something crucial about the man and his art. He believed deeply in America and the American people and their life, their pace and their tempo. For him, modernism was not a remote or obscure

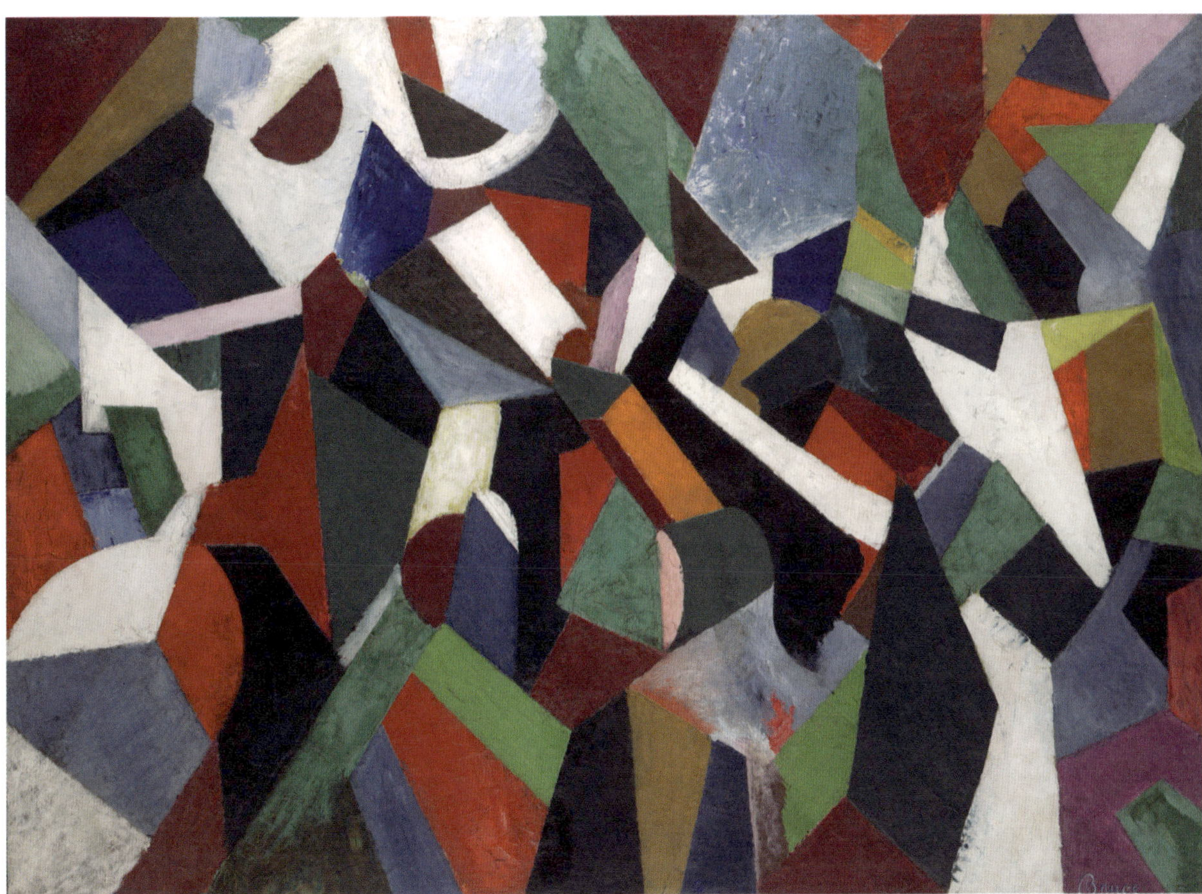

65

enterprise; it was always a populist and democratic art, intended to embody the essence of modern life, its speed, movement, flux, and its essential vitality and optimism, a particularly American version of Bergson's concept of *élan vital* (that spiritual force or energy that underlies reality and influences matter).

Daugherty became an active participant in the artistic life of New York, exhibiting at the MacDowell Club and the Whitney Studio Club, when his art and life took a dramatic and defining turn. He had rented a studio at 8 East 14th Street, when in 1915 another young American artist, Frost, moved in next door. The son of the famous American illustrator of the same name, Frost had recently returned from a long stay in Paris, where he had become close friends with Bruce. In New York, Frost immediately set out to teach Daugherty the principles and techniques of colour theory and colour painting. Daugherty himself was surely no stranger to colour. He would have been made aware of it in Hind's book and he would have seen the many paintings of intense colour, including works by Van Gogh and Matisse, at the Armory Show. Indeed, his Futurist works, *Cabaret (Café Chantant)* of 1914 among them, were marked by sequences of strong, bright colour, adding to their expansive, rousing mood. However, Frost's passionate belief in and understanding of the possibilities of colour quickly convinced Daugherty. He became a receptive and diligent student and was soon applying these ideas to his own work, first in figurative manner, then increasingly in works of greater abstraction.

Daugherty and Frost were concentrating on the prismatic hues, raised to their highest value, when some time in late 1916 or early 1917 Frost received the shipment of six *Compositions* that Bruce had produced in Paris. Daugherty later recounted that Frost was thunderstruck by the use of black in these works, for since Impressionism it had been banished from the artist's palette. A basic modernist law had been reversed, with powerful and effective results, by increasing and heightening the range of colour expression. Frost immediately set about repainting a large abstraction on which he had been working, and soon Daugherty, too, began to include such passages in his own work; it became a practice that would inform Daugherty's art for the rest of his life.

We often think of American modernism as behind the times, but this was not always true, for by 1916 New York had become a vital part of the hybrid internationalism of modern art. In that year on East 14th Street, these two young artists were helping to define some of the most advanced ideas then current. The newest colour theories, published in 1916 by Wilhelm Ostwald, had established black and white as primary colours, according them equal status with the familiar hues of red, blue and yellow. The use of black and white was quickly adopted by Matisse and was soon evident in the work of Mondrian, among others. It was Bruce, Frost and Daugherty who brought the practice, which had broad implications for painting, into the vocabulary of American art, simultaneously with its spread in Europe. They were at the cutting edge of new ideas in world art, even more so since they were among the first artists whose art delineated a shift that by 1918 permeated advanced Western Art

Daugherty took up the cause of teaching colour abstraction and passed on the principles of colour painting to his circle of friends, including such artists as Jay Van Everen (1875–1947) and Alexander Couard (1891–1926), who in turn created a body of early abstract colour painting. Daugherty had become the leader of a small but influential group of painters, an intrinsic part of avant-garde painting in America, important even if overshadowed by the more famous circle around Alfred Stieglitz.

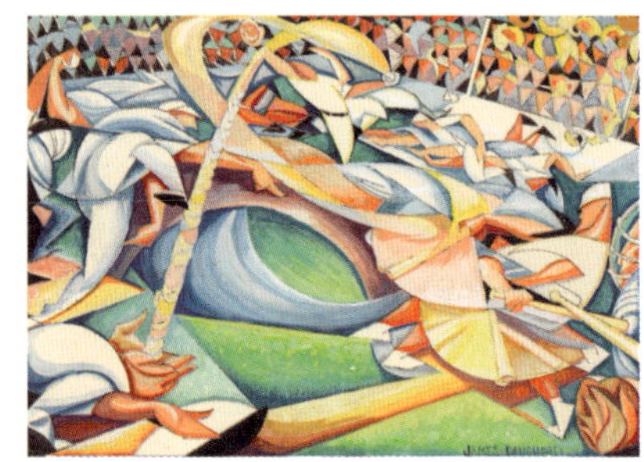

66

66 James Daugherty, *Three Base Hit*, 1914. Pen and ink and opaque watercolour on paper, 39.4 × 48.3 cm (15½ × 19 in). Whitney Museum of American Art, New York

67 Marsden Hartley, *Portrait of a German Officer*, 1914. Oil on canvas, 173.4 × 105.1 cm (68¼ × 41⅜ in). The Metropolitan Museum of Art, New York

Modern Art in America

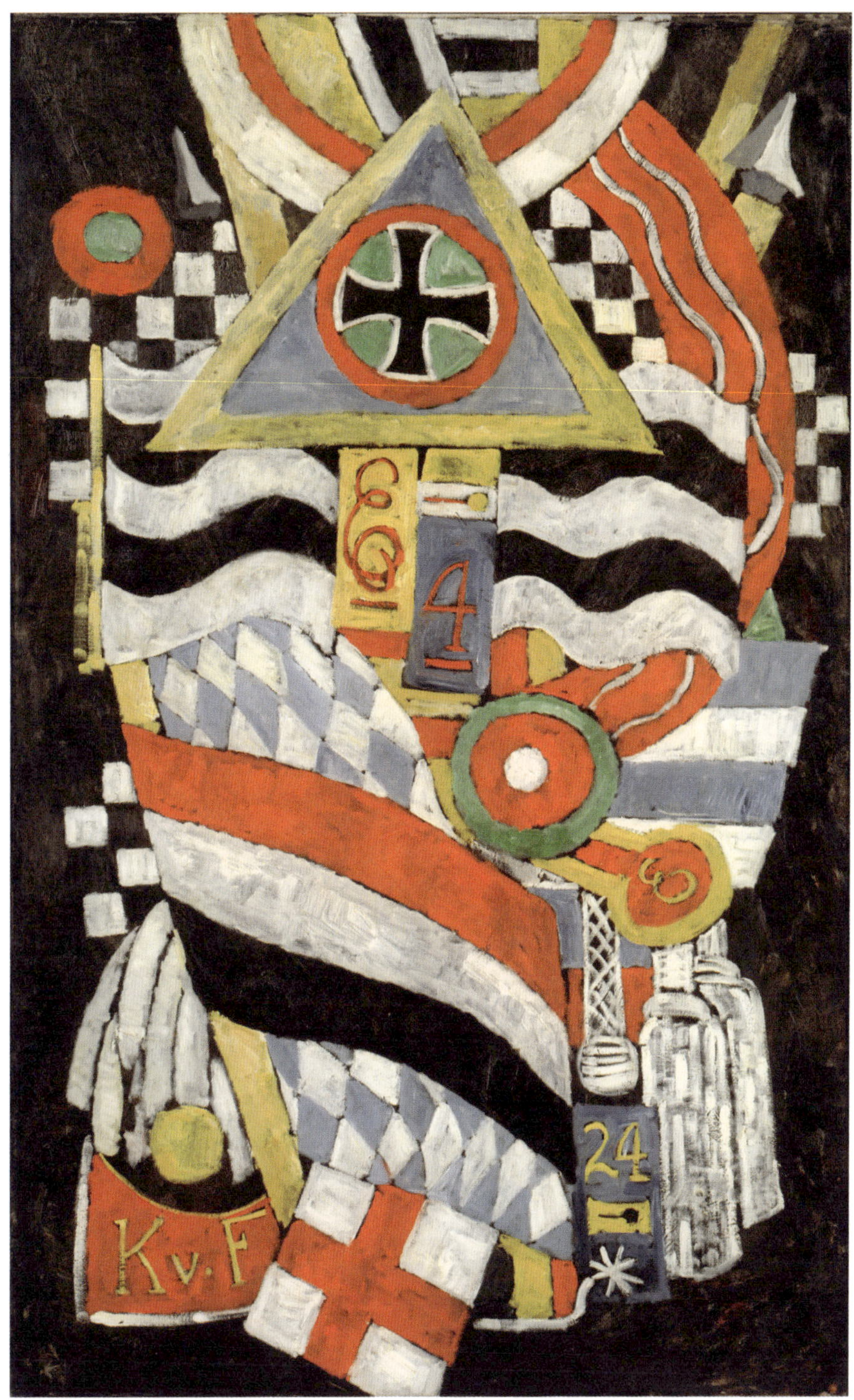

67

Another artist who should help us to reconsider the old bias against American art as lagging behind the times was Marsden Hartley, who had also spent considerable time in Europe and was well aware of the change of mood there. Indeed, he had lived it first hand, through the loss of a dear friend (and presumed lover), the dashing young German officer Karl von Freyburg, who was an early casualty of the war, killed in October 1914. The mood of the dazzling colour and pageantry he had captured in his brilliant, thrilling paintings of pre-war Berlin shifted overnight to one of loss and elegy. But in a terrible irony of the sort that only war can bring, it led to the creation of his German military series, including *Portrait of a German Officer* (1914) [67], surely the greatest painting of his life and among the most accomplished works done by any artist in the first half of the twentieth century.

It is a large, vertical work of painterly and emotional depth, the largest Hartley ever did, standing before us in a presentational mode and, although abstract, a virtually literal embodiment of von Freyburg himself. We meet him as if he were present with us, or as if he were beside Hartley, still living. It is an object-portrait, with a discernible head and body, composed of the Iron Cross, the emblems of his unit and his age, '24', knitted together in a type of Cubist grid or design, presenting the awful facts of war so that we cannot help but come face to face with them. The hues are strong, deep and rich but not blazing as they had been; they are muted by their setting against a funereal black ground, an elegy for the lost friend and love, for the loss of life wrought by the war, a loss of a connection with a loved culture, and finally the loss of an old order, for the world was never again the same. The casualties suffered by the English, French and Germans were horrendous, amounting to millions and millions of deaths and virtually wiping out an entire generation of young men.

Georgia O'Keeffe (1887–1986) later commented that seeing this series of paintings at 291 in 1916 was like listening to a brass band in a closet. From these paintings came the inspiration for her outburst of colour in 1917, which marks her as one of America's best colour artists. O'Keeffe had met Stanton Macdonald-Wright and was impressed by his use of colour, which was, in addition to Hartley's, a catalyst for the change in her work from dark charcoals to brilliant, spectral hues that launched her as an important contributor to American colour painting thereafter. Her watercolours of this time, such as *Evening Star III* (1917) [69], are original and exceptional, distinguished for the sheer beauty of the hues. These were applied directly to the paper, soaking in as watercolour does, forming an indivisible bond with the support, so the clarity and colour remain pure, uncluttered by any build-up of excess pigment. This method of direct application in watercolour came to be a source for later painting, known as colour-field painting, which emerged in the 1950s.

In 1916, Hartley's art also changed dramatically. No longer were his canvases crowded with high-keyed hues; his colour shifted to a darker

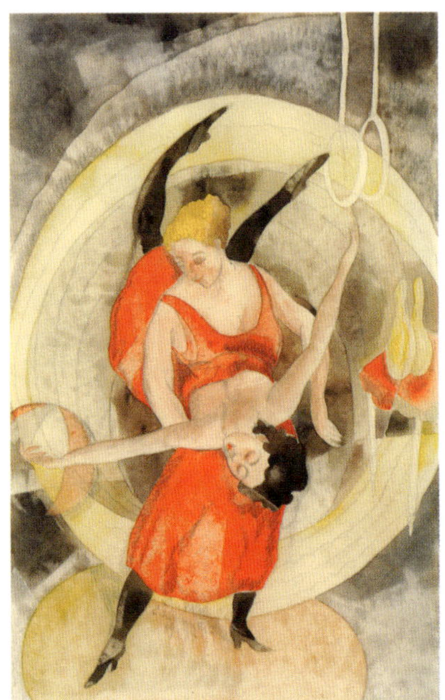

68

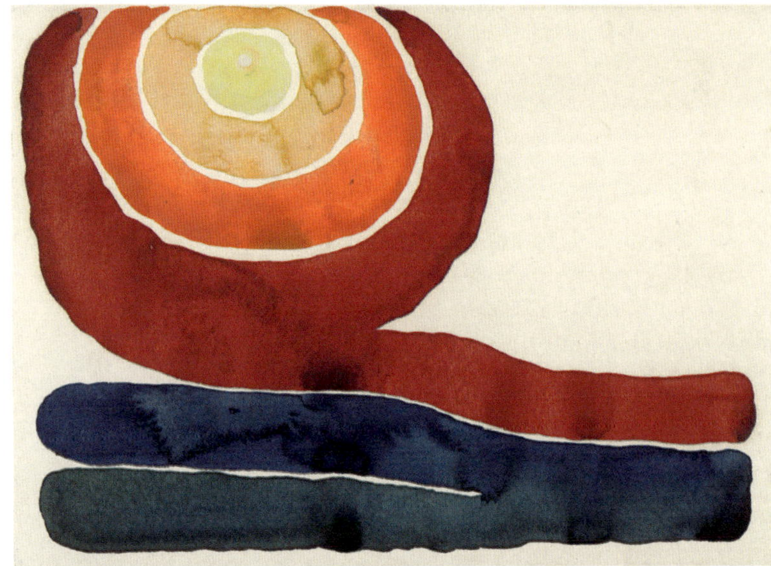

69

68 Charles Demuth, *Tumblers*, 1917. Watercolour and pencil on paper, 33 × 20.3 cm (13 × 8 in). Private collection

69 Georgia O'Keeffe, *Evening Star III*, 1917. Watercolour on paper mounted on board, 22.7 × 30.4 cm (8⅞ × 11⅞ in). The Museum of Modern Art, New York

70 Marsden Hartley, *Movement 1 (Provincetown)*, 1916. Oil on board, 50.8 × 40.2 cm (20 × 15¹³⁄₁₆ in). Philadelphia Museum of Art

71 Charles Demuth, *Bermuda No. 2, The Schooner*, 1917. Watercolour and graphite on paper, 25.4 × 35.2 cm (10 × 13⅞ in). The Metropolitan Museum of Art, New York

Modern Art in America

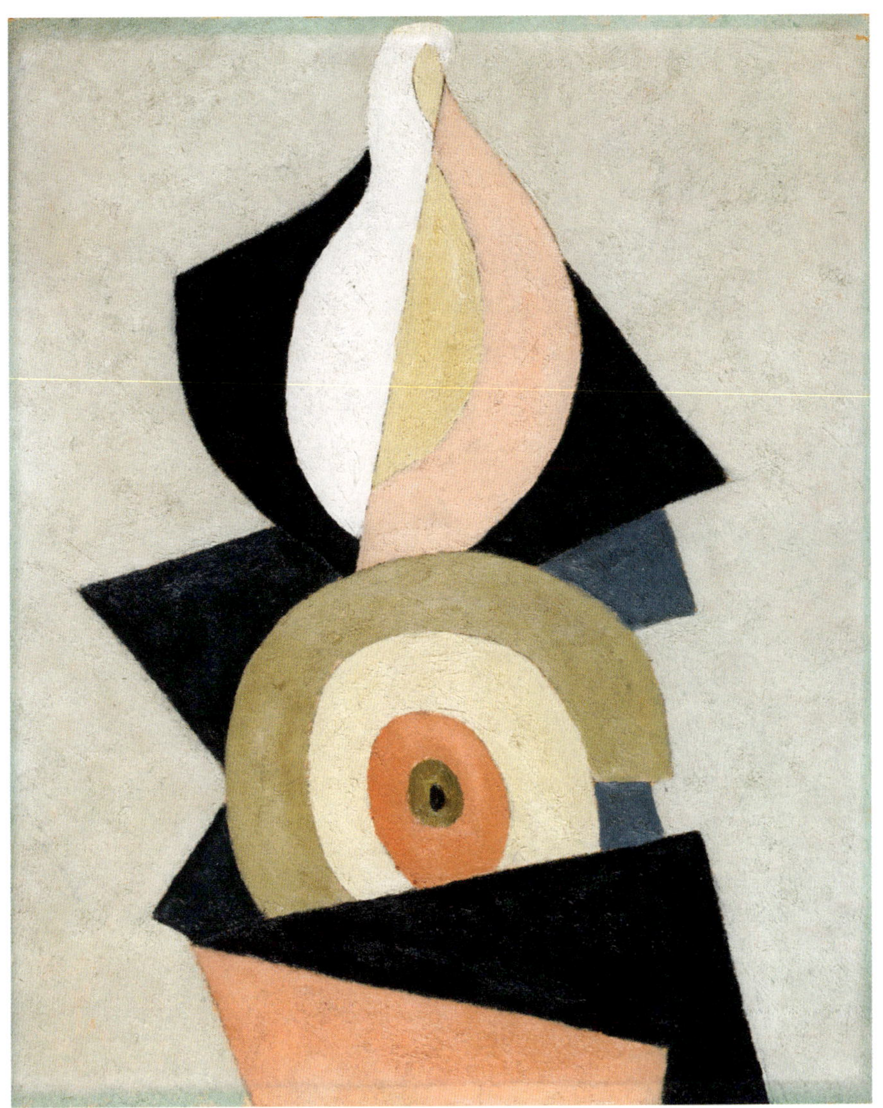

70

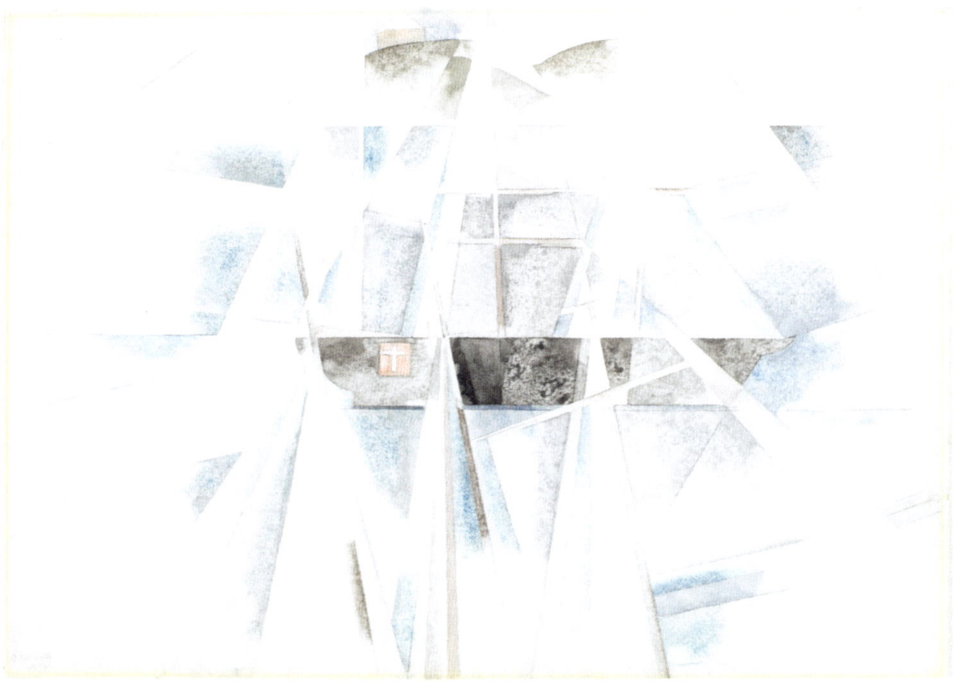

71

palette, of blacks, browns and greys, muted and sombre, arranged in a reductive Cubist format of fewer, broader and clearer shapes than the earlier work [70]. His darker colours surely reflected the sombre mood of the war, and its emphasis on a formal and emotive discipline, a sense of a solid foundation, that we see in Bruce's paintings of the same year.

In 1916–17, the art of Charles Demuth (1883–1935) moved from full painterly surfaces to a more controlled and focused structure, as did Charles Burchfield's. Working with Hartley and Albert Gleizes in Bermuda, Demuth developed his thinly painted, razor-sharp angular watercolours, which belong to the first phase of Precisionism[71]. They are refined, controlled and balanced, with clear, open forms and hues, and as such are part of the drive to a new classicism undertaken by Bruce and Hartley. In works like *Tumblers* (1917)[68], broad swathes of circles bathe the performers in light, certainly forms that acknowledge the intersecting patterns of Synchromism and Orphism.

Although Synchromism no longer existed as a formal movement, its principles lived on. Macdonald-Wright, like many artists, had returned to America when the war began. His art, as in *Still-Life Synchromy* (1917)[72], for example, became fuller and more complex, and even more nuanced and subtle than it had been before. Here, his painting is filled with dazzling passages of colour that seem directly descended from Renoir and the atmospheric space of Turner, two artists whom he deeply admired. The painting seems veiled, as though in another world altogether, making it difficult to read. But we can see at lower right a jug on a table, an apple floating above it and two figures, difficult to discern, emerging from the background. All elements are fractured and grouped around a central cluster of Orphic circles common to colour painting of the time; here they serve as the generating core from which the artist orchestrates the overall composition. The figuration is not surprising, since even the more abstract paintings such as *Arm Organization* (1914)[73] were based on Michelangelo's *Dying Slave*[74] in the Louvre, a work that Macdonald-Wright and Russell had studied so closely. However, both American and European artists used the figure more often after the war started, as a way to a more stable and firmly constructed painting. The two figures here are a man behind a reclining woman, probably a seduction scene, signalled by the broken vessel, an old symbol of lost maidenhood, as is the apple, pointing to the original sin of Adam and Eve. It is a spectacular work, done when Macdonald-Wright was not yet thirty, telling us of his precocious facility as a painter.[7]

Ernest Percyval Tudor-Hart had taught Macdonald-Wright and Russell a complex scheme of relating specific colours to particular musical notes in varying octaves. The two Americans had simplified Tudor-Hart's system by way of a simple analogy of the twelve-tone musical scale with the twelve colours of the standard colour wheel, perhaps paralleling Arnold Schoenberg's use of the twelve-tone scale. If one moved around the colour wheel in set intervals the way one would play a musical scale on the piano, one could arrive at an analogous colour scale. *Still-Life Synchromy* is painted in the scale of red, which is comprised of tonic red, followed by orange, yellow, yellow-green, blue-green, blue-violet and red-violet. Macdonald-Wright wrote: 'red is the great energetic contrast scale. It is beautifully harmonized, is simple and honest, but to see and to feel the beauty of this scale requires more sensitivity than for most scales.'[8] But we need only see and relate to the sheer technical skill of colour and brush to appreciate the body of work that Macdonald-Wright created.

72 Stanton Macdonald-Wright, *Still-Life Synchromy*, 1917. Oil on canvas, 56.4 × 76.2 cm, (22⅛ × 30¼ in). Private collection

Modern Art in America

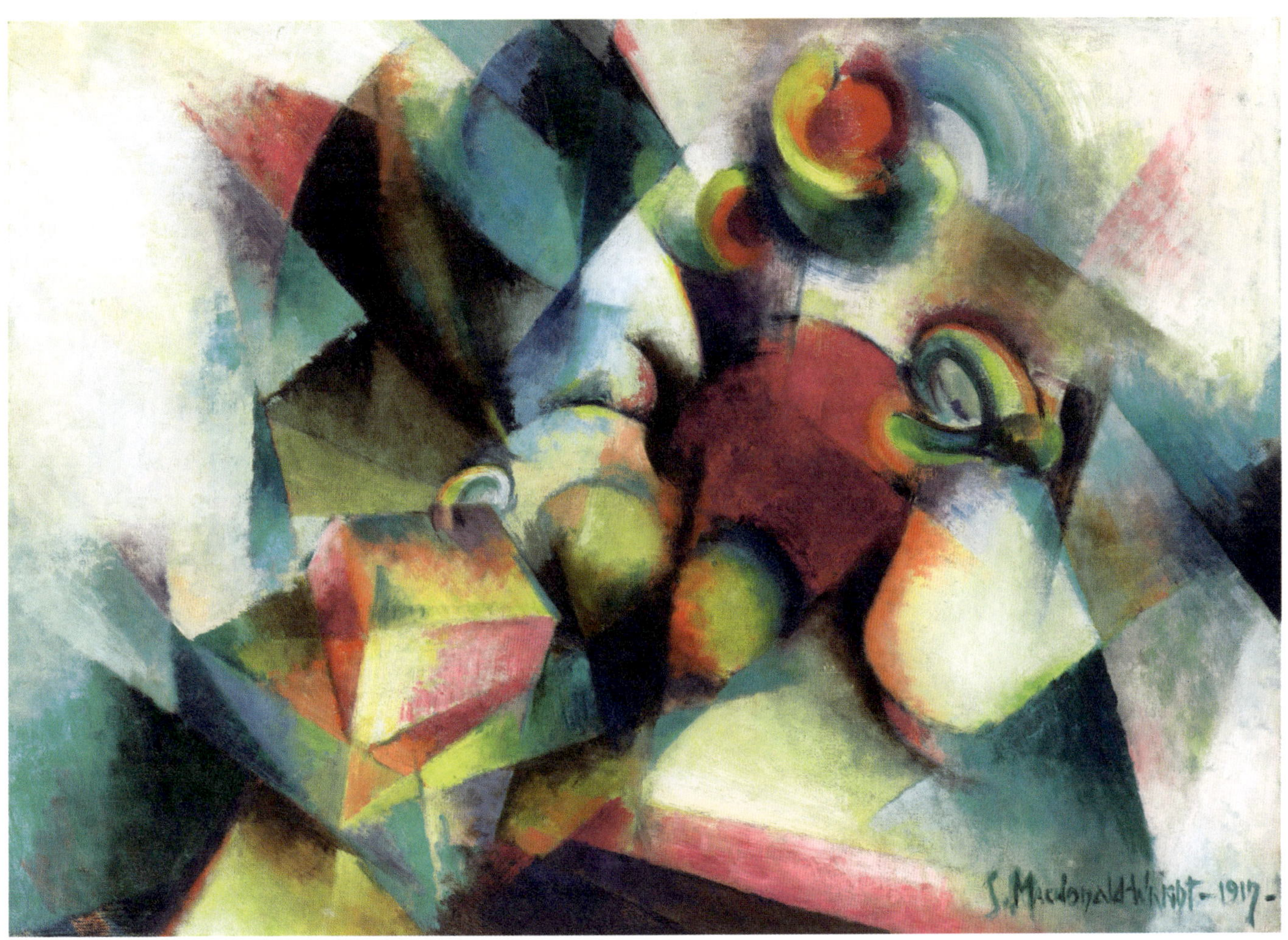

72

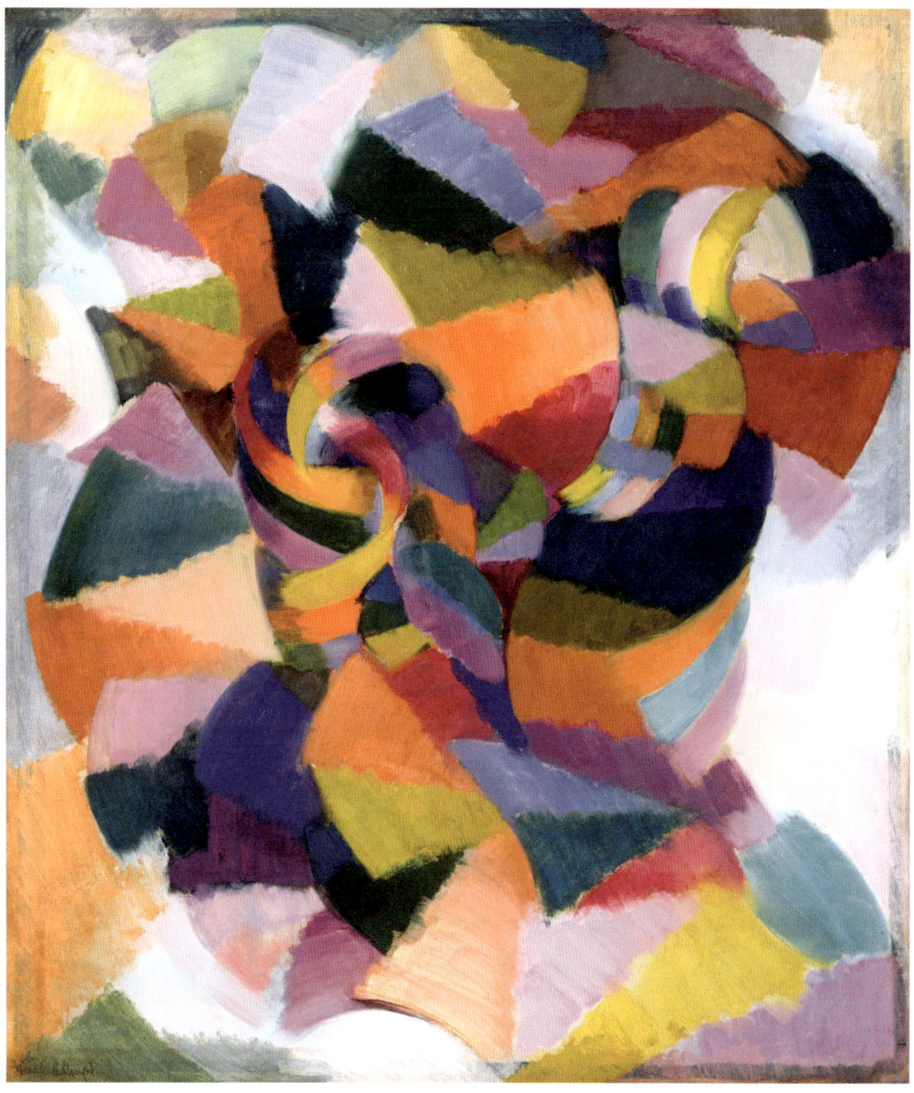

73

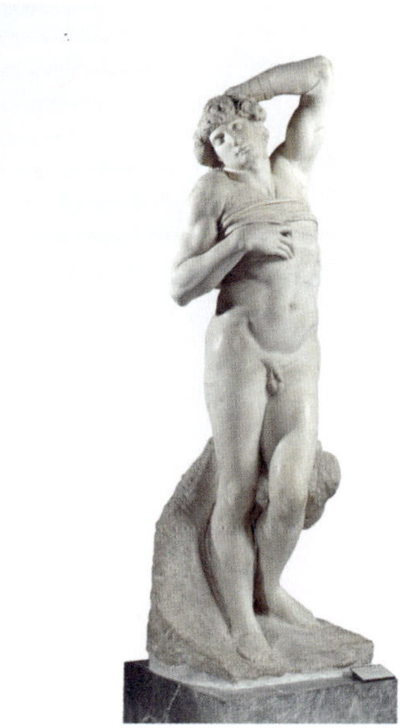

74

73 Stanton Macdonald-Wright,
Arm Organization, 1914.
Oil on canvas, 91.4 × 76 cm
(36 × 30³⁄₁₆ in). The Museum
of Fine Arts, Houston

74 Michelangelo, *Dying Slave*,
*c.*1513–15. Marble, height:
2.3 m (7½ ft). Musée du
Louvre, Paris

75 Thomas Hart Benton,
Constructivist Still Life,
1916–17. Oil and tempera
on canvas, 31.7 × 20.3 cm
(12½ × 8 in). Private collection

76 John Marin, *River Scene
from Weehawken*, 1916.
Oil on canvas, 50.2 × 59 cm
(19¾ × 23¼ in). Karen and
Kevin Kennedy Collection,
New York

Thomas Hart Benton, America's most famous regionalist, a painter of the Midwest, had started in Paris, in 1910, as a student of Macdonald-Wright, from whom he learned about Impressionism, Cézanne and abstraction. In 1916 and 1917 he made a series of abstract still lifes[75] that were based on Macdonald-Wright's colour principles. These colour chords merged into his art after 1920 and became a staple of his painting, most especially in his later murals. His baroque, twisting contortions, his 'bump and hollow' method as it was known, were also derived from Macdonald-Wright's teachings of Baroque art; the same in-and-out movements can be seen in *Arm Organization*. Looking ahead, we recall that Benton was Pollock's teacher in the 1930s, and the churning gestural movements at the heart of Pollock's iconic all-over paintings of 1947–50 can be traced in good part to the baroque rhythms first developed by Macdonald-Wright. Further, colour was far more intense in and important to Pollock's work than has been acknowledged, confirming once more that Synchromism and early colour abstraction had a deep and long-standing impact.

Prior to 1916–17, John Marin had developed a gentle, lyrical style of watercolour painting, primarily landscapes after his visits to Paris, the earliest in 1905. By 1912, he had mastered a focused, condensed and powerful mode in both oil and watercolour that places him at the forefront of those working with colour. His watercolour of 1912 *Sunset* is composed

Modern Art in America

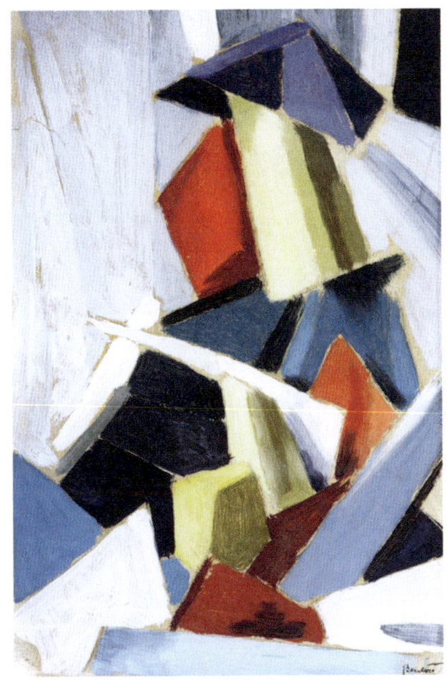

75

around a strong band-like arrangement of sky, middle distance and foreground, flattened into a single plane that will remind us of the classic images of Mark Rothko after 1949. These early works were perfectly pleasant, but in 1916–17, Marin's art underwent a radical transformation, shifting into an intense, explosive expressionism of dense strokes and colours. Whether this came from his reaction to the war has never been discussed, but it is a possibility. Known as the 'Weehawken' series [76], these works seem to be the product of another artist altogether. But it is from this date that Marin truly emerged as a first-rate artist and a major force in American art until his death in 1953.

Marin's explosions of rapid strokes of intense hues may have been a response to the 1916 Forum Exhibition of Modern American Painters organized by Macdonald-Wright with his brother Willard, and with the collaboration of other art-world figures, specifically to demonstrate how colour had taken hold in American art. In addition to Macdonald-Wright, Russell and Benton, artists such as Arthur Dove were included (a stretch, since Dove's colour was still limited). William Zorach was represented with landscapes of high colour, making one wish he had stayed with painting rather than devoting himself to academic sculptures for the rest of his career, the worst of a retro classicism that would plague American art for years to come. The exhibition was also compromised by Macdonald-Wright's editing of the artists' statements, in some cases making them virtual inventions.[9] However, the point was made: colour could provide the means to a dynamic type of art. Macdonald-Wright's art was even more in evidence in 1917 after his exhibition, at Alfred Stieglitz's Gallery 291, and at the Daniel Gallery in March of the next year.

Joseph Stella and Early Precisionism

Joseph Stella (1877–1946), one of America's most diverse, unpredictable artists in terms of style and theme, also participated in the development of the thin, sharp, crystalline linearity of early Precisionism. In fact, Stella

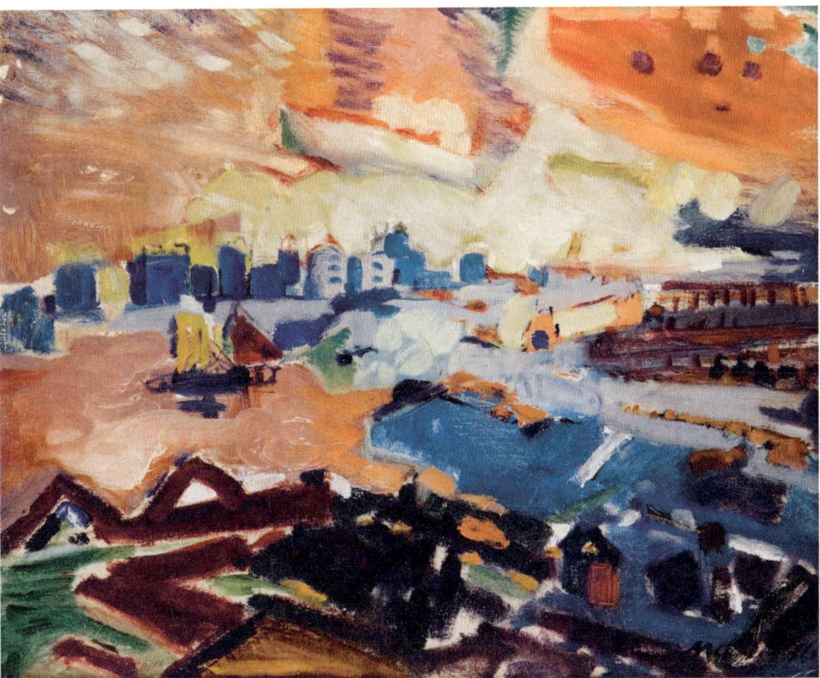

76

gives full evidence of the transformation of artists from pre-war free-form abstraction, in which planes and lines interact simultaneously, to a more focused, stable and centred format, and, in Stella's case, a more figurative style as well.

Stella had made his mark early on with his Futurist paintings based on Luna Park at Coney Island, filled with seemingly limitless prismatic shafts and beams of light breaking and shattering into myriad forms. He had also been drawn to the Brooklyn Bridge[77] as no other American artist had been. He took it almost as a personal icon, a towering, monumental symbol of the best of American architecture and engineering. For years after its opening in 1883–4, the bridge was the largest structure not only in New York, but in America as well. In effect, it was really an early skyscraper, or actually two, with its span swooshing across the East River, seemingly starting from nowhere and shooting into a limitless space. It was America's Eiffel Tower, pre-dating the feats of Charles Eiffel in France, and that was the way it was depicted in early paintings and prints: as almost a cosmic force unto itself. It was surely everything the Futurists loved. Stella was particularly taken with the bridge at night. He started depicting it around 1918, from a distance, in a Futurist manner, with lines of force speeding across the surface and intersecting continuously with others. He then gradually focused the image until it was centred, the suspension wires brought into balance and control, the arches forming virtual altarpieces, as if we were up close and on the bridge itself, moving towards the object of devotion like a twentieth-century pilgrimage to a mechanical idol. He later transformed the bridge as part of a five-panel piece, *The Voice of the City of New York Interpreted* (1920–2), depicting New York, again like a central altar and its wings. As French artists such as Duchamp-Villon and the Delaunays had venerated the Eiffel Tower, seeing it as a modern reincarnation of the glories of French gothic cathedrals, especially Chartres, so Stella saw the bridge as a modern urban cathedral, a kind of pilgrimage church.

De Stijl and post-Russian Revolution Constructivism

The destruction wrought by the war changed the course of art in manifold ways throughout the Western world.[10] In the Netherlands, Mondrian and the De Stijl (The Style) movement, founded in 1917, sought a structural type of art that could literally build a new world, architecturally, artistically, morally and spiritually. De Stijl could be applied to all aspects of art and life, and thus called for a new cohesion of the artist with the broader world, a joining of art to the pulse of life itself. This aim was generated and deliberately set as a reaction against what was seen as the overly individualistic and self-centred practice of pre-war art. From then on, art had to be an intrinsic part of life, and had to serve society. This was the same course set by the Russian Constructivists after the Revolution of 1917; art and life were viewed as inseparable. Art was meant to build a new society after the chaos of the war and the revolution, and every citizen could be an artist in this effort. Art was no longer an elitist affair, a private practice, but was to be directed towards improving society at large. This art and life debate runs throughout the century; here, art is a function of life, to be undertaken by everyone, so as to improve and build society. In the United States, these abstract movements would not make an impact until the 1930s, when Josef Albers brought their principles from the Bauhaus to America, first at the avant-garde school Black Mountain College in North Carolina (see pages 230–1).

77 Joseph Stella, *Brooklyn Bridge*, 1919–20. Oil on canvas, 215.3 × 194.6 cm (84¾ × 76⅝ in). Yale University Art Gallery, New Haven

Modern Art in America

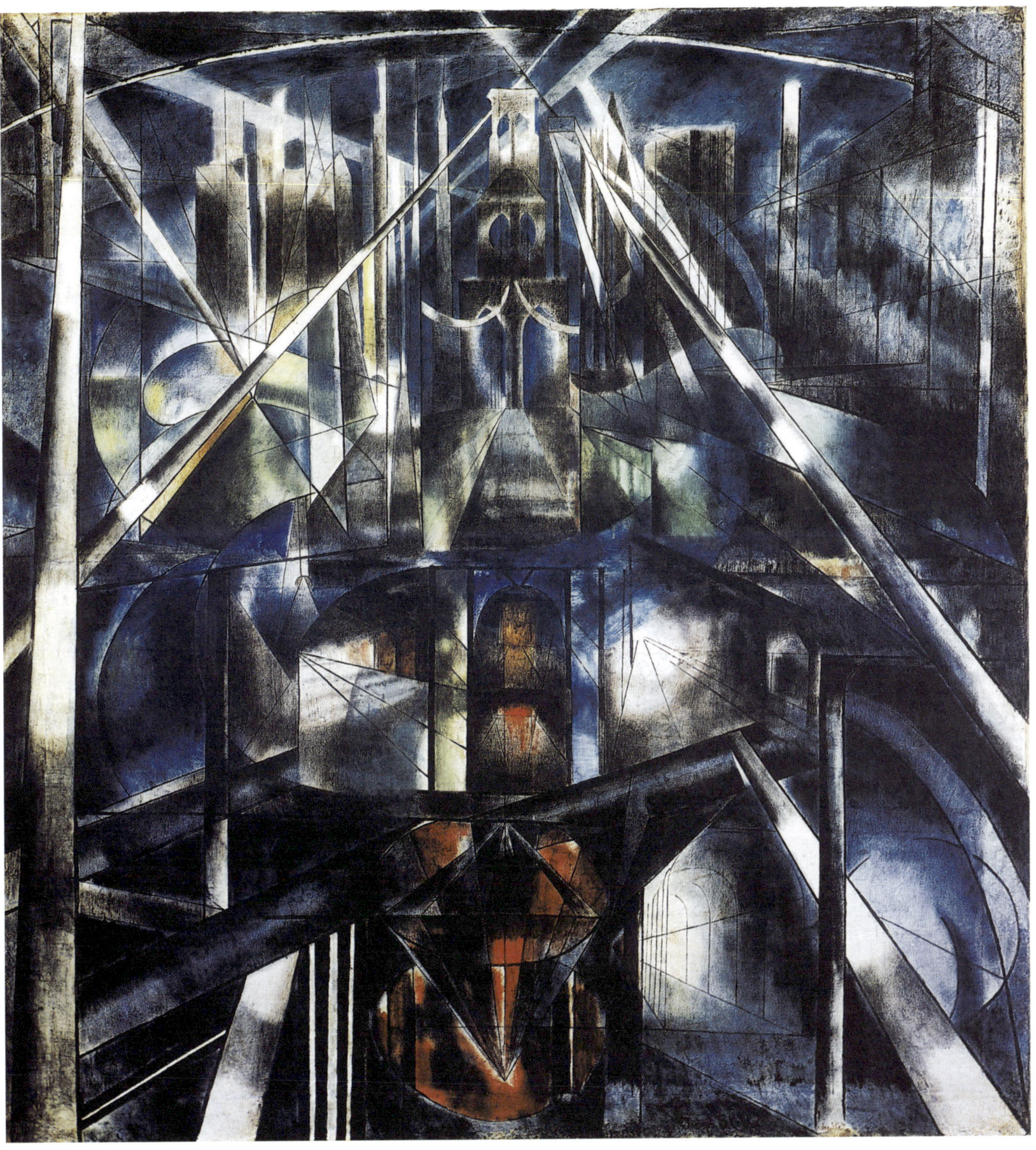

77

THE ROOTS OF DADA IN AMERICA

A third direction, which we can now see was the most far-reaching of all, was the development of the multifaceted Dada movement. Dada was officially born in 1916, in Zurich, but its roots can be traced to America, and specifically to New York, as early as 1912, well before the outbreak of war; in fact, New York can be said to be the epicentre of the movement, and the city might well be the real birthplace of Dada. For in 1913, Marcel Duchamp's *Nude Descending the Staircase* at the Armory Show was one of the most notorious works seen there, and his very presence in the city announced a new attitude towards high art. It is one of the hallmarks of the modern sensibility that a reaction to the existing art and attitudes sets in almost immediately. Duchamp's poke at the classical nude, now rendered as a clanking machine contraption, was perhaps the first, well-known jibe at the existing tide of painterly abstraction, whether based on colour or on Cubism, which formed the high art of the day. We see this type of reaction throughout this book, whether in the early 1950s or the mid-1960s, in reactions first to Pollock, then to Donald Judd.

The full-blown Dada spirit as we know it arose in protest against the war, in effect proclaiming that if that were where our rational minds had brought us, to nothing less than disaster, then we must start exploring our

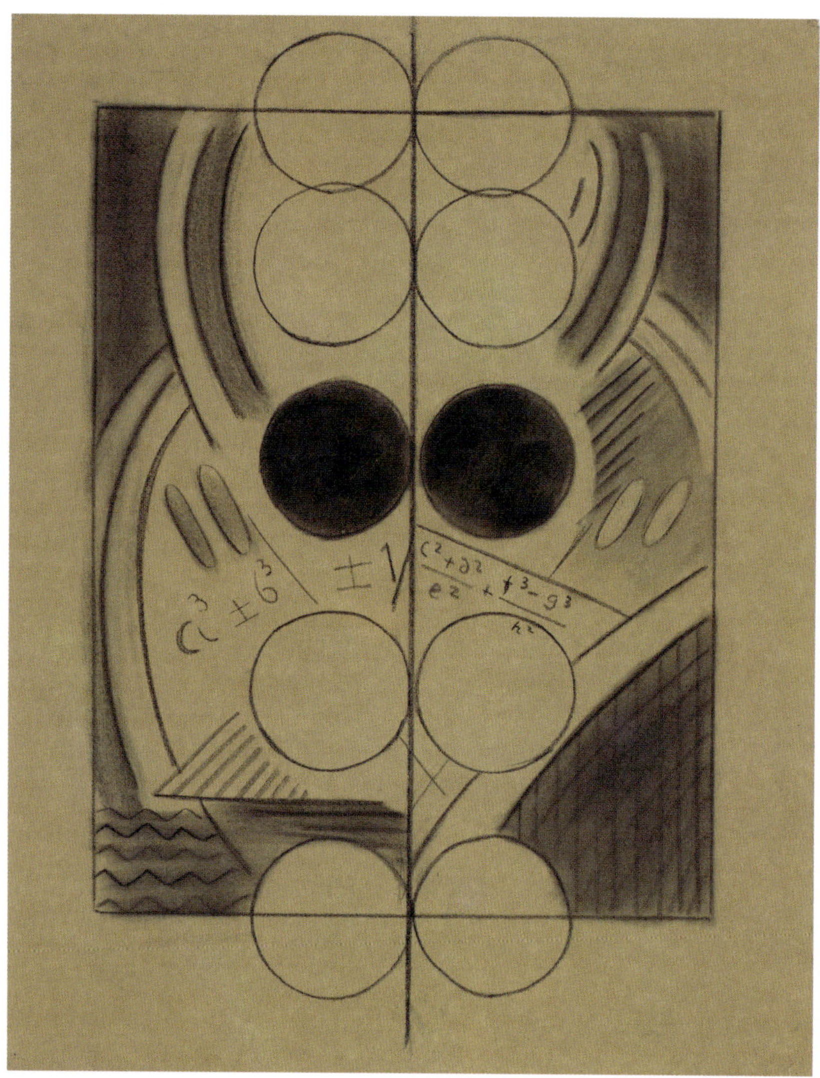

78 Marius de Zayas, *Alfred Stieglitz*, c. 1912–13. Charcoal on paper, 62.2 × 47.6 cm (24½ × 18¾ in). The Metropolitan Museum of Art, New York

Modern Art in America

other side, the irrational as the source of life. If high art was the equivalent of our most exalted institutions and leaders, then it must be subjected to serious and sustained critical examination. Indeed, one Dada artist said: 'Dada tried to destroy not so much art as the idea one had of art, breaking down its rigid borders, lowering its imaginary heights – subjecting them to a dependence on a man, to his power – humbling art; significantly making it take place and subordinating its value to pure movement which is also the movement of life.'[11]

But in fact, the core of Dada rebellion had started as a protest against the increasing materialism and sanctity of American life and art. Interestingly enough, it began within the ranks of the Stieglitz circle, best known for its role as the centre for advanced and abstracting modern art. Benjamin de Casseres (1873–1945) and Marius de Zayas (1880–1961) were both friends of Stieglitz and editors of the magazine *Camera Work*. They were the first to launch a full-scale attack on the canons of art and morality and thus to define the attitudes of what later became known as Dada. De Casseres is still little known, and has not received full credit for his early and intense assaults on established institutions. In the July 1910 issue of *Camera Work*, he published a systematic disavowal of bourgeois rationalism:

> *In poetry, physics, practical life there is nothing…that is any longer moored to a certainty, nothing that is forbidden, nothing that cannot be stood on its head and glorified…*
> *Anarchy? No. It is the triumph of discrimination, the beatification of paradox, the sanctification of man by man…*
> *Nothing which lasts is of value…That which changes perpetually, lives perpetually…*
> *I find my supremest joy in my estrangements…I desire to become unfamiliar with myself…I cling to nothing, stay with nothing, am used to nothing, hope for nothing. I am a perpetual minute.[12]*

In April 1912, de Casseres explicitly invoked the Dada litany of revolt when he stated: 'All great movements begin with the gesture of hate, of irony, of revenge…There is a re-evaluation going on in the art of the world today. There is a healthy mockery, a healthy anarchic spirit abroad…No art is perfect until you have smashed it.'[13] He was soon joined by de Zayas, a Mexican artist and writer working in New York, who in the July 1912 issue of *Camera Work* lamented the artist's loss of contact with the unknown, foreshadowing and even defining Dada's interest in the primitive and irrational side of human behaviour, urging a new participation in the untrammelled instincts of the child's world. De Zayas concluded with what became the familiar Dada cry, 'Art is dead', with which de Casseres concurred the following year.[14]

Picabia in New York

When Francis Picabia (1879–1953) arrived in New York in January 1913 to visit the Armory Show, he no doubt came into contact with de Zayas and de Casseres, all of which surely quickened the pace of his dissent. We know he was quickly in touch with Stieglitz, meeting him and other members of the 291 circle almost daily, before returning to Paris in April. The chant of de Casseres's 'healthy anarchic' spirit echoes throughout Picabia's 'Manifeste de l'école amorphiste' published in the June 1913 issue of *Camera Work*, one of the first Dada announcements in the world. Picabia's manifesto included diagrams of two blank canvases entitled *Femme au bain* (*Woman Bathing*) and *La mer* (*The Sea*), which were signed 'Popaul Picador'.[15] By parodying these two standard themes of painting, Picabia denounced what he took to be the impoverished idealism of Western thought and art. His use of a pseudonym (as with Duchamp's adoption of the female alias Rrose Sélavy in 1920) established the Dada questioning of the relevance of personal identity to the work of art. In turn, we can trace this as the source for the wholesale shift in art to questions of identity during the 1990s in America.

The interaction between these artists may have encouraged de Zayas to pursue his anti-art gestures. In a series of abstract caricatures, still little known[78], he reduced portraits of public figures and members of the Stieglitz circle, including Picabia himself, to invented forms punctuated by mathematical equations. Like Picabia's blank diagrams, they repudiated the portrait 'likeness', long a mainstay of Western art. In its stead, de Zayas introduced a new symbolic-associative language, which was a forerunner of Picabia's object-portraits of 1915–17. One of the most famous of these was Picabia's disrespectful 'portrait' of Stieglitz, *Ici, C'est Ici Stieglitz Foi et Amour*, as a broken-down camera[79].

291 Magazine

The collaboration continued for several years, with the founding in New York of *291* magazine in March 1915. Edited by de Zayas and Paul Haviland, and published by Stieglitz in conjunction with his gallery of the same name, *291* was a continuing source of Dada images and ideas, although it lasted for only twelve issues, until February 1916. In it appeared some of Picabia's most famous Dada creations, such as the spark plug labelled *Portrait d'une jeune fille américaine dans l'état de nudité* (Portrait of a Young American Girl in a State of Nudity) (1915). The publication of *291* was the last phase of the Stieglitz circle's Dada activities. The rupture was caused in part by strong disagreements between de Zayas and Stieglitz over what role commerce should play in current art – Stieglitz was resistant to it, de Zayas all for it. But at heart, Stieglitz was more truly given to American painting and photography that moved in an abstracting manner, often with a strong spiritual underpinning. He preferred Dove, Marin, O'Keeffe and his own art to Dada diagrams and puns. This unlikely fusion of supporters and artists, however, had yielded a rich vein for American art, and is one more clear sign that it was far from behind the times or provincial, the tired clichés that we have heard for so many years.

Arensberg Salon

But Dada was far from finished in New York. Indeed, American Dada lasted longer than we have understood, actually longer than in Europe. It can be traced from 1912 to 1930, the date of the last collages done by Arthur Dove that were inspired by Dada, especially by the collages of Kurt Schwitters, often on view in the galleries of the Société Anonyme. By 1916, its locus had shifted to another circle and salon, still less known and appreciated than Stieglitz and his group, for he has rightly commanded the most attention. From 1915 to 1920, the avant-garde salon conducted by Walter Conrad Arensberg (1878–1954) and his wife Louise in their apartment on West 67th Street in New York was the source of many of the most far-reaching ideas injected into America up to that time.[16] It included Duchamp, Picabia and Man Ray, as well as a diverse group of artists who added to the body of Dada art in ways still little known, or yet unrecognized.

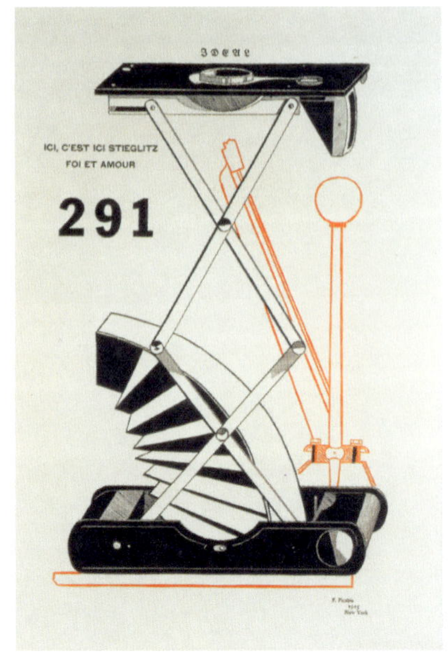

79

79 Francis Picabia, *Ici, C'est Ici Stieglitz Foi et Amour*, 1915. Relief print on paper, 44 × 28.9 cm (17⁵⁄₁₆ × 11³⁄₈ in). National Portrait Gallery, Smithsonian Institution, Washington, DC

That there was even such a thing as a body of Dada work in the United States went unacknowledged for a long time, primarily, one supposes, because Dada seemingly went against the grain of American innocence and optimism, its faith in order, reason and logic. That changed dramatically after the events of 1968, so that today we can understand more clearly the nuances of the American character and its history, including its profound cynicism and corruption, allowing perfectly for the contrary spirit of the Dada attitude.

Arensberg – poet, critic, patron and collector of the first order – and his wife Louise were warm and congenial hosts. Their salon should be considered as important as the Steins' in Paris and those around Stieglitz. The nucleus of their circle consisted of Duchamp and Picabia and, soon after, Man Ray, who had met Duchamp after his arrival in New York in May 1915. The group attracted other lively artists, and by early 1916 the Arensberg apartment was the scene of endless activities and discussions carried on at all hours of the day and night.[17] Until the Arensbergs moved to California in the early 1920s, their salon was one of the most extraordinary in American history, and was visited by authors Henri-Pierre Roché, Walter Pach, poet William Carlos Williams, dancer Isadora Duncan, composer Edgard Varèse, and artists Albert Gleizes, Jean Crotti, Joseph Stella, Marsden Hartley, Katherine Dreier, Charles Demuth, Charles Sheeler, Morton Livingston Schamberg, John Sloan, John Covert, George Bellows, and, quite possibly, Arthur Dove. The art of most, if not all, of the visitors was sooner or later touched by Dada, especially in the use of non-art materials and the embrace of machinist imagery, in one manner or another. Of inestimable value was the remarkable collection that Arensberg assembled, since it included important works by Picasso, Braque, Brancusi and Picabia, and the most comprehensive selection of Duchamps that could be found anywhere. In effect, it was an early, mini-museum of modern art; today it forms the heart of the modern collection, one of the best in the world, at the Philadelphia Museum of Art.

Unlike European Dada, the movement in America was not deeply literary, but its spokesman was Arensberg, a Shakespeare scholar who composed Dada poems and is credited with having written the only American Dada manifesto, which was published in the French magazine *Littérature* in May of 1920.[18] Although it was subsequently discovered that the text was not actually written by Arensberg (but rather by another Dada provocateur in Paris), it claimed that Dada belonged to America as much as it did to Europe and the world. This was really a statement of fact, and certainly not an empty boast. In addition, Arensberg offered considerable support to the three Dada magazines that appeared in New York: two issues of *The Blind Man*, in April and May 1917, a single issue of *Rongwrong* (May 1917) and one of *New York Dada*, in 1921.

From this circle issued some of the most important Dada art in the world, surely making New York a true centre of Dada, and for the time, of modernism. It was in New York that Duchamp conducted his famous debunking of supposed liberal artistic freedom by submitting in 1917 the notorious urinal *Fountain*, signed 'R. Mutt', to the newly formed Society of Independent Artists in New York. This organization, founded and run by artists, promised a new age of freedom, and proclaimed open admission for all, with no jury. One look at *Fountain*, however, and all that went out of the window in a New York second. Duchamp, Picabia and Man Ray were the three major full-time Dada artists working in New York. Indeed, Duchamp can be considered an American artist by this time. He loved America and New York, and was deeply touched by the city and the country, drawing continued inspiration and creative energy from them. But he was not recognized as such for a long time, even though he became an American citizen in 1955, mostly perhaps because the Whitney Museum of American Art disapproved of his shenanigans, which seemed un-American in their subversion. This too has obscured the obvious connections to the work of myriad Americans who followed in his wake. None of them adopted the full Dada attitude of rejection and rebellion, yet all were quick to see the possibilities in the Dada embrace of non-art materials and images. Those Europeans who came to the United States and became in spirit, outlook, and approach distinctly American are an important chapter in its history.

American Machinery and Precisionism

The first American after Man Ray to produce work that was directly indebted to Dada was Morton Livingston Schamberg. After his full-colour paintings of 1913–14, Schamberg turned to the precise linear drawing of Duchamp as found in his *Chocolate Grinders* (1913 and 1914) [80] and in the *Large Glass* (1915–23). Leave it to Duchamp to jump to an opposite pole from the trend towards painterly abstraction, to the exact *disegno* championed by the Renaissance artists – a contrary move apparently, but actually in keeping with the desire of many artists to continue the structural firmness of Old Master art. Nothing is easy or obvious with Duchamp, so that what seemed a move of rebellion was actually an affirmation of the art he was supposedly trying to destroy. This, too, can be seen as being a result of the dramatic shift in 1916 to a more classical art brought on by the destruction wrought by the war. But in Schamberg's case, it confirmed his early impulse, in his studies before 1910, to seek an art as sure and clear as that of the so-called Italian primitives.

In 1915 and 1916, Schamberg created his Dada-related machinist abstractions that had moved from the Cézanne-Matisse tradition to a detailed exactitude that is the true beginning of Precisionism, although its start is generally credited to Sheeler.[19] Their clarity also related to the new classical drive found in world art from 1916 onwards, a drive to a new solidity and stability, an art that would fit the needs of the new world to be ushered in after the war. However, Schamberg agonized over the war, and his optimistic belief in the machine as a progressive instrument was quickly eroded. To achieve his goals of a modern art based on solid structure, he turned once again to Cézanne, who by then was fully enshrined as a master of classic proportion and importance, the equal of any seventeenth-century artist. His one surviving late work is a beautiful drawing, *Fruitbowl* (1917) [81], done in a full-blown Cézannesque manner that tells us worlds about the shift in art brought about by the war. Schamberg clearly felt the need to reassert the primacy of drawing and the Old Masters, sure and solid, a metaphor for a new and more rational society that was foreseen for the world after the war. The fullness of the drawing embodies the very idea of the monumentality, order and stability of the classical past that could be a model for this new world.

Were it not for the schematic edge of the plate partially delineated in the foreground, we might well mistake the drawing for an image similar to the rocks and mountains that Cézanne loved to depict. The forms seem permanent, even timeless; in writing on Cézanne in 1913, Schamberg stated that when we add a consideration of 'weight, pressure, resistance, movement, as distinguished from motion', we are speaking of a fourth dimension.[20] In keeping with the desolate climate of the war, Schamberg limited himself to the stark contrasts of light and dark of the Conté crayon,

80 Marcel Duchamp, *Chocolate Grinder no.1*, 1913. Oil on canvas, 61.9 × 64.5 cm (24⅜ × 25⅜ in). Philadelphia Museum of Art

81 Morton Livingston Schamberg, *Fruitbowl*, 1917. Conté crayon on handmade Japanese tissue paper, 27.9 × 38.1 cm (11 × 15 in). The Albert Pilavin Memorial Collection of Twentieth-Century American Art, Museum of Art, Rhode Island School of Design, Providence

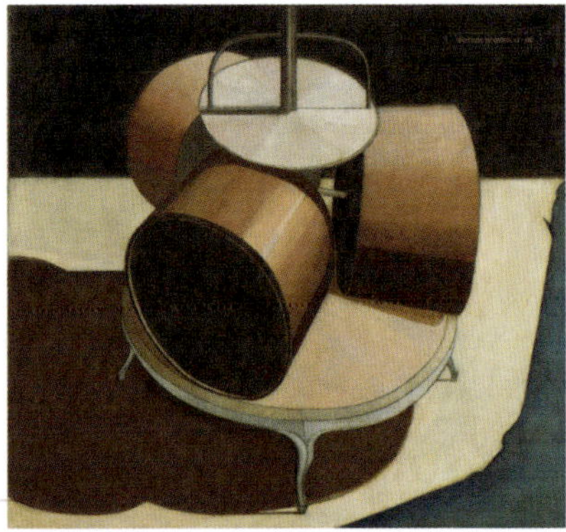

80

Modern Art in America

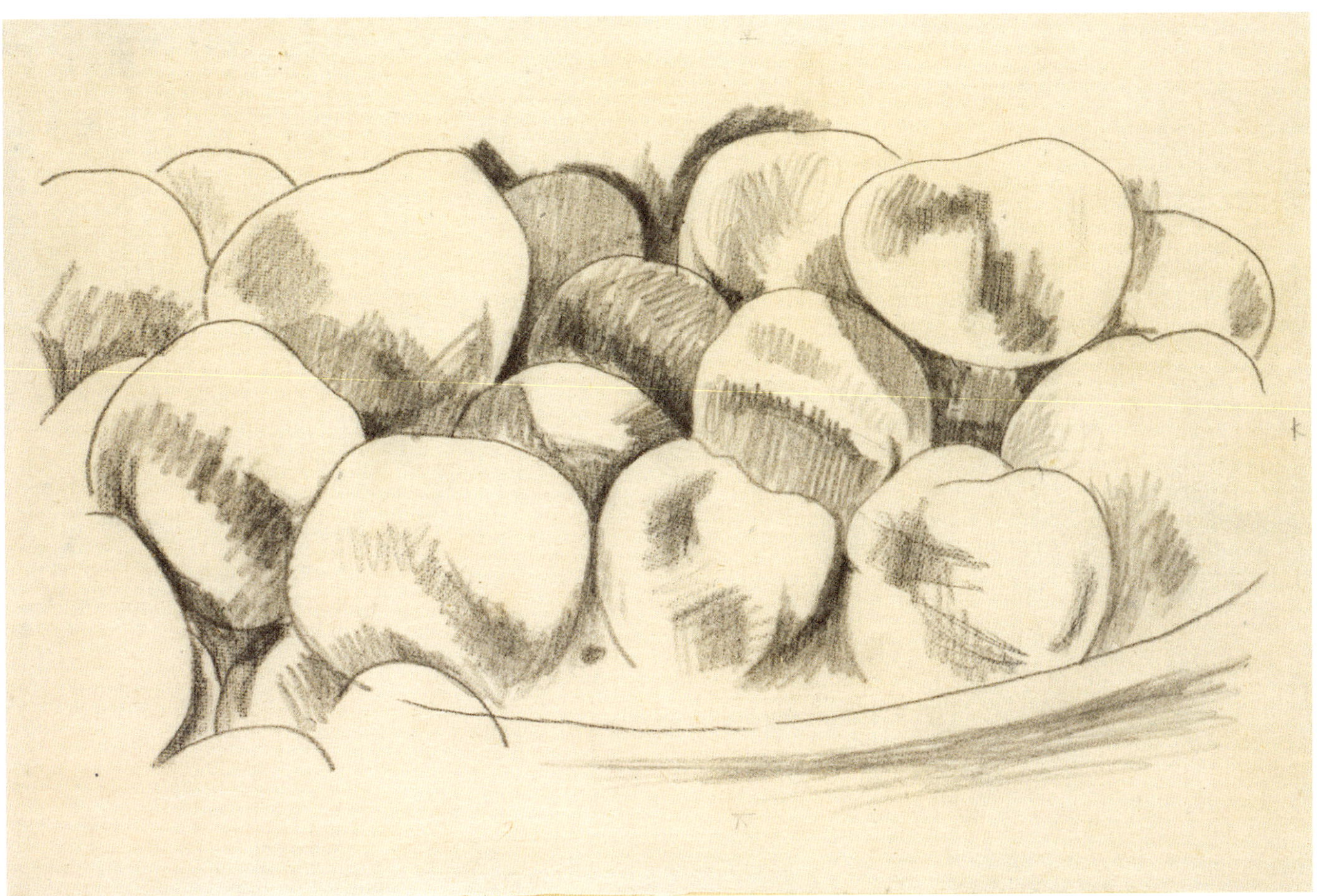

81

a tool that gives a waxy, tactile surface materiality. Schamberg makes the crayon darkest at the top from the apex of the triangular or pyramidal structure, as Cézanne often did in his watercolours and drawings. We then read the areas of the untouched paper as 'lighted volumetric form',[21] as colour itself, accentuating the depth and substance of the black marks. The fruits – if that is what they are – are so generalized that specific identification is impossible, giving a more abstract feel to the drawing. The abstract is thus made concrete and solid, transforming the 'chaotic into the purely architectural plastic', as Max Weber had written in his note on Cézanne for the catalogue of the show held at Montross Gallery, New York, in 1915–16.[22] This exhibition no doubt spurred interest in Cézanne to even greater heights and was doubly relevant given world events of the time.

Duchamp and Picabia had discovered American machinery and revelled in it, describing it as the true art of America. Urban views incorporating all manner of modern machines were commonplace in American art by 1916, most successfully, perhaps, in the work of John Sloan and George Bellows. However, the focus on a single machine, seen up close, in detail and in isolation, as the only element in the painting was new – another Dada pictorial discovery. In Picabia this was a diagrammatic usage, but in Duchamp it was a beautiful rendition, as it was for Schamberg in his machine images of 1916. Some of these machines, like the bookbinders depicted in the Yale and Philadelphia paintings, were still used by printers for years afterwards, demonstrating the typical predilection of American artists for the immediate, known world around us, the actual, particular facts. Another was formerly identified as a camera and flash, but in fact is a textile-splicing machine, used in the manufacturing company of Schamberg's father, something close to the artist. Schamberg has been credited with later making a Dada machine contraption (a plumbing fixture mounted on a box) with the ironic title *God* (1917), but most likely it was actually done by a true Dada personality, Baroness Elsa von Freytag-Loringhoven, who dressed and lived in a spirit of total anarchy. This precise type of drawing reintroduced by Duchamp is the true source of Precisionism, and Schamberg was in fact the first Precisionist proper, as can be seen in his *Painting* (formerly *Machine*, 1916)[82]. Although Schamberg died in the flu pandemic of 1918, his innovations were at the heart of the machine imagery rendered in a tight linearity that marked a large portion of American art in the decades to follow.

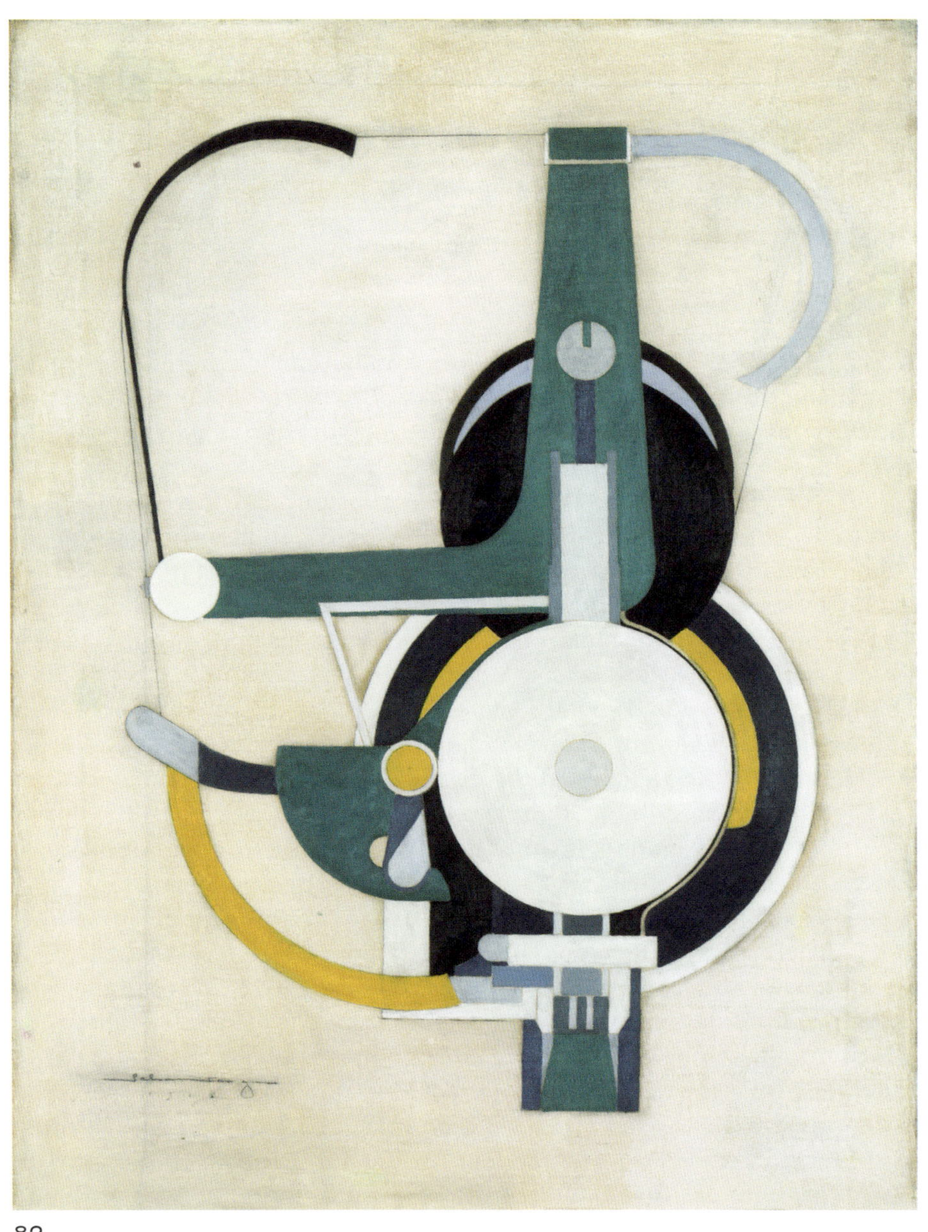

82

82   Morton Livingston Schamberg,
Painting (formerly *Machine*),
1916. Oil on canvas,
76.5 × 57.8 cm (30⅛ × 22¾ in).
Yale University Art Gallery,
New Haven

     Modern Art in America

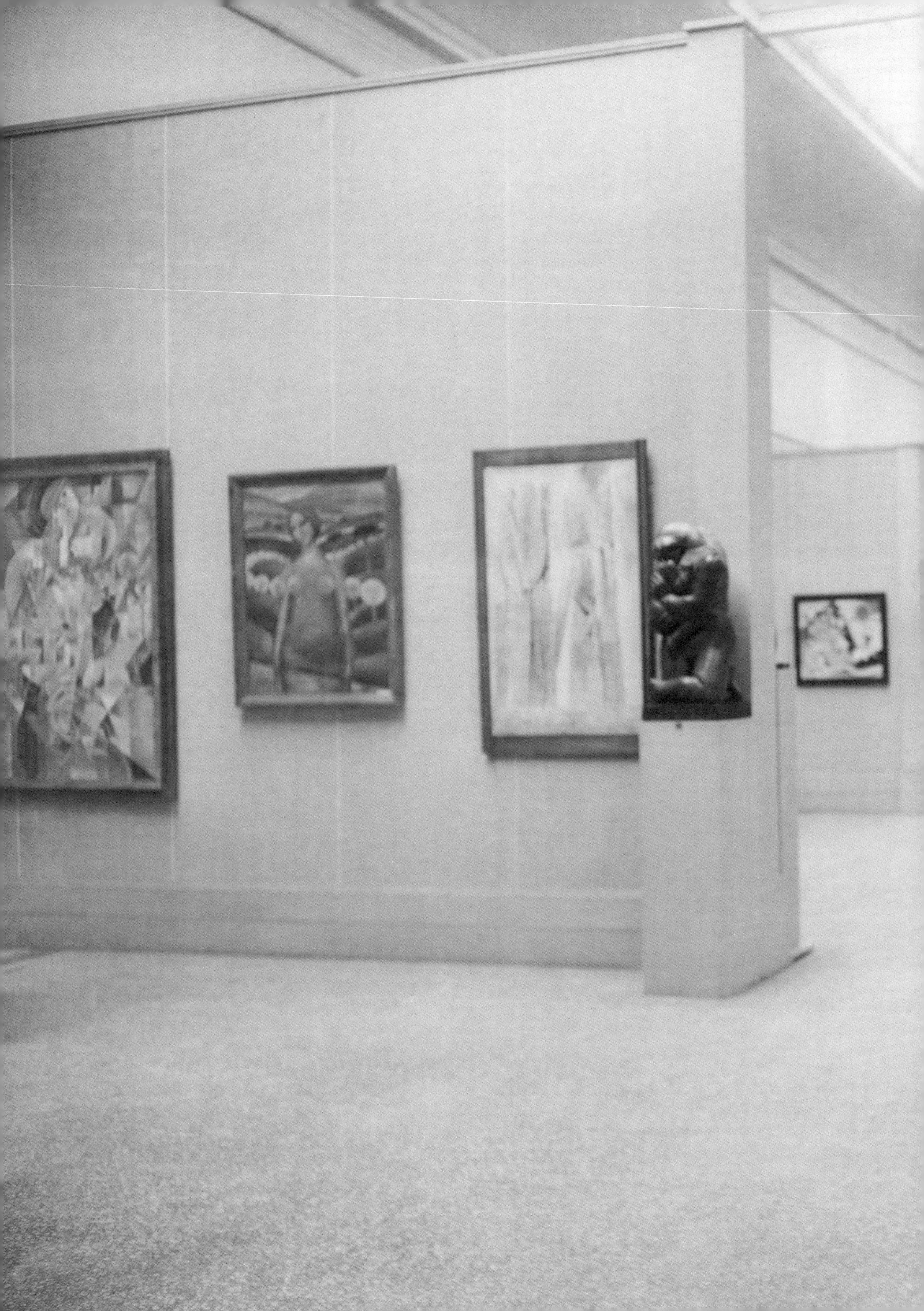

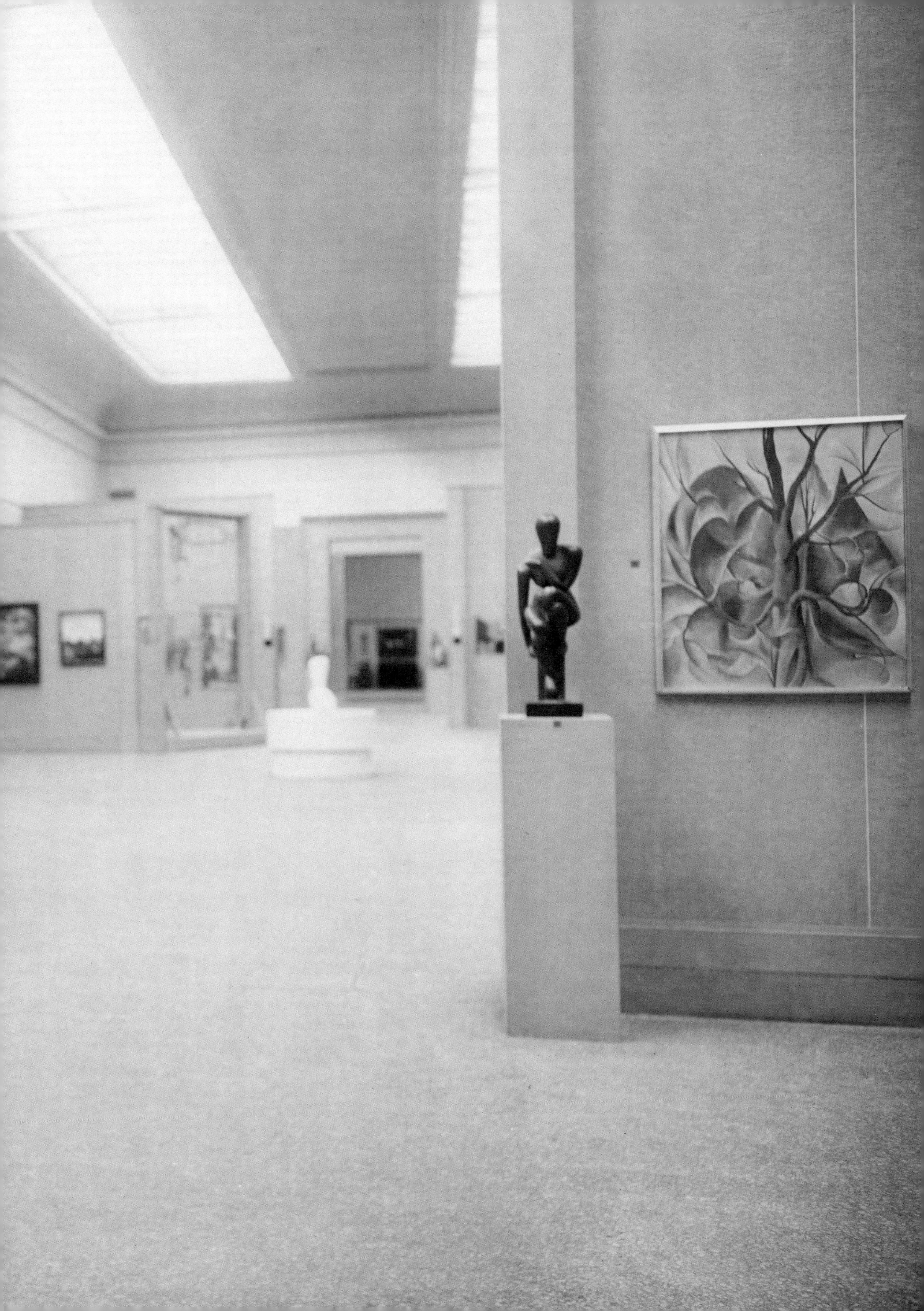

NO RETREAT: ADVANCES IN MODERN AMERICAN ART

1919 —29

Whatever group cohesion there had been in the modern movement in American art before 1914 began to dissolve during World War I, and continued to do so thereafter. However, this is not to say that after 1918 modernism slowed down or disappeared in the US, as has so often been claimed. We have seen how new groups had formed, and how artists like Dove and Davis continued to develop. But their activities were often dispersed, both formally and geographically, leading to the mistaken idea that modernism had lost its momentum. There were losses: Frost had died in 1917 owing to fast-paced living that his frail body, weakened by TB, could not sustain. Schamberg had died in the flu pandemic in 1918. New York had overwhelmed Macdonald-Wright by 1918, and he moved on to California, where he remained for the rest of his life while becoming a central figure in the development of modern art there. Affected by the soft, diffused light of California, his painting became more open, more transparent, with almost pastel-like hues, evident in the California version of Impressionism still widespread in the 1920s. Demuth, plagued by illness and infirmity, travelled between his mother's house in Lancaster, Pennsylvania, and New York, drawing artistic sustenance in each place. Dasburg retreated to Taos, New Mexico, where he worked with great effectiveness in a nuanced range of hues based on a Cézannesque Cubist structure. Most famously, O'Keeffe also took up residence in New Mexico, where she became closely identified with the imagery of the southwest. Dove lived in Long Island, on a boat, then moved to Geneva, New York, for five long years before returning to the water he loved, on the sound in Centerport, New York. The most restless of all was Hartley, who, it seemed, could never find peace and was always uncomfortable in his own skin. He worked for short periods in Mexico, New Mexico, Germany and France, before finally settling in his native state, Maine, in the late 1930s. Thus, for years, until the late 1930s, American modernist art was widely dispersed across the country, but its thrust continued, even when overwhelmed in number by Depression-era art.

Bruce's Late Still Lifes

Two pioneers of colour, Morgan Russell and Patrick Henry Bruce, stayed in France, where they had long ago settled. Russell continued to make colour abstractions into the 1920s, but then turned to a figuration that tried to recapture a classical tradition of Renaissance religious art. This move to a modern classicism was actually widespread. But for Russell it did not bode well; his art fell off precipitously after 1925 into an awkward religious and classical mode, and he never regained his former touch.

On the other hand, the art of Bruce continued apace, growing with deep, rich paint surfaces and increasingly complicated colour passages of related and contrasting hues and values. His format had evolved by 1918 from the last of his *Compositions* into architectural, often monumental still lifes based on those of Cézanne that he had studied so carefully twenty years earlier. This represented one form of Cézannism that became wide-spread in Europe and America in the years after World War I, following his model but now extended into a purist type of semi-abstraction. The complex colour passages in the still life were also based on the principles that Matisse had extrapolated from Cézanne. However, Bruce took them to new complexities, gained from his long practice and experience.

As with his earlier pictures, Bruce's late work depends to a great extent on principles such as gradation, the laws of harmony of contrasts and harmony of analogy, of simultaneous contrasts, and the use of triads to form chords conceived and constructed much as the composer creates music. Only twenty-five of the late paintings are extant, because Bruce destroyed many of them. When he exhibited them in Paris, he titled them either *Peinture* or *Nature Morte*; because none of these paintings are dated, one cannot be sure which works carried which title, so each has been

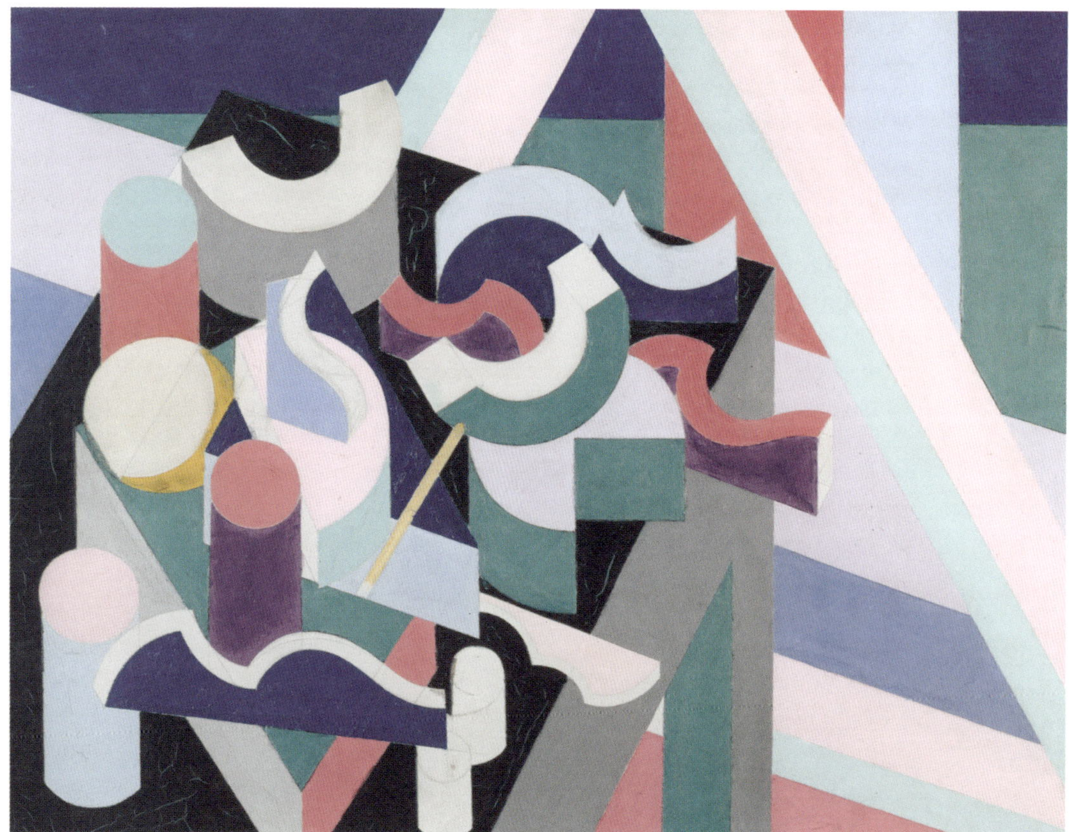

84

Modern Art in America

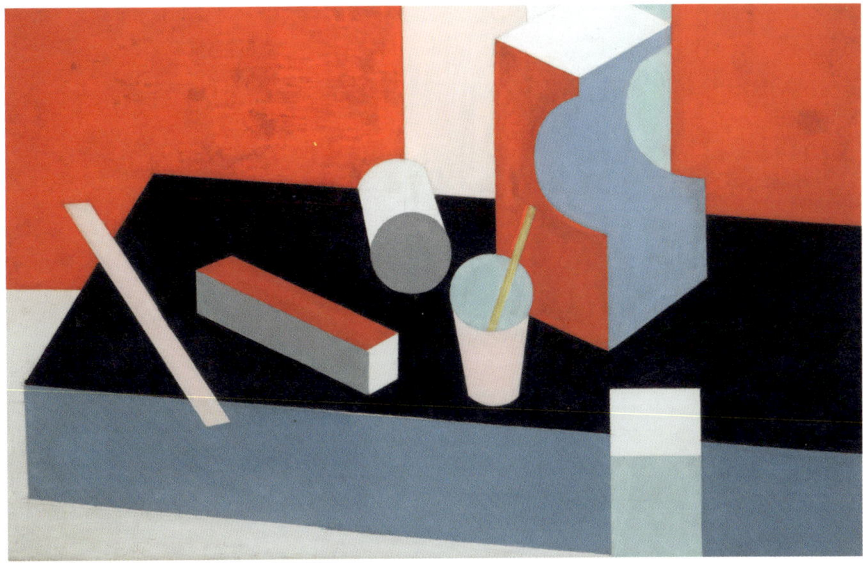

85

given both. They began with relatively simple formats, containing multiple forms of similar architectural elements of 'collapsed beams', then became progressively more complex, but by 1930 they shifted into reductive compositions of just a few elements: a glass, a ruler, a piece of fruit on a spare table top. At their most complex, they are extraordinary orchestrations of multiple hues and their gradations. Bruce laboured over the paintings, building and then changing areas, so that there are sometimes five or six layers of pigment. In *Peinture/Nature Morte* (c.1924)[84], the painting in the Addison Gallery collection, Andover, blue is taken as the starting point and over the surface at least ten variants of the hue appear, ranging from a light pastel blue to an almost pure black, as well as red and green. By contrast, Bruce left open areas of bare canvas and rich graphite drawing, which give a particular resonance to the hues and the material fullness of the laboriously painted and repainted forms.

Fortunately, the Andover still life has the original graphite drawing intact. Many of the late works suffered egregious errors of conservation in the mid-1960s, which erased the drawing, an intrinsic part, apparently to make them look more finished. These paintings depict Bruce's immediate and intimate world, the content of his studio apartment: glasses, fruit, wedges of cheese, a pencil and scrolled pieces of wood taken from the antiques he collected and that filled the apartment [85]. He constructs the work through the complex joining of myriad, precipitously stacked objects that simultaneously seem frozen in space and threaten to spill off the table. The apparent use of perspective in the rendering, a seemingly antimodernist device, is deceptive. He employed not classical perspective but isometric and oblique projections, the techniques of the mechanical draughtsman. For Bruce, they were a means to emulate the fullness and solidity of the Old Masters without exactly duplicating them. These methods account for the abstract illusionism of the picture – the look of the three-dimensional is projected, but in fact nothing actually recedes, and all elements stay on the surface. Bruce both reinforces and counteracts the illusion by showing us the actual support in the areas of bare canvas.

The complexity of the painting is unrelenting, with a constant tension between movement and stasis, order and ambivalence, harmony and conflict. Bruce sought to recall a classical world, first suggested to him by the Jeffersonian ideals that he had admired as a youth. But it was now a

84 Patrick Henry Bruce, *Peinture/ Nature Morte*, c.1924. Oil and graphite on canvas, 73 × 92 cm (28¾ × 36¼ in). Addison Gallery of American Art, Phillips Academy, Andover

85 Patrick Henry Bruce, *Painting*, c.1929–30. Oil on canvas, 60.3 × 92.4 cm (23¾ × 36⅜ in). The Museum of Modern Art, New York

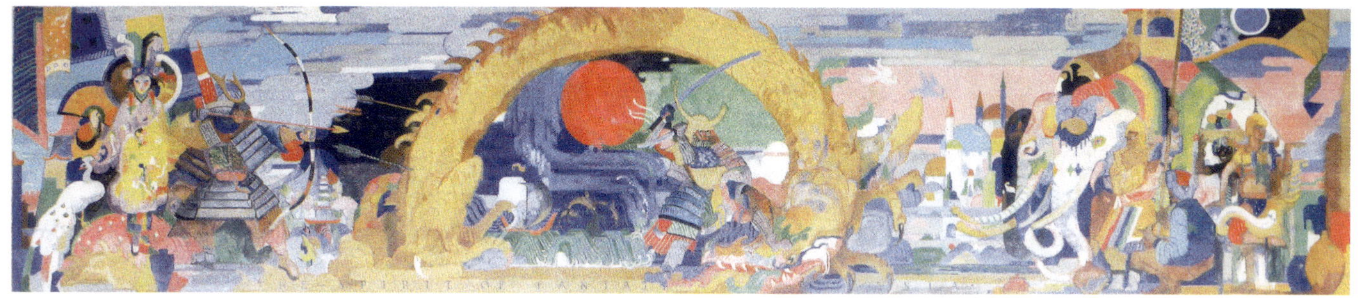

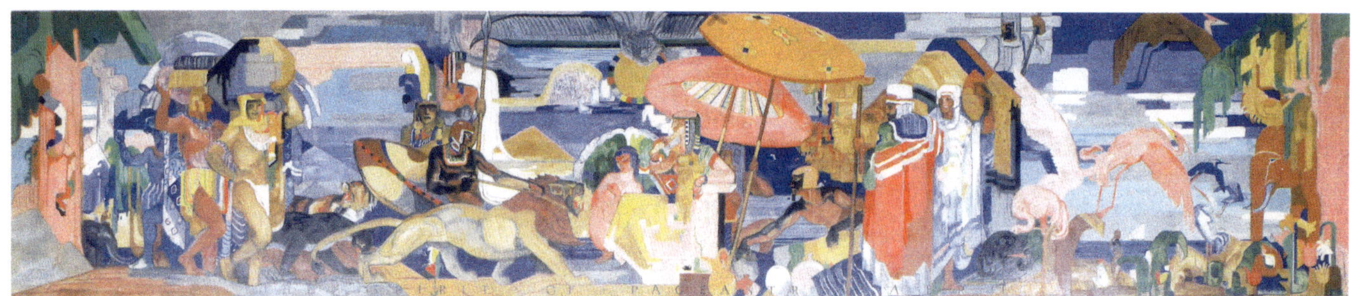

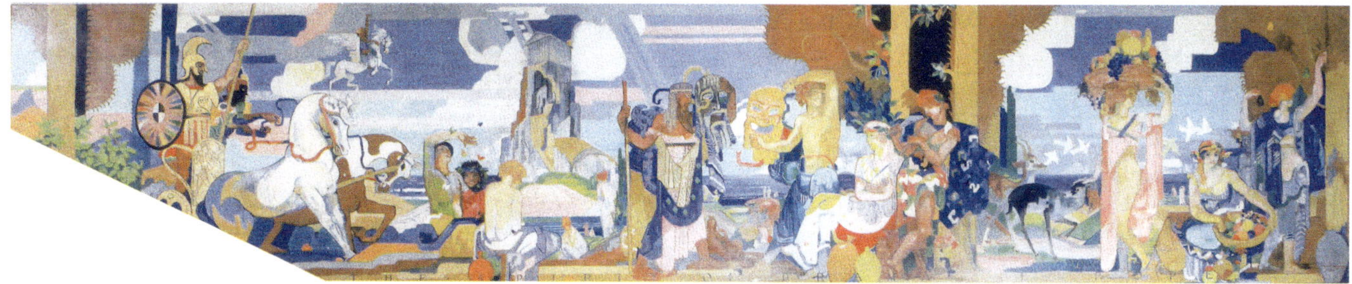

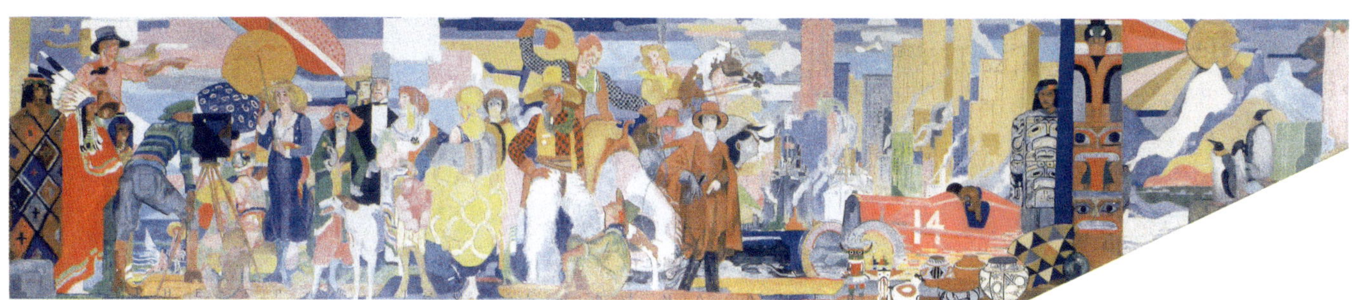

86

world in which he saw classical values profoundly altered, with absolute clarity replaced by uncertainty and contradiction, with the appearance but not the substance of classical order in place. In this tension, Bruce captured the very essence of the modern condition. That he could resolve these conflicts in an elaborate pictorial puzzle was an act of affirmation of the power of painting to convey authentic experience and feeling. In the 1920s, however, in a world that sought harmony and stability in the wake of the Great War, it was little wonder that his work, with its apparent irresolution, went without recognition. It was not until the 1960s, when artists such as Al Held, Ron Davis and Frank Stella began to explore the possibilities of abstract illusionism, that the radical and far-reaching implications, as well as the sheer audacity of these pictures, could be grasped.

Once an active member of the Parisian avant-garde, after the war Bruce became increasingly reclusive (that old American habit) staying alone in his studio apartment and painting only the objects around him in abstracted shapes. His work was known and respected by few people, and he rarely exhibited the paintings. In some ways, Bruce and his art are emblematic of American modernism – working at a high and accomplished level of achievement, producing major art, but isolated and hardly known until years later. His isolation was such that he grew despondent, finally taking his own life in 1936, an all-too-common story of American modern art in those years.

A Modern Approach to Classical Themes

For decades, the 1920s were thought of as a kind of dark age in American modernist art, a hiatus of sorts between the initial forays into abstraction prior to 1914 and the shift to the United States as the centre of world art after 1945. Too often, art writing followed the clichés about 1920s life and society, seeing it as a retreat into isolationism, more or less bereft of major advances. But art does not follow the course of politics and sociology exactly. In fact, the decade saw a new flourishing of major and innovative art on the part of both older and newer artists. Hartley, Marin, Dove and others of the pioneering generation reached even higher peaks of achievement, and a wide variety of progressive younger artists established themselves as important figures. While there was a move towards a more conservative, classicizing art, newer realms of pictorial exploration made their presence felt. Modern art moved on apace.

A group of works by James Daugherty that are among the glories of American art of the 1920s force us to revise our thinking about that period. During the war, the Navy had employed Daugherty to paint camouflage on warships, an experience he used when making a series of large-scale figurative paintings depicting tumultuous battle scenes. Their sheer size prepared him to undertake in 1920 a commission for a set of four vast murals in the lobby of Loew's State Theatre in Cleveland [86]. This was not an uncommon motif, but the execution was extraordinary – huge murals done in a symphony of brilliant colour unequalled in the United States, then or now. Although figurative, they are not a retreat into tradition nor evidence of a loss of confidence, as so much American art of the time has been commonly viewed. Part of the shift in the world view of artists after the war was prompted by the desire to integrate art and life more closely, to relate modern art to a larger audience. The most direct way to achieve this was through figurative imagery, and there was no better medium for this imagery than the large public mural, so much in evidence during the 1920s and 1930s in America. The vast Cleveland murals, each forty-six

86   James Daugherty,
The Spirit of Pageantry – Africa
The Spirit of Fantasy – Asia
The Spirit of Drama – Europe
The Spirit of Cinema – America,
1920–1. Oil on canvas, each
panel 3 × 14 m (10 × 46 ft).
State Theatre, Cleveland

feet wide, retreat from nothing. They blaze forth into new and unknown domains, dazzling and unfurling across the walls; their likes were not seen again until the large murals done for the Paris International Exposition of 1937 by Robert and Sonia Delaunay. The works in Cleveland, as well as a large-scale two-sided canvas completed in 1922, mark Daugherty as a key artist of the 1920s. He continued as a major mural painter on the government art projects during the 1930s. Without knowing his history, it was easy enough to think that his wall painting of the 1930s followed in the wake of those of Thomas Hart Benton, but we now know that he was an accomplished muralist long before Benton was.

New Museums for New Art

Serious interest in modernism gathered steam throughout the 1920s. American collectors – including the four Steins and Claribel and Etta Cone of Baltimore in Paris – had helped to determine the rise of an American taste for new art by the start of World War I. After the war, Katherine Dreier, a painter herself since 1910, continued her work and in addition became a serious collector and patron of the arts, forming one of the most significant bodies of work ever assembled in the country. Deeply impressed by the Armory Show, particularly Duchamp and Picabia, she began a study of modern art that led to a long and close relationship with Duchamp. Her 1918 *Abstract Portrait of Marcel Duchamp* [87], like Picabia's many portraits of the period, reduced the subject to a series of mechanical elements and conveyed the spirit so convincingly generated by Duchamp in New York. By 1920 Dreier had assembled a collection that rivalled Arensberg's in its depth and importance. It was particularly strong in New York Dada and could count among its resources major works by Duchamp, Man Ray and soon Picabia, Max Ernst and Kurt Schwitters. However, she was also alert to the best colour painters of the time, including Bruce and Daugherty, and she quickly acquired Bruce's *Compositions* for her collection.

Dreier's commitment to modern art had convinced her of the value and need for an organization devoted to educating the public in its principles. She enlisted the aid of Duchamp and Man Ray and in 1920 they founded the Société Anonyme, the first museum devoted to modern art, one of the most important institutions in American history, which continues even today at Yale University, and to which Dreier donated her collection in 1941. They opened galleries on 47th Street and organized a full schedule of purchases, shows (including travelling exhibitions), symposia and publications that

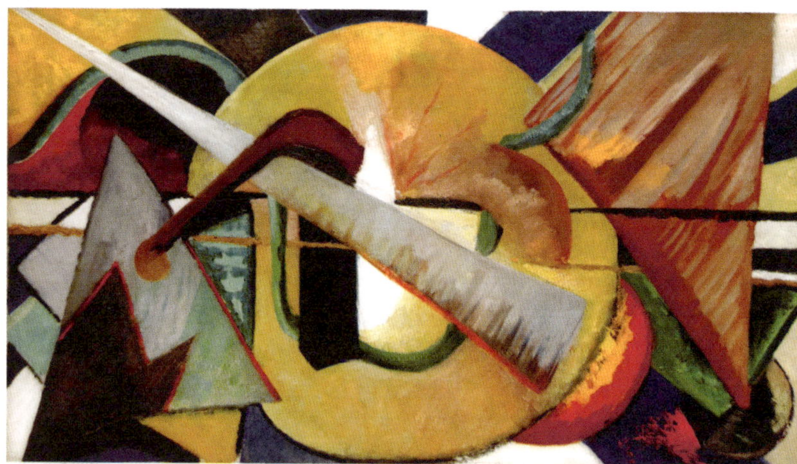

87

Modern Art in America

were invaluable in extending the knowledge and practice of modern art throughout the 1920s. In its first three years of operation, the Société was a hotbed of Dada, after Duchamp and Man Ray had left for Paris in 1921.

The exhibitions held at the Société's galleries at 19 East 47th Street were part of a broad educational thrust launched by Dreier that lasted until she gave the collection to Yale in 1941. Daugherty and other colour painters were collected and exhibited by Dreier, so that Bruce and the related group were seen far more widely and had a larger impact on developing art than has been imagined. Indeed, the existence and activities of the Société Anonyme in the 1920s was a major factor in the continued development of colour painting and of modernism in that decade. A programme of exhibitions and intelligent catalogues were presented in New York and were circulated in museums, thus furthering a wider public knowledge of modernist art. Virtually simultaneously in Washington, DC, the collector Duncan Phillips opened a gallery of modern art in memory of his father and brother. Despite the elegiac tone of its founding, the Phillips Collection was from the start a home for some of the best and most radical colour paintings of modern art.

When the Newark Museum relocated in the 1920s, under the direction of John Dana Cotton, it placed a new emphasis on American art. Together with the founding of the Museum of Modern Art in 1929, the Whitney Museum of American Art and the Addison Gallery of American Art, both in 1931, America demonstrated a more serious interest in modern art than any other country. Perhaps most importantly, artists could now study and learn from the best of modern art, no doubt a prime reason why American modernism could grow at the pace it did.

When MoMA opened in 1929, for some it meant the end of modern art. 'You can be a museum, or you can be modern, but you can't be modern and a museum at the same time', Gertrude Stein famously said.[1] Under the guidance of the Founding Director, Alfred H. Barr, Jr., however, the museum gave modernism a history – just as Renaissance or nineteenth-century art had been presented as a canon – and thus credibility as a real field of serious study. However, as we have seen, American modernism was a 'problem' for the museum that, to this day, it has failed to solve. In the 1930s and 1940s, Barr did a commendable job, organizing exhibitions of the most important moderns including Hopper, Marin, Demuth and Davis. But from the start it was Eurocentric, and after Barr's gradual retirement, American modernism seemed to disappear altogether. Recently there have been encouraging signs of revived interest, but even now the discourse mostly revolves around the 'problem', as if the museum still believes that American modernism struggles to hold its own.

Further Growth of Colour Painting: O'Keeffe and Demuth

Colour painting increased in its sophistication in the 1920s, to which older as well as younger artists made a contribution. Georgia O'Keeffe's brilliant *Grey Lines with Black, Blue and Yellow* (c. 1923) [88] ripples as it plays on the chords of the colour wheel, a perfect foil for the almost literal depiction of female anatomy, a symbol of sexual energy, the very joy of life itself. The work bespeaks sexuality, birth and rebirth, the passage from conception to a newborn being in the world. Colour movement and gradation of hues spark energy and movement. The size and scale of the painting make it appear almost like a landscape, as if we are moving through something larger than the anatomy itself. It is a proud declaration of O'Keeffe's sex, her female identity, done with the kind of poetry that could be equalled

87 Katherine Dreier, *Abstract Portrait of Marcel Duchamp*, 1918. Oil on canvas, 45.7 × 81.3 cm, (18 × 32 in). The Museum of Modern Art, New York

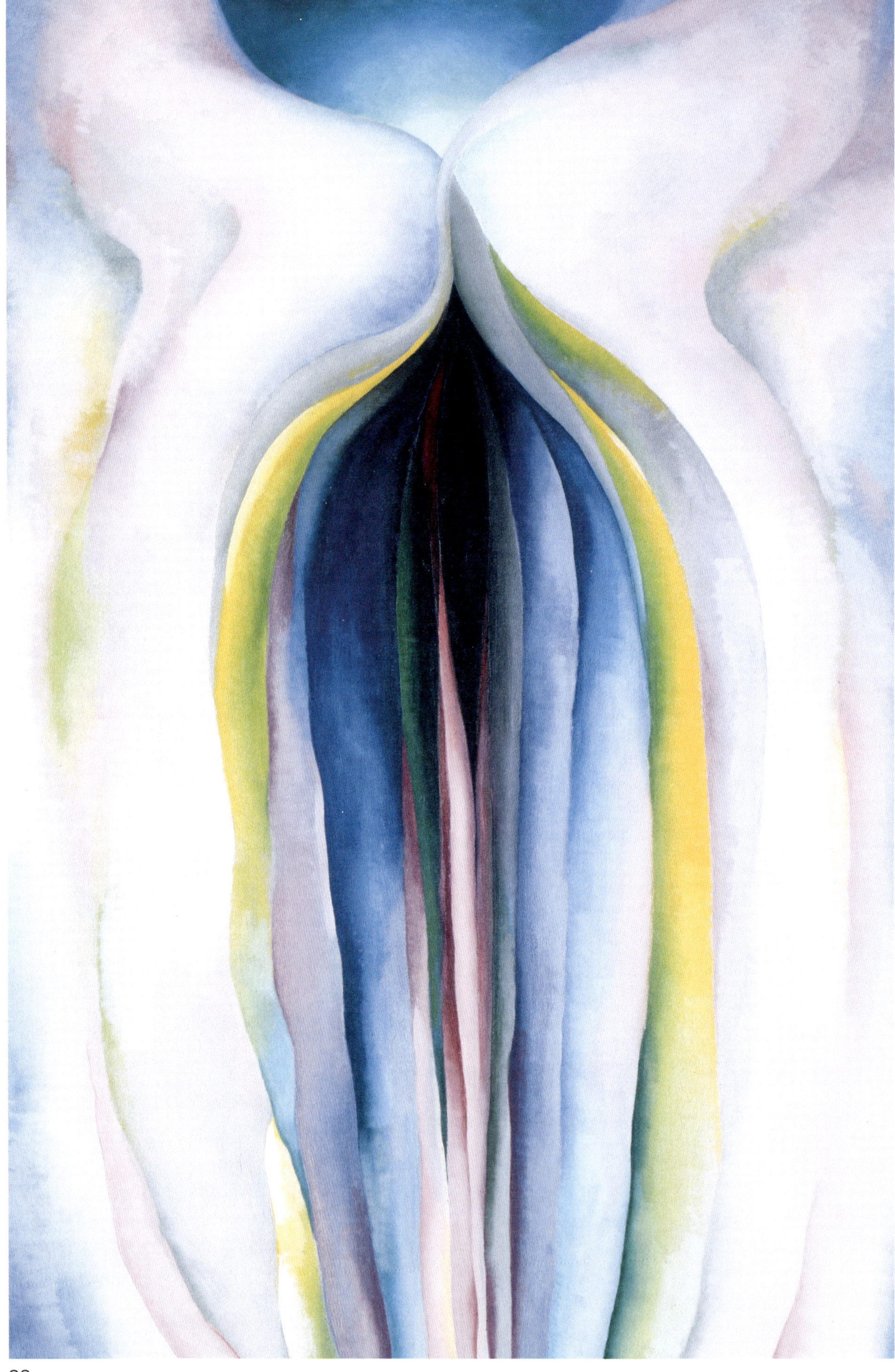

88

only by Dove. She was praised by critics for the female attributes of her art, to which she later objected, as has a younger generation of feminist writers. Yet it is clear that O'Keeffe revelled in the forthright depiction of the female body, making her proud statements in the face of the overwhelming masculine tenor of society and the art world.

THE IMPORTANCE OF BEING DADA

Demuth and Duchamp

Charles Demuth and Marcel Duchamp were good friends and respected colleagues in New York, and Demuth's paintings of the 1920s show that he had drawn from the linear machine images developed by Duchamp and Picabia before the war. Demuth plays on *Nude Descending a Staircase* in his beautifully rendered *Stairs, Provincetown* (1920) [89], which includes no nude, but rather focuses on each stair as an independent form in its own right. His *My Egypt* (1927) contains Dada irony in its very title (like Sheeler's similar vein in *Classic Landscape*), for the grain elevators are a symbol of American prosperity, its true monuments, rather than pyramids or other classical sites. They have as their ultimate source both Duchamp and Picabia, although they are now blown up to an outsize American scale; and as so much American art has done, Demuth translates new pictorial devices into a depiction of the American scene.

Duchamp's fascination with sequential motion, inspired by the loco-motion photography of Étienne-Jules Marey,[2] was the ultimate source for one of the most famous paintings of American modernism, Demuth's dazzling *I Saw the Figure 5 in Gold* (1928) [90]. It was inspired by his good friend William Carlos Williams's poem *The Great Figure*, composed after his experience on his way to visit Marsden Hartley in his studio. The best approach to this work is to listen to the poem being read aloud while standing in front of the painting. Each line accords, exactly, with a particular shape, line or colour in the painting. Each section in the painting is short, clipped and crisp, as is each line. We pick out each, as we see each, in a perfect correspondence.

> *Among the rain*
> *And lights*
> *I saw*
> *the figure 5*
> *in gold*
> *on a red*
> *fire truck*
> *moving*
> *tense unheeded*
> *to gong clangs*
> *siren howls*
> *and wheels rumbling*
> *through the dark city*

It is a fusion of urban realism, Dada, Precisionism and Futurism, all in one, a typical American choice of a variety of elements, taking and using what is needed to make a personal and powerful painting, empirically, with no reliance on doctrinaire theory or manifesto. Is the fire truck moving past us and down the street, or is it coming towards us? Traditionally, it has been read as disappearing into the distance, but the proximity of the

88 Georgia O'Keeffe, *Grey Lines with Black, Blue and Yellow*, c.1923. Oil on canvas, 121.9 × 76.2 cm (48 × 30 in). The Museum of Fine Arts, Houston

89 Charles Demuth, *Stairs, Provincetown*, 1920. Watercolour and pencil on board, 59.7 × 49.5 cm (23½ × 19½ in). The Museum of Modern Art, New York

90 Charles Demuth, *I Saw the Figure 5 in Gold*, 1928. Oil, graphite, ink and gold leaf on paperboard (Upson board), 90.2 × 76.2 cm, (35½ × 30 in). The Metropolitan Museum of Art, New York

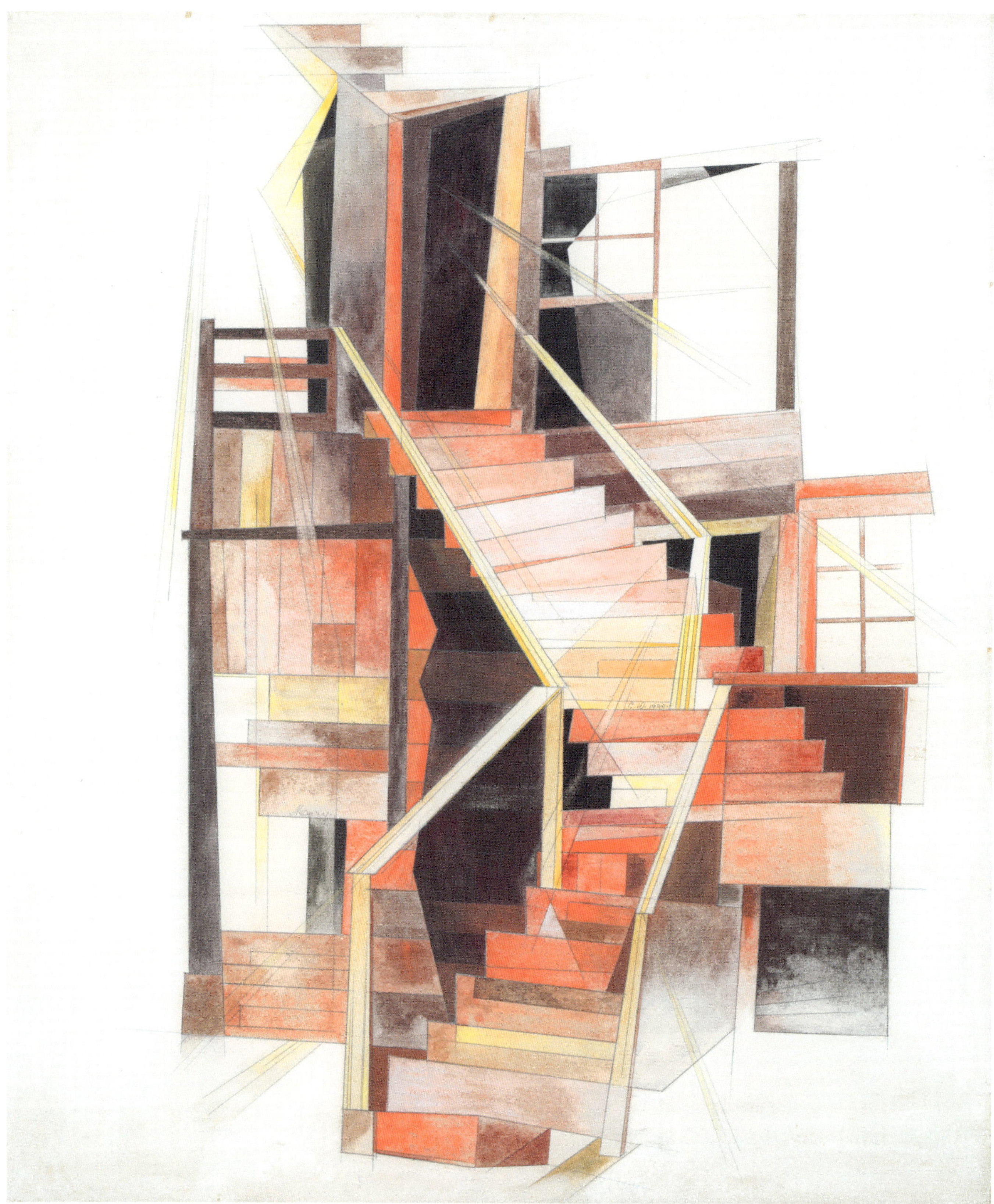

89

Modern Art in America

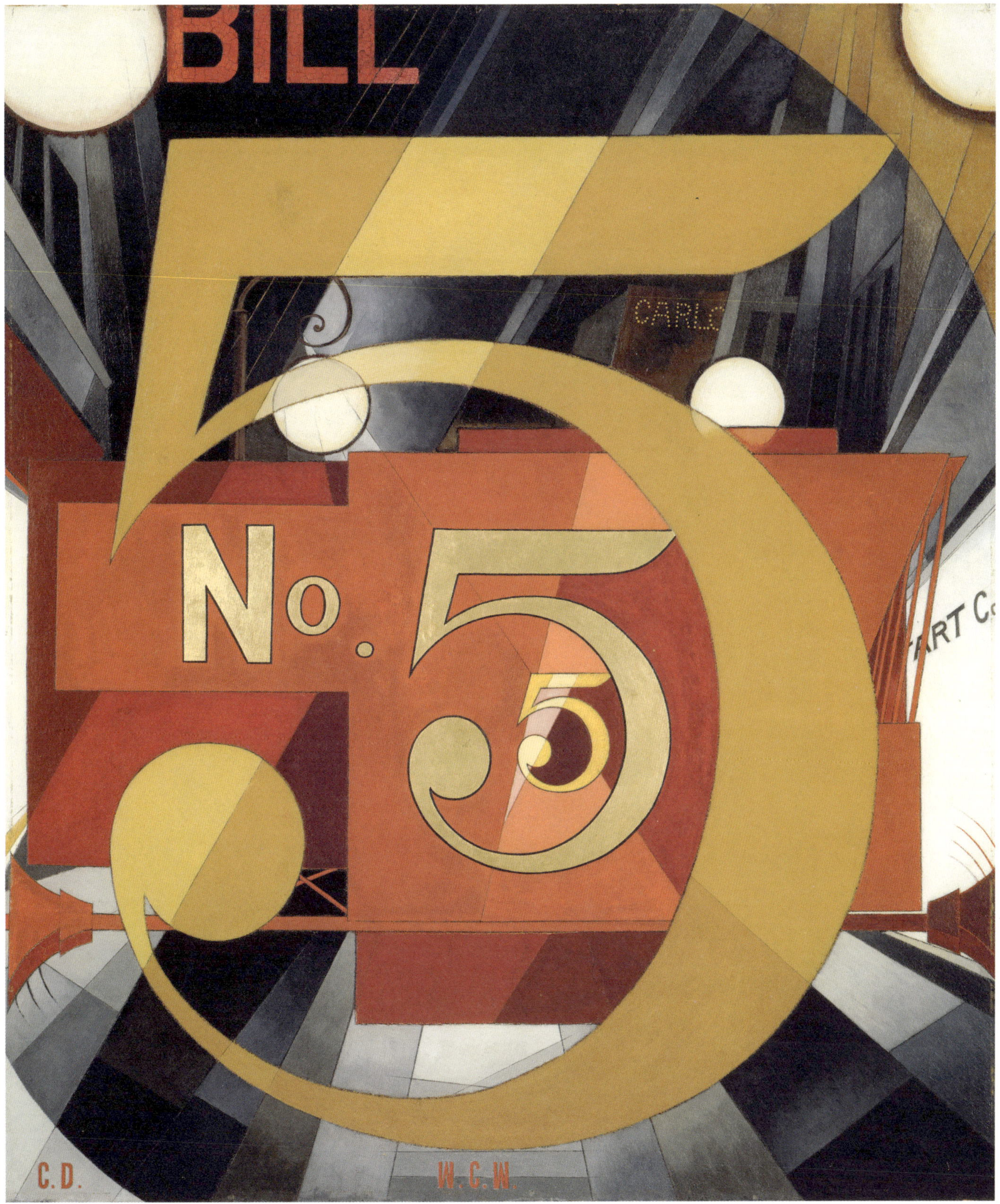

90

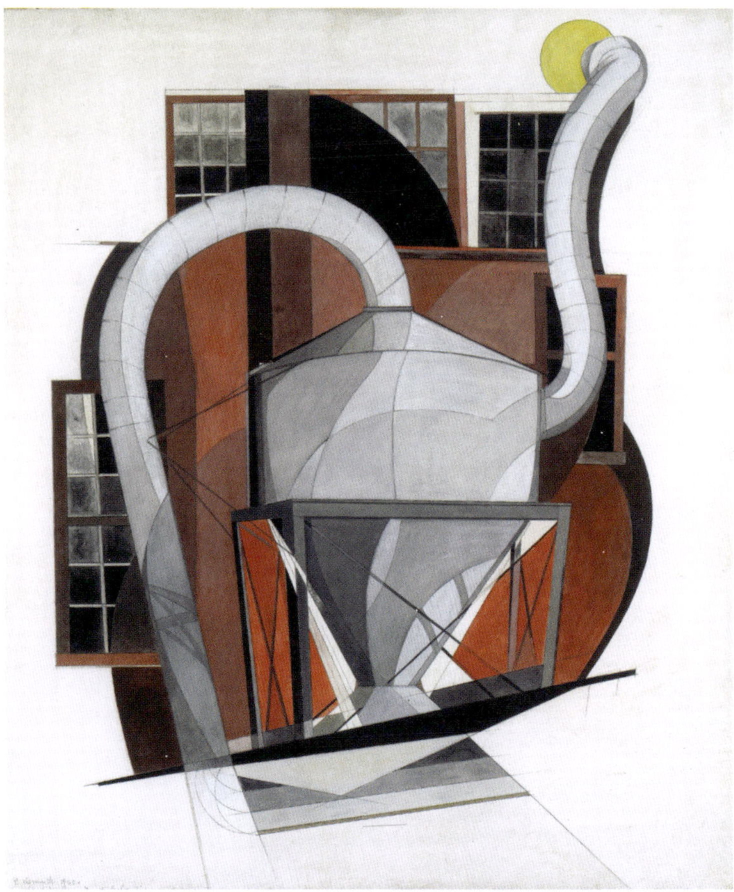

91

largest and nearest section of the figure 5 in gold makes one feel as if it is virtually on us, a metaphor of how the urban experience can engulf and overwhelm us.

Demuth demonstrated extraordinary versatility and range as an artist: dynamic city scenes, delicate watercolours of landscape, unflinching depictions of gay bathhouses, and some of the purest, most beautiful straight painting in his still lifes that one can find in American art. He has been pegged as an 'outsider' because he was gay and because he spent much time at his mother's house in Lancaster, Pennsylvania.[3] This is clearly nonsense. He was an integral part of New York City's art life, close to many of the artists, including Duchamp, who all respected and admired him and fully accepted his sexuality. He was also one of many artists who found it fruitful to partake of city life but then retreat to a distance to renew themselves and their work. We need only think of David Smith, Stuart Davis and Jackson Pollock in this regard. The admiration for Demuth has continued to grow, and *The Figure 5* has become an iconic image, used and transformed by artists such as Robert Indiana and Jasper Johns in the 1960s.

These urban encounters recall Stuart Davis's famous statement: 'I am an American born in Philadelphia of American stock. I studied art in America. I paint what I see in America, in other words I paint the American scene.'[4] The fascination with America itself extends from the early nineteenth century, and throughout the twentieth. The fascination with machinery, although first pointed out by the Dada artists, ran deep in Demuth's art as well as in the work of numerous other Americans. Think also of Demuth's *Machinery* (1920)[91] and *Paquebot Paris* (the title is another Dada play on words), both giant blow-ups of French intimate scale. To this we can compare Sheeler's similar use of steamboat engines.

91 Charles Demuth, *Machinery*, 1920. Gouache and graphite on paperboard (Beaver board), 61 × 50.5 cm (24 × 19⅞ in). The Metropolitan Museum of Art, New York

92 Charles Demuth, *Poster Portrait of Georgia O'Keeffe*, 1924. Oil on panel, 59 × 48 cm (23¼ × 18⅞ in). Beinecke Rare Book and Manuscript Library, Yale University, New Haven

93 Gerald Murphy, *Watch*, 1925. Oil on canvas, 203.4 × 199.4 cm (79 × 78½ in). Dallas Museum of Art

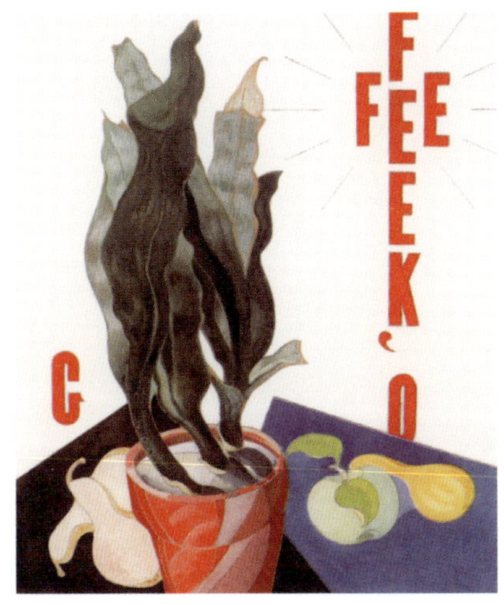

92

Picabia's object-portraits of 1915 found a new outlet in Demuth's poster portraits of 1924, which depicted artists by means of their well-known images – such as the use of flowers to depict O'Keeffe [92] – just as Picabia had depicted Stieglitz as a camera.

Gerald Murphy and the Machine

In one form or another, the machine was everywhere. The large canvas called *Watch* (1925) [93] by Gerald Murphy (1888–1964), and his enormous *Engine Room* (1922), with its Piranesi-like jumble of pistons and shafts, cannot help but recall the machinist imagery of Duchamp and Picabia, as in the latter's *Réveil Matin* (Alarm Clock, 1919), now taken to an enormous, American-type scale and size. Sadly, Murphy's career was cut short by the tragic death of not one but both of his young sons, bringing about another loss to American art of considerable consequence.

Murphy was the wealthy scion of the owner of Mark Cross Company, educated at Andover and Harvard, with no art background. He and his wife Sarah moved to Paris to find a new way of life, away from America and its values. One day he came across works by Picasso and Léger and was so struck by them that he decided he wanted to start painting. He studied with Natalia Gonchorova (1881–1962) and was soon making works of startling originality and impact. His paintings were defined by sharp, clear forms, as was much of 1920s art, and was directed towards machines and machine-like compositions.

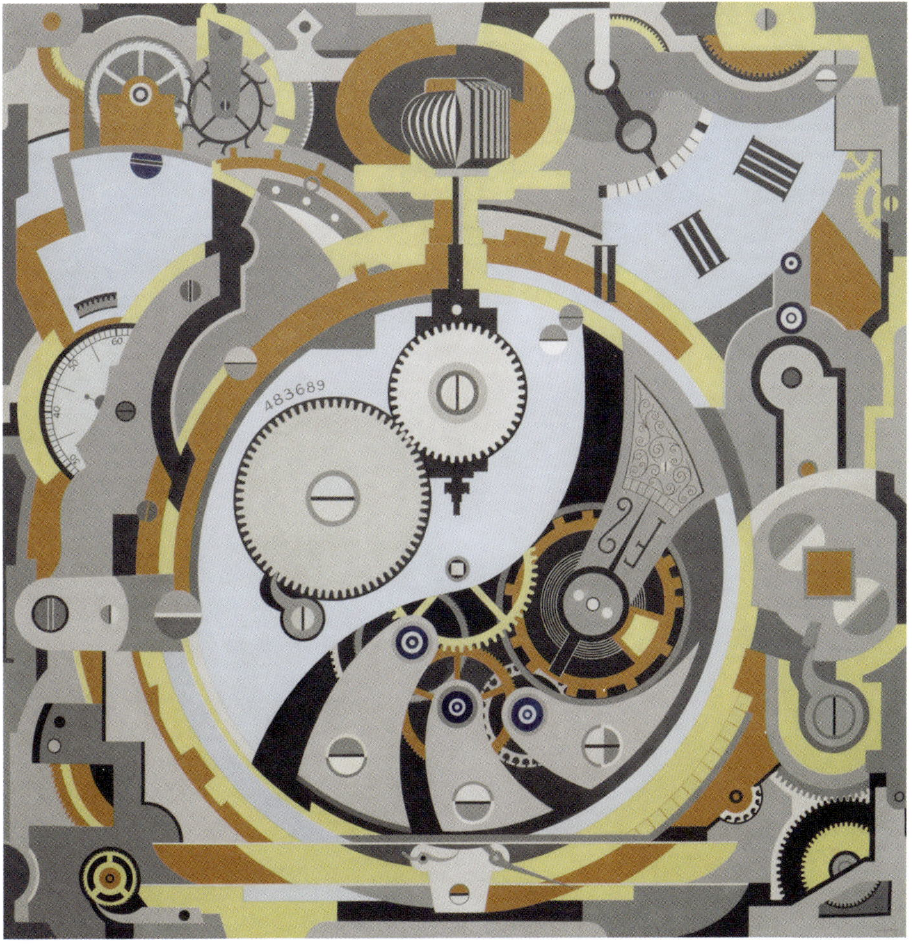

93

Although, like other Americans, his corpus was small, Murphy's was a major addition to world art. We know of only sixteen works by him, and eight of these through photographs. They are all major works, overshadowed for years because Murphy was best known for his biography – a dashing American, living the high life with his family in Paris and on the Riviera, where they lived in a large house in Antibes. The Murphys were close to Picasso and Léger and a friend of F. Scott Fitzgerald (Gerald was the model for Dick Diver in *Tender is the Night*), John Dos Passos (who termed them 'international chic') and Ernest Hemingway – the romance of the 1920s personified. Regrettably, recent writing has focused unnecessarily on the social aspect of Murphy's life, whether or not he was gay, and if his wife slept with Picasso. However, the painting *Watch* lives on in American culture, for surely it was a prototype for the famous engine room in Charlie Chaplin's classic film *Modern Times* of 1936.

Murphy made remarkable and rapid progress in his art, and almost overnight it seemed he had hit full stride. His range, even in such a small body of work, was wide, both thematically and expressively. His striking painting *Villa America* (c.1924)[94] served as the signpost to the entrance of his home. Painted in red, white and blue, as well as gold and black, it seems to be a proclamation of all things American, a plug for American art and culture as a presence in France, not so long ago almost unthinkable. The five stars are for the five members of his family, united within the large star as a close and loving group.[5] The letters of 'Villa America' are split up, so that it might be read 'vil âme' (meaning 'villa soul', not 'vile spirit' as has been suggested)[6] in French, and 'la rica', meaning 'the rich one' in Spanish. L'Âme, the soul, the spirit, signals an awareness of something beyond the material pleasures denoted in La Rica, and the gold paint was perhaps suggested by the Byzantine religious art that Murphy had seen in Venice – the richness of a higher order.

The layouts of Murphy's painting are carefully ordered and balanced, part of the classical orientation of so much art of the 1920s. In paintings such as *Doves* (1925)[95], the classical references are made explicit in the Greek architectural elements, drawn from a church he had seen in Genoa, in which pigeons had nested. Indeed, the soft grey tones, which Murphy called 'ghosted', make the painting seem as if remembered in a dream, telling us that the artist was well aware of the new movement of Surrealism.

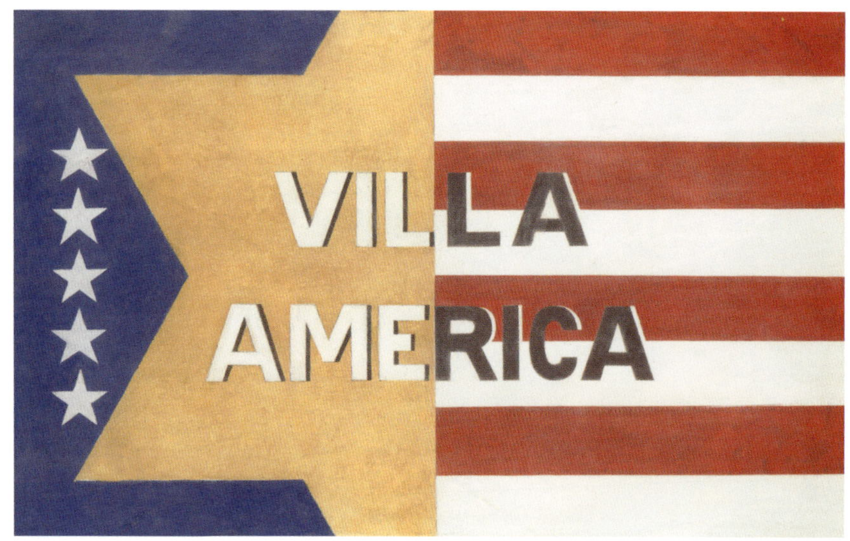

94

94 Gerald Murphy, *Villa America*, c.1924. Tempera and gold leaf on board, 36.8 × 54.6 cm (14½ × 21½ in). Myron Kunin Collection of American Art, Minneapolis

95 Gerald Murphy, *Doves*, 1925. Oil on canvas, 123.5 × 91.4 cm (48⅝ × 36 in). Private collection

Modern Art in America

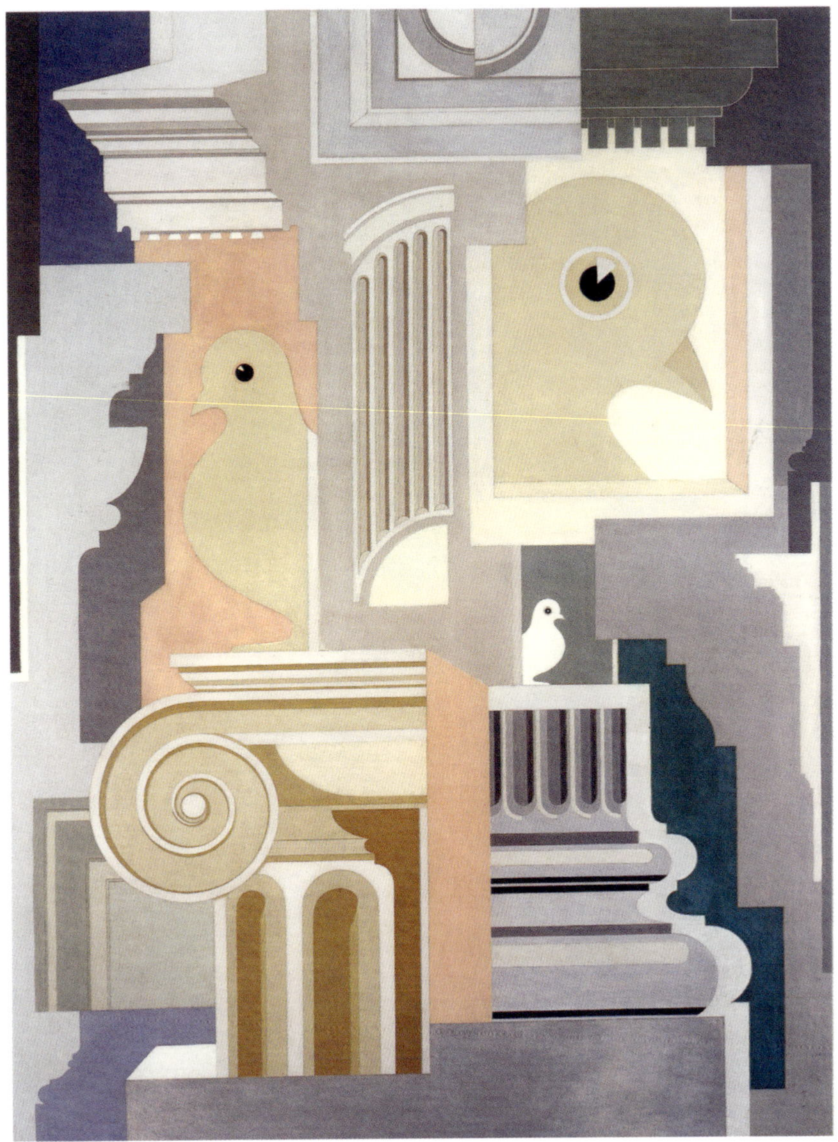

95

The painting has been lovingly constructed part by part, as if it were a fine piece of furniture; or as if Murphy had read Apollinaire's call in 1916 for making a painting like a machine, in order to stabilize art, avoiding the undisciplined freedom of expressionist abstraction that had characterized pre-war painting.

Reconsidering Marsden Hartley's Middle Years

Although his work—with one exception—shows no overt signs of Dada, Marsden Hartley, possessed of an inquisitive and venturesome intellect, caught the Dada spirit of freedom. His *Portrait of a German Officer* (1914) (see page 95) represented this new form of portraiture most frequently associated with Picabia, namely the object-portrait. Hartley called regularly at the Arensberg apartment, knew the artists there and was an active participant in the Société Anonyme's lecture and exhibition programme. In his book *Adventures in the Arts* (1921), Hartley included a chapter titled 'The Importance of Being Dada', which perhaps best summarizes the non-doctrinaire, non-political nature of American Dada.[7] Hartley embraced Dada for reuniting art and life and for restoring to art the free and

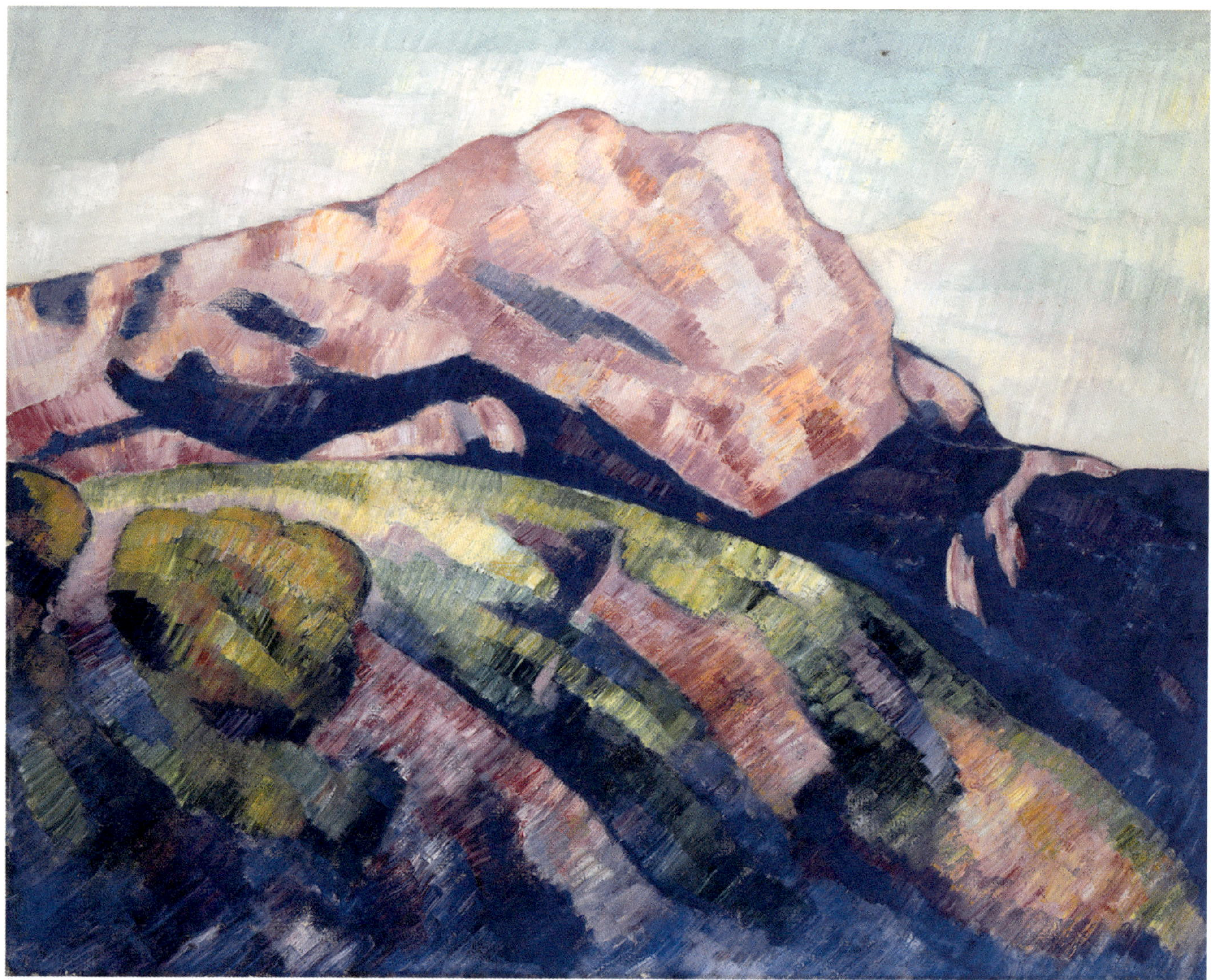

96

unbridled expression of the individual. In a country still governed too much by convention and orthodoxy, Dada provided a welcome and much-needed infusion of experimentation. Once more, as they have throughout the country's history, the pragmatist American artists took what they could use, adapted it to their own needs, and let go of the rest.

Hartley is often judged as an exceptional painter for the years prior to 1914, and also for the last few years until his death in 1943, but as not so good a painter in between. This needs careful reconsideration, for he produced a great deal of remarkable art in the intervening years. The problem seems to have been that this work is marked by multiple shifts in geography, subject and style, making it difficult to identify and grasp, something like Hans Hofmann's dilemma years later (see pages 164–5). We like artists to keep it simple, to stick with one look that we recognize quickly and without effort. But art rarely works in that way.

Hartley's colour once blossomed again in the 1920s, especially late in the decade, when he returned to France. There he sought to begin again with the roots of modernism, with Cézanne, as if to restart himself by going back to his original impulses. In 1927, he went to Aix, to Cézanne's famous site Mont Sainte-Victoire, and recast his painting in Cézanne's image as it were, but in a distinctly personal idiom. These works are made with the parallel brushstrokes of Cézanne, in a manner so literal that their originality

96 Marsden Hartley, *Mont Sainte-Victoire*, 1927. Oil on canvas, 81.3 × 100.3 cm (32 × 39½ in). Private collection

97 Kurt Schwitters, *Merzbild 25 A, Das Sternenbild*, 1920. Oil, string, wood, sheet metal, mesh and paper on cardboard, 104.5 × 79 cm (41¼ × 31¼ in). Private collection

98 Joseph Stella, *Chiclets*, c. 1920. Collage on paper, 20.3 × 16.5 cm (8 × 6½ in). Weatherspoon Art Museum, Greensboro

Modern Art in America

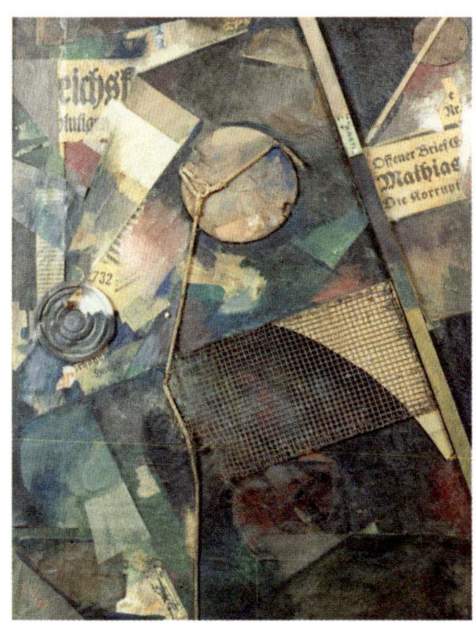

97

may come only slowly to light[96]. They are an act of homage, to be sure, but the results are startling: the touch is rougher and the image more compacted, and above all the colour becomes arbitrary and even fantastic, filled with intense light, a far cry from Cézanne's greens and blues. Hartley's works here may be truly called late Fauve, for they are almost florid, with multiple gradations of red, pink, yellow, blue and purple, a new height of intensity in his long engagement with colour. Because of the subject, critics often think the works are derivative, not understanding why the artist was compelled to go to the mountain. In fact, these paintings are among the glories of American art of this time.

COLLAGE

The absence left by Duchamp and Man Ray when they left New York in 1921 was filled by a new concentration on Kurt Schwitters, an artist whom Dreier deeply admired, with special emphasis on his collages, which were shown in November 1920 and March 1921. These collages[97], which Schwitters called 'Merz' to distinguish them from other Dada art, were a primary example of the worldwide drive to abolish art as a remote discipline and reunite it with the world around us. Schwitters used scraps of paper, ticket stubs and other cast-off ephemera, derelict mementos that re-created an entire autobiographical world.

Their presence was manifest in the remarkable series of collages done by Joseph Stella. In one of the best of these, *Chiclets* (c. 1920)[98], he arranged three mutilated and stained gum wrappers in a vertical composition with all the presence of a pure abstraction. This was but one of about three dozen collages he did from the early 1920s into the early 1930s, in which he worked with disparate fragments of matchbooks, leaves, theatre programmes and blank, bleached paper.

John Covert: Dada Principles

Another artist of considerable if brief accomplishment was John Covert (1882–1960), still not well known in histories, but an early exponent of the collage. He experienced Dada directly in New York, for Arensberg was his cousin and thus he was a frequent visitor to the apartment on West 67th Street. There he met Duchamp and others in the circle, and by 1919 he had begun to incorporate Dada principles in his art. In *Brass Band*[99] of that year, Covert defined the planes and spatial direction by attaching string directly to the composition, just as Duchamp had attached lead wire to the *Large Glass* and in *Tu m'* (1918). In *Vocalization* (1919), Covert mocked the pure planes of Cubism by gluing wooden dowels to the surface in much the same way that Picabia had used macaroni in *Le Midi* (c. 1924-5). Covert's most fertile and inventive embodiment of Dada was in *Time*[100], also 1919, in which he employed upholstery tacks interspersed with equations and mathematical drawings to create surface divisions that rejected traditional techniques. (Think of Eakins's *Professor Henry A. Rowland*, 1897). Covert soon gave up art and returned to business, as Gerald Murphy was also forced to do.

Dove's Search for the Real

The most important group of collages created in America before 1955 were those executed by Arthur Dove in the 1920s. They number only twenty-five, but together form one of the most radical and daring bodies of work undertaken in the country, or anywhere else for that matter, at the time.

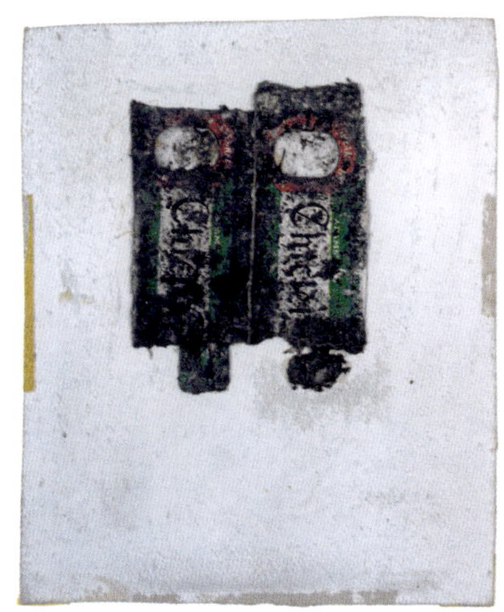

98

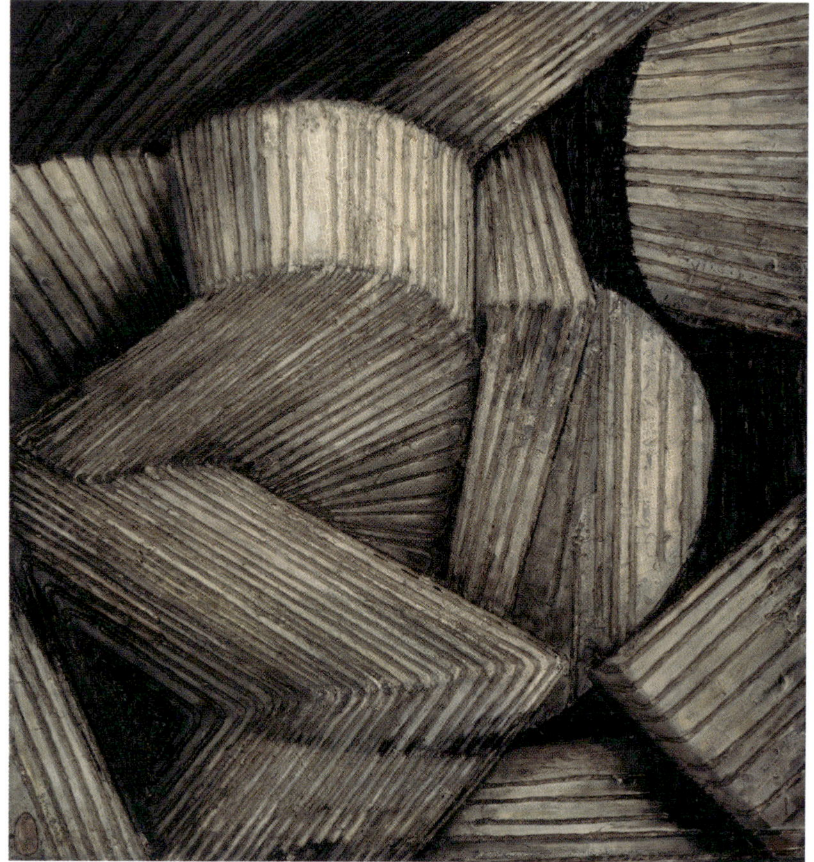

99

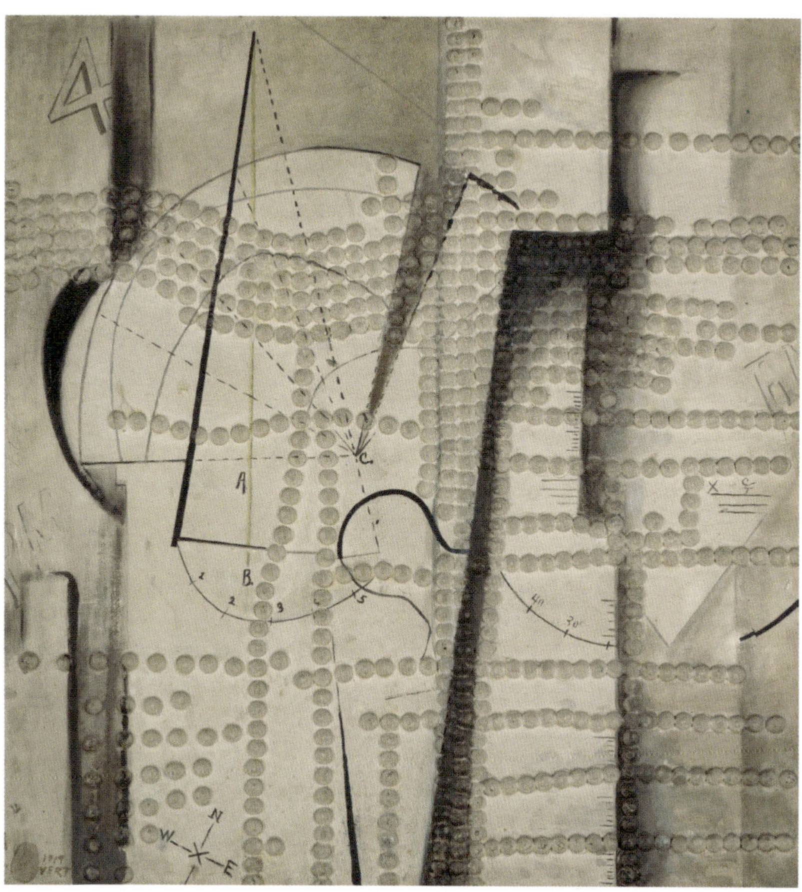

100

99 John Covert, *Brass Band*, 1919.
Oil, cord (probably sisal fibre),
nails and tempera over gesso,
on commercial pieced wood,
covered on both sides in
cardboard, 66 × 60.5 cm
(26 × 23¹³⁄₁₆ in). Yale University
Art Gallery, New Haven

100 John Covert, *Time*, 1919.
Oil, carpet tacks and tempera
on commercial pieced wood,
covered on both sides
in cardboard, 61 × 61 cm
(24 × 24 in). Yale University
Art Gallery, New Haven

101 Arthur Dove, *Portrait of Alfred
Stieglitz*, 1924. Assemblage
of lens, mirrored glass plate,
springs, steel wool, glue
and nails mounted on board,
40.3 × 30.8 cm (15⅞ × 12⅛ in).
The Museum of Modern Art,
New York

 Modern Art in America

In terms of their impact and sheer inventiveness they can be challenged only by those of Robert Rauschenberg thirty years later. They are still little known and have been generally avoided or disregarded in the Dove literature, primarily dismissed as aberrations. However, they fit perfectly and logically into the course of Dove's art, for they are a physical embodiment of his lifelong search for the real – not realistic, but real – true, authentic, without artifice, palpable, a search that has driven American artists. Davis, for example, sought an art that was real in itself, an independent self-generating object with a life of its own, obeying not the laws of nature but its own needs and demands. Hofmann's essay 'Search for the Real' of 1948 proposed that the life of the painting was in its very materials, but finally, for him, the real was a matter of seeking – finding – a spiritual order to life and art,[8] a goal echoed by Josef Albers.

Dove's search for the real occupied him throughout his life. He had made a promising start in his work in 1911–12, shown at Gallery 291 in 1912, but then seemed to have retired to Westport, Connecticut, to run a chicken farm. This was a move born of desperation, so anxious was he to be financially and emotionally independent from his family, who had virtually disowned him for his pursuit of a career in art. He did little artwork for years, for his quest for independence had in fact cost him his freedom, as well as his calling. Yet Stieglitz, virtually a surrogate father, never lost faith in Dove and his abilities, perhaps because his own art was in a fallow period. Stieglitz gently prodded and encouraged him: 'No painting for you in sight?'[9] until Dove finally gave up farming and resumed painting in the summer of 1921. He was exultant when he wrote to Stieglitz in August that 'It is great to be at it again, feel more like a person than I have in years.'[10]

While Dove's collage of 1924 *Portrait of Alfred Stieglitz* [101] recalled Picabia's portrait of Stieglitz as a camera, its assemblage of separate elements including a camera lens and photographic plate is closer to Schwitters's constructions, which would have been known through exhibitions at the Société Anonyme. Even closer to Schwitters's use of old junk are the magnifying glass, chicken bone and scale combined in *The Intellectual* (1925), a Dada mockery of the limitations of reason and intelligence, an attack repeated in Dove's collage of *The Critic*, also 1925. Here, the ridiculously pompous figure in a top hat, tux and monocle whizzing along on roller skates tells us just how closely he looks at art, and exactly what his attitude is towards that art.

These collages have often been considered as native folk art, related somehow to 'Americana'. This completely misses Dove's sophistication as an artist, his awareness and appreciation of developments in modern art. The collages were carefully conceived – they were not accidents made from chance materials. We know from Dove's journals that he went on purpose to the dime store to search out the exact materials for *Miss Woolworth*, his first collage in 1924.[11] It is a parody of how he and his wife Reds lived so frugally, seeking out bargains wherever they could. In these works, Dove found as wide an expressive and formal range as he did in his paintings. Some verged on total abstraction, as in *Monkey Fur* (1928), where the only possibly discernible image is the vestige of a head or face under the fur and tinfoil and rusted iron, all taken to be an unmanageable shock of hair. The purest collage, and a radical work, is the untitled vertical piece [102] consisting of cork, plaster and wire meshing a work so complete in itself that it rivals the self-contained purity of Brancusi; it is no coincidence, then, that when Brancusi saw it he told Stieglitz that it was 'handsome'.[12]

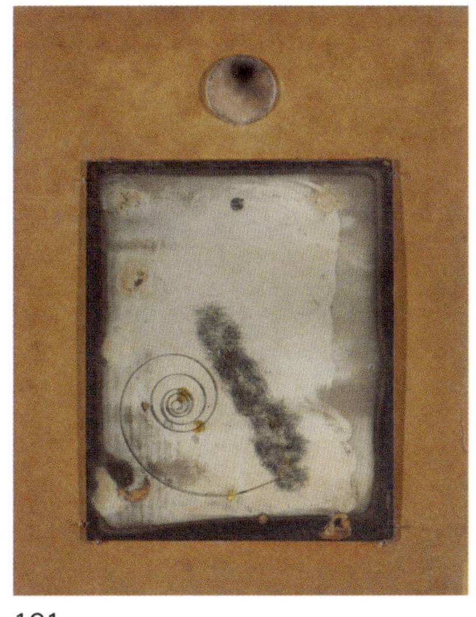

101

The image of Dove as a loner, a kind of Thoreau in the woods, is in part true, but he was no recluse or hermit oblivious to the world around him. In the 1920s he lived on the water in Centerport, Long Island, an easy commute to New York City, which he did with regularity. He also read widely in world and American literature and art. His fusion of up-to-date ideas in art is no better demonstrated than in the complex collage called *Goin' Fishin'* (1925) [104]. It seems at first to be an abstract compendium of elements such as the bamboo, overalls and tar-covered post that point to something, rather like an object-portrait, with which Dove was familiar. However, it is not only an amazing assemblage of diverse materials but also a compendium, a virtual history of older and modern American art and the forces driving it. The subject matter is in accordance with the work's title: a man sits on a pier, casting his bamboo fishing rod back and forth, in perpetual motion, leaning out then back, as a fisherman will do. Therefore it refers to nineteenth-century genre painting, creating an image of serenity, even lassitude. It might be read as a racial dig at the mythical lazy black man, but it was a scene Dove knew well, so it is more accurate to call it an up-to-date, rural version of urban realism. Dove lived on a boat, docked at the pier from which the locals fished, as he did himself, for he and his wife lived off the bounty of the land and the waters, as his journal makes clear. It is no fantasy then, but rather a depiction of a common, shared experience, for Dove was a man of the people, a humble, modest person who appreciated and was grateful for the world around him. Indeed, he recorded the temperature and the weather every day in his journal, and was deeply in touch with nature, whether the landscape, a bird, a sunrise or the mood of a day.

The pieces of bamboo, so American and folksy, should also be seen as Cubist planes defining space and form, now made real, as can the denim and the wood, a special kind of American Cubism, adapted to American needs. This literal depiction of time and movement refers to Bergson and his ideas of time as *la durée*, an object seen in past, present and future, as it moves through space, changing as it goes. Bergsonian thought, we will remember, was a constant topic for Duchamp and the other artists of the Puteaux group, now indelibly transferred to New York. In the use of sequential motion, Duchamp and the *Nude Descending a Staircase* also come to mind, for Duchamp confirmed that indeed the sequential photographic diagrams and photos found in Étienne-Jules Marey's *Movement* were the precise source for his famous image.[13] The tangential encounter between the reclusive mavericks and former illustrators and caricaturists František Kupka and Duchamp, who for a brief period lived on rue Caulaincourt in Paris and met through Duchamp's brother Jacques, is one of these magical, ephemeral and seminal moments in art history. It gave birth to two iconic paintings deeply indebted to the kinetic typographies of Marey, while all at once transcending the current preoccupations of Cubism and Futurism: the Czech's *Woman Picking Flowers* of 1910–11 [103] and the Frenchman's *Nude Descending a Staircase* of 1912, just before the former went on a journey to Pure Painting via Symbolism and the latter to the pure objectivity of the readymades via Cézanne.[14] With this in mind, it is easy to see why Katherine Dreier, in her important book of 1926, *Modern Art*, referred to Dove as the 'only American Dadaist',[15] an overstatement, perhaps, but a revealing, contemporary account of an attitude and spirit long overlooked. American Dada never had the bitterness or nihilistic urges of its European counterpart; it was more sanitized, and looked primarily to the possibilities of non-art materials in new formats rather than to an overriding world

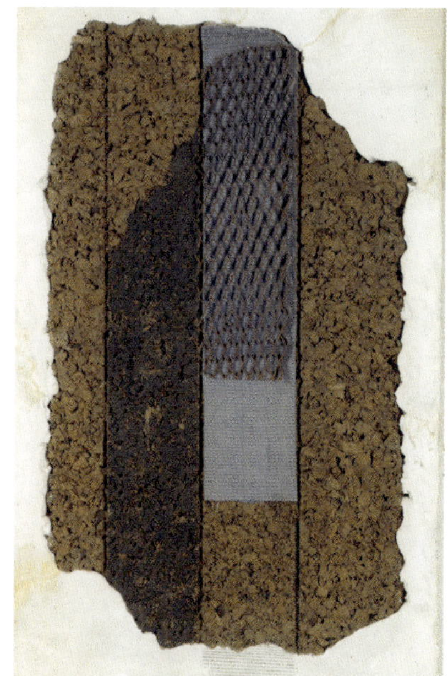

102

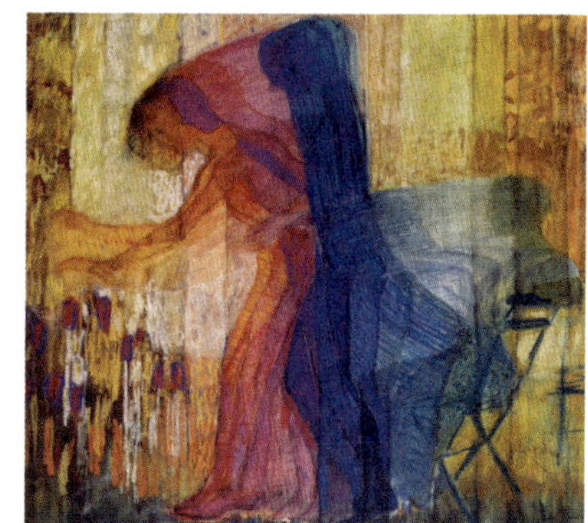

103

102 Arthur Dove, *Untitled*, c.1925. Crayon and graphite on plaster, wire mesh, cloth and cork, 54.9 × 34.3 cm (21⅝ × 13½ in). Amon Carter Museum of American Art, Fort Worth

103 František Kupka, *Woman Picking Flowers*, 1910–11. Pastel on paper, 48 × 52 cm (18⅞ × 20½ in). Musée National d'Art Moderne, Centre Pompidou, Paris

104 Arthur Dove, *Goin' Fishin'*, 1925. Assemblage of bamboo, denim shirt sleeves, buttons, wood and oil on wood, 53.9 × 64.7 cm (21¼ × 25½ in). The Phillips Collection, Washington, DC

Modern Art in America

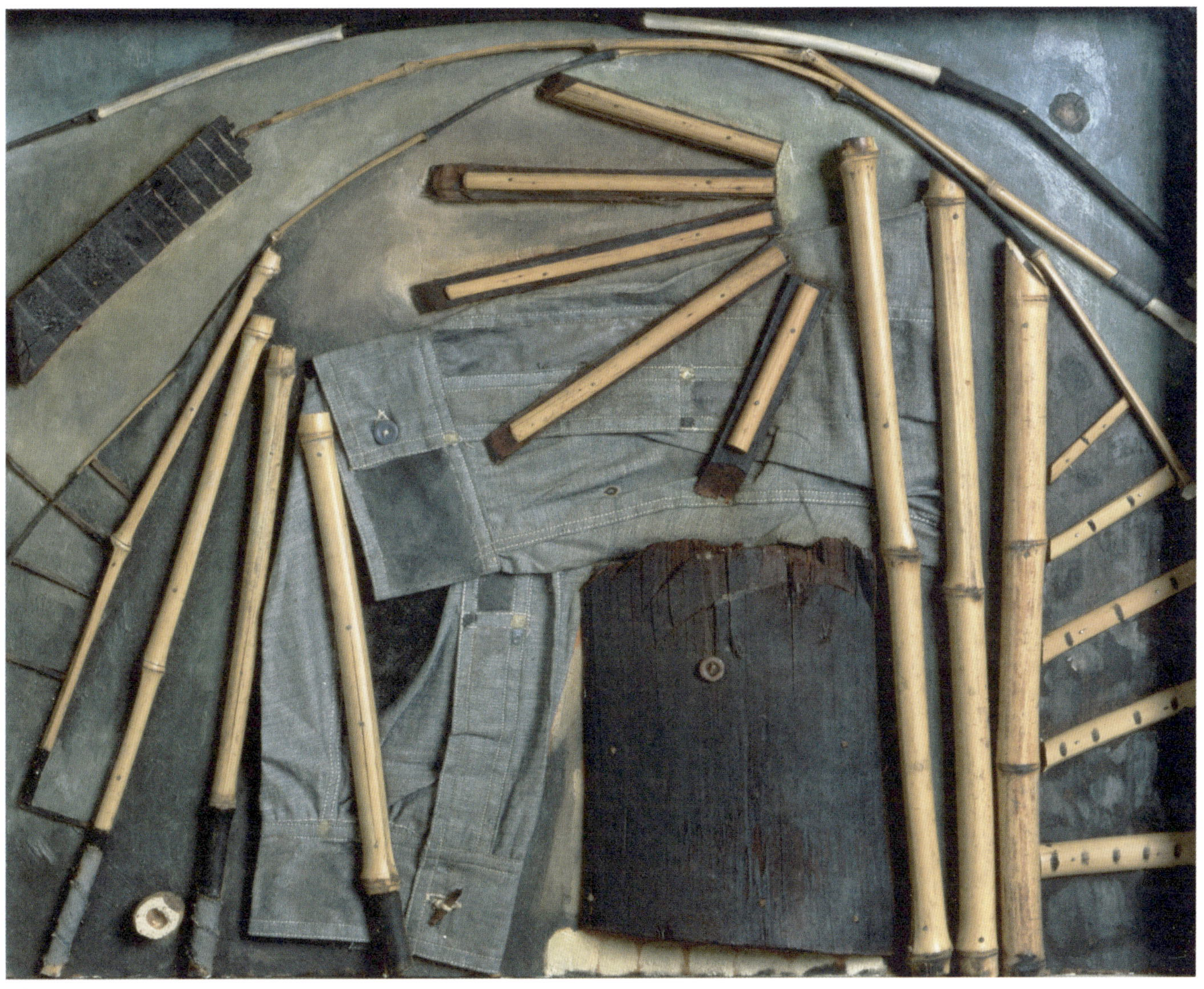

104

view. It is another example of American empiricism, of artists taking what they could use and dropping anything extraneous in order to make their own, personal idioms.

Dove often concentrated on the landscape, especially the water, and the sun, which he frequently painted rising, as in *Sunrise: Milwaukee* (1924), a glorious burst of light and colour suggesting not just the dawning of a new day, but the constant rebirth of the self and the world. The image is reminiscent of Van Gogh; the means and the colour come from Matisse and Cézanne. In a carefully plotted system of colour and paint application, a fusion made through contiguous, tightly knitted parallel brushstrokes that recall Cézanne's technique of *passage*, the expansive bursts of light are translated into something concrete. Dove continued this method throughout much of his career. In late works such as *Flour Mill II* (1938) we still see his debt to Cézanne's pure colour patches and complete forms.

Life on the water was not easy, however – Dove's boat was leaky and the motor unreliable, requiring constant attention. There was always an adventure to be had, with considerable hazards involved. In his painting *Moon and Sea II* [105] done in the late autumn of 1923, he recorded one of his most perilous journeys. It was done shortly, if not immediately, after a fierce gale had passed over the waters of Long Island Sound on 23 and 24 October. The event was vividly recorded by Dove in a letter written to Stieglitz during the course of the storm in the early hours of the 24th. Dove and his new companion, Reds, had weathered the storm on their new boat, the *Mona*, while moored in Manhasset Bay after a difficult journey from the Hudson River. The storm had severely tested the boat, as well as the new partnership of Dove and Reds, but they had survived, stronger and with a new 'unity of interest'. Dove related to Stieglitz that he had been 'trying to memorize the storm all day so that I can paint it. Storm green and storm grey.' That morning, he added a postscript: 'Storm breaks…What a relief!' It is precisely that 'relief' and its aftermath that Dove painted, not the storm itself.[16]

The painting exudes a calm that speaks volumes about Dove. The serenity marks his freedom from backbreaking farm labour, from his father (who had recently died) and from an unhappy marriage, and his joy with a new partner. Finally, the painting itself, confident and fully realized, marks his return to painting, his true passion. It is something of a private icon, symmetrically composed with a lyrical simplicity. Its vaulted sky speaks of a personal altar, one formed in and by nature. The artist stands before the vastness of the cosmos, with which Dove felt a new unity. The image of the moon over the water seems to speak of a transcendent world of another sphere, in a higher domain, themes that appeared throughout his art. It relates to a long tradition, referring to the whole history of Romanticism, from Caspar David Friedrich to the sun and moon images of Van Gogh, an artist whose work Dove loved deeply.

STUART DAVIS: AN AMERICAN CUBISM

Stuart Davis (1892–1964), the youngest artist to exhibit in the Armory Show, was still feeling his way from Ashcan Realism and through post-Impressionism in the early 1920s, when he caught the Dada spirit. Although not a member of the Arensberg circle, he responded to the work of Duchamp, Picabia and Man Ray. He said of this group that they 'couldn't help broadcasting revolution wherever they went'.[17] For Davis, Duchamp's *Fountain* worked like a 'time bomb' in his consciousness: 'Duchamp's suggestion worked slowly. Unaesthetic material, absurd

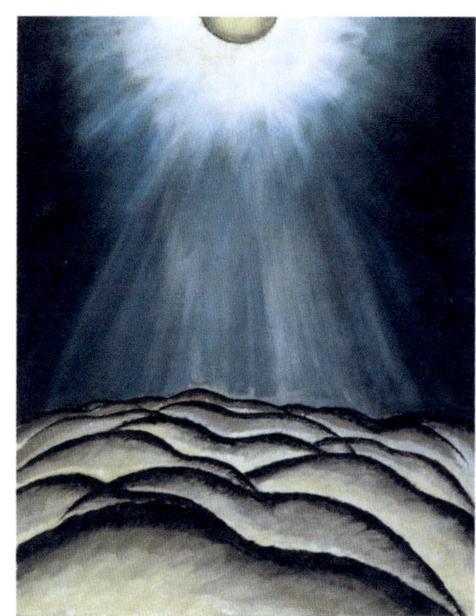

105

105　Arthur Dove, *Moon and Sea II*,
1923. Oil on canvas,
61 × 45.7 cm (24 × 18 in).
Crystal Bridges Museum of
American Art, Bentonville

106　Stuart Davis, *Lucky Strike*,
1921. Oil on canvas,
84.5 × 45.7 cm (33¼ × 18 in).
The Museum of Modern Art,
New York

material, non-arty material – ten years later I could take a worthless eggbeater, and the change to a new association would inspire me.'[18] He acknowledged that Picabia's macaroni and feather in *Le Midi* (c. 1924-5) made it easier for him to 'sew buttons and glue excelsior on the canvas without feeling any sense of guilt'.[19] In fact, Davis incorporated collaged elements in his *Itlksez* of 1921 to create a stick figure that mocked Western figure painting. The shorthand word of the title, reading 'It looks easy', was a comment on the difficulties of making art of importance and authenticity. As an emerging young artist finding his way, he was still learning just how great those difficulties were.[20]

In 1921 – the year in which the Société Anonyme opened and sparked a renewed interest in Dada – Davis produced several paintings, such as *Cigarette Papers* and *Lucky Strike* [106], that emulated collages of the discarded, non-art materials of Dada; in both these cases cigarette wrappers were an early taste of pop imagery in American art. These and other works in a similar vein enabled him to go beyond the last of his rich, painterly landscapes of high colour, done during 1919 in the vein of Van Gogh, and move from what he called 'percept' art to 'concept' art. It is the first use of this word, I believe, in American art, but Davis was thinking in Cubist terms, saying that the real subject of a landscape was 'a mental concept derived from various sources and expressed in terms of weight and light … Cubism is the bridge between percept and concept.'[21] It was here,

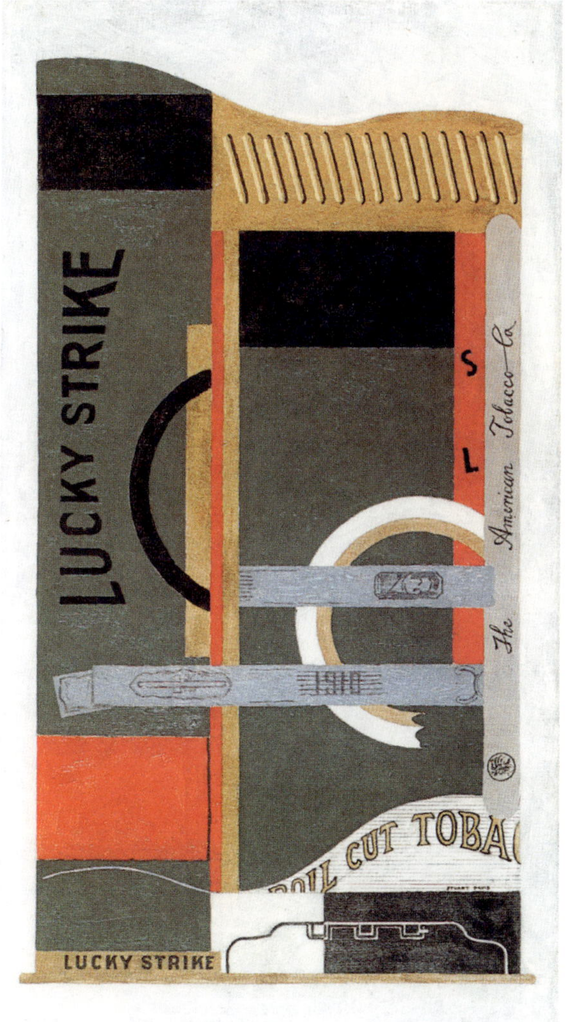

106

in the broad planes of these forms, that Davis began his most profound contribution to modern art, the development of a full-blown, original Cubist vocabulary that took many distinct turns throughout his life. At the same time, we must remember that he had an impact on, and was in turn affected by, virtually every movement in modern art, from Ashcan Realism to Dada, Cubism, Matissean colour construction, mural painting, Abstract Expressionism, colour field, and Art and Language, in a career that extended from 1910 until his death in 1964.

During the course of the 1920s, Davis's colour sense, sheer inventiveness and brilliance, and structural soundness, grew ever stronger. Just as important was his development of a personal, American type of Cubism, which provided the structural basis for his art for the rest of his life. After a trip to Cuba, he returned to America in 1920 and settled in with a new resolve. At this time he began a journal filled with notes and drawings, primarily of a theoretical nature, that he maintained until his death.[22] They are rich and revealing, but one feels they were often post-facto observations, intended to work out on paper what he had already worked out on canvas. Davis knew well, then and later, that 'The theory must be burned in the fires of reality before it comes alive.'[23] From 1921 to 1924, he urged himself to make his paintings as clear and direct, as impersonal and simple, as possible, but always respecting 'the life of the medium he is working in'.[24]

In 1922, Davis was just turning thirty; he had been an artist for fourteen years, but he had as yet no clear direction. He urged himself to:

Loosen up. It is now that we draw in paint, taking for granted all we have learned in the last two years. Our purpose is now to paint with as much bragaashio [sic] as our training will permit. Good luck. Starting now I will begin a series of paintings that will be rigorously logical, American not French. America has had her scientists, her inventors, now she shall have her artist.[25]

Over the next several months, he produced a series of some twelve Cubist still lifes, his most sustained and accomplished series to date, that represent a breakthrough in his art. They are also part of a second, more sustained wave of American Cubism that extended into the 1930s in the work of Bruce, Maurer, Graham, Carles, and the young Arshile Gorky. The series began with a group of small, loose, painterly works and, as Davis gained confidence and skill, moved to larger, more complex formats such as that of *Still Life with Dial* (1922)[107]. They point to the influence of Picasso, his guide throughout, but also to the *guéridons* of Braque.

In the summer of 1922, Davis continued in the direction of greater complexity in his *Landscape, Gloucester*, where he spent summers until 1940. But still the clear, sharp geometry is there. That summer, he would comment, 'The effort will be to attain a style both realistic and abstract that can be applied successfully to all subjects'[26]–in effect, his working credo for a lifetime.[27] The fusion of abstract and realist predicts and reflects Picasso's famous statement in 1923 that either could be used, according to the means of expression needed.[28] Thereafter Davis could put his efforts to a whole battery of Cubist subjects, from the hard-edged *Apples and Jug* (1923)[108] to *Supper Table* (1925), in which he employs a pictorial X-ray vision within the linear structure, seeing through supposed solids to new layers. They are all original and compelling contributions to American and world Cubism.

There is no question that the Dada spirit of exploration and challenge deeply impressed Davis. In the summer of 1923, the spirit was still there when he went to Santa Fe at the behest of John Sloan, his early mentor.

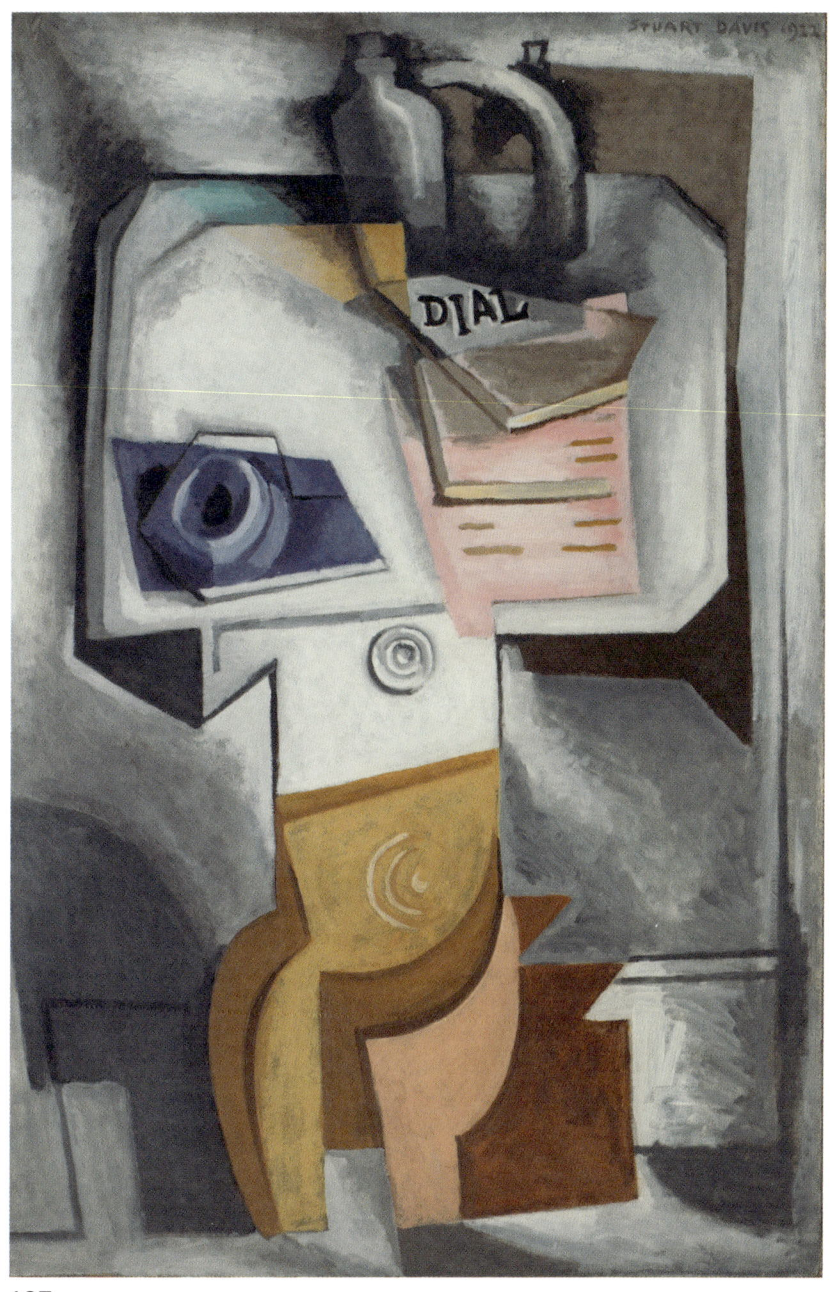

107

107 Stuart Davis, *Still Life with Dial*, 1922. Oil on canvas, 127 × 81.3 cm (50 × 32 in). The Vilcek Foundation, New York

Sloan, an honoured figure in Santa Fe, arranged to set him up in a choice studio in the Palace of the Governors, the epicentre of the town. Davis did not take to the town, however, finding its setting, its history and its archaeology to be contrary to his urban spirit, too overbearing and too filled with tourist art. Clearly still infected by the Dada urge to rebellion, Davis literally turned his back on the spectacular landscape, and instead went down into the basement to find his material. There he painted old tin cans, a rusty saw and other junk that became the subject of a series of paintings that are among his best, most original works of the 1920s, complex amalgams of non-art images. In *The Saw* (1923), the tool appears as a giant, looming machine, but if the painting is viewed sideways, it seems to be a crawling extraterrestrial conveyance or an outsize mechanical bug. The good mayor of Santa Fe was upset by Davis's snub of the famous landscape. In order to pacify him, the artist went out and dashed off a dozen or so landscape paintings, which can fairly be termed the least interesting of his life. One painting bearing the name of the place was

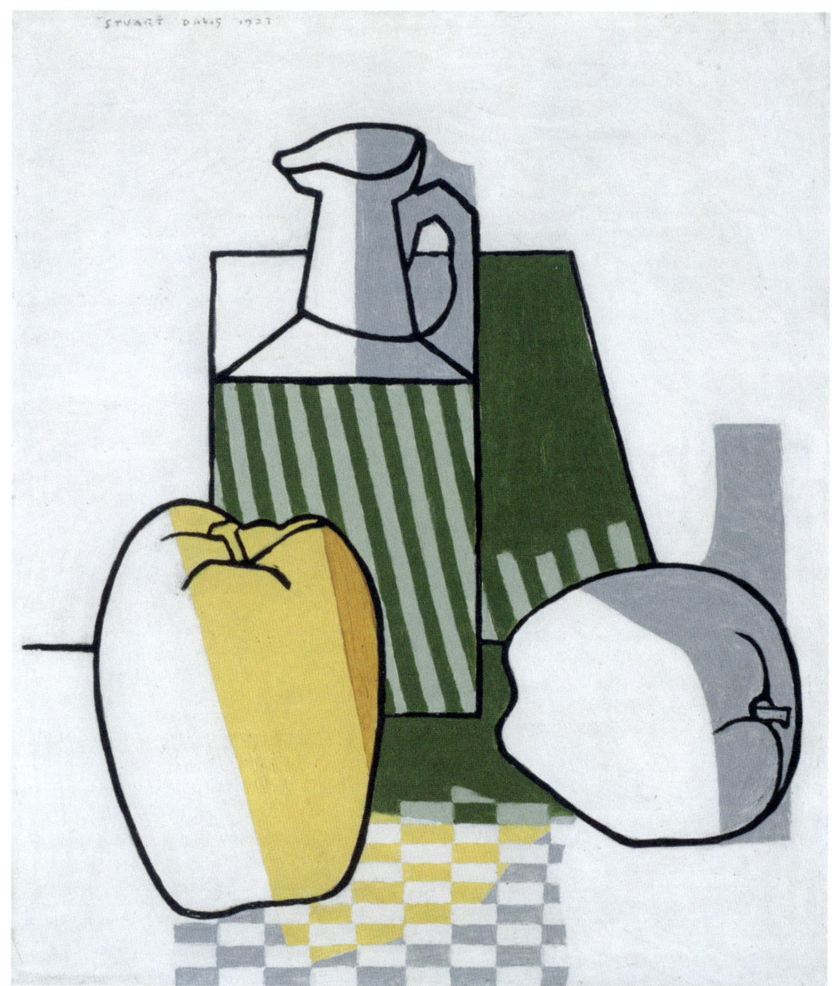
108

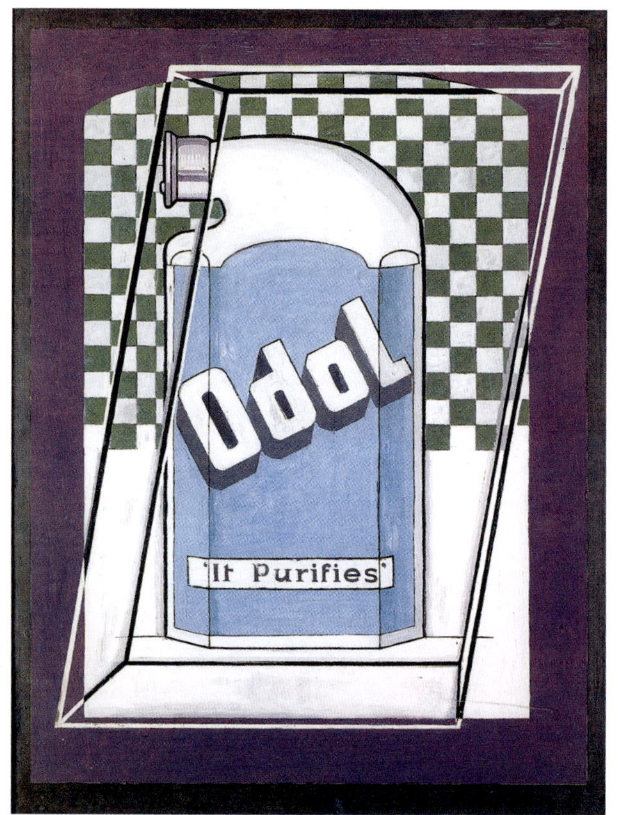

109

Modern Art in America

his *Taos Tea Bags*, also of 1923, done in the tight precisionist drawing style that defined much of the Dada-related art of the time.

In a journal entry of 11 March 1921, Davis had affirmed that 'imitation is sentimentality. Let us rather use an alphabet of letters, numbers, canned goods labels, tobacco labels, in a word, let these well-known, purely objective things be used – to make a direct impression on the spectator.'[29] Labels were a way out of his painterly work of the late teens, a means to gain a more overt structural clarity, a personal entry into the post-1916 drive to a more architectural, more solid way of painting. In part also, as we have seen, the use of these non-art materials and subjects can be traced to Duchamp and Schwitters. Davis's most famous use of commercial sources is *Odol* (1924)[109], often the one painting used to illustrate the entirety of his art, and especially loved because it casts him as a kind of historical proto-Pop curiosity. This is in part true, of course, but it hides the real and full complexity of the artist.

In *Odol* we are taken by the brand itself, a cleansing agent, with its bold graphic image. But it is how this image and the painting are constructed that is of deeper interest. It is situated within a sophisticated Cubist frame, a kind of linear cage reminiscent of Russian Constructivist art, or at the very least an original adaptation of American Precisionism. Equally powerful in the painting is the black-and-white chequerboard pattern – is it a kind of Cubist device? A spatial inversion of a bathroom floor? Or does it refer to a Mondrian pattern seen in his work in 1917? The last is unlikely, since Mondrian was not shown in the United States until the International Exhibition of Modern art organized in 1926 by Katherine Dreier at the Brooklyn Museum.[30] These are just a few of the questions that accrue to *Odol*, showing that it is a far more layered and even mysterious painting than we may think at first glance.

In his famous 'Egg Beater' paintings of 1927–8[110], Davis reached a new height of complexity and achievement; no other Cubist paintings are quite like these, and they should be recognized as genuine American additions to world art. They ushered in a new type of distilled, lean geometric art, based on Cubism, that lasted in America until Mondrian's death in New York in 1944. Davis claimed that in these paintings he had done nothing but nail an eggbeater, a rubber glove and a fan to a table and focus on nothing but them. Typically, he is misleading us, trying to divert us from the full import of his paintings. He took an eggbeater, first used in 1923, and perhaps suggested by a photograph of the utensil done by Man Ray in 1918; a rubber glove, possibly suggested by Giorgio de Chirico, all non-art materials that he said were inspired by Duchamp's revolutionary approach to art. But they are impossible to identify with any certainty in any of the four versions, or in their preparatory drawings and gouaches. We have taken Davis's word for it that they are present, but so hard have we tried to find them that we have missed altogether the architectural structures in which they are housed. Clearly there are objects on a table within a large room distorted by a linear Cubist perspective, which is further located within an urban landscape indicated by the tops of buildings at the highest edge. What we have, then, is an abstract still life in a large room, in turn within a city of tall buildings, a format unique in world art or Cubism, save for one known Picasso work of the early 1920s. Here the still life, usually depicted as a hermetic, isolated subject, is opened up and elevated to being a part of the modern urban world.

The space frame in the *Odol* and the flat clear geometric planes of his works of 1924 such as *Lemons*, in which each form takes an autonomous identity, is the result of Davis's constant demands on himself, to seek a

108 Stuart Davis, *Apples and Jug*, 1923. Oil on composition board, 54.3 × 45 cm (21⅜ × 17¾ in). Museum of Fine Arts, Boston

109 Stuart Davis, *Odol*, 1924. Oil on canvas board, 60.9 × 45.6 cm (24 × 18 in). The Museum of Modern Art, New York

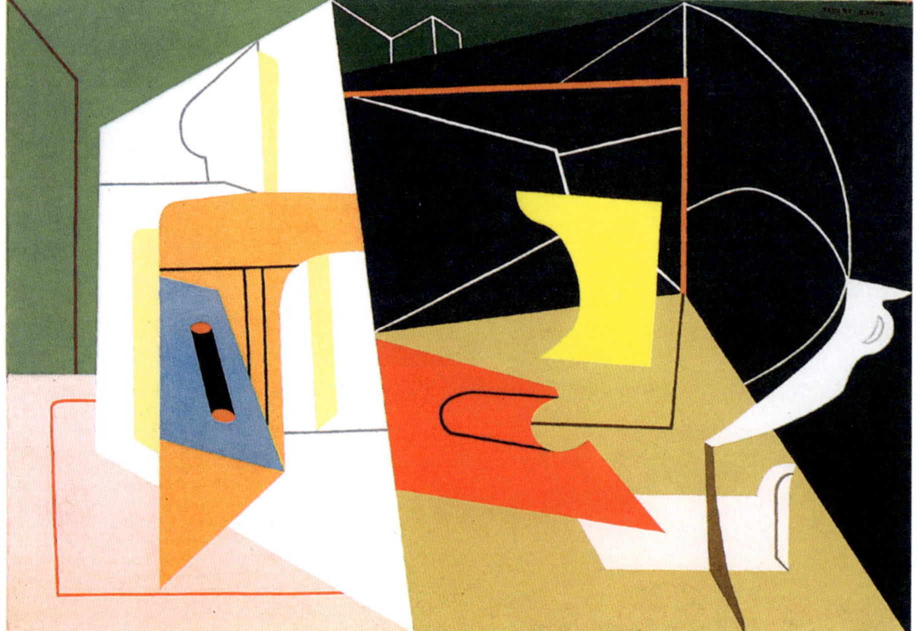

110

'fuller clarification' as a pictorial necessity. The vivid colours are closely identified with each plane, helping to stamp the paintings with a new unity. Davis later witnessed the work of Mondrian and El Lissitzky at the Brooklyn show organized by Dreier in 1926, from where he would have derived the additional possibilities apparent in their lean, linear geometries.

Given the spare geometry of the *Egg Beaters*, the paintings that Davis made in Paris during his stay there in 1928–9 have generally been taken as a 'retreat' from his earlier work – primarily, one supposes, because they are more overtly figurative. But they are not a let-down, unless we dogmatically take abstraction as inherently better than figuration, which it is not. We must also remember that no matter how abstract his work, Davis always asserted that he was a realist artist, and to miss that was to misunderstand his approach. He insisted on the underlying quality of the painting as an independent object, with its own reality, obeying its own laws, made up of the tangible materiality of paint and canvas. Davis had challenged himself in 1922 to do both abstract and figurative paintings, as if he were deliberately setting out to prove that there was no real difference. The paintings seem to challenge the ubiquitous tourist-souvenir canvases he would have seen in Paris, reversing their clichés into serious and advanced compositions. One thinks of his love of jazz, especially Earl Hines who, Davis said, 'had the ability to take an anecdotal or sentimental song and turn it into a series of musical intervals of enormous variety', a practice that was important to Davis 'to formulate my own aspirations in painting'.[31]

Davis loved Paris and, like any good tourist, enjoyed nothing better than to walk its streets, soaking up their sights and sounds. He chose a wide range of sites to sketch and later paint, both picturesque and historic or of no apparent archival or visual interest. The city's architecture provided a foil for his 'structural approach' and the walls of buildings lent themselves perfectly to a Cubist planarity. He described the great variety in Parisian houses and how they were 'all different in regard to size, surface, number of windows, etc.'[32] This is exactly what he reproduced in his paintings of Paris. Each plane, whether the Place des Vosges or the Porte Saint-Martin, has a different angle or geometry, a different colour, surface texture, touch,

110   Stuart Davis, *Egg Beater No. 4*, 1928. Oil on canvas, 68.9 × 97.1 cm (27⅛ × 38¼ in). The Phillips Collection, Washington, DC

111   Stuart Davis, *Rue Lipp*, 1928. Oil on canvas, 81.3 × 99.1 cm (32 × 39 in). Michael and Fiona Scharf Family Collection

feel or hue, some new and inventive even by Davis's standards. These are well-known and easily identifiable sites, but at the same time Davis could throw us off from what he was actually looking at. His *Rue Lipp* (1928) [111], for example, has nothing to do with the Brasserie Lippe on the boulevard Saint-Germain, a famous tourist and artist spot; rather, Davis depicts a spot in the fifth arrondissement near the École Polytechnique. There he sits in a café (still there) behind the table with his mug of beer, looking out on to an unnamed, open square. The École is on his right and the Hotel Belle France on his left, at the head of the rue de la Montagne Sainte Geneviève, where four streets run together.[33] Davis collapsed the multiple planes of these streets into a stage-set kind of structure, enclosing the space around, even as he had first done in *Consumers Coal Company* (1912) (page 57). It is a new kind of Cubist complexity for Davis, conjoined with a beautiful coloration of multiple hues. He returned home to New York in late August of 1929, but the spirit of Paris stayed with him.

ALFRED MAURER'S FINAL YEARS

From 1928 until his death by suicide in 1932, Alfred Maurer also brought a Cubist idiom to new heights, in still lifes that Clement Greenberg thought might even go beyond Paris Cubism.[34] That Greenberg was surely right is demonstrated by *Still Life with Red Bowl and Black Bottle* (c.1929–30) [112]. Maurer uses an old-fashioned subject but turns it into a modernist statement. Its tactile surfaces, the sublime touch and application, were rivalled only by the still lifes of Picasso and Braque of 1911–12. Maurer fused surface and depth, integrating parts with the whole through a grid system that unified the structure while allowing each part to retain its distinctive character. The overlapping of shapes was in line with established

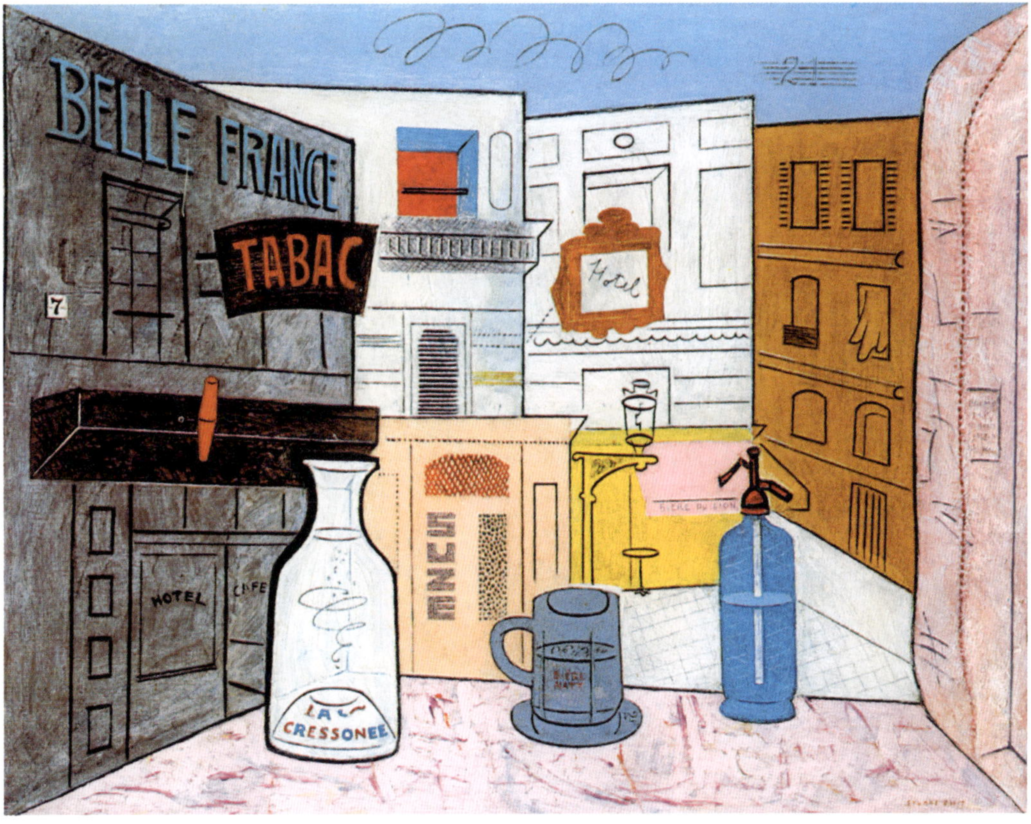

111

Cubist practice, but Maurer achieved something unique by means of his extraordinary glazing, the building-up of the surface, in which there is a literal, physical overlapping, not just the fictive, illusionist overlapping found in most Cubist painting. Maurer's still lifes of the time are marvels of the art of painting, reminding us of Meyer Schapiro's memorable description of still life as a meditative practice, as the artist moves objects here and there, in various relationships, like a 'solitary pictorial chess'.[35] They are meditations on colour, as well, fused with a Cubist structure, a hallmark of American art from the 1920s well into the 1960s. Here, colour is form, fulfilling in a new and more abstract manner Cézanne's famous and influential dictum that 'Form is at its fullest when colour is at its richest.'[36] So rich is the colour in these paintings that Joshua Taylor once described them as 'paintings to be in, rather than paintings to look at'.[37]

Sadly, in 1932, Maurer took his own life, apparently driven over the edge by the continued rejection of his father. But later artists would appreciate Maurer, such as Hans Hofmann, who wrote in an introduction to a show of Maurer's art in 1950 that he was forerunner of a 'true and great American tradition' that was then being carried on by 'the vanguard of modern artists'.[38] Hofmann was right – perhaps even more so than he understood. It is also now apparent that he took a great deal from Maurer's rich layering of paint in his own work after 1935.

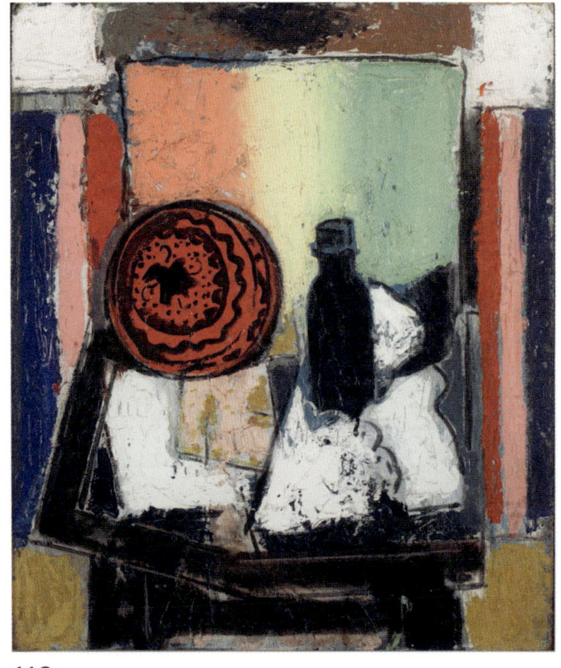

112

112 Alfred Maurer, *Still Life with Red Bowl and Black Bottle*, *c.*1929–30. Oil on gessoed board, 57.8 × 46 cm (22¾ × 18⅛ in). Tommy and Gill LiPuma Collection

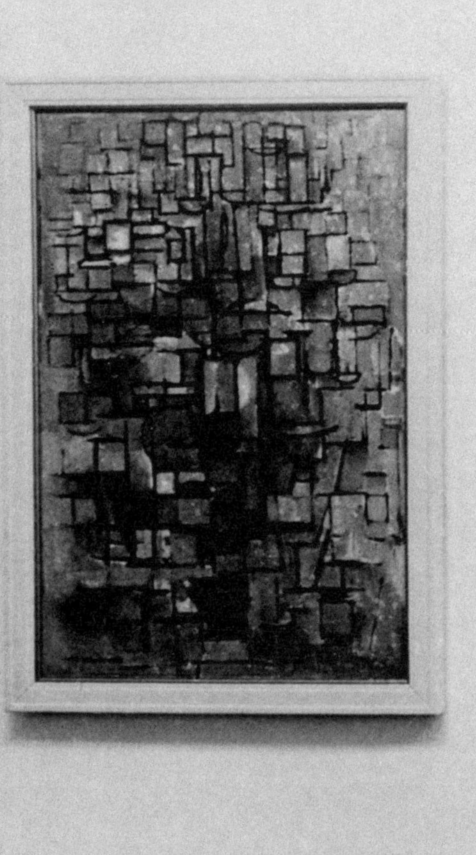
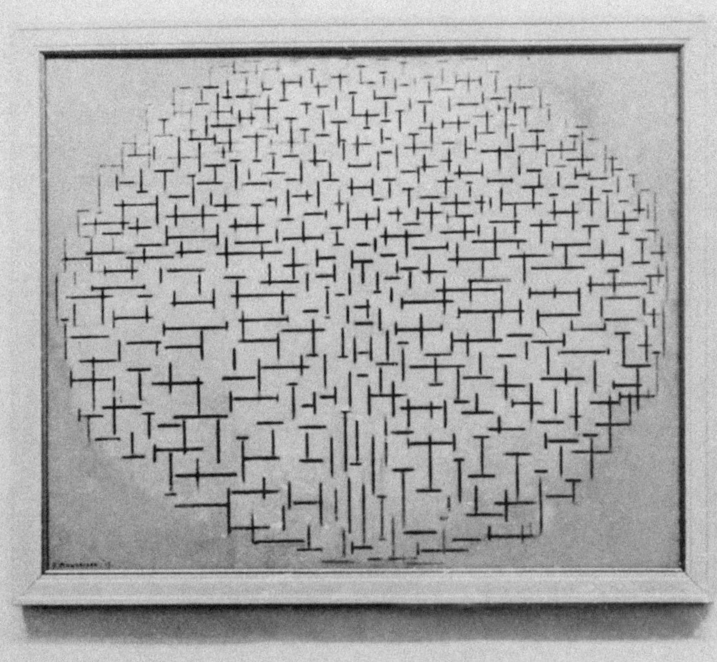

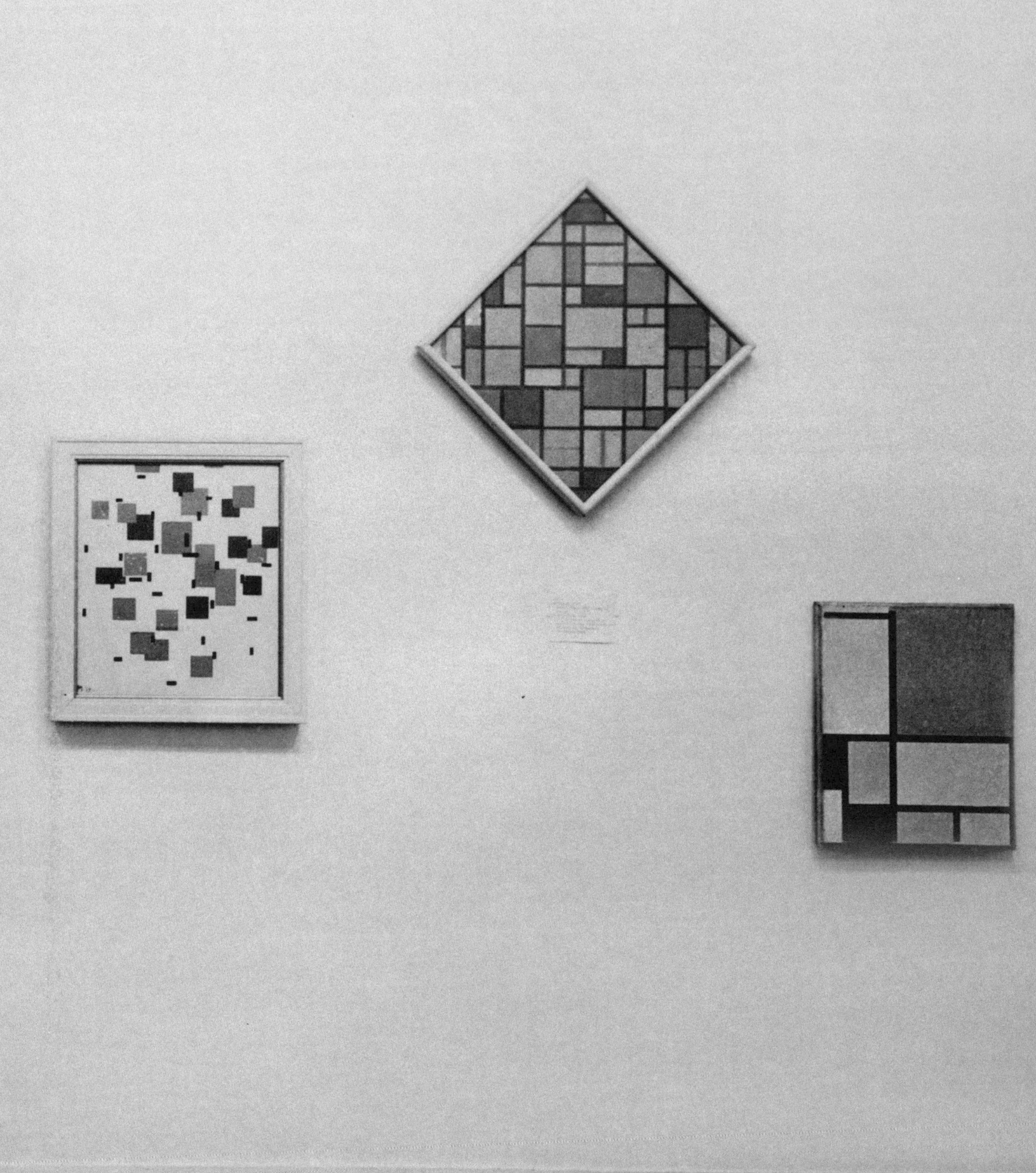

MODERN ART MARCHES ON

THE 1930s

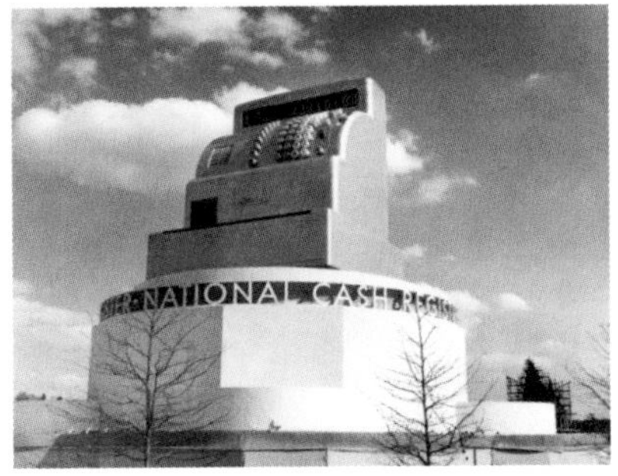

114

113   Installation of 'Cubism and
Abstract Art' exhibition at
the Museum of Modern Art,
New York, 2 March–
19 April 1936.

114   National Cash Register
Pavilion with huge replica
of a cash register on top of
a building at the New York
World's Fair in 1939.

The art of the 1930s is still often thought to have constituted a full retreat from modernism, and to have been entirely given to depicting the social and economic disasters of the Depression.[1] But contrary to received opinion, modernism carried on in new ways and developed new avenues that formed a continuity between early and later art in America. The turbulent forces of the period – the Great Depression, the rise of Fascism and Communism, the approaching world war, radical politics – did seem to put advanced art in the background, since numerous artists wanted to create an art that reflected the social and political ferment in which they lived, or sought an 'art of the people' by portraying the heartland of their native America. And much art that addressed these subjects featured at the forefront of public and critical awareness. Yet this was only one aspect of American art in the 1930s. The decade was in fact a rich and infinitely complex period. A spirit of optimism and hope for the future ran through American art, as witness the faith in technology, modern communications and education so prominently on display at the new Rockefeller Center, and then again at the New York World's Fair of 1939. Indeed, a note of Pop optimism was embodied in the National Cash Register building at the fair[114], for the building was topped by a giant cash register that predicted the single-object sculpture of Claes Oldenburg twenty-five years later. The 1930s was a watershed, the point at which old problems met the newer currents that were to emerge in the great flowering of America after 1945. Some painters and sculptors, although in the minority and virtually unknown until now (art history is never determined by numbers, only by quality), were working in ways divorced from the political and social currents of the time. Many of them were, however, passionately involved with contemporary topics and events. Here, Stuart Davis is the shining and most prominent example. He was involved in all the political issues of the day, was head of the Artists Union and the Artists Congress and the editor of *Art Front*, yet (with two minor exceptions) it never shows in his art. Many, including Davis, were committed to a modern abstracting mode, but attached a revolutionary interpretation to their work and saw it as an act of social change. These are equally artists of their times, even though their art was not conceived as a direct instrument of political action. 'We were all poor,' de Kooning said, 'and worried only about the work.'[2]

Almost never considered in appraisals of the 1930s is the older generation, which consisted of the artists who in the main had been responsible for the first wave of American modernism prior to 1920. They did not stop painting for the duration. On the contrary, artists as familiar as Dove, O'Keeffe, Demuth, Marin and Davis, or as forgotten as Bruce, John Storrs and Arnold Friedman, were at the height of their powers during this period. Their accomplishments are among the finest of the 1930s, although they have nothing to do with politics.

Social Protest, Regionalist and American Scene painting were the three paths that the public and critical demand for a 'socially conscious' art followed, and all reached their point of highest concentration in the 1930s. It is a mistake, however, to suppose that they were 'movements' in any sense of the word, or that they were 'born' in the 1930s. These painters were part of a generation that reacted both in the US and in Europe against what they felt was the excessively private and remote Cubist and Cubist-derived abstraction of 1914. Like the European Dadaists and Surrealists – who were also for the most part born in the 1890s – they desired to reintegrate art closely with life in terms that would more directly incorporate man's common experiences. In this sense, we might view them as a later part of the shift in approach that had occurred worldwide during and after World War I. American Scene painting, of which Regionalism is a geographic subdivision, has a long history in the nineteenth and twentieth centuries. Its distinguishing characteristics in the 1930s had been well defined by Charles Burchfield and Thomas Hart Benton by the mid-1920s. Social Protest painting really began with Dada in Berlin in 1919–21. George Grosz, a leading member of the Berlin group, transplanted its spirit to the United States when he emigrated there in 1932. The work of the Mexican muralists José Clemente Orozco and Diego Rivera in the 1920s also provided a major impetus for Social Protest painting. It is important to keep this historical background in mind if we are to understand that the 1930s was not a monolithic period, either stylistically or conceptually.

Surrealism and Magic Realism attracted a great deal of attention in the US during the 1930s. The first waves of American artists drawn to the movement – Man Ray, Joseph Cornell, Peter Blume, Ivan Albright and O. Louis Guglielmi – concentrated almost exclusively on the 'dream image', rendered with a photographic realism, that formed one pole of Surrealist art. The 'abstract' phase of Surrealism, which derived from André Breton's conception of psychic-automatism, never created a body of painting per se in America during the 1930s. Rather, its forms, techniques and attitudes were adapted in generalized ways in the late 1930s and 1940s by those artists who reached their full maturity after World War II. Vital to the development of Surrealism was the long line of artists such as Giorgio de Chirico, Salvador Dalí, Yves Tanguy, Roberto Matta, Pavel Tchelitchew and others who either visited America or stayed there for extended periods.

The tradition of Russian Constructivism and Dutch De Stijl that emerged at the Bauhaus in Germany also made an important imprint on abstract art in America. At the time of his arrival there in 1933, Josef Albers, although not thought of as a 1930s artist, was producing work of superb quality. His teachings were widely influential in spreading the principles of a non-objective art based on clarity and strict economy of structure, volume and colour. Mondrian's work was known in America by the early 1930s

                                                     Modern Art in America

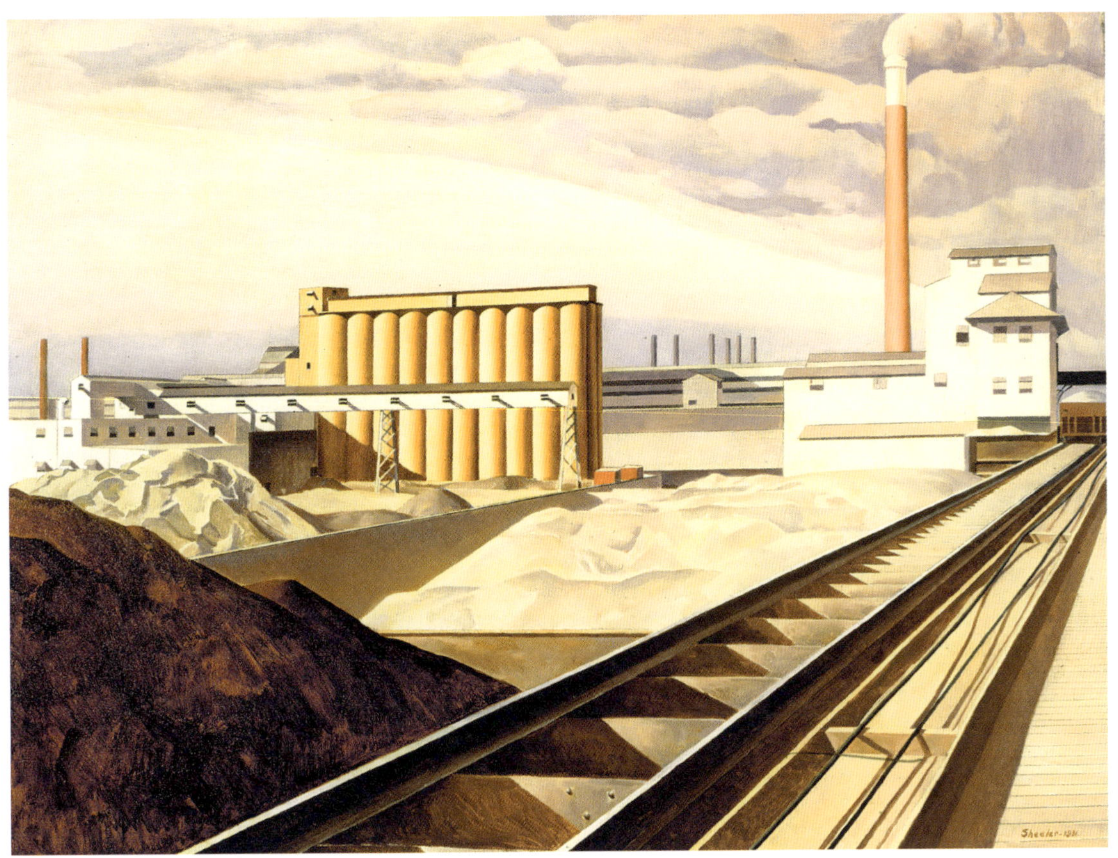

115

through the paintings in the Gallery of Living Art at New York University, an important showplace for abstract art, collected by Albert E. Gallatin, himself an artist of considerable accomplishment. Mondrian had a decisive and immediate effect on Burgoyne Diller and Harry Holtzman, and later, as will be discussed, on a wide group of artists after he arrived in New York in 1940. Balcomb Greene, first chairman of the American Abstract Artists (founded in 1936) as well as Fritz Glarner and Ilya Bolotowsky, both members of the group, also produced 'structural' abstractions.

What might be termed Precisionist Abstraction – marked by sharp, formal delineations and hard, flat colours and derived from Synthetic Cubism, Léger and Jean Hélion – accounted for a considerable segment of painting in the 1930s. The brilliant abstractions of the garish American urban landscape done by Davis, the advancing and receding forms of John Ferren and the optical sensations in the work of the young Ad Reinhardt should all be considered in this context. Charles Sheeler is also associated with Precisionism, especially in his images of the River Rouge plant in Detroit, icons of 1930s painting. He often expressed his admiration for Duchamp and would later state that the *Large Glass* was the 'picture of the century'.[3] Indeed, it was no accident that he entitled one of these iconic images of industry *Classic Landscape* (1931)[115], for although it depicts contemporary industrial America, the buildings and machines are viewed as if they were Greek monuments on the Acropolis that have been there through the ages. Here, Duchamp and the Puteaux artists are invoked, for the tracks come out of the darkness and move into the light, as if from a murky past into the dawn of a new day and even age. The light is filled with promise, moving us towards the glorious future brought on by the towers of industry rising high above, replacing the Church as the centre of society and the New World. The painting recalls nineteenth-century landscape art, for example Thomas Cole's *The Oxbow* (1836),

115   Charles Sheeler,
Classic Landscape, 1931.
Oil on canvas, 63.5 × 81.9 cm
(25 × 32¼ in). Collection
of Barney A. Ebsworth

where the dark woods of the primeval past give way to the sun-filled land of promise as man settles the continent. It is a classic, American rendition of the Bergsonian depiction of time. Related to this linear sharpness, confirming and reinforcing its effectiveness, was the photographic practice developed before the war by both Schamberg and Sheeler, at first only as a means to make a living but gradually developed as an art form in itself. By the end of the 1930s, Sheeler's painting and photography were inextricably united, a fusion that has been a hallmark of modern American art.

The 1930s were also marked by a more painterly and expressionist vein rapidly developing under the influence of Matisse, Cubism, Miró and Surrealism. It can be traced in the work of Milton Avery, Arshile Gorky, Hans Hofmann, Mark Tobey, Willem de Kooning, Jackson Pollock, George McNeil, Karl Knaths and John Graham. These artists were an integral part of the 1930s, not because they became well known at a later date, but because they were all strong artists whose work of the time stands on its own.

Sculpture in America began the decade in an impoverished state and entered the 1940s with a glowing promise, and is thus emblematic of the dynamic shifts within the 1930s that belie the one-sided assumptions about the period. The ranking master of American sculpture until his death in 1935, Gaston Lachaise was perhaps the only figurative sculptor who could embody his deepest and most personal emotions in a consistently inventive and convincing art. Other sculptors of the figurative tradition, such as Hugo Robus, William Zorach and John B. Flannagan, sought a more indirect and symbolic content that would convey principles of birth, the stages of life and the regeneration of the spirit. With this symbolism, as well as through the highly polished volumes of Robus and the direct-carve and truth-to-materials methods of Zorach and Flannagan, 1930s sculpture demonstrated its profound debt to Brancusi.

From 1915 until the early 1930s, the only American to keep alive the possibility of an abstract sculpture was John Storrs, a vital and accomplished figure. Thereafter, a younger generation of Americans began the path that was to fulfil the promise held out for sculpture by the methods of Cubism and Constructivism. By 1932, Alexander Calder had produced his first motorized, free-standing sculptures, and by 1934 he had made a series of suspended mobiles that contained all the wit and lyricism that has characterized his art ever since. At the same time, Joseph Cornell was creating the objects and boxes that mark him as the most personal and poetic of any Surrealist-influenced American. By the late 1930s, Ibram Lassaw had effectively adapted the biomorphic, floating shapes of abstract Surrealism to his cage enclosures related to Alberto Giacometti's sculpture. David Smith, whose importance to the 1930s we now understand, also learned from Giacometti and, most significantly, from the welded-iron sculpture of Picasso and Julio González. Although it still bears strong evidence of its debts, Smith's sculpture of this time is exhilarating for the unmistakable power and range of expression and composition that would soon establish his position as the greatest of all American sculptors until his death in 1965.[4]

No study of the 1930s can ignore the momentous influence exerted by vanguard European artists. It is one of the paradoxes of the time that a period generally considered totally isolationist in historical terms learned so much from Picasso, Matisse, Miró and Léger, and found in their work the basis for a new and original art. The primary European source for Americans looking to the mainstream of modern art at this time was Picasso, although he was not there; Matisse, almost as influential, more so after 1945, made only two brief visits in 1930. Léger, however, was in the US in 1931, 1935, 1938–9 and 1940–6. Not only was his presence a stimulating force, but he

Modern Art in America

in turn was deeply affected by the pace of American life and virtually became an American in outlook and spirit. American art was infinitely enriched by those who came and stayed: Grosz, Albers, Glarner, Berman, Tanguy; by those who stayed for extended periods: Matta, Hélion and Tchelitchew, as well as Léger; and by those such as Dalí who visited briefly, but who had a wide influence. Their arrival prefaced the great influx of the 1940s (Mondrian, Max Ernst, Jacques Lipchitz, André Masson and others), to which one can trace in part the change of artistic climate in America.

Abstraction and Figuration: John Graham and The New Artists

By 1932, a new and younger group of artists had emerged that were vital to the period and planted the seeds for the explosion of painterly abstraction after 1940, while producing a body of work of exceptional quality that allows us to see the 1930s in an altogether new light. The group formed around the brilliant and eccentric John Graham (1887–1961), born Ivan Gratianovitch Dombrowski, who had arrived in 1920 from Russia; he can be considered the first émigré after the war who was to enrich American art enormously. In Russia he had served in the cavalry and had visited the Shchukin Collection, where he saw important paintings by the modern masters, especially Picasso. He may also have seen the vanguard exhibitions held prior to 1914 in Moscow, and he seems to have known some of the advanced Russian artists. He had drawn since childhood, but received no formal art instruction until he arrived in America and enrolled in John Sloan's drawing class at the Art Students League in 1922. He soon distinguished himself as an outstanding draughtsman, an artist of talent and high promise. An outgoing and compelling figure, he met a wide assortment of artists and collectors, including the Cone sisters and Duncan Phillips, who began to acquire his work, with Phillips becoming something of a patron. After 1928, Graham went annually to Paris, where he showed his work and absorbed the latest developments in modern art, bringing news back to his American friends. He became a collector and art advisor, with special knowledge of African art, and in 1937 published *Systems and Dialectics of Art*, in which he set out certain principles for modern art: that it should be abstract in nature, it should find its source in the unconscious, and it should 'contain news, surprises and enigma', ideas that took root in a younger generation.[5] Graham had met Davis, Smith, Gorky and de Kooning, and the group soon formed a true avant-garde in New York. The circle also included Jan Matulka, Dorothy Dehner, Adolph Gottlieb and later Jackson Pollock. In 1942, the multitalented Graham would organize the exhibition 'French and American Painters' at McMillen Gallery, New York, and include many of these artists; it was the first time that Pollock, one of the group that Graham called the 'young outstanding American painters', exhibited publicly.[6] It is no wonder, then, that de Kooning insisted it was Graham who had discovered Pollock. Indeed, Graham should be seen as a mentor and teacher in the tradition of Eakins, Henri, Stieglitz and Sloan.[7]

Most important, though, was the art that Graham produced, some of the finest done in America at this time. He was especially gifted and original in the mode of Cubist still lifes from c.1928–32, and along with Davis and Maurer gave strong impetus to the second wave of American Cubist painting. His *Still Life with Pipe* (1929)[116], done in whites of varying shades, mixes, textures and thickness of paints, is sublime, a masterpiece of Cubism. Also of special interest in Graham's art is a small, fully abstract painting in the Musée Zervos in France, *Composition* (1929)[117], consisting of a few shapes

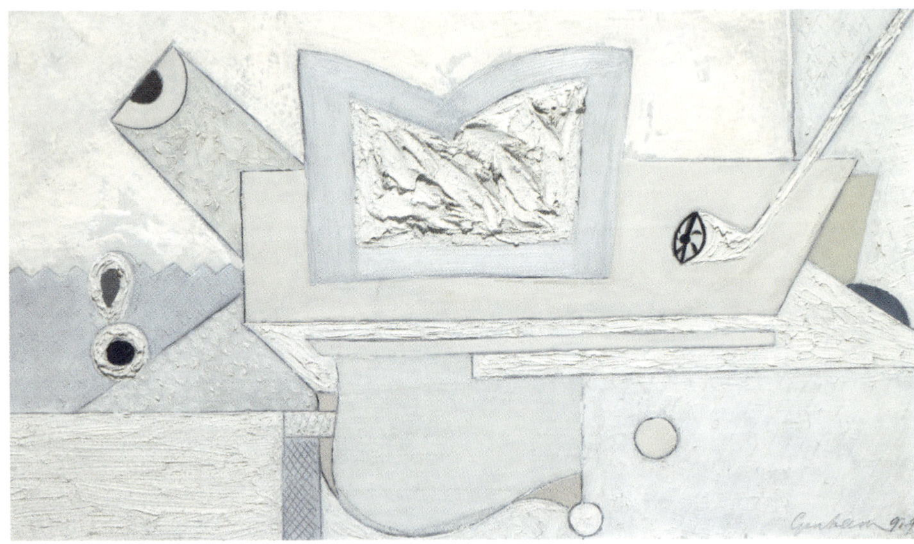

116

frontally arranged, representing what he called 'minimalism'. The varied surfaces of these paintings clearly relate to the Paris works of Stuart Davis, for they were both in Paris at that time. Graham was insisting on maximum clarity of image and surface, a call that Davis answered in his series of open, linear black-and-white works of 1932. These interactions were also paramount in the early Cubist paintings of Arshile Gorky, which reached a peak in his *Organization* (1933–6)[118], based on Picasso's studio series of 1927–8, but totally original in its final state. Gorky was often told that his work looked like Picasso's – his reply was 'Thank you', for he saw this as a great compliment, much in the mode of the Old Masters, to whom young artists were apprenticed.[8]

The understanding of modern and avant-garde to mean abstract, abstracting and non-objective art must be rethought when we consider Graham, de Kooning and Gorky. Some of their best work was based on the figure, grand compositions that were meant to – and often did – rival the art of the past. By 1942 Graham had turned from Cubism and concentrated on large compositions of bulky figures, usually women, a move that has been interpreted as a renunciation of modernism. We can now say that it was in fact a turn to another kind of modernism. In the twentieth century, modern art never abandoned the figure per se; Graham turned to these modes in the 1940s, away from abstraction, to recall the grand figures of Ingres and the classical nudes of Picasso done in 1917–24, or a monumental mural. So, too, de Kooning never really left the figure, and Gorky often disguised figures in his last years, from 1943 until his death in 1948. Nor should we be shocked when Pollock proclaimed: 'I'm very representational some of the time, and a little all of the time,'[9] especially when we consider how Thomas Hart Benton had taught him to study and recast Old Master drawings in the late 1930s.

In this propensity to use both abstract and figuration in their art, we have yet another example of American willingness to pick and choose certain elements, without concern for theory or correctness. It is best embodied in de Kooning's urge to paint like Soutine and Ingres – both at the same time – in order to make something new.[10] De Kooning, Graham and Gorky were émigrés who had arrived in the 1920s, and they all felt a new freedom here, unbound from Europe and not tied to the dictates of the prevailing American aesthetic provincialism. Freed from the burdens of history, they could make use of what they found, ripe with promise, including

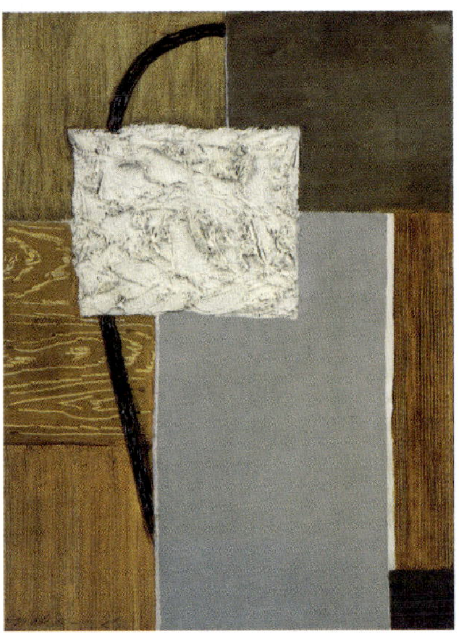

117

116 John Graham, *Still Life with Pipe*, 1929. Oil on canvas, 33.7 × 58.4 cm (13¼ × 23 in). The Museum of Fine Arts, Houston

117 John Graham, *Composition*, 1929. Oil on canvas, 46 × 33 cm (18⅛ × 13 in). Musée Zervos, Vézelay, France

118 Arshile Gorky, *Organization*, 1933–6. Oil on canvas, 127 × 152 cm (50 × 59¹³⁄₁₆ in). National Gallery of Art, Washington, DC

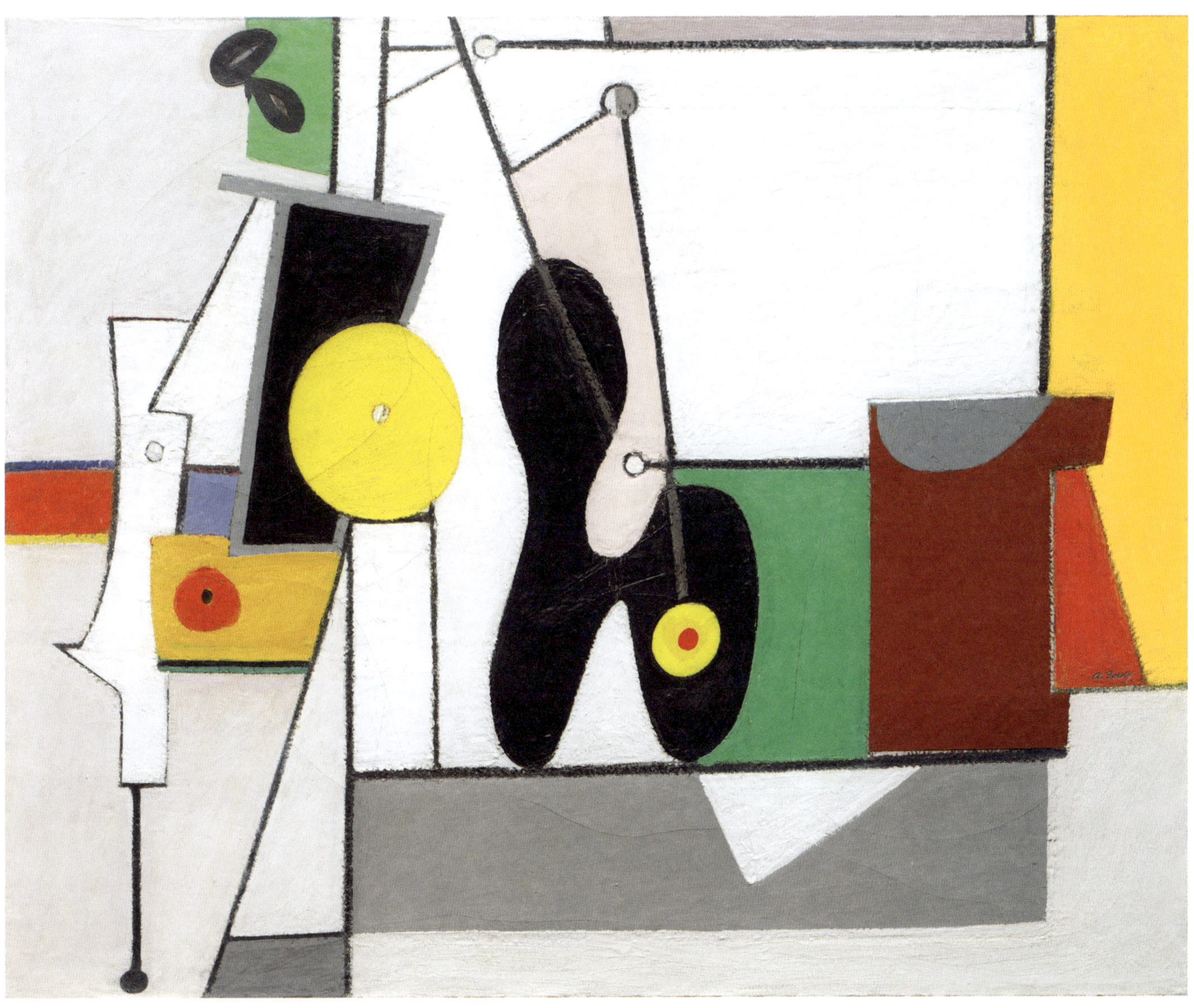

118

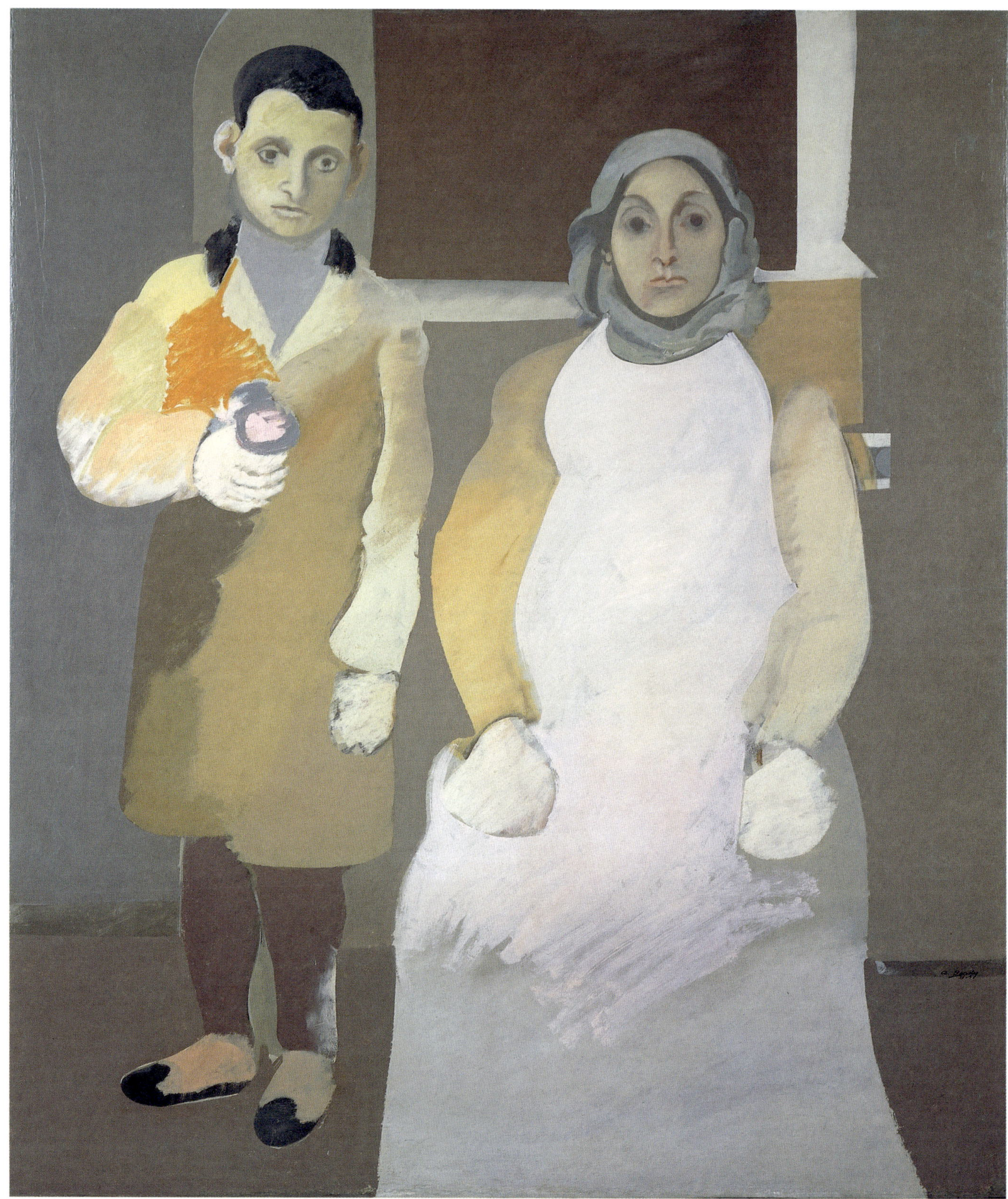

119

Modern Art in America

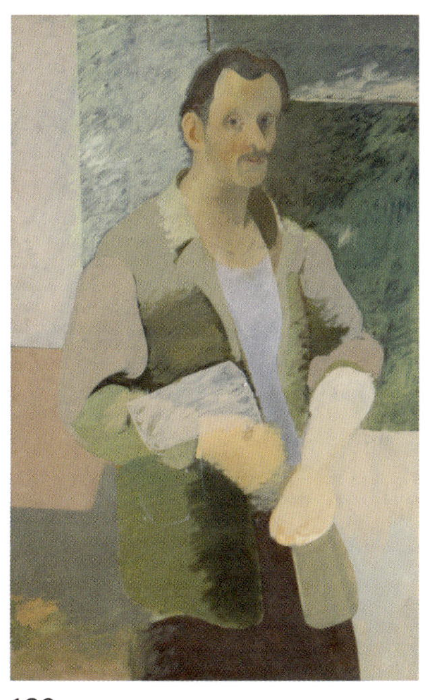

120

the art of the past. Picasso, so important to Americans in the 1930s, had given permission when he said in 1923: 'If the subjects I have wanted to express have suggested different ways of expression I have never hesitated to adopt them.'[11]

As we have seen, after 1916 and the devastation of World War I, the very conception of modernism changed and expanded significantly. A new wave of Classicism came to the forefront, viewed as the way to restore the world to a stable harmony. This took many forms, and it was open and flexible. It could refer to ancient Greece and Rome, as with Picasso's massive figures, started when he visited Rome in 1917 and done until 1924 as one part of his work simultaneously with major monuments of later Cubism, the most notable being *Three Women at the Spring* (1921). Such works set an example for the Americans, but, as Graham said, he and the group around him were seeking an art that must be 'something original, purely American'.[12] These three émigrés – de Kooning, Graham and Gorky – coming to America to make something of themselves, found a new artistic and personal freedom and forged new identities as artists and as men, thus adding a rich and important dimension to society.

The artistic freedom to oscillate between abstraction and figuration is no better exemplified than in the work of Arshile Gorky (1904–1948). His story is well known: he had lost his mother to starvation in Armenia during the Turkish genocide when he was twelve years old, and after emigrating to the United States, taking a new name and turning himself into a modern artist, he essentially spent his life trying to recapture his past, his family, his homeland. His famous *Portrait of the Artist and His Mother* (c.1926–36)[119] was his first major attempt to memorialize, to make present, his family history. Its importance to him – and his difficulty in realizing it – is clear from the long period he spent working on it, off and on for ten years, from about 1926 to 1936. It began with a photograph, then a close-up preparatory drawing of his mother's head, a haunting evocation of a painful recollection. In its sheer skill and emotional depth it is surely one of the best paintings of the modern age. As Gorky intended, it also stands with the Old Masters, recalling Ingres for its sureness and conviction of touch. While the heads are drawn with exactitude, the bodies are loosely, even roughly and summarily brushed in, and thus the painting has been deemed unfinished. But it is finished enough to engage us in the profound pathos of the figures, and perhaps the unfinished aspect is part of that pathos, a search unfinished. The bodies seem like ghost images that Gorky was trying to locate and pin down, to make material, and thus alive. They are elusive, and there is a probing, searching quality evident in the paint and surface, a record of his ongoing and frustrated search to find, and to bring back, his early life. The very touches of paint seem to embed a seismograph of feeling, just as they would in his later abstract painting. The means are as radical, as modern and as moving as any abstract painting.

The qualities of this and other portraits by Gorky in this period show an ever-increasing confidence in his abilities, and a new self-assurance as an artist and as a man finding his way in a foreign, alien country.[13] Gorky, de Kooning and Graham haunted the museums of New York, gaining a knowledge of Old Master art that few, if any, American artists could rival. Gorky's *Self-Portrait* (c.1937)[120] has the grandeur of a seventeenth-century work, and begs for a comparison with Rembrandt's late self-portraits. It is clear that in the later 1930s a renewed interest in the grand figure tradition had come to the fore. Think of Marsden Hartley's heroic figures of New England men, rendered in outsized scale, that bring to mind the Greek *kouros*, and the work of Piero della Francesca and Michelangelo.

Walt Kuhn (1877–1949), a fine but under-appreciated artist, also made
a series of what we can call Americanized Renaissance figures. Kuhn's art
only got better as he aged, and his painting *Roberto* (1946)[121] is strong
and compelling. In an exhibition at the New-York Historical Society entitled
'Swing Time: Reginald Marsh and Thirties New York', it dominated by
means of its bold assertion of the physical presence of its subject, a circus
acrobat, almost literally in our space. The facture is strong, rough and dense,
but at the same time controlled and nuanced. In any show of post-war art,
it would stand out. It is a synthesis of Michelangelo, Watteau and Cézanne,
of an ancient and modern theme, the circus performer, there to entertain
others, constantly relocating, never settling, an old American trait and
pattern: that of finding isolation and independence by never sitting still.
Indeed, the acrobat seems to be not so much sitting, as about to spring
up and off from his perch, to launch himself up and in motion, for we feel
how tightly he grips the bench, how taut his muscles are, poised for
momentary release from his pose, staying only long enough to engage us
briefly. Independent and physically powerful from years of labour at his
craft, he is also focused and centred; but he will not remain there for long.
This is the best of old-line American figure painting, conservative perhaps,
but still a work of immense potential, with sublime physical and psychological strength. In this sense, *Roberto* may be seen as a symbol of America
itself, poised after the end of war to undertake great feats. It was as if the
best artists, young and old, were issuing a challenge to the mass of weak
and insipid figure painting of the period, to make it American, yes, but
primarily to make it strong and of the highest order – a figure painting that
could rank with the work of Copley, Eakins and Homer.

Willem de Kooning (1904–1997) once said that Gorky was a 'Geiger
counter of art',[14] who always pointed out the best artist, the best work, the
best passage in any painting in any room they entered. De Kooning himself
had developed his latent taste and affinity for Old Master painting since
he had come from Holland, where oil painting had been invented. It is no
wonder, then, that de Kooning never really left the figure except for a few
years in the late 1950s, although he was the most widely emulated artist
in the so-called Abstract Expressionist group. His figure paintings are the
most ambiguous and haunting of any in the Graham circle. The male
figures of the late 1930s[122] are unusual, even unsettling. They have a kind
of indeterminacy, an elusiveness that keeps the painting from cohering
into a clear, single focus for the viewer; they seem to keep slipping away
from us. They are ghost-like at points, yet real both physically and
emotionally. Their reddish colour reminds us of the murals from Boscoreale
at the Metropolitan Museum, by which de Kooning and Gorky were
intrigued (as was Rothko). They exude a mournful, melancholy feel, a
certain sadness, hidden, as it were, in a shifting, indefinable space, again
both physical and psychological. They are perplexing and fascinating,
a kind of challenge to the generic realist painting of the 1930s.

These figures turned into his *Women* of the early and mid-1940s,
with parts drawn like Ingres, others akin to Soutine, an idiosyncratic fusion
unique to de Kooning. He was in essence merging the old and the new,
a kind of new American experimentation, a type of empiricism raised to
the level of a working methodology. No one understood better than de
Kooning that 'there is a train track back into the history of art that goes
back to Mesopotamia…Duchamp is on it, Cézanne is on it. Picasso and
the Cubists are on it, Giacometti, Mondrian, and so many, many more –
whole civilizations.'[15] He was, by his own admission, conservative, 'more
in tradition', while trying to 'change the past'.[16] It is no wonder that in 1951

121 Walt Kuhn, *Roberto*, 1946.
Oil on canvas, 101.6 × 76.2 cm
(40 × 30 in). Myron Kunin
Collection of American Art,
Minneapolis

Modern Art in America

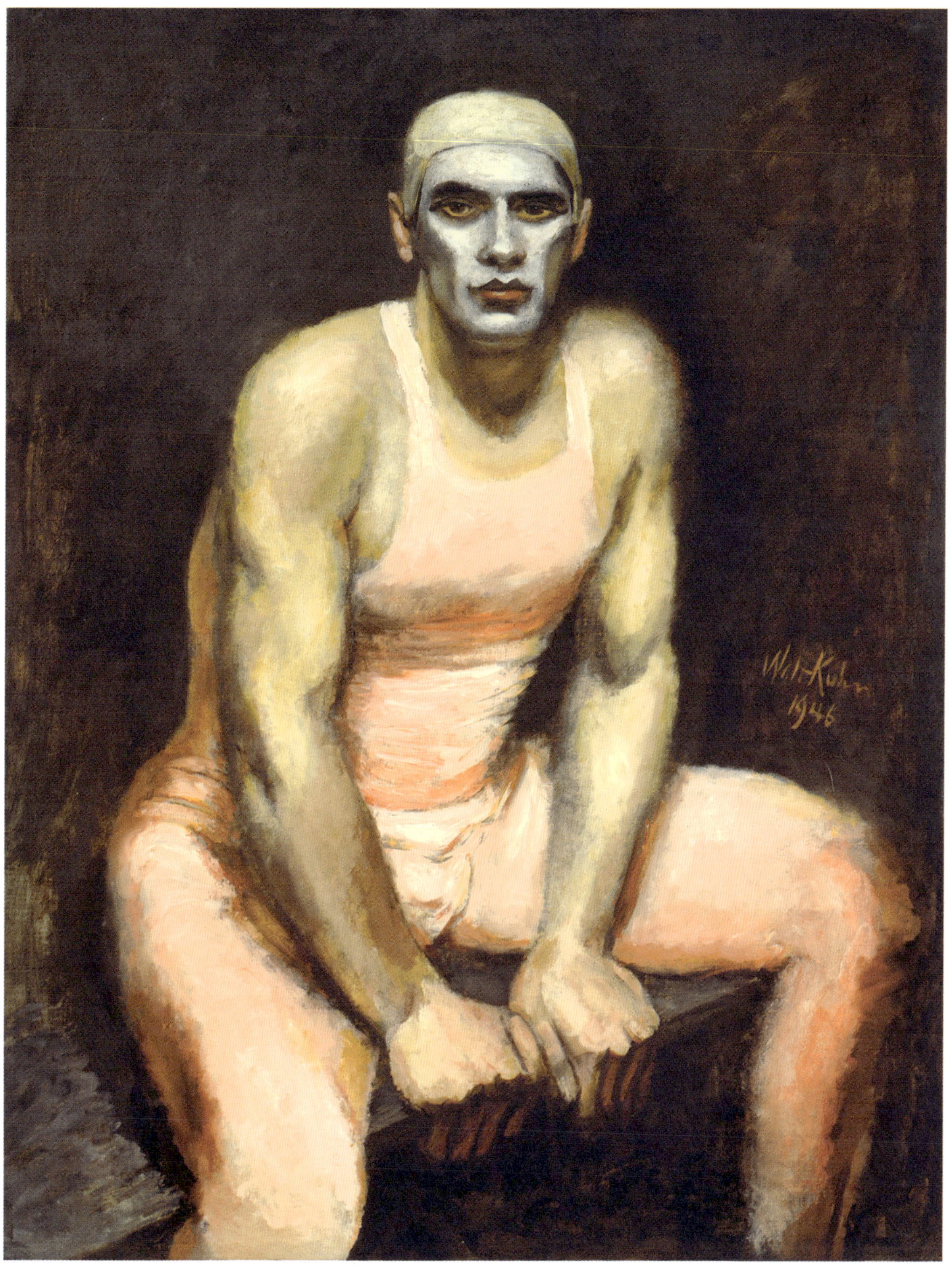

121

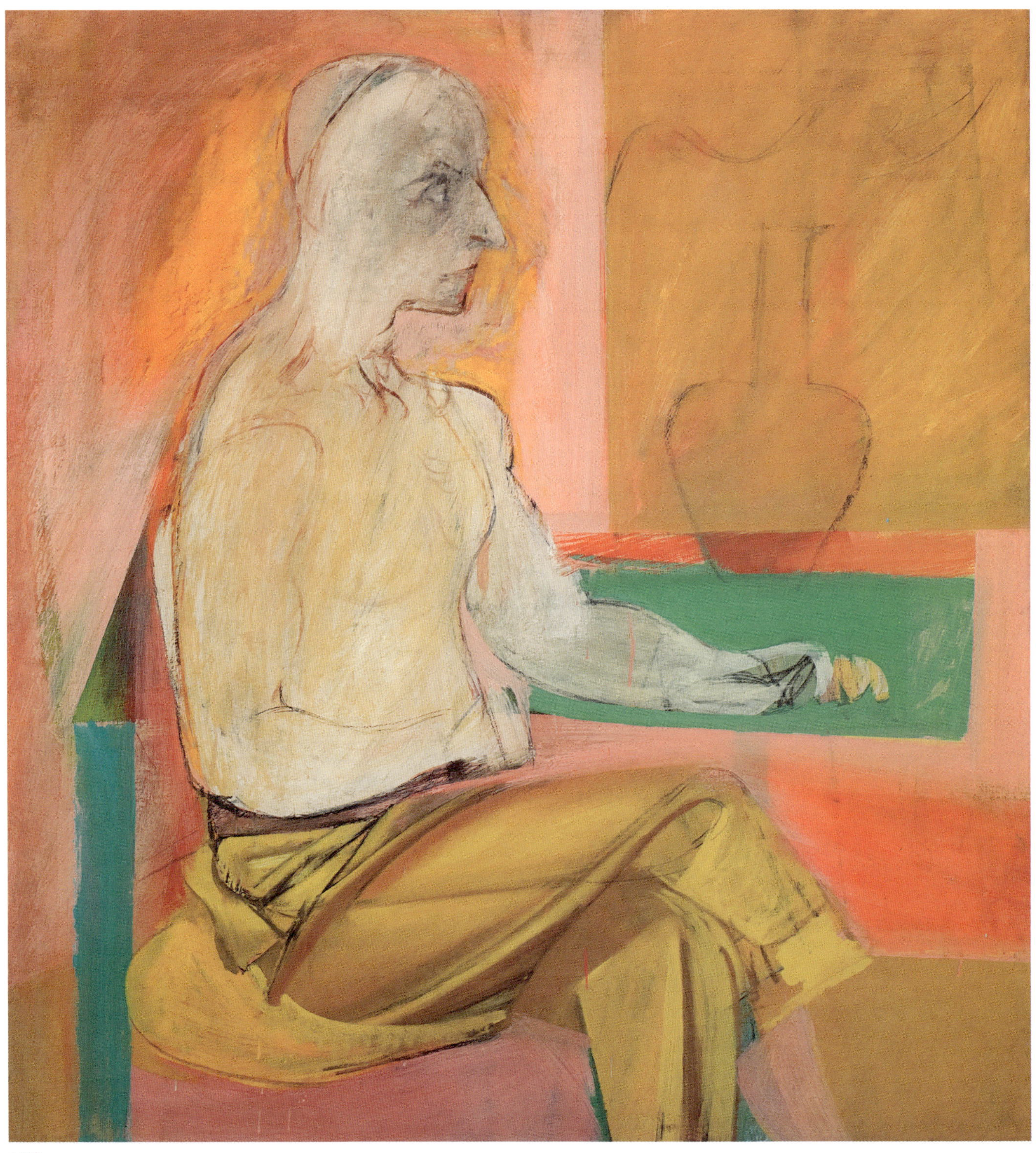

122

he would write his famous contribution to MoMA's symposium *What Abstract Art Means to Me* with the title 'The Renaissance and Order'.[17]

De Kooning's course was one of constant change and searching, leaving 'wilful pentimenti' as a kind of ghost map.[18] Both his and Gorky's figures embody Graham's dictum that a painting's brushstrokes are authentic records of an artist's reactions, his moods and his feelings. The sense of search, of discovery, of revealing something quickly then having it virtually disappear, recalls de Kooning's comment that 'content is a glimpse of something, an encounter like a flash'.[19] These figures speak of something past, dimly remembered, of the attempt to recall them in the present. At the same time, they have a dark feel to them, the mood of the Depression years made palpable, like looking through a dirty window in a tenement or studio downtown. They recall John Sloan's painting *Sunday, Women Drying their Hair* (1912) (page 63), with their buxom flamboyance, as well as the Rubenesque figures of Kenneth Hayes Miller in the 1930s and especially the wanton openness of the shop girls in Reginald Marsh's famous New York scenes of the period. As these grim years receded, in the 1940s, de Kooning's women figures took on a brighter, more rambunctious mood, reminding us of the strip joints and saloons made famous by the Ashcan artists, while pointing to the brazen females of the 1950s, and after, to the flamboyant women of Pop art.

Honest Vulgarity: Downtown New York and its Crowds

For years art history held that after 1945, American artists reacted against and discarded the Social Realism of the 1930s. This is not true. De Kooning surely would have related to Reginald Marsh (1898–1954) and his love of the 'honest vulgarity' of the burlesque shows he frequented. There is something appealing about this Ivy League preppie, a son of money, a graduate of Andover and Yale, who was drawn like a magnet to the underclasses of New York, to the Bowery, saloons, flophouses and the teeming mass of bodies on 14th Street.

Marsh was not alone in these pursuits. Photographers also gravitated to the visual circus of downtown New York, feasting endlessly on the life of the streets. Weegee, Berenice Abbott, Walker Evans, Lisette Model, Ben Shahn and Marsh himself, an accomplished photographer, took countless photos of the down-and-outs, ordinary men and women working, career-office employees, subway riders. For they, and the painters, understood that in the 'ordinary, there is the extraordinary', as Fairfield Porter later put it;[20] that the beauty of America was in the pace, the speed and the energy of the people themselves; that those who came there had been forced to struggle, whether on a farm or in a hardscrabble urban existence.

Marsh's attraction to flesh, the shop girls, the strippers, the hookers, was deep-seated and compulsive. His art can be said to presage the sexual awakening of America in the 1960s. Many of his figures came from his photographs and were then rendered with the mass and contrapposto of Michelangelo and Rubens, Géricault and Delacroix, that Marsh had avidly studied in Europe in 1925–6 and, we may be sure, at the Metropolitan Museum. It is there – the stamp of Old Master authenticity – in the voluptuous line-up in *Ten Cents a Dance* (1933)[123], low-life America front and centre. Once again, American artists take what they need for whatever reasons they need it and use it in brash new contexts. Some have thought that Marsh's figures are 'stereotypes', or that he created a 'fictional world'.[21] But if we look at the paintings and his photographs, we see that it was anything but. It was real, and it was authentic, and we can still experience

122 Willem de Kooning, *Seated Man*, c.1939. Oil and charcoal on canvas, 97.1 × 86.9 cm (38¼ × 34¼ in). Hirshhorn Museum and Sculpture Garden, Smithsonian Institution, Washington, DC

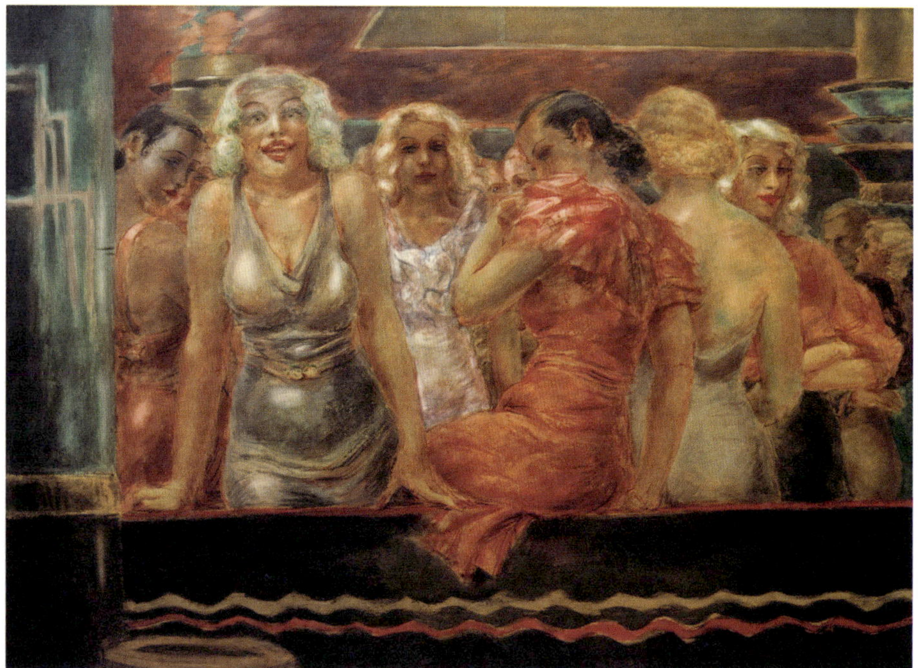

123

it, if in a somewhat higher mode as we traverse the packed streets of New York. The speed, energy and pace of American life can be seen through the paintings of Franz Kline and de Kooning, as in the latter's vivid *Gansevoort Street* (c.1949) (page 212) and the compacted and shredded figures of his monumental *Excavation* (1950). This is also visible through the spread of endless signboards that mark cityscapes, especially in New York, that were an old American fascination, starting in the nineteenth century and continuing in Sloan and Davis, reaching full bloom in the 1960s Pop world of Andy Warhol and Robert Indiana.

Nor was Marsh's work mere slumming; he was not a Baudelairean *flâneur*, nor was his fixation on strippers misogynistic and emotionally detached, as has been claimed.[22] He saw and vividly depicted the despair of the unemployed, the down and out, the penniless, the drunks and the starving that haunted urban landscapes all over the country. In his etching of 1932, *Bread Line*, Marsh depicted an endless queue of the unemployed and the hungry. There seems to be neither a beginning nor an end to the line, or to the composition. It is like a classic pediment frieze, depicting not the gods but the forgotten of New York's slums, and yet each face is different and rendered as an individual. So, too, the layered density of bodies in Marsh's painting *BMT 14th Street* (1932), or *In Fourteenth Street* (1934), finds no equal until Pollock's *Mural* (1943), or the de Koonings of 1949–50. In these paintings, Marsh makes sharp class distinctions, as in the well-dressed women at right in the former, making an abrupt exit from the scene, an emblem of his own class background. In the latter, the young woman in the middle wearing bright, stylish clothes is clearly apart from the rush of the crowd. Racial issues abound in *Twenty Cent Movie* (1936)[125], in which the two entrances house two races, and two classes. On the left, white, well-dressed and well-attended women are set apart from the figures at the right, black hustlers, pimps and hipsters.

Raphael Soyer (1899–1987) was another artist closely associated with 14th Street and its crowds. There is something modest about his art; it depicts not the flamboyant nudes of Marsh, but something more personal, even intimate. Take his *Window Shoppers* (1938), for example[124]. It seems

123 Reginald Marsh,
Ten Cents a Dance, 1933.
Tempera on composition
board, 91.3 × 121.8 cm
(36 × 48 in). Whitney Museum
of American Art, New York

124 Raphael Soyer, *Window
Shoppers*, 1938. Oil on canvas,
91.4 × 60.9 cm (36 × 24 in).
New Jersey State
Museum, Trenton

125 Reginald Marsh, *Twenty Cent
Movie*, 1936. Carbon pencil,
ink and oil on composition
board, 76.2 × 101.6 cm
(30 × 40 in). Whitney Museum
of American Art, New York

                          Modern Art in America

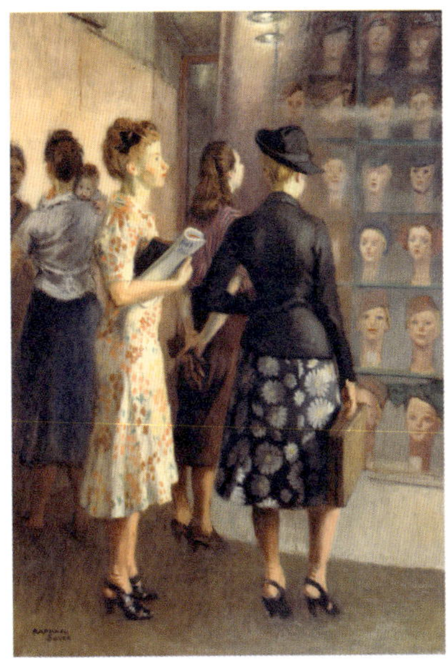

124

but another view of women shopping, nothing exceptional. But when we look more closely we see three women, all of different demeanour and dress, staring into a window full of hats on mannequin heads. What do they see? Themselves, as they are, or as they wish to be? This, again, cannot help but recall Picasso's *Girl Before a Mirror* (1932), made famous when shown in MoMA's epic exhibition 'Fantastic Art, Dada, Surrealism', held just the year before. Further, the women all represent different stages of life and of circumstance. The one nearest to us seems unsure, not knowing where to look, even as she holds a newspaper, no doubt advertising job possibilities. In the centre is a figure more certain of herself, but not fully settled; and at right a woman of accomplishment, dressed for business, doing well, carrying at her side that badge of success, a briefcase. Finally, at left is a woman with a baby, suggesting life in a constant state of change and rebirth. But what of the space they are in, especially to the left of the shop? It seems a kind of undefined, dream-like space that may suggest Surrealist overtones of reverie. And is it an early, proto-feminist tract, since these are all women managing and looking after their own welfare, unaided, even in a world on the verge of collapse. The painting cannot help but move and touch us; it is born of the 1930s, but nevertheless timeless.

EUROPEAN SETTLERS: HANS HOFMANN AND JOSEF ALBERS

If John Graham was the first major European artist to settle in America, he was soon followed by two others who also deeply affected the course of modern art in America. Hans Hofmann (1880–1966) and Josef Albers (1888–1976) were not only accomplished artists, but were also famous teachers who shaped the course of art instruction in America. Their common denominator was colour – to be specific, Cézanne, to whom Hofmann always referred, insisting in his own work that when colour is at its richest, form is at its fullest. They contributed two very different bodies of colour art that

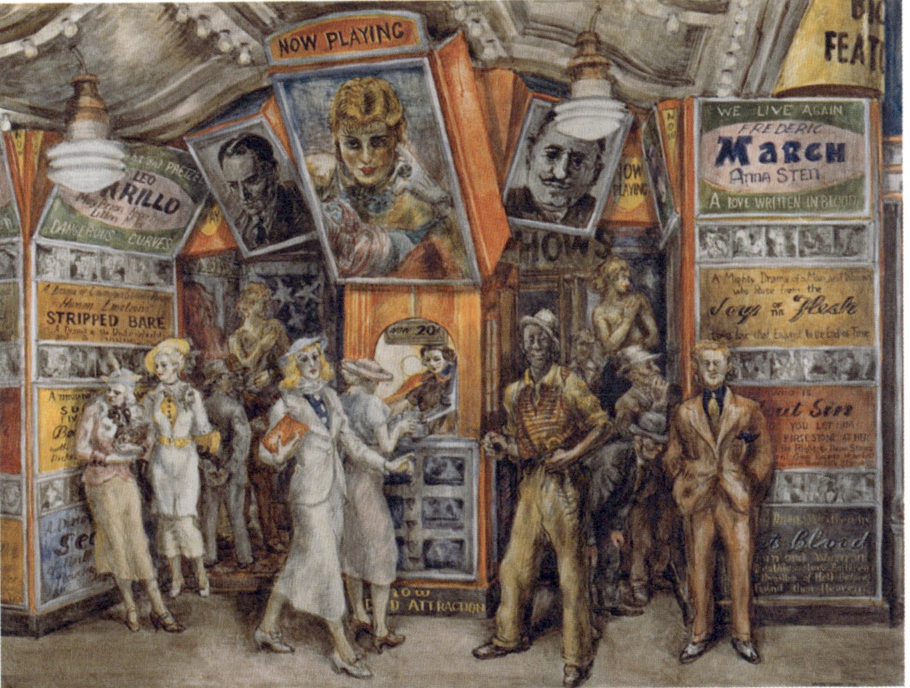

125

immeasurably enriched American abstract painting. Hofmann arrived first, in 1930, at the invitation of Worth Ryder, to teach at the University of California, Berkeley. Ryder had known of Hofmann's considerable reputation as a teacher at his school in Munich, which he had opened in 1915, and getting him to America resulted in an instant upgrade of the teaching of modernism there. Hofmann taught that summer and returned in 1932; he continued to teach until 1957, transferring the vast body of knowledge of modernism he had accumulated over more than thirty years in Europe.

Hofmann was born in 1880, thus being a year older than Picasso. He was in Paris by 1903, and later claimed to have taught Robert Delaunay the essentials of colour and colour painting. In Paris, Hofmann witnessed the monumental Cézanne shows of 1905–7 and Cézanne's lessons of structural colour, especially his conception of planes of pigment as forms in themselves, remained at the heart of Hofmann's approach to colour throughout his life. In Paris, when illness forced him to cease painting, Hofmann also met Arthur B. Carles. The latter was an ongoing example and inspiration to Hofmann, who always appreciated the pioneers of modernism in America, who understood the continuity and connection between the younger and older American modernists. Others did, too, as we shall see, thus showing us that the barrier between pre- and post-1945 art has been an artificial construct of historians.

Almost none of the work done by Hofmann before the mid- and late 1930s has survived, thus putting him in a strange historical position as a member of an older generation who began to emerge only with the artists of a younger age. Yet his impact was national: his mark was long felt in the Bay area, despite his short time there, and he began teaching in New York in the autumn of 1932 and in Provincetown, touching the direction of many artists who would soon make their contributions to American art. Clement Greenberg famously remarked that by the late 1930s, in Hofmann's class one could learn more about Matisse's colour than one could from Matisse himself.[23] Hofmann also taught hundreds of students the elements of Cubism. We now know of his early career in some detail, and we can understand how his enormous range of colour came to be. But it was not until the later 1930s that his own work developed in any depth, so it is no wonder that he was – and still is – often regarded as more of a teacher than an artist, a judgement that is far off the mark, for his work is one of the high points of American art in the years after 1935.

Hofmann began to teach in 1915, and made little art except drawings until 1934. Why? The war intervened, for one thing, and for another Hofmann said he had to make a living. But all artists have to make a living, and they manage as best they can while doing their chosen work. Possibly there are other reasons for his delay. Hofmann, like Dove at the same time, had difficulty getting to his talent, perhaps reluctant to face it directly. He seemed to know he needed time to grow into it, that he wasn't ready to take a full plunge into serious painting; it had to be all or nothing for him – that was his nature. His teaching was his pulpit, as Bartlett Hayes said,[24] and he was preaching to convince himself as much as his students. He had to be sure, confident in his beliefs about art, fully ready to take on the task of making ambitious art that could stand with the best of his time. Frederick Wight put it well: 'His painting therefore was not only what he did, but what he was forced to believe';[25] by teaching, he could account for and justify his faith in his slow absorption of the past, growing out of a tradition that gradually became his own.[26] In the course of time, Wight added, Hofmann moved from 'anguished uncertainty to boundless assurance'.[27] Part of this may be the emigrant's breaking loose

Modern Art in America

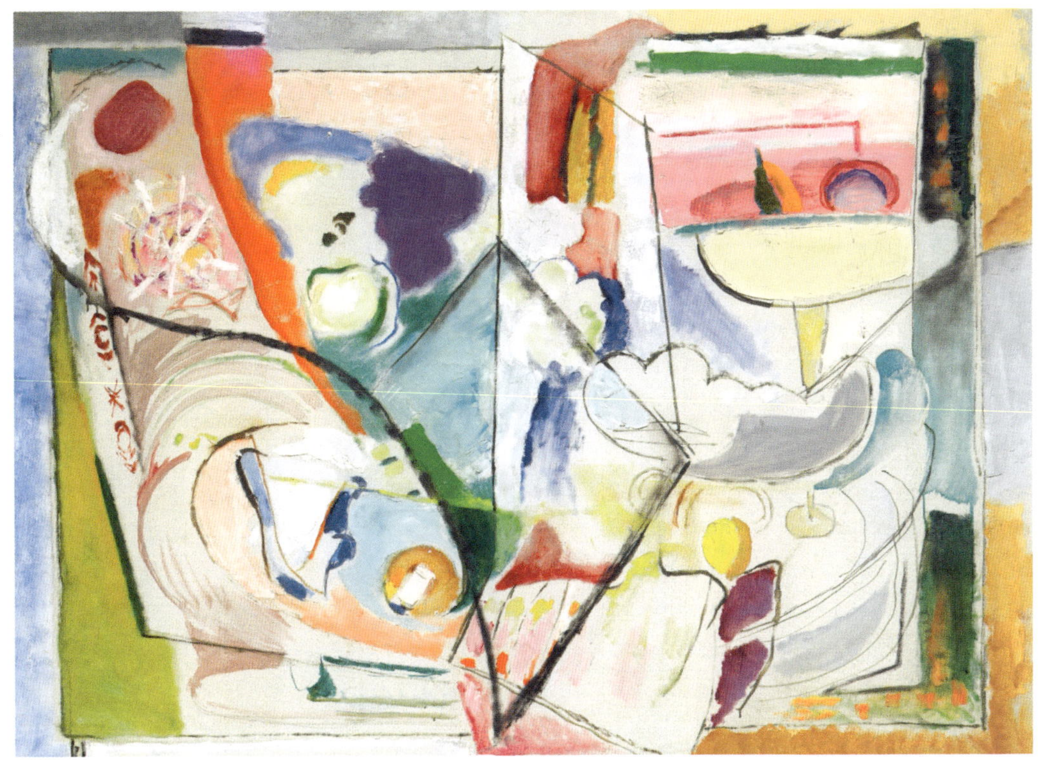

126

from the hierarchies of European art and life, and acclimatizing to the unrestricted freedom of America. Think of Emerson's dictum: 'build therefore your own world.' Hofmann moved, we might say, from doubt to total certainty, to the most fecund and exuberant pictorial imagination of any artist in the twentieth century. By 1934 he had settled in the United States, and, he soon established his famous schools in New York and Provincetown. He was so depressed, however, that he was only drawing and not painting. Carles and his daughter Mercedes, herself a painter, inspired Hofmann to find his way back to painting.

Carles's work of the 1930s was powerfully expressionist and intensely coloured, a kind of fusion of Matisse's colour and Picasso's Cubism, something akin to what Hofmann himself worked towards throughout his life. Barbara Wolanin has pointed out that Hofmann particularly admired Carles's painting *Composition* (1935–7) [126], a work that might almost pass for a Hofmann of the 1940s or 1950s.[28] The same is true of Carles's dynamic *Abstraction (Last Painting)* (1936–41) [127] – a work of such pictorial energy that it too surely suggested rich painterly possibilities to Hofmann.

By the 1930s, colour poured on to, down and across Hofmann's paintings of interiors [128] as if a torrential flood of paint had been let forth from the depths of body and soul. Indeed, it had been. He was fifty-five at the time, but the colour and drawing had the exuberance of a young man let loose from an anguished, pent-up confinement. These glorious paintings are a manifestation of what Hofmann himself said about painting: 'The heavens opened up and what comes down is colour, sound, and music',[29] all readily apparent in his studio paintings of the late 1930s.

If Hofmann had emerged from the painterly expressionist tradition of modern France, the geometric compositions of the Bauhaus produced the other German master of colour, Josef Albers, who escaped the Nazis and came to America in 1933. Like Hofmann, Albers had a long and distinguished teaching career, both in the States and in Germany, where pedagogy and painting went hand in hand; in America, historians have thought a person

126 Arthur B. Carles, *Composition*, 1935–7. Oil on canvas, 110.5 × 150.5 cm (43½ × 59¼ in). Private collection

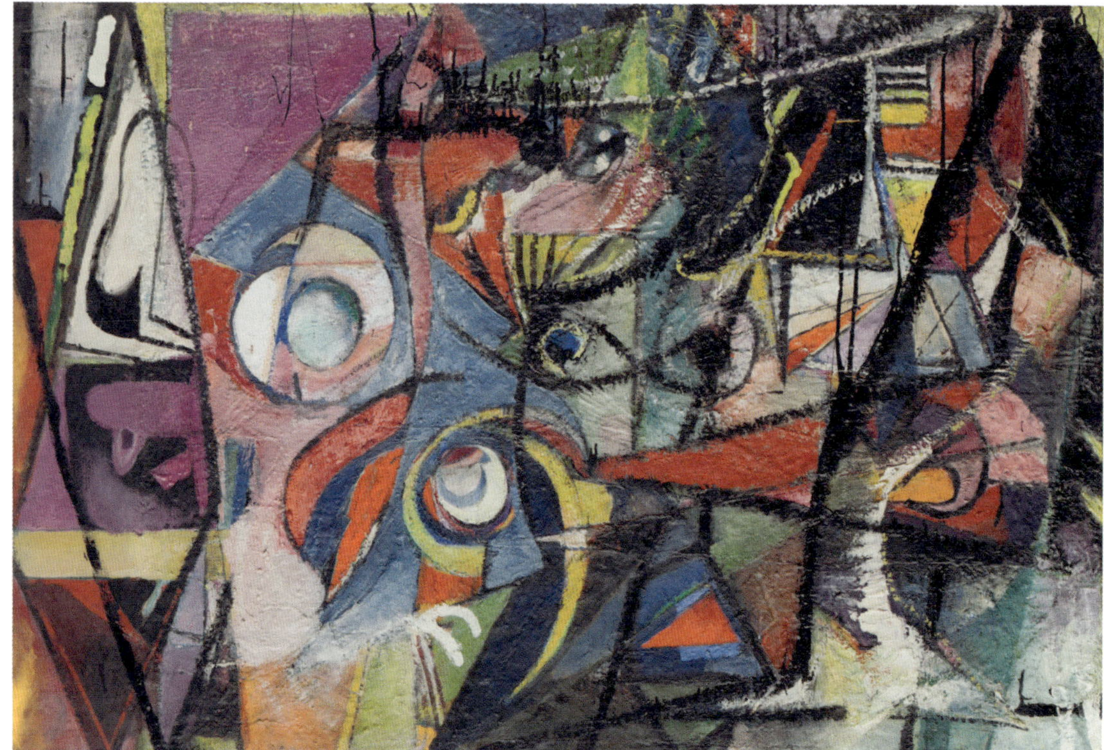

127

could be one or the other, but not both and certainly not at the same time. Thus, both men have suffered neglect as painters. If Hofmann's surfaces were charged with energy, Albers's were a model of clarity and stability. His later paintings were based on a grid that he had learned from his teacher at the Bauhaus, Paul Klee, himself a master of colour, whose influence was later manifest in artists as apparently far removed as Kenneth Noland. Yet we must remember that Albers's famous colour squares can be tracked to – who else? – Cézanne, of course. In 1908, Albers encountered Cézanne's *The Quarry at Bibémus* in the collection of Karl Ernst Osthaus at the Folkwang Museum in Hagen, Germany, a famous collection now housed in Essen. We can visualize how in essence Albers isolated those solid planes of colour and developed them, finally, into his *Homage to the Square* series, begun in about 1950 and continued until his death. During his Bauhaus years and into the late 1930s, he developed a repertoire of colour combinations in a variety of materials, including glass. Unlike Hofmann, perhaps, Albers was a steady producer all along, but like Hofmann, he did not reach his peak until the early and mid-1950s, and thus we will discuss their art in greater detail later in the book.

THE ONGOING WORK OF OLDER ARTISTS: DOVE, MARIN, FRIEDMAN AND AVERY

The arrival of Hofmann and Albers alone should alert us to the faulty premise that American modernism was on the wane during the 1930s. Add to them the ongoing work of Dove, Marin, Hartley and Demuth in the 1930s, and we can see that modernism had not in the least diminished its force and progress.

Arthur Dove's colour reached new heights of pitch and intensity, as did his painting in general in the 1930s, and extended until his death in 1946. Only recently has much attention been paid to his late work, as with other artists, because we tend to think of modern art as a series of

127 Arthur B. Carles,
Abstraction (Last Painting),
1936–41. Oil and paper
on canvas, mounted on wood,
102.5 × 146 cm
(40⅜ × 57½ in). Hirshhorn
Museum and Sculpture
Garden, Smithsonian
Institution, Washington, DC

128 Hans Hofmann,
Interior Composition, 1935.
Oil and casein on panel,
110.2 × 89.9 cm (43⅜ × 35⅜ in).
University of California,
Berkeley Art Museum and
Pacific Film Archive

                    Modern Art in America

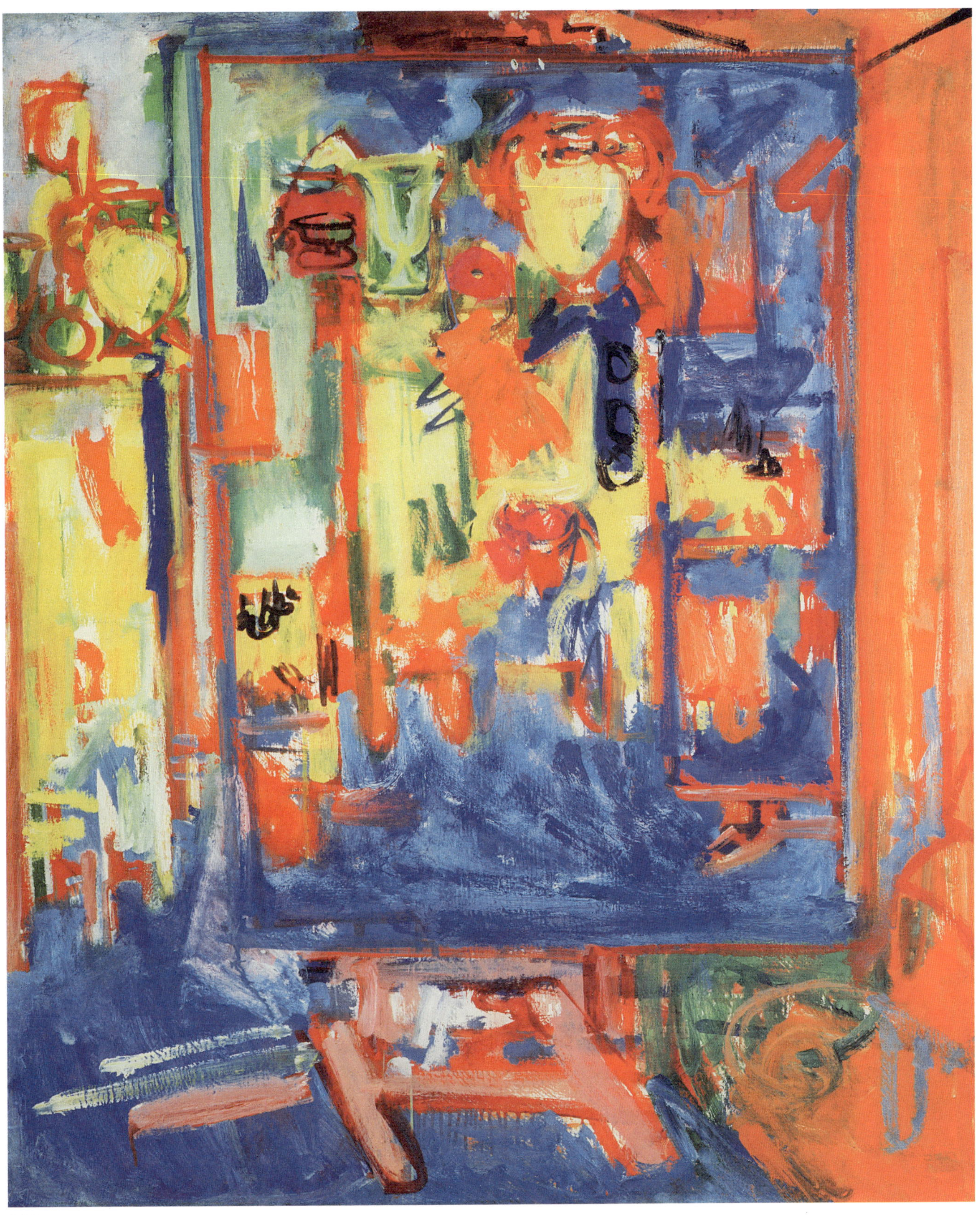

128

innovative movements launched by young, radical artists, while forgetting
the continuing achievements of older artists, late in life.[30] Dove was slow
to realize his talent, and he was sixty before he reached his full powers.
His series of *Sunrise* paintings[129] of 1936–7 ranged from deep, rich,
golden tones to brilliant yellows, so intense that it is as if we are witnessing
the sunrise before our own eyes. His imagery and colour take the natural
world around him to exalted spheres of art, and have made him America's
most cherished modernist.

John Marin was always one of America's most consistent and
accomplished artists. He had made his mark with his watercolours as
early as 1910, working in a fluid, expressionist style of high colour. Over
the years he interjected a rough Cubist frame or latticework to give his
colour an architectural support; the framework was always secondary to
the brush and its intense coloration, so it is hard to call him a true Cubist
at any point. He began working in oil as early as 1913, but watercolour
was his primary medium for years, and today he is still better known as a
watercolourist than as an oil painter. In the late 1920s, however, when he
was almost sixty, he returned to oils. Just why is unclear, but when he did,
he seems to have approached them with a new intensity, with sheer joy in
fact, almost as if he were discovering oil paint for the first time. Returning
to Maine – to the place closest to his heart, the landscape of rocky coasts,
open sea and crystal air – seems to have had a liberating effect on him.
In paintings *Rocks and Sea, Maine* and *Small Point, Maine* (1932)[130], he
reduced the geometric Cubist superstructure that could restrict his brush
because it seemed imposed, not composed.[31] In these oils of 1932, he
appears to take a pure, sensual delight in the pigments, the physicality of
thick oil paint, as if he had found a long-lost friend, or as if he could now
let loose and enjoy a long-suppressed aspect of his work. This is the sign
of a mature, experienced artist who can trust his talent, his instincts, his
latent gifts, now nurtured through long experience. The materiality of the
paint, arranged in adjoining and parallel squares and patches, suggests
Cézanne's late work while at the same time looking forward to the dense
paint in Hofmann's.

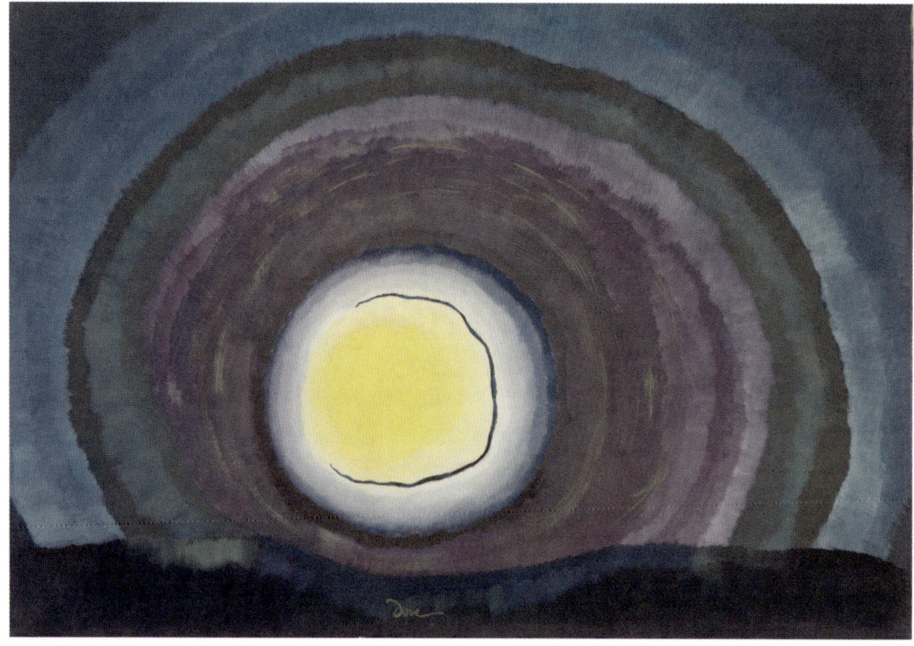

129

                                    Modern Art in America

By 1940, in paintings such as *Cape Split* [131], now a favourite motif, Marin's hand and touch had become free and open, letting the pigments fill the entire canvas, with no reliance on a supporting grid. The painting is a fully organic entity, responding to its own inner dictates, and to the ocean and rocks before him. Pigments are thick, most of all in the crashing waves, so that the frothy foam is as concrete as the rocks, showing the power of the sea in a way no artist had since Winslow Homer. Whether small, circular or broad, thick or thin, the strokes mesh almost seamlessly, indicating an artist now in full control of his medium. Such works are masterpieces of expressionism, a powerful tradition in American art, and look forward to the new energies of Abstract Expressionism, while recalling the turbulent surface movements of Leonardo and Van Gogh.

Other older artists working with colour in new ways by the 1940s had also appeared in the 1920s and 1930s. Among them was Arnold Friedman (1874–1946), who had made a series of abstract colour paintings in the teens that related to Synchromism and Orphism. The story of his life and his art is highly unusual, even in a field that seems made up of nothing but unusual stories. Living quietly and modestly in Flushing, Queens, then largely rural, he supported his family for forty years by working as a postal clerk until he retired in 1933.[32] He had been a well-known and respected artist early on, having studied with Robert Henri at the beginning of the century. He was not an outsider or a Sunday painter, even if he worked at nights and weekends before 1933. In 1908 or 1909 he had travelled to Paris, where he immersed himself in Impressionism, then in the art of Seurat, and he certainly saw and absorbed much in the Armory Show. In the 1920s, he embarked on a series of classicizing figures, as many Americans did, but his colour even here was strong, if restricted, defined by flat, linear shapes.

By the late 1920s, Friedman's art was described as having the 'luminosity of Seurat' – high praise indeed.[33] He was exhibiting regularly in prestigious galleries and was a well-known figure in American art. After retiring from the Post Office in 1933, he was able to devote himself to his painting, and it is no surprise that his work took off, in scope and ambition. By the late 1930s he had reached new heights of achievement, through another kind of painting altogether, described by one critic as a 'new abstract vision of nature'.[34] He turned from his earlier classical nudes and portraits to sites immediately surrounding his house by Flushing Bay, and to fields in the country, where he took his family on weekends. His art was transformed.

Friedman's new, more open means of execution was apparent in paintings such as *The Basin* (1938–9) [132], a site built for the New York World's Fair of 1939 that was close to the artist's home. His old love of deep, rich greens appeared once more, but in this work it is modulated by a more active surface, especially in the moving cars that seem to be activated by almost Futurist lines of motion within them. Of special note is the contrasting surface in the upper portions of the painting, which is rendered with what may have been Friedman's first use of thickly applied impasto, which would become the most salient aspect of his work after 1940. There was an even more rapid acceleration of movement in the cars depicted in the *Park Avenue* paintings (for example, *Park Avenue at 62nd Street*, c. 1939–40) [133], in which the cars seem to whizz by in a blur, rendered almost as ghost images with a pronounced delicacy of colour and open, cursive handling of paint. These urban images may even suggest Camille Pissarro's fast-paced views of Paris done around 1900, another aspect of late Impressionism that had clearly intrigued Friedman. 'Every painter

129 Arthur Dove, *Sunrise III*, 1936–7. Wax emulsion and oil on canvas, partly coated in gesso, 63.5 × 89.1 cm (25 × 35⁵⁄₁₆ in). Yale University Art Gallery, New Haven

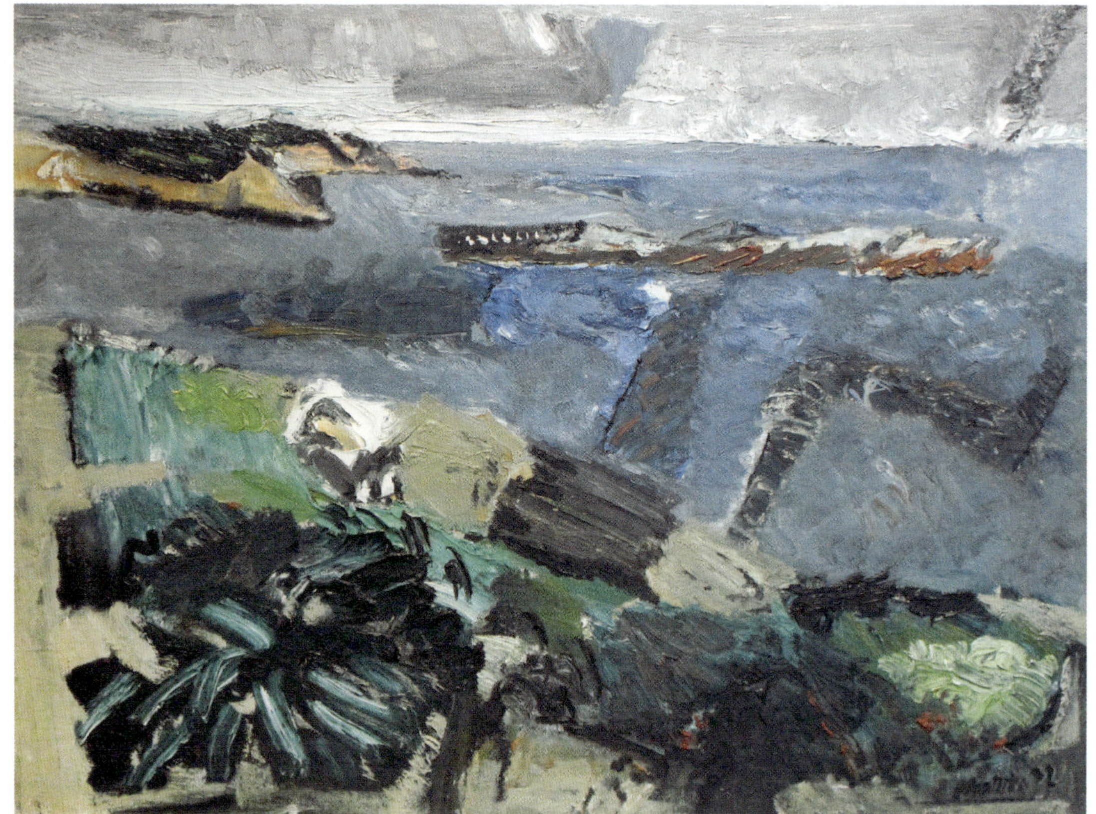

130

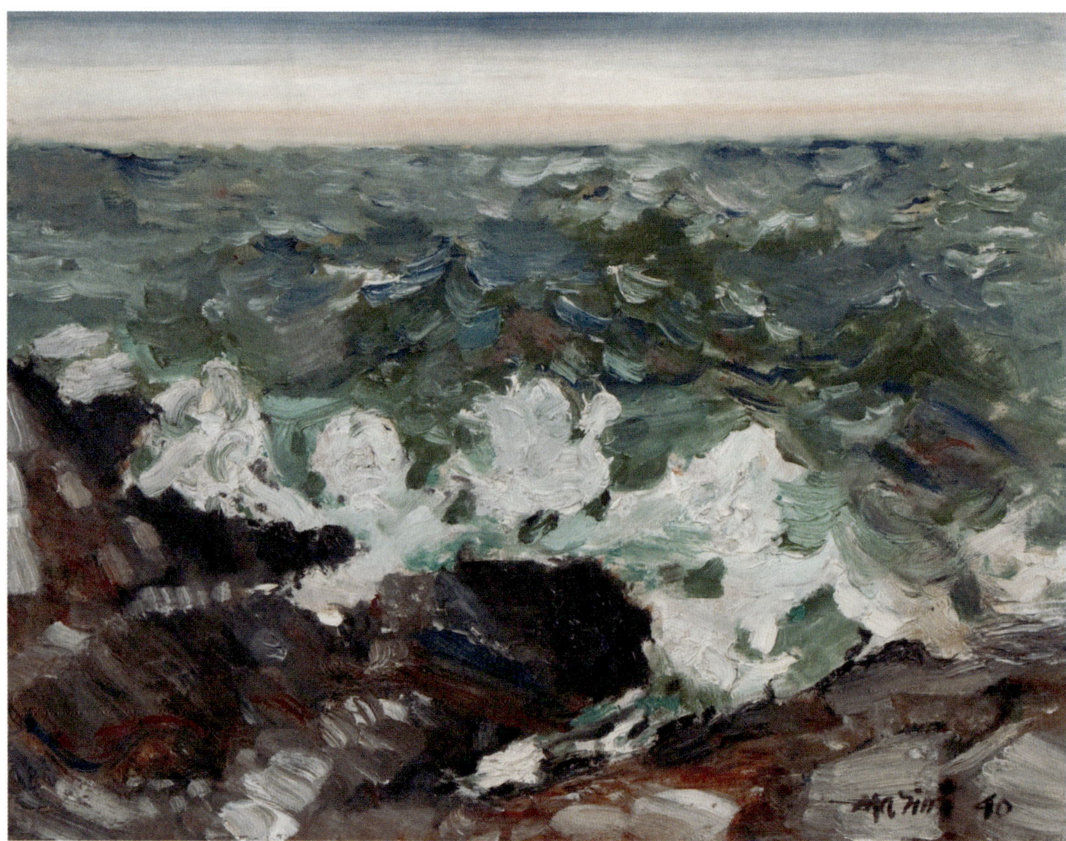

131

130 John Marin, *Small Point, Maine*, 1932. Oil on canvas, 55.8 × 71.5 cm (22 × 28¼ in). Private collection

131 John Marin, *Cape Split*, 1940. Oil on canvas, 55.8 × 71 cm (22 × 28 in). Private collection

132 Arnold Friedman, *The Basin*, 1938–9. Oil on canvas, 60.9 × 50.8 cm (24 × 20 in). Private collection

133 Arnold Friedman, *Park Avenue at 62nd Street*, c.1939–40. Oil on canvas, 46.5 × 63.5 cm (18¼ × 25 in). Collection of Lucy Beck, Vermont

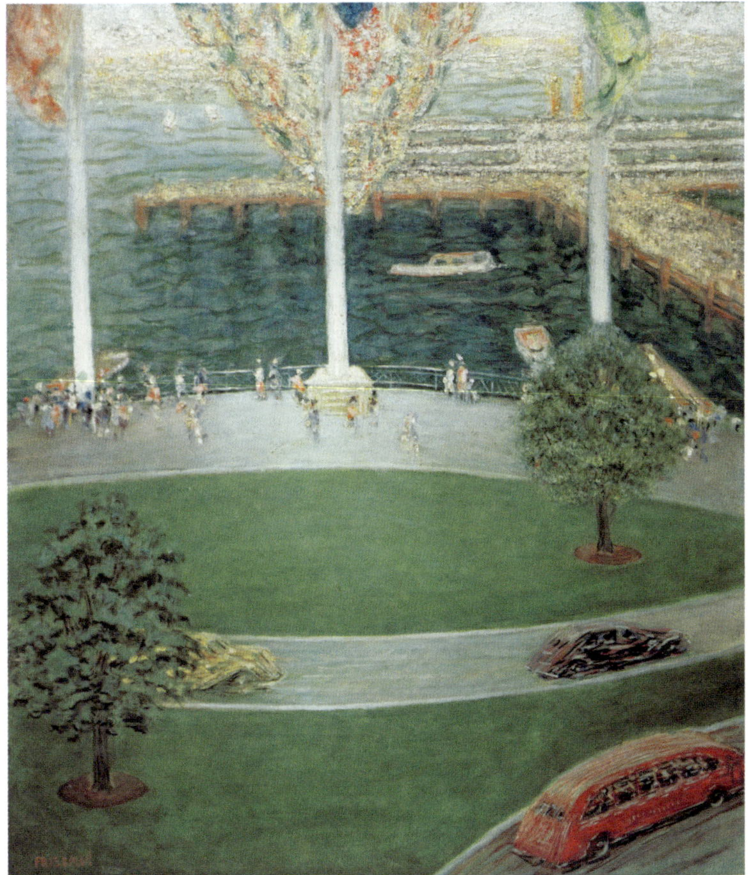

132

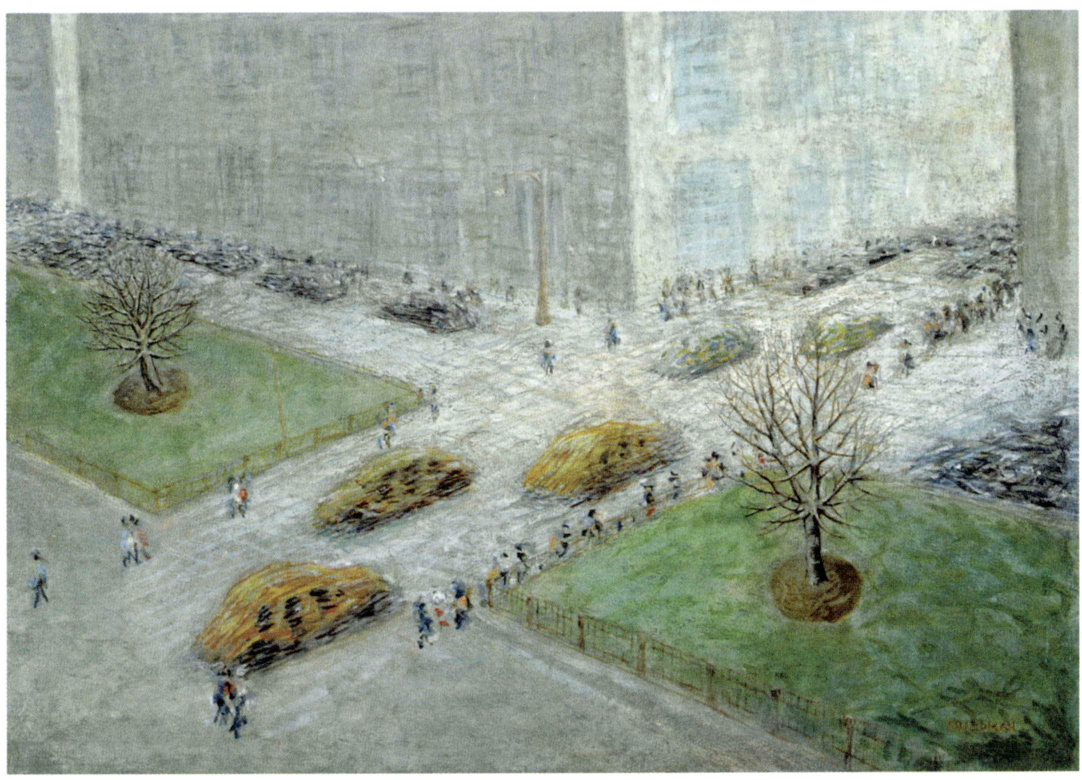

133

must learn his own trade,' he wrote on the back of a painting, or else 'be consigned to the ranks of the "dime a dozen" so dear to the dime a dozen essayist the New York art critic'.[35]

Friedman's work blossomed fully in the 1940s, in paintings in which there is a new glow, a richer internal luminosity that suggests the atmospheric effects of J.M.W. Turner and, later, Impressionism. But the atmospheric effects constitute what we might call an 'Old Master Impressionism', for the hazy skies and land masses, especially in *Bay and Balustrade* (c.1944–6) [134], are suffused with a new, palpable materiality of deep, golden-brown hues that call to mind first the landscape artists of the Barbizon school, and then no less an artist than Rembrandt himself. Clearly, Friedman had spent his time well in the Metropolitan, absorbing the lessons of the greatest masters, to put them in the service of a modernist art. The surface is now built up, with a new tactility, evidencing extensive use of a palette knife that gives a new weight to the painting. In this and subsequent canvases, until his death in 1946, it is as if Friedman had literally heeded Cézanne's dictum to make something solid and substantial out of Impressionism, 'like the art of the museums', and had gone one better by actually employing Old Master effects. The built-up particles of paint in these late works may also suggest an extension of Seurat's system of coloured dots. The net result seems to have been nothing less than to outline a procedure by which he could embody the whole history of landscape painting, from seventeenth-century Dutch artists through to nineteenth-century Impressionism and post-Impressionism. Friedman was well aware of this, for on the back of one canvas, a still life, possibly from the same year, but no later than 1942, he beckoned us with this inscription: 'Psst! Psst! Don't look now mister but your Impressionism is showing! – Thanks!'[36]

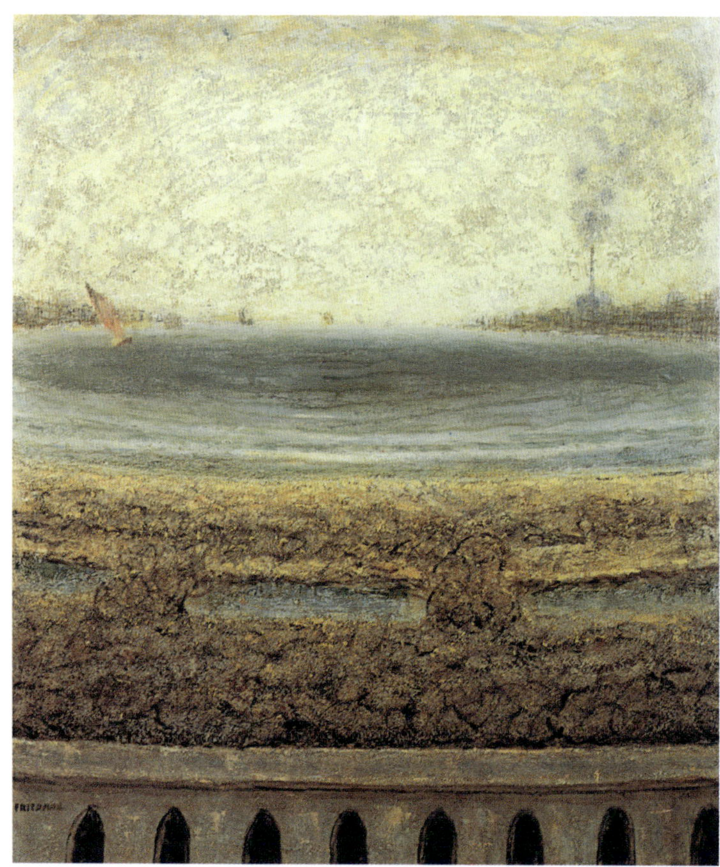

134

Modern Art in America

While Friedman did not work in situ, the painting *Bay and Balustrade* is surely based on one or several locations near his house, but perhaps altered and structured for the sake of the surface and its composition. From around 1940–1 we find a correlation between structure and content, as in *Shore Path* (c.1942–6)[135], where the curve echoes, in fact, *is*, the movement of the bicycle riders. So, too, the paint quality is the nature of the surface: the bicycle path is fairly smooth, but the adjoining gravel path is grainy and pebbly, so that the particles of paint are fully coeval with the stones. Gravel is not depicted; it is synonymous with the paint. Similarly, the waves and ripples are not depicted, but are the paint surface itself, as is the grass and foliage on the bank. These areas become a single large mass, rendered with a thousand variations of surface touch and colour, echoing the movement of the water itself. The work achieves an all-over density of surface, for even the wisps of smoke and atmosphere at the upper left have the same painterly weight as the rest of the painting. To achieve this overall intensity was part of a long-standing modernist ambition, which in the 1940s in America was undergoing a resurgence, most famously promulgated by a younger generation of emerging artists; but it was an ambition that Friedman helped to propel in no small measure. His art of the 1940s is every bit as radical and innovative as theirs.

In his review of Friedman's one-man show in April 1944 at the Marquié Gallery, Clement Greenberg pointed out that Friedman was capitalizing on what Bonnard and Vuillard had shown, namely that there were possibilities in Impressionism that the nineteenth century had 'failed to exhaust'.[37] Friedman's exhibition, Greenberg wrote, 'demonstrates that something can still be said with atmospheric envelopes, complementary colours, and optical mixtures', and that in his successful pictures, 'vibrating colour surfaces move toward and away from each other like incidents in a well-told story.'[38] The atmospheric envelope noted by Greenberg is especially apparent in *September Marshland* (1944). The painting evokes an even, golden atmosphere of Barbizon tones, its elements centred but modulated by curving areas of the marshes themselves, rendered by heavily encrusted surfaces, so that, like the very strata of the landscape they depict, they constitute a distinctive chapter in American art.

By means of a pictorial alchemy, Friedman transformed what seems to be inert matter into a field of light and colour. 'The result is complex, ripe, wistful, atmospheric, and at the same time, solid and monumental,'[39] Greenberg stated. These works can be described as a distinct and original variant of late Impressionism – one, as Greenberg commented, that was more radical than Bonnard's.[40] Some of the very last works even seem to be a new embodiment of the Fauve intensity of arbitrary colour. But it is a colour now in the service of an increasingly abstract vision of the natural world. In his last paintings, the surface of the land takes up more and more of the canvas, until the land is the entirety of the painting, and dissolves into pure surface and colour. In *Sunset* (c.1942–6)[136] the reds fill and virtually become the painting; we are hardly aware of the landscape, for it is as if the whole world has become suffused with light and colour.

The 1930s also marked the appearance of another major American colour painter, Milton Avery (1885–1965). His work would bloom fully in the 1950s, but his career was long and varied, and by the mid-1930s he was making all-over colour paintings, especially of idyllic landscapes[137]. Even earlier, we have recently discovered, he was doing remarkably strong paintings of industrial and urban sites. They are worked in the darker hues and values of the spectrum, reminding us of the richness of colour available to artists working in this other key. This should not have

134 Arnold Friedman,
Bay and Balustrade,
c.1944–6. Oil on canvas,
76.2 × 63.5 cm (30 × 25 in).
Private collection

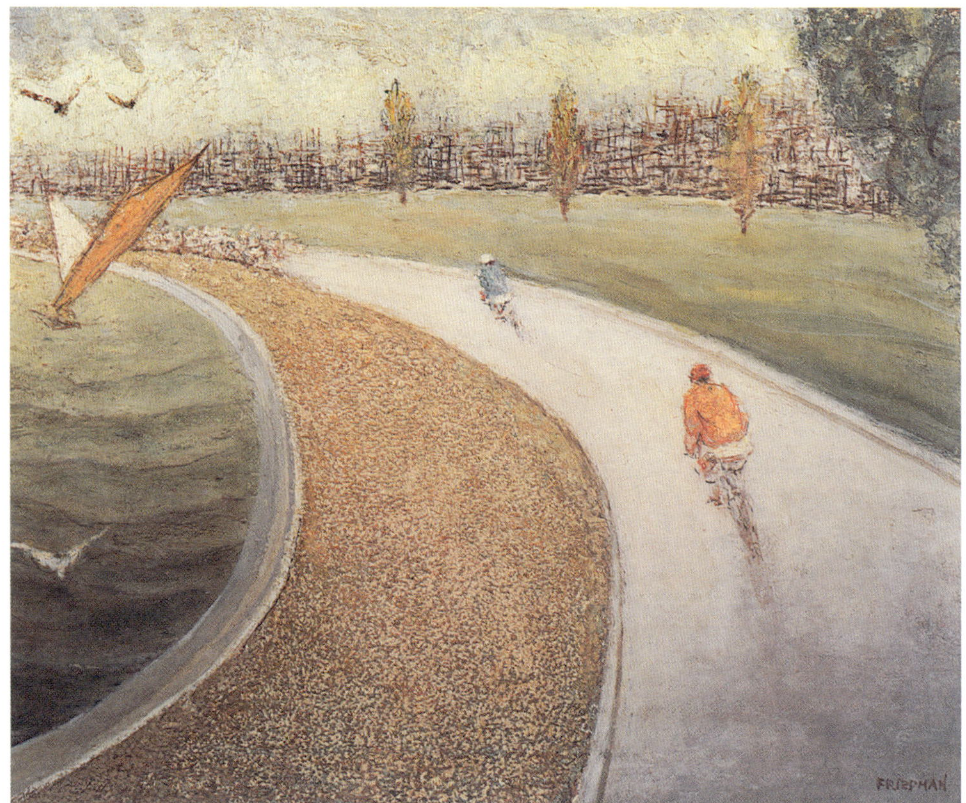

135

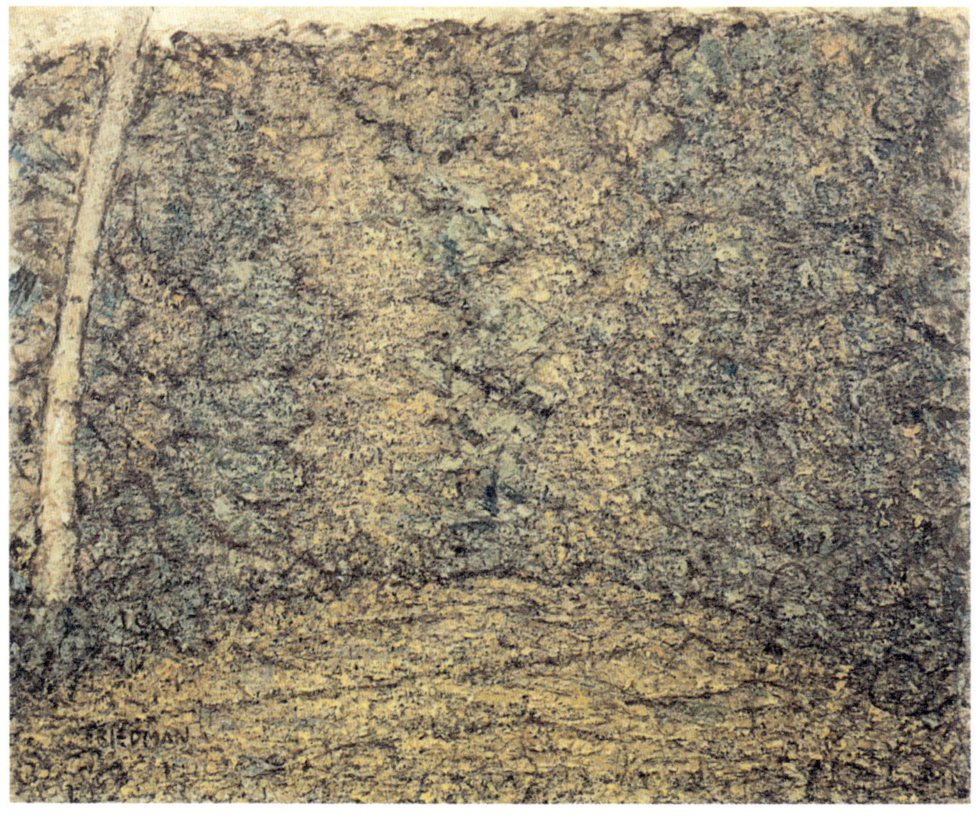

136

     Modern Art in America

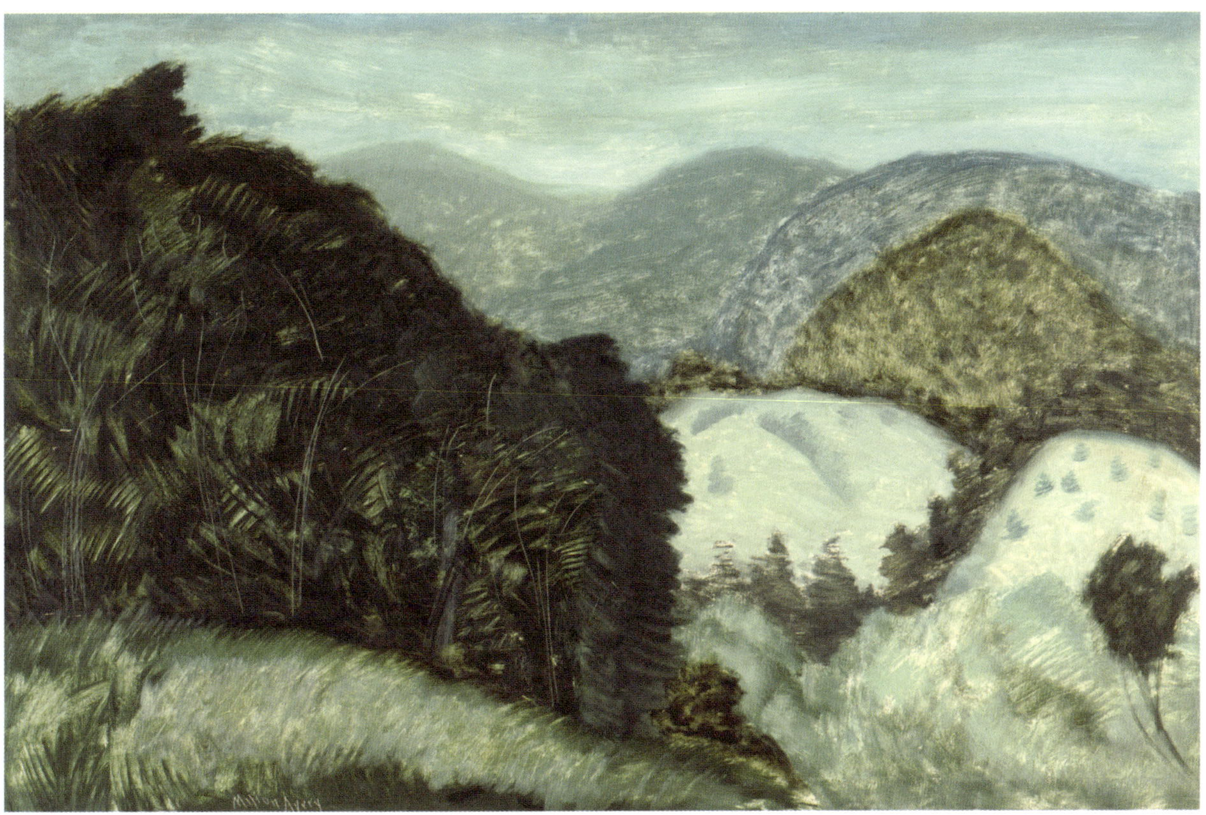

137

135 Arnold Friedman,
Shore Path, c.1942–6.
Oil on Masonite,
53.3 × 64.8 cm (21 × 25½ in).
Private collection

136 Arnold Friedman,
Sunset, c.1942–6.
Oil on board, 25.4 × 30.5 cm
(10 × 12 in). Private collection

137 Milton Avery,
Vermont Hills, 1936.
Oil on canvas, 81.3 × 121.9 cm
(32 × 48 in). Rose Art
Museum, Brandeis University,
Waltham, MA

surprised us, since he was born in 1885, eight years earlier than he had
said, a fact that places him as part of the older generation of Dove and
the pioneer modernists, so that his work had plenty of time to develop.
The darker range of colours may well remind us of Dove's similar palette
in the 1920s, and suggest that Avery had assimilated something of the
Symbolist mood of veiled mystery. Duncan Phillips recognized his early
promise, and acquired a painting by Avery in 1929; there is good reason
for the exceptional quality and depth of the Phillips Collection.

Avery was often termed the 'American Matisse', coinciding with the
resurgence of Matisse's reputation in the 1940s and 1950s. This is partly
true, but Matisse was not his only source, for the pale, chalky colours
owed a great deal to Thomas Dewing, John Twachtman, James Abbott
McNeill Whistler and Puvis de Chavannes, whose murals had been recently
completed at the Boston Public Library, within easy distance of Hartford,
where Avery had lived and worked. (For sheer intensity, vitality and sense
of hue invention, the term 'American Matisse' might more properly belong
to Stuart Davis.) But Avery, like Matisse, was a teacher, and under his
tutelage two younger artists, Mark Rothko and Adolph Gottlieb, learned
much about being professional artists. The Averys looked after them, almost
as surrogate parents, and Avery nurtured them to artistic maturity, for which
they were both deeply grateful. At Avery's funeral in 1965, Rothko could
say: 'Avery is first a great poet. His is the poetry of sheer loveliness, of
sheer beauty. Thanks to him, poetry of this kind has been able to survive
in our time.'[41] Poetry is the word that comes to mind when we look at his
colour orchestrations in late works of the 1940s.

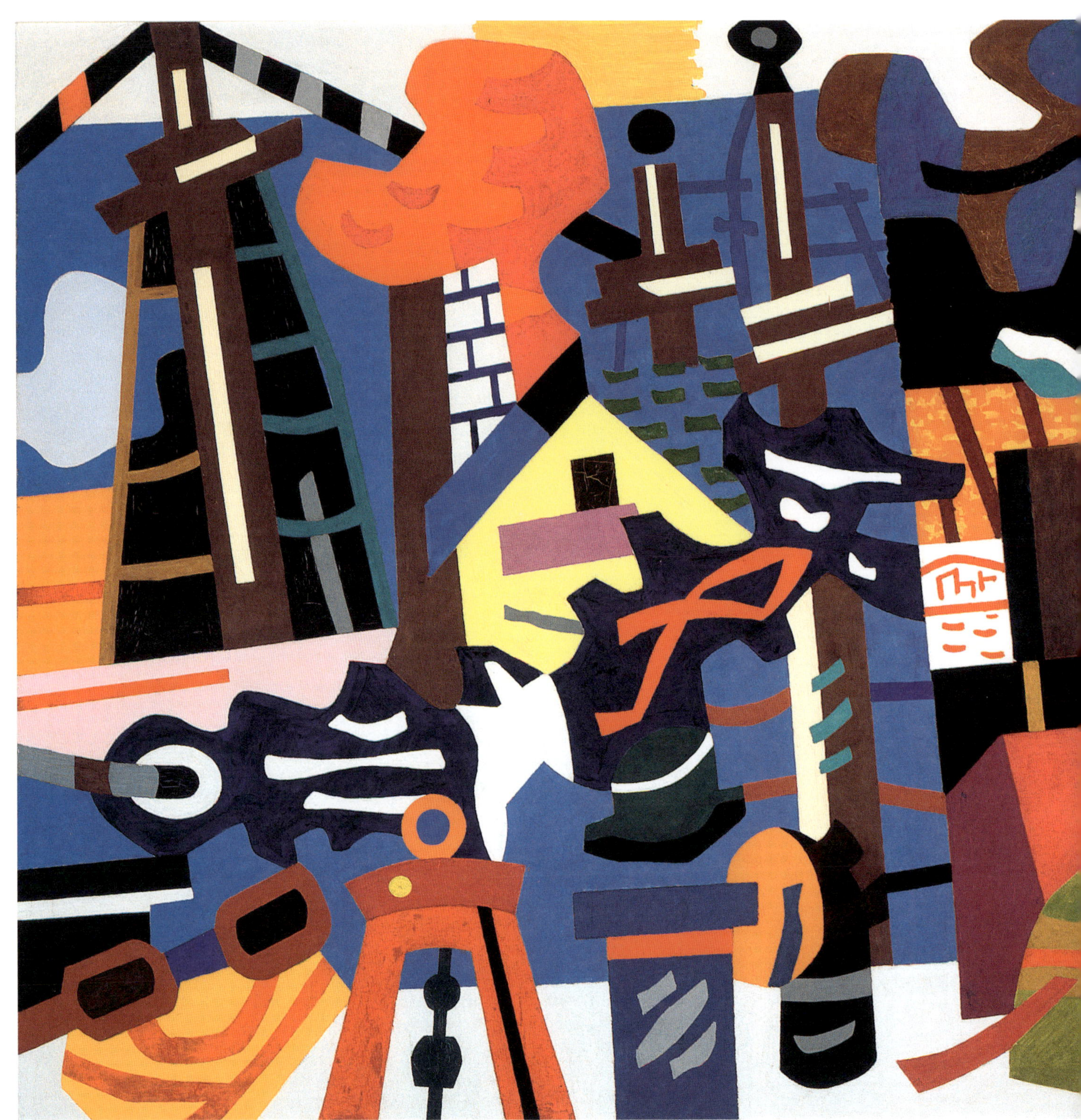

138

Stuart Davis, *Swing
Landscape*, 1938. Oil on
canvas, 220.3 × 439.7 cm
(86¾ × 173⅛ in). Indiana
University Art Museum

Modern Art in America

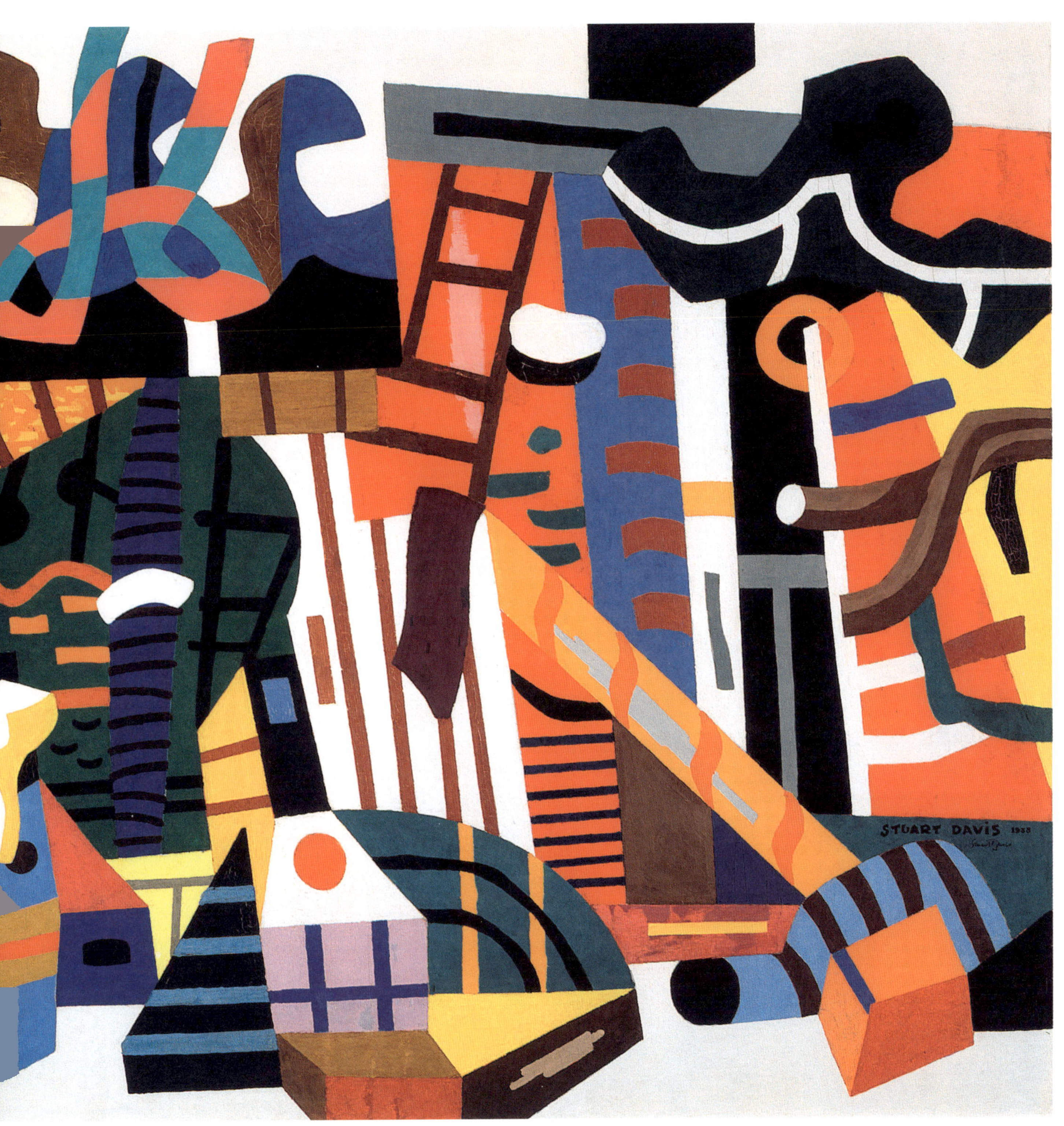

STUART DAVIS AND THE MEXICAN MURALISTS: *SWING LANDSCAPE* (1938)

Early American modernism had thus reached new heights of accomplishment in the work of these artists. A high point in the history of painting, especially colour painting, in American and indeed in Western art, was the completion of the large mural in 1938, *Swing Landscape* by Stuart Davis[138]. Between 1921 and 1957, Davis undertook nine mural projects; seven were completed as full-blown works for public spaces, one was never installed, and two remained as large studies. The one that was never installed (for reasons still not entirely clear), was *Swing Landscape*. It measures some twelve by fourteen feet and was arguably Davis's greatest painting to date, possibly the best work done for the Mural Division of the Federal Art Project of the Works Progress Administration, and one of the most accomplished large-scale paintings executed in the twentieth century, prior to Pollock's *Mural* of 1943 and four mural-size paintings of 1950, and Matisse's large cut-outs. Indeed, John Graham called the Davis work the 'greatest American painting'.[42] It was commissioned by the WPA, for the Williamsburg Housing Project in Brooklyn, a fact that has caused egregious misreading of it as an abstract scene of the Brooklyn streets.[43] It is no such thing: it is an abstracting depiction of the docks at Gloucester harbour, where Davis had been summering since 1916. The subject was the culmination of a favourite motif of his that had appeared frequently in his art since at least 1924.

Swing Landscape has only rarely been seen outside its home at Indiana University. To see it is thus likely to be a stunning surprise for the viewer, especially since its recent restoration to its original glory. Based on a tripartite arrangement, almost invisible at first glance, the mural seamlessly integrates colour, form, line and space with its subject matter. Abstract though it may be, it depicts the boats and schooners moored at a dock and the baggage and crates on the pier itself. For Davis was what he said he always was: a realist artist. *Swing Landscape* enabled him to develop his powers of colour construction in a new size and scale. The primaries dominate and are at the heart of the painting; they are then varied in seemingly infinite sequences, an orchestration of colour indeed. Colour creates form and space, it *becomes* form and space, in keeping with Davis's theory that he had formulated at this time. The mural is lyrical, upbeat, an affirmation of American art, in a welcome contrast to the hundreds of overwrought polemics and social diatribes made by so much mural and easel painting in the United States during the 1930s.

Meyer Schapiro likened *Swing Landscape* to a 'brass band',[44] and it was indeed a parallel to the big-band sound in America, Davis's homage to the jazz he had loved all his life. He joins the long tradition of artists equating painting with a musical composition, from Whistler, Gauguin, Matisse and Kandinsky to Pollock and Ray Parker. *Swing Landscape* can be usefully compared to Dove's painting *Swing Music (Louis Armstrong)* [139], also of 1938, a homage to Louis Armstrong, and in its linear energies a forerunner of the drawing found in Abstract Expressionism. In some ways, it even looks ahead to Mondrian's iconic *Broadway Boogie Woogie* (page 195), another painting-cum-musical composition that drew on the energy of the American experience. The rectangles of interspaced vibrant colour in the mural also point to the alternating bright hues in the Lego pieces done by Donald Judd in the 1980s – and indeed we know that Judd knew and respected the work of Davis. The mural is pure American scene – but done in a more universal style, as Davis liked to say.

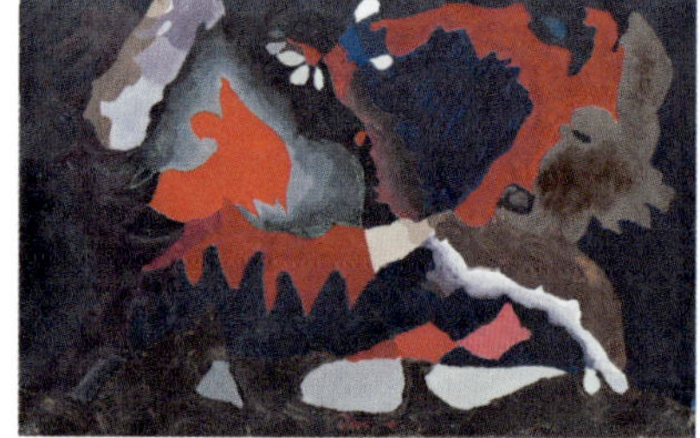

139

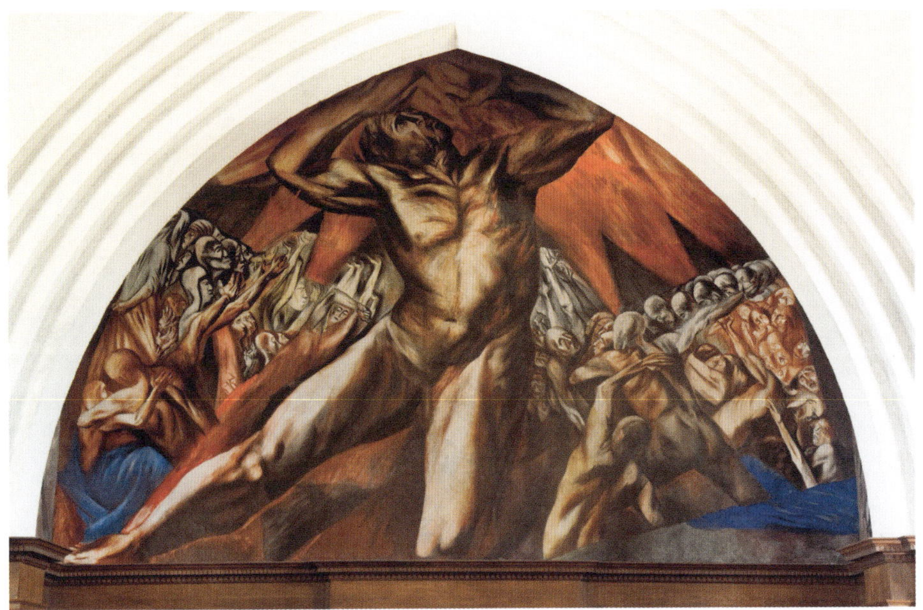

140

We might say that Davis had responded to the accomplishments of the Mexican muralists in New York and California, and in far more distant places, such as Dartmouth College, New Hampshire. Indeed, MoMA had organized an exhibition of proposed murals by Americans in 1932, precisely to counter the Mexican monopoly on murals in the country. The first in the United States was Orozco's powerful expressionist and formal mural for Pomona College, California, installed in 1930[140]. The subject is Prometheus, symbol of wisdom, depicted just as he brings fire to earth, the force that propels life, imbuing man with the power to create, to bring forth the marvels of the world. Two young American artists (and no doubt many more), Jackson Pollock and Philip Guston (then Goldstein), saw the mural, which introduced a scale and a way of painting and seeing the world that had a decisive influence on much of American art for the next ten years. In works such as *Gladiators* (1940)[141], Guston depicts epic forces at work in a type of figuration that reappeared in his painting after 1967. We see its drama and physical force in Pollock's art from the late 1930s well into the mid-1940s; there the human figures are rent asunder by enveloping powers that virtually engulf and absorb the half-human, half-mythic personages and fuse to become an all-over flow of expressive dynamics.

Pollock also made the long trip to Dartmouth College to see Orozco's cycle of frescoes, *The Epic of American Civilization* [142], in the reading room at the Baker Library there. Between 1932 and 1934, Orozco installed a spectacular suite of thirty-two separate panels that tell the story of the Americas from the migration of the Aztecs to modern industrial society. It is one of the most compelling monuments in the United States. The sheer power of expression, the pictorial forces that are unleashed throughout the cycle, as well as its environmental feel and atmosphere, were all surely of major importance in the development of American art after 1940. The Mexican contribution, including the murals of Rivera and Siqueiros, has only recently begun to be acknowledged in this respect. So, too, American murals by Benton and, earlier, James Daugherty have been thought of as period pieces, with no continuing importance. But Pollock, who studied with Benton, took much from his teacher, although he never gave him the credit he deserved for transmitting the powerful, swirling, baroque energy that is at the heart of Pollock's classic pour paintings of 1947–50.

139   Arthur Dove, *Swing Music (Louis Armstrong)*, 1938. Emulsion, oil and wax on canvas, 44.8 × 65.7 cm (17⅝ × 25⅞ in). Art Institute of Chicago

140   José Clemente Orozco, *Prometheus*, 1930. Fresco, 609.6 × 622.3 cm (240 × 245 in), Frary Hall, Pomona College, Claremont, CA

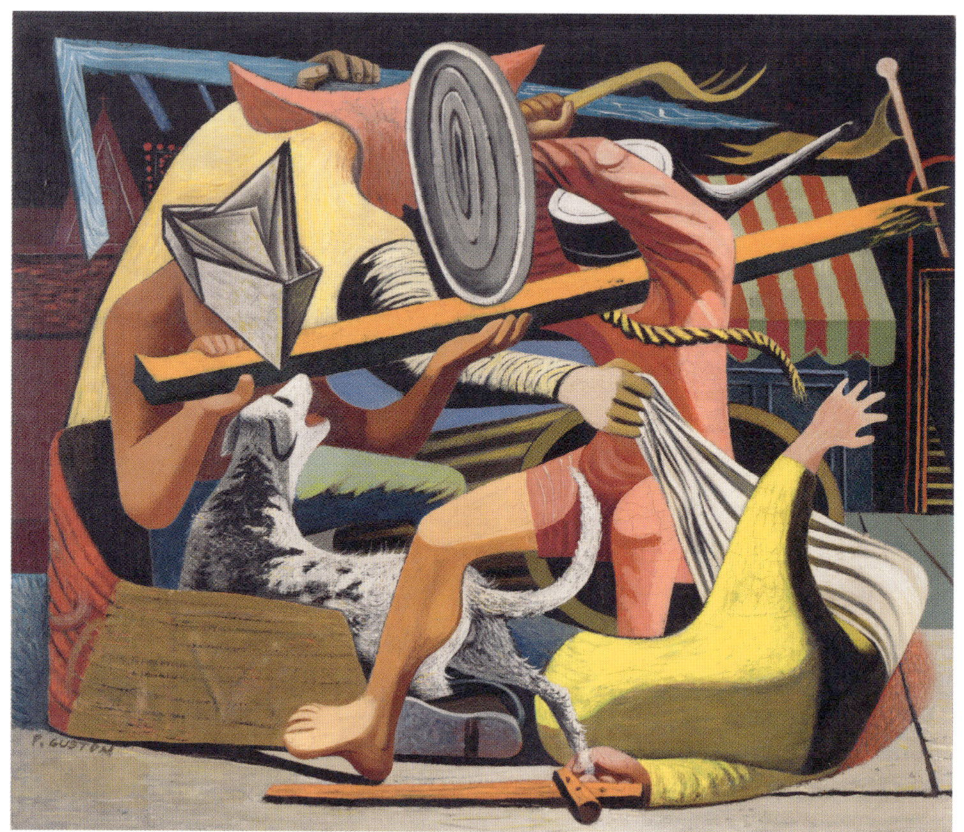

141

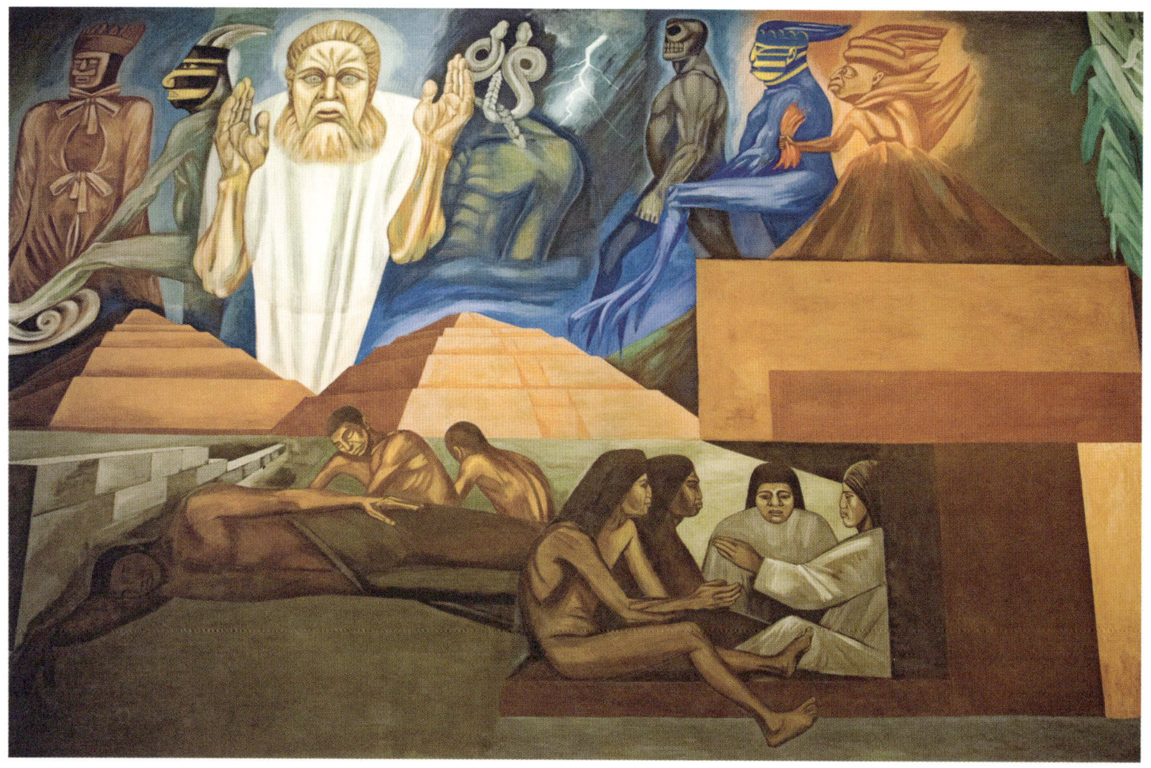

142

Modern Art in America

The Mexican and American mural movement has been seen as a kind of footnote, a minor element compared to the noble European ancestry of Picasso and Miró that has been claimed by scholars of Abstract Expressionism. Of course, the same has been true for American art itself. Historians have wanted an epic, high-class pedigree for the 'triumph of American art', not some out-of-the-way, less heralded art. Even the social and political context of the Mexican contribution has seemed somehow apart from the developments in Europe that spawned so much art after 1918. However, the Mexican Revolution of 1910–20 is actually part of the broad age of revolution that changed Europe, and its art, in the same years.

The Return of Sculpture

By no means was the domain of painting alone in its development at this time. Sculpture had lagged behind painting in terms of exploration and innovation, and by 1930 had been relegated to an arcane practice, reserved for a few neo-classical sculptors of note such as Aristide Maillol and Paul Manship. The mass and weight of traditional sculpture simply could not match the speed and dynamics of space, drawing and colour of modern painting, which had far outpaced the old methods of sculpture. Carving and modelling, the domain of sculpture, were simply too laborious and slow. Sculpture had to be transformed, somehow, so that it could keep pace with painting.

Picasso, as he had done so often, started the process of reinventing sculpture for modern needs. He began with his *Guitar* of 1912, now more open and penetrated by space, through his use of thin, malleable materials. However, he put the idea down until 1928, when he joined with his compatriot Julio González, a sculptor and jewellery designer who was an expert in welding. This process, with the acetylene torch, revolutionized the art of sculpture. It let artists open up sculpture, make it lighter, more flexible, and get it up in the air, off the pedestal, by working with tensile materials such as iron and steel that could be bent and shaped. Picasso and González worked with this method in the 1930s to great effect. However, it took the inventive spirit of two Americans, Alexander Calder and David Smith, to liberate sculpture truly, and make it something new, by drawing from ideas currently available in advanced painting.

In Paris, in 1930, Calder (1898–1976) moved beyond his *Cirque Calder*, with which he had entertained the Parisian art community since 1926, but which had as much to do with high art as bell chimes have to do with Zen Buddhism.[45] Calder was the first American who was deeply impressed by Mondrian, fascinated by the large, brightly coloured sheets of paper that the painter had up in his studio, making an environment of colour that surrounded the visitor. Calder consulted Mondrian and expressed his desire to make the colour planes move, but the latter demurred, saying they had enough motion already. Calder went ahead anyway, and from these planes of colour, his mobiles were born[143]. Using primary, even secondary colours, Calder connected biomorphic shapes with thin metal wires in intuitive ways. He was also among the first Americans to be integrated fully into the Parisian avant-garde, an artist who thereafter held a unique position in affecting American art for forty years and more. As such, he became as important as Matisse and Picasso, Miró and Léger for American art. Alexander Rodchenko had floated an open sculpture from the ceiling, but he never fully developed the practice. The floating mobiles of Calder, in red and black, combined sometimes with blue or yellow, gently moving with any kind of breeze, as if colour were made solid and

141   Philip Guston, *Gladiators*, 1940. Oil and pencil on canvas, 62.2 × 71.4 cm (24½ × 28⅛ in). The Museum of Modern Art, New York

142   José Clemente Orozco, *The Epic of American Civilization*, 1932–4. Mural, 24 panels, detail showing *The Coming of Quetzalcoatl*. Hood Museum of Art, Dartmouth College, Hanover

sent into the space around us, have become a symbol of what modern art was. The mobile – and his 'stabiles', with the same sources – has enriched our urban environment, but its inherent limitations meant that it became a set format and could only be taken so far. To Calder's credit, however, he was one of the first to find a solution to the age-old problems that had plagued sculpture: its static, floor- or pedestal-based qualities.

In that same year, 1930, Smith, a painter who became close to other leading artists of the day (Graham, Davis, de Kooning and Gorky among them), was absorbing the recent lessons of modern art, fusing strong colour and Cubist design. He needed something more physical, more literally real. He added elements to the surface, letting the painting morph into a relief, and from there let thin wire describe a figure in space, literally a three-dimensional drawing. He was as much a painter as he was a sculptor, and his goal was to make sculpture as dynamic as painting, so that there was no difference except one of dimension. For this alone, Smith deserves accolades. For thirty years thereafter, he proved himself to be a towering figure.

143 Alexander Calder, *Untitled*, 1939. Painted sheet aluminium and steel wire, 37.1 × 22.8 × 27.5 cm (14⅝ × 9 × 10⅞ in). The Museum of Modern Art, New York

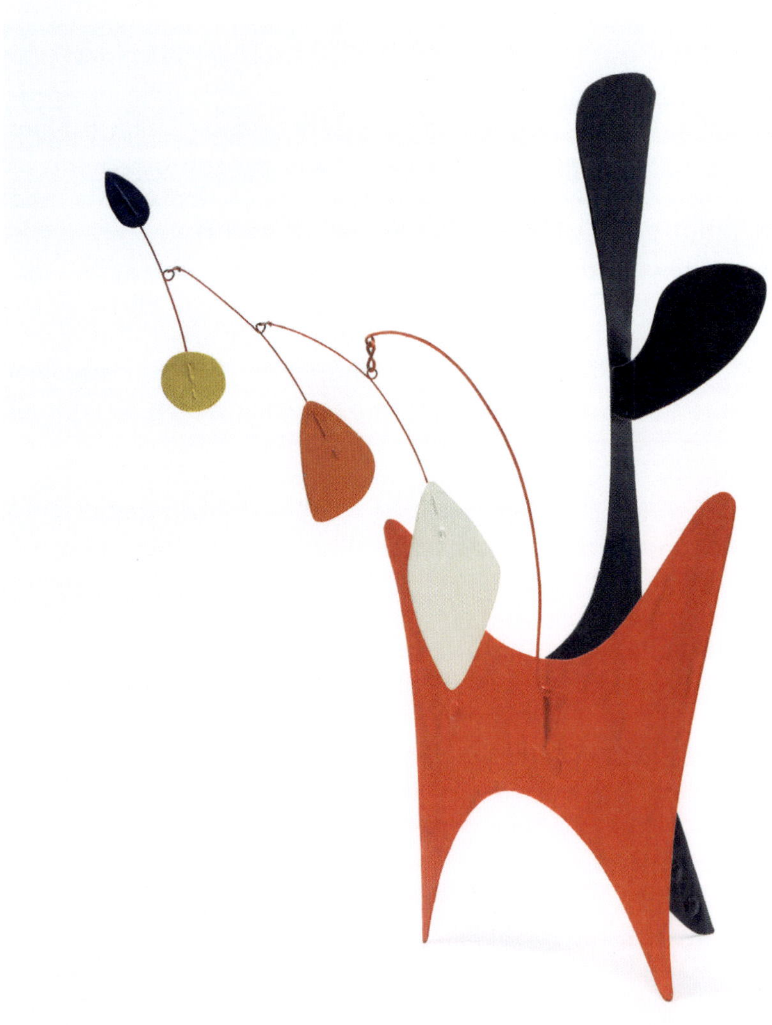

143

    Modern Art in America

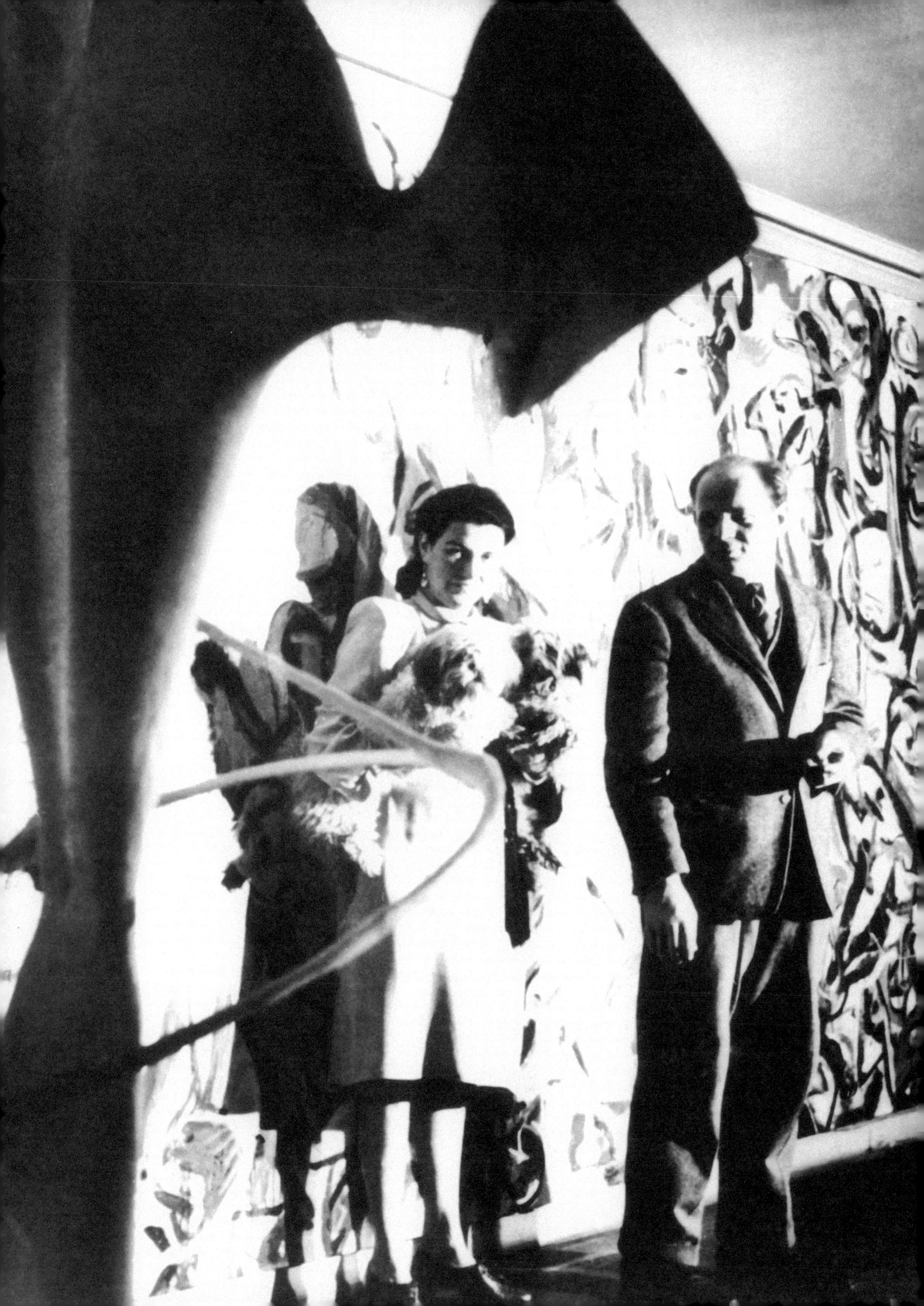

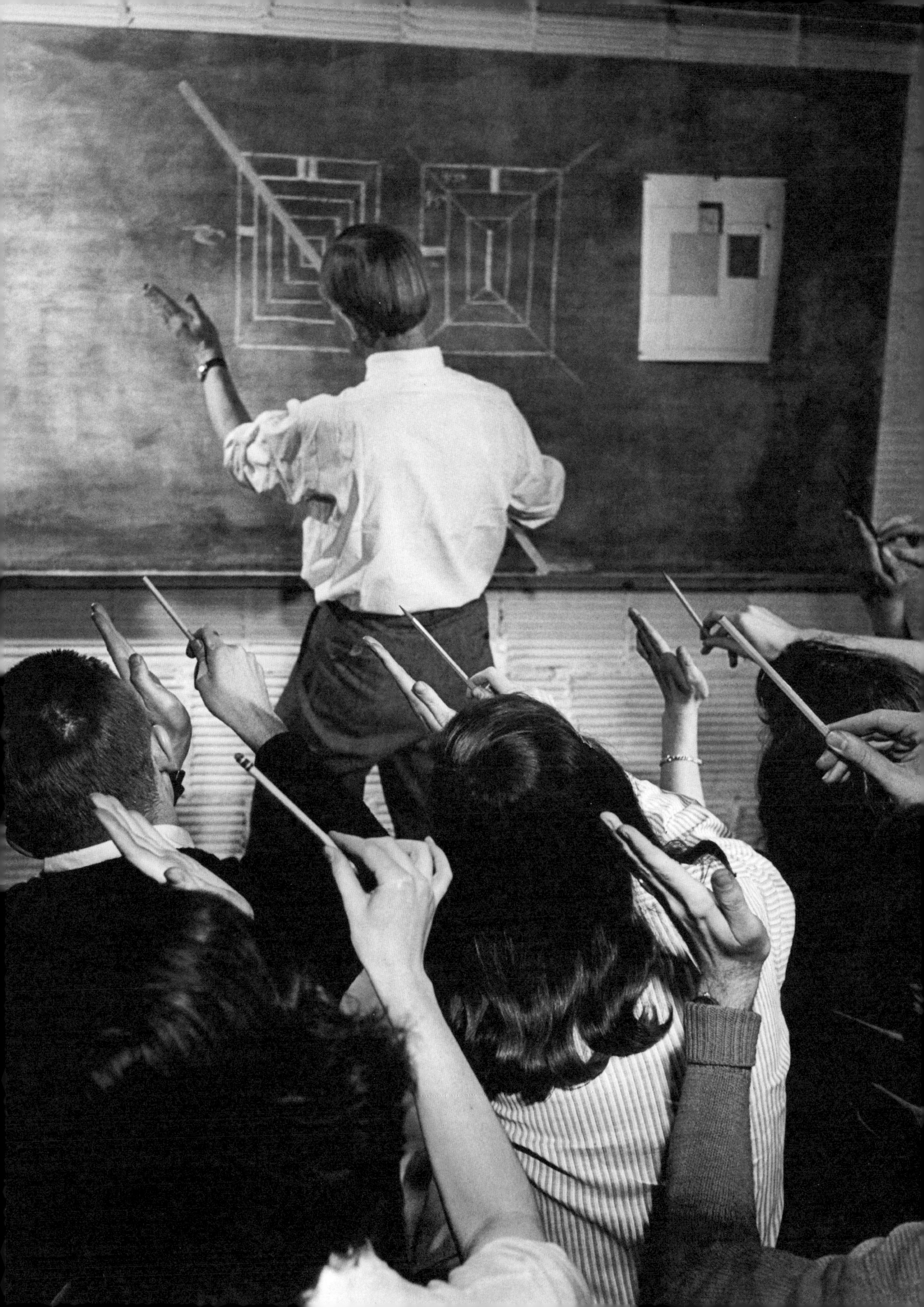

A NEW WORLD ORDER

THE 1940s

144 Peggy Guggenheim and
     Jackson Pollock in front of
     Mural, in the hallway of her
     town house at 155 East
     61st Street, New York, *c*.1944.

145 Josef Albers with his
     class at Black Mountain
     College, 1949.

By 1940, America had reached another turning point. This time, culture and history were in sync. With the fall of Paris to the Germans in June, France, except perhaps for Picasso and Matisse, was never a force again. America had made great strides in developing an art that was maturing rapidly and that was truly modern, and growing deeper, while embodying the experience and character of the country. Colour had been a major factor in shaping the new American painting, and it continued to do so in the years thereafter. America was poised to assume a new stature in world history. It could take any number of forms and ways of making work, as is best exemplified in the art of four artists: Stuart Davis, Arthur Dove, John Marin and Edward Hopper, who had all reached their full power. Curiously, none, except occasionally for Marin, is ever discussed in histories of post-1940 painting; they are thus relegated to positions as pioneers, their careers as important artists frozen in the 1920s. But in fact, the four were the seeds and first plants of three traditions in America that had begun early in the century and reached full bloom during the early 1940s and then after 1945. They show the wide range and depth of quality in American art, its rich modalities, abstract and figurative: Davis in the hard-edge geometric mode, Dove and Marin the organic, and Hopper the figurative and abstract. America continued in these modes of intersecting movements, but after 1945, in the rush to proclaim the triumph of American painting, the focus was only on the organic and painterly of a younger generation. The others were basically forgotten, as if they had stopped working in 1940, or sooner. We need to go back, retrace and recapture this historical multiplicity to develop a more inclusive history since 1940, now thankfully the aim of contemporary scholarship in the field.

Stuart Davis: An All-over Colour

In 1940, in a uniquely potent work titled *Report from Rockport*[146], Stuart Davis synthesized the multiple developments that had marked one side of American art of the twentieth century to date. Its brilliant, all-over colour that he loved so much has built on Matisse, taken to a high pitch. It is structured around Cubist planes and is animated by Surrealist-related biomorphic shapes that swim across the picture. The planes descend from Picasso, but Davis makes them his own, in a personal, original type of Cubist-Constructivism. The flying forms show the influence of Miró and other Surrealists, and these too are original adaptations. (There is no denying Miró's importance, although the development of biomorphism came from other directions as well; he was absorbed into American art well before the advent of Abstract Expressionism.) The colour gives Davis's work an energy and intensity that announce the emergence of a new depth in American art. The pigment is thick, something rarely noted in Davis, as if an omen of the heavy surfaces soon to come in American art. But he is never thought of as a source for post-1945 art.

For all its abstractness, however, *Report from Rockport* is a uniquely American scene, a street and a gas station, descended from the realist tenets of Robert Henri, who had urged his students to paint the world around them. The painting depicts the main road into Rockport, Massachusetts, on Cape Ann, just north of Gloucester, where Davis had summered for twenty-five years. The buildings are composed of the familiar Cubist planes that he had developed in his Paris paintings of 1928–9, and here order the otherwise frenetic activity of the painting. It is as if we are peering through the windscreen of his car, which he loved, as he drives down into the main street of the fishing village to report on what is happening, that is, to show us what he has been up to in his art. A lot, as it turns out, for the painting speaks of colour intensity, a new, broader Cubism, and a distinctly new Surrealist imagery. To this day, nothing much has changed in this town, including the gas pumps and traffic beacons and directionals, although a convenience store has replaced the old gas station. As such, it embodies a main tenet of American modernism – adapting current modern styles to depict the essence of America and American life – and thus Davis is reporting on American art as well as on himself. His work tells us that America has come of age, that the modern vocabulary has replaced the omnipresent tourist souvenirs for which Rockport had long been noted, that a new kind of intensity now informs American art.

Edward Hopper: A Conservative Modernism

Edward Hopper's painting, *Gas*[147], also done in 1940, represents what we might call a more conservative aspect of American modernism. But it is one of the most impressive American paintings. It has virtually the same subject as the Davis, an urban scene with a gas station, the very symbol of American progress and mobility, but what a different picture! Hopper's composition is filtered through the experience of French Impressionism and modern America. His colour is based on light in all its possibilities, the legacy of the artists whom he had studied so carefully on his three trips to Paris in the early years of the century. Hopper said it took him a long time to get over Paris, but in truth he never really did: it was assimilated into his own personal style and outlook. We do not think of him as a colourist, but since light and colour are coeval, then he is certainly a first-rate colourist. In *Gas*, light is rendered masterfully in virtually all its

146 Stuart Davis, *Report from Rockport*, 1940. Oil on canvas, 61 × 76.2 cm, (24 × 30 in). The Metropolitan Museum of Art, New York

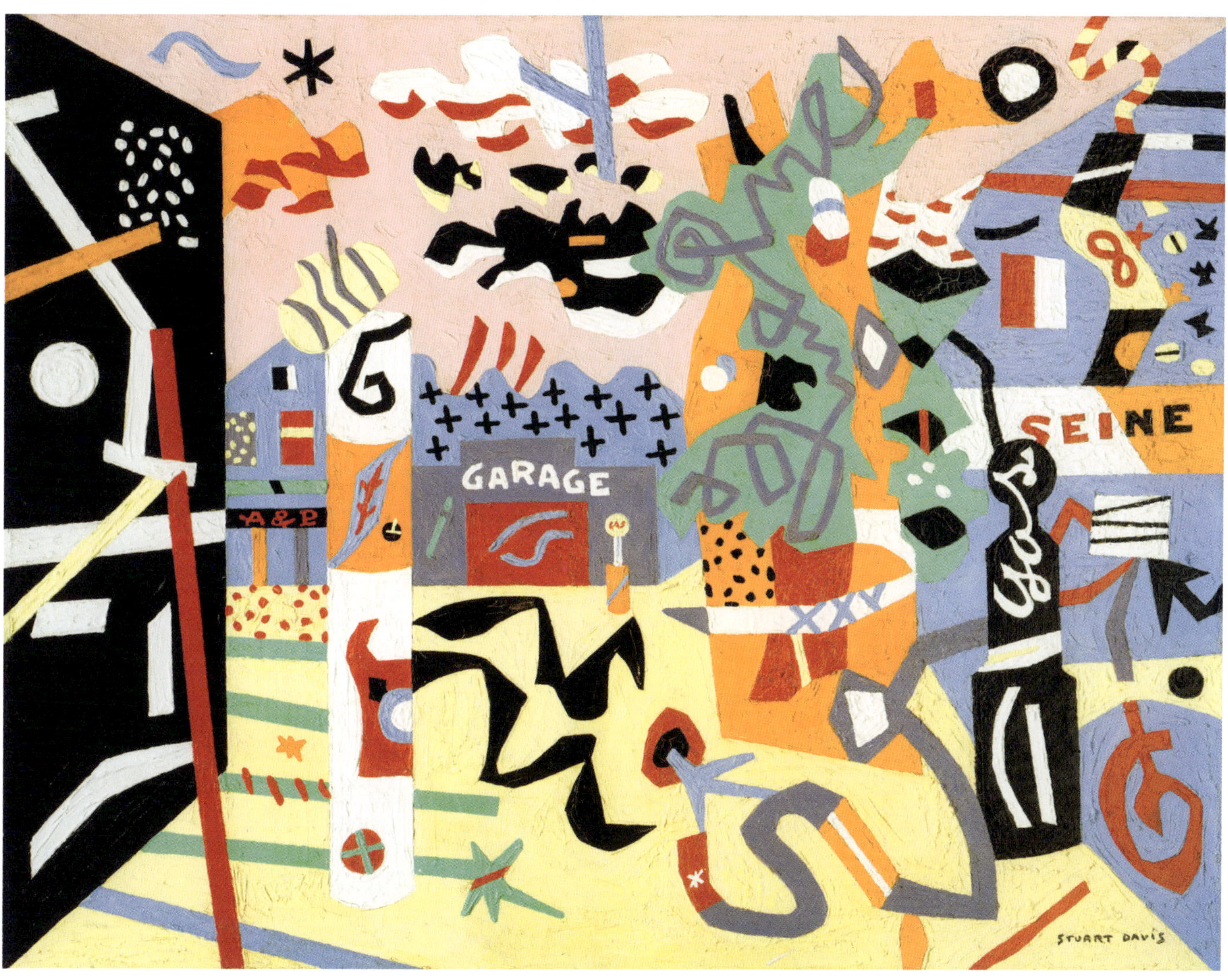

146

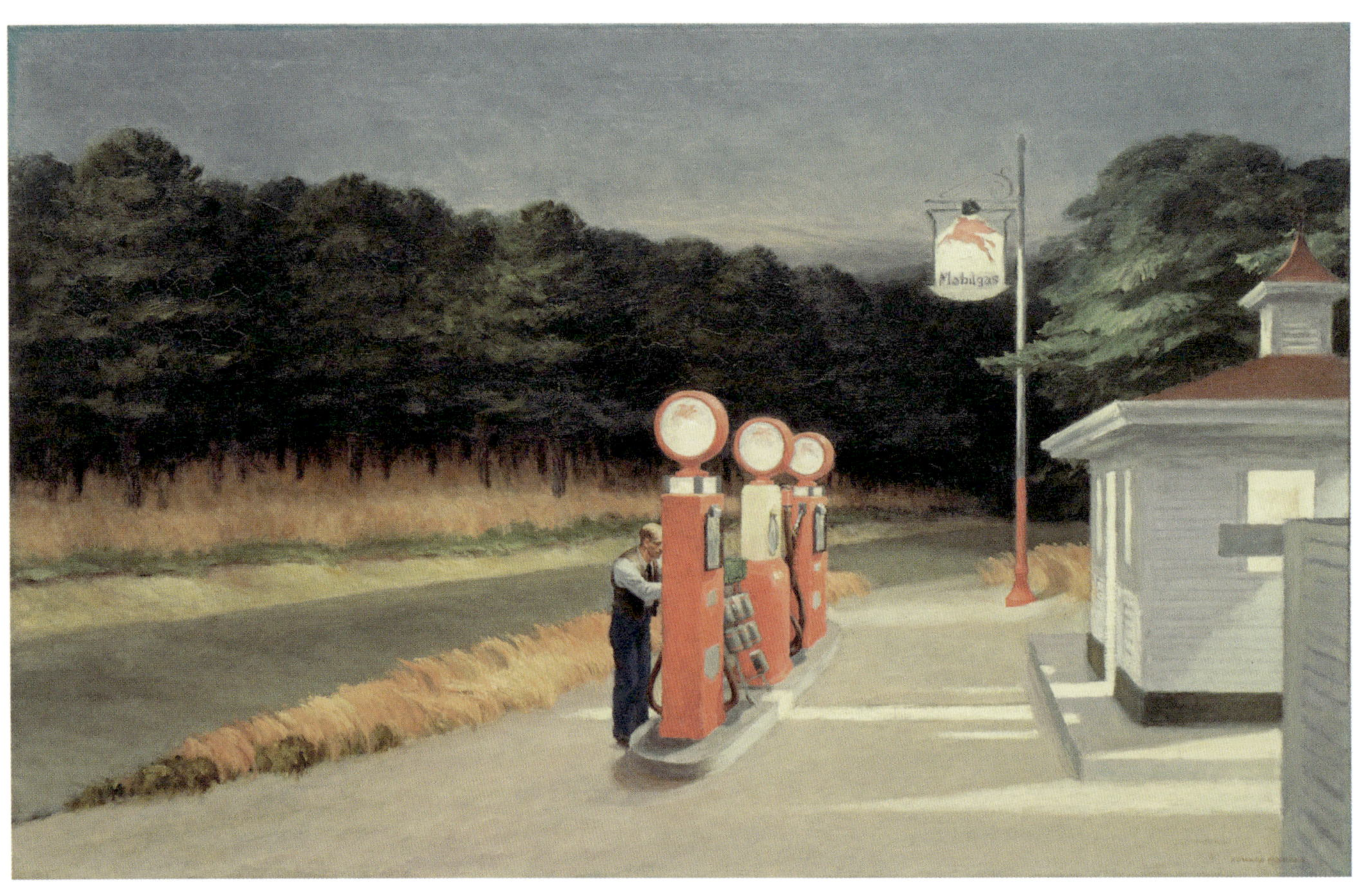

147

Modern Art in America

modes. Hopper said it was hard to paint both inside and outside light, and so it is, but he loved the challenge and responded brilliantly to it. There is the twilight of the sky, the light fast disappearing, the already impenetrable dark of the New England woods, a special kind of darkness that only Hartley could equal in his late Maine landscapes. It is the fading light of an era now lost with the coming of war. There is the natural light on the station itself, a kind of half-light, of long, late summer evenings. And there is the artificial illumination, first outside, the light of the lamp, then the glare on the Mobil sign and the flying horse, Pegasus. This is complemented by the artificial light on the inside of the office and the way it spreads outside, affecting interior and exterior space at the same time.

It is a tour de force, proving that Hopper was a far greater artist than we have given him credit for, since we have mostly seen him only as a purveyor of alienation, one of the most overused and misconceived clichés in American art history. This label has come about because his figures are usually pictured alone. This is too easy, even simple-minded. If we are by ourselves, we are alone, but not alienated. We are inside ourselves, in our thoughts, as in Hopper's *New York Movie* (1939)[148].[1] We may be feeling down or elated or anxious, but we are not necessarily alienated. The usherette is a model of quiet contemplation, with the solemnity we associate with an Old Master devotional scene. Indeed, in this and in most of his paintings, there is an overwhelming feeling of quietude, of stillness and silence, a quality that links Hopper to much of nineteenth-century landscape painting as so well described by Barbara Novak.[2] Hopper relished this interior mode, and it is no accident that the one person in the audience we can see clearly is the head of the large, half-bald man, surely a self-portrait. Hopper himself loved the theatre and the cinema, performances in which we can lose ourselves, travel to other worlds, not become alienated. The usherette, perhaps, is in a similar mode of pensive dreaming.

Greenberg commented in 1946 that Hopper was a bad painter, but that this was exactly what made him a superior artist, one who should have a special category for the kind of art he made.[3] One can quarrel with the

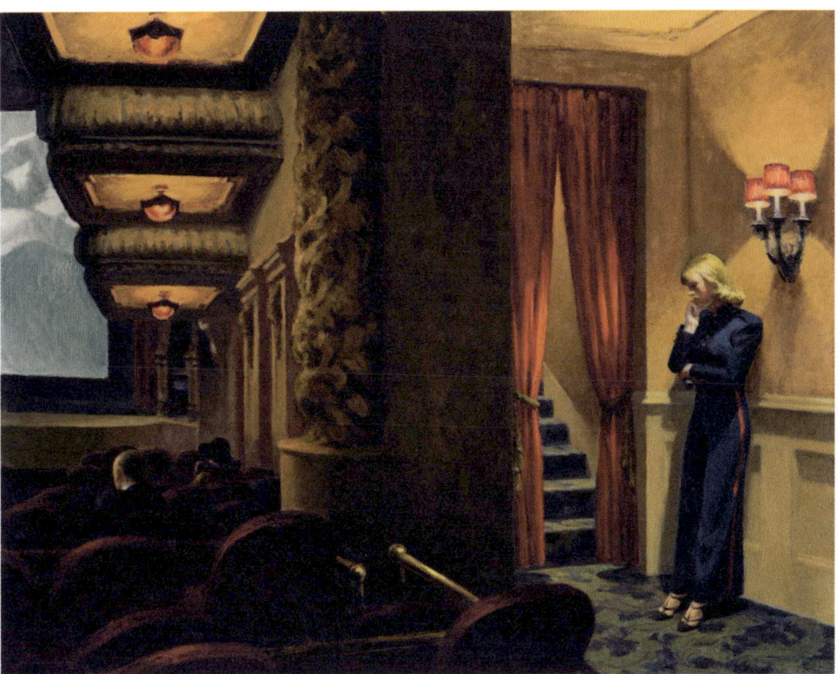

147 Edward Hopper, *Gas*, 1940. Oil on canvas, 66.7 × 102.2 cm (26¼ × 40¼ in). The Museum of Modern Art, New York

148 Edward Hopper, *New York Movie*, 1939. Oil on canvas, 81.9 × 101.9 cm (32¼ × 40⅛ in). The Museum of Modern Art, New York

148

first point, but not with the second. Earlier historians and critics could only see Hopper as a simple, homespun realist, simply recording what he saw in front of him. There is truth in this, but for Hopper that is barely the start. His sources and the implications of his art are as manifold, diverse and complex as those of any American artist. He began with the Impressionists, especially Degas and his multiple angles of space and architecture. Hopper's roots are also in Symbolism, and his embrace of Symbolist literature and poetry[4] is evident in the twilight mood, and the literal twilight of the road, sky and woods, which induces a feeling of melancholy, uncertainty and even anxiety in the face of the vast unknown space of this continent.

The road, as in a Degas, goes on past us, and past the isolated human island of the station, where to and for how far we cannot be certain – a kind of road to perdition or loss, as the country heads towards a world war. The attendant has apparently just reconnected the hose, implying that he has only now finished filling up a car, which has gone on its way to who knows where, just like the country as it prepares for the oncoming war. The single figure, frozen like those of Giotto and Manet,[5] stands 'alone in a sea of space and of change', as John McCoubrey has put it.[6] This is also a recurring theme in American art, from the nineteenth-century vistas of the Luminists to Hopper, and then to David Smith, whose photos of his work emphasize the single figure alone facing the vastness of the land. That the image on the sign (another reference to classical art) recalls Carl Jung's understanding of Pegasus as a source of spiritual energy that could give access to Mount Olympus, suggests that Hopper was calling man and his country – or at least himself – to renewed and heroic efforts in the near future. Hopper lamented the fall of Paris to the Nazis,[7] for he knew it meant, if not the end, the twilight of a long tradition of painting that had nurtured and sustained him over these many years, as it had sustained Western art itself. This painting is a picture not of alienation (despite the single man) but of an impending dark cloud, indeed of loss, even doom. He is alone, as the country was then alone, close to a road that led to an uncertain destination. American art, Hopper also seems to have comprehended, stood alone, obliged to forge its own path, without the help of French art.

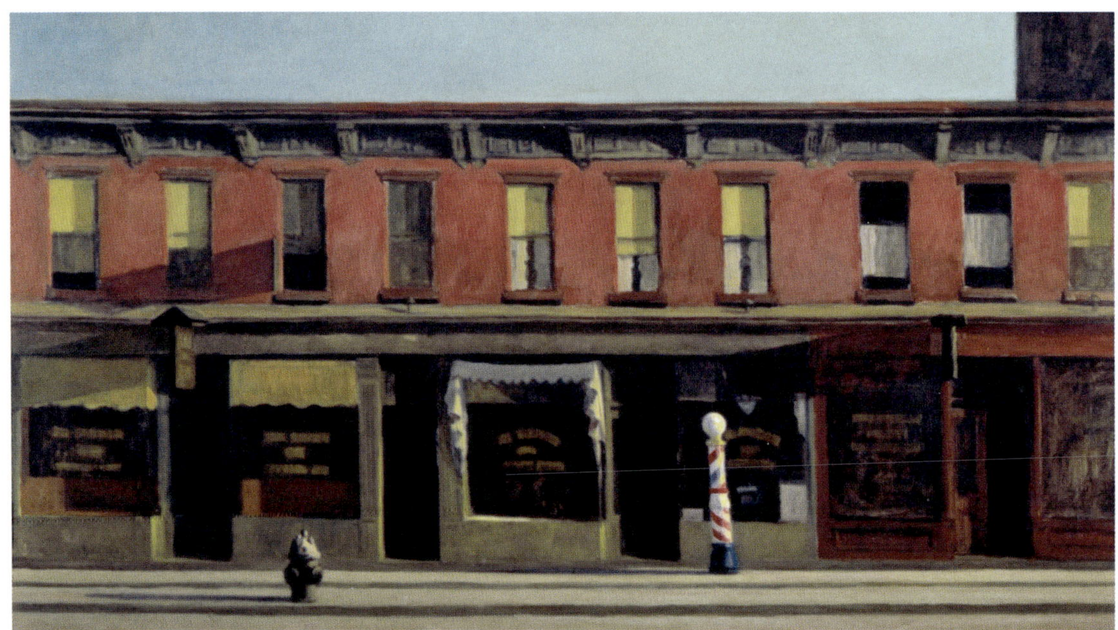

149

　　　　　　　　　　Modern Art in America

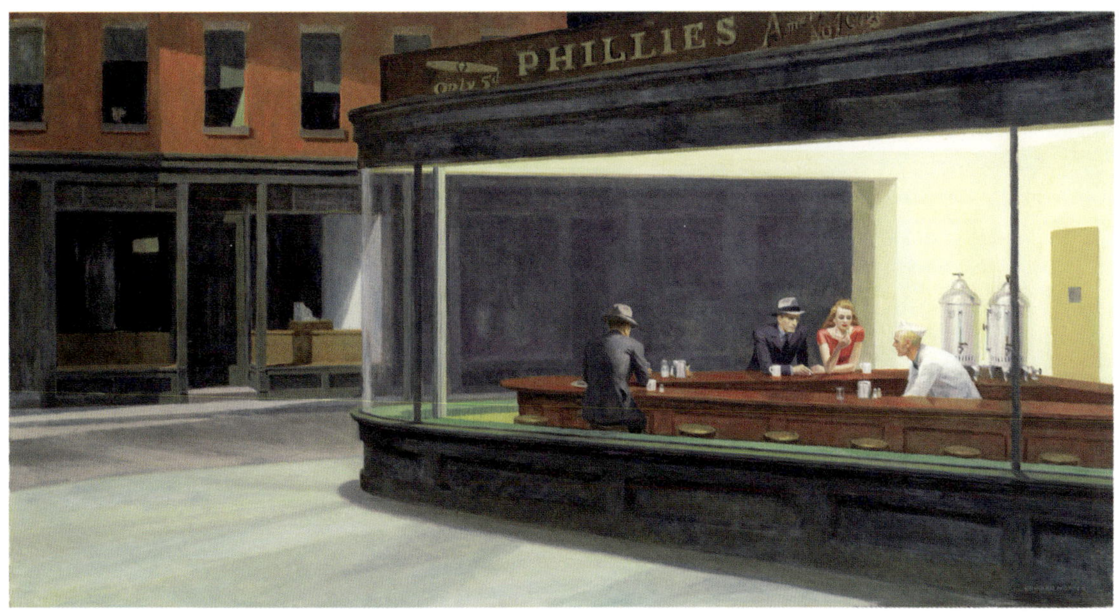

150

Light is the source of power in Hopper's paintings, most famously in his iconic *Early Sunday Morning* (1930)[149], in which the sun comes up in the city, with the promise of a new day that fills the scene with a new and eternal hope. 'The elation of sunlight', the artist called it.[8] It is this light that especially marks him as an artist of the first rank, and that continued, as we shall see, to the end of his life. After 1950, his art changed, as America's did, and in his late work light becomes a physical, palpable presence that lets his paintings stand side by side with the post-1950 work of Mark Rothko. The structure of this early painting – its repeated verticals and its sequence of rectangles – has been compared with Rothko and with Pollock. We are just coming to understand and investigate these modernist aspects of Hopper. I have compared Hopper's structure to a proto-Cubist mode, following the reference to Cubism by Alfred H. Barr, Jr., when discussing *Office Windows at Night* (1929) in the catalogue of the 1933 Hopper show at MoMA.[9] Barr alone understood Hopper's modernist impulses, and it is no coincidence that the first painting to enter the museum's collection was Hopper's *House by the Railroad Tracks* (1925). Barr's voice was a singular note in the otherwise overwhelmingly critical views that saw Hopper as a humble American realist, working in a simple, uncomplicated way.

The influence of modernism is also clear in Hopper's famous *Nighthawks* of 1942[150], done when Mondrian was in New York and all manner of artists were responding to his geometries and his presence. The vertical supports of the diner and its windows illustrate another American adaptation of a European structural system that appears over and over again after 1940, when Mondrian arrived in New York. The garish, brilliant yellow of the interior walls also points directly to Mondrian. At the same time, the rendering of illuminated light on both indoor and outdoor surfaces, animating the dark of night, tells us once again how intriguing Hopper was as a painter. When we contrast this painting with an outdoor daylight painting such as *Early Sunday Morning*, we see Hopper creating his own cycle of the course of life from day to night.

149 Edward Hopper, *Early Sunday Morning*, 1930. Oil on canvas, 89.4 × 153 cm (35³⁄₁₆ × 60¼ in). Whitney Museum of American Art, New York

150 Edward Hopper, *Nighthawks*, 1942. Oil on canvas, 84.1 × 152.4 cm (33⅛ × 60 in). Art Institute of Chicago

Arrival of Mondrian: 1940

One of the most important events in this period of the war was the arrival of Piet Mondrian (1872–1944) in 1940 in New York, where he lived until his death in early 1944. His presence there, and his art, were enormously influential. He was a primary form-giver of the twentieth century, and his clarified grid structure, a kind of late Cubism, gave countless American artists a way to a concrete structural foundation on which to build a personal abstract art. Not the least of Mondrian's contributions to American art was colour. His art was not on public view in America until 1926, in the International Exhibition held at the Brooklyn Museum, but from 1932 on, it could be seen at the Gallery of Living Art, the collection of Albert E. Gallatin, housed at New York University on Washington Square East. MoMA's landmark exhibitions, especially 'Cubism and Abstract Art' of 1936, showed Mondrian's work in some depth, as well as corollary movements. The flat planes of the intense primaries in his classic works of the 1920s and early 1930s offered good examples of what a large, undiluted area of two primaries, contrasted with black lines and strong white areas, could do to activate a painting. In the late 1930s, his paintings became more complex, with multiple lines, a revolutionary change for the deliberate Mondrian. But coming to America changed his vision and produced new and radical work, for the freedom from the war and the fast pace of New York let him open up in ways that would have been previously unimaginable.

In *Broadway Boogie Woogie* (1942–3)[151], Mondrian moved away from the strict grid of black lines and adapted a new, freer structure composed of squares and rectangles of brilliant primary hues that seem to pop and gyrate over the surface. Now he had made a painting of nothing but colour, with no constricting lines, and as such it is a pivotal point in the history of colour painting. Blacks are gone, and thus the value and hue intensity seems doubled and able to pull away from the surface, appearing to resolve itself in our space, in front of the canvas, a phenomenon that the psychologist of perception David Katz called 'film colour'.[10] The entire canvas is composed of the primary colours, divided into small rectangles, and thus it may be termed the first colour-field painting.

Mondrian moved even further in his new direction in his last painting, which is perhaps unfinished, perhaps not, but certainly finished enough. *Victory Boogie Woogie* (1944)[152] brought him to a new conception of painting, a fusion of the linear and the painterly, for the surfaces are built up of pigment and paper, dense, like a relief. The painting represents an intersection of older European art with the painterly expressionism of the younger Americans just then emerging into the public sphere. In particular, it points to the recognition of Jackson Pollock by the elder Mondrian as a leading force in the wave of new art, the American art of the future, even then beginning to assert itself. Mondrian had seen and admired Pollock's art at Peggy Guggenheim's gallery Art of This Century, calling the *Stenographic Figure* (c.1942)[153] the best he had seen in New York. Why was Mondrian so taken with Pollock? Surely he saw the possibilities of the new painterly surfaces of American Expressionism, a way beyond his own self-restricted type of structure and colour. He loved New York and its pace – and for him the speed of the Pollock would have embodied the very essence of the city and the country. In *Stenographic Figure* we see marks of shorthand that resemble the plus and minus signs of Mondrian's work of 1913–14, paintings that Pollock himself admired. Pollock's marks were perhaps a way for Mondrian to reach back and use his own past, updating it in accordance with the most advanced art of the day. It was a new and

151 Piet Mondrian, *Broadway Boogie Woogie*, 1942–3. Oil on canvas, 127 × 127 cm (50 × 50 in). The Museum of Modern Art, New York

152 Piet Mondrian, *Victory Boogie Woogie*, 1944. Oil and paper on canvas, 127 × 127 cm (50 × 50 in). Gemeentemuseum, The Hague

Modern Art in America

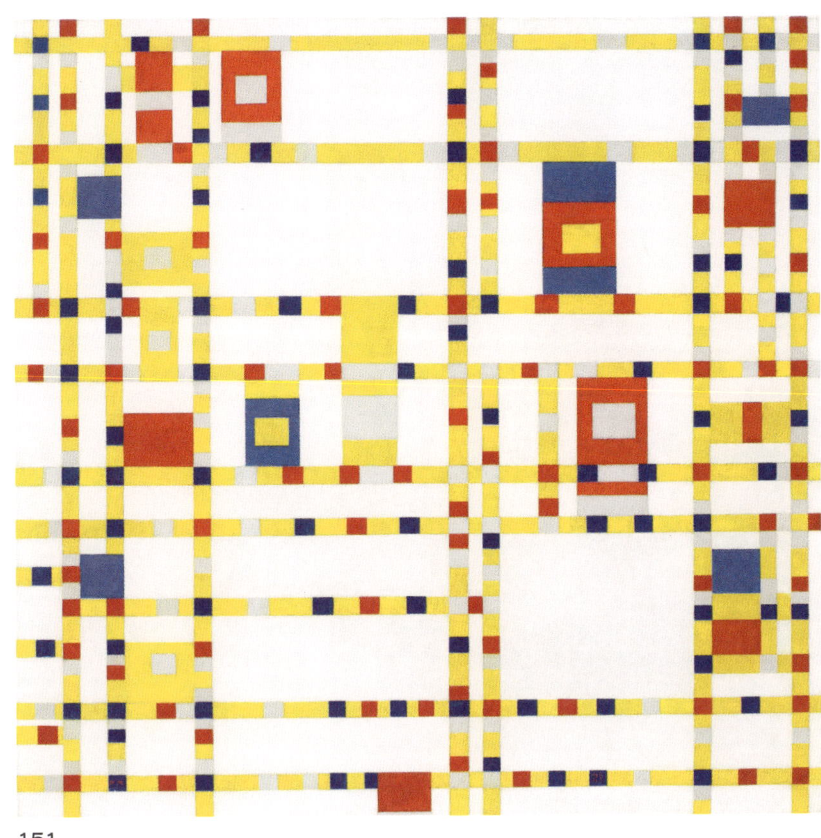

151

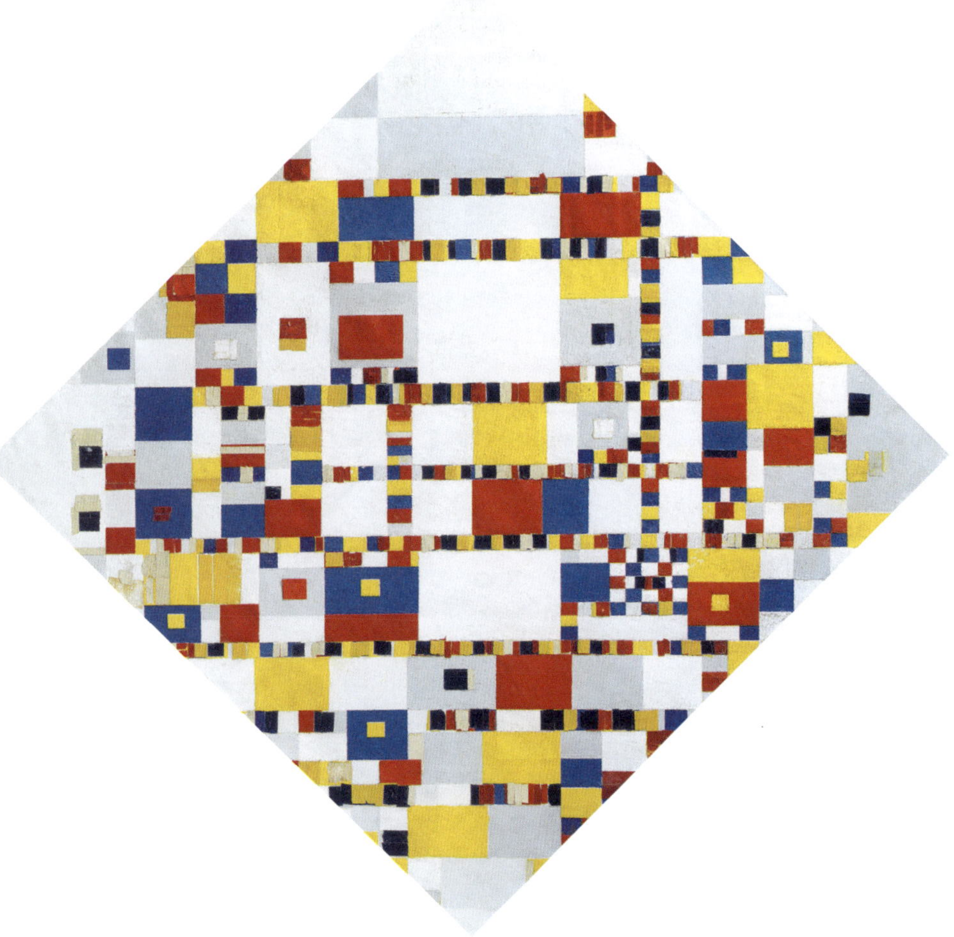

152

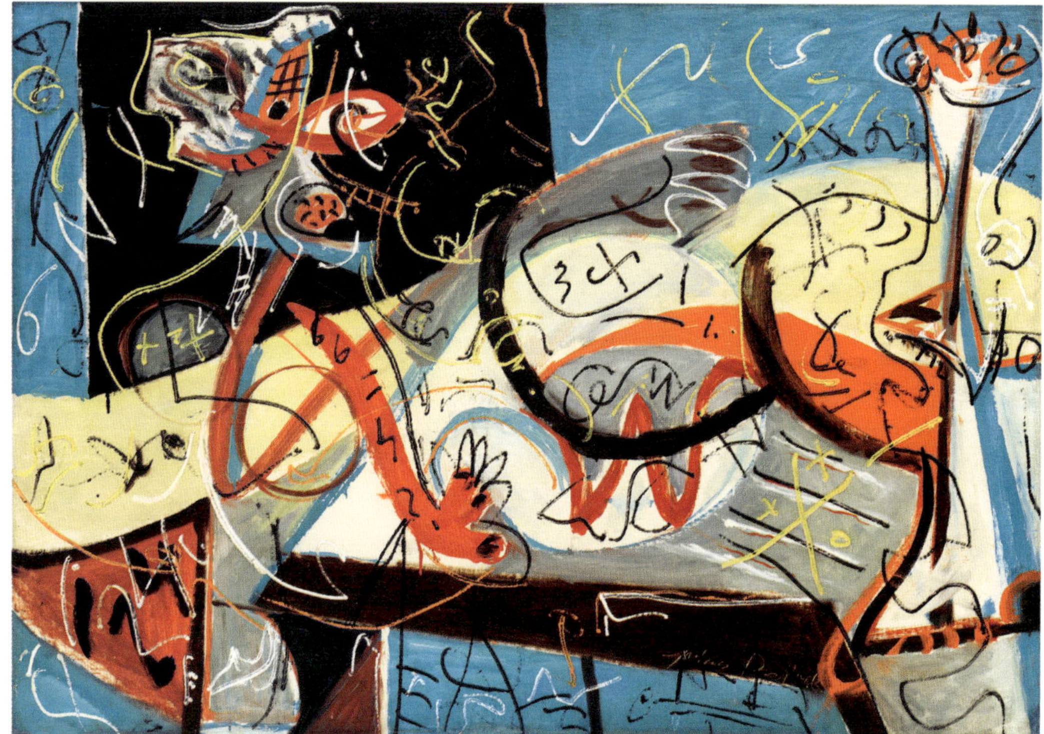

153

radical shift for him; one of his close friends and followers, Charmion von Wiegand, who worked in a Neoplastic manner, perplexed at seeing the new painting, asked, 'But what about the theories?' Mondrian smiled, and in his quiet way replied: 'Painting first, my dear, then theories.'[11]

Mondrian's colour – as well as its structure – quickly made itself felt in New York. Motherwell's painting *The Little Spanish Prison*[154] was done in 1941, not long after Mondrian's arrival, then reworked in 1944. Its irregular columns of yellow, set off by a red rectangle, intermixing with greyed whites, demonstrated early on the idiosyncratic uses that could be made of Mondrian's early, pristine geometry.

After Mondrian's death, Stuart Davis painted two critiques of the late artist, *For Internal Use Only* (1945)[155] and a smaller version, a kind of study, *G and W* (1944). This was a favourite practice of Davis, taking on the masters as he had taken on Matisse in 1917, and as he continued to do, in an ongoing study of Matisse, and then younger artists, Pollock and de Kooning among them. In 1944 he seems to have been inspired by the all-over colour of Matisse, now taken to even higher intensities, fused with the structural rigor of Mondrian, the grid now cast askew. Inside the grid, Davis inserts abstractions of Popeye and Wimpy from the comic strip that appeared in July 1944, thus introducing an American pop phenomenon inside the exalted, spiritually based spaces of Mondrian. Mondrian loved American culture, jazz and the pace of the city, but this was something else. Because we have tended to see Davis primarily as a precursor of Pop, a kind of historical curiosity, we have not understood his importance as an innovator of colour construction (and Cubism), where his real importance rests. The pure imagination of Davis's hues, their intensity, as in the yellows for example, are as high-keyed and unique as that of any colour painting we can find in the twentieth century up to this date. Interspersed as it is with infusions of other powerful hues, *For Internal Use Only* is a painting that functions in great degree on the sheer power of colour alone, and might well be considered an early example of colour-field painting.

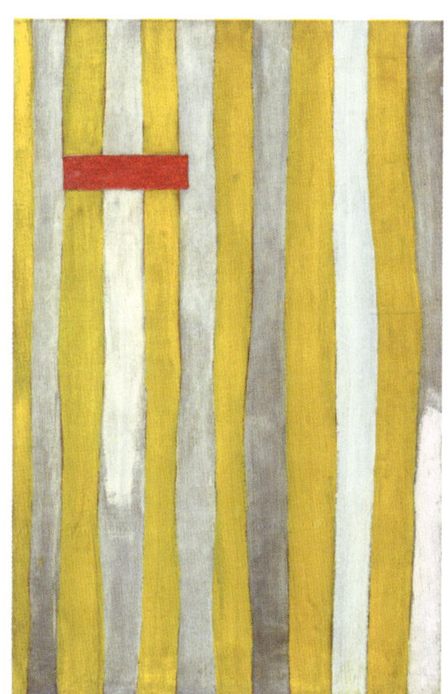

154

Modern Art in America

153 Jackson Pollock,
     *Stenographic Figure, c.*1942.
     Oil on linen, 101.6 × 142.2 cm
     (40 × 56 in). The Museum of
     Modern Art, New York

154 Robert Motherwell, *The Little
     Spanish Prison*, 1941–4.
     Oil on canvas, 69.2 × 43.5 cm
     (27¼ × 17⅛ in). The Museum
     of Modern Art, New York

155 Stuart Davis, *For Internal Use
     Only*, 1945. Oil on canvas,
     114.3 × 71.1 cm (45 × 28 in).
     Reynolda House, Museum
     of American Art, Winston-
     Salem, North Carolina

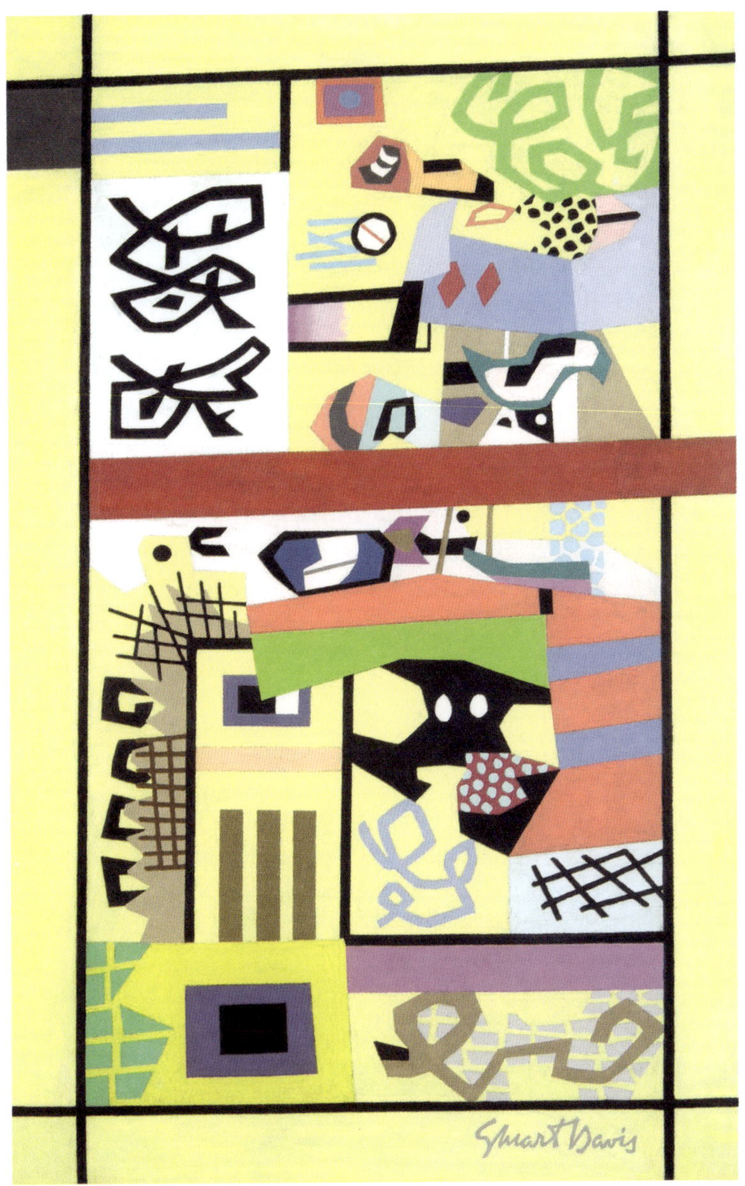

155

ABSTRACT EXPRESSIONISM: THE PRECURSORS

John Marin: A Proto-Abstract Expressionist

A famous and obvious early American artist whose work continued
after 1945 was Marin, who can be considered a kind of proto-Abstract
Expressionist. He was widely recognized as such and was celebrated
through countless awards, exhibitions and publications in the post-war
years, until his death in 1953. A poll conducted in February 1948 by *Look*
magazine among museum directors and artists declared Marin to be
America's 'Artist No.1'.[12] More critical acclaim came in December when
Clement Greenberg stated: 'If it is not beyond all doubt that he is the best
painter alive in America at this moment, he assuredly has to be taken into
account when we ask who is.'[13] If there were any lingering doubt about
Marin's standing, it was put to rest by Alfred H. Barr, Jr., director of MoMA,
who included Marin in the prestigious Venice Biennale of 1950, side by
side with Pollock, de Kooning and Gorky.

Marin had returned to Maine, close to the sea and rocks, the place he had always cherished. No artist since Homer had so powerfully captured the power of the sea. His works are in the tradition of Van Gogh in their surging pictorial energies. We think of Marin as the 'painter of Maine', but this should not be taken as a limit to the reach of his powers, or suggest that, as a recluse of sorts, he was unaware of the world of art around him.[14] He was open to new modes of expression and had responded to Mondrian, whom he deeply admired for his ability to build a painting like a boat. Indeed, we see Mondrian's grid in Marin's 1944 *Related to Hurricane*[157], a structural device that centres and holds in place the rocks and crashing seas. Here and later, Marin began to move to a more open surface, away from the density of his earlier oils, as if to open it to the Maine air and let the canvas breathe, in joyous appreciation of the water. He loved paint, its materiality and physical presence, but as he loosened up his surfaces he transformed the painting into liquid, transparent areas of paint that seem to embody the forces, not just the forms, of nature. His move away from reproduction included his use of colour, which became more and more arbitrary and intense – 'Colour is life', he said, and indeed we feel it in these late works.[15] His line became more open and energetic, even frenzied at points, in ways that both echoed and surely influenced the gestural artists. He reminded himself that he 'must go into the picture and live'.[16]

In *Sea Piece* (1951)[156], Marin found a new openness, away from his early dense surfaces and also away from the total density of Pollock and de Kooning in 1950; thus he should be seen as part of the movement towards clarity that set in just as Abstract Expressionism was reaching its peak of intensity. The surface is opened and defined by floating rectangles of yellow and blue, a clear homage to the purity of Mondrian. They also refer to the sun and sky, so much a part of American art in the nineteenth and twentieth centuries, pointing to a bucolic Maine day on the water, filled with peace (a pun intended in the title's 'Piece'?) and serenity, of being one with himself and the world.

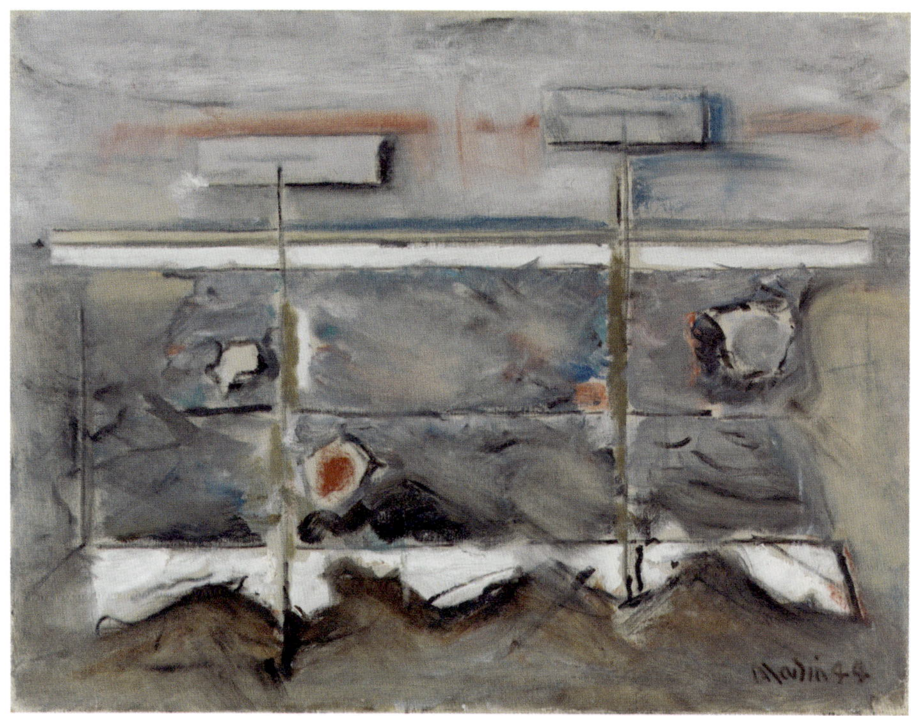

156

157

     Modern Art in America

156 John Marin, *Sea Piece*, 1951.
Oil on canvas, 55.9 × 71.1 cm
(22 × 28 in). Private collection

157 John Marin, *Related to
Hurricane*, 1944. Oil on canvas,
55.8 × 71.1 cm (22 × 28 in).
Private collection

158 Mark Rothko, *Multiform*,
1948. Oil on canvas,
155 × 118.7 cm (61 × 46¾ in).
National Gallery of
Australia, Canberra

159 John Marin, *New York Fantasy*,
c.1912. Watercolour on paper,
43.8 × 36.8 cm (17¼ × 14½ in).
Private collection

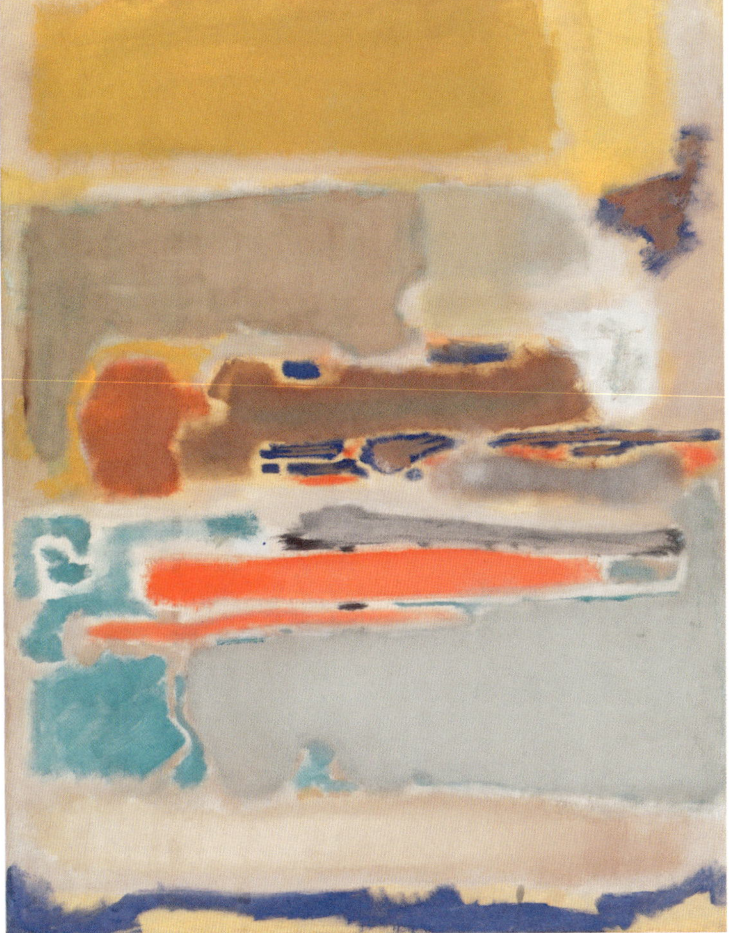

158

Marin's Influence on Mark Rothko

Marin's line is not his only connection to Abstract Expressionism. Indeed,
Mark Rothko (1903–1970) had looked carefully at Marin in the 1920s, as
evidenced in his wooded landscapes of the time that show Marin's touch
and pooling of pigment in his watercolours. The way Rothko pulls together
these liquid pools appears again in his *Multiform* (1948) [158], which also
have the feel of Marin's skies. The landscape references are clear here,
as they are in his zonal treatment of horizontal rectangles of floating
colours in his mature, post-1950 work. In fact, the Marin watercolour
New York Fantasy (c.1912) [159] could almost be mistaken for a Rothko, a
miniature Rothko at least, by means of the identical ways in which the
colour areas are stacked as abstract signs of foreground, middle ground,
distance and sky. Rothko was not alone in his landscape references – we
need think only of Pollock's titles, which included *Autumn Rhythm*, *Sounds
in the Grass*, *Accabonic Creek* and many other familiar references.

The range and sheer quality of Marin's art from beginning to end
make clear that Greenberg was not exaggerating in his praise. And the
critic had been pre-empted in 1922 by Paul Strand, who said that Marin
was 'one of the few whose work is the supreme proof of the actuality of an
American painter, of the possibility of American painting'.[17] No wonder,
then, that Greenberg could state in 1948 that the new talents of Pollock, de
Kooning and Gorky, as well as the consistently high standards set by Marin,
demonstrated that 'the main premises of western art have at last migrated
to the United States.'[18]

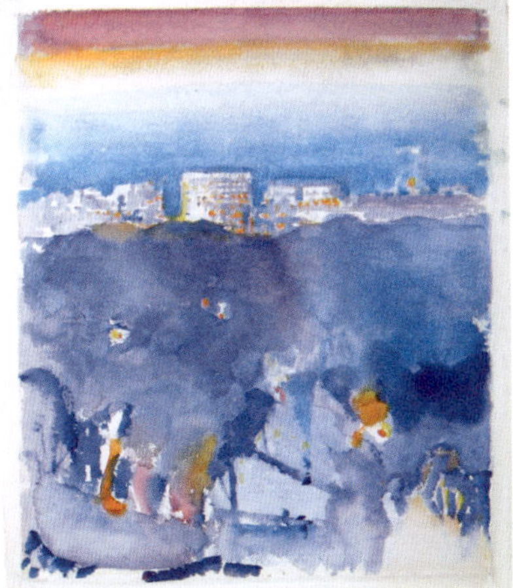

159

Dove, Maurer, Carles and Tack:
An Expressionist Tradition

We must also credit Arthur Dove, Alfred Maurer and Arthur B. Carles with pointing the way to Abstract Expressionism. They were more than precursors; they were actually early practitioners in an expressionist tradition that had deep roots in America and Europe, a tradition that became known in New York during the 1940s as Abstract Expressionism. They were earlier kindred spirits, working in the same direction, but without the large scale and size of their younger successors. They were father figures, Abstract Expressionists *avant la lettre*, but often, as Marin, they were fathers working alongside their sons and daughters. They understood and believed in continuity, and would have no use for Newman's idea that painting was starting from scratch. Like Fauvism and Cubism, and later Minimalism, Abstract Expressionism is a misleading name, for much of it is not really abstract, and much is not really expressionist, at least in the traditional sense of the word as applied to the German Expressionists. The best term and description is perhaps 'painterly' (*malerisch*), for it is the one thing that all the artists (except for Newman) had in common – brushed, broken surfaces, coloristic in the Venetian sense of *colore*.

Arthur Dove has often been seen as a forerunner of Abstract Expressionism, or even as the first Abstract Expressionist, for his biomorphic imagery, his painterly coloration and his exceptional linear tracing. As early as 1953, Robert Goldwater,[19] one of our most important scholars, cast him in this light, and subsequently equally well-known writers have sung his praises and extolled his role. Helen Harrison,[20] Frederick Wight, Alan Solomon, Barbara Haskell, Elizabeth Turner, Barbara Buhler Lynes and others, as well as countless artists, have written eloquently on Dove and his art in a virtually continuous dialogue that has not ceased.[21] Therefore we cannot say that Dove has been neglected in the least since his death; no earlier American modernist has been more in public view. But the specifics of these connections and his continuing influence, down to the present day, have not yet been examined in full detail.

Theodoros Stamos, Barnett Newman and William Baziotes certainly drew on Dove's organic nature forms, but he must be put into an even broader context. If we consider painting-collages such as *George Gershwin – 'Rhapsody in Blue', Part I* (1927)[160], composed while he listened to the music, we can identify close parallels with the automatic writing of the Surrealists and a rapid type of drawing that points to gestural abstraction, especially that of Pollock. This fast-paced 'writing', in which line takes on a generating force, is also at the heart of such key works as *Orange Grove in California, by Irving Berlin*, also 1927, and *Seagull Motif (Violet and Green)* (1928). All have the surging linear energy that we associate with the later work of Pollock. In addition, *Rhapsody in Blue* is so close to Newman's early pieces, such as *The Song of Orpheus* (1944–5)[161], that one feels Dove did it first. There is little if any distinction between the works. Further, Newman's *Genesis – The Break* and *Pagan Void* (both 1946)[162] are direct descendants of Dove's 'Sunrise' series of 1936–7. So, too, Newman's famous zip is clearly anticipated in several paintings by Georgia O'Keeffe, among them *Blue Line* (1919) and *Blue and Green Music* (1921); the configuration of his *Broken Obelisk* comes straight out of its spitting image in a Rudolph Bauer painting of 1934, *Blue Triangle*. So much for Newman's claim to 'have started all over'.

By the same token, Dove's sense of the land and space, as well as the crackling forces of natural phenomena like lightning and rain, as seen

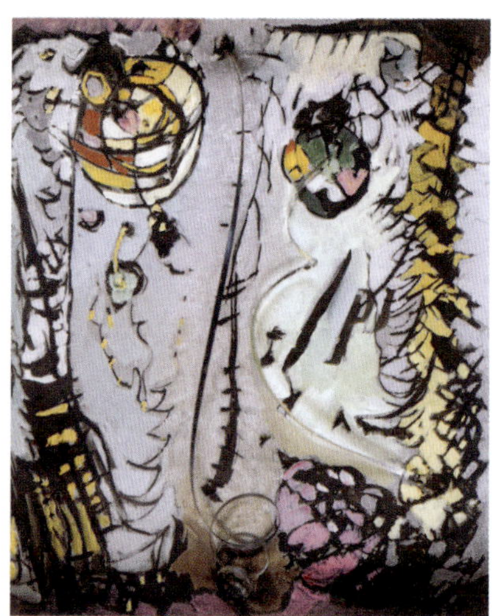

160

Modern Art in America

160 Arthur Dove, *George Gershwin – 'Rhapsody in Blue', Part I*, 1927. Oil and metallic paint with clock spring on aluminium support, 30 × 24.8 cm (11¾ × 9¾ in). Michael and Fiona Scharf Family Collection

161 Barnett Newman, *The Song of Orpheus*, 1944–5. Oil, oil crayon and wax crayon on paper, 50.8 × 37.8 cm (20 × 14⅞ in). The Metropolitan Museum of Art, New York

162 Barnett Newman, *Pagan Void*, 1946. Oil on canvas, 83.8 × 96.5 cm (33 × 38 in). National Gallery of Art, Washington, DC

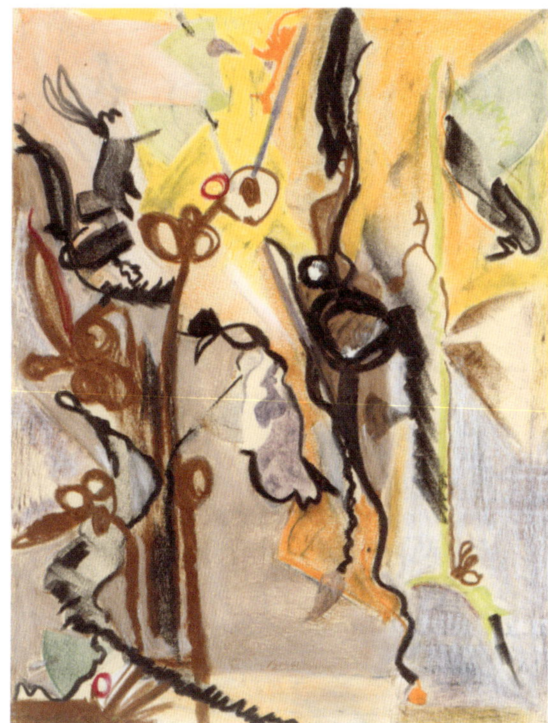

161

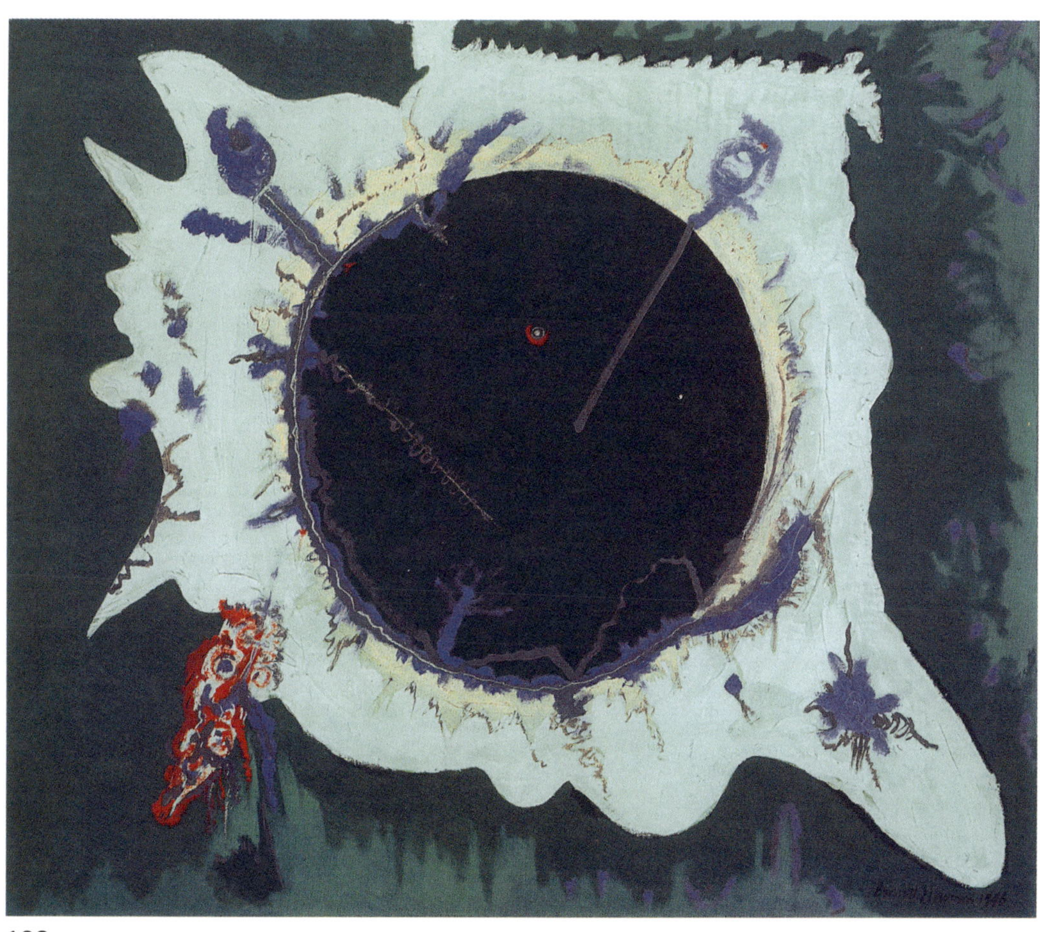

162

in his *Thunder Shower* (1940)[163] are a virtual prototype for later colour-field abstractions. Here the storm and lightning seem to explode across the surface, causing a virtual fissure in the earth. The shapes are organic, but with an edge, and the space is vast. The work looks back to nineteenth-century Luminists such as Albert Bierstadt and Martin Johnson Heade, while looking ahead to the crackling cuts of colour in Clyfford Still's paintings and then to the earth works of Walter De Maria, especially, of course, in his *Lightning Field* (1977), located in the otherworldly setting of west central New Mexico.

This similarity in approach to the wonders of nature suggests once again that there were more connections between Dove, his generation and the younger abstract artists that emerged after 1943. Dove worked in two modes, one organic and the other more stable and geometric, influenced by his contact with Mondrian and Constructivist art in the late 1930s and 1940s. His organic paintings flourished until the end of his life, as in *Dancing Willows* (c.1944)[164]. Based on the tree in his yard – he needed to go no further – the painting is a brilliant series of intersecting yellows, blues and greens, gradated as recommended by the nineteenth-century colour specialists, so that the hues – which could make the heart lift up, as one critic described Dove's colour[22] – like the leaves and the very movement of the tree itself, flow together in perfect accord. Indeed, the fusion of colours and planes reminds us of Morris Louis's floral paintings of 1960, such as *Point of Tranquillity*. In the later types of painting, Dove's colour could be deep, rich, evocative, adding to the aura of stillness and mystery in nature. Colours were reduced in number, a few hues forming single, independent planes, as he strove for what he called 'pure painting'.[23]

This culminated in Dove's last major work, done before his increasingly poor health fully caught up with him in 1945. The work, entitled *That Red One* (1944)[165], is almost a perfect painting, a sunrise viewed from his house on the harbour in Centerport, New York, on Long Island Sound, not far from the city itself. The painting is remarkable for its sure, frontal qualities, its directness and immediacy, composed with broad colour planes of the primaries: red, yellow, blue, with two or three gradated variants. As simple as can be, centred perfectly before us, balanced as we balance ourselves on this earth, without extraneous and unnecessary forms, all is taken to its fullest possibilities. Yet its effect is majestic, a last homage to the

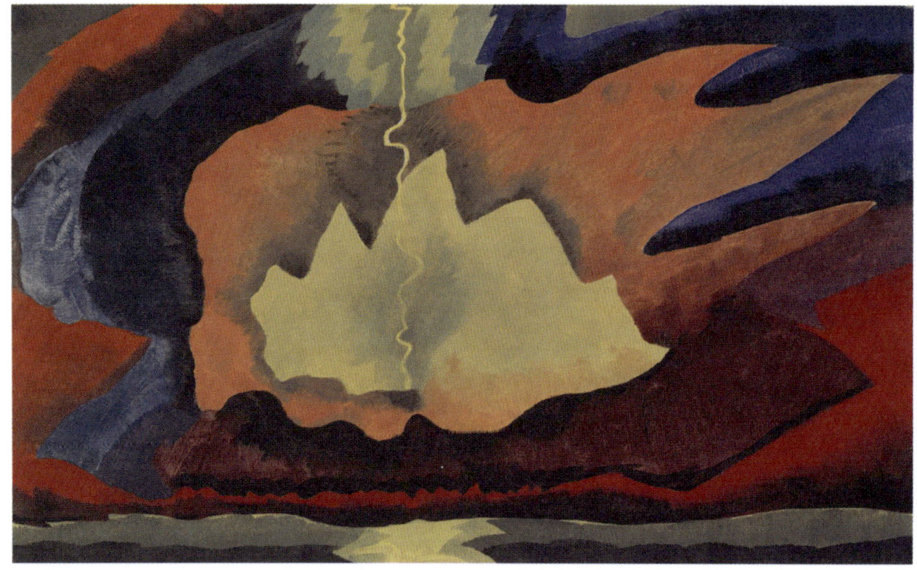

163

163   Arthur Dove, *Thunder Shower*, 1940. Oil and wax emulsion on canvas. 51.4 × 81.3 cm (20¼ × 32 in). Amon Carter Museum of American Art, Fort Worth

164   Arthur Dove, *Dancing Willows*, c.1944. Oil and wax on canvas, 68.6 × 91.1 cm (27 × 35⅞ in). Museum of Fine Arts, Boston

165   Arthur Dove, *That Red One*, 1944, Oil and wax on canvas, 68.6 × 91.4 cm (27 × 36 in). Museum of Fine Arts, Boston

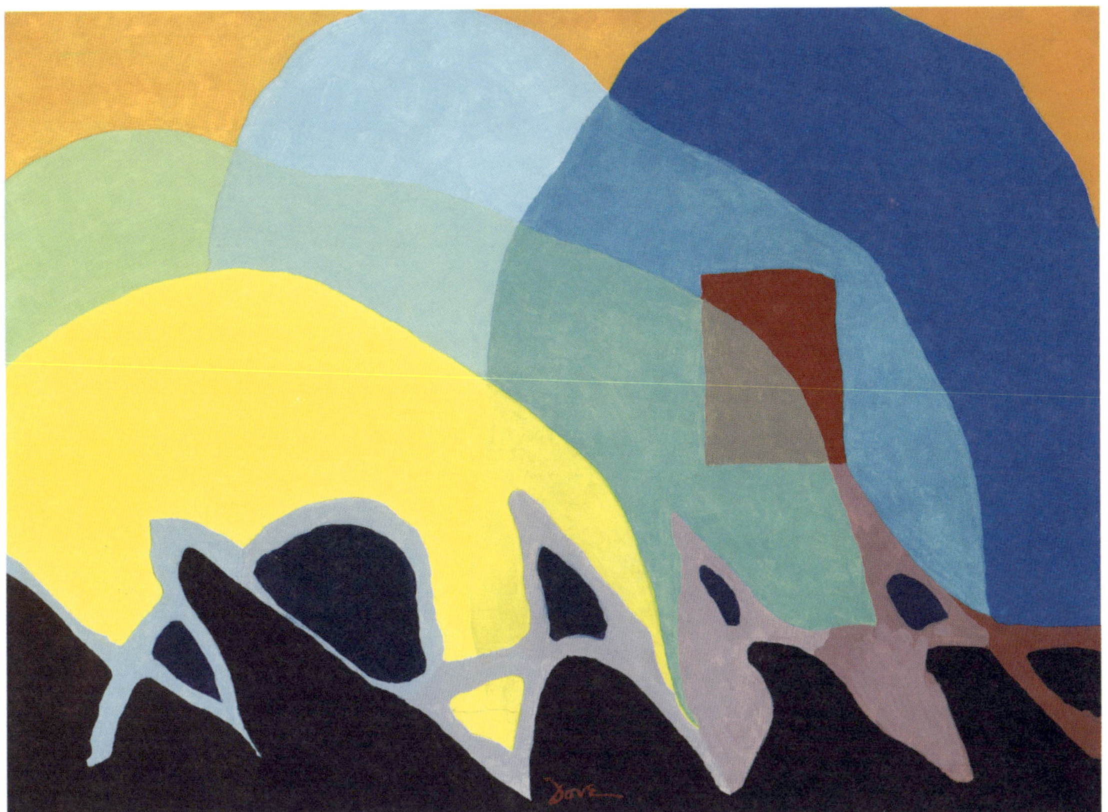

164

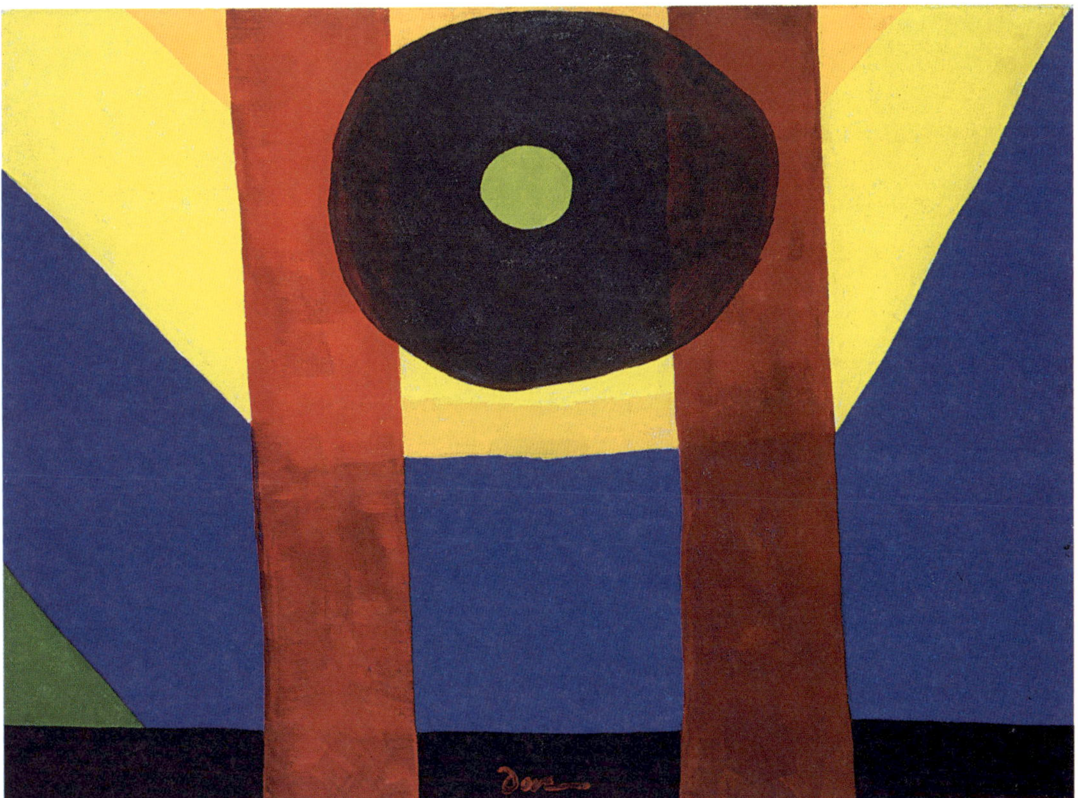

165

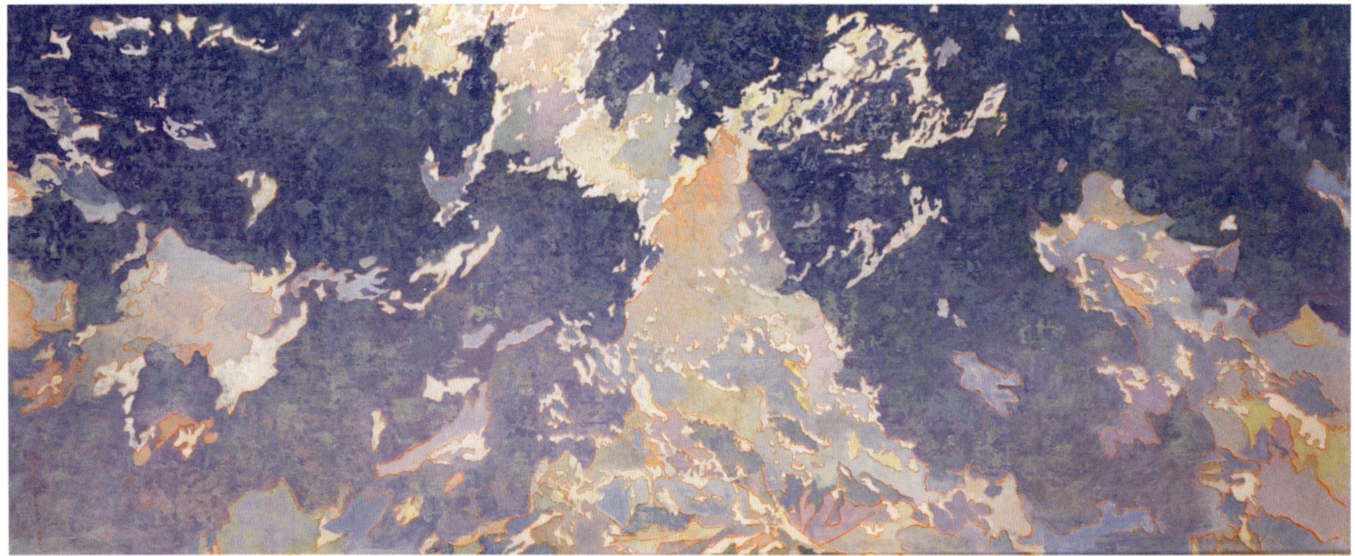

natural world that Dove loved, in the spirit of Van Gogh, who, like Dove, sought 'something of the eternal'.[24] It is a personal, American, original and unique adaptation of Mondrian and Constructivist art, the best the country produced in the early years of modernism, and should be considered as the equal of the early work of a younger generation of artists just then emerging.

Frank Stella also felt Dove's impact, for he was a great example of an authentic, honest, abstract painter. 'I loved Arthur Dove when I was young, and I still think he was a wonderful painter,' he said. 'I would like to be a successor … by following in that tradition.'[25] To this day, Dove and his circles of the universe reverberate in the work of contemporary artists such as Nancy Haynes (b.1947) and the German-born Tomma Abts (b.1967). In 1924, Paul Rosenfeld had characterized Dove's art as 'still rather more the prelude than the symphony', the art of a man not able 'to give the power in him the chance of manifesting itself in all its altitude'.[26] In the decades that followed, Dove more than answered the challenge, finishing at an 'altitude' not often approached by artists in their last years.

In 1950, in a preface to an exhibition of Alfred Maurer's work, Hans Hofmann wrote that Maurer was the forerunner of a 'true and great American tradition' that was then being carried on by the vanguard of modern artists.[27] Since Hofmann was really a member of the early modernist generation, it is not surprising that he understood the continuities between the older and younger artists. Greenberg, often considered to be staunchly disinclined to American modernism, also thought highly of Maurer, who he believed had enormous talent. He stated in 1950 that Maurer's early figure compositions were close to 'perfection', and that his later work (his still lifes, not the Cubist heads) was one of the few original contributions to American painting. At his best, in Greenberg's view, Maurer was 'more than a very good painter'.[28]

In 1993 Judith Zilczer, then the curator at the Hirshhorn Museum, underlined the close relation of Arthur B. Carles's *Composition* of c.1935–7 (page 165) to Abstract Expressionism by installing it as the lead painting in that group's section of works. It absolutely fitted and made perfect sense, since it and other works in this series were crucial in establishing a painterly, fluid abstraction that presaged Abstract Expressionism as we have defined it. Intense and powerful, they are filled with cross-currents and intersecting patterns of what seems the pure energy of nature itself.

166 Augustus Vincent Tack, *Time and Timelessness (The Spirit of Creation)*, 1943–4. Oil on canvas, 99.7 × 216.5 cm (39¼ × 85¼ in). The Phillips Collection, Washington, DC

167 Mark Tobey, *Broadway*, 1935–6. Tempera on Masonite, 66 × 48.9 cm (26 × 19¼ in). The Metropolitan Museum of Art, New York

Another older artist who should be considered when discussing the birth of Abstract Expressionism is Augustus Vincent Tack (1870–1949). He was of the previous generation, to be sure, but in 1944 he produced a large curtain for the auditorium at George Washington University[166], the culmination of his earlier work, that makes him worthy of a place as a proto-Abstract Expressionist along with Dove, Marin and Carles. Tack is one of America's most confusing – and intriguing – artists, a mix of the hack portraitist and the benighted cosmic visionary. For years he produced commissioned portraits of no interest for well-heeled clients while doing abstractions with distinct landscape origins that seem to explore a higher order in a celestial environment far beyond earthly realms. The shapes are organic, of golds and blues, rough-edged and cut from colour and space, wending through a series of canvases called *Dunes* (1935). Others clearly aspired to reach the heavens with titles like *Aspiration* (1931) or *Flight (Fugue)* (1930), early interpretations of the landscape from above, in a plane. In a letter to a critic, Tack wrote of his experience in the Canadian Rockies, of how in 'a valley...walled in by an amphitheatre of mountains as colossal as to seem an adequate setting for the Last Judgement, glacial lakes lay like jewels on the breast of the world'.[29] He nurtured old Symbolist values, but now tailored to the New World. Nature's patterns and processes were dear to him, as they were to Dove and O'Keeffe and later to Rothko and Still.

Pollock's Predecessors:
Hartley, Tobey, 'Grandma' Sobel

In the late 1930s and early 1940s, Marsden Hartley concluded his deep and rich career with rugged portraits, most notably a series of some twenty 'portraits' of mountains, interpretations of Mount Katahdin in north central Maine. They have been seen as actually being portraits of himself – large, looming, hulking – a mountain that is hard to approach, and can appear as if from nowhere like an apparition, and with many moods and looks. The works are done with an expressionist, painterly handling that sets the stage for the surface actions of the nascent Abstract Expressionist path. They follow his powerful Maine landscapes, in which the clouds are like rocks or mountains, and whose lively surfaces surely affected Pollock's work from the mid-1930s right through to his mature period.

The 'white writing'[167] of Mark Tobey (1890–1976) – formed by dense calligraphic signs, developed in the 1930s and continued well into the 1950s – was certainly a prototype for Pollock's poured paintings. Also of special interest in relation to Pollock's all-over approach is the work of Janet ('Grandma') Sobel (1894–1968). She had emigrated to the United States and had only taken up painting when she was forty-three, and yet produced a series of all-over paintings as early as 1944, as in for example *The Burning Bush*[168]. Greenberg and Pollock saw them when they were exhibited at Peggy Guggenheim's Art of This Century Gallery in 1944, and both were impressed. Greenberg said they were the first all-over paintings he had seen. To be sure, they belong to the history of Abstract Expressionism, yet because Sobel was an amateur and a woman, they have been largely discounted. Tony Smith, Pollock's best friend, meanwhile reported that Pollock was struck by the possibilities of Mondrian's *Apple Tree* series, seen in the Mondrian show at MoMA in 1945, in which the branches increasingly spread out over the surface to make a dense patterning of all-over line.[30]

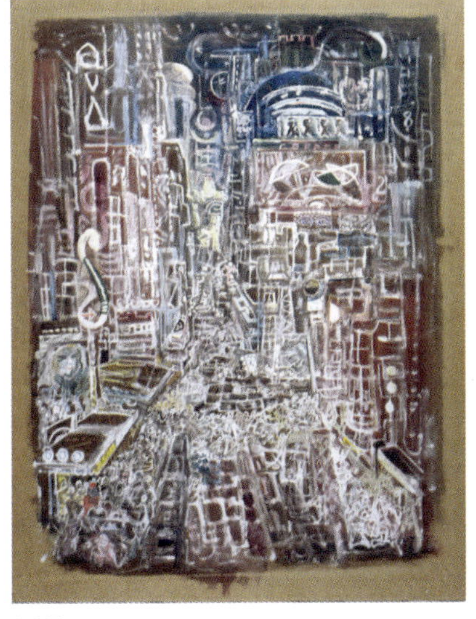

167

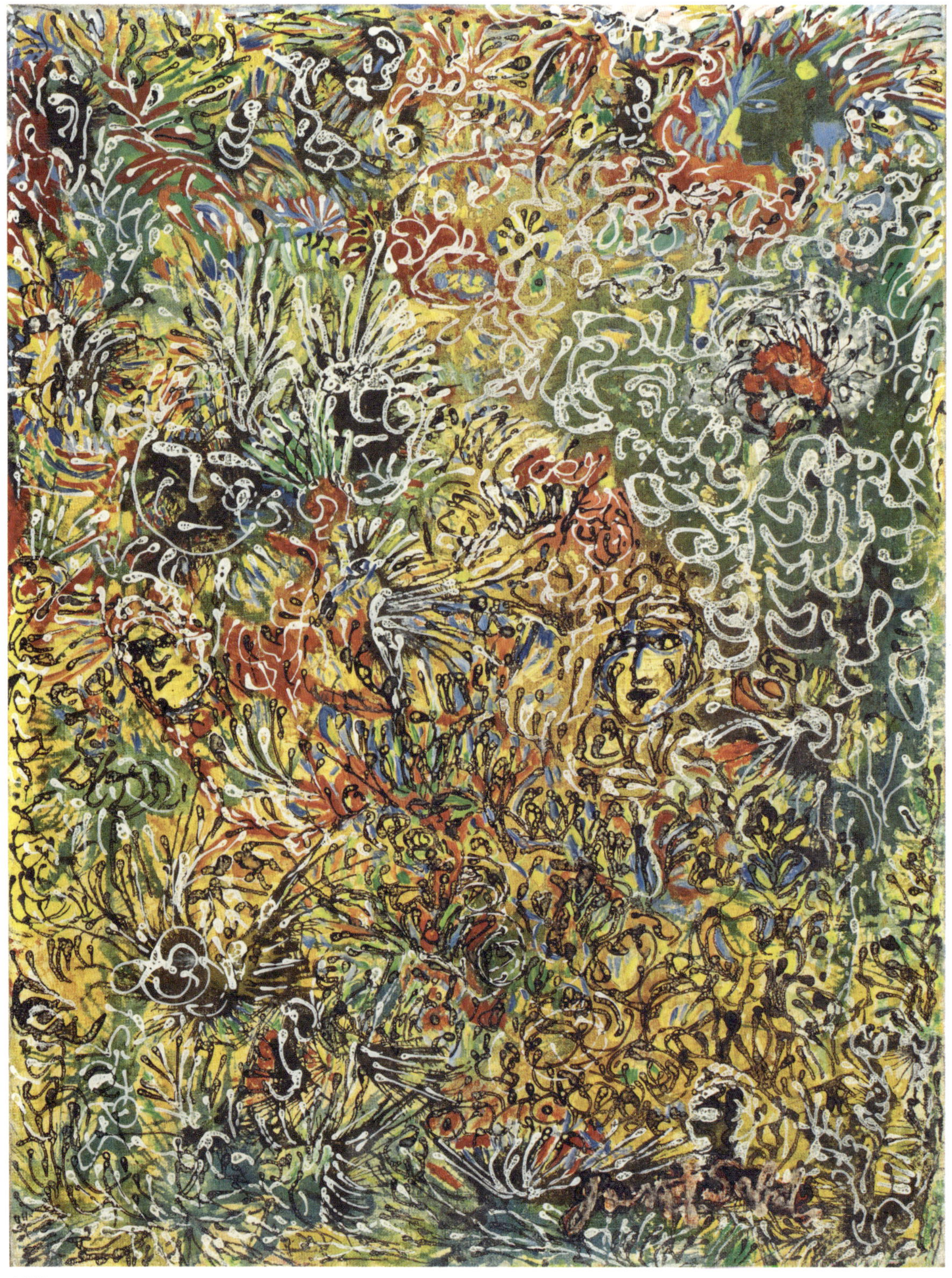

168

During the war years 1940–5, art did not stop for the duration; the period was filled with significant events in American art. Indeed, we can say that in these years, especially in 1943, a new generation of younger American artists – all born after 1900 – came together as a very loose group that we have come to call the Abstract Expressionists. In 1942, John Graham had organized an exhibition of French and American artists at the McMillen Gallery in New York, and had included Pollock and de Kooning, perhaps providing the first inkling of something new emerging, roughly as a group. The year 1943 is the key year – not 1945, which contained epic historical events, but not art-historical ones. As a matter of convenience, rather than from real thought, textbooks on this period have invariably been called *Art Since 1945*, or some variation thereof. The advent of the atom bomb in 1945 caused deep concern for the world, including for artists, but it was not the animating force of American art since then down to the present day, as has been suggested.[31] Art did not start anew as if it had never existed prior to this date, as Barnett Newman claimed, and nor was this group the only artists who practised art-making during and after the war. Newman, who was considered primarily a writer by the other artists, an advocate for their work, was typically trying to build a case and context for himself, almost alone, as the true creator of a new American art, perhaps due to the fact that when he first showed his work, in 1951, it was treated negatively. Only in the late 1950s did he gain respect as an artist, not from his peers but from a still younger generation, notably Donald Judd and Dan Flavin, who admired the clarity of his work.

The group was not short on egos. Mark Rothko, Adolph Gottlieb and Clyfford Still were also guilty of self-aggrandizing propaganda, pumping up their work as the new art in a post-war world. All played the Existentialist card of the time: lonely man pitted against the world, standing by himself, with no history, using his powers to make a new destiny. In this way they could disavow any influence from past or current art, American or European. It was instant destruction of past, older American art, with the young artists now the conquering heroes of the New American Painting, soon to be heralded as *The Triumph of American Painting*,[32] as if it had emerged from a dark, medieval past. Adding to this negation of the past, in 1946 Clement Greenberg wrote a strong attack on O'Keeffe and Alfred Stieglitz and his circle on earlier modernism as if to wipe out their memory in order to pay more attention to recent art.[33]

A New Post-War Internationalism

The young emerging artists wanted no part in the nationalistic American jingoism of Regionalist chauvinism, led by Thomas Craven and Thomas Hart Benton. With the end of the war, artists were determined to shed this cant, proclaiming themselves part of a drive towards an international endeavour, beyond the limiting confines of a single country. In her foreword to the 'Fourteen Americans' exhibition held in 1946 at MoMA, the curator Dorothy Miller went out of her way to state that in the show, 'The idiom is American but there is no hint of regionalism or chauvinistic tendency. On the contrary, there is a profound consciousness that the world of art is one world and that it contains the Orient no less than Europe and the Americas.'[34] In his statement for this exhibition, Motherwell made clear that 'modern art is related to the ideal of internationalism.' He was the best,

168 Janet Sobel, *The Burning Bush*, 1944. Oil on canvas, 76.2 × 55.9 cm (30 × 22 in). Los Angeles County Museum of Art

most intelligent writer of the group, with a far more balanced view than the self-serving Newman. 'Art is not national,' Motherwell said, 'to be merely an American or a French artist is to be nothing.'[35] Internationalism, he continued, cannot be willed, but arises instead from following 'the true nature of reality, by taking things as they are, whether native or foreign'.[36] With this insight, Motherwell concluded that 'nationalities become accidental appearances.'[37] But try as they might, artists – nor any other American – could not cast off their roots.

As we have seen, the dispersal across the United States of the pioneer modernists, as well as other crucial sources, such as the Mexican artists Orozco and Siqueiros and even classical Old Master art, never came to the critical fore in the search for a pedigree for the new art. That is not to discredit the art of the young, emerging group. They all (mostly) produced art of high quality and world importance, and there is no doubt that Pollock was one of the two foremost American artists, then and now. Nor is it to disclaim the roles of Picasso, Miró and Matisse in their formative years and after. It is to say that this is only part of the story, that they did indeed continue on the path of the artists who had come before them, who had paved the way for a modern, often abstracting art that set the stage for their emergence.

1943–4: Art of This Century

In 1942, as we have seen, John Graham organized an exhibition of French and American artists for the McMillen Gallery in New York. It was a landmark show, for it included Pollock and de Kooning, among others. It marked another fusion of French and American art, showing that the Americans could stand up to close scrutiny alongside the more veteran Europeans. Peggy Guggenheim took up the direction when she opened her gallery Art of This Century in the autumn of 1942, and until she closed it after the war it was a place of enormous influence and importance. In 1943, she gave shows to Pollock, Hofmann and Still, among others. We can fairly say that this was the epicentre, the grounding point of the new generation of talented artists who were now emerging and creating work with a depth that the country had never known before. It was part of the unleashing of an enormous torrent of talent in America both during and after the war that extended into all the arts.

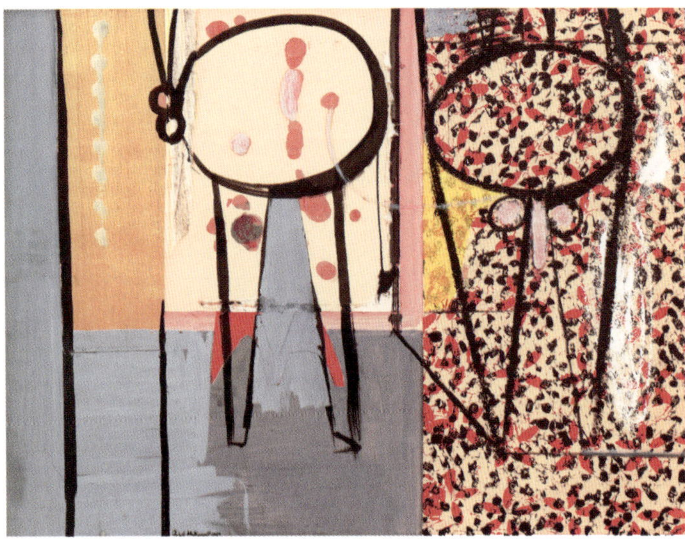

169

169 Robert Motherwell, *Pancho Villa, Dead and Alive*, 1943. Cut-and-pasted printed and painted papers, wood veneer, gouache, oil and ink on board, 71.7 × 91.1 cm (28¼ × 35⅞ in). The Museum of Modern Art, New York

170 Arshile Gorky, *The Liver is the Cock's Comb*, 1944. Oil on canvas, 191.1 × 254.9 cm (75¼ × 100⅜ in). Albright-Knox Art Gallery, Buffalo, New York

171 Hans Hofmann, *Fantasia*, 1943. Oil, duco and casein on plywood, 130.8 × 93 cm (51½ × 36⅝ in). University of California, Berkeley Art Museum and Pacific Film Archive

     Modern Art in America

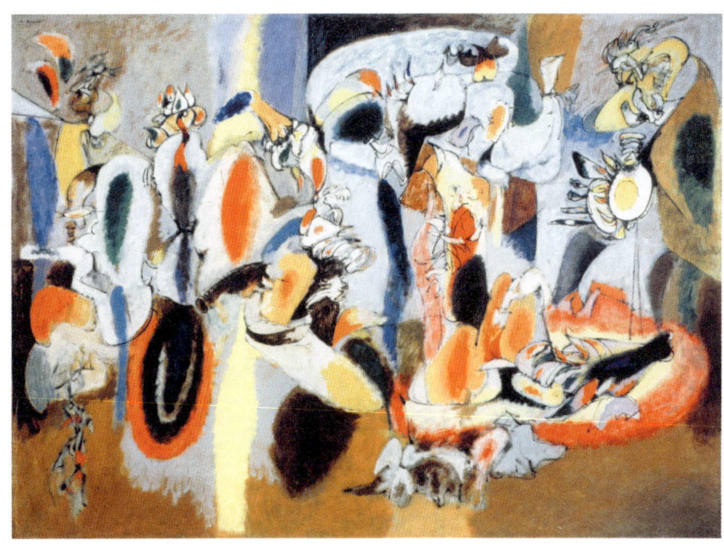

170

In the same year, John Marin and Arthur Dove attained an intensified focus, and in 1944 Georgia O'Keeffe brought a new expressive power to her work, both in the handling and the emotive range of her New Mexican scenes. Marsden Hartley had reached renewed peaks in his late work, then shown at the Paul Rosenberg Gallery. Also in 1943, Katherine Dreier lent Duchamp's *Bride Stripped Bare by her Bachelors, Even (The Large Glass)* (1915–23) to MoMA, where it had an immediate impact on Roberto Matta, as well as on Rothko, especially in his early surreal masterpiece *Slow Swirl by the Edge of the Sea* completed the next year (page 227).

Other art events in 1943 included the show 'Americans 1943: Realism and Magic Realism' at MoMA and the museum's purchase of Motherwell's *Pancho Villa, Dead and Alive*[169]; the arrival of Léger and other émigrés in New York; Joseph Hirshhorn's purchase of sixteen paintings from Arshile Gorky; the appearance of an article by Robert Coates in *The New Yorker* later in 1946, in which he singled out Hofmann for praise and dubbed the art 'Abstract Expressionist'.[38] New talent was appearing, including new curators and writers such as James Thrall Soby and James Johnson Sweeney, who added much-needed critical firepower.

But most importantly, in 1943 and into 1944, art itself came together in a new depth of talent, and that art provides the most important documents and criticism of all. Thomas Hess, a champion of the Abstract Expressionists at that time, commented that 'Newman, Gottlieb, Rothko and Still each thought (and thinks) himself the greatest painter in the world. That one might owe a debt to another becomes not a matter of simple ordinary fact, but a major issue of debate – like a trial for high treason. They made a tactical alliance, not a team, nor a group style, nor even a tendency.'[39] This warns us about how we should approach the rhetoric. But in fact there were a few tendencies that came together; mostly they shared a common painterly quality to their brushwork, an opposite to the hard edges of Mondrian or the Precisionists. Some reached new heights of accomplishment and imagination. Pollock's *Mural* for Peggy Guggenheim of 1943[172] presages all the characteristics of his mature style.[40] Gorky in *Pirate I* and *II* of 1943 achieved a new looseness and openness of touch common to the group, and the next year, 1944, brought his masterpiece, *The Liver is the Cock's Comb*[170]. Motherwell's *Pancho Villa, Dead and Alive* was quickly recognized as a breakthrough piece. Hofmann reached a degree of abstraction in paintings such as *Fantasia*[171], including an all-over dripping that allied him with this group. At the same time, Rothko, Gottlieb

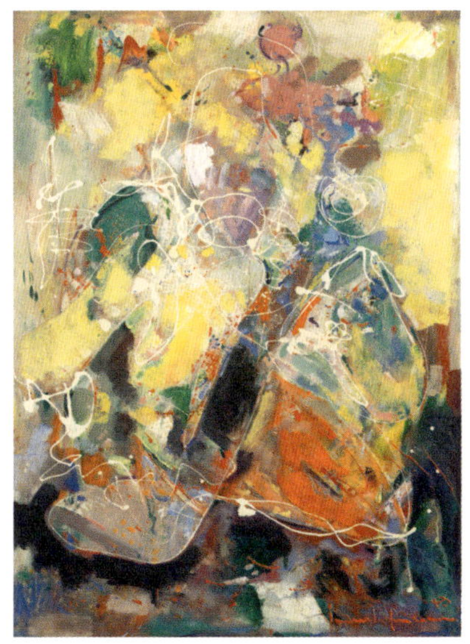

171

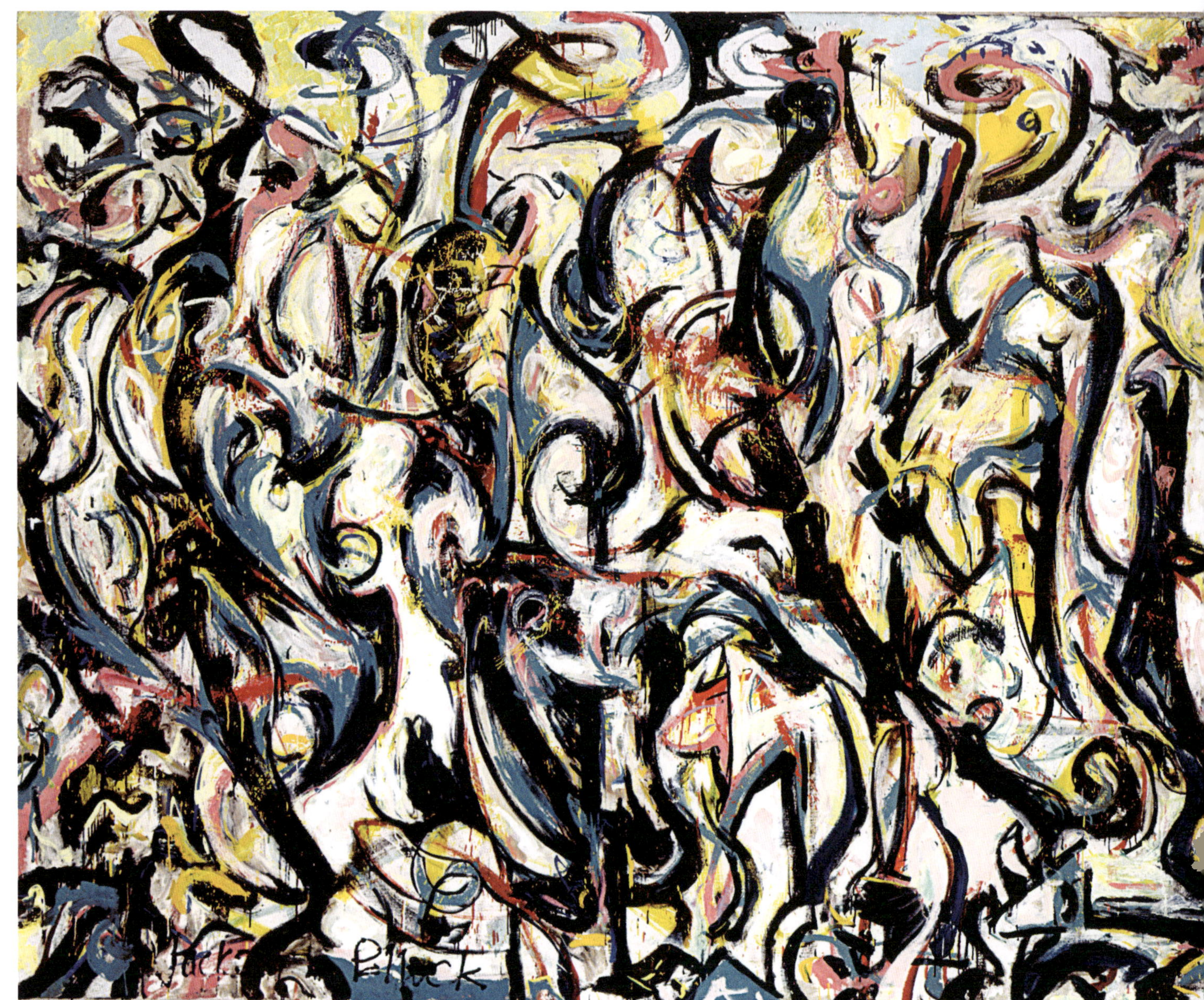

172

Jackson Pollock, *Mural*, 1943.
Oil on canvas, 247 × 605 cm
(97¼ × 238 in).
The University of Iowa
Museum of Art, Iowa City

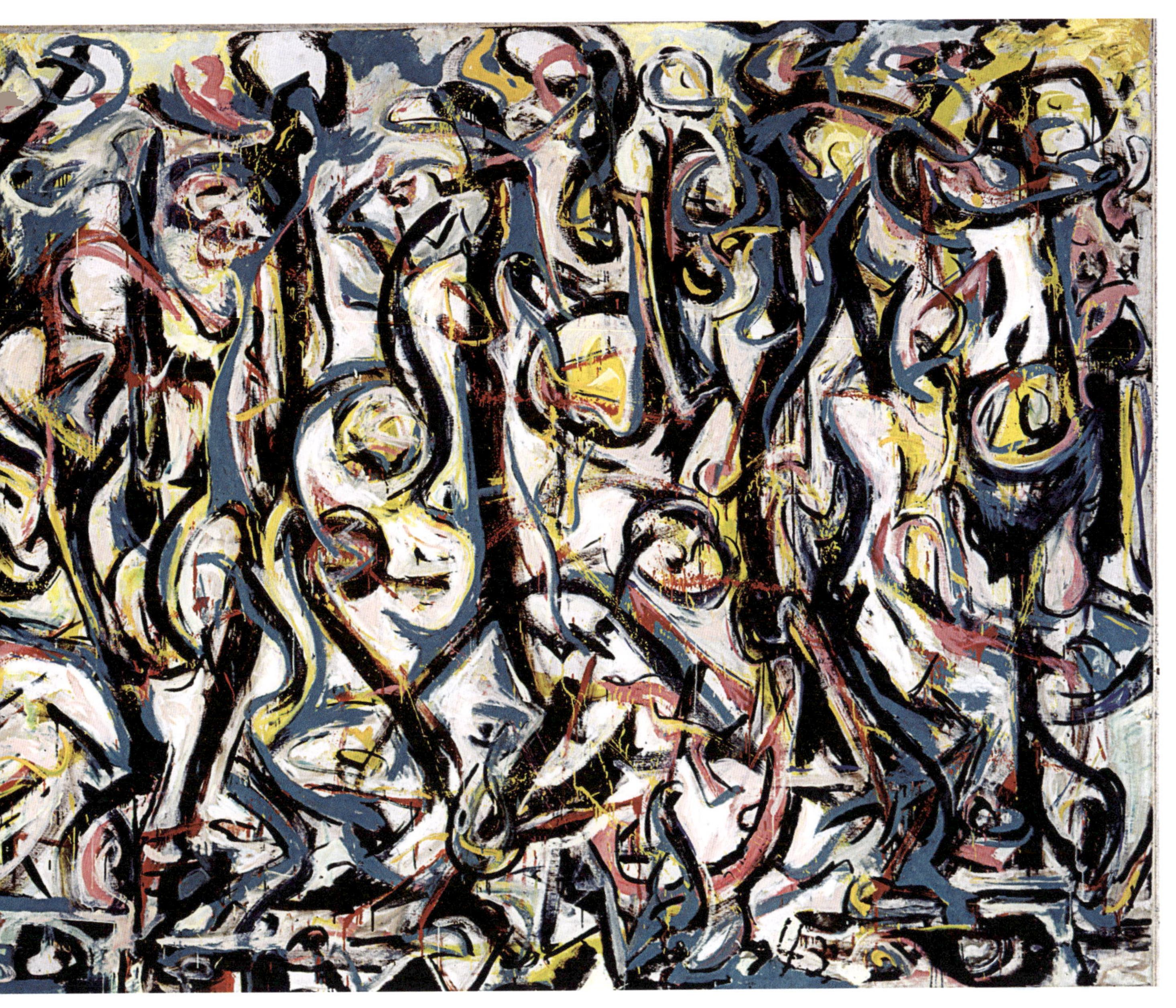

and Avery all continued apace. But so did other Americans, such as Davis and Marin, who must be considered part of the history at this time if we are to fulfil our goal of a more complete and inclusive account.

Colour in Abstract Expressionism: Pollock, de Kooning and Gorky

The gestural artists of the budding Abstract Expressionism movement – Pollock, de Kooning and Gorky especially – are not generally considered colourists. But on the contrary, a use of colour of real interest and originality in the younger generation begins in the late 1930s, in de Kooning's series of portraits of men, seemingly in distress, refugees from the Depression, lost and adrift in an indeterminate environment. They seem a kind of nod to the Social Realist art then current in America, seen in the figuration of Raphael Soyer, Isabel Bishop and others, but now made more modern. Their coloration is notable, a mix of muted reds and dull greys that suggest the murals from Boscoreale that de Kooning knew well from his frequent trips to the Metropolitan Museum of Art. The portraits make us feel seem as if we are actually looking into the past to discover these figures.

They were but a prelude to de Kooning's coloration in his series of women from c.1940 to 1945. The *Women* series was always his preoccupation, its subjects seeming at once like Broadway floozies and characters in ancient myths, a modern and personal interpretation of the Surrealist *personage* that was then occupying many artists of the emerging generation. The acid yellows, greens and reds are unique in American painting, as if de Kooning was seeking his own interpretation of the high coloration of Matisse and, closer to home, of Stuart Davis. In *Pink Angels* (c.1945)[174], based on Titian's *Diana and Actaeon* (1559), de Kooning reached a beautiful fullness of oranges and yellows that surely suggests Matisse, and might actually be counted as among his first forays into a type of colour painting. In works such as *Gansevoort Street* (c.1949)[173], an intense red screams out at us, a mark of the passions and human actions that defined the intensity of city life. De Kooning's art demonstrates the fact that colour was sometimes as important to the gestural branch of Abstract Expressionism as for the colour-field artists.

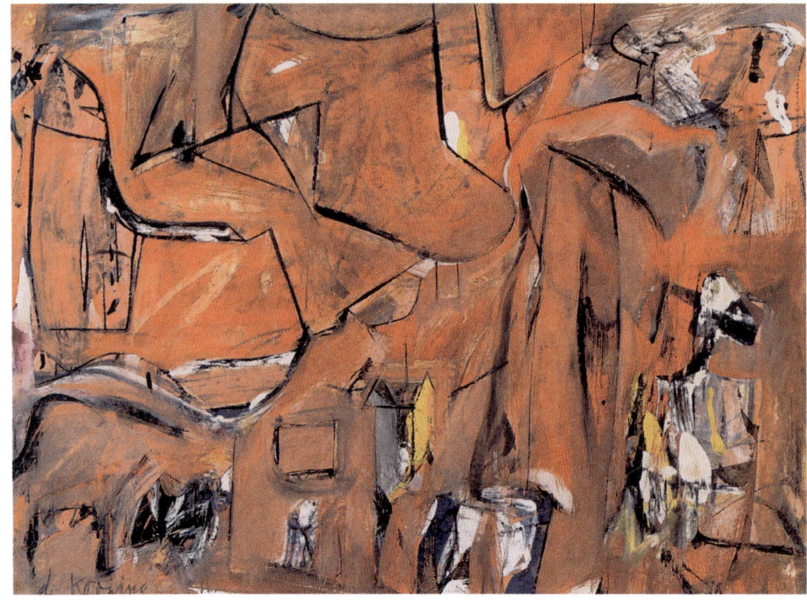

173

173 Willem de Kooning,
Gansevoort Street, c.1949.
Oil on paper mounted on board,
76.2 × 101.6 cm (30 × 40 in).
Collection of Harry W. and
Mary Margaret Anderson

174 Willem de Kooning,
Pink Angels, c.1945.
Oil and charcoal on canvas,
132.1 × 101.6 cm (52 × 40 in).
Frederick R. Weisman Art
Foundation, Los Angeles

                    Modern Art in America

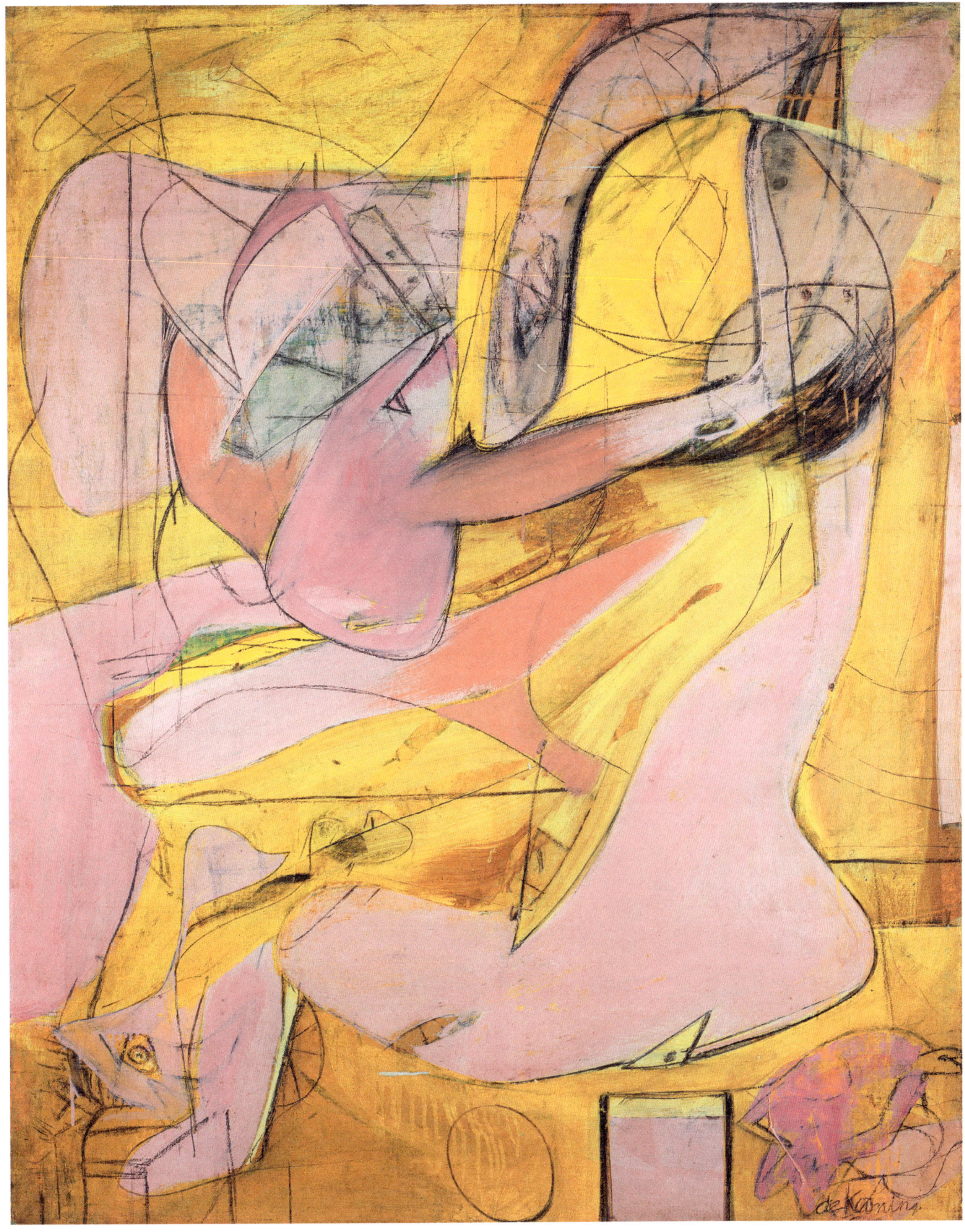

174

Arshile Gorky often reached great heights of colour effectiveness. We first notice this in his *Waterfall* (1943–4), with its flowing greens that seem to embody the columns of water near his house in Connecticut. His first peak of high colour came in his brilliant painting of 1944, *Water of the Flowery Mill* [175], filled with glowing reds, oranges and yellows that animate and illuminate the lush foliage near the mill, also not far from his Connecticut home, at a time when he was filled with the joy of life and family. Gorky surely had in mind a painting that could challenge Kandinsky's fluid coloration and biomorphism, such as that in *Improvisation 27 (Garden of Love II)* (1912) (page 75), owned by Alfred Stieglitz in New York. However, when one tragedy after another befell him, his mood changed dramatically, as one can see in the dry, airless reds suffusing the picture *Agony* of 1947 [176], believed by some to be a prelude to his suicide of the next year. These paintings tell us how colour can seem to embody feelings, emotions and states of mind, for there is no mistaking the moods that they clearly bring forth.

Jackson Pollock's colour is primarily as colour surface, as material in and of the paint itself, applied directly in the all-over paintings of 1947 and after. Donald Judd, writing later, understood how important Pollock's colour was, that the paint itself is the colour, standing sometimes as part of a maze, at other times as independent line and shapes. He emphasized its particularity, its singularity and physical presence. [41] We see a strong, rich mix of reds, blacks and yellows coming forth in the pivotal *She Wolf* (1943), an early but effective step in the maturation of his art. Like all great artists, Pollock could achieve many different types of painting, works that often pointed to other artists. His colour increased in intensity after his experience of Mondrian, whom we know he admired and respected. By 1945-46, his interest in colour was evident in works such as *The Key*, where he incorporated the brightness and openness of colour used by Matisse, who was enjoying a resurgence of interest among younger artists as his

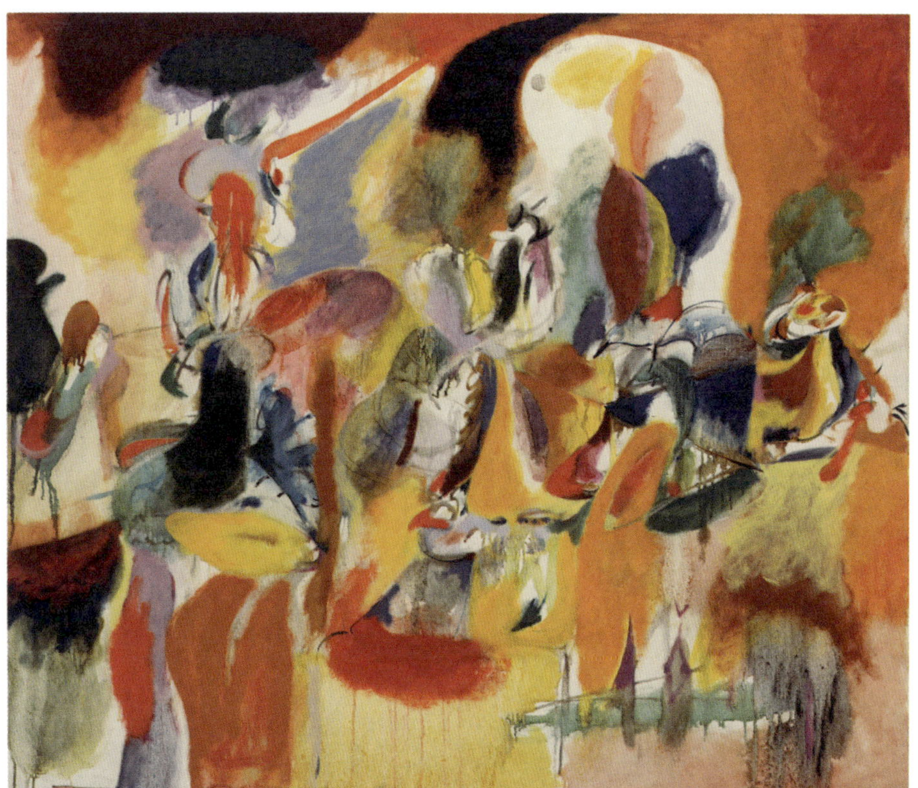

175

175 Arshile Gorky,
Water of the Flowery Mill,
1944. Oil on canvas,
107.3 × 123.8 cm
(42¼ × 48¾ in).
The Metropolitan Museum
of Art, New York

176 Arshile Gorky, *Agony*,
1947. Oil on canvas,
101.6 × 128.3 cm (40 × 50½ in).
The Museum of Modern Art,
New York

     Modern Art in America

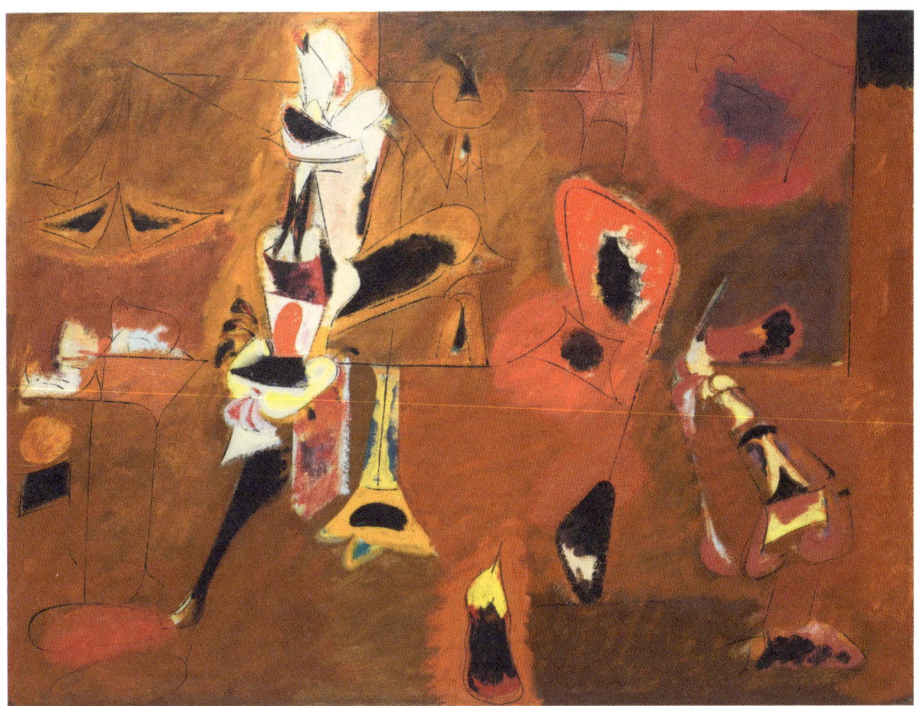

176

brilliant late paintings and cut-outs became known in the United States. Here, the reds even suggest *The Red Studio*, where it could have been seen by De Kooning, Gorky and possibly Pollock at the Bignou Gallery in New York between 1942 and 1949. The key in the title – seen at the upper right corner – may mark a turn in Pollock's life and art, for it could well be the key to his new house in Springs, New York, on the eastern end of Long Island. In his works of 1946, *Shimmering Substance*[177] and *Sounds in the Grass*, Pollock became almost an Impressionist artist, his work filled with a light and sun and air that recall Renoir and Bonnard, no doubt a result of his new relation to nature and the glorious landscape around him, where he was clearly affected by the light, the water, even the tall grasses and the marshes that led from his house down to the edge of Accabonac Harbor. Here, Pollock was anything but overwhelmed by the atom bomb. In the mid-1940s, people in the eastern United States were more scared of polio than of the bomb; by the early 1950s, they were more worried about Korea and McCarthyism and the Senator's witch-hunt for the 'Commies'.

Pollock often depicted the mood, the weather, the sky and the wind of the East End, so special for its particular light, which seems to be in constant flux. In *Phosphorescence* (1947)[178], he captured a natural phenomenon, the strands of phosphorescence that could sometimes drift over the wetlands behind his house and across Accabonic Creek. This same phenomenon could be seen in the water at night as he waded or swam, and Pollock had learned the trick of creating phosphorescent effects by passing his hand over wet sand.[42] He also captures what is the signature colour of the eastern island – grey – the deep greys of the ocean and bays, water and sky and light, seeming as one, and that can turn to fog or dark skies. In turn, the dense grey is punctuated by streaks and hits of colour, as we see in the painting in small areas of red, blue and yellow. So dense is the colour and paint that we are in the presence of something that can be called a field of colour,[43] a form of colour-field painting, from an artist not usually associated with colour at all, certainly not colour-field painting in the sense of Rothko, Kenneth Noland and Morris Louis.

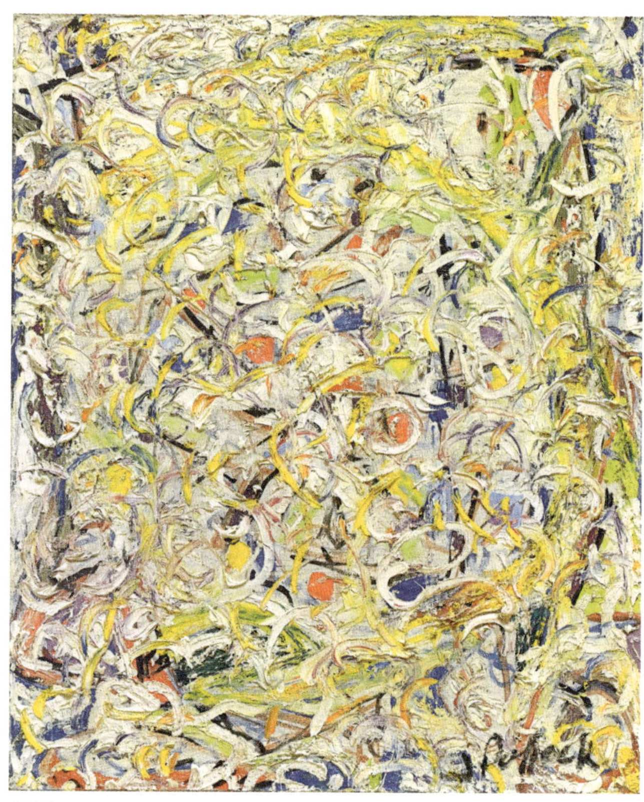

177

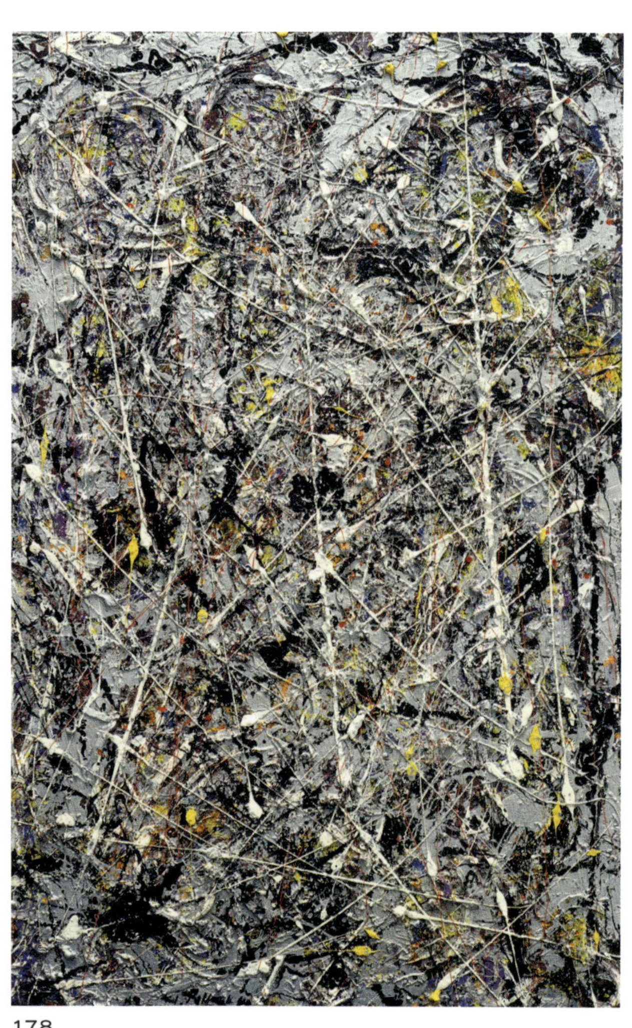

178

177 Jackson Pollock, *Shimmering Substance*, from the 'Sounds in the Grass' series, 1946. Oil on canvas, 76.3 × 61.6 cm (30⅛ × 24¼ in). The Museum of Modern Art, New York

178 Jackson Pollock, *Phosphorescence*, 1947. Oil, enamel and aluminium paint on canvas, 111.76 × 71.12 cm (44 × 28 in). Addison Gallery of American Art, Phillips Academy, Andover

179 Jackson Pollock, *Number 1, 1950 (Lavender Mist)*, 1950. Oil, enamel and aluminium paint on canvas, 221 × 299.7 cm (87 × 118 in). National Gallery of Art, Washington, DC

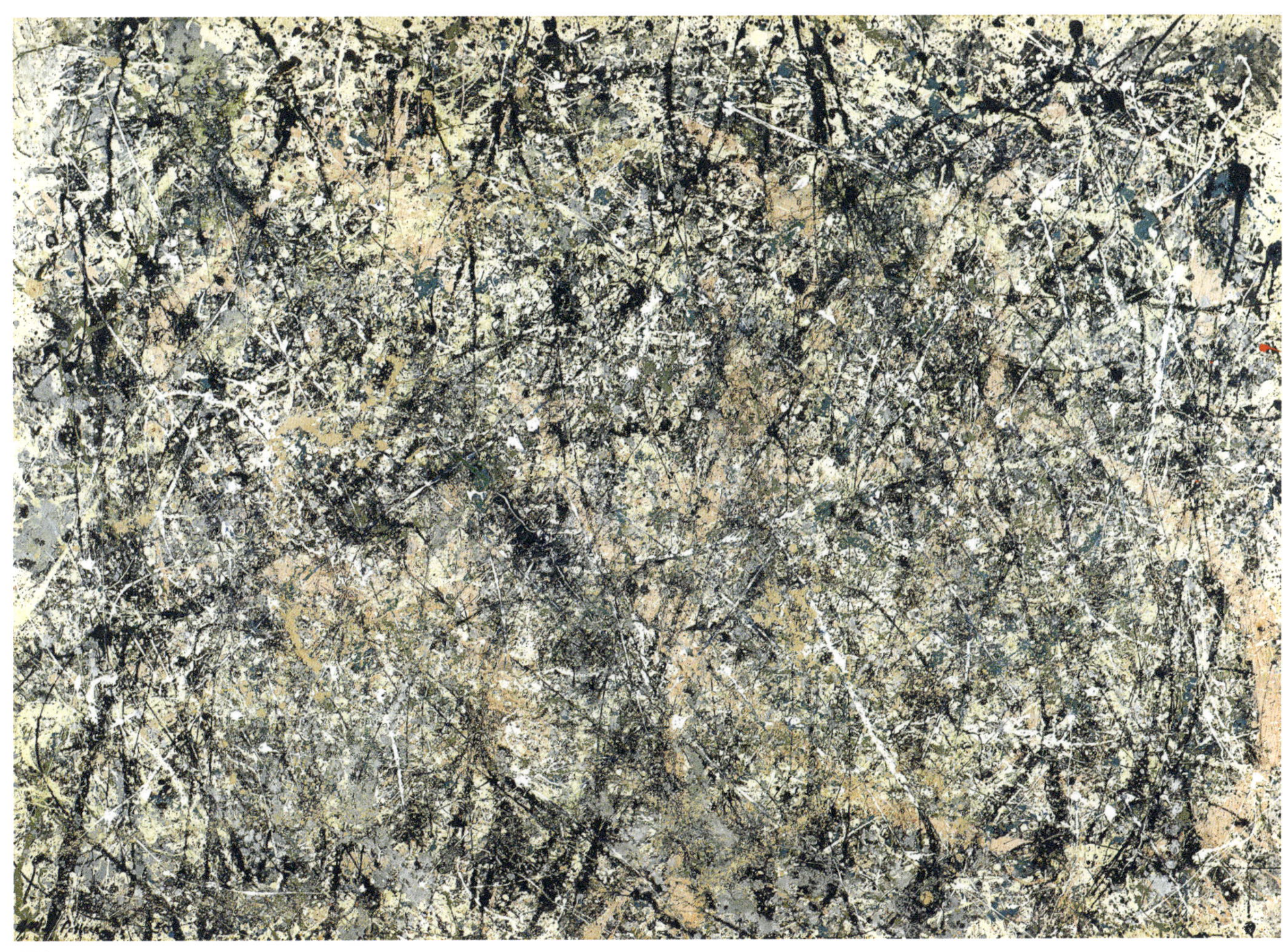

179

The greys are transformed into an intense silver because of the use of an aluminium paint that comprises most of the surface, a paint first used in American art by Arthur Dove some twenty years earlier, but not seen in such quantity again until Frank Stella in 1960. The streaks of white also suggest frost, or sleet, and recall Dove's great painting *Rain or Snow* (1943) [180], which in turn suggests the lines of rain in Van Gogh's painting of that title of 1889. We feel the sun emerging from the grey sky, just as we do in Winslow Homer's *Eight Bells* (1886), truly the starting point of what we might call the abstract seascape in American art. Indeed, the deep banks of clouds over the churning seas in Homer's – and John Marin's – paintings point directly to the dense surface of Pollock's grey painting.

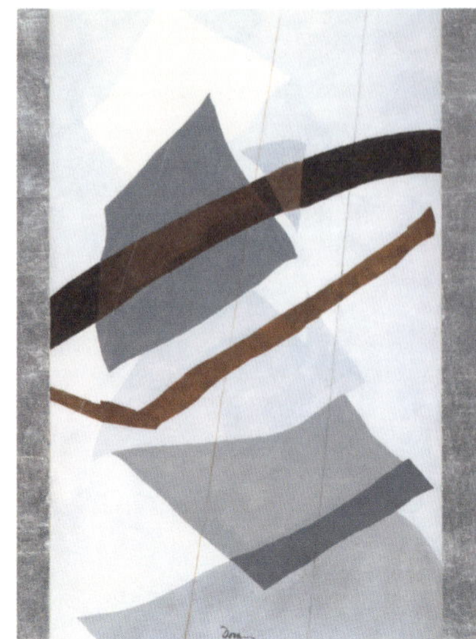
180

Phosphorescence is a brilliant painting and was described by Clement Greenberg as an 'overpowering surface … stalagmited with metallic paint [that] will in the future blossom and swell into a superior magnificence; for the present it is almost too dazzling to be looked at inside'.[44] Its brilliance is such that it rivals nature itself (can this be taken as another meaning of Pollock's comment to Hofmann that 'I am nature'?).[45] This is convincing evidence that Pollock's works, after 1945 at least, were often landscapes, as were those of many of his Abstract Expressionist colleagues, including Hofmann, de Kooning and Gottlieb, even Rothko and Still, as well as the sculptors David Smith, Herbert Ferber and David Hare. Among the pioneers, this would also include Dove and Marin, whose late work fuses with that of the younger generation by 1945. It has frequently been claimed that Abstract Expressionist art had gone beyond the natural landscape, but this assertion does not hold up when carefully examined. It was no accident that Pollock's show at the Parsons Gallery in New York in 1948 took the theme of the four elements, air, fire, earth and water, the very elements embodied in his painterly surfaces.

Mood, feel, even the taste of an early spring day, with its first softness and warmth, are palpable in *Number 1, 1950 (Lavender Mist)* (1950) [179], a mural-sized canvas that recalls the fragrance of rococo painting, as in a Watteau, for example. In 1953, in his much-discussed late masterpiece *Blue Poles*, one of his large-scale paintings, Pollock's density of surface and depth of hue, a spectacular experience to confront, become a large mass of colour, a slab of pure pigment that Richard Serra described as a '*wall* of colour',[46] perhaps making it one source for the sculptor's massive walls of steel.

COLOUR-FIELD PAINTING

Hans Hofmann: Controlled Explosions of Colour

Thus, in a full account of colour-field painting – painting literally as a field of colour – we can include Pollock and, we will remember, Mondrian in his *Boogie Woogie* paintings of 1942–4. By 1944, Hans Hofmann moved to a more abstract type of work. In paintings such as *Shapes in Black* (1944) [181], we see the controlled explosions of colour, as his art has so often been described. It seems to be a kind of galactic Fourth of July fireworks display, or a depiction of his own universe expanding into the dark reaches of multiple galaxies, looking into and beyond Van Gogh's *Starry Night* (page 64), those intense motor-impulse swirls to which Pollock's all-over patterning can also be traced back. We may even detect a rough circular shape, with spokes, suggesting the wheel of a chariot as it races across the fiery sky as we interpret the intense reds at the upper left. Hofmann's sense of the cosmos relates to that of other early American

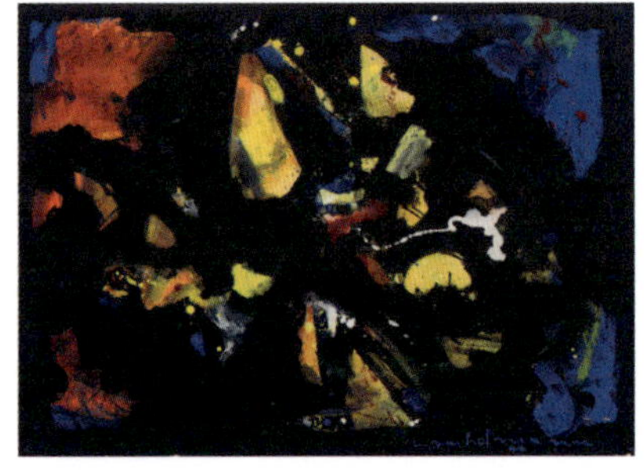
181

     Modern Art in America

180 Arthur Dove, *Rain or Snow*, 1943. Oil and wax emulsion on canvas, 88.9 × 63.5 cm (35 × 25 in). The Phillips Collection, Washington, DC

181 Hans Hofmann, *Shapes in Black*, 1944. Oil on panel, 77.5 × 100.4 cm (30½ × 39½ in). Private collection

182 Hans Hofmann, *Exaltment*, 1947. Oil on canvas, 151.8 × 121.3 cm (59¾ × 47¾ in). Addison Gallery of American Art, Phillips Academy, Andover

modernists. This point in his art coincides with the moment when Gorky, Pollock, de Kooning and others were moving into a new type of painterly abstraction that defined the emergence of Abstract Expressionism. We may also note that Hofmann's use of black coincides with the start of an extensive run of black and white undertaken by artists such as Motherwell, Kline, Reinhardt, Pollock, de Kooning, Davis and then by Frank Stella in the 1950s. He may have been a late bloomer, but he was far ahead in other respects, making his relation to Abstract Expressionism all the more puzzling.

In 1947, in paintings such as *Exaltment* [182], Hofmann became a virtual colour-field artist. For here, the large open areas and planes of strong red and yellow, forming an abstract version of one of his earlier table paintings, cover much of the surface. The painting is emotive and intuitive, yet we can see that the old principles of gradation and the harmony of analogous and contrasting colours are at work, now in a modern kind of art. Two of the primaries, red and yellow, are closely gradated, then contrasted with variants of blue, the third primary. These variants are a light blue, then a dark purple, all set off by a discordant hue, green, a secondary colour. Together they form a vibrant colour chord, in effect adding to Hofmann's body of what he called 'symphonic painting'.[47] His legacy was continued in Stella's work with baroque scrolls done after 1968.

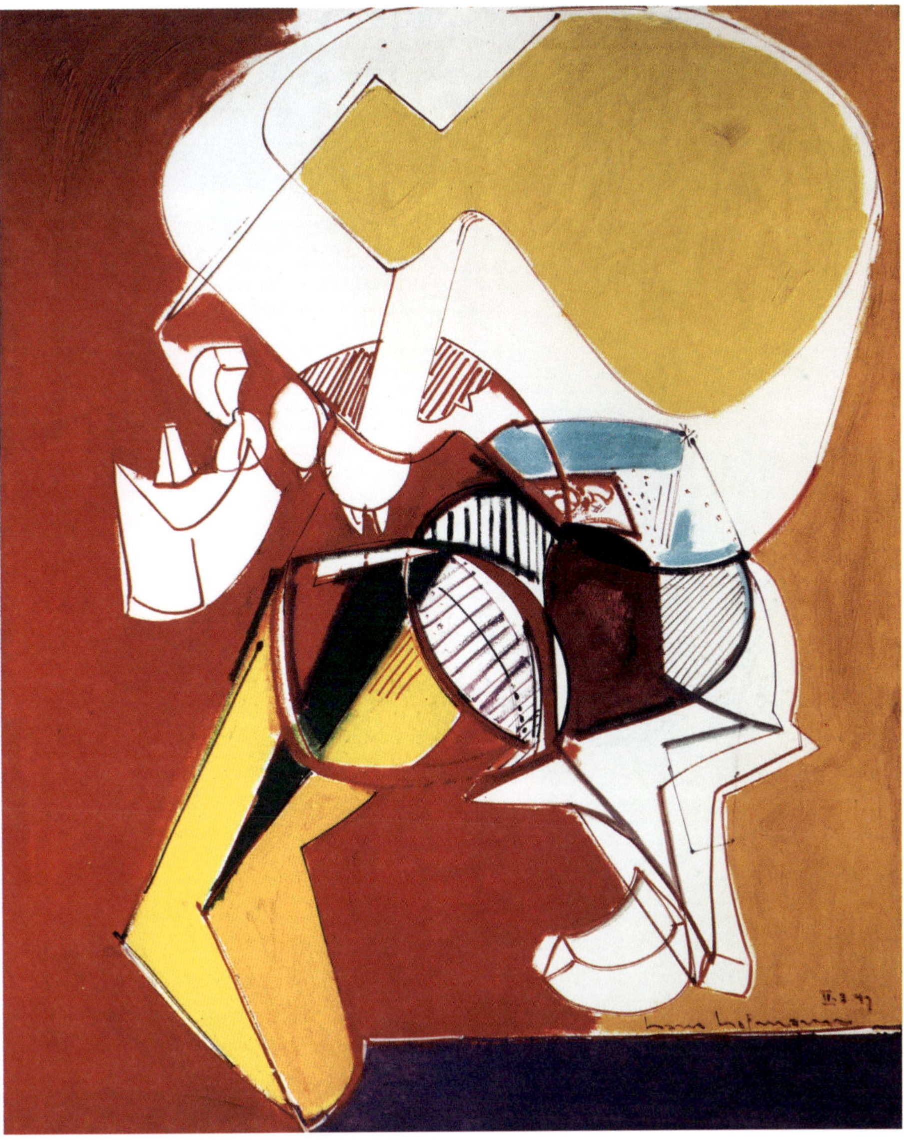

182

Clyfford Still: The First Colour-Fields Paintings

Perhaps the first fully fledged colour-field artist of the younger generation was Clyfford Still, an artist crucial to this period, and later. Until 2011, when the Clyfford Still Museum opened in Denver, the majority of his art had been hidden away in his estate, so that his full corpus was invisible. Now that the Still Museum has begun the long task of fully unveiling its riches,[48] we can begin to see the range and depth of his art. This is perhaps the most remarkable discovery in American art in forty years – we have re-found an artist whom we thought we knew, but who in truth is just now revealing himself to us. In effect, we have discovered a new artist, and one of the highest accomplishment and importance.

We now also have full and reliable accounts of his art and life. Because he dropped out of the art world in 1951, he tended to be pictured as something of a crank, inhospitable and withdrawn, who had assigned ambitious dates to his paintings. Now we can see him whole, as a man and an artist, no more difficult than countless other artists in a generation haunted by mammoth egos. We can say with full confidence that by 1943 he was spreading deep, rich, thick paint over the entirety of his surfaces, a fact that places him in the advance guard of painterly abstraction. In this sense, he now stands with Pollock, Gorky and Motherwell as one of the artists who, in 1943, pushed figuration into the abstracting modes that we now understand as being at the core of what we have defined as Abstract Expressionism. His art, we can now see, was at the forefront of a painterly and emotive intensity unmatched by others of his generation, with the exception of Pollock. We can now understand Pollock's comment: 'Still makes us all look academic.'[49]

Still was good from the start, even in the late 1920s. He could draw well, unlike most of his contemporaries. He knew art and art history, and had a keen sense of the best of older art, dating at least to Rembrandt. His Master's thesis was on Cézanne, knowledge that appears in his art over and over again, sometimes in the form of thematic references, at others in the form of technical passages of paint. His early work is far better than all except perhaps Gorky and at points de Kooning, and his landscapes and figure paintings of the 1930s are among the stand-out accomplishments of that decade.[50]

Still maintained that his work always stemmed from the figure, but just as often it emphasized the vast open spaces of Canada and Washington State, where he grew up on a farm. We cannot help but feel in our bones the isolation of the plains in his landscapes, their barren, frigid expanses, as in *PH-782* and *PH-443* (1927)[183]. It is in the paint itself, thick, rough, spread with deep-seated emotion, rendering the skies as palpable as the grain silos themselves. They are regionalist paintings, but with a big difference, expressionistic to their core, far more intense than those of Benton, Joe Jones or Grant Wood. We need only note these skies to see the source of his mature abstract works, fields of colour that evolve, literally, from fields.

On the other hand, scenes of railroads, mills and wire poles can be squeezed and forced to one side, creating a tension and compression that make us feel the discomfort of life there. Still never forgot this experience, and in the late 1960s he did a series of memory drawings to recall and retain how it felt to live and work in such conditions, a kind of reverse continuity. He knew what hard work was, and that makes itself painfully evident in his grotesque and deformed figures from 1934–5 on, that at once bear resemblance to Rembrandt, Van Gogh, primitive art, Dorothea Lange's unforgettable photographs of plains farmers and their poverty-sapped families, on the bare edge of existence.

183 Clyfford Still, *PH-443*, 1927. Oil on canvas, 85.1 × 91.4 cm (33½ × 36 in). Clyfford Still Museum, Denver

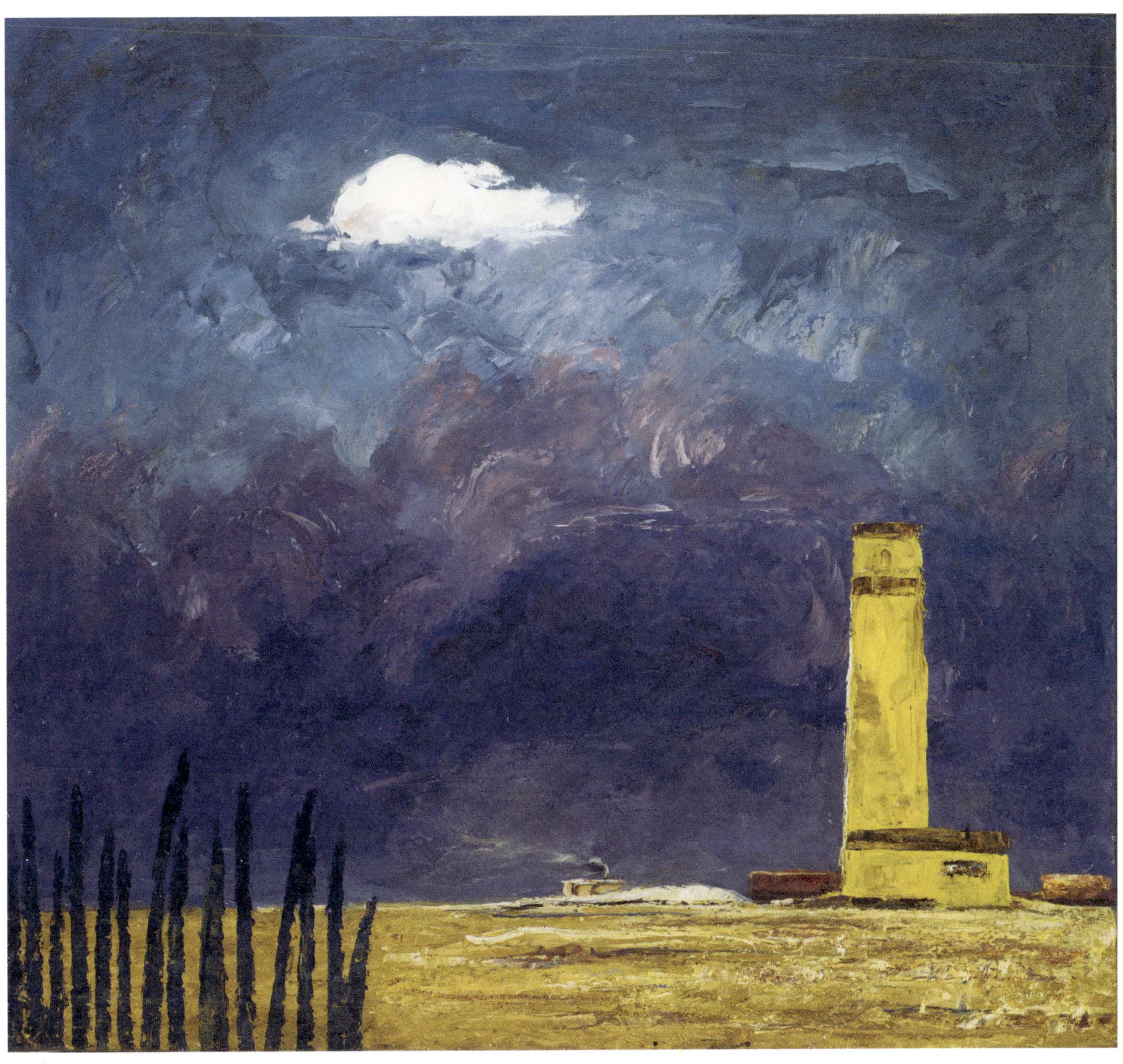

183

184

185

Modern Art in America

In 1936, Still did his own version (*PH-418*) of Van Gogh's *Night Café*, here a desolate western bar and restaurant, as well as a variant (*PH-81*) of the *Potato Eaters* the year before. In at least a few works, the intense yellows of Van Gogh's sun and sower paintings had clearly influenced Still in the intensity of their yellows, especially in *PH-163* of 1954[184]. This marks Still as one of the foremost American artists to take direct and continuing inspiration from Van Gogh, a tradition that started with Dove and O'Keeffe as early as 1913, and extended into the work of Pollock and later Robert Smithson, whose *Spiral Jetty* (page 330) takes as its basis the spirals of *Starry Night*. Still's figures were progressively elongated and stretched into abstract, vertical patterns of the most brilliant, resonant colours one can imagine, or they go to the other end of the spectrum into weighty blacks that can feel otherworldly in their depth and mystery. Their variety of hue, touch, stroke, paint application, configuration, size and scale is endless. Their sense of vast space seems broader than that of any artist of his generation. Still's configurations seem to know no bounds: dense and massive, or open and flickering, blips of yellow across a large, mostly blank canvas, as if we were in the air ourselves, suspended in the midst of the flecks of sunlight moving across the sky.

Paintings such as *PH-241* (1949)[185] are dramatic, in part deep, stormy skyscapes, suggesting an abstract version of Constable's studies of clouds, here an almost all-black field, cut into by streaks of red and red-orange, like flashes of lightning suddenly cutting across distant views. They are dramatic also because in the early paintings, streaks of colour have to fight their way into the field to make their presence felt, bespeaking human dramas of conflict and opposition. These are intensely emotive paintings, and in a sense hark back to the vast panoramas of nineteenth-century paintings of the American West. We can also trace a tradition of abstracting landscapes back to the work of Dove, as in his fissures in *Red Tree and Sun* (1929)[186] and *Thunder Shower* (page 202) or the intermingling of colour shapes, reflecting the shadows of a canyon and desert in the work of Tack, championed at the Phillips Collection, Andover, Massachusetts.

Still was perhaps the most consistent of his group and, in good health, he worked until his last years, longer than those devastated by alcoholism and fear, whose lives ended before their time. Seen this way, Still (and de Kooning) can be considered the Old Masters, inspiring a younger generation to learn from them, but the early loss of so many of the group deprived this generation of such mentors. Perhaps that is one reason why art changed so radically after 1968.

Matisse's Cut-Outs

By 1949, it was clear that American art had reached a new level, not least because of a now highly developed use of colour. From the early exposure to Matisse some forty years before, American artists had rapidly absorbed the possibilities inherent in pure colour as an expressive and formal ingredient that had brought forth some of the best art in the world. Matisse's reputation had been somewhat eclipsed in the 1930s by Picasso, especially by *Guernica* (1937), but by the late 1940s Matisse's work had undergone a marked rejuvenation. The colour and design in his post-1945 paintings were certainly stronger, but the real surprise came from his new, revolutionary colour cut-outs.

Matisse had been rendered an invalid as a result of a near-death experience with stomach cancer, saved only by a drastic operation that forced him to work in bed much of the time. Paradoxically, he reacted to his

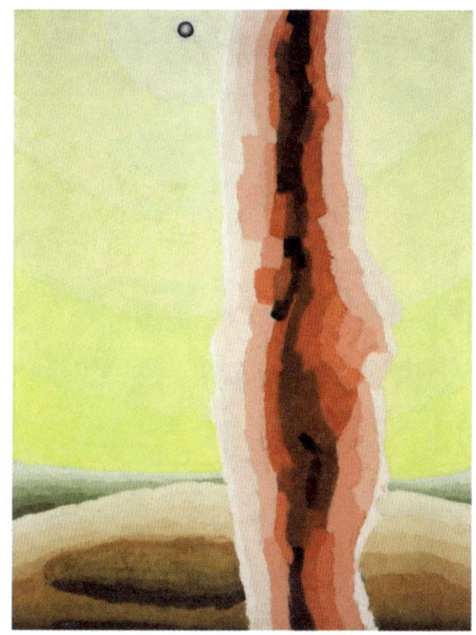

186

184 Clyfford Still, *PH-163*,
     1954. Oil on canvas,
     243.9 × 182.9 cm (96 × 72 in).
     Clyfford Still Museum, Denver

185 Clyfford Still, *PH-241*, 1949.
     Oil on canvas, 172.7 × 148 cm
     (68 × 58¼ in). The Museum
     of Fine Arts, Houston

186 Arthur Dove, *Red Tree and
     Sun*, 1929. Oil on canvas,
     73.7 × 54.6 cm (29 × 21½ in).
     Alfred Stieglitz Collection,
     co-owned by Fisk University,
     Nashville, and Crystal
     Bridges Museum of American
     Art, Bentonville

new situation by letting his creativity overflow, with no constraints, an attitude that led to an essentially new way of making art that had a wide and deep influence on world art, especially in America. Matisse took sheets of already coloured paper, or paper to which paint was added, and cut directly into them, letting his hand go where it would, cutting out shapes of flowers, animals, figures, whatever came to mind. He was like a sculptor, carving directly into his material, in this case, pure colour, as the Renaissance sculptor had cut into his marble block. The coloured paper became Matisse's material; his scissors became his drawing tool, like a pencil or charcoal, or even a paintbrush, tracing the invented forms. Once these shapes were created he could, with assistance, place them on the wall or canvas and begin moving them as he wished. Photographs show that his rooms became an enormous, all-encompassing environment of colour in a multitude of shapes and forms, of different sizes and scales, a kind of chromatic paradise created by a man who at the age of eighty, virtually crippled, made art with the energy and vision of someone half his age. It is one of the greatest feats of old-age art the world has seen, and unlike those of Michelangelo, Rembrandt and Cézanne, his late and last works are about nothing but pure joy, celebrating art and life to the very last.

Colours can stand alone, as in the 'Blue Nude' series, made all the more intense by the vibrant contrast of the white grounds; or they can be part of a symphony of orchestrated hues reminiscent of Hofmann's late work, especially his 'symphonic' paintings. Their impact was as strong and as pervasive as the first in-depth appearance of Matisse's paintings in 1913 at the Armory Show. They had begun as a method of study for composing and executing the Barnes mural, which was to reach a length of forty-five feet. To formulate the movements and placement of the dancers (a homage to Cézanne's bathers, the paintings that had so deeply affected him years earlier) Matisse had to use large paper collage elements to study the layout and the juxtaposition of the colours – grey figures against pink, blue and black grounds. The resulting murals – the first was too small – are among the triumphant moments of Western art. They are a grand conclusion to the Barnes collection, once mocked by Philadelphia, now eagerly grasped by the city for its own purposes, for the collection is itself a history of colour from Impressionism and Post-Impressionism through to Matisse and his later art.

In his use of pinks and blues, and in the Cubist format, Matisse was clearly reassessing his work. The hard edges were new, as were the colour schemes. They remind us of the hues found in the later paintings of Patrick Henry Bruce, Matisse's student twenty years before, an artist whom Matisse still respected. We know this because on his way back to France in 1930, after visiting Barnes and surveying the building, Matisse encountered the American painter and writer George L.K. Morris. At lunch, Matisse inquired of Morris if he knew the work of his former student Bruce; Morris said that he did, but that he found it dry or cold. In reply, Matisse snapped, 'That doesn't make any difference!'[51] In fact, the only precedent for Matisse's colours in the Barnes murals was Bruce's abstract still lifes of the 1920s and early 1930s, demonstrating that the connections between America and Europe ran deeper, and reached further, in the years before 1945 than has been imagined. There is a bridge, but we need to remember that bridges go both ways.

The idea resurfaced in 1938 in a trial cut-out, then flourished into a full working method after Matisse underwent surgery. The works were widely distributed in 1947 with the publication of *Jazz* [187], a volume reproducing one hundred of the cut-outs in print form. It has never been

187 Henri Matisse, *Icarus*, plate VIII from *Jazz*, 1947. Pochoir plate, 65.5 × 42 cm (16½ × 10¼ in). Scottish National Gallery of Modern Art, Edinburgh

          Modern Art in America

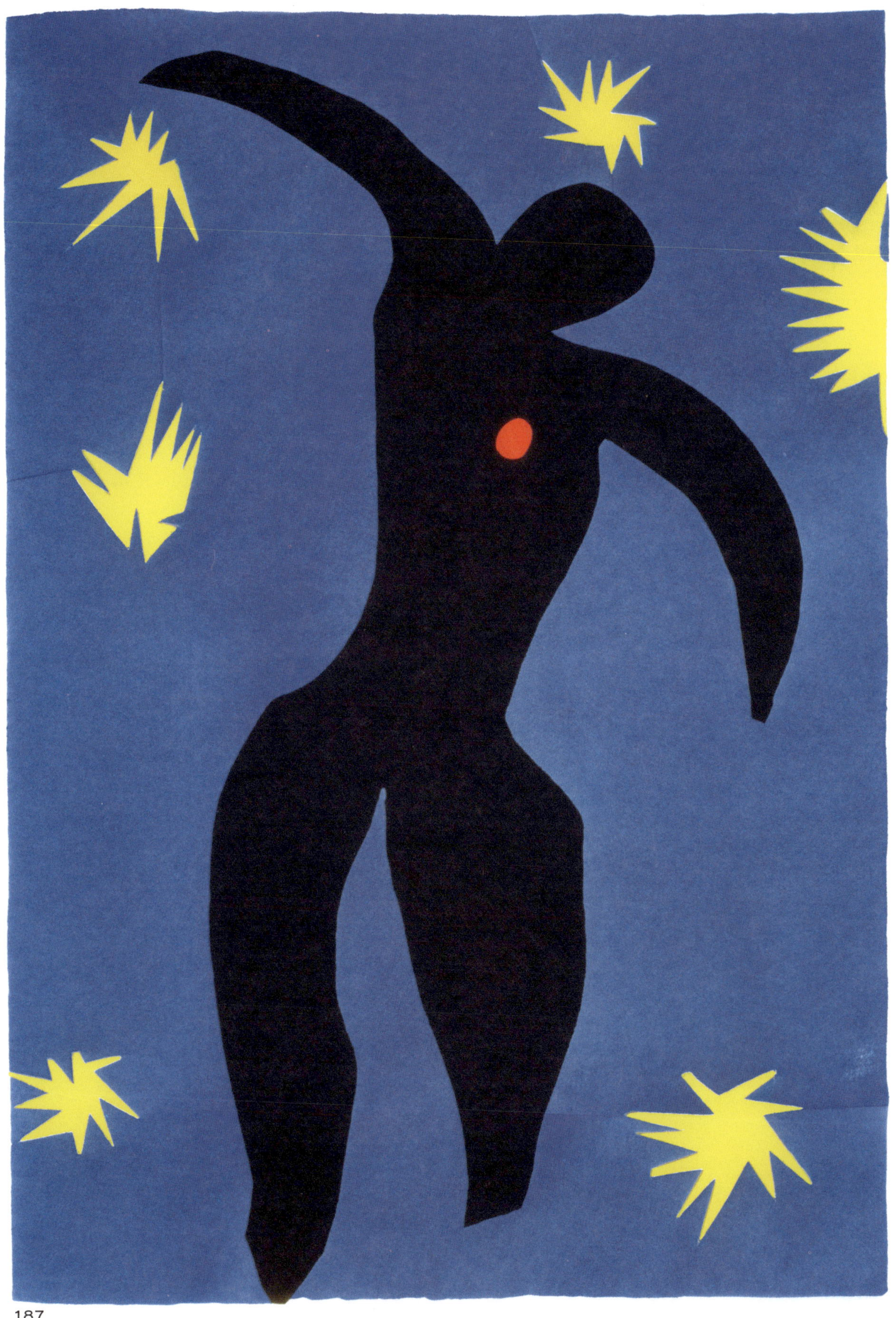

187

out of print since and, as with the Barnes collection, we can only guess how wide its influence has been. The first actual cut-outs to be seen in America appeared in 1949 in an exhibition at the gallery run by Matisse's son Pierre in New York. American art would never be the same again.

Return of *The Red Studio* in 1949

That same year, MoMA acquired *The Red Studio* [188], which had virtually disappeared from public view since 1942, when the painting was purchased by George Keller of the Bignou Gallery in New York. Its reappearance, coupled with the coloured cut-outs, again had an indelible impact on American art, and its effects – the total field of colour, a chromatic continuum – appeared as the fundamental compositional element in the styles of one American artist after another. The most famous and most dramatic instance, although certainly not the only one, was Rothko's discovery of the painting that same year. His palette had advanced significantly in the two years prior to this, and was already flourishing in his multiforms, composed of various colourful biomorphic shapes floating in rich and many-hued fields. But Rothko's aim was to clarify, to eliminate any form or idea between the artist and the painting, and between the painting and the viewer, to make it as direct as possible. The problem then was how to keep the colour but eliminate the multiple shapes. Rothko looked intently at *The Red Studio* every day, he said, for six weeks.[52] In it he found his solution – the full surface of red that covers the painting from top to bottom, side to side, from the floor to the ceiling of the room. From this, Rothko could break into his mature signature style of broad, lateral rectangles of glowing and rich hues, which formed their own type of total field. The compositional prototype of varied and stacked rectangles he might also have gleaned from other Matisse paintings, such as *Bathers with a Turtle* (1907–8), which he may well have known.

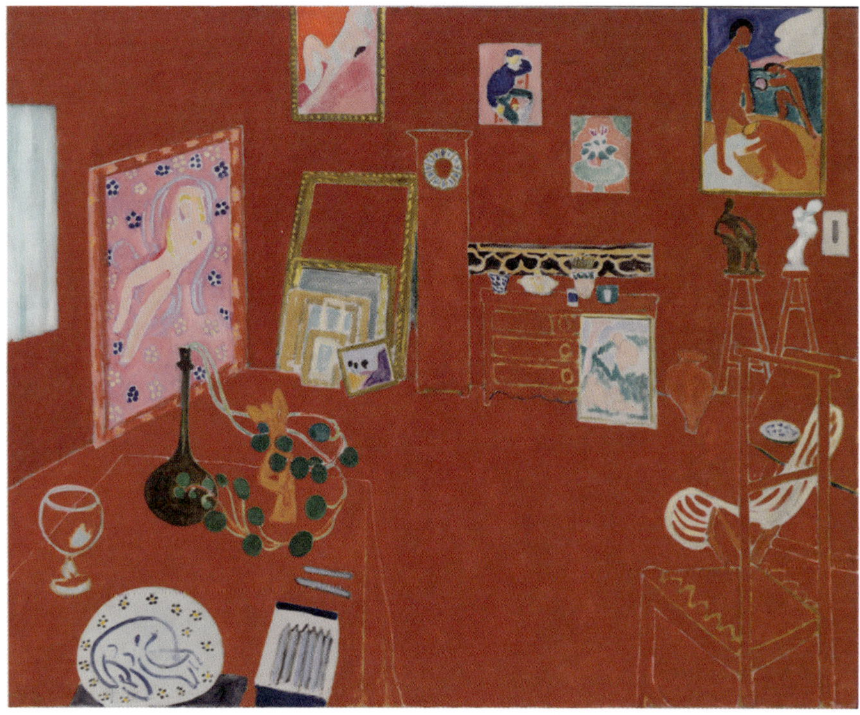

188

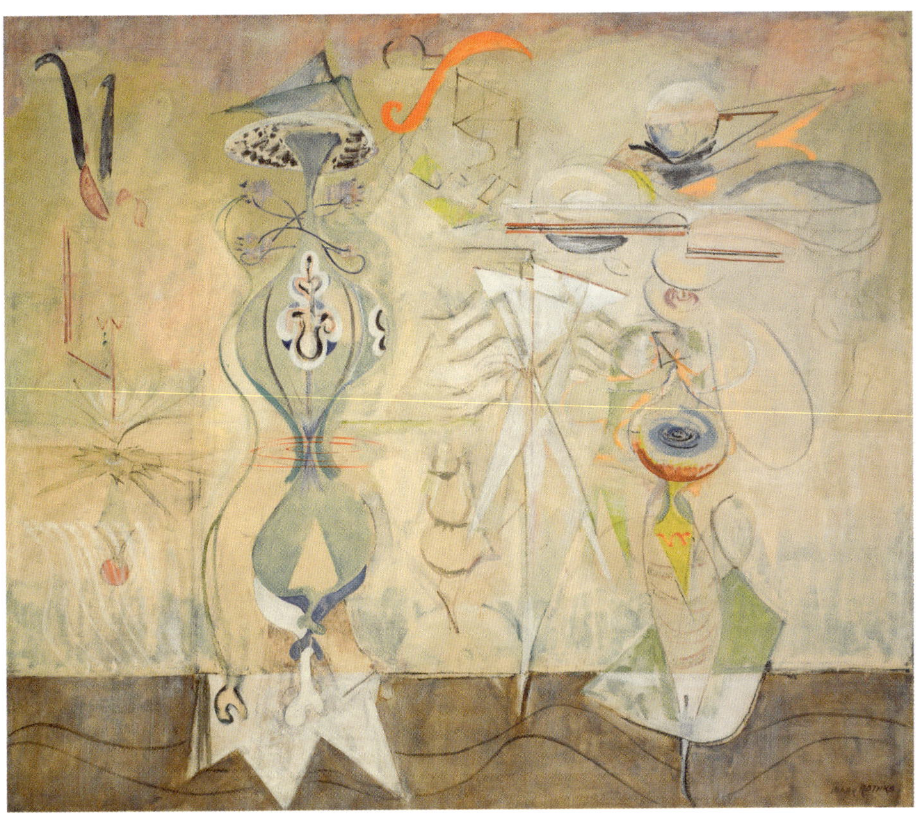

189

Rothko's landscape themes

Closer to home, though, was the work of Marin, whose art Rothko knew well and had worked through in paintings of the 1920s and 1930s. This suggests that Rothko's experience came from landscape painting, both in the United States and his place of birth, the vast spaces of Russia that would have lingered in his memories. We should look at his Surrealist masterpiece of 1944, *Slow Swirl by the Edge of the Sea* [189], to understand how landscape/seascape themes permeated his work, for these figures emerging from the sea on to a protean landscape move in just such a space as occurs in his mature work. 'It is a widely accepted notion among painters that it does not matter what one paints as long as it is well painted. This is the essence of academism,' Rothko wrote in a joint statement with Gottlieb.[53] 'There is no such thing as good painting about nothing. We assert that only that subject matter is valid which is tragic and timeless. That is why we profess spiritual kinship with primitive and archaic art.'[54] We should bear this in mind when we interpret these images – his colours can be found in nature herself.

Sam Francis and the Emergence of West Coast Colour-Field Painting

Further evidence of the landscape motif – sky, water and land – at the heart of Rothko's work is found in the emergence of the colour-field painting of Sam Francis on the West Coast. Francis (1923–1994) had been severely injured in a test flight while in service. He was in hospital for two years, much of the time in a full-body cast that confined him to bed. He was given paints to relieve the tedium – like Matisse, who also started as an artist while recuperating – and found that he enjoyed painting and was good at it.

188   Henri Matisse, *The Red Studio, Issy-les-Moulineaux*, 1911. Oil on canvas, 181 × 219.1 cm (71¼ × 86¼ in). The Museum of Modern Art, New York

189   Mark Rothko, *Slow Swirl at the Edge of the Sea*, 1944. Oil on canvas, 191.4 × 215.2 cm (75¼ × 84¾ in). The Museum of Modern Art, New York

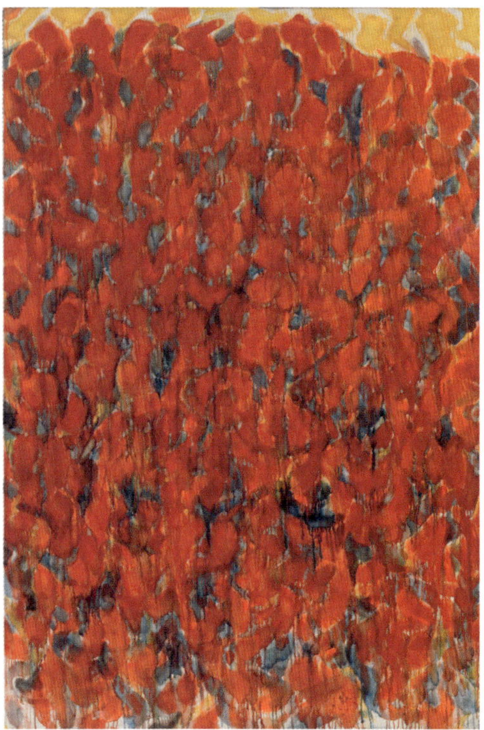

190

Thereafter he literally painted his way back to health, for he found in colour and light nothing less than his salvation. He progressed rapidly and by 1949 was moving towards abstraction, a format based on the elements of air, sky, water and land, the only things he could see from the hospital on San Francisco Bay.

Francis evolved a layering of the curves of these basic elements in the world around us. He painted the night or the late evening, as well as the atmosphere created by the bright Californian sun. He had been influenced by Rothko, who taught in San Francisco in the summers of 1947 and 1949. But Rothko took as much from California and West Coast artists as he gave. The atmosphere and colour of Edward Corbett's white paintings had impressed Francis and may well also have touched Rothko.[55] It is at this point that we encounter again the interaction between east and west that we can trace to Macdonald-Wright's move to California in 1918. Macdonald-Wright had been a painter of the soft and luminous, a tendency that was increased by the California sun and space, giving far different effects from those of the east and New York. The glowing hues of Rothko's floating rectangles might thus come from a series of sources, including the light of San Francisco, much closer to home than Matisse, all part of an American experience, here the cross-fertilization of both coasts.

In 1950, Francis moved to Paris, searching for the memory of his mother who had been highly educated in French culture. His paintings there took on a soft, cloudy, grey quality, often traced to the atmosphere of Paris. This was certainly true to an extent, but the grey-white paintings also recall the light of San Francisco that he had known since he was a boy. These paintings also remind us of Rothko, but we should not discount the possibility that Rothko had seen and been influenced by them, rather than the other way round, for they quickly commanded wide international acclaim and success.

By 1952, Francis had returned to the layering that he had developed earlier, which spoke in brilliant hues of the elements of water, sky and earth. His paintings now included biomorphic shapes recalling the work

190 Sam Francis, *Big Red*, 1953. Oil on canvas, 303.2 × 194 cm (120 × 76¼ in). The Museum of Modern Art, New York

191 Ad Reinhardt, *No.15*, 1952. Oil on canvas, 280.8 × 107.9 cm (110½ × 42½ in). Albright-Knox Art Gallery, Buffalo, New York

of Gorky in the 1940s. *Big Red* (1953)[190], an early masterpiece by Francis, is a sheer, dense curtain of layered red globules that seem to pour down the surface, fused by dripping and poured streaks of colour. The title hints at a link to *The Red Studio*. *Big Red* certainly shows the evidence of Francis's immersion in the culture of French painting, which he quickly came to know and love in Paris. Monet, Cézanne, Bonnard and Matisse were artists whose works he could see and study close at hand. *Big Red* forms its own kind of wall of intense colour; it is a field, to be sure, and should be counted as one of the most effective works in the body of colour-field painting that we have been tracking. His fusion of French and American art was unique at this time, not only in its open embrace of a culture from which most young Americans were distancing themselves, but also for the high achievement of the paintings he produced.

The discussion of Rothko's glowing rectangles, and their references, will go on. However, what cannot be denied is that by 1950 Matisse and Rothko together had an immediate and profound effect on the use of colour in American art. In that year, major artists adopted the curtain of sheer colour as a field, either in its own right or as a support for other pictorial activities; they did in personal ways, but the sources are clear.

Developments in Colour Field: Davis and Reinhardt

By 1949, Davis was near death because of his heavy drinking; by a miracle, friends were able to get him sober, or at least pull him back from total self-destruction. He made a comeback, and in subsequent paintings until his death in 1964, he worked in an intensity of hues worthy of Matisse, surely from looking at *Jazz* but also by reconnecting with his early, vivid impressions of Matisse at the Armory Show. Indeed, *The Red Studio* can be seen as reappearing in his late art.

At the time, the ascendancy of Abstract Expressionism meant that critically Davis was passed over, since he seemed to be looking back to an earlier type of geometric art. But we see now that painterly abstraction was not the only new art being made, and that Davis, late in life, was still contributing to the new advances in contemporary painting. 'There should be applause,' said Donald Judd, reviewing Davis's one-man show in 1962. 'At age sixty seven he is still a hot shot.'[56] Indeed he was, like Matisse late in life, making art with joy and vitality. If we were to mount an exhibition of American hard-edge art from 1945 on, an alternative history of post-war art, but one without painterly abstraction, it would be impressive and illuminating.

In 1950, colour-field art came to full bloom in the work of Ad Reinhardt and Barnett Newman. Although famous for his all-black paintings after 1960, Reinhardt (1913–1967) also came from a study of hard-edge abstraction of the 1930s, particularly that of Davis. He sought continually to clarify his compositions, working towards a minimum of shapes. But this was hard-won, and came only after he had worked through a painterly vocabulary of multiple, rich forms in 1947 that remind us of Picasso and Braque in 1911–12, and of Mondrian in his work of 1914–15. From there, by 1950, he could move to a few solid blocks of close-value colours floating in a full colour field; they are remarkable paintings, some of the best done by any American in the hard-edge mode[191]. In his quest for an ultimate purity, he then moved into his all-black series in which the demarcation of areas is barely visible. They are intense, even mesmerizing works, but for this writer, finally more of a conceptual process than true paintings.

191

THE GEOMETRIC, HARD-EDGE TRADITION

Josef Albers: Homage to the Square

Albers had matured as a colourist by 1940, and in paintings such as *Bent Black (A)* (1940)[192] he was already making major abstract paintings, even if here he limited himself to blue, black and white. However, by 1950 he had developed his famous 'Homage to the Square' series, which occupied him for the rest of his life. Within ten years he had found a new, focused and clarified format that was ideally suited for his colour to reach its full powers. The format of three and four concentric squares had its ultimate source in the colour blocks, solid and pure, that he had discovered in Cézanne back in 1908 in the Folkwang Museum in Hagen. These were thinned out, distilled and brought into a highly defined composition that revolved around the centre of the painting, just as the Renaissance painter found the exact centre of his altarpieces. In retrospect, these were very simple means, but it was not so easy to get there, since Albers had no idea what the conclusion would be while he was working through the process. Although the means were simple, the possible effects were limitless, as he liked to say. He worked with high- or low-keyed tones, intense and deep or open and light; he could use one basic hue and gradate it from light to dark, either at extremes or within a narrow range; he could employ contrasting colours in the most unexpected ways that can set us on edge, or the hues could be soft and melodic, carrying across the surfaces like a gentle wind.

The 'Homage' works often carried a secondary title, which signalled the note Albers wished to sound. Frequently they were cosmic, deeply spiritual in intention and effect, pointing to the cycles of day and night,

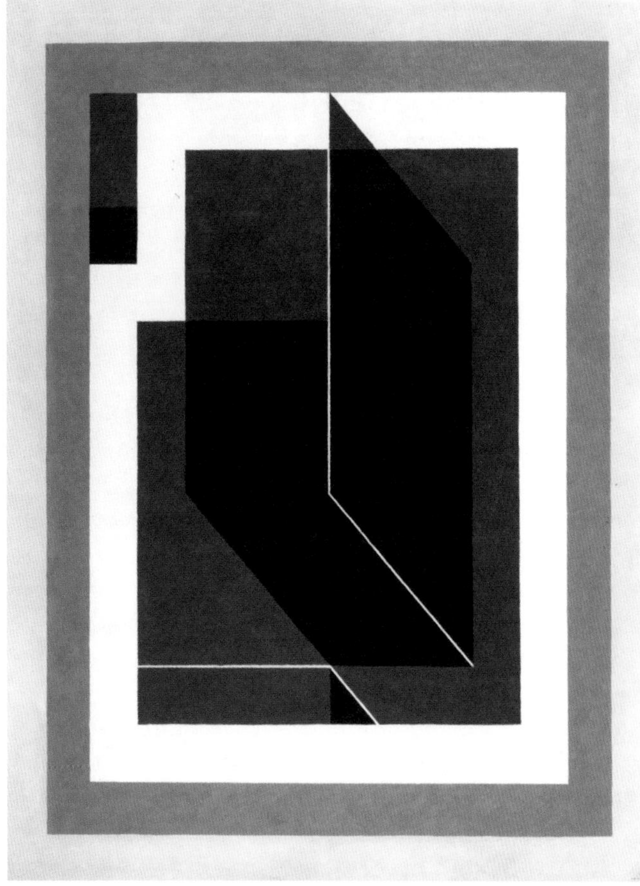

192

192 Josef Albers, *Bent Black (A)*, 1940. Oil on Masonite, 95.3 × 70.5 cm (37½ × 27¾ in). Addison Gallery of American Art, Phillips Academy, Andover

193 Josef Albers, *Homage to the Square: Joy*, 1964. Oil on board, 121.9 × 121.9 cm (48 × 48 in). Crystal Bridges Museum of American Art, Bentonville

193

sunrise and sunset, the cycle of life itself. He painted as if he wished the sun were behind the canvas, filling it with intense and spreading light. Albers had deeply admired the early version (1912–13), of Edvard Munch's large mural painting, *The Sun*, which he had first seen in Berlin at the Herbstausstellung of 1913. Here, the sun does indeed seem to be in the painting itself, its rays of light animating the world as represented in the canvas. It might be said to be a northern counterpart to Matisse and his joy-of-life works of the time. Munch's mural would be a reference point for the sun paintings of O'Keeffe, Dove and Noland, whether they knew it or not. It is a universal force for Thoreau at Walden, as well as for the Luminists, O'Keeffe in New Mexico, and Dove, who kept a daily record of the weather in his diary, and whose art is rooted in the sun and earth.

This cycle of life, both physical and emotional, also has an impact on Albers's art. We find it throughout his work, especially in such paintings as *Homage to the Square: Joy* (1964) [193], in which the strong yellow at the centre pushes outwards through gradations of oranges and reds, mimicking the course of the sun; we can read it either as sunrise or as sunset, from in to out, or from out to in. Albers spoke to me of the joy in the light of the day, repeated on a daily basis, the rhythms of nature, and our existence. Such paintings remind us that for him, as for Hofmann, the ultimate reality was spiritual in nature. Postmodernism viewed Albers (and Mondrian) as 'a cold, impersonal formalist'[57] but this is an ill-informed reading. Geometric painting is as deeply felt, as filled with 'meaning' as any other type of art. When we realize this, we might finally get over the idea that while Albers was a famous teacher he was not a great artist. In addition, a full and proper exhibition of true colour-field art would have a prominent place for him.

Ralston Crawford: Pictorial Puzzles

Others were working in the geometric, hard-edge tradition, among them Ralston Crawford and Ilya Bolotowsky, both of whom had also developed a pictorial colour construction by 1950. Crawford (1906–1978) is a major artist, but his place and the reach of his long career, have been overshadowed by the (mis)fortune of creating a series of signature paintings early on that has frozen our view of him. By 1940, his images of the *Overseas Highway*[194] and *The Whitestone Bridge* had brought him renown for their daring perspectives that seemed to take viewers into an infinite space, in an unknown future that would carry them from the Great Depression into a new, golden age of unlimited possibility. So famous were these works for their fusion of Precisionist drawing and Surrealist space that anything after them was probably doomed to be thought of as lesser, particularly since Crawford's art became progressively abstract. Not helping the situation was his fecundity, his prolific output in literally every medium, for he was also an accomplished photographer and printmaker. By the same token, he was a compulsive traveller who explored every aspect of the world. Nothing could sate his curiosity. But he never relied on sentimental subjects or romantic views to carry him. 'I make pictures', he simply said.[58]

And what pictures they are. They often focus on subjects he had explored in photography, or he made the photographs after painting the site. The relationship between the same subject as rendered in the different media was often tenuous at best, again adding to the complexity and diversity of his art. *Third Ave El*[195], for example, was photographed in 1949 from underneath, looking almost straight up, a novel and dramatic shot at the time, with the sky virtually covered by the steel structures of the overhead El. These views recall the paintings of similar scenes done by Sloan earlier on, but this photograph is particularly vivid. One cannot help but wonder if Franz Kline knew these pictures, for they certainly suggest his bold black-and-white forms that shoot across the canvas, just as the tracks do. It is all gritty, starkly light and dark. Compare this to the painting of the theme and we find instead a lyrical abstraction of separate but connecting

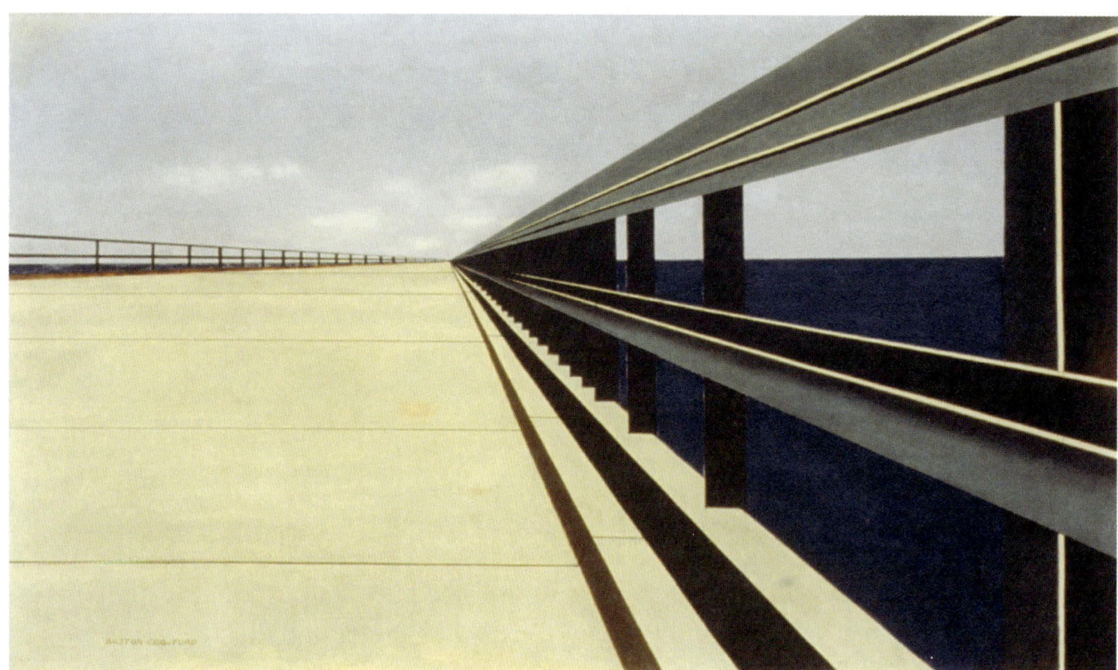

194

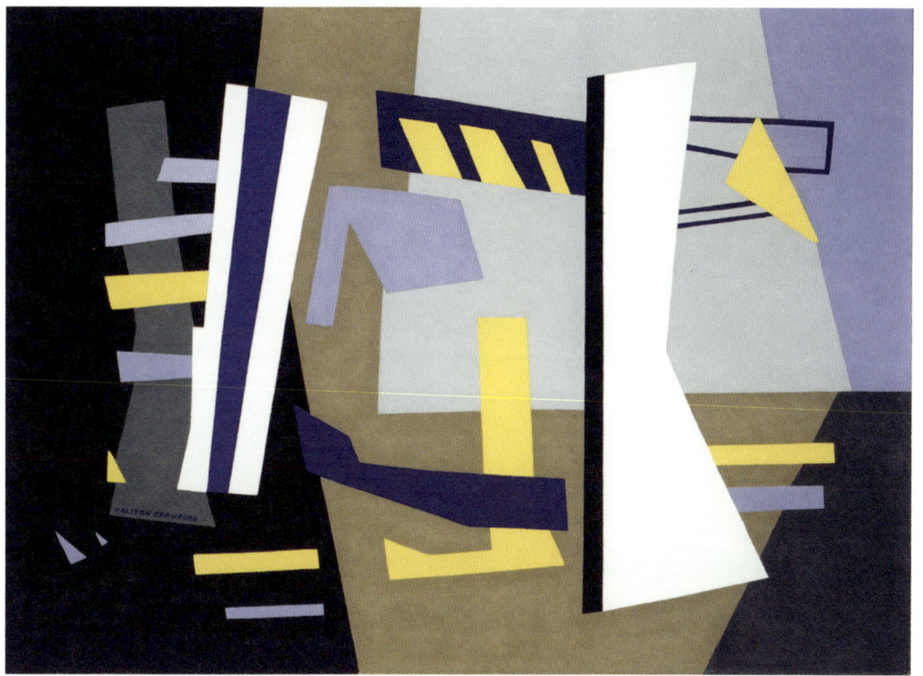

195

hard-edge forms, dark at the edges, but mellowed by the softening yellows and blues, more suited to a rural landscape we might think. Virtually the only similarity we can recognize is the spaces between the tracks, now rendered in almost pastel hues, plus white, that give the painting a bucolic look and feel. How can one make head or tail of the series? But that was Crawford, ceaselessly exploring, shifting, experimenting, moving on, finding the most ordinary subjects and turning them into dazzling, intricate pictorial puzzles. It is as if both he and Davis used hard-edge styles to create surface actions and patterns as complex as any done by Pollock or de Kooning at the same time. Might we even call them hard-edge action painters in a parallel history to Abstract Expressionism? This history would need to be traced back to Copley, John James Audubon, many of the Luminist painters, Schamberg, Sheeler, Bruce and numerous others before and after 1914. To trace them would help us to see an unbroken tradition, and might thus help us finally to break down the Iron Curtain between the periods.

Burgoyne Diller and the WPA Mural Division

This geometric type of painting can seem as if it had been easily appropriated from existing European models. But for all these artists, it was attained only through a hard-won evolution over years of diligent application. So much was true for Albers, and for Burgoyne Diller, whose art can look as if it came directly and easily from Mondrian. It clearly owes much to that artist, but this occurred only after long study, first in 1932–3 with Hofmann, who identified Diller then as 'one of the most promising of the young American painters'.[59]

Diller was among a handful of artists in the early 1930s who helped to continue the tradition of an abstracting type of art in America. As director of the WPA Mural Division, he saw to it that abstract artists such as Davis and Gorky could aspire to, and actually make, large murals that could stand up to and co-exist with the Mexican muralists of the time. This mural tradition, as we have seen, was an important factor in the emergence of ambitious American painting, especially that of the young painterly

194   Ralston Crawford, *Overseas Highway*, 1939. Oil on canvas, 45.7 × 76.2 cm (18 × 30 in). Private collection

195   Ralston Crawford, *Third Avenue El*, 1949. Oil on canvas, 77.2 × 102.4 cm (30⅜ × 40⁵⁄₁₆ in). Walker Art Center, Minneapolis

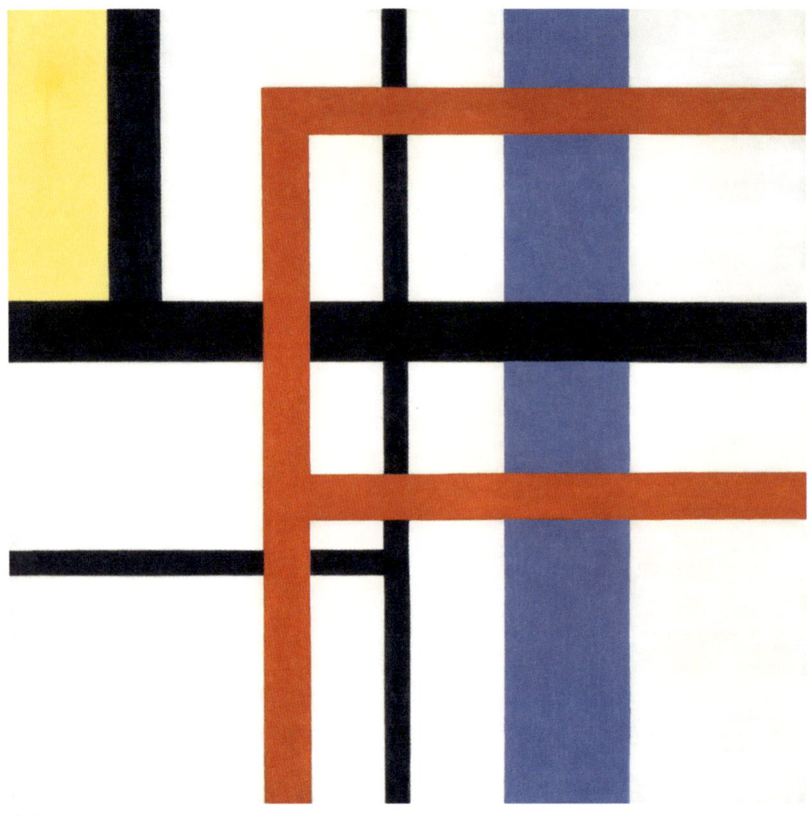

196

artists after 1945. But only after serious study could Diller submit to the
principles of Mondrian and his group. By 1940, he had developed a
geometric style that differs in telling ways from Mondrian, as in *Second
Theme* (1938–40)[196], which included primary hues plus black and white
lines and areas of various widths and shapes, a practice never found in
Mondrian. Later, in the 1960s, Diller broke through and beyond Mondrian
with a powerful series of vertical bar paintings, red, yellow and blue
intermixing with a black ground that made a distinctive and original
addition to the modern body of geometric painting.

Monet's Blue: Ellsworth Kelly and Sam Francis

Younger artists working in a flat, linear and hard-edge art had also
appeared by the early 1950s. Foremost among them was Ellsworth Kelly
(b.1923), who was living in Paris at the time, and is a part of the complex
story of Americans in Paris still to be told in all its fullness. Kelly had gone
there directly from Boston and was unaware of the new expressionist
painting then developing in New York. He looked instead to the old
Constructivist tradition of European painting and was developing an
abstraction based on the pure shapes suggested by the architecture of
Paris, such as bridges, windows and shadows, a kind of visual feast distilled
into strong and affecting shapes and compositions. In *Colors for a Large
Wall* (1951)[197], his colour opened up in a wide array of hues, primaries
and secondary colours, unlike anything he had done previously. There are
sixty-four panels, each separate and independent forms, but joined
together to create not a picture, but a wall itself, something quite different
from a painting as usually understood. It can be seen as akin to a mural,
although not a fresco, on the wall and almost *as* the wall itself. In this,
Kelly's work is a continuation of a French tradition of wall painting designed

196 Burgoyne Diller,
Second Theme, 1938–40.
Oil on canvas, 76.5 × 76.5 cm
(30⅛ × 30⅛ in).
The Metropolitan Museum
of Art, New York

197 Ellsworth Kelly,
Colors for a Large Wall, 1951.
Oil on canvas mounted
on sixty-four panels,
240 × 240 cm (94½ × 94½ in).
The Museum of Modern Art,
New York

       Modern Art in America

to bring art more directly into the public sphere. That tradition can be traced to the Art Nouveau movement, then into the Bauhaus, where collective and public art was taught, as was the kind of geometric art that informed Kelly from the start. It continued after World War II.[60]

In the *Colors for a Large Wall* (1951), we can detect a kinship with Mondrian, and especially *Broadway Boogie Woogie*, as well as the colour-grid paintings of Paul Klee – a master at the Bauhaus who had mentored Albers – and, further back, even the colour patches of Cézanne, now made fully autonomous. But for all its European ancestors, it is distinctly an American painting. There is first its size – 8 × 8 feet – and its scale, with everything taken to its all-out maximum; it is a lively, bouncing painting in constant movement, in keeping with Kelly's desire to imbue all his works with 'good spirits',[61] to give his shapes their own space and freedom as separate entities. It is American optimism at its fullest, with the zing of a big-band swing orchestra that recalls Davis and his monumental mural *Swing Landscape* of 1938. Indeed, *Colors for a Large Wall* should be considered a cornerstone of abstract colour painting in American art, a midpoint between early Orphic-Synchromist art and, say, the enormous protractor canvases of the late 1960s by Frank Stella. It is said to have been done by chance arrangement, something like Hans Arp's Dada-orientated collage of 1917, also supposedly arranged by chance. There will have been no fully programmatic composition to follow, but there are also no accidents. Kelly is one of the first at this time to institute a practice of using prearranged or ready-made forms in order to avoid making new and original compositions every time, a sticking point in expressionist practice. De Kooning and his *Women* of 1950–5 is another instance, as is Rauschenberg by the same time, and Johns by 1954 in his use of the flag and targets. Black and white predominate (there are twenty-six whites, fifteen blacks), a practice that Kelly had already mastered;

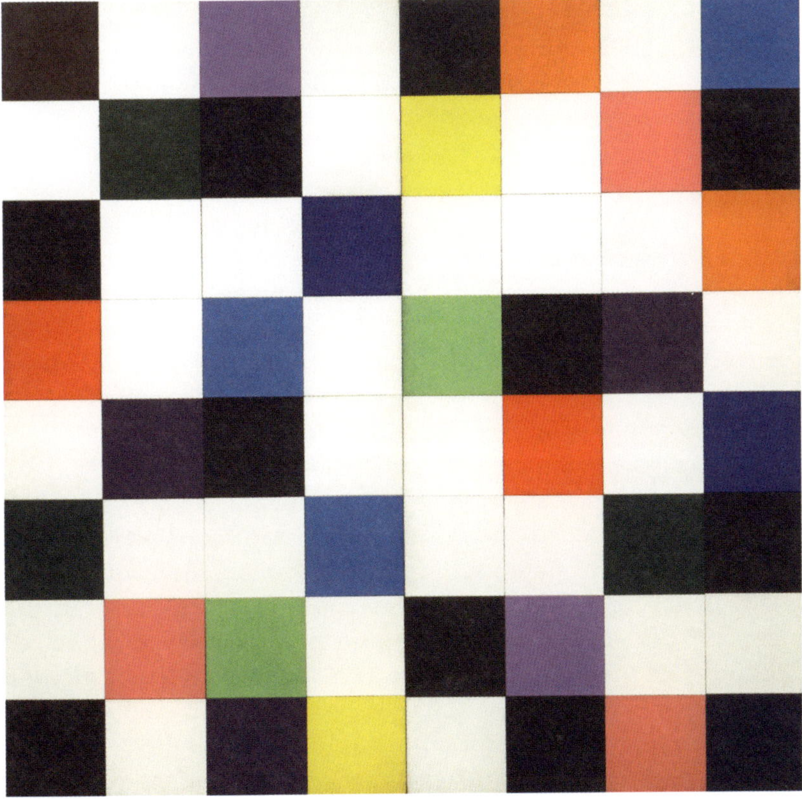

197

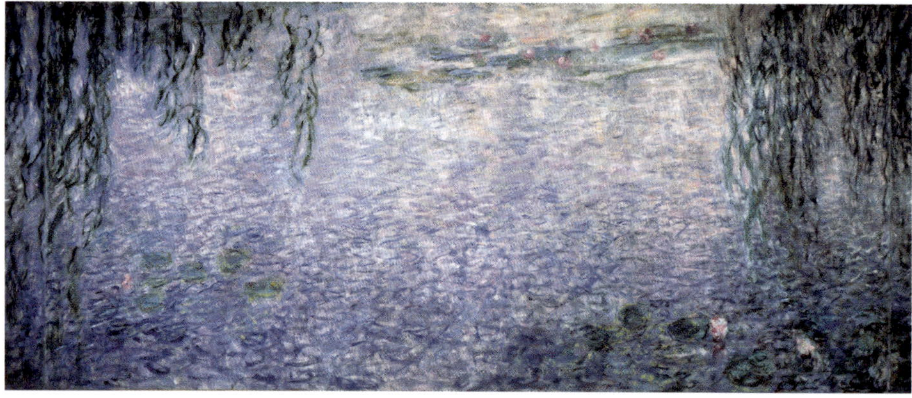

198

its use goes back to Matisse and Wilhelm Ostwald in 1916 and it was subsequently incorporated by Bruce, Frost and Daugherty into their work of that year and after. There are sequences of shades of blue, based on the colour principle of gradation and harmony by analogy, as well as triads and pairs of colours throughout, also an old colour practice from early twentieth-century art, as is the use of complementary hues such as red and green, placed side by side. And, sure enough, there at the top and bottom centre are the intense yellows, nothing less than representations of the sun, at high noon and sunset or sunrise. Although done in Paris, this painting points to and is part of an old American tradition, dating to the Luminists and the nineteenth century, of the sun blessing the activities of Americans as they go about their lives. The juxtapositions and the total effect are the result of a master of colour – one who must be included as a major field-of-colour painter.

In 1953, Kelly, like many other artists then in Paris, discovered Monet, and especially Monet's blue. The occasion was the reopening in that year of the Orangerie, which had been closed during the war, the site of Monet's two oval rooms filled with the *Nympheas* murals[198] that he had given to the state in the late 1920s. For young artists, Francis and Kelly among them, to enter these rooms was to enter a world of misty hues, infusing the air itself. It seemed nothing less than an environment of atmospheric colours, and in particular an environment of a multiplicity of blues that ran the gamut from light to dark. It was a catalyst for Kelly to brighten, enliven and deepen his flat shapes with a range of hues, often blue.

These blues also rekindled Kelly's early memories of the large blue shape of the water in Cézanne's *Gulf of Marseilles* (c.1895), which he had seen as a child in the Met. Wherever we look we find Cézanne at the heart of artists' pictorial journeys. Who later said that Cézanne was the father of us all? Matisse, of course. When it comes to colour, Matisse is always the final source, and Kelly is no exception. In his late cut-outs from 1950–4, the best art made anywhere in the world at the time, Matisse used the wall as the site for his work, spreading the intense hues, or simply white and blue, across his bedroom and house. They were no longer pictures, but virtual environments, as most famously in *The Swimming Pool*, which filled the four walls of the dining room.[62] In his cut-outs, Matisse solved the long-standing historic dilemma, the question of Florentine *disegno* vs. Venetian *colore*. Cézanne had joined the two, but Matisse took it even further, for there is no difference at all – as he cuts into the colour he is drawing while forming the purest of pure colour volumes. From Matisse, Kelly could finally learn to trust entirely in colour and its power of expression – how a single panel of colour on a wall could set up a vibrant pattern of

198 Claude Monet, *Les Nymphéas: Le Matin clair aux saules*, 1914–26. Oil on canvas, triptych, central panel, 200 × 425 cm (78¾ × 167¼ in) overall. Musée de l'Orangerie, Paris

199 Theodoros Stamos, *Full Moon*, 1948. Oil on canvas, 50.8 × 60.9 cm (20 × 24 in). The Phillips Collection, Washington, DC

Modern Art in America

visual complexity and delight, perhaps the ultimate extension of Matisse's method of placing one colour on a blank canvas at a time and responding to the excitations then set up, as outlined in his *Notes of a Painter* of 1908. These walls, both Matisse's and Kelly's, come out of the ideas developed in the wake of World War I, then reiterated after 1945, that art must turn from ego-driven, individualist painterly abstraction, and reunite itself with society at large, becoming an art for the public good.

From there, Kelly expanded his vocabulary of squares, rectangles and curves of high colour into ever larger forms, so that by the late 1960s, he had made huge wall panels of intense hues that ran through the colour spectrum and back again. Here, we are also in a kind of environment, with space permeated by light and colour. It is a prime example of the constant drive to clarity and directness that we see throughout modern art. Kelly stands as one of the greatest American artists to emerge after 1945; it would be revealing to put this large wall next to a Pollock, a de Kooning and a Rothko of the same year, and see what happens. My guess is that the Kelly would more than hold its own.

For Sam Francis, the discovery of the Monets, and thus blue, was also transformational. From that year until well into the 1960s, his art revolved around blue, often as if in sheets, although yellows and reds frequently dominated the picture. In his art of the early 1950s, Francis became a pioneer of colour-field painting, with lush patterns of deep and rich pigments that seemed to fuse the French tradition and the new painterly art of America. He is most often identified as a 'second generation' Abstract Expressionist, since he was born in the 1920s rather than the 1910s, but it is from this group of younger artists that colour-field art emerges in the form in which we most conventionally know it, after Rothko and Still and the other pioneers, Matisse and Mondrian. This is the painterly expressionist branch, working in loose, fluid, open and organic shapes, coming out of Abstract Expressionism and developing into a new form.

By the early 1950s, as Abstract Expressionism spread widely, it increasingly began to be seen as prone to overworking the paint, the brushstrokes too dense and thick, even mannered, with the look of something rather than the real substance. As Pollock declined in the 1950s – his heavy drinking recurred, leading to less work and fewer important or

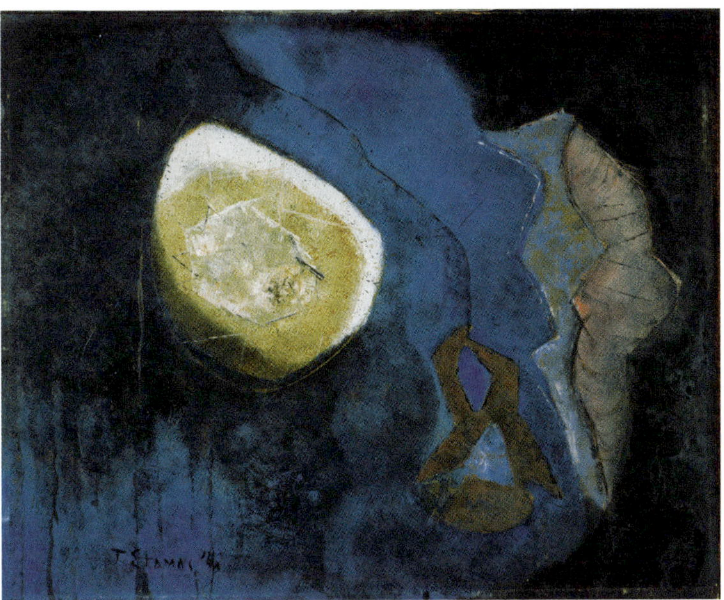

199

even successful paintings – younger artists rethought the process, wishing to clarify, to open up and lighten the surface and let the paint breathe again, to take in colour and air and light. This is precisely what we see in Francis's work of the 1950s, which James Johnson Sweeney called among the most 'sensuous and sensitive'[63] of any painting of the time.

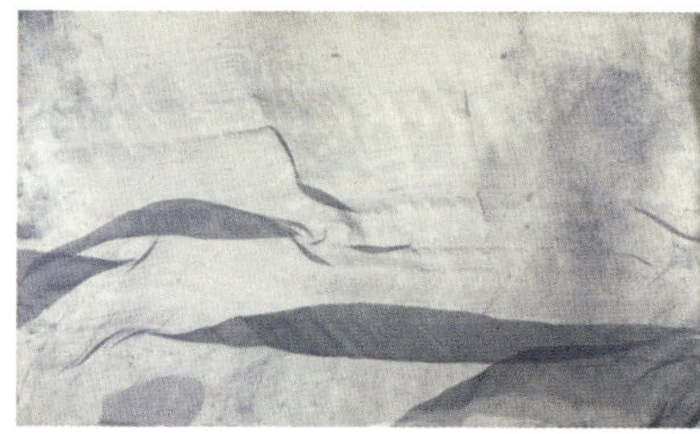

200

Theodoros Stamos and William Baziotes

Not all younger artists conformed to Newman's bogus claim that they had started painting again from scratch. Theodoros Stamos (1922–1997) was a gifted painter and something of a child prodigy. By 1943, his organic, soft, primeval shapes continued directly from the work of Arthur Dove and were at the heart of a series of exceptionally moving paintings – including *Full Moon* (1948)[199]. He had been one of the few to visit Stieglitz's gallery An American Place in the late 1930s and early 1940s, and there he had discovered the work of Dove and his close friend and colleague, O'Keeffe. Stamos was not able to sustain this high level after 1950 because he tried to move into the vein of Rothko's colour fields, a misdirection for him, since he abandoned his early, best instinct to work in Dove's lyrical manner that created private worlds, seemingly unknown to all except the artist. But many artists work at their peak for only a few years; think of Pollock, and certainly Kline, who had no more than seven or so good years.

In this same mode we can place William Baziotes (1912–1963), one of the many in this group who died early. He nurtured soft poetic forms, such as those in *Aquatic* (1961)[201], which seemed to swim in an indeterminate sea, gently, serenely, much like the biomorphic shapes of Dove's collage *Sea II* (1925)[200]. For these artists, there was no break at 1945; rather, they understood themselves as part of an ongoing continuity.

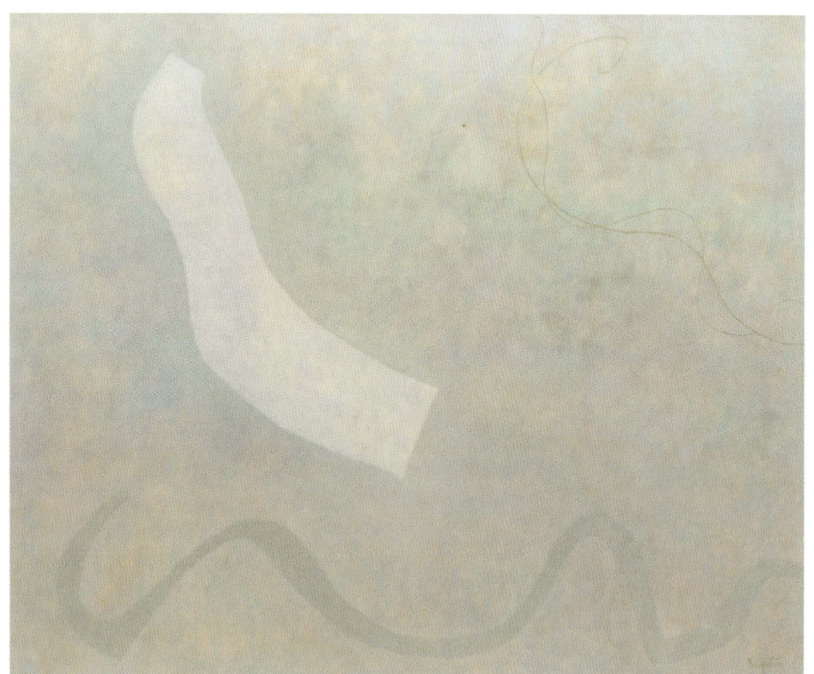

201

200 Arthur Dove, *Sea II*, 1925.
Chiffon over metal with sand,
31.8 × 52.1 cm (12½ × 20½ in).
Collection of Barney
A. Ebsworth

201 William Baziotes, *Aquatic*,
1961. Oil on canvas,
167.6 × 198.4 cm (66 × 78⅛ in).
The Solomon R. Guggenheim
Museum, New York

Modern Art in America

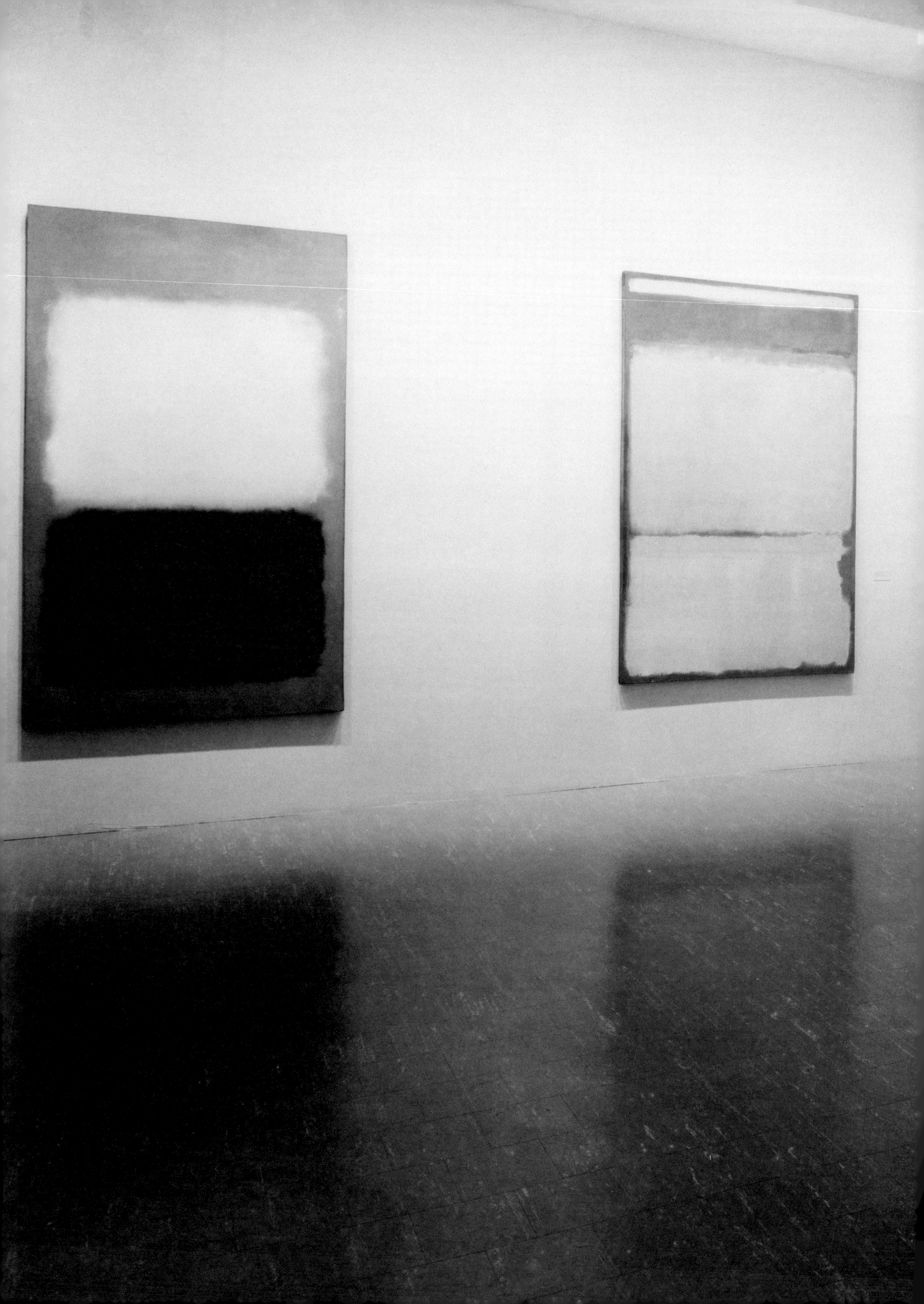

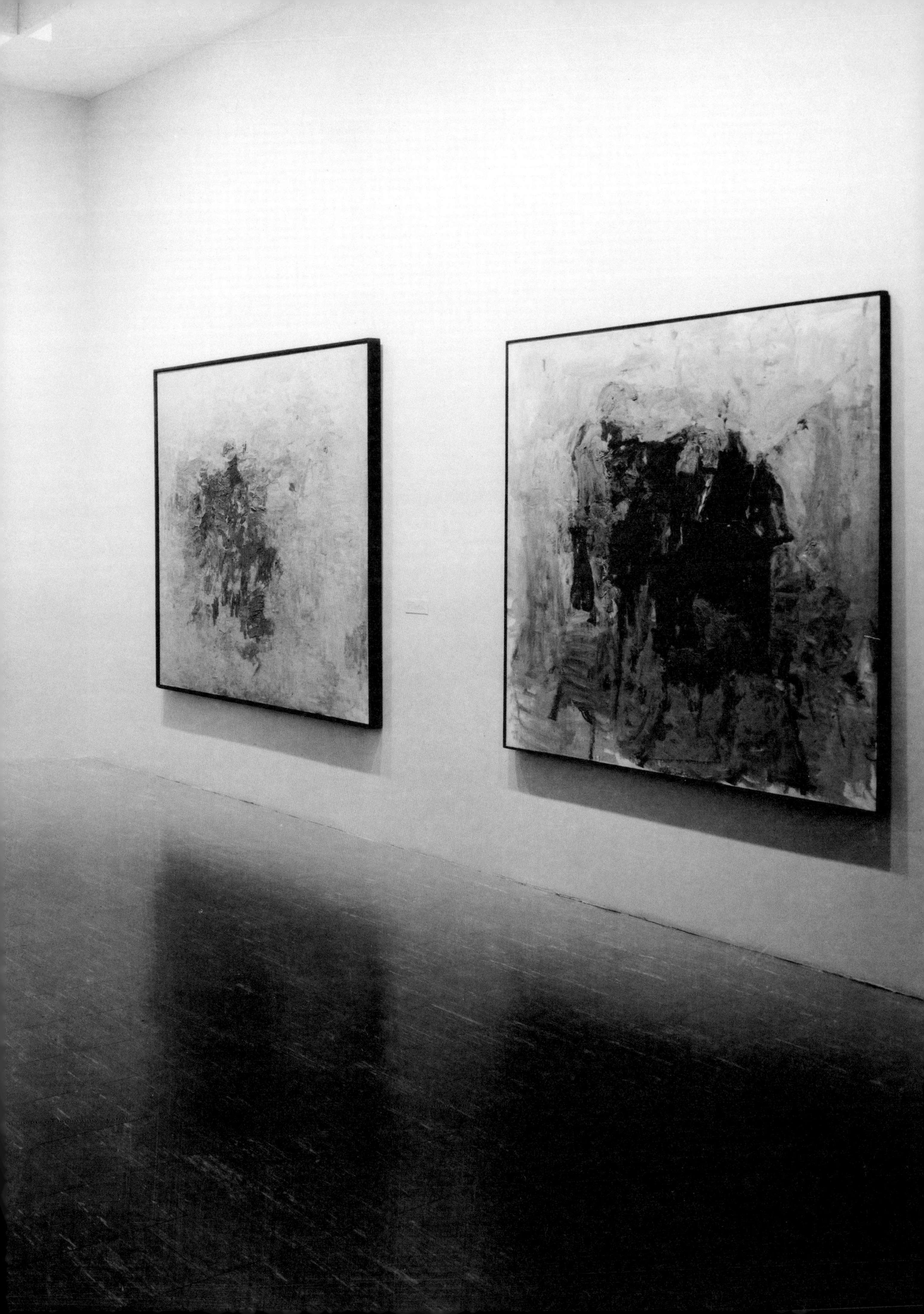

A NEW DEPTH IN AMERICAN ART

THE 1950s

Painterly abstraction was in the ascendency by 1950. Pollock, de Kooning, Rothko and Still had all reached a peak of achievement and were doing work that brought America acclaim, and countless artists appeared to be joining the ranks of the fledgling Expressionists. America's art seemed exclusively defined by the members of this group, but art is never so neat and tidy, and is always a complex intertwining of diverse currents. For around the same moment, 1950, there reappeared two familiar figures: Stuart Davis and Edward Hopper, with new works that will be discussed in detail in this chapter. Just as they had in 1940, Davis and Hopper again insisted, in their striking new compositions, that they be accorded a prominent voice in contemporary art alongside the younger generation.

Philip Roth called the 1950s the time 'America became America'.[1] The decade has been called the era of the silent generation, because the leaders of the 1950s had served in the war, had seen enough of strife and horror and now wanted only to get on with their work and their lives. But this was surely not true of art in America at this time of profound change and high accomplishment. By 1956, younger artists had emerged who dramatically changed the very conception of what art could be. The depth and quality of the arts, whether painting, theatre or jazz, had never been higher. It was a golden age in many ways. It was also the last time the country could speak of itself as 'we', as sharing a common core of values and identities, the last time America could be seen as a unified country.

By any measure, 1950 was a watershed year for artists across the spectrum. Pollock reached his peak with the four mural-sized paintings – *Number 1, 1950 (Lavender Mist)* (page 217); *Number 28, 1950; One: Number 31, 1950* [203]; and *Autumn Rhythm (Number 30)* – all with a new harmony and balance, away from his old expressionist ferocity. Gottlieb did the last of his primitivizing pictographs and moved into a more reduced, settled series of imaginary landscapes, made of far fewer forms. So, too, Rothko completed his shift from the multi-forms into his mature format of floating rectangles, directly confronting the viewer, so as to give the most

202 Installation view of the exhibition 'The New American Painting' (which toured Europe, 1957–9), The Museum of Modern Art, New York, 28 May–8 September 1959.

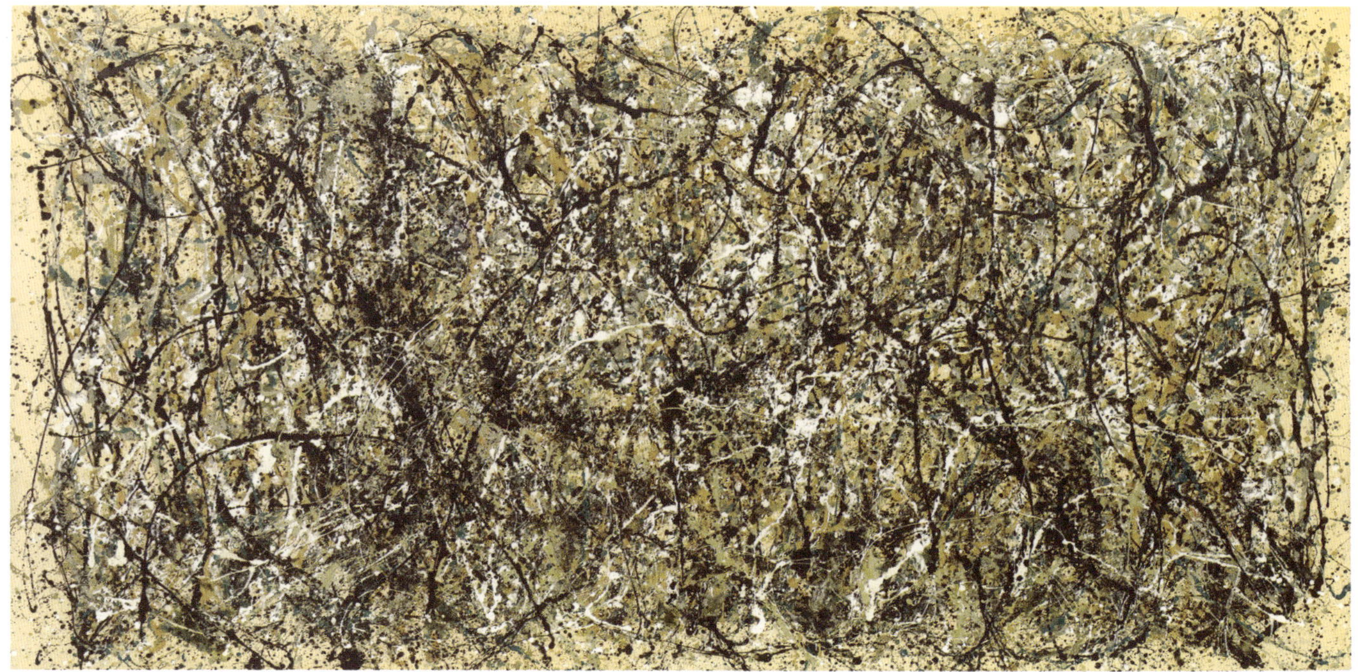

203

direct possible connection between the artist, the painting and the viewer. By 1950–1, Newman had enlarged the format in a new simplicity in his zip paintings, large, meditative expanses of silent space divided and punctuated by his vertical stripes. Motherwell did the first of his *Elegies*, also based on large verticals moving across the canvas, very different from his earlier, more densely populated collages and canvases. These works should be grouped with Davis's new style and the emergence of Kelly as a first-rate artist.

As at other times, older artists did not stop working. The re-emergence of Davis and Hopper in 1950–1 is an important episode in American art, although it has never been treated as such in textbooks. Indeed, it has never been mentioned, since the late work, post-1945, as well as that of numerous other Americans, has been ignored. To incorporate late work into our understanding of the period makes the art all the more rich, complex and diverse.

Hofmann's *Push and Pull*

Hofmann was a master colourist, to be sure, but he had also absorbed Cubism into his very pictorial being. In 1950, he began introducing broad planes of intense colour that can be said to be a unique fusion of Matisse and Picasso, but in an art all his own. In *Push and Pull III* [204] and *Composition No. 5*, both of that year, he essentially developed a new kind of Cubism, one of large, broad colour planes that went beyond anything Cubism had done to date. Cubism was supposed to be on the decline, finished as a vehicle for important art. Hofmann tells us otherwise, reminding us once again that the artist, not the critic, points to where art is going. Hofmann reinvigorated Cubism as a conduit for art of the highest reach both then and until the end of his life. Once again, he is in the vanguard, for with the work of Davis and Sheeler, his paintings made Cubism the catalyst for new and fresh art. The broad Cubist planes of all three opened up the surface and let it expand. Here, too, Hofmann is in the vanguard, for in 1951 Pollock and de Kooning moved to open the dense surfaces of their paintings, Pollock in his black pictures, de Kooning in his *Women*.

203 Jackson Pollock, *One: Number 31, 1950*, 1950. Oil and enamel on canvas, 269.5 × 530.8 cm (106⅛ × 209 in). The Museum of Modern Art, New York

204 Hans Hofmann, *Push and Pull III*, 1950. Oil on canvas, 91.4 × 121.9 cm (36 × 48 in). Private collection

The title of Hofmann's 1950 painting introduced his theory of push-pull, one of the basic principles in his art. It has caused a lot of confusion. That light colours advance and dark ones recede has been basic to Western painting, first postulated by Leonardo in his 'Perspective of Colour' (*Prospettiva di colore*). By balancing forces that come forward – the strong yellow – with a darker hue, blue, which tends to recede, Hofmann asserts the reality of the picture plane as a two-dimensional surface. By doing so, he participates in the modernist drive, evident since Manet, to move beyond the Renaissance system of perspective that depicted the illusion of three dimensions on a flat surface. Thus the painting becomes a reality in itself. On this surface the artist is then free to create his own worlds, which is exactly what Hofmann cherished more than anything. In his Germanic way, Hofmann wrote extensively, often making his art seem more difficult to get to than it really is. Theory can do that; but art, like life, is real, not a theory, and it depends on direct and immediate experience.[2] Modern science now tells us that there is a counter force to gravity, an anti-gravitational force that is called dark energy, exerting a push-pull effect throughout the universe. In fact, scientists now tell us that the three-dimensional world is an illusion, that our world is really a two-dimensional surface. So maybe Hofmann's idea is not a theory at all. Further, we are learning of the Higgs particle, the theory that even the emptiest of spaces is filled with a substance capable of bestowing mass upon particles. So space is not a fictive pictorial supposition, but a living, breathing presence that surrounds us.

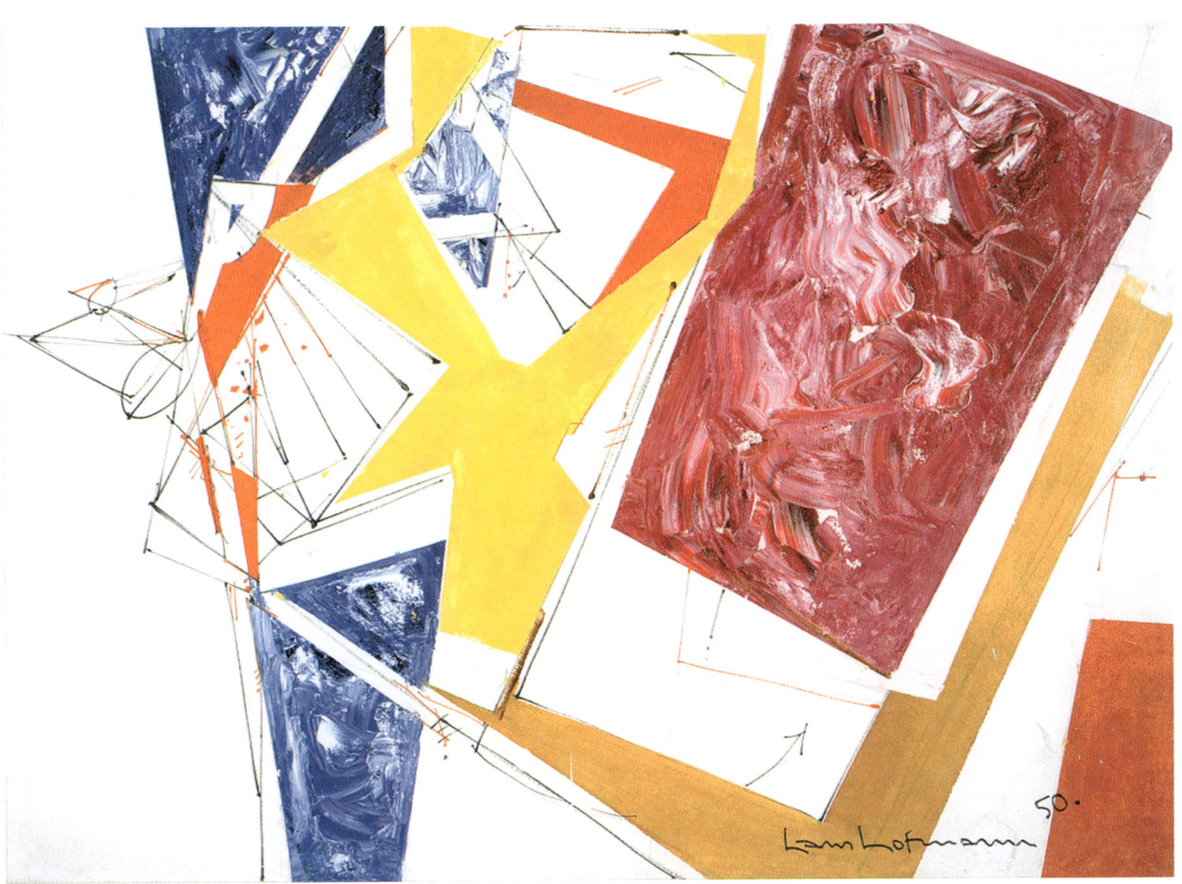

204

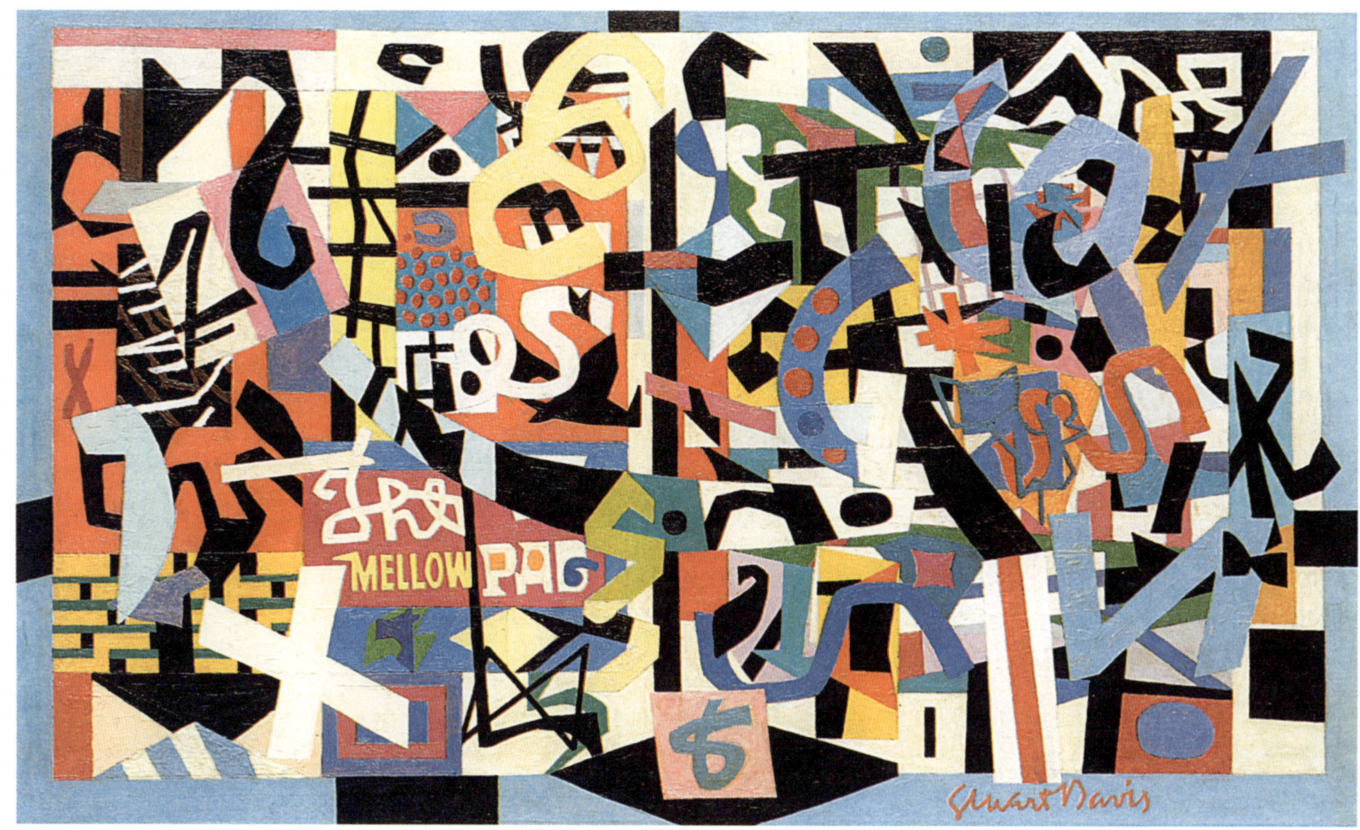

205

An Explosion of Culture

If sculpture and painting had developed a new depth in the 1950s, that should be seen as part of the enormous release and explosion of pent-up energy after the end of World War II, which brought a blossoming of American culture as never before and still remains a high point. It covered all the arts. The post-war years were the golden age of American theatre[3] and of Broadway musicals.[4] Never again have we seen this kind of concentrated brilliance, which remains a high point of American culture. Stories and metaphors for the country itself run throughout these productions.

Jazz, so important to so many American artists, flourished as never before; the art of Dove, Davis, Pollock, Noland, Parker and Ryman, to mention only a few, had been inspired, directly or indirectly, by the music that Davis felt was the only art (beside the new painting) to be truly American. Jazz is of the here and now, the essence of an inborn experience, unlike opera, which is based on distant cultures and times.

The American novel also flourished: Vladimir Nabokov, George Orwell, Robert Penn Warren, Sinclair Lewis, Norman Mailer, William Faulkner; Ernest Hemingway, Jack Kerouac, Ralph Ellison, J.D. Salinger, James Jones, Saul Bellow, James Baldwin, John O'Hara, James Agee (a distant relation), and then the first appearance, in 1959, of Philip Roth with *Goodbye, Columbus* all contributed to a depth of literature that paralleled the growth of the visual arts. This is worth our attention, for in literature we find some of the themes that are discussed in this book. The ongoing dialectic between the sources of art itself – drawing from the immediate world as opposed to those who see art as removed from the world and in a higher order – also marks the modern novel and literature. Jack Kerouac, Allen Ginsberg and the Beat poets, for example, embrace the actuality of life

205　Stuart Davis, *The Mellow Pad*, 1945–51. Oil on canvas, 66.7 × 107 cm (26¼ × 42⅜ in). Brooklyn Museum, New York

206　Stuart Davis, *Visa*, 1951. Oil on canvas, 101.6 × 132.1 cm (40 × 52 in). The Museum of Modern Art, New York

with the fervour of the Ashcan artists, directing us back to Emerson and Whitman, who urged the American artist to sing of himself and the commonplaces of American life. They all point to the American sense of individualism; or, in another vein, the American as an isolated, lonely soul, an island unto himself, as described by Melville in *Moby-Dick*.

Stuart Davis: A New Campaign

Davis had recovered enough from his near-death episode in 1948–9 to begin a new campaign of painting. He had finished what he called his 'killer' picture, *The Mellow Pad* (1945–51) [205], a confused and overworked painting that appears to be an attempt to rival the density of Pollock's all-over compositions.[5] Davis was well aware of Pollock, de Kooning and Kline, and understood them to be his most serious challengers, despite his apparent dismissal of Abstract Expressionism as a 'belch from the unconscious',[6] another example of how he took pleasure in misdirecting his audience. The question he posed was, could he match them in their power and density, but in a way that could retain his way of painting in a clear, hard-edge manner? After *The Mellow Pad*, he put this challenge aside for several years and took on the younger artists on his own terms, using the brilliant colour of Matisse that he had emulated since the Armory Show of 1913, and his brand of open planes of a personal late Cubism.

Davis's post-1950 paintings can be said to be a corrective to his own earlier work, as well as to the most acutely visible style of the Abstract Expressionists. In his new paintings he announced his return as a contending artist, back in the mainstream. He claimed that the word 'Champion', which he used prominently in works of 1950–1, was based on a spark-plug ad on a matchbook, and that is true on one level. But this too was a typical Davis deflection. The painting *Visa* (1951) [206] has a far more personal and pungent reference that personifies Davis's core personality and experience. It surely refers to the hit film, *Champion* (featuring the young Kirk Douglas), then playing on Broadway, its title emblazoned in giant illuminated letters,

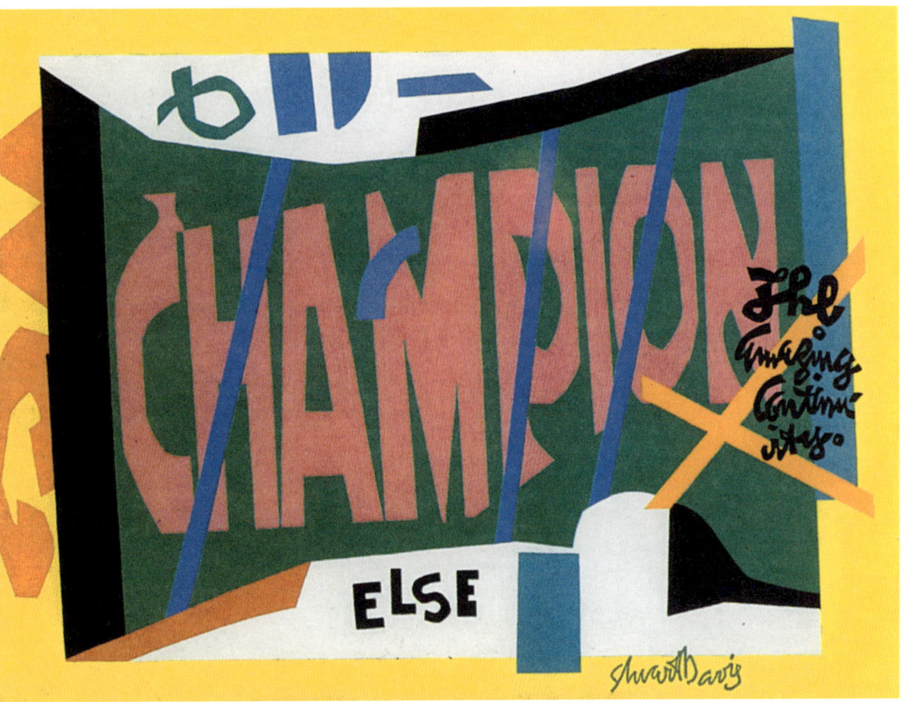

206

moving on a slight path upwards as in the painting itself. The sign would have dominated the Broadway area, and the film itself garnered wide critical praise. It told the story of the rise and fall of Midge Kelly, champion boxer, who had fought his way to glory only to lose it because of pride and arrogance. Davis loved boxing; he was the only one in his circle of friends to own a TV, so they came to his house to watch the Friday night fights. His love of the boxing scene no doubt goes back to Bellows's famous fight scenes and the hard-drinking days of the Henri school, where Davis learned the joys of the city, when boxing was still illegal. In his paintings he tells us that he is still champ, unlike the protagonist of the film.

These paintings also announce the continuation – and expansion – of the Cubism that Davis had himself done so much to develop and extend into American art, as a viable, continuing mode for new, original and important art. This is a crucial fact, since many critics thought Cubism to be a defunct, retrograde style, now permanently displaced by the painterly gesturalism of Abstract Expressionist art. The artists themselves did not think so – including Davis, Sheeler, Smith, Hofmann, George L.K. Morris, Crawford, Bolotowsky, Diller and many more who continued to work in a Cubist manner after 1945. Cubism was, in effect, a counter to the expressionism of de Kooning and Pollock; it offered correctives to what they saw as the undisciplined, over-painted and uncontrolled surfaces of painterly abstraction that for them had hidden, or even buried, the surface. It was the start of the drive that took many forms but extended through the 1950s until the hard-edge surfaces of the early 1960s took prominence in America.

It is the new brilliance of Davis's colour that is the most striking. His late work signals the importance of Matisse's colour cut-outs for America then and certainly throughout the 1960s. It offered a solution to the already perceptible problem of the overworked surfaces of Abstract Expressionism, but largely contains the same intensity of line and pictorial energy as his earlier work.

Visitors to the Davis retrospective at the Minneapolis Museum in 1957 would have been particularly struck by a painting that announced this shift in his work, as if it had been timed to fit the emerging art. Indeed, the exhibition brought Davis renewed attention and admiration, as well as presenting an example of how art might proceed. Fittingly enough, the painting was entitled *Premiere* [207], and had been done just that year. It was even bolder than his previous work – with high-keyed, intense hues, including a brilliant yellow and strong accents of white, red and black – using a minimum of colours, just as Mondrian had done. (In fact, Davis had consulted Meyer Schapiro on Mondrian's colour theories, and he confirmed that Mondrian believed five colours were enough.)[7] The picture is structured around an off-centre, irregular Cubist grid that also pointed to Mondrian. A series of large words pop out from the surface: PAD, FREE, 100%, JUICE, NEW, as if on a billboard. The painting had been commissioned by *Fortune* magazine as part of a series of artists' impressions of walking through the new giant supermarkets, just then appearing in America. It was therefore an early example of work drawing on commercial packaging, soon to be a staple of contemporary art.

Davis approached the assignment by gathering various products, taking them home and arranging them in a Cubist/Mondrianesque type of still life. They were not literal depictions; only words from their labels were used, a play on Cubist signs that Davis had employed as early as 1917 with the word 'Garage' prominently displayed in a scene done in Gloucester. The words seem to embody the new experience of the large

207 Stuart Davis, *Premiere*, 1957. Oil on canvas, 147.3 × 127 cm (58 × 50 in). Los Angeles County Museum of Art

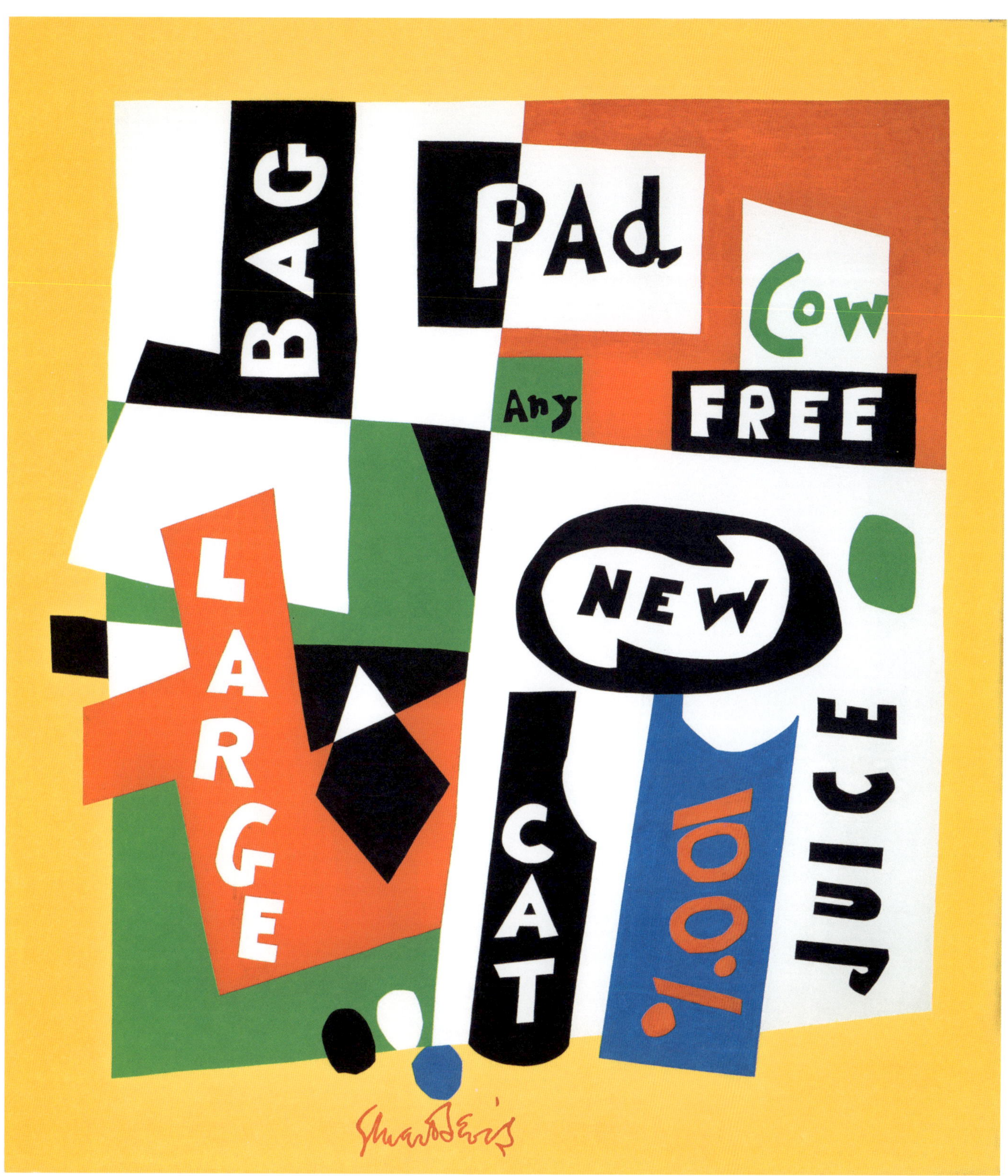

207

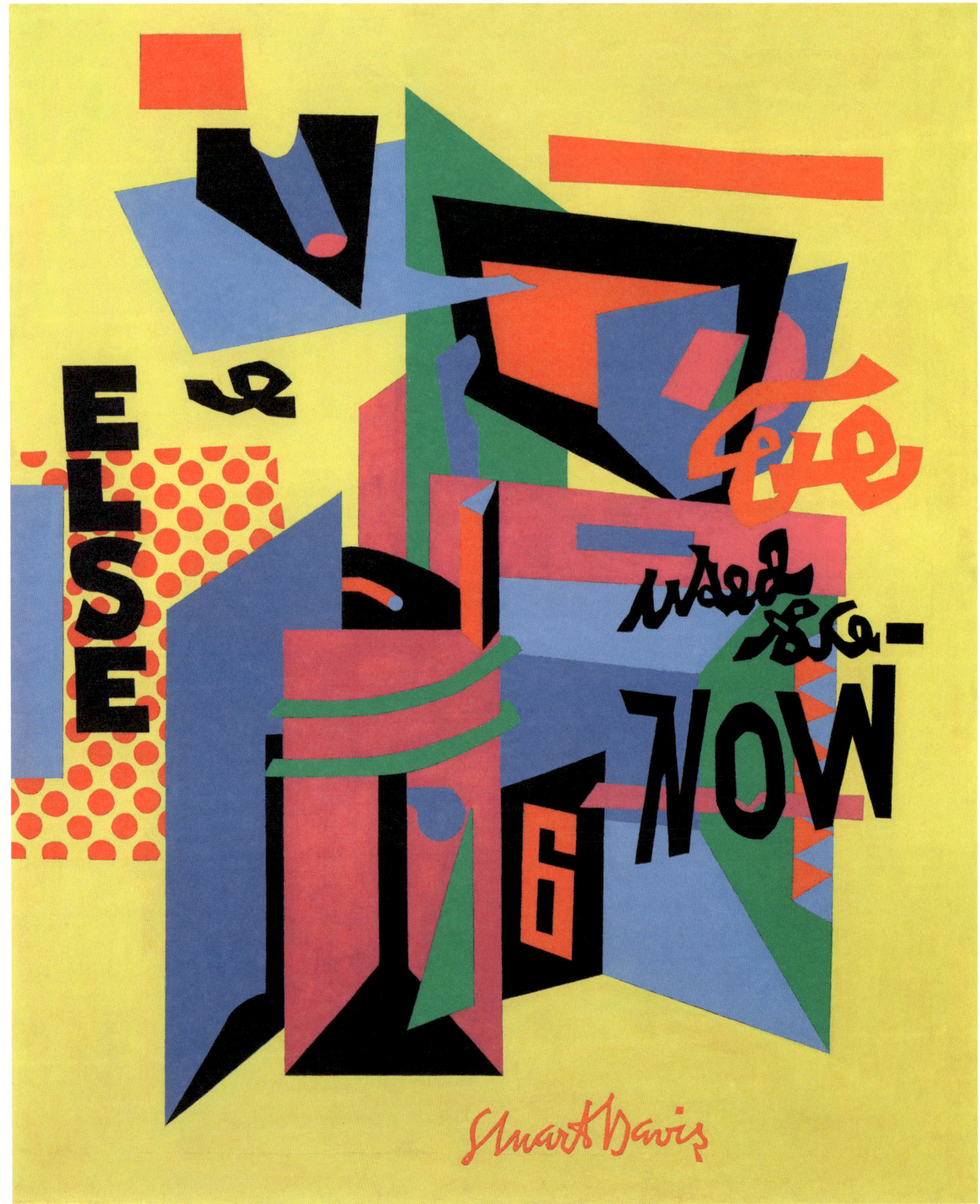

208

supermarket, but, typically of Davis, there are other meanings as well. He tells us he is working in a NEW direction; he is FREE in pursuing this direction and his art; he is doing it in his PAD, which for him is the painting itself; he is giving it all the JUICE needed; he is working in an all-out manner, in a 100% effort. It is the beginning of a series that he pursued until the end of his life, in which he sent these blatant but still hidden messages. But even here, it is clear that Davis had made stunning advances in his old stylistic ventures: a new and vibrant use of Cubism; colour intensity fit to match Matisse; and clarity and use of words, a forerunner of the Art & Language movement of the 1960s. In her review of the show, Elaine de Kooning got it just right when she said that in the midst of so much vague, hectic work, Davis's art came as a 'sock in the jaw'.[8]

Davis never went far from Matisse. Indeed, in the 1950s he appears to have re-examined *The Red Studio*, the work that he had seen in the Armory Show and of which he had done his own version in 1917. Matisse had used the painting to record his life as an artist. We can identify all but one of the paintings hanging in the studio, as well as the sculptures, and we also see the tools of the draughtsman. It is an autobiography of an artist. Davis did the same in his own version, inserting his current state of mind and artistic thought. This practice began with the 'Champion' series, into which he placed his own story, and it becomes more explicit in *Owh! In San Paõ* (1951) [208], where he interjects an abstract diagrammatic version of an earlier work, in this case his painting *Percolator* of 1927.

In *Cliché* (1955) [209], Davis uses the full red curtain (although the red is more towards an orange) just as he did in his *Studio* of 1917, his first take on Matisse. Then, within it, as he now did continually, he makes a reference to an old work, in this case especially difficult to read but finally decipherable

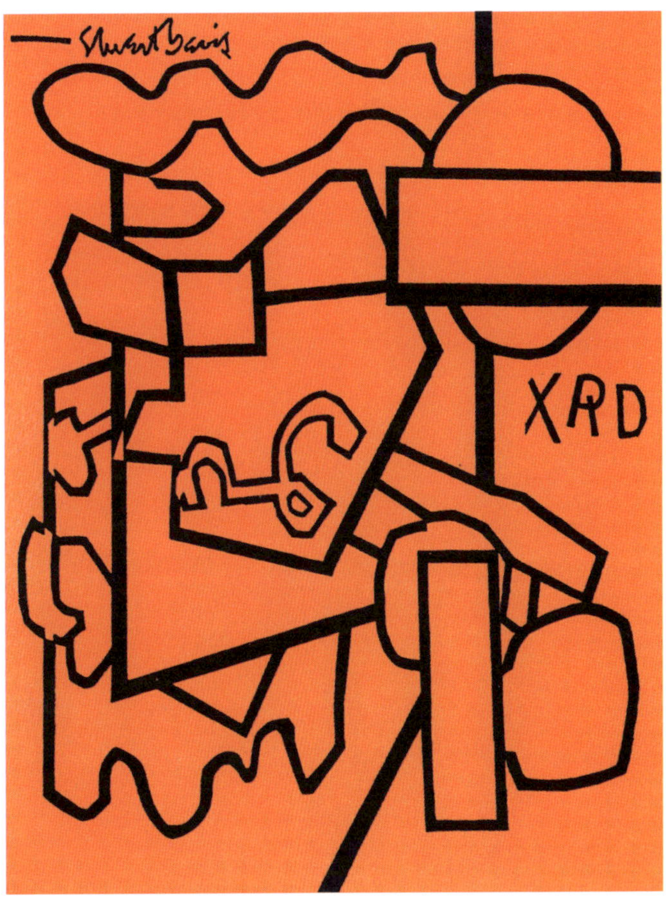

209

208 Stuart Davis, *Owh! In San Paõ*, 1951. Oil on canvas, 132.6 × 106.7 cm (52¼ × 42 in), Whitney Museum of American Art, New York

209 Stuart Davis, *Cliché*, 1955. Oil on canvas, 142.9 × 106.7 cm (56¼ × 42 in). The Solomon R. Guggenheim Museum, New York

as a composition from 1922.[9] The painting may well have been intended as
a homage to the grand master, who had died the year before. In *The Red
Studio*, Matisse had shown us his place of comfort, his pad as it were,
and Davis also tells us in *Premiere* that his pad is his studio and the single
work of art. Davis emulates Matisse by using only a red curtain, incised with
a pattern of lines, the essential ingredients of *The Red Studio*.

Edward Hopper's Resurgence

We can see Hopper's resurgence after 1950 as part of this drive to a new
clarity. His work had somewhat stagnated since 1945, but it underwent a
rejuvenation in 1950. His paintings after this date are reduced, distilled,
with fewer elements than before, with planes broader and clearer and
more open, often including a single, isolated figure. In *Rooms by the Sea*
(1951)[211] there are no figures; a prominent rhomboid of light is the
central presence, almost as a substitute for a human form. The view is
allegedly based on a house on Cape Cod, but the abrupt division between
house and water seems almost like a Surrealist juxtaposition; Hopper is
known to have admired Surrealism, including Magritte and even perhaps
Pierre Roy. The calm and the silence are eerie, rendering the painting at
once ominous and serene. The most compelling element is the block of
light, as physical as the architecture. The painting cannot help but recall
Rothko, whose mature style of floating rectangles of light had just come
to fruition. This canvas – and others – shows that Hopper was not a kind
of off-beat curiosity, but a member of mainstream art as much as any
other artist. Rothko would not have disagreed, and a small study,
Composition 1 (1929–31) [210], is a virtual paraphrase of Hopper's *Chop
Suey* [212] of 1929.[10] In 2010, the Yale University Art Gallery installed
Hopper's *Rooms by the Sea* on a single wall, side by side with two abstract
Cubist paintings of the same time by Crawford and Sheeler, a daring and
revealing juxtaposition, for all three are similar in their composition, in
fact almost seem to be based on the same angular design.

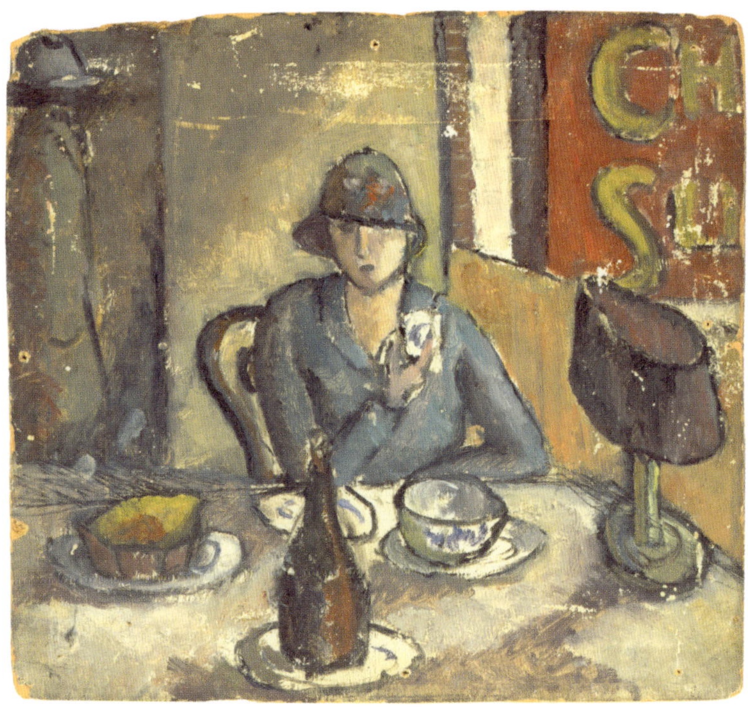

210

210 Mark Rothko, *Composition 1*
      [recto], 1929–31.
      Oil on board, 32.7 × 34.9 cm
      (12⅞ × 13¾ in). Collection
      of Kate Rothko Prizel and
      Christopher Rothko

211 Edward Hopper, *Rooms by
      the Sea*, 1951. Oil on canvas,
      74.3 × 101.6 cm (29¼ × 40 in).
      Yale University Art Gallery,
      New Haven

212 Edward Hopper, *Chop Suey*,
      1929. Oil on canvas,
      81 × 96.5 cm (32 × 38 in).
      Collection of Barney
      A. Ebsworth

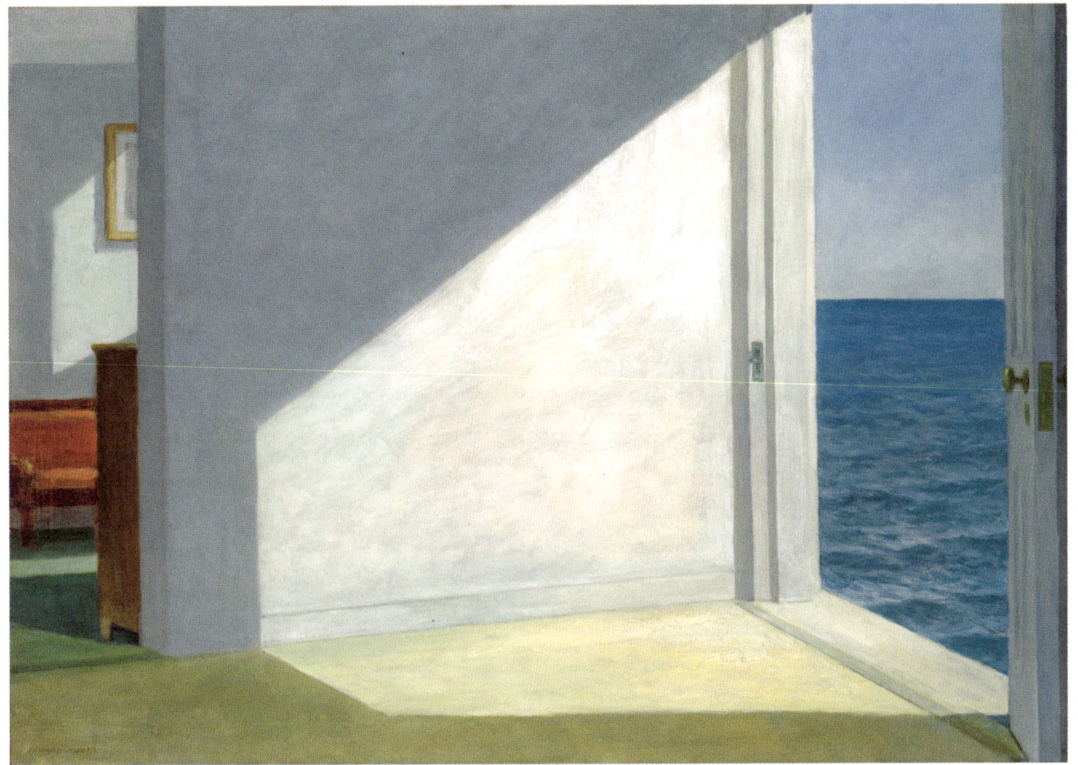

211

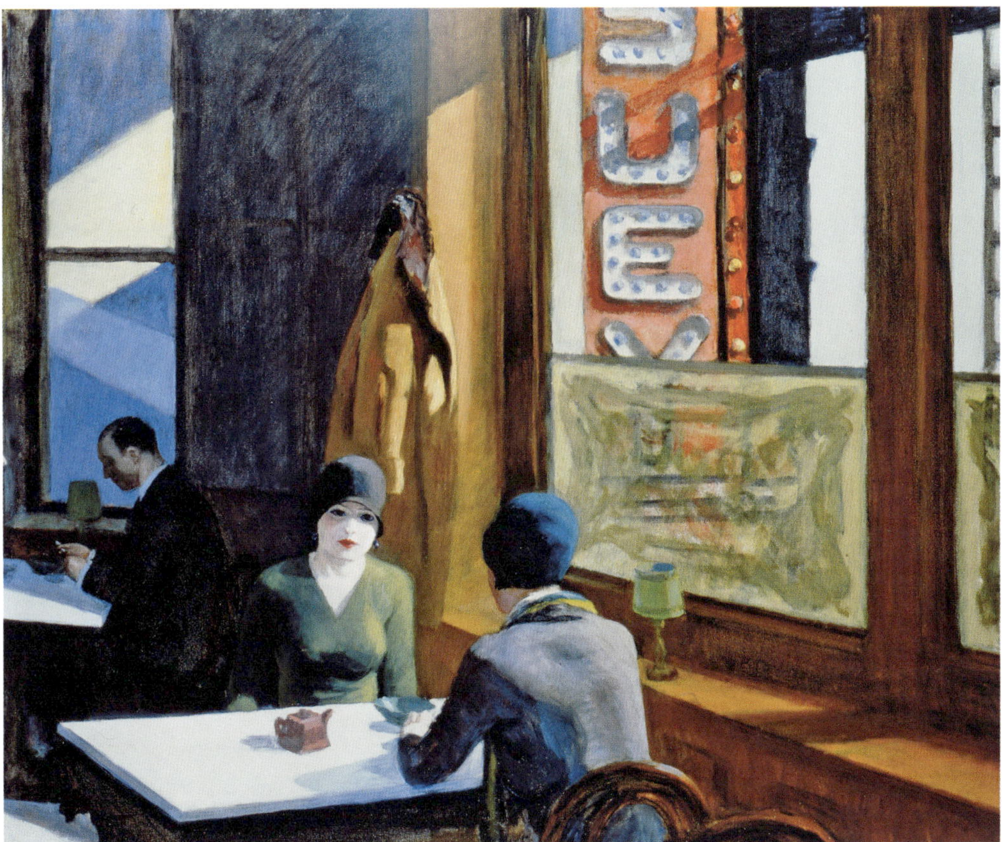

212

De Kooning and the 'Pre-Determined'

From the start, de Kooning had worked with the figure. That is not surprising given his background and training in northern Europe, the area where oil painting was invented, and which had stamped him with an indelible attachment to the Old Master tradition. By 1949–50, in *Attic* and *Excavation* (two of his most famous paintings), de Kooning had shredded the figure into myriad parts interwoven like a jigsaw puzzle, the most complex paintings he had ever done. In 1950–2, however, he too saw the need for greater clarity, as Pollock had, and returned to a full-blown figure composition. His *Woman I* of 1950–2 [213] introduced a series of front and centre ferocious females pressed close to us and the picture plane, as if intruding on our space. These paintings caused a sensation, even for the mere fact that they seemed to revert to figuration in the midst of what was thought to be an unremitting drive towards abstraction. But de Kooning had always been a figurative painter at heart. If this marks him as 'conservative', in the sense that he looked to the past, there was never a more flexible, inventive, far-seeing conservative. His gift for paint and paint manipulation, his sheer abandon in materials, were unequalled at the time, even by Pollock. Nothing seemed impossible for de Kooning with a brush in his hand. He could recall Rembrandt, as in *Woman V* (1952–3), while at the same time pictorially defining what we might take as a modern angst in *Woman and Bicycle* (1952–3). He was not anti-women by dint of the disjointed female forms – if he was, as one writer quipped, then how did he feel about bicycles, here depicted as a twisted mash?[11]

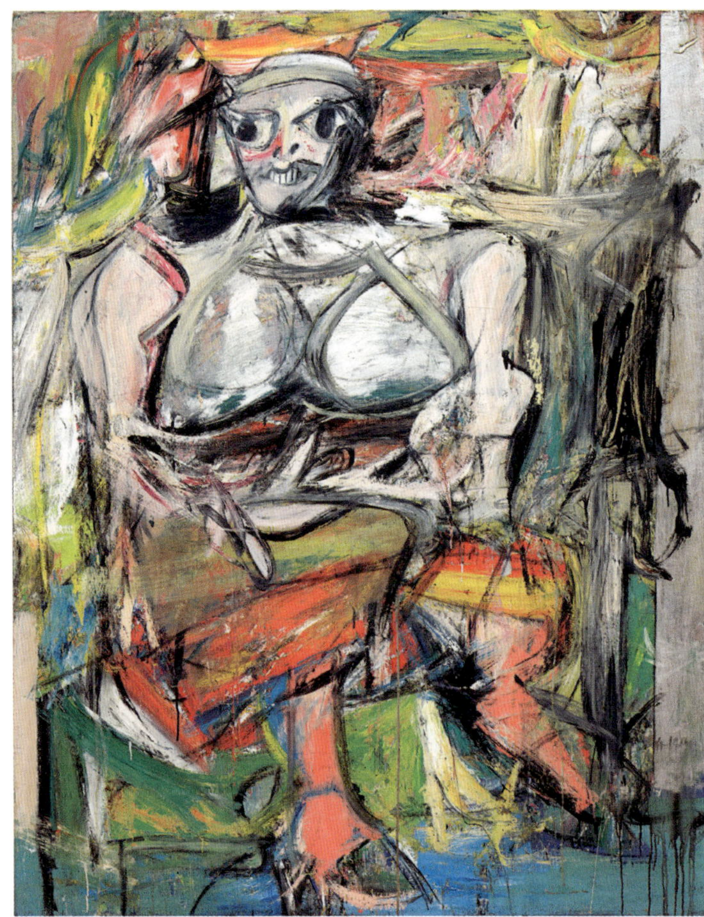

213

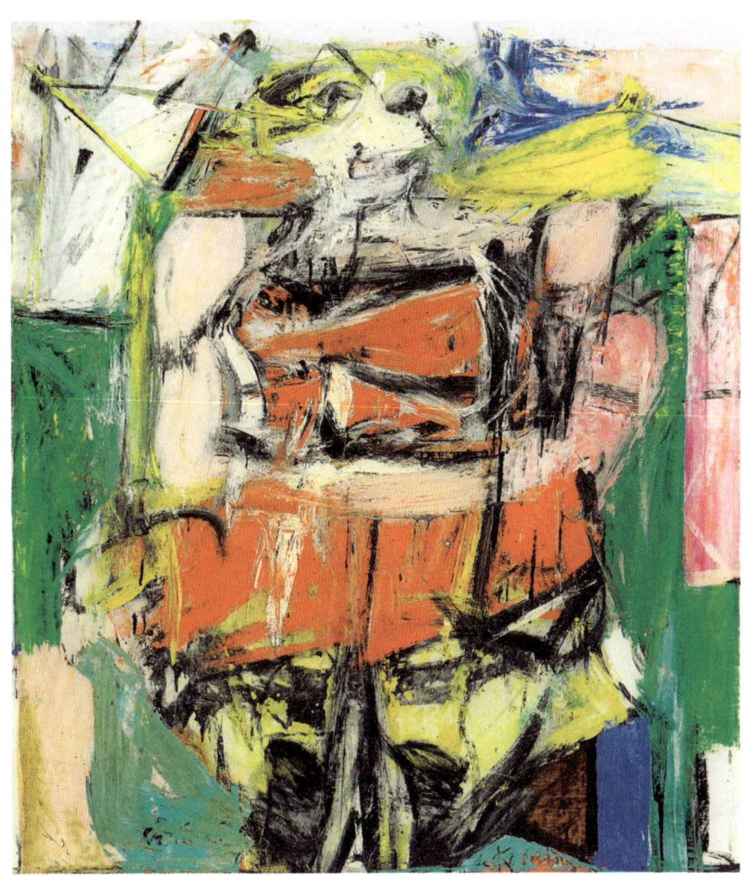

214

213 Willem de Kooning, *Woman I*,
1950–2. Oil, enamel and
charcoal on canvas,
192.7 × 147.3 cm (75⅞ × 58 in).
The Museum of Modern Art,
New York

214 Willem de Kooning, *Woman VI*,
1953. Oil and enamel on
canvas, 174 × 148.6 cm
(68½ × 58½ in). Carnegie
Museum of Art, Pittsburgh

De Kooning's move to a full figure should also be seen as another important and early part of correcting what were viewed as problems with the art of this generation. The figure opened up the canvas, giving it more breathing space – de Kooning's understanding of a necessary, higher degree of clarity and legibility. Using the figure also provided a given for the artist, a sure way to get the picture going, thus avoiding the necessity of inventing a new and original composition every time, a demand that had grown tiresome for de Kooning. In 1951, he stated that using the *Women* motif 'eliminated composition, arrangement, relationships, light – all this silly talk about line, colour, and form' and concluded that 'I put [the image] in the centre of the canvas because there was no reason to put it a bit on the side.'[12] This last is especially important, for it speaks of focusing head on the image, which could then be used pictorially in myriad ways. The structure is a given, with no arrangements or relationships, a composition that is pre-determined.

We must ask what it was about 1950–1 that wrought this seismic change. This leads us to look ahead a mere two or three years to the pre-determined formats of Jasper Johns, which introduced a turning point in the drive to clarity in the mid-1950s. In the last of the de Kooning 'Women' series, *Woman VI* (1953) [214], the figure is fully squared away, frontal, occupying most of the canvas, a precursor of the shift to broader and clearer forms that had appeared by 1957 and was to define the look of the 1960s. The squared and true format in these de Koonings also echoes the influence of Albers's frontal structures. Indeed, this move in the mid- and late 1960s indicates a growing awareness and respect for the geometry of Albers.

Colour-Field Painting in the Early 1950s: Frankenthaler

Helen Frankenthaler (1928–2011) took another path to clarity altogether
by closely studying the watercolours of Marin and the open, soft colours of
Gorky, and by seeing how Pollock's colours often soaked directly into the
surface of the canvas, thus reducing the physical presence of pigment
and offering an inherent opening-up of the surface. The colour remained,
but without the increasingly clogged surfaces of overabundant paint that
marked the work of many of the second-generation Abstract Expressionists
also born in the 1920s. Essentially, Frankenthaler was introducing a new
way of working that could reconcile the drawing of Pollock with the
openness and colour of Gorky, Marin and others. It was these elements
that were the foundation of the development of colour-field painting in the
early 1950s, and she is the artist most closely associated with its inception.

Here, it is important to understand the difference between colour-field
painting and fields-of-colour painting, two separate types of art that are
central to this book and the history of colour. As we understand it today,
colour field is the term we use to describe the direct stain process, of
thinned paint soaking into the canvas; Frankenthaler was the pioneer of
this method, often associated with Greenberg and his taste. But there is
a much broader use of the term, as found in this book: fields of colour,
covering the canvas, but not necessarily stained in. Indeed, the paint is
often thick, but the effect is of a field or fields of total colour that carry
the picture. This can be traced to Matisse and *The Red Studio*, in which
the whole surface is covered in an envelope of thin colour. It would include
pioneers such as Newman, Still and Rothko, then Alfred Jensen and others.
The distinction is crucial. Direct stain stemmed from Pollock, Gorky and
Marin but was brought to fruition in the later 1950s and 1960s by
Frankenthaler, Noland, Louis and others of the Washington Colour School.
This type of painting is often coeval with the rise of second-generation
Abstract Expressionism; certainly it applies to Frankenthaler, but also to
artists such as Sam Francis, who was instrumental in direct-stain colour-
field art. The fact is that second-generation colour field is often, but not
always, synonymous with second-generation Abstract Expressionist.

Frankenthaler's breakthrough canvas, the work that established her
artistic identity and announced the arrival of a prime innovator, is *Mountains
and Sea* (1952)[215]. It has long been recognized as an American icon – a
bridge between past and future that changed the course of abstract art,
and her own work, by means of an essentially new technique. It is a work
of mesmerizing beauty, a marvel of modern landscape painting. Large in
size, it is nonetheless intimate and inviting. Frankenthaler created *Mountains
and Sea* when she was only twenty-three, a precocious newcomer to the New
York art world. She had studied at Bennington College, at the Art Students
League and with Hofmann, one of the founding fathers of advanced art
in America. She was well acquainted with the masters of modern art,
especially Pollock, Gorky and Marin among them. She quickly adapted
the openness and free movement of Abstract Expressionism. In August
1952, she travelled to Nova Scotia, where she continued her practice of
making small landscapes, showing once again how important landscape
painting was to Abstract Expressionism. She painted in watercolour and
oil on paper, working freely from nature. These studies helped to keep her
limber and flexible, like a dancer or athlete warming up, or – as was the
case here – a painter preparing for a major new effort.

On the afternoon of 26 October, back in New York, she tacked
a large – roughly 7 × 10 foot – piece of canvas to the floor of her studio

215 Helen Frankenthaler,
Mountains and Sea, 1952.
Oil and charcoal on canvas,
220 × 297.8 cm
(86⅝ × 117¼ in). Collection
of the Helen Frankenthaler
Foundation, on extended loan
to the National Gallery of Art,
Washington, DC

Modern Art in America

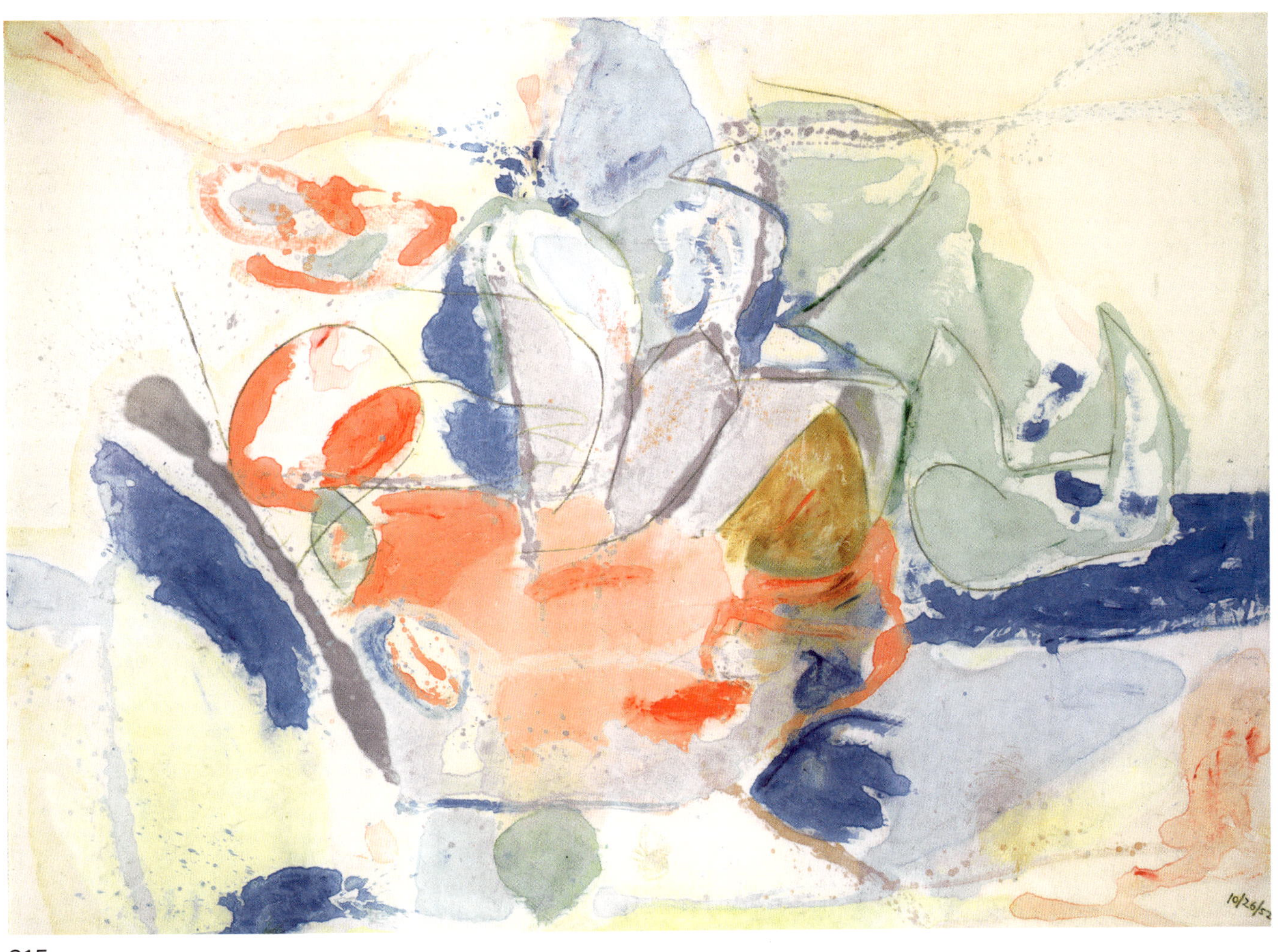

215

to begin the biggest painting she had ever undertaken. Her mind was filled with memories of the spectacular Cape Breton landscape. After roughing in a few charcoal marks as an initial guide, she poured highly thinned oil paint from coffee cans directly on to the canvas, as if she were drawing with colour. She had no plan; she just worked, with control and discipline. At the end of the afternoon, when she had finished, she climbed on a ladder and studied the painting. She was not yet sure what she had done; she was 'sort of amazed and surprised and interested'.[13] It soon became clear that what she had done was invent a new way of making art.

Frankenthaler's painting method, and *Mountains and Sea* itself, had not appeared out of the blue. Like Pollock, she had worked directly on the floor. But Pollock had used enamel paint, which stayed on the canvas surface when it dried. She wanted something more liquid, watery. Still, there was no concentrated effort to find a new technique. 'I didn't try staining per se', she later recalled. 'I was trying to get at something … I didn't know what it was until it was manifest.'[14] By working as she did, she allowed the pigments to settle into the weave of the fabric itself, joining them as one. This application gave her a freedom, openness and flexibility that allowed colour to move and expand in liquid pools, under the control of her hand and her arm, as if the surface were a giant watercolour. This avoided the dense paint and tactile weight that could often clog the surface. In its place, by staining directly into the canvas, Frankenthaler could introduce a new lyricism and an idyllic setting that recall the Venetian pictorial tradition of the pastoral.

From this point on, staining became the basis of her art and pointed to new directions for others. It also restored colour to its old grandeur, a departure from the dark, angst-ridden hues of so many Abstract Expressionists. *Mountains and Sea* invokes an unfolding drama of space, light and movement. Each colour tracks its own course, free, independent and leisurely. It becomes a pastoral landscape of a type familiar in Venetian painting of the Renaissance, as well as in more modern works such as Matisse's *Bonheur de Vivre* (1905–6), a bucolic idyll that seems to recall a golden age, a garden of paradise.

Although the colour and canvas are bound together on a totally flat surface, our eye moves, in her words, 'miles back and forth'[15] through the fictive space she creates out of her large, open washes of colour. We almost lose ourselves in the fresh Canadian air, as if on a fine summer's day. Indeed, we feel the topography of Nova Scotia is clearly suggested, as the mountain-like peak at the apex descends to the 'sea' at centre right. The hues themselves are not loud but mellow, limpid. Pale blues and light greens suggest sky, water and forest, modified by areas of bare canvas that become colours and shapes in their own right. The painting has a pastoral and lyrical quality, fusing the colour and drawing of the two poles of Abstract Expressionism, but free now from its dense, overworked surfaces. This in itself pointed to a new direction. Her painting looked both backwards and forwards, like a Janus-faced monument.

Mountains and Sea received barely any notice when it was shown the following year. But in the spring of 1953, two little-known artists from Washington, DC, Morris Louis and Kenneth Noland, visited Frankenthaler's studio in New York. Both were promising artists, but they could not find their way out of Abstract Expressionism and into something personal of their own. *Mountains and Sea* was a revelation for both, 'the bridge between Pollock and what was possible', as Louis later said.[16] They adopted Frankenthaler's technique, found their own directions and became central figures in the colour field school of painting of the late 1950s and early 1960s, a great chapter in American art. Nor was that the extent of Frankenthaler's influence. Her technique also started a drive towards an overall clarity and directness of colour that informed much of the best art of the next fifteen years, from the older Hofmann himself to younger artists such as Ray Parker.

Noland, Louis and the Colour Field School

This narrative of Frankenthaler, Louis and Noland demands a broader context, for art never happens that quickly. Louis and Noland had been working through Abstract Expressionism in the late 1940s and early 1950s, trying to find something that was truly their own. In fact, Noland was a very good painter in the Abstract Expressionist, painterly style, but later he stopped showing these paintings, which are only rarely seen in public.[17] We are missing an exceedingly accomplished body of work. Both artists were well aware of Pollock's black paintings and the way the paint soaked into the canvas, just as Frankenthaler's had. Noland had studied colour with Bolotowsky at Black Mountain College, and knew the colour masterpieces at the Phillips Collection – which he and Louis visited every Sunday, a ritual that for them was like going to church.[18] There he looked closely at the work of Paul Klee – Albers's teacher – and admired the way in which he could join the colour and the surface as one, the very thing Noland himself sought and soon achieved. Noland and Louis also looked carefully at the American modernists there, especially Dove and O'Keeffe. They took note of the soft, diffused colour and the circular compositions of their work.

By 1956, Noland had made paintings of thin, stained and open colour, still painterly in look and feel but now with an arbitrary circle drawn into the surface, to give it focus and clarity. Thereafter the circles became more pronounced, the centre and primary element of the canvas. At first the outer edges were still jagged and painterly, clearly Abstract Expressionist in origin, the very image of painting in transition; by 1958 the painterly sections had virtually disappeared, and then by 1959 concentric circles, clearly drawn, of varying widths and hues dominated. This shows once more that colour-field art came out of and evolved from Abstract Expressionism. The progression was in full swing by 1955–6, when Pollock's death announced a new era in painting, and his legacy was widely discussed, most notably by Allan Kaprow. 'The King is dead! Long live the King! But things will change!' seemed to be the order of the day. So they did, marking 1956 as a key date in the history of American art.

The colour-field work of these three artists is closely associated with Clement Greenberg, the critic who more than anyone had championed their art. Greenberg has been condemned by many who have seen him as espousing a cold impersonal formalism, without real meaning. What this is actually saying is that Greenberg focused on painting as an art, a practice, a discipline, which it has always been. It is not cold and empty – the exact words Stalin used to condemn Russian avant-garde art; it has meaning – it has to have human content since it is made by human beings, and thus it is humanistic by definition. Greenberg was not interested in extra-pictorial content, only painting. But we can extend that to a fuller understanding of Noland and his art.

For example, Noland chose the exact centre of the canvas as the core of his circles, like a bull's-eye, or the centring of the Madonna's head in a Renaissance painting, with perfect symmetry. That brings full attention to the painting, focusing us on the work. For Noland, this was

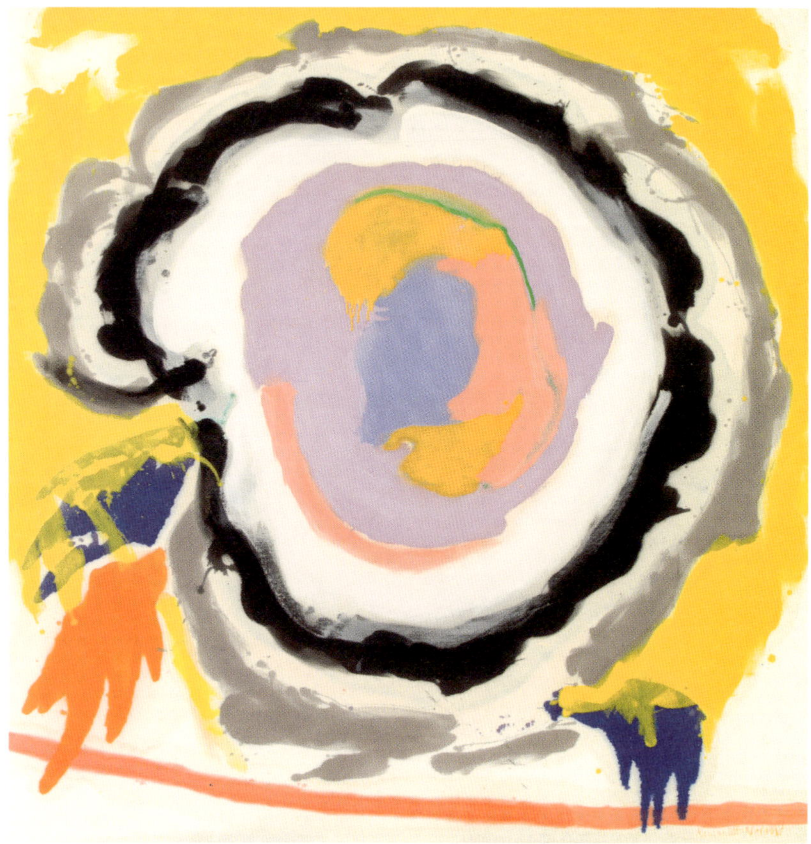

216

the best way to locate and stabilize the body's kinaesthetic centre as the spectator confronted the painting; by implication, the middle of the canvas was also the site of the viewer's emotions and psychological stability. That is, we centre ourselves to locate our emotions and feelings, and to stabilize ourselves in the world around us. Many of the early circles contain embryo-like shapes, referring to the birth of the world and to a human. *Ex-Nihilo* (1958) [216], 'out of nothing', seems to refer to the making of something, of the world and human life, that can be compared to Dove's 'Sunrise' series of 1936–7. For Noland, the circle was not simply an appropriated design, but in fact came from what he had observed in much modern art, the tendency for a painting to enclose itself, to gather itself, the better to keep the focus on the centre. He saw this in Cézanne's grand bathers, the figures there posed like bookends and the trees bending as arches. The circle, rough as it is, is implied in Pollock's compositions, in the large-scale murals and in smaller but no less powerful works such as *Phosphorescence* (page 216). There is no doubt that Jasper Johns's 'Targets' also had an effect for Noland.

In 1957, Adolph Gottlieb introduced his clarified format in the 'Burst' paintings, consisting of two elements, an irregular rough circle at top and a burst of rough strokes at the lower part of the canvas. They are clearly landscape paintings, as in *Mist*, 1961 [217], which can be traced to such works of Arthur Dove as *Moon and Sea II* (1923). So, too, Noland is often a landscape painter, frequently with cosmic overtones, as in his painting *Lunar Episode* (1958), which depicts a moon moving through the sky and pays homage to Dove's sun and moon paintings of the 1930s (work that Noland knew well from his visits to the Phillips Collection). The intense heat in the painting of that title, and the burning summer sun of the oranges in *Noon Afloat* (1962) [218] or the cool colours of *April* (1960), convey the chill beginning to warm in the sun of the middle of an early spring day.

     Modern Art in America

This mood continued in the 1960s. In *East-West* (1963) [219], for example, we feel the sun as it follows our journey from east to west, from the high yellows of morning to the deep reds of the sunset. The rising sun is surely invoked in paintings such as *Cadmium Radiance*, also of 1963, in which the rays rise from the centre at the low horizon of the picture plane. While visiting the artist in California to prepare his exhibition, I found that he loved the water, the sky and the land. We walked on the beach twice a day, and Noland took innumerable photographs along the way. I understood, finally, and blurted out that he was a landscape painter. He looked at me, smiled and said 'I'm glad you understand.'

The early paintings of Morris Louis, such as *Charred Journal: Firewritten V* (1951) [221], done with a personal Abstract Expressionist handling of paint, make clear references to barbed wire and the death camps in Germany, a vivid reminder of the atrocities just past. This in itself tells us that Louis, like Noland, was not immune to an art of personal and emotional references, especially to nature and the world around us. He, too, seems to refer to the spread of colour of the distant horizons in his 'Veils', or the dawning of a new day, a new world in the majestic spreads of the 'Florals' [220] and then the 'Unfurled' series. In the 'Florals' we have suggestive images of nature, of huge trees and their branches, as in Dove's masterpiece of colour *Willows* (1935), in which the broad movement of branches and leaves causes them to intersect and fuse in blues and yellows.

Finally in his late work, the vertical stripes [222], Louis's colours seem to shoot down to earth from above, as if sent by Zeus as thunderbolts of pigment from on high. But at the same time they are more purely structural, in keeping with the 1960s drive to a new clarity, which took

216 Kenneth Noland, *Ex-Nihilo*, 1958. Magna on canvas, 170.2 × 162 cm (67 × 63¾ in). Private collection

217 Adolph Gottlieb, *Mist*, 1961. Oil on canvas, 182.9 × 121.9 cm (72 × 48 in). The Solomon R. Guggenheim Museum, New York

217

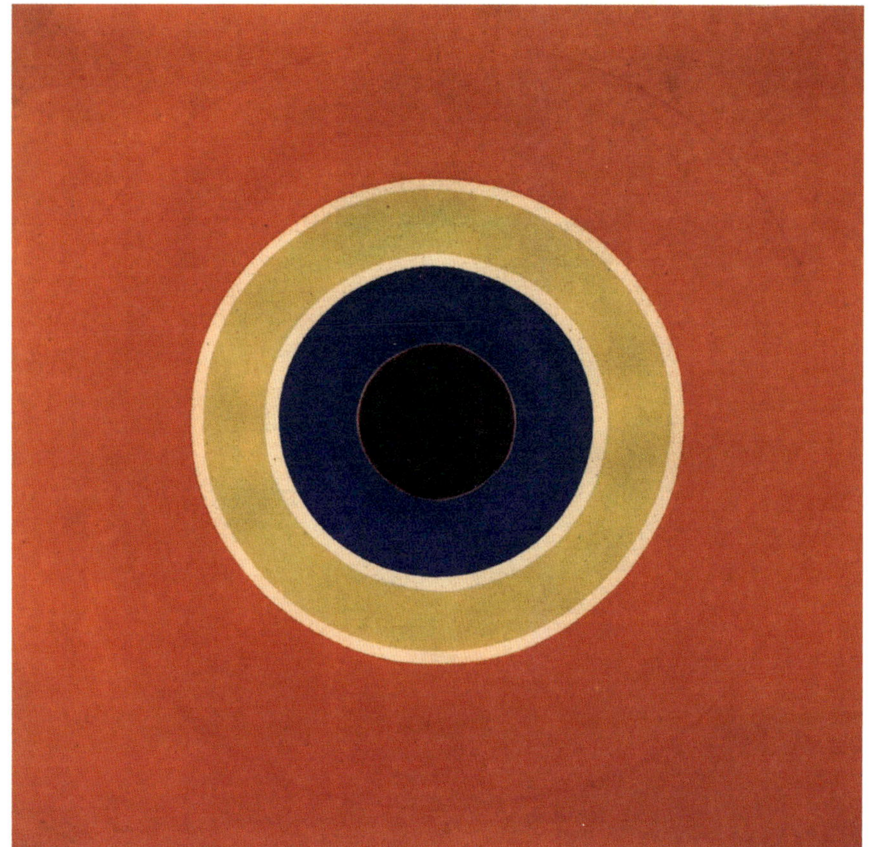

218

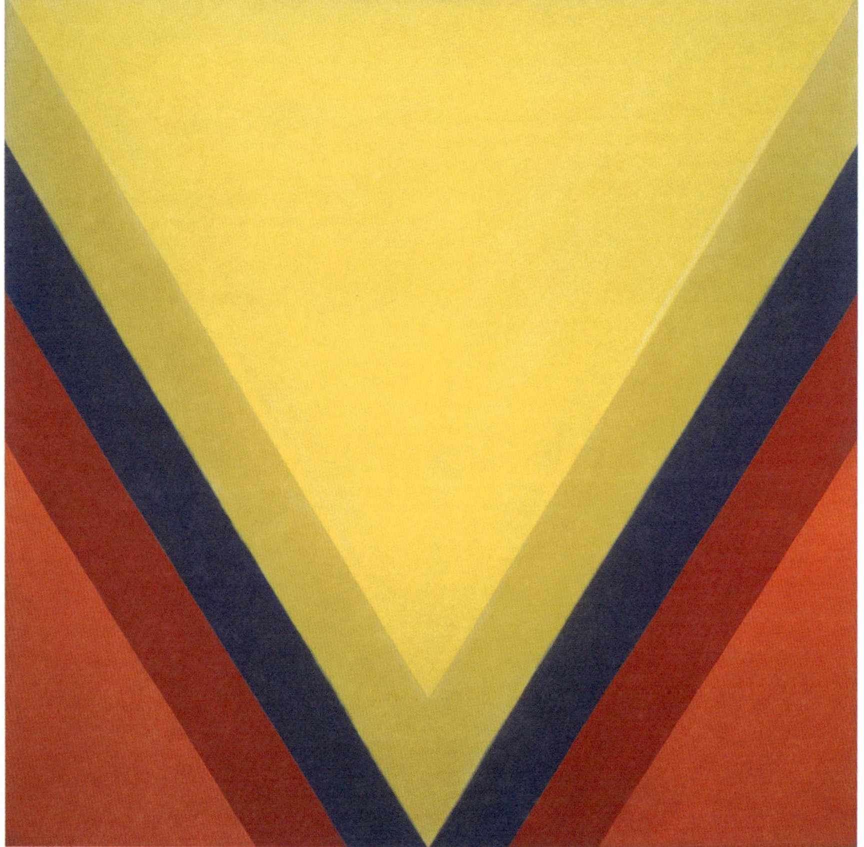

219

Modern Art in America

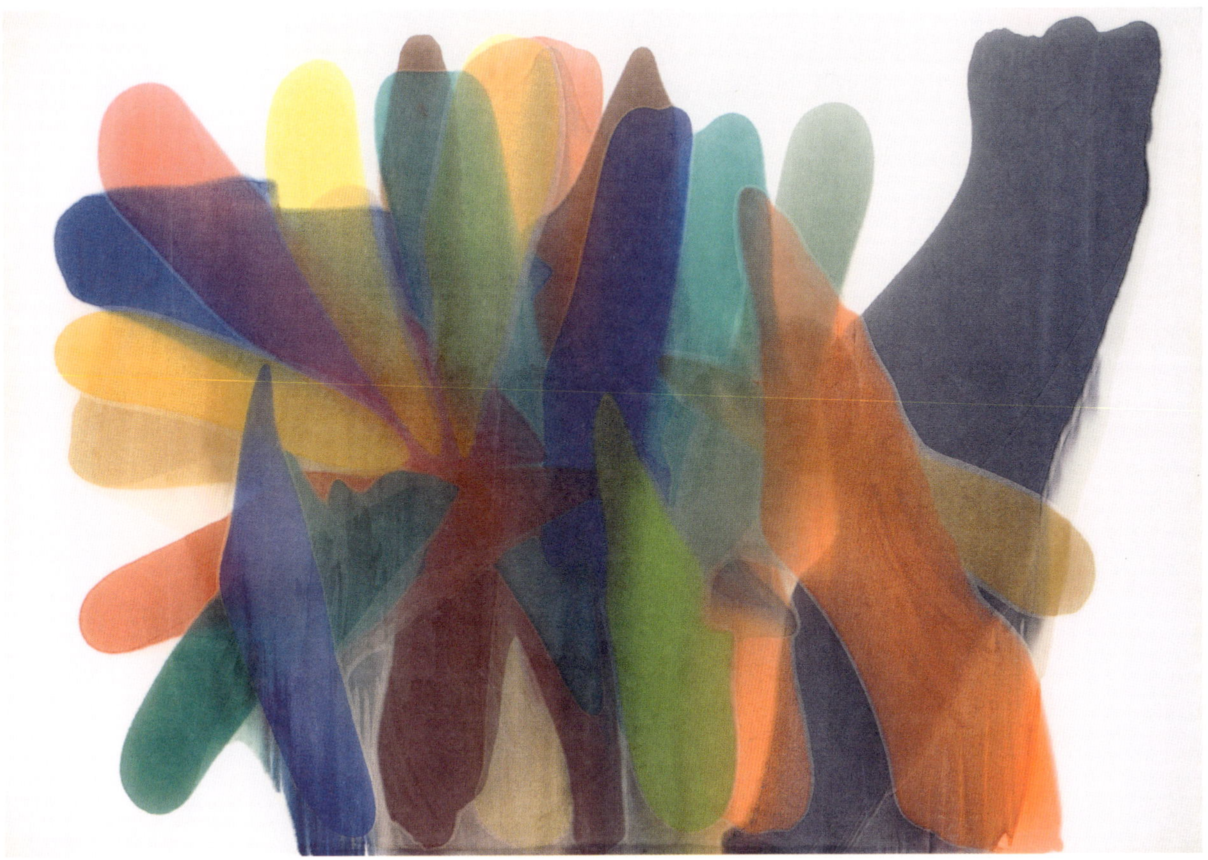

220

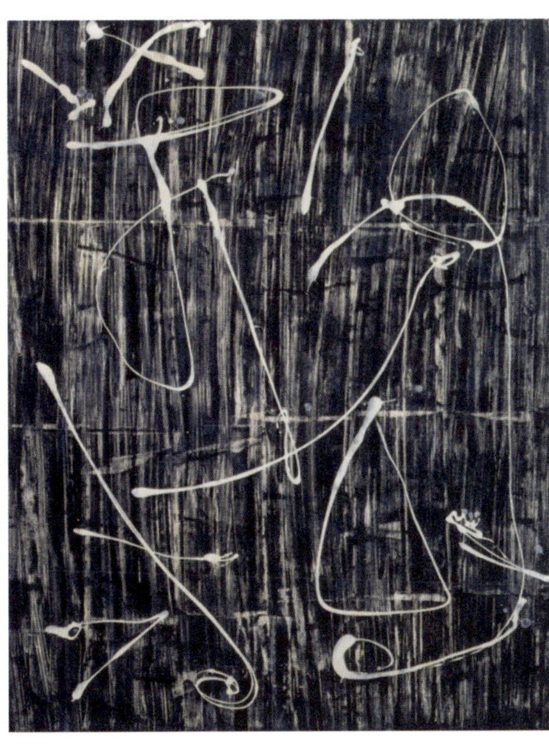

221

218 Kenneth Noland, *Noon Afloat*,
     1962. Acrylic on canvas,
     121.9 × 121.9 cm (48 × 48 in).
     Collection of André and
     Susanne Emmerich

219 Kenneth Noland, *East-West*,
     1963. Acrylic on canvas,
     178.4 × 176.5 cm (70¼ × 69½ in).
     Private collection

220 Morris Louis, *Floral*, 1959.
     Acrylic resin (Magna)
     on canvas, 261.6 × 360.7 cm
     (103 × 142 in).
     Private collection

221 Morris Louis, *Charred Journal:
     Firewritten V*, 1951. Acrylic
     resin (Magna) on canvas,
     86.4 × 66.0 cm (34 × 26 in).
     The Jewish Museum, New York

many forms. This was aided by Noland and Louis's experimentation with new water-based paints that helped to keep the colour flat and fast-drying, giving it the kind of intensity not possible with oil paint, and with much less surface so that the colour seems disembodied and independent, referring only to itself. Broad areas of intense hues are placed separately and directly on the paper or canvas in open compositions that surely point to the later work of the two artists.

Louis and Noland were not alone in exploring colour in Washington. Indeed, an entire generation of talented artists came of age in the area, and together made paintings based on pure colour that added a distinctive chapter to the history of American art. They included older artists like Jacob Kainen and Alma Thomas, along with younger artists such as Paul Reed, Gene Davis and Tom Downing. One answer to the question of how it came to be that Washington developed into a centre for colour art, what nurtured it and how it spread so extensively, can be found in the Phillips Collection,[19] where from the start the founder concentrated on colour, from Renoir and Cézanne to O'Keeffe, Klee, Dove, Diebenkorn and Rothko.

Georgia O'Keeffe: A Brilliant Blue Ascending

We find a similar use of colour in the early watercolours of Georgia O'Keeffe, c.1917–19, especially in her *Light on the Plains* series and her oil *Sunrise* of 1924 in the Phillips Collection. In *Series I – From the Plains* [223], her surfaces are nothing less than planes of intense colour, nuanced reds and oranges, in which the western sky itself seems to appear as a modern update of the flaming sunsets of the Luminist painters in the nineteenth century. O'Keeffe's colour had then waned in the 1940s, but after 1950 she seems to have rediscovered it and she pursued it once again, to the limits of its possibilities. In her cloud paintings of the 1960s she took up on a grand scale her husband Alfred Stieglitz's songs of the sky of the 1920s, while also paying homage to Dove, her dear friend. Before that, in *In the Patio IX* (1950) [224] she had also looked to the skies above, a brilliant blue ascending, a statement of humility and awe before the universe itself. In this, she fulfils her own early efforts in colour, transforming them in mature and experienced full-scale paintings that mark her as a pioneer but also as a full-blown colour-field painter who must be counted as an important contributor to this aspect of later American painting.

Jasper Johns's Flags: Composition Built In

In his famous *Flag* of 1954–5 [225], Johns, in the spirit of de Kooning, turned from the Abstract Expressionist idea of always making a new and original composition to well-known, immediate images that seemed almost prosaic, yet induced a sense of mystery, uncertainty and questioning that has lasted to this day. The image of the flag comes with the composition built in, in fact it *is* the composition. It is a serial image, a succession of horizontal stripes and forty-eight stars in a row, immediately obvious to us, but even now elusive and strange. Johns retained the facture of painterly abstraction, but now with a care and precision that had seemed to be missing from later Abstract Expressionist art. Indeed, it is a beautifully painted picture, its touch sublime, equalled only by Picasso and Braque in 1911. In a way, Johns demonstrated what could still be wrought from Abstract Expressionism. The flag set the tone for the coming format of the late 1950s – stripes, circles, squares, geometric designs, all clear, open compositions the better to focus and control paint and especially

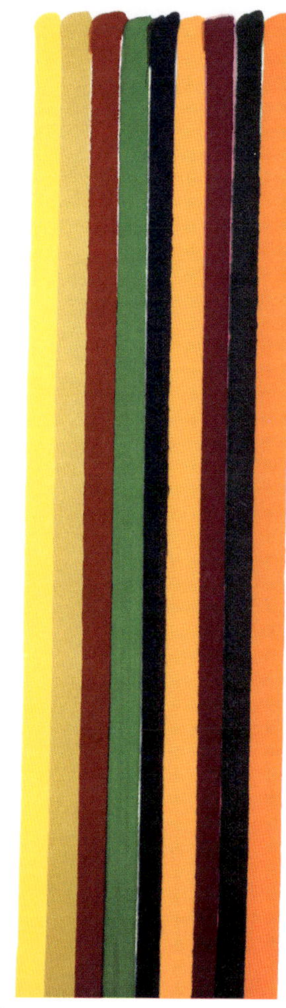

222

222 Morris Louis, *Number 25*, 1962. Acrylic resin (Magna) on canvas, 203.2 × 83.8 cm (80 × 33 in). Private collection

223 Georgia O'Keeffe, *Series I – From the Plains*, 1919. Oil on canvas, 68.6 × 58.4 cm (27 × 23 in). Georgia O'Keeffe Museum, Santa Fe

224 Georgia O'Keeffe, *In the Patio IX*, 1950. Oil on canvas mounted on panel, 76.2 × 101.6 cm (30 × 40 in). The Vilcek Foundation, New York

Modern Art in America

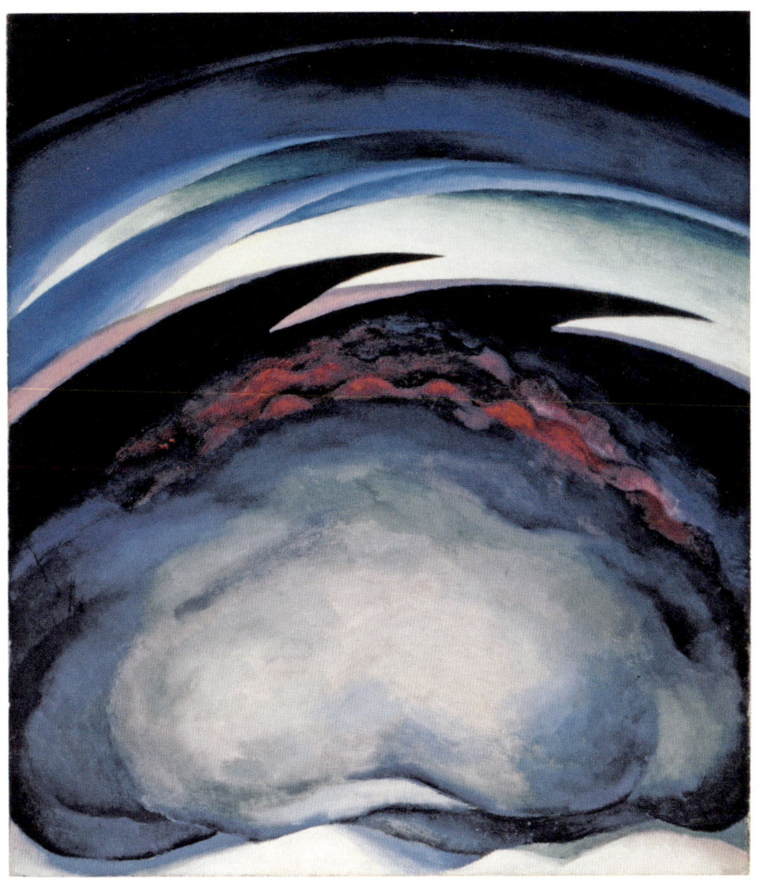

223

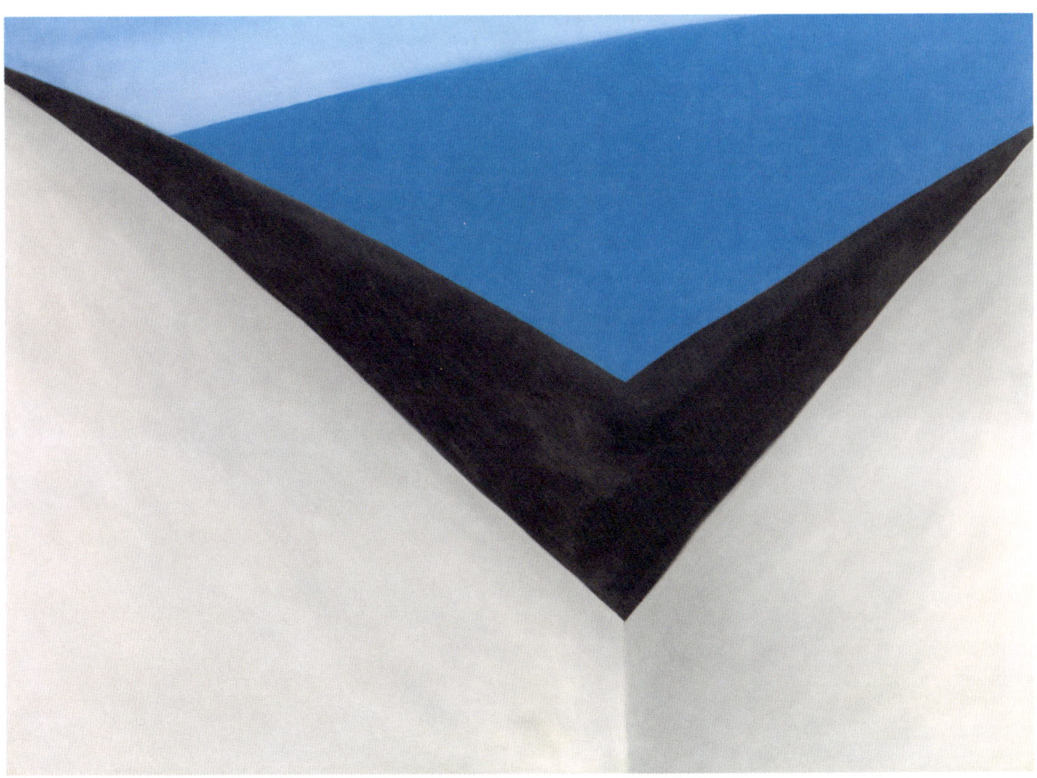

224

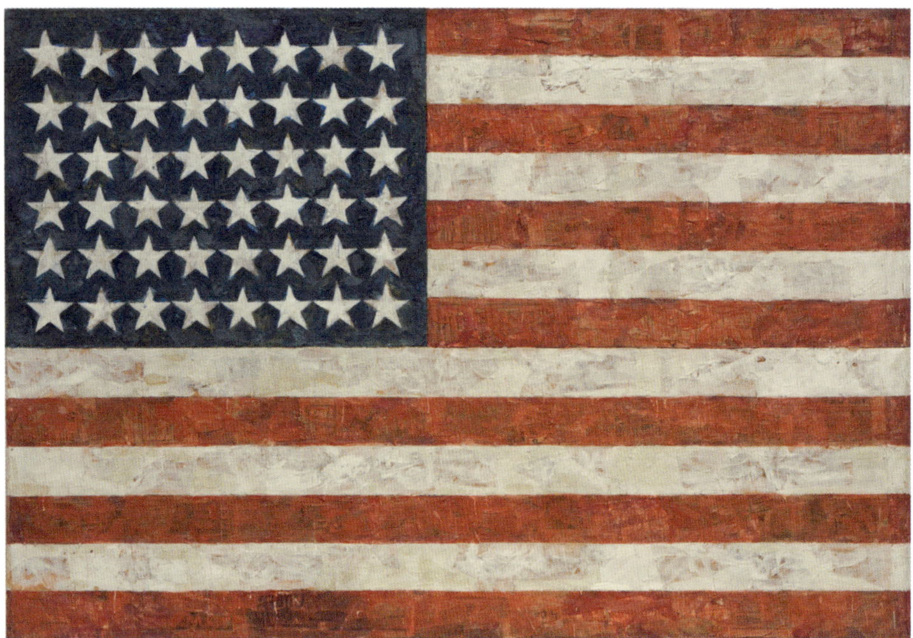

225

to deliver colour in pure, large, undiluted areas. It is a working illustration of Ockham's razor, the scientist's urge to discover the most direct and elegant solution to a problem. It is a matter of 'distillation … An actualized sense of the tenor of the times being presented … in concentrated form, in visual synecdoche', as Peter Plagens put it.[20] *Concentrated form* is the key. The best art always has this, whether it is by Pollock or Judd; there are no unnecessary or extraneous parts; everything is realized to its fullest potential, no more, no less; take the chaos of the modern world and channel it into 'rigorously intelligible art'.[21] As Judd always preached: complicated is not the same as complex.

Robert Rauschenberg's Stripes

The first use of orderly and ordering stripes (unless we count Charles Sheeler's photograph *White Barn, Bucks County, Pennsylvania*, 1914–17) is found in Robert Rauschenberg's (1925–2008) painting *Yoicks* (1954) [226], a still mostly painterly, even messy composition that is nevertheless structured around a series of centred, horizontal stripes that make the work a historical marker. Rauschenberg was a radical figure at the beginning of the 1950s. His 'White' series, then the 'Black' series of 1950–2, were virtually mono-chrome pictures, a kind of jab at, and answer to, Newman's large-scale paintings of 1950–1 that were exhibited in both 1951 and 1952, and provoked a wide critical reaction, mostly negative. In Rauschenberg's all-white paintings, visual incident was formed solely by the shadows caused by viewers moving in front of them, a kind of Dada gesture, a retort to the primacy of paint and its movement, of the power of the painter's hand. By 1955, he had begun his 'Combines', in which actual objects were introduced into the painterly surfaces [227], thus becoming three-dimen-sional pieces that interacted in real space. The objects – a taxidermy goat, a rubber tyre, a tennis ball – were all so commonplace that many thought them unsuitable as art. But we recall Rauschenberg's statement: 'Painting relates to both art and life; neither can be made. I try to act in the gap in between.'[22]

225 Jasper Johns, *Flag*, 1954–5.
Encaustic, oil and collage on
fabric mounted on plywood,
three panels, 107.3 × 153.8 cm
(42½ × 60⅝ in) overall.
The Museum of Modern Art,
New York

226 Robert Rauschenberg,
Yoicks, 1954. Oil, fabric and
newspaper on two canvases,
243.8 × 182.9 cm (96 × 72 in)
overall. Whitney Museum of
American Art, New York

227 Robert Rauschenberg,
Monogram, 1955–9. Oil,
paper, fabric, printed paper,
printed reproductions, metal,
wood, rubber shoe, heel and
tennis ball on canvas, with
oil on Angora goat and rubber
tyre, on wooden platform
mounted on four casters,
106.7 × 160.7 × 163.8 cm
(42 × 63¼ × 64½ in). Moderna
Museet, Stockholm

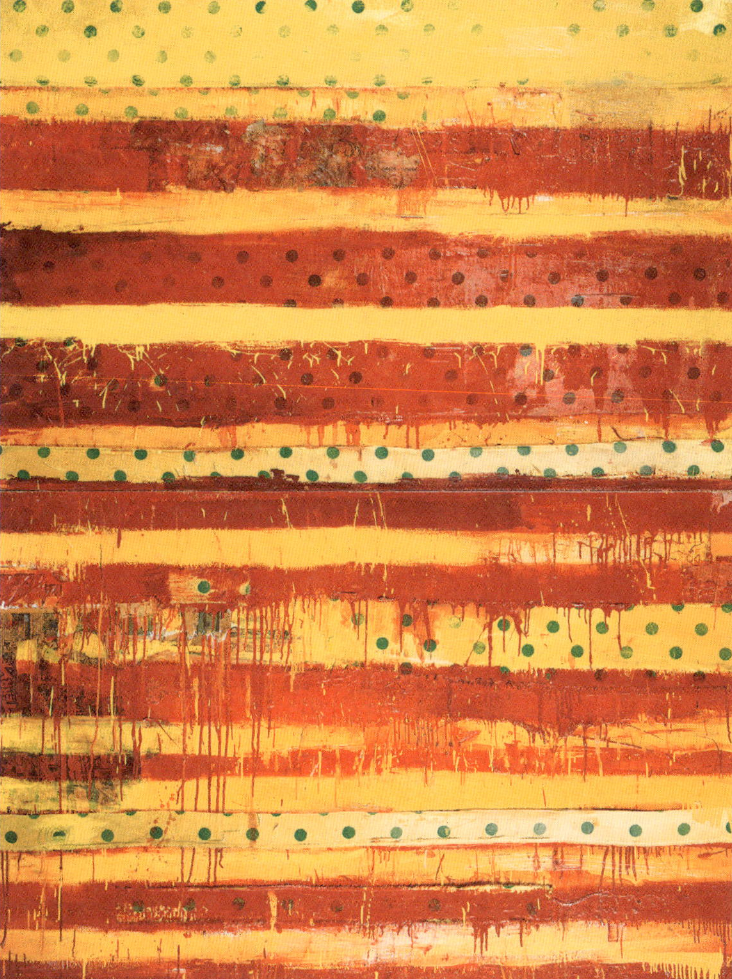

226

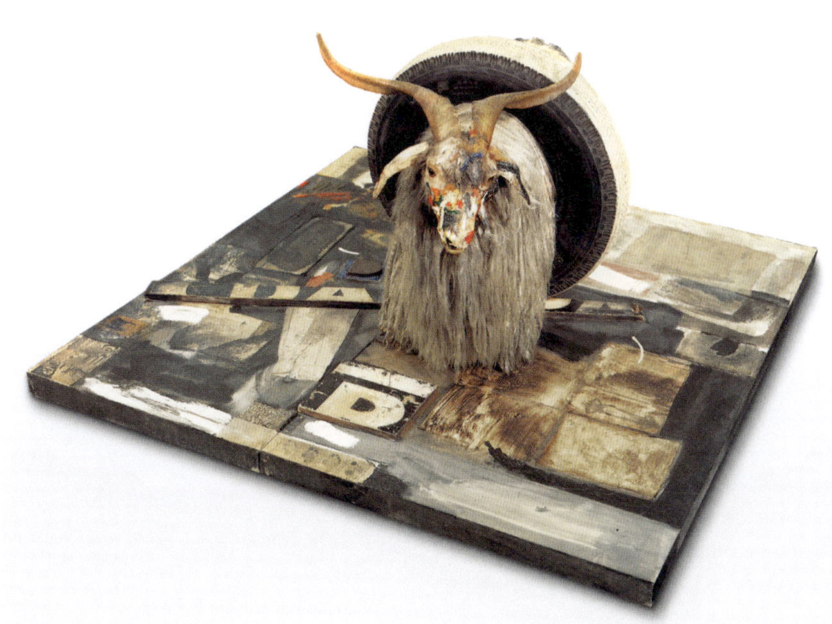

227

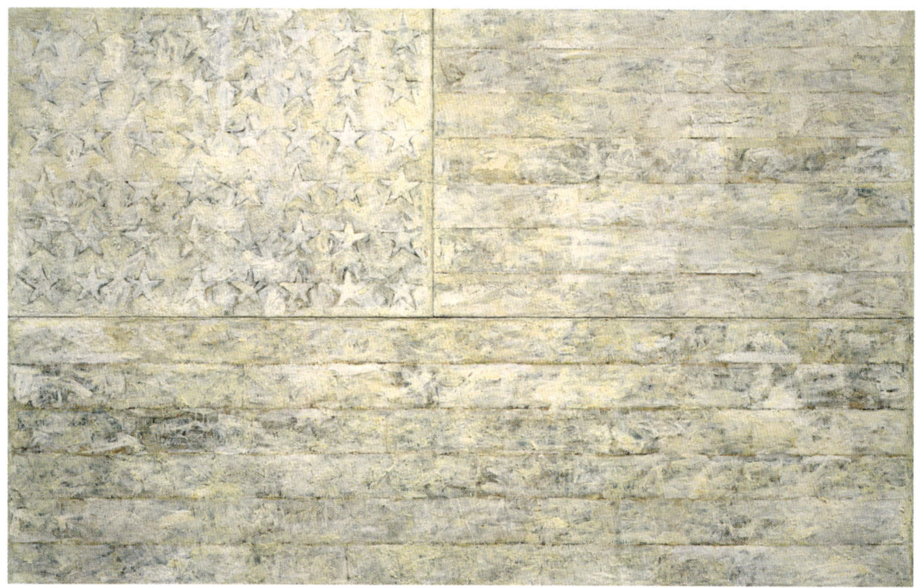

228

Black and White

In 1955, there appeared another kind of colour-field painting altogether: Jasper Johns's monumental *White Flag* [228], purely Abstract Expressionist in touch, and with a thousand variations of stroke and hue and value that take an almost mesmerizing grip on us. This painting may have been at least partially inspired by Rauschenberg's white paintings of 1951, and in turn may have inspired Robert Ryman, who by 1957 had launched his series of all-white paintings, still being done today, that offered limitless possibilities of size, shape, touch, handling, support, surface, mood and feel.

The opposite of the spectrum, black, had been used in the late 1940s and 1950s to great effect. Picasso's *Guernica* set an example, and in Matisse's post-1945 paintings, black is often a powerful force. In 1946, he published the short article 'Black is a Colour', which attracted much attention.[23] Blacks used intensively can be traced back to Goya, then to Manet's work, which Matisse referenced in his article. In his black series of 1948, de Kooning was certainly a pioneer in its use. By 1950, Kline was using it in his bold black-and-white compositions, as was Still, and soon afterwards, Rothko, who introduced it to offset criticism that he was only a 'decorative' artist when he used bright colours.

In 1951–2, Pollock did a series of all-black paintings in which he included distinctly figurative references. Younger artists focused on black, such as Rauschenberg in his black paintings of the early 1950s, and by 1952 Ad Reinhardt had introduced his mysterious, 'ultimate' black paintings, thus renouncing a fine gift for colour that he had been developing since the late 1930s. The black-on-white tiles in Matisse's Chapel of the Rosary in Vence may also have inspired its use; indeed, an interesting question is whether Pollock knew of the Chapel when he began his black-and-white series in 1951,[24] or Kline when he made *Wotan* (1950) [229], based on an off-centre rectangle, or Davis in his post-1953 black and white paintings. The most famous use of black emerged in 1958–9 in the black stripe paintings of a still younger artist, Frank Stella [230]. They seemed to many, especially older artists, to mark the end of painting, thus constituting a form of Neo-Dada. But when we see them in the context of Still and Reinhardt and the 1950s, they make perfect sense, an ongoing part of a tradition that was by then well established.

228 Jasper Johns, *White Flag*, 1955. Encaustic, oil, newsprint and charcoal on canvas, 198.9 × 306.7 cm (78¼ × 120¾ in). The Metropolitan Museum of Art, New York

229 Franz Kline, *Wotan*, 1950. Oil on canvas mounted on Masonite, 139.7 × 201 cm (55 × 79⁵⁄₁₆ in). The Museum of Fine Arts, Houston

230 Frank Stella, *The Marriage of Reason and Squalor, II*, 1959. Enamel on canvas, 230.5 × 337.2 cm (90¾ × 132¾ in). The Museum of Modern Art, New York

   Modern Art in America

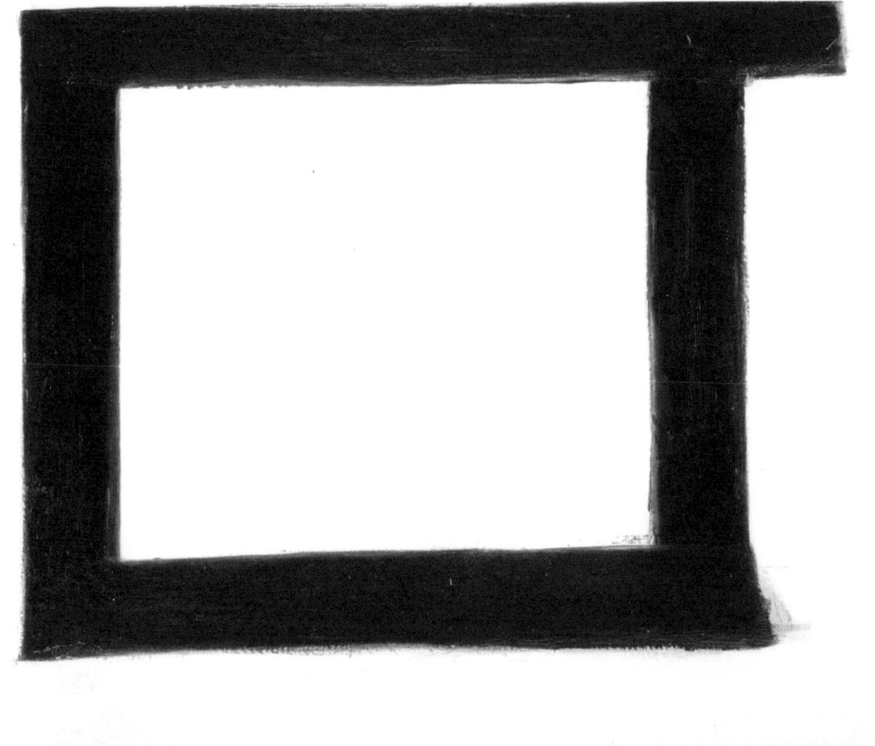

229

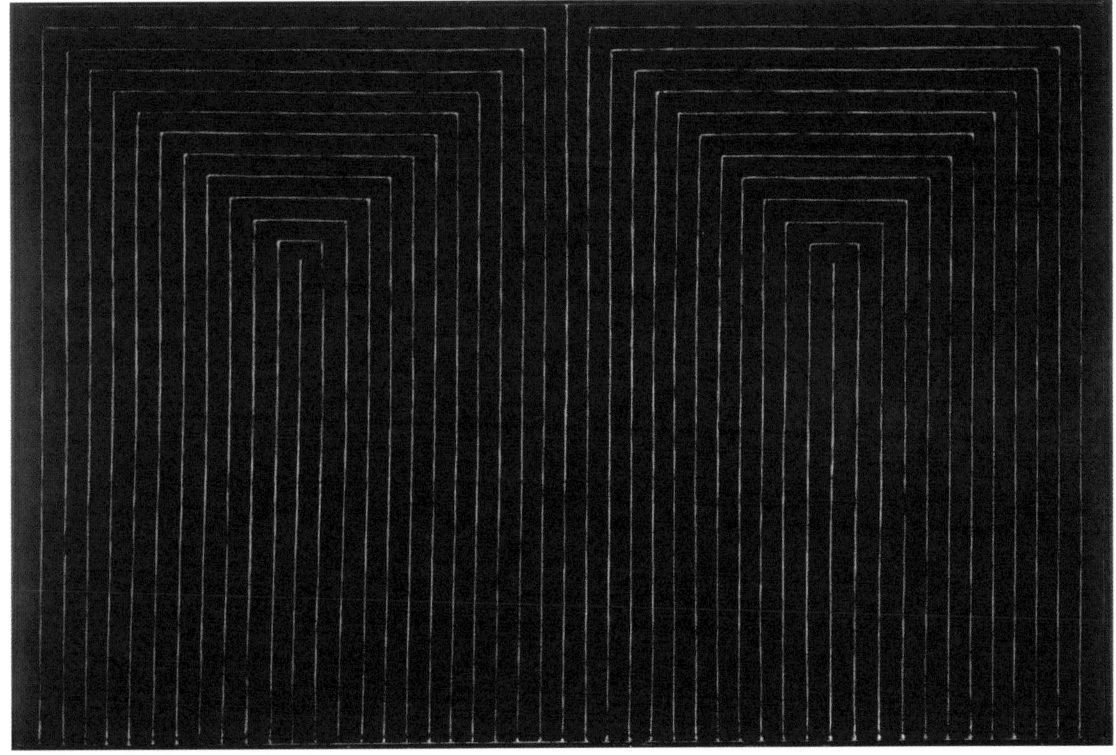

230

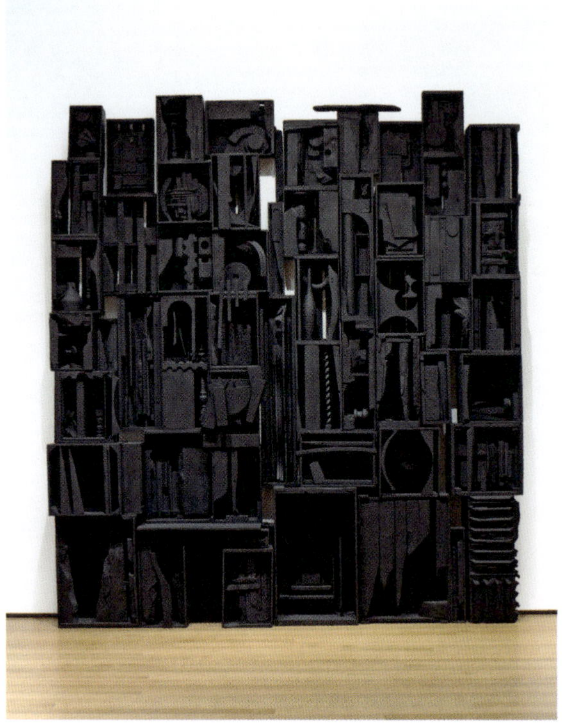

231

By 1962, Tony Smith's *Die* and subsequent sculptures, all a deep monochrome black, established the colour as a powerful element in defining the massive bulk of three-dimensional objects, as had Louise Nevelson's wooden structures, painted a profound, rich black. Nevelson's wooden box sculptures [231], many of large and imposing scale, were famous in the 1950s and were often seen, suggesting environments of dark and mysterious places. Black had been a special challenge for artists since at least Goya – see his painting in the Frick Collection, *The Forge* (c.1817) – then Manet, Maurer, O'Keeffe, Malevich and others prior to 1950.

'The Legacy of Jackson Pollock': Kaprow's Turning-Point Essay

An old modernist question asks where does art come from? For the Abstract Expressionists, it seemed to come from and be caused by forces of the universe. As David Anfam has written, they sought a 'world elsewhere'.[25] For Rothko, it is a journey into unknown places, far away, and is undertaken only by those willing to venture forth. Pollock thought art came from the unconscious. Newman's rhetoric saw art as the creation of the first man. In the predictable pattern of art and artists, a younger generation, all born in the 1920s and 1930s, saw this as too remote. For this generation, art was right before them, in the everyday common-places of mundane experience, born of the here and now.

The most forceful statement of this situation was written by Allan Kaprow, an extraordinarily visionary and articulate artist and writer whose essays should be required reading for us all. Just after Pollock's death in August 1956, he drafted one of the most important and far-seeing essays of the period. Although not published until 1958, 'The Legacy of Jackson Pollock'[26] stands as a turning point in the history of mid-century art. 'Where does Pollock leave us?' Kaprow asked. He summarized the situation as he saw it. It was a given for him that art had to continue on the ground-

Modern Art in America

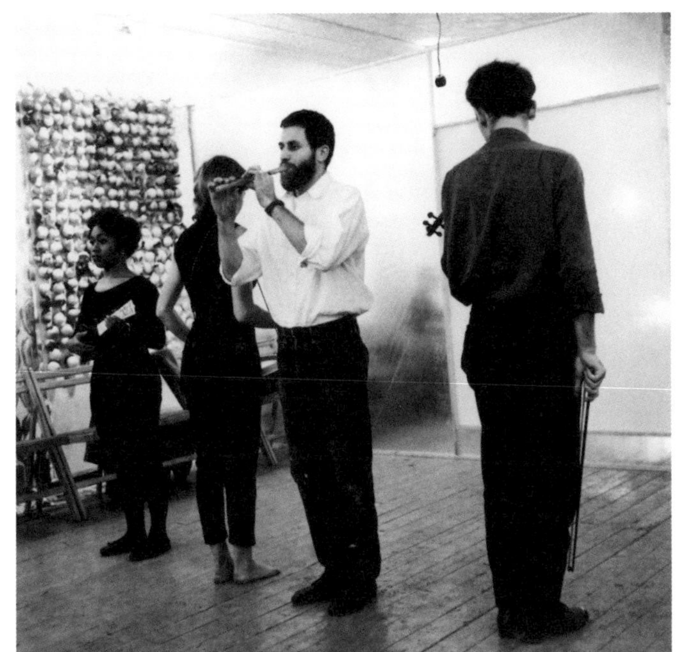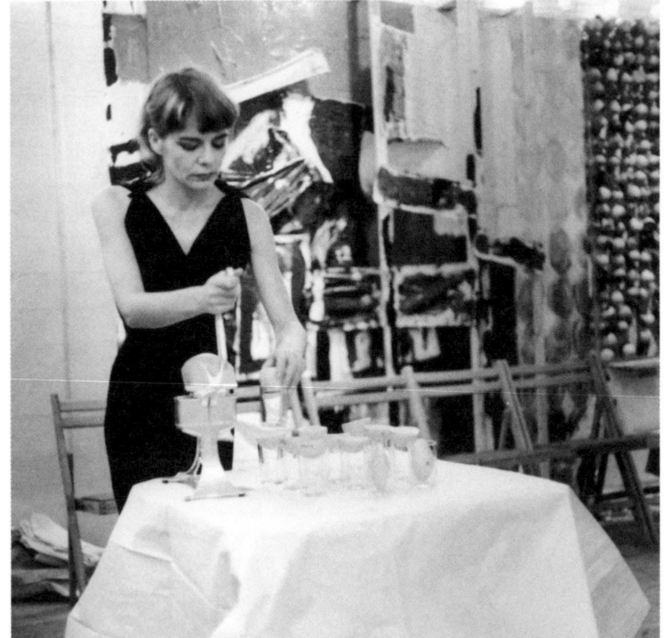

232

breaking path set by Pollock's work. To do so, there were two options. One was to continue in his style and methodology, but Kaprow rejected that as a retrograde activity that would go nowhere. The second possibility was to take the qualities of Pollock's work, its overwhelming sense of space and reality, and extend them into a literal three-dimensional space, our space in which we live and move. In so doing, art could then encompass anything: it could be part of 42nd Street, as it were, part of life itself. From then on, Kaprow added, there would not be painters or sculptors, but simply artists, orchestrating and composing work wherever they went. It was an essay that changed the course of history. Within a year, in *18 Happenings in 6 Parts* [232], Kaprow had staged the first performance event, with minimal directions, within a makeshift setting, and it became a major force in America. It was the source for today's spectacles, of huge spaces and multiple media, in which art and life fuse. Looking back, we can see that this relates to Robert Henri's admonition to look to the streets, to the immediate world around the artist, a dictum that had early on shaped the work of artists as diverse as Stuart Davis and Edward Hopper.

Hofmann's Late Great Work

231 Louise Nevelson, *Sky Cathedral*, 1958. Painted wood, 343.9 × 305.4 × 45.7 cm (135¾ × 120¼ × 18 in). The Museum of Modern Art, New York

232 Allan Kaprow, *18 Happenings in 6 Parts*, 1959. Left: the artist (second right, in white shirt) rehearses with fellow performers Shirley Prendergast (left), Rosalyn Montague (second left) and Lucas Samaras (right). Right: artist Rosalyn Montague squeezes lemons as part of the performance at the Ruben Gallery, New York, 4 October 1959.

Also in 1956, Hofmann was finally able to retire from teaching and devote himself full-time to his painting. From that point on until his death in 1966, he reached the height of his powers as an artist. His work blossomed, with one masterpiece after another, in those ten years. His paint and colour burst forth, colour producing light, and light generating colour, as if one and the same, and for him in fact they were indistinguishable. He had always told his students to be bold with colour, and to use plenty of it, a dictum that he now followed in his own work. He worked primarily in two ways: one with coloured rectangles and squares, the other in a free-flowing organic expressionism.

Hofmann's late great works – such as *Cathedral* (1959) [233], consisting of brilliant hues arranged in rectangles and squares of varying thickness of paint – were a stimulus of untold importance to new directions in American art, most especially in the attention given to colour. By 1955, and certainly

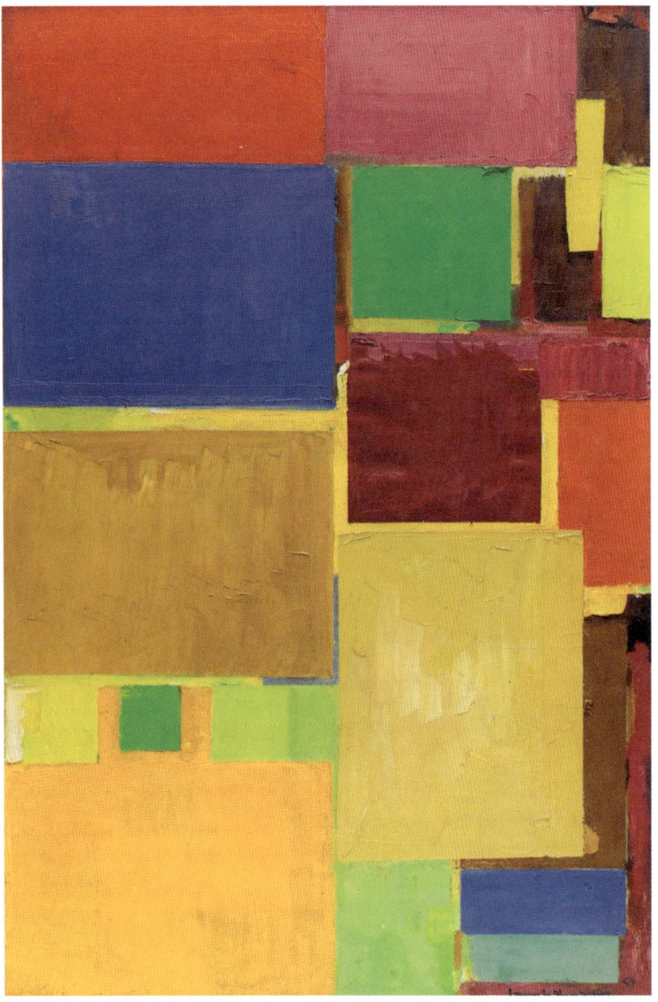

233

by 1956, he had introduced stabilizing planes of colour at least tentatively
to posit a way past what by then was seen as the overworked surfaces of
painterly abstraction. By 1957–8 the process was fully under way in his
work. In *Cathedral*, the colour radiates on us like light through a glorious
rose window, speaking of a spiritual power. That tradition continues to
this day, as in the work of Stanley Whitney [234].

Sheeler's Rejuvenation

By 1957, only a year after Pollock's death, the effects of his loss at the age
of forty-four were widely felt. Cubism underwent a deep resurgence with
the work of Hofmann and Davis, as we have seen. Even earlier, by 1946,
Sheeler had undergone a startling rejuvenation by developing his own
brand of Cubism. By 1940, his work had run dry, used up by his dealer's
insistence that he keep his painting and his photography clear and distinct.
But the fusion of the two was the core of his gift, and he could no more
ignore one than the other. His rejuvenation came at the hands of Bartlett
Hayes, then the director of the Addison Gallery of American Art, Andover,
the locus of so many important works. In 1946, Hayes invited Sheeler to
spend six weeks at Andover; he did not have to teach and he was free to
do as he saw fit, but Hayes promised he would do his best to acquire a
new work by the artist for the collection, one he hoped would be stimulated
by the environment, with a direct connection to Andover. It was a tonic.
Sheeler explored the area with new enthusiasm, often making notes with

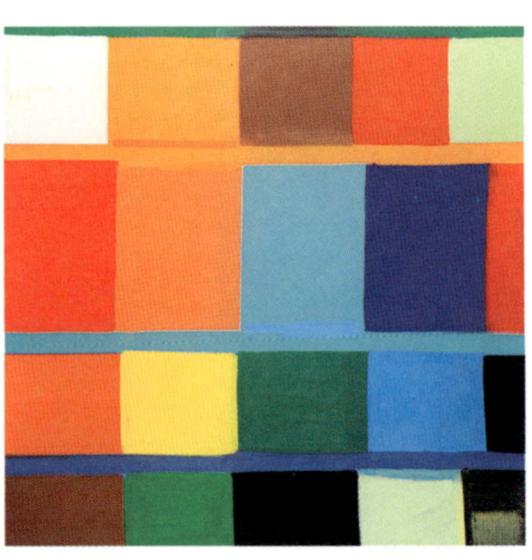

234

     Modern Art in America

his camera. He discovered near the campus in an area called Ballardvale a group of abandoned mill buildings, and took a series of photographs of them from various angles, just as he had done years before of barns in Pennsylvania. He saw buildings as representing something important from the American past, and in his painting, *Ballardvale* of 1946, he depicts the subject as if it were a soaring cathedral, with the same kind of grandeur as when he had photographed Chartres or the Ford plant in the 1930s. The colours are strong and vibrant, recalling the colour of Matisse that Sheeler had admired as early as the Armory Show and was now finally letting flow in his art. The tower soars as in triumph,[27] a metaphor for his sense of the past but also now his renewed energy and ambition as an artist. His Cubism is more vigorous than ever before, and here and in other versions it is coupled with, and created by, a shifting, superimposed variety of photographs and negatives taken at the site, a brilliant fusion of painting and photography, producing the best work of his career.

In *New England Irrelevancies* (1953) [235], Sheeler even combined views of Ballardvale with those of the mills of Manchester, New Hampshire, where he had also done first-rate paintings. Fusing the two in time and space was his answer to Duchamp, especially his *Large Glass*, which Sheeler thought was the picture of the century. His work of the time was the first salvo of post-1945 Cubism that only concluded in the mid-1960s with the deaths of Davis, Smith and Hofmann.

233 Hans Hofmann, *Cathedral*, 1959. Oil on canvas, 188 × 122 cm (74 × 48 in). The Museum of Modern Art, New York

234 Stanley Whitney, *Bodyheat*, 2012. Oil on linen, 243.8 × 243.8 cm (96 × 96 in). Private collection

235 Charles Sheeler, *New England Irrelevancies*, 1953. Oil on canvas, 73.7 × 58.4 cm (29 × 23 in). Museum of Fine Arts, Boston

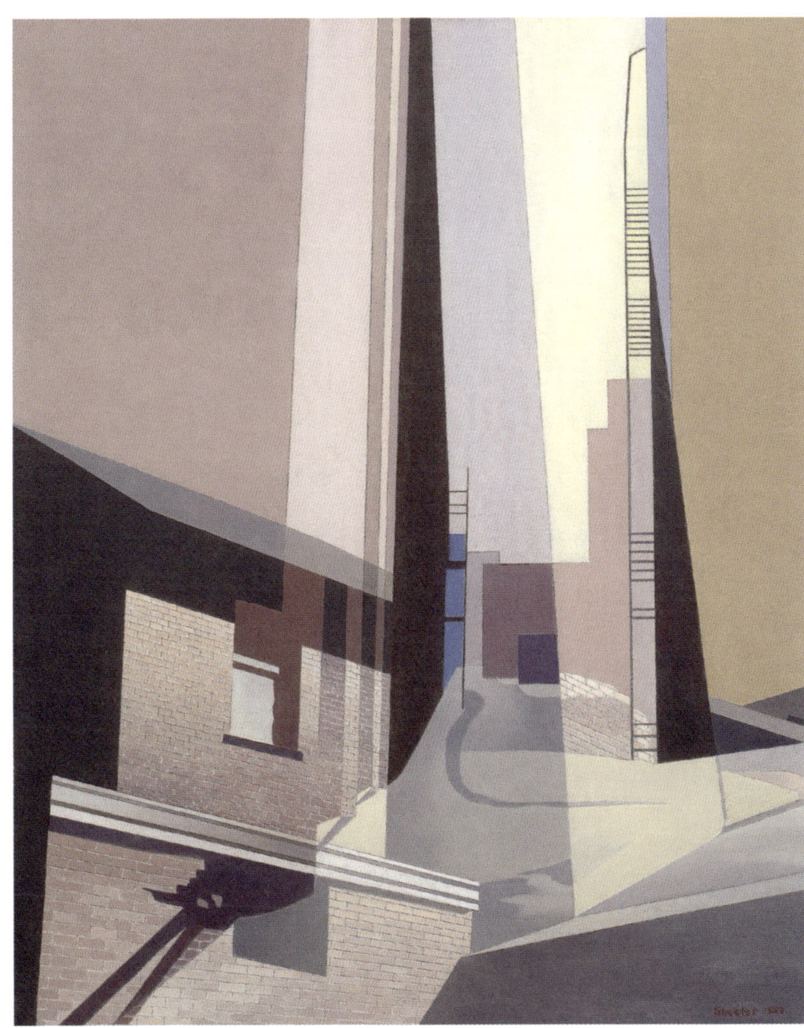

235

The Return of Figure Painting: Fairfield Porter

In 1957 a new wave of exceptional figure painting appeared that can be seen as a response to Pollock's death, as if his loss required a rethinking of art, especially abstract art. At that point, it would seem, artists of all persuasions realized, once again, that pure abstraction was not the sole destination of modern art or the modernist impulse. (Postmodernism had a fatally mistaken reading of avant-garde art.) The new recognition of Hopper as a major, complex painter also surely provided inspiration for a host of artists who saw the possibilities of the figure. As it had for de Kooning, the use of the figure provided a compositional given, a base from which the artists could then proceed.

Two of the most talented of these artists were Richard Diebenkorn and Alex Katz, who had by 1950 started working in an abstract mode, but had come to believe that figuration was their best path at the time. Diebenkorn had admired both Hopper and Matisse, and the strong architectural structures of both are fully evident in his work, as is Matisse's unparalleled use of high colour.

However, perhaps the best – at least the most consistently committed to the figure over his lifetime – was Fairfield Porter (1907–1975), an important artist often disparaged because his art seems too genteel, at least in its subject matter. He has been termed a realist artist, but that does not represent his true concerns. He understood that the difference between realism and abstraction is not as simple as it seems, and how elusive those terms are, commenting: 'The realist thinks he knows ahead

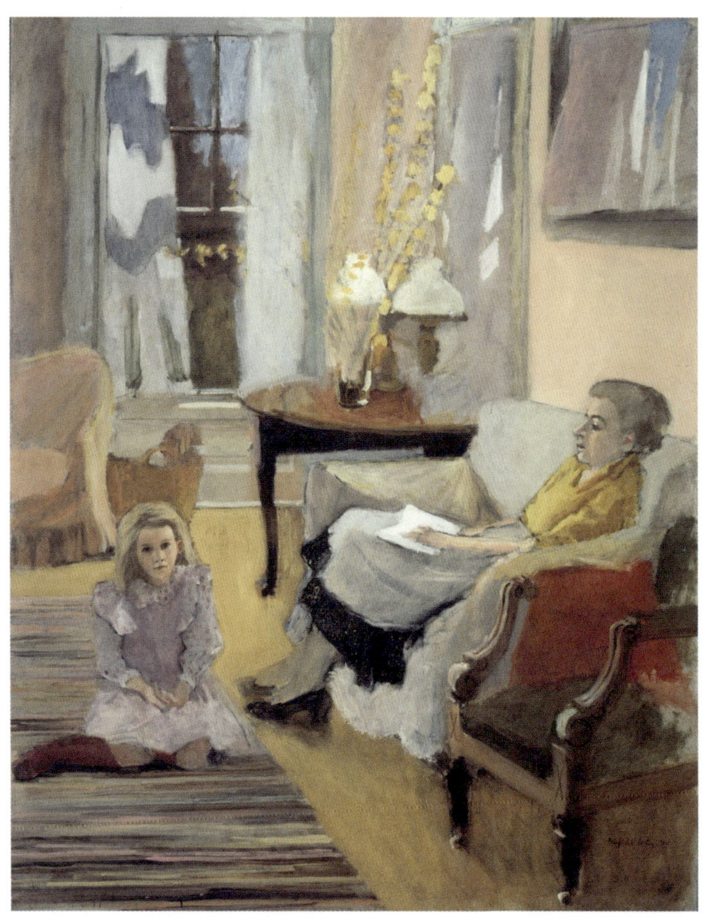

236

236 Fairfield Porter, *Katie and Anne*, 1955. Oil on canvas, 203.5 × 157.7 cm (80⅛ × 62⅛ in). Hirshhorn Museum and Sculpture Garden, Smithsonian Institution, Washington, DC

Modern Art in America

of time what reality is, and the abstract artist what art is, but it is in its formality that realist art excels, and the best abstract art communicates an overwhelming sense of reality.'[28]

Porter's landscapes convey a strong and clear sense of place, and his portraits a strong and clear sense of the sitter's presence [236]. However, the literal transcription of what he saw before him was not his concern: the subject per se is of little importance. Rather, it was in the paint itself that he found the life of the work, its wholeness and its vitality. In Porter's painting, the abstract, formal qualities always come first, and make up the true subject. When he worked, he tried not to see the object as it was, but 'to see only concrete shapes which have no association except as themselves',[29] and to see only where one thing ends and another begins. His lack of interest in realist transcription explains why he was often a blunt and awkward painter, for frequently things seem off or wrong in his work. Rendering his experience by means of an abstract interlocking surface was the idea. In this we are often reminded of the monumental figure paintings of de Kooning and Gorky of the late 1930s, in which anatomical shapes diverge radically from accurate description, and in which the artists' probing search for unity and harmony takes precedence. Indeed, de Kooning was his major influence, and Porter's procedure was to fuse the broad and physical paint handling of de Kooning with Vuillard's intimate world. In the same way, he admired the smooth flow of paint in the art of Velázquez.

Porter proceeded directly and empirically, more like the Abstract Expressionist than the realist, and let his eye and brush dictate his next move. He was alert and open to the surprise encounters of composing with paint and colour. There were no rules of construction. The only rule was to preserve the life and vitality of the picture, which was its essential content. The experience of the tangible stuff of painting is everywhere apparent; a patch of Maine fog becomes as solid, as real, as an adjoining land mass, which can be arbitrarily cut off, according to the needs of the composition. Air and space become real and weighty; and the connections and relations between things, rather than their description, the most meaningful. Porter refused to make any concessions to canons of taste, finish or agility, did not hide his 'mistakes' or the bluntness of his pictures under painterly guises, and was content to retain the record of his struggle with the medium and the painting.

This, too, is in line with a long American tradition. Porter is distinctly American because of his insistence on the concrete and the specific, rather than on the European heritage of the ideal and the general. He worked empirically, an approach deeply rooted in American culture, and through his insistence on the real and concrete nature of life and experience — on the distinctness and diversity, even the arbitrary nature of facts — he proclaimed the triumph of the individual over technocracy and the state, the singular over the general, the real and vital over the standardized and the routine, the natural over the artificial. His love of the land — he was a staunch environmentalist before it was a movement — is also in line with a long American tradition, a love shared by innumerable artists in the country.

In Porter's view, art does not stand for anything outside itself. It is measured by its interior intensity, and by its capacity to compel our imagination. Paint is as real as nature, and the means of painting can contain its ends. When reviewing a de Kooning show in 1959 — he was an excellent critic and writer — Porter summarized his views of what art can be when 'everything is at its own limits of possibilities … the picture presented of released possibilities, of ordinary qualities existing at their fullest limits and acting harmoniously together — this picture is exalting.'[30]

Influential Exhibitions of the Late 1950s

In 1957–8, two major exhibitions gave added stimulus to the new developments in hard-edge and colour art, shows that demonstrated ways of painting alternative to Abstract Expressionism. In 1957, the Minneapolis Museum organized a large retrospective exhibition of the work of Stuart Davis, his first major museum show since his exhibition at MoMA in 1945. It travelled to New York, where it would have been a revelation, presenting his clean-edged, clear colour forms in an engaging, dynamic style that seemed to show no sign of the Abstract Expressionist rhetoric about the unconscious and the end of the world that by then had grown tiresome and irrelevant to younger artists. It was bright and bold, with no existentialist angst, and it opened up – or reopened – new avenues of exploration.

The next year, in 1958, MoMA organized a comprehensive show of the work of Georges Seurat that also opened the eyes, or confirmed the nascent ideas, of the emerging artists.[31] Seurat's place as both an heir of Impressionism and the major artist to have introduced a much-needed corrective and stabilizing order to its principles, coincided exactly with the position of artists who were seeking a way out of Abstract Expressionism. Seurat was the apotheosis of ordered, stable, even frozen compositions, creating a clarity in which each dot of colour was independent and visible (in theory, at least). He did not rebel against or try to overthrow the previous art styles; he admired what had come before and incorporated the primary elements of the earlier art. He kept the colour and direct application of Impressionism; the young Americans kept the size and scale, the directness and power of Abstract Expressionism. But each sought something of his or her own, something new and adventurous, building on what had come before in a process of 'visionary reconstruction', as Smith termed it.[32] Seurat's legacy was apparent in the thick pointillist dots in the circle paintings of Richard Pousette-Dart (1916–1992) [237], works with a deeply spiritual bent, in the Pop images of Roy Lichtenstein, with their Ben-Day dots, and the grids of the younger colour-field painters who emerged in the late 1960s, such as Sanford Wurmfeld.

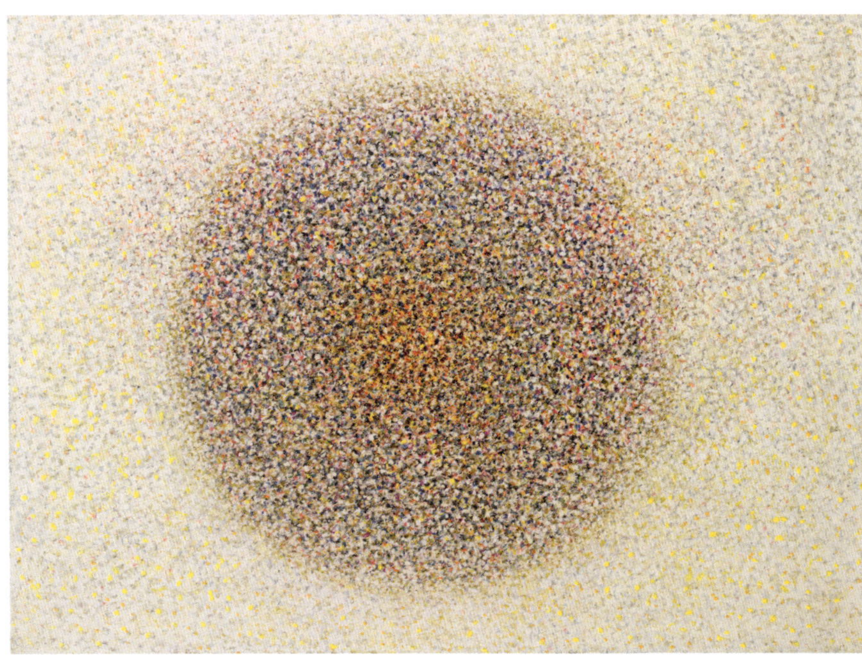

237

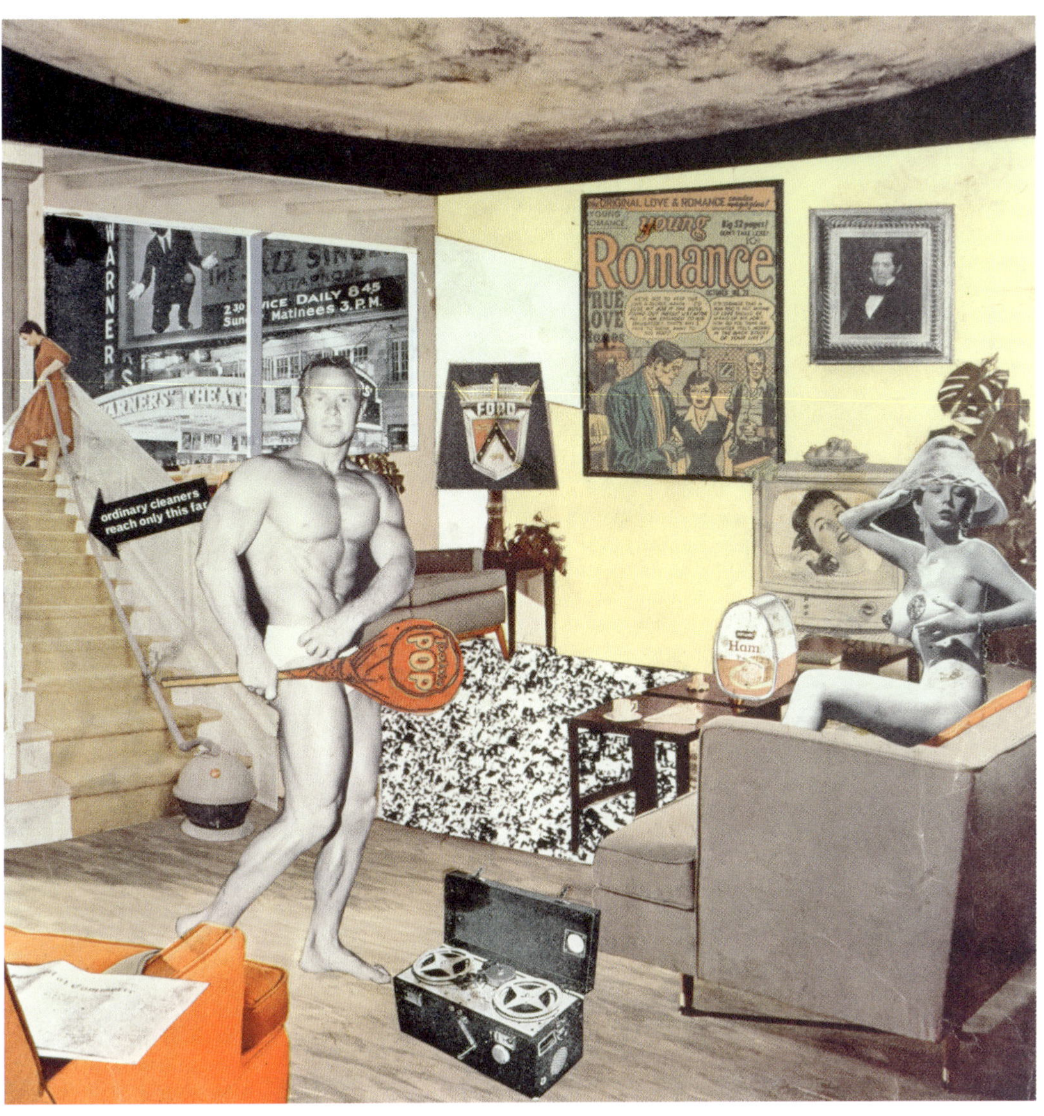

238

Pop Art's Origins

By 1959, the first images taken from popular culture had appeared in the US in the work of Andy Warhol, Claes Oldenburg and Roy Lichtenstein. However, Richard Hamilton in London had actually done the first real Pop artwork, *Just What Is It That Makes Today's Homes So Different, So Appealing?* (1956) [238]. It is a curious fact that what has seemed so purely American had its origins in London, with a group of artists and critics so bored with the dreary post-war life there that they turned to the glitter of American culture. It was the reality of American consumerism, the glitz and glamour, the ordinary objects of the American household, kitsch such as comic strips and pin-ups, that compelled the British and then a younger generation of Americans, all born in the 1920s, to seek a new everyday reality. It was the flow and pace of America, its teeming hordes in the cities, continuing Walt Whitman's embrace of the country, that caught the imagination of the new realists. Like Whitman, the brilliant poet and curator Frank O'Hara was captivated by the vulgarity, the rush of the city and captured it in his poems, as if in an extension of Ashcan realism. Like Whitman, he proclaimed that Americans should experience life, dip in and out of it at will, find the extraordinary within the ordinary, and embrace the everyday.

237 Richard Pousette-Dart,
      Radiance, 1962–3. Oil and
      metallic paint on canvas,
      183.3 × 244.4 cm
      (72¼ × 96¼ in). The Museum
      of Modern Art, New York

238 Richard Hamilton, *Just
      What Is It That Makes Today's
      Homes So Different,
      So Appealing?*, 1956. Collage,
      26 × 25 cm (10¼ × 9¾ in).
      Zundel Collection, Kunsthalle
      Tübingen, Germany

De Kooning and the Tradition of American Abstract Landscape Painting

In his *Merritt Parkway* series of 1959–60, de Kooning turned to the natural landscape as his source. He had spent more and more time on the east end of Long Island, and in 1963 he moved there permanently. The bracing tonic of the sun and water deeply affected him, just as it had Pollock when he had moved there some fifteen years earlier. In this series, which includes *Door to the River* (1960) [239], de Kooning moved into a full-blown mode of abstract landscape painting. The works are filled with a bright light unique to Springs and the East End, filled with the yellows of the intense sun, the blues of the glorious sky, the endless movement of the light on the water, and the water itself. The broad, sweeping strokes recall the swoosh of Homer's brush in his *West Wind* (1891) (page 29). It is in the American grain, this sweep of the land and its air and space. De Kooning, as had Eakins, captured the reality of the American continent in the paint itself. His turn away from urban and quotidian pressures to a 'world elsewhere' places him, along with Pollock, Gottlieb, Rothko, Still and others, squarely in the long tradition of American abstract landscape painting, which goes back even further to an old Romantic tradition of landscape, both in Germany and in America, with the Luminists.[33]

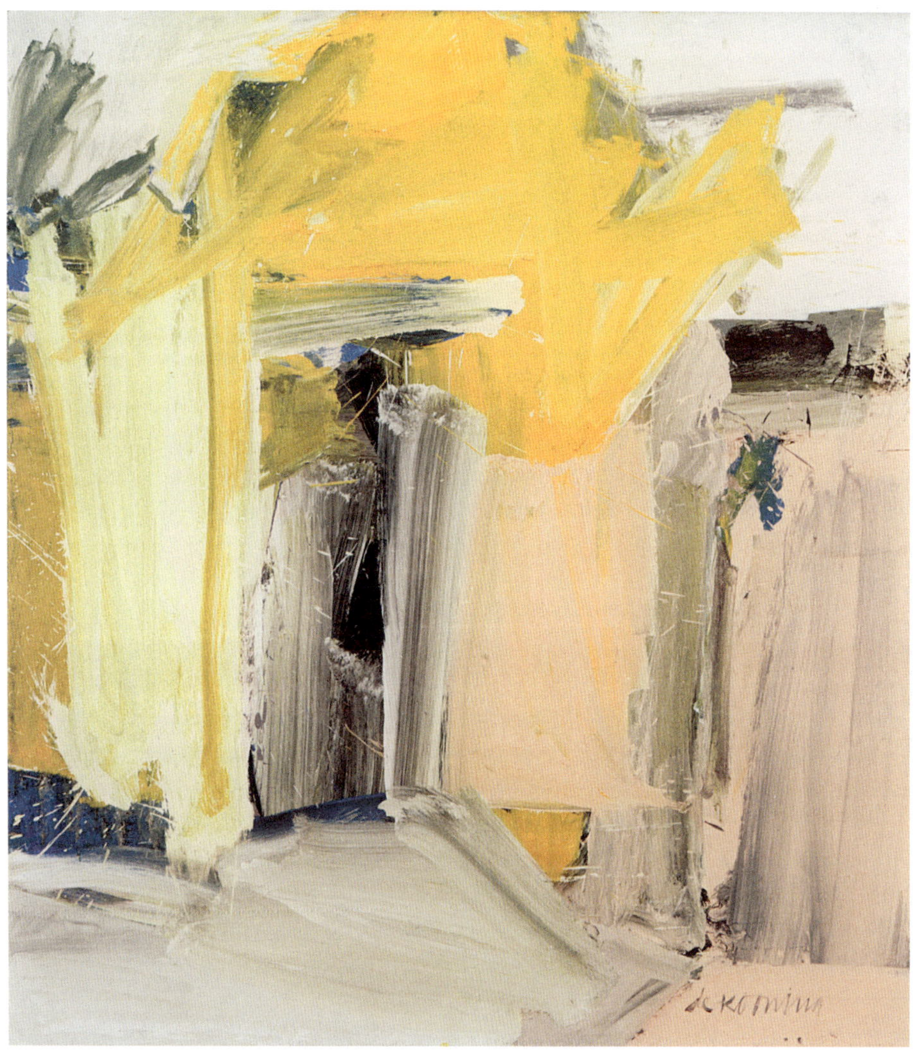

239

The broad strokes form a central rectangle – a door – through which we feel we can step into the open horizon of the land and sea. Its rough but clear geometry stabilizes the painting for us, centres it, so we can find our own centre and our bearings in the vast landscape. This painting can be compared to Kline's *Wotan* (page 269), and to David Smith's late masterpiece *Cubi XXVII* of 1965, also known as *The Gate*. This last work has a similar geometry, a rectangle or a square, an open frame or door that leads out to the vast expanse of the Adirondacks mountains, where Smith lived and worked. The two had surely met in the 1930s through John Graham, and had now got to know each other again – de Kooning visited Smith in Bolton Landing. Indeed, one of his most powerful paintings of this period is *Bolton Landing* (1957), based on the severe geometries of Smith's late work. Thus both artists became part of the 1960s generation. We can also surmise that the squares in Albers's 'Homage' series played an increasingly important role in this move towards a broad pictorial geometry.

Alfred Jensen's Systems and Surfaces

As part of the move in American art towards a new sense of clarity and openness, away from the impacted surfaces of Abstract Expressionism, we must pay close attention to the paintings of Alfred Jensen (1903–1981), who was something of an anomaly in his time. Born in Guatemala and of Danish descent, Jensen travelled the world, studying art before settling in New York in 1951. He belonged by birth to the generation of Abstract Expressionists, but while he befriended many of them, especially Rothko, he was not of their artistic persuasion, for he had arrived late to their milieu. Like Newman, Jensen was more closely aligned with a younger generation, both artistically and philosophically. He had little use for what he called the large empty canvases of his peers, and looked for something with a more specific reality. That reality was colour, and he soon orchestrated it to spectacular effect. He had studied modernism carefully and in depth in Europe, including the tradition of colour painting, dating back to Impressionism. But, possessed of a boundless curiosity, he had also immersed himself in ancient non-Western cultures, including the Maya and the Chinese. His colour was often used to embody in his work complex number systems that are still a mystery to most viewers. This made him seem something of an outsider, but he saw himself as a mediator between past, present and future art.

His long interest in colour had led him to investigate Goethe's important treatise *Zur Farbenlehre* (*On Colour*), which, coupled with his close study of modern masters, led him to his first personal works. In 1957, Jensen initiated a series of works based on concentric circles, almost at the same time as Noland did. While they are very different types of paintings, Jensen's mark him as one of the artists who, in his own way, introduced a type of art that embodied the thick impastos of Abstract Expressionism but spread out over the surface in even patterns dictated by the preordained layout of the composition. Jensen always retained a painterly quality, with a distinctive feel of the hand carefully building up surfaces. He would use circles again, with outer bands done in black and white. They emphasized the dualities of the world, even life and death, elements of colour that he had learned from Goethe, for Jensen insisted that his art should relate directly to life. By the early 1960s, his immersion in the palpable physical surface was such that his paint became thicker and thicker, at points resembling a low relief, the antithesis of the thinly stained canvases of Frankenthaler, Louis and Noland. These works

239 Willem de Kooning, *Door to the River*, 1960. Oil on canvas, 203.2 × 177.8 cm (80 × 70 in). Whitney Museum of American Art, New York

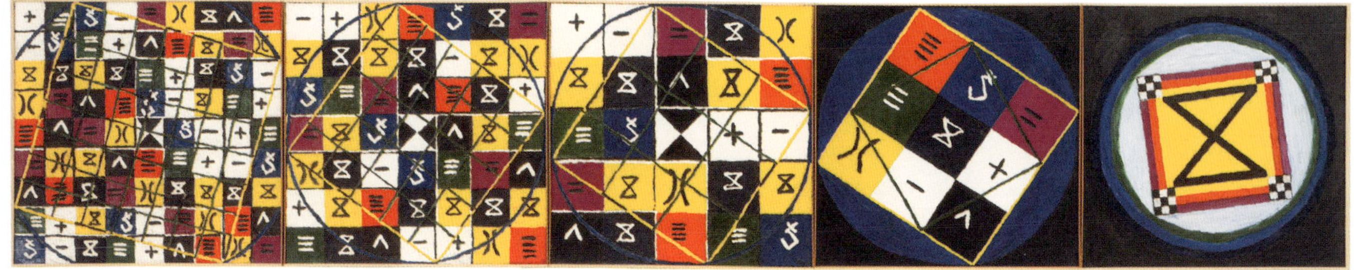

240

embodied completely the old modern dictum that a painting should be a full and independent object in its own right, not a depiction of something but a living, organic object with its own properties and laws, and its own range of references, both near and far.

If slow in coming, Jensen's breakthrough and subsequent development arrived as a veritable torrent, built up through thirty-five years of preparation. By 1960, as in *Square Beginning – Cyclic Ending, Per I–V* [240], the scale, size and complexity of his paintings had undergone a quantum leap forward, almost as if his imagination could no longer be contained within the boundaries of a single canvas. This mural-sized painting measured more than 20 feet across; consisted of five panels, and many of his works were of similar size, although they were never intended as public murals. Jensen also introduced a new complexity of elements, using early Chinese mathematical systems taken from Shang oracle bone inscriptions (a dense surface patterning within an inscribed circle representing the female, and a square, the male), then moved to an ever-simplified format, ending with a frontal, highly clarified structure. It is as if he were mimicking and demonstrating the course of art from the 1950s into the 1960s, from relative multiplicity to a higher, clearer definition of elements. Never has there been such a large or complex colour-field painting, a dense field of pigment. His use of signs, symbols and numbers seems to constitute an encyclopaedia of ancient wisdom, garnered through a lifelong study of world cultures, virtually unique in twentieth-century art.

By the early 1960s, Jensen had attracted a good amount of critical interest from all quarters of aesthetic outlook and interest. In 1963, Judd and Kaprow, surely polar opposites in their outlooks on art, each reviewed Jensen's show at the Graham Gallery in March of that year. Judd, as usual, got right to the point: 'Now and then a chance occurs for a narrow, substantive, categorical statement: Jensen is great. He is one of the best painters in the United States.'[34] Jensen's marks and numbers meant little to Judd, who commented that 'His theories are important to him and irrelevant to the viewer.'[35] Later that year Kaprow was effusive in his praise of Jensen, saying that 'the contemporary vanguard looks to Alfred Jensen with an interest that is accorded few other older artists.' For Kaprow, moreover, Jensen's myriad cultural references made him a 'metaphysical artist, his vision cosmic'; the numbers were nothing less than an attempt at a 'theory of the universe, a world view'.[36] It is clear that Jensen was one of the most difficult, intriguing and purely beautiful of America's painters.

Interpretations of The Real: Judd and Kaprow

The interpretations of Judd and Kaprow, apparently so disparate, do in fact continue an approach in art that has marked the country for two centuries: the deep vein of American realism, translated by the two men, in their different ways, as The Real. Both their views of the real came directly from

240 Alfred Jensen, *Square Beginning – Cyclic Ending, Per I–V*, 1960. Oil on canvas, five panels, each: 127 × 127 cm (50 × 50 in); overall width: 6.4 m (21 ft). Private collection

their experience of Pollock's work. For Kaprow, it meant moving beyond painting or making physical objects, into the wider world of expanding space, performing acts more like the shaman or magician than the painter, beyond precise measurement. For Judd, Pollock's surfaces demanded an extension out into real space; there, he was to make concrete forms that he termed 'specific objects'.[37] They were not paintings or sculptures, but something in between, as physical, precisely measured three-dimensional pieces. 'Things that exist, exist', he said, and 'We can only know what we can know; things are as they are.'[38] Reading Judd is akin to watching William Harnett or John F. Peto describing in paint the objects in front of them, 'the material poetry of the country'.[39] Like much realist painting, Judd's objects seek a state in which they look much lighter and more open than they actually are. They are airy, precise, recalling Brancusi's carefully defined shapes or Demuth's thin, sharp lines. There is no illusionism – that was the way of old European hierarchies and, for Judd, the first task of the American artist was to get past Europe.[40]

For Kaprow, once Pollock got him past the picture plane and into space, almost anything could go into the work, including the abstracting figuration that exists in some of Jensen's work of the early 1960s.[41] Kaprow saw Jensen in terms of the Symbolist tradition, opposed to systematization, open to a kind of metaphysical dreaming that could reference the world and its cultures and rituals. Kaprow sought a unity of all the arts, as in the medieval age, with artisans of all sorts rather than the singular artist. To be sure, Judd sought unity too – of a single piece, and a single space in which all parts went to make a single environment – but for Kaprow that unity ranged over the history of the world, to which Jensen's art surely pointed. Jensen's work constantly shifts before our eyes as we focus on one aspect or another, one reference or another, yet it always holds together. For Kaprow, only change was really enduring. Judd wanted art that you could see instantly, like Stella's 'what you see is what you see',[42] although he ascribed deep theories of philosophy to his work. Jensen – and Kaprow – welcomed the ineffable, the difficult, beyond immediate analysis. Jensen knew his work was hard to understand, that it would take a long time to absorb, but that was fine with him, since art lasts beyond our times. This may seem utopian, and perhaps it is, but the best artists are visionaries. Judd addressed this while building his museum in Marfa, Texas, now a major art destination, when he asked 'Why was it idealistic to want to do something new and beneficial, practical also...? Is it practical to let the civilization become as gross as it's becoming, to let it become stagnant, and then try to aerate it?'[43]

A Renaissance for Sculpture:
Ferber, Lassaw, Hare, Bourgeois, Snelson

Smith and Calder were the two most famous American sculptors to have emerged in the 1930s and 1940s, but they were far from the only ones to appear after 1940. In fact, American sculpture at that time underwent something of a renaissance. The method of open construction in new materials led the way, as did Smith's insistence that sculpture could be as free and inventive as painting. After all, he had stated that he belonged more with the painters than the sculptors.

Herbert Ferber (1906–1991) was one of the most talented and, after Smith, may well have been the best sculptor of his generation. He had started in the 1930s, working in modelled three-dimensional figures with a decidedly socially conscious tone. Then in the early 1940s, he learned from Henry Moore to take his work into more extended, thinner sculptural forms, as demonstrated in his *Three Legged Woman* (1945). Ferber began to draw compulsively, making countless sketches, usually with a Surrealist flavour, particularly like that of Miró, helping him to realize shortly thereafter his versions of 'drawing in space', the term often used to describe the open-form work of his generation. By 1948, he had attained a new degree of open forms, organic in nature but often spiked with the menacing points of Surrealist savagery, as in *Hazardous Encounter* (1947).

Sculpture is more physical and technically demanding than painting, and thus Ferber and others of the time did not evolve as quickly as the painters. But by 1954, in *Roof Sculpture with S Curve II* [241], his forms had become larger, more extended and more flowing, although to be sure still protected by piercing linear forms that keep us back, discouraging us with their threatening presence from becoming too familiar or cosy with the sculpture. But here was the beginning of two ideas that became unique to Ferber. The roof, supported by the vertical swords, contains the seeds of an enclosed space, an environment that Ferber realized for Rutgers University some years later, in 1966, perhaps his version of the implications of Pollock's mural paintings extended into our physical space. An even more fruitful result of the roofed sculpture was his series of cage sculptures, developed from a work by Giacometti, which provided an open environment, as it were, a structure in and from which lofty organic shapes could twist and turn, in a quiet, meditative kind of modern baroque composition. Sadly, because sculpture is difficult to move and show, let alone collect, many sculptors of this generation are fast disappearing from our view.

Ibram Lassaw (1913–2003) worked in a quieter, even gentler mode, by using a three-dimensional grid structure [242] that can be traced to Picasso and early Mondrian, as well as to Giacometti's cage. He worked his surfaces

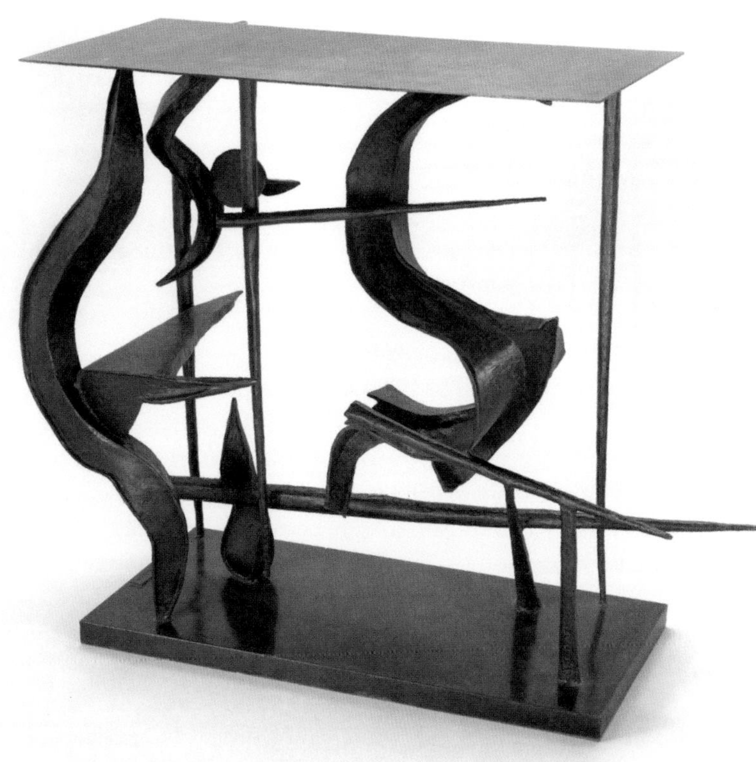

241

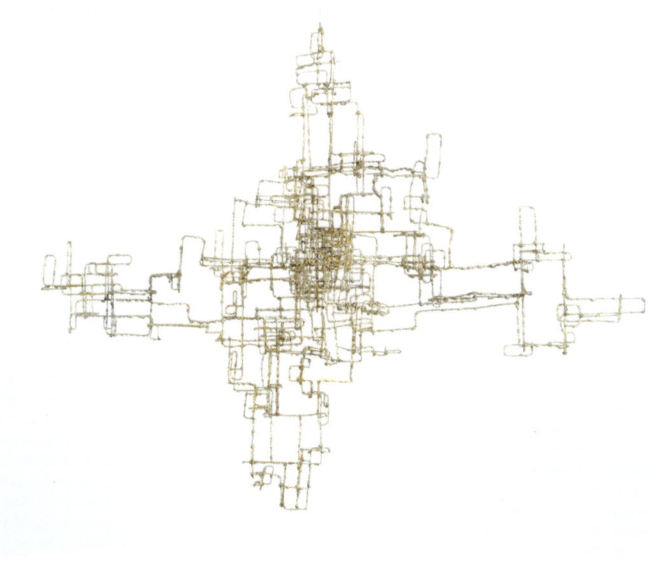

242

like the painterly equivalents of Philip Guston's abstractions of the early 1950s, with their similar references to the grid, another reminder of the lasting influence of Cubism well after its supposed demise. Similar grids were used by Peter Grippe (1912–2002), a sculptor now almost entirely forgotten, but one who merits serious attention [243]. Working out of Mondrian and Cubism, Grippe developed elaborate structures defined by multiple shapes, all of which embraced the simultaneity of life in the modern city – while at the same time reminding us of the primitive, distant cliff dwellings of long-lost nations. In his series on this theme, Grippe showed marvellous inventive power in constructing three-dimensional equivalents of the movement, immediacy and unceasing activity of human life, whether ancient or modern. At their best they are fascinating and compelling, for they demonstrate an ambition, technical mastery and sheer visual power rare for any artist, especially among modern sculpture.

David Hare (1917–1992) was well known and an active presence in the New York art world, noted for his connections to Surrealist practices and the Europeans then living in exile in New York. His touch in sculpture-making was exquisite, truly refined and articulate, allowing him to make open works of such finesse that they seemed almost beyond the reach of three dimensions. Yet in his landscapes of the early 1950s, Hare showed how the medium could in fact incorporate these themes with clarity and strength. The works were to be suspended, thus getting sculpture off its restricting pedestals and exposing it to the air, where it could now breathe with the freedom of the aesthetics of painting. Calder had pioneered this practice, but artists like Hare gave it extensive formal and emotive powers. As such, Hare and Smith joined the numerous painters of the 1940s and 1950s who openly embraced landscape themes and the forces of nature [244]; such themes are often denied by the artists themselves, yet there they are, in plain sight.

Louise Bourgeois (1911–2010) was little known and hardly recognized at the time her work first appeared, in the 1940s, but by 1980 she had become a famous artist, recognized the world over for her large-scale environments and elaborate constructions. Born in Paris, she moved to the United States in 1938, where she studied at the venerable institution that nurtured so many young artists, the Art Students League.

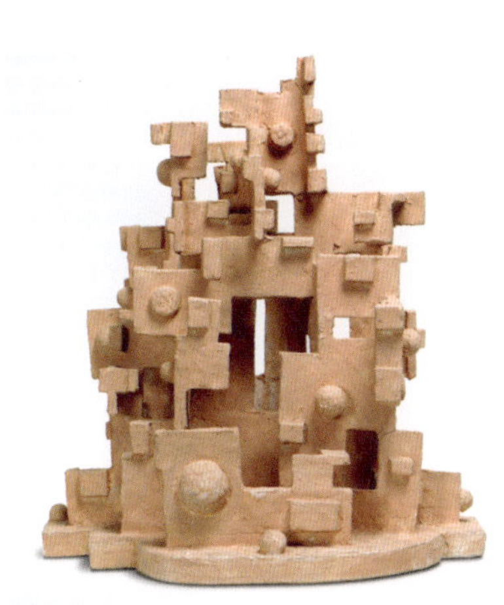

243

241 Herbert Ferber, *Roof Sculpture with S Curve, II*, 1954 (cast 1969). Bronze, 125.4 × 152.4 × 67.8 cm (49⅜ × 60 × 26¾ in). The Museum of Modern Art, New York

242 Ibram Lassaw, *Nebula In Orion*, 1951. Welded bronze, 73 × 86.1 × 50.7 cm (28¾ × 34 × 20 in). The Museum of Modern Art, New York

243 Peter Grippe, *City Music*, 1945. Terracotta, 45.7 × 38.1 × 38.1 cm (18 × 15 × 15 in). The Allentown Art Museum

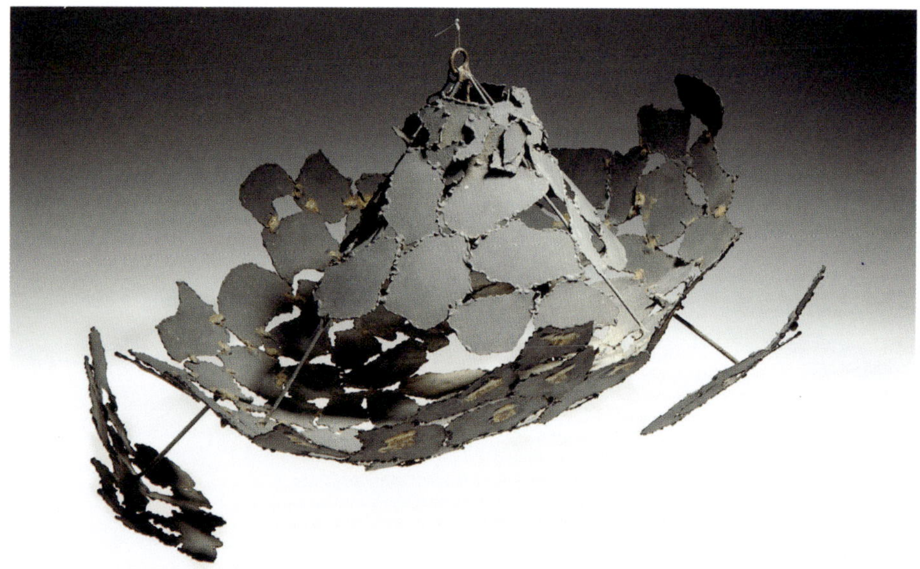

244

Bourgeois's first sculptures were fragile standing figures, plays on the Surrealist image of the *personage*, part human, part mythic, that was so often a feature of 1940s art in America. They were carved from light, fragile balsam, tipping off centre, making them delicate and precarious, perfect metaphors for her own fragile memory and psyche, as well as for her standing in the art world. She was mocked for this work by the officials at MoMA in the late 1960s, who accepted gifts of her art from her only because they would cost them nothing. But they were beautiful, resonant in their silent eloquence, for those who cared to look and take in their quiet, compelling aura.

She stayed the course, however, and her work became physically and emotionally tougher, more visceral, as can be seen in sculptures such as *The Quartered One* (1964–5) [245], which could suggest vaginal openings roughly abused, or a slaughtered cow hanging from a rack. The organic is taken to new extremes even at a time when more reduced, condensed structures were appearing to great acclaim. She investigated her memories of childhood, which for her could be magical or intensely painful, opening up gaps and hollows and crevices that suggested the scarring of the human mind and soul as well as the body. She also had a sensuous side, loving forms of voluptuousness and sexuality, rendered abstract but recalling the swelling breasts and hips sculpted by Gaston Lachaise in the 1930s. She led the way in the now fashionable search for personal identity (as if art was ever anything else), but she did it on her own terms, working it out through her art over decades.

Although his work became known only in the 1960s, Kenneth Snelson (b.1927) deserves serious attention. His sculpture *V-X* [246] is made of reflective stainless-steel 'poles' held in acute tension, at diverse angles, another kind of open sculpture. His particular kind of tension-construction reminds us of Richard Buckminster Fuller, but in fact Snelson himself taught Fuller the principles while studying with him. He speaks of nature and its forces, and makes patterns of the physical dynamics of the world. We can say, then, that he is also a landscape artist, depicting in shimmering light the electric impulses of the world around us. Indeed, the linear aspect of the supporting wires surely owes a debt to Pollock's all-over tracings of his own landscape drawing and patterning.

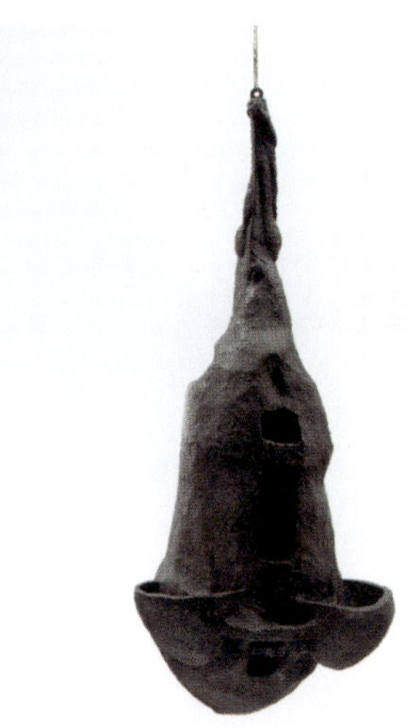

245

     Modern Art in America

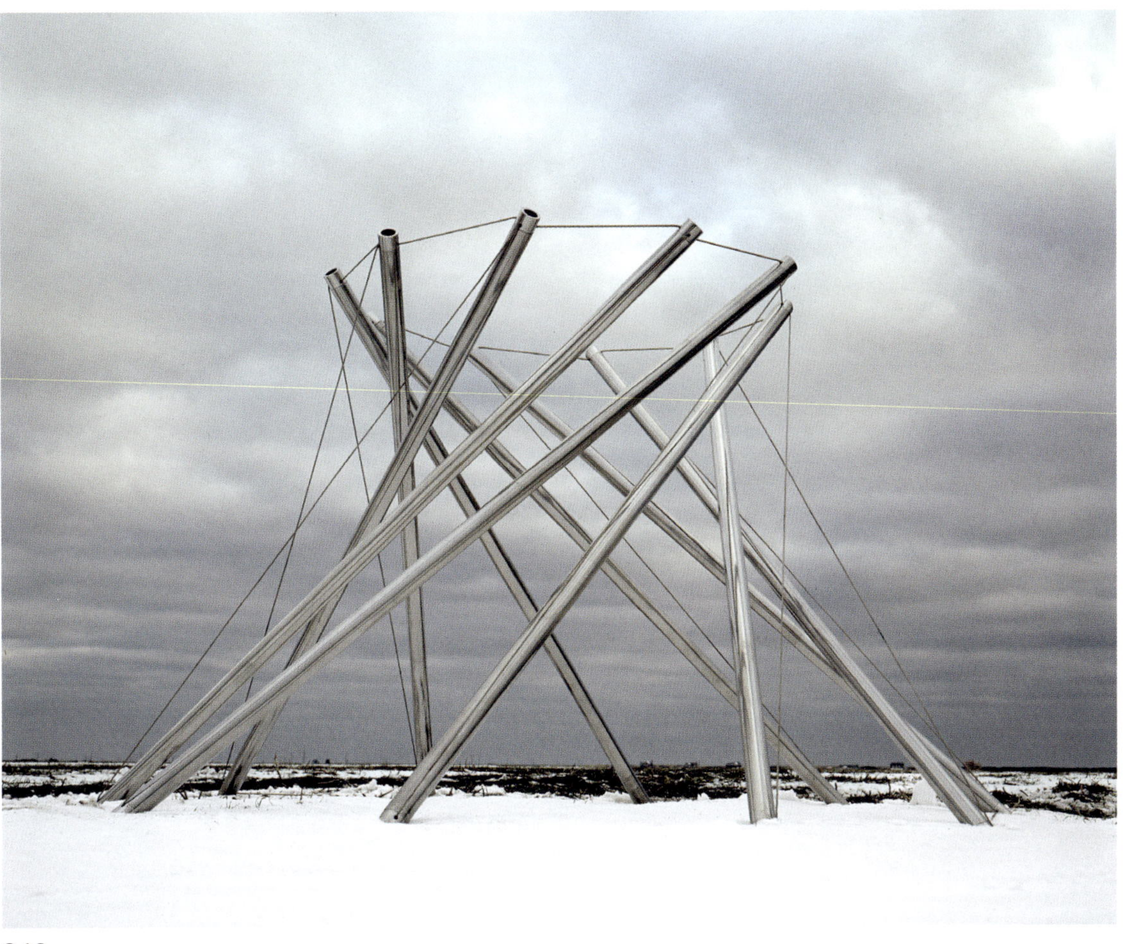

246

Smith and Colour

David Smith (1906–1965) had been in close contact with Davis in the 1930s, and surely took him as a strong example as to the possibilities of colour. Echoes of Davis are there from the start, first in his painting, then in his early reliefs of 1930–2. *Helmholtzian Landscape* (1946), a work that paid homage to the nineteenth-century pioneer of colour science, clearly referenced Davis, and marked the start of pronounced colour in his mature work.

Smith used colour off and on until the late 1950s, perhaps most lyrically in the pinks of *Study in Arcs* (1957)[247], a vertical drawing in space of a large figure leaping and extending beyond reach. This linearity was matched by the strong hues of frontal, Cubist planes in vertical works of the early 1960s such as *Three Planes* (1960–1) and *Zig II* (1961). By this time, Smith had become close friends with the colour-field artists, Noland and Frankenthaler among them. Working virtually side by side with them, he opened up his colour as if to show that he could match with sculpture what the painters were doing. In his *Three Circles* (1962), for example, Smith clearly referenced Noland's concentric circles, but he extended them out and across a considerable distance. It was as if he were creating literal, physical parts of the landscape, as viewed at his home and studio in upstate New York, thus reinforcing his ongoing reference to the landscape, perhaps most famously evident in *Hudson River Landscape* (1951)[248].[44]

The circle was also the main and central element in Smith's extraordinary and perhaps greatest piece using vivid colour, *Bec-Dida Day* (1963)[249]. The piece embodies his two beloved daughters and, as Edward Fry, the late Smith scholar, noted, it 'fully resolved for the first time

244 David Hare, *Cloud and Rain*, c.1950. Welded and painted bronze and steel, 26 × 52.2 × 50 cm (10¼ × 20½ × 19⅝ in). Smithsonian American Art Museum, Washington, DC

245 Louise Bourgeois, *The Quartered One*, 1964–5. Bronze, 149 × 72 × 54.1 cm (58¾ × 28⅜ × 21⅜ in). The Museum of Modern Art, New York

246 Kenneth Snelson, *V-X*, 1968. Stainless steel, 182.9 × 304.8 × 304.8 cm (72 × 120 × 120 in). Columbus Museum of Art

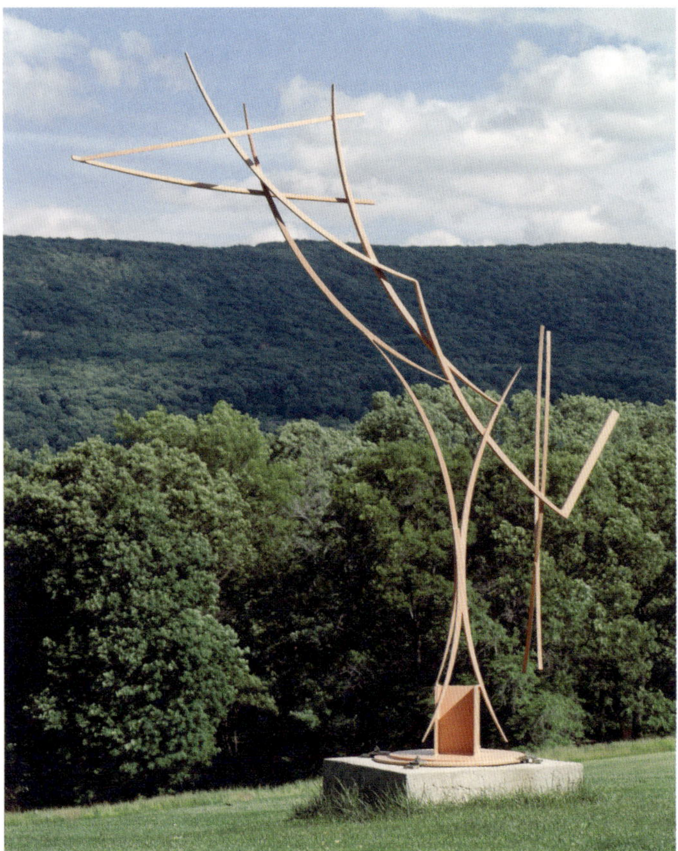

247

the problem of using colour in sculpture for purposes other than those of cubist pictorial aesthetics'.[45] Fry had more to say on the work, and his words are worth quoting in full:

> The huge tank end, assuming the role of torso in a roughly anthropo-morphic composition, is painted blue within and yellow on its rear, converse side; the fact of this other side is emphasized through the yellow on the rim of the tank end; and this yellow is inescapably visible unless the viewer is very near the sculpture and directly in front of it. Similarly, the steel 'I' beams at top and bottom (where the beam was cut and welded so that no break is visible) are polychromed in such a way that emphasis is given not only to their finite, separate existence within the sculpture as a whole, but also to the fact of their own three-dimensional structure. Hence the 'I' beam on top is brick red within its recessed channel but black elsewhere, including the ends and the entire reverse side. In similar fashion, the recessed channel of the lower 'I' beam is painted the same yellow as the reverse, convex side of the tank end, but elsewhere it is black, as on the upper 'I' beam; while on its opposite side Smith painted the recessed channel the same brick red that he also used on the upper 'I' beam. From almost any position the viewer consequently is provided with infor-mation concerning the existence and structure of that which he cannot perceive directly, as well as that which is immediately visible to him; and thus the organization of colour on what is structurally a thin, frontal composition invites a three dimensional apprehension of Bec-Dida Day exceeding that offered by much free standing sculpture composed deliberately in the round.[46]

247 David Smith, *Study in Arcs*, 1957. Steel, painted pink, 335.3 × 293.4 × 105.4 cm (132 × 115½ × 41½ in). Storm King Art Center, Mountainville, NY

248 David Smith, *Hudson River Landscape*, 1951. Welded painted steel and stainless steel, 123.8 × 183.2 × 44 cm (48¾ × 72⅛ × 17 5/16 in). Whitney Museum of American Art, New York

249 David Smith, *Bec-Dida Day*, 1963 (with *Volton XX*, 1963). Painted steel, 226.1 × 165.7 × 45.7 cm (89 × 65 × 18 in). Yale University Art Gallery, New Haven. Photograph by the artist at Bolton Landing

     Modern Art in America

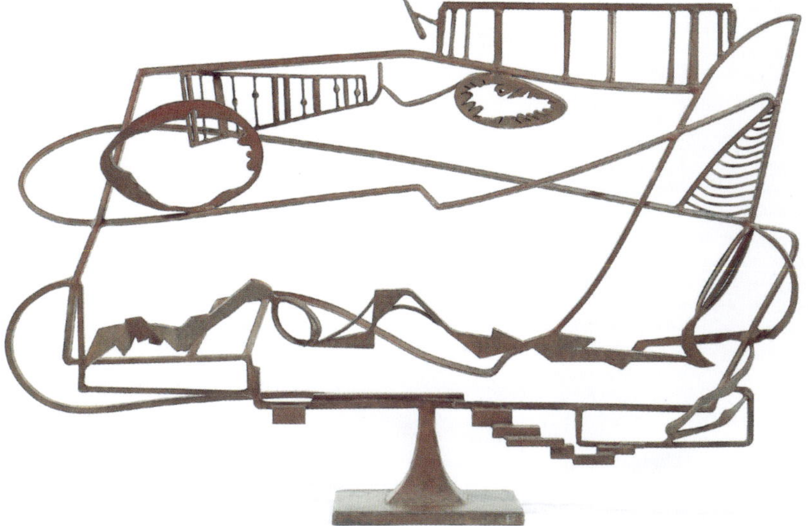

248

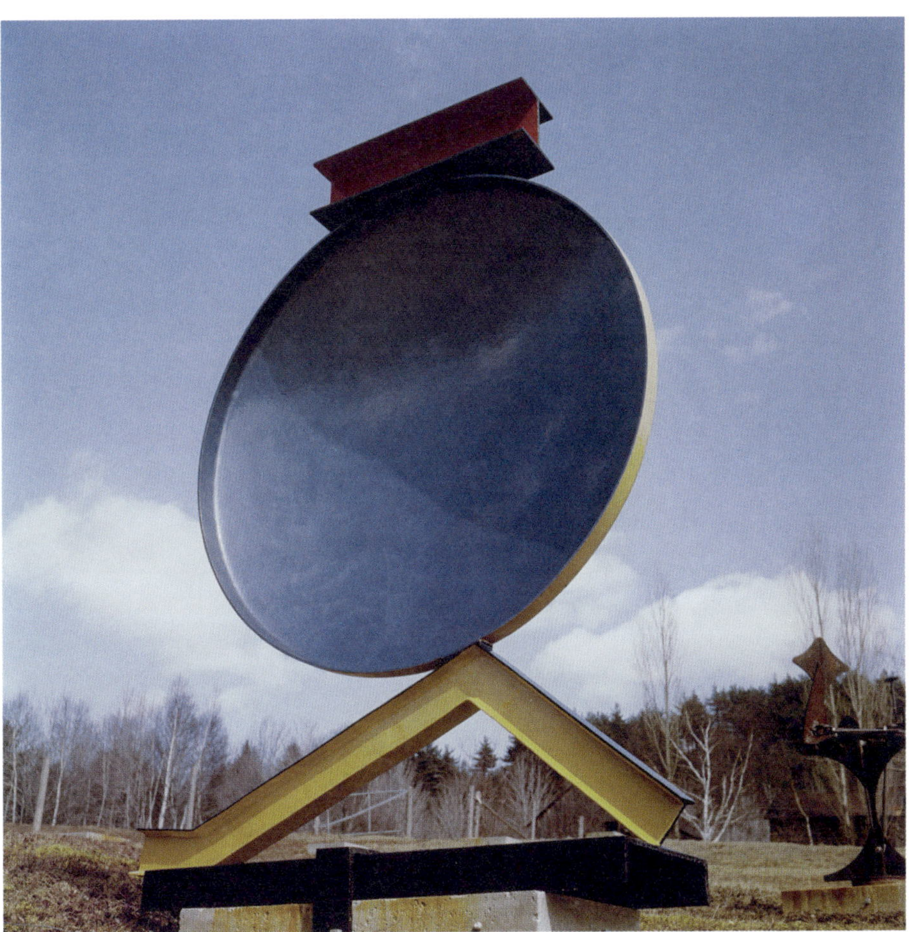

249

Until the early 1960s, Smith had used colour as an applied surface, a material on top of another. It was clearly an additive process, effective though it was. Possibly he was inspired by the painters to find a way to make colour and light intrinsic to the surface, as the colour-field painters had let the paint soak into and become coeval with the canvas. In the *Cubis*, his monumental series of twenty-eight pieces begun in 1961 and continuing to his death in 1965, he found the sculptural parallel, if not equivalent, of colour staining. In these majestic works, Smith fused colour and light from and in the material itself – stainless-steel elements – by buffing them to a highly reflective surface and then burnishing them with a grinder. This process created painterly surfaces that fairly glistened and covered the entirety of the surface, a kind of all-over patterning analogous to the surfaces of Pollock's classic poured paintings. Encountering one of these sculptures bathed in the direct sunlight of early morning is a transcendental experience.

Yet, modern as he was, Smith also paid attention to classic art forms and structures, as many of his generation did. This process has been well described,[47] and it has been pointed out how the majority of these works were standing abstract figures with references to Greek, Etruscan and Roman art. The sculptures often loom over us and before us like a guardian figure from Greek or Roman mythology. We can well imagine *The Hero* (1950), a rigid vertical figure of quasi-geometric bearing, deriving from a classical temple of ancient times. This sculpture, as we have seen, introduced a new formality into Smith's work after the drawing-in-space curvatures of the linear pieces *Australia* and *Hudson River Landscape*,

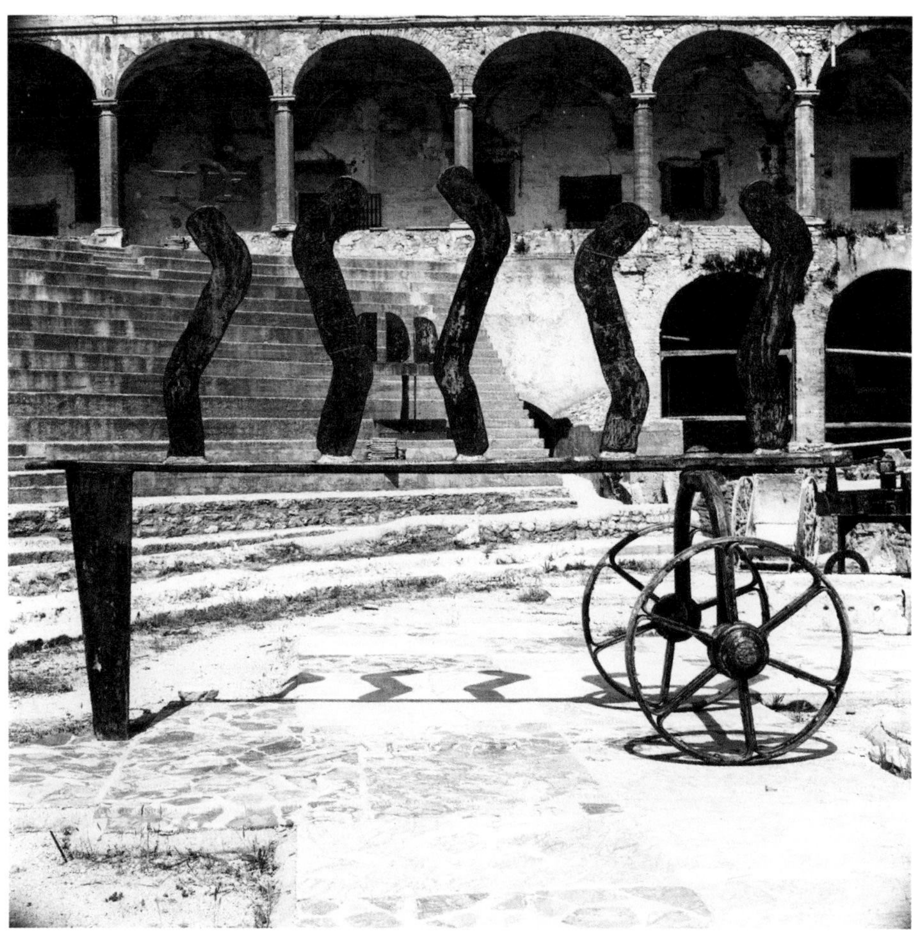

250

250 David Smith, *Voltri VII*, 1962.
Steel, 215.9 × 311.2 × 110.5 cm
(85 × 122 × 43½ in).
The National Gallery of Art,
Washington, DC. Installed
at the Roman amphitheatre,
Spoleto, Italy, with *Voltri IV* in
the background. Photograph
by the artist, 1962

251 The Guggenheim building
in its opening year, 1959,
New York

both highly expressive gestural works from 1951. Smith's shift to a new frontality corresponds to de Kooning's large-scale women of the early 1950s, as well as to Pollock's figures of the same time. So, too, in 1950 Rothko had entered his mature style of a few frontally orientated rectangles floating in a circumscribed space, a more formal art than his multiforms of 1947–8. Smith's work emits a new calm, a new sense of balance and serenity – classical values now updated in a modern idiom. This staunch verticality marks much of his work in the 1950s. In his piece *Superstructure on 4* (1960), an early stainless-steel work, the figure is based on a classical post-and-lintel configuration, topped by two heads, suggesting a pair of guardians at the gate.

Smith's connection with the classical world was made real in 1962 when he was invited to Spoleto, Italy by the art historian and collector Giovanni Carandente to take part in an exhibition named 'Sculpture in the City' for the Festival of Two Worlds. He was one of thirteen sculptors to participate. Smith and the others were asked to send pieces and make works for the show. Smith sent *Cubi IX*, a stainless steel sculpture he made the year prior. He was given a few choices of factories to work in, and he chose the farthest one from Spoleto, in Voltri, where he worked for a month in the abandoned steel factories. The factories were a treasure trove for Smith: he used old tools, benches and wheeled tangs for transporting buckets of molten metal; he worked out of the materials he found there, letting them suggest the forms and mood, a concept that can be traced to Stieglitz and Matisse in the early years of the twentieth century. What followed was a great creative burst, for Smith made twenty-two pieces in thirty days, many of monumental proportions, after misunderstanding that he was only supposed to make one or two works.

In *Voltri VII*, Smith forged a rough equivalent of an ancient 'chariot', as the artist himself called it. To a two wheeled bar, used to insert and remove hot steel, he attached a 10-foot-long horizontal iron bar. Atop this, he welded five S-shaped forgings that he had also found in the Voltri factory. Placed sequentially in a regular A-B-A-B-A pattern, these shapes recall a frieze with S and reverse S shapes called 'strigilation' that often appears in antique art as carved fluting patterns, on the sides of stone sarcophagi. Placed on the chariot, they suggest a sarcophagus being borne on a wagon in a Roman funeral procession. The figures were placed around the steps of the amphitheatre in Spoleto, positioned as if looking at *Voltri VII* at the centre, as at a funeral oration. At the end of the festival, Smith welded some of the scraps and tools and had them shipped to his studio at Bolton Landing in the United States, where they provided the basis of much of his best work. He used this material in all of his *Voltri-Bolton* and *Volton* sculptures.

The Guggenheim Museum, 1959

One of the great achievements of American creativity in this decade, and indeed in the century, came from the field of architecture, just as it had some fifty years earlier. In 1959, the Guggenheim Museum opened its new building[251], on upper Fifth Avenue in New York, designed by Frank Lloyd Wright, perhaps America's earliest, most influential architect. Years later he was still a radical presence, for the building received as much strong reaction and comment, praise and disdain as any monument, painting or building ever has in the United States. The experience of visiting the Guggenheim is thrilling – we wind around as we ascend, viewing art and spectators before us and across the space; and we peer up into a dome that is nothing less than magisterial. This experience still seems so contemporary that it is nothing less than timeless. The concept of the building was first developed and worked out in Wright's studio, which he had built for himself in 1898 in Oak Park, Illinois. When we see that building we fast-forward to the Guggenheim, a continuity from past to present in the most palpable sense.

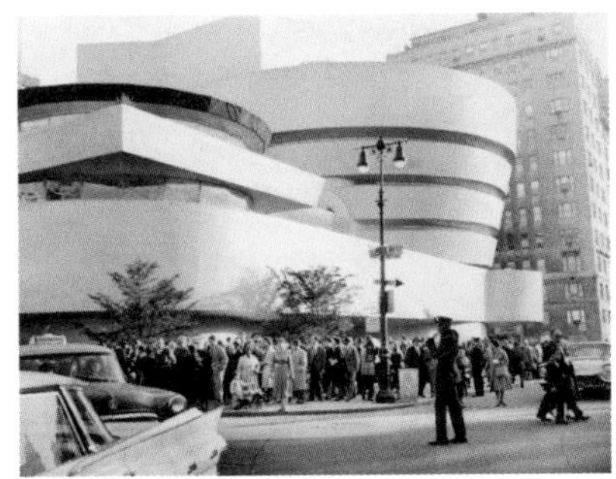

251

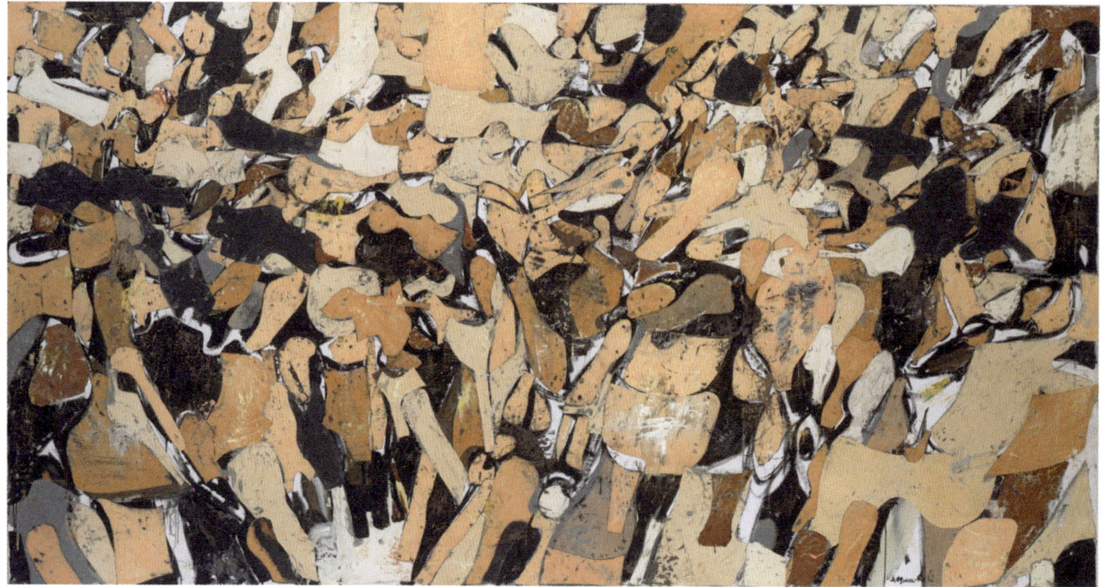

252

The New American Painting:
Conrad Marca-Relli and James Brooks

The proliferation of new and rising talent in post-war American painting and sculpture was primarily based in New York, and thus came to be loosely known as the New York School. That name has hidden the enormous diversity in technique, theme, background and approach that characterized what has also been called The New American Painting, named after an influential exhibition organized by MoMA and widely circulated in New York in 1958–9. Its origins have been traced mostly to Picasso and Miró, but this is not the half of it.

Consider Conrad Marca-Relli (1913–2000), who often worked in New York but whose art took its basic feel and character from the classical past he had inherited. True, his achievement rested on a new and expanded use of collage, which of course can be traced to Picasso and Braque, but he extended it into a practice without precedent. The colour, surface, texture and placement of his forms all seem to stem from ancient Rome, his heritage made present, and another example of how classicism in multiple forms stayed true to the course of American art.

The surface agitation of his ripped forms will recall the paintings of de Kooning, but Marca-Relli's collages always retain a certain classical stability of careful placement and always point to the colour and texture of the ruins and palazzos of Italy, which he had known from frequent visits there as a child, as well as other sunlit Mediterranean countries. To walk through a room of his collages is like walking through the stones of the Roman Forum, a trip back to the distant past perhaps, but an essential aspect of the artist's experience as an inveterate traveller. They also make reference to the adobe villages of Mexico, where he also explored the past.

Marca-Relli did not give up the figure in the 1950s, although it was condensed and abstracted in many cases. He had always admired the pictorial complexities of the great Italian murals, especially the famous *Battle of San Romano* by Paolo Uccello. In his multiple-figure composition *The Battle* (1956) [252], with exacting lines of sight and space, he continued his obsession with the 'architecture of the figure', as he termed it.[49] Each figure is conceived and structured as if Marca-Relli were a Renaissance or Roman architect placing each element until the whole was completed to

252 Conrad Marca-Relli,
The Battle, 1956. Oil cloth,
tinted canvas, enamel paint
and oil on canvas,
179.1 × 331.5 cm (70½ × 130½ in).
The Metropolitan Museum
of Art, New York

253 James Brooks, *Aviation*,
1940. Mural in the Marine
Air Terminal of La Guardia
Airport, New York.

his satisfaction. Given its multiple bodies, he could call such an endeavour the 'architecture of an event'.[50] Gone was any semblance of the free-form, automatic writing that we often view as the basis of the art of the 1950s. His work had matured somewhat later than that of the more canonical figures of the time, placing him in the realm of the so-called second generation. It is a term of dubious distinction for many, and has tended to hide the real quality and achievements of numerous artists who matured after 1950.

James Brooks (1906–1992) was a major painter for years, yet he is little known today because he did not get on to anyone's official list. This happens all too often – but it should not prevent us from bringing him to full light. Like virtually all the New York School, he was a provincial, from St Louis, and came to the city to better himself. By the late 1930s he had made his mark as a muralist of the WPA Federal Art Project Mural Division (headed by Diller) for his mural *Aviation* at LaGuardia Airport [253], in the Marine terminal, which he finished by 1940. It has been restored and can still be seen in the Rotunda (a space now virtually empty, affording ideal conditions for viewing it), to understand the optimism and ambition that the Mural Division put out to further the cause of advanced American art. The mural encircles the entire rotunda, surrounding us with an epic history of flight. Part is figurative but other areas are abstract, a fine mix of sequential movements that take us through time and space into the present. We often ignore the WPA, but the chance it gave artists to live a decent life and to develop their talents was an unmistakable boon to art in America. So, too, the chance to work at this size and scale had a considerable impact in moving post-1945 painting into realms it had never known before, resulting in the mural-size paintings done from 1950 onwards. Brooks was also a pioneer in using direct stain, which appears in his art by 1949, telling us that Pollock was not alone in developing the technique widely adopted by the colour-field artists in the late 1950s and 1960s.

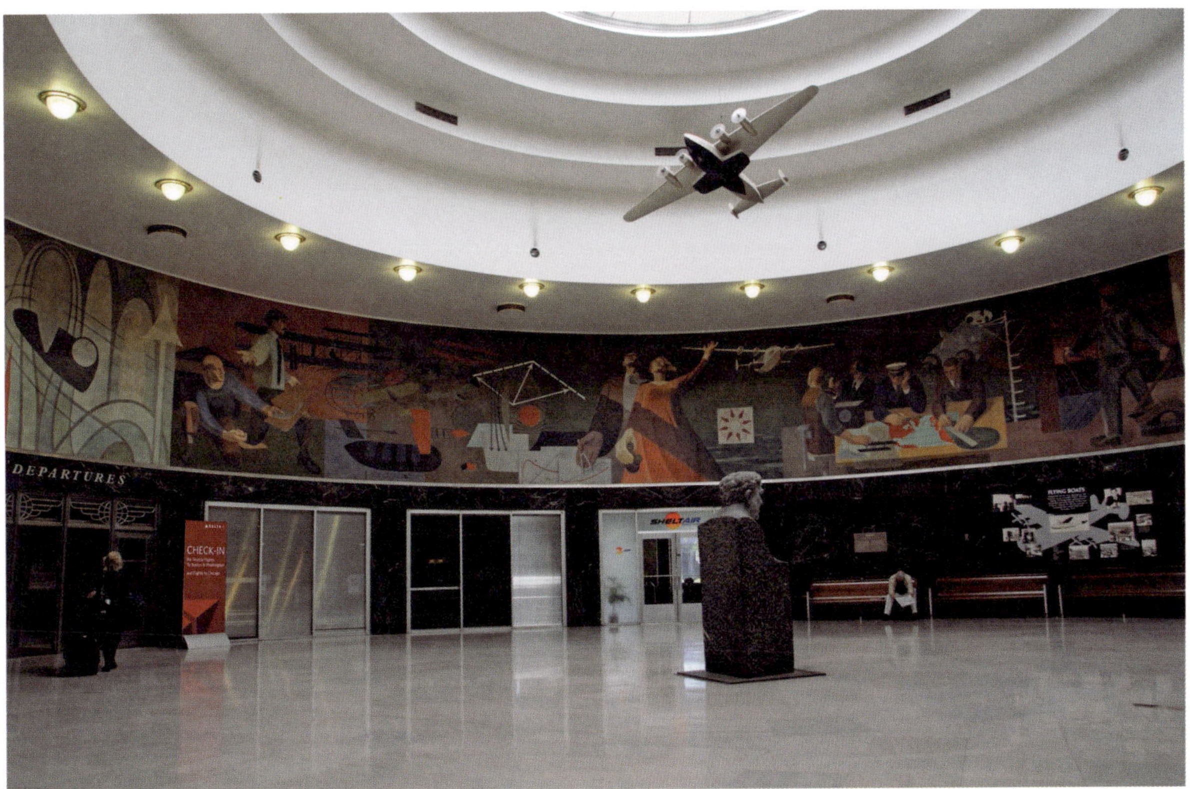

253

The American in Paris in the 1950s: Norman Bluhm

New York may have been central to American art, but another old tradition was not only revived but given new impetus: the American in Paris, so basic to US history since the eighteenth century. By virtue of one of the most inspired actions ever taken by a government, and inconceivable today, Congress passed the G.I. Bill of Rights, by which if a man had fought for his country he deserved to have an education, paid for by a grateful America. Countless Americans were given the chance to improve themselves, no doubt a prime factor in the boom in American life after the war. If you stayed home, or if you went abroad, and if you enrolled in a legitimate school, the government paid for the costs and gave you $75 a month to live on. This encouraged numerous artists to see what they could do, and how far they could take it. To be in Paris with this kind of stipend was like a dream come true, so off they went in numbers not seen since the first decade of the century.

Among them was Norman Bluhm (1921–1999), who was joined there by Joan Mitchell and Sam Francis, among others. Bluhm was from Chicago and had first studied architecture (another old practice of Americans, among them Bruce, Marin and Bluemner) with Mies van der Rohe. After leaving the service, however, he took to painting[254], and what better place than Paris, where the rich, flowing, natural forms of the great French tradition of colour painters could be fused with new concepts of direct, even automatic responses to the stimulus of nature. Bluhm later collaborated with Frank O'Hara on a series of painting-poems in which one artist reacted to the other's actions, creating a painterly update of old practices that stemmed from Apollinaire, and Dada and Surrealism. O'Hara preached on the importance of the surface in poetry, just as the painters of his generation had pushed towards heavy, dense layers of paint that could make the picture almost a palpable relief. His presence in his many roles in New York was a godsend for artists, critics and curators. His insight, his eye, his sensibility and his sense of loyalty, support and encouragement to all were one of the richest sources of creative energy in the city – his tragically young death at forty cut off a wealth of ideas and creativity still missed by many today. He would have been a calming influence amid the societal collapse of the late 1960s.

254 Norman Bluhm, *Black & Red*, 1953. Oil on canvas, 88.9 × 115.6 cm (35 × 45½ in). Michael Rosenfeld Gallery, New York

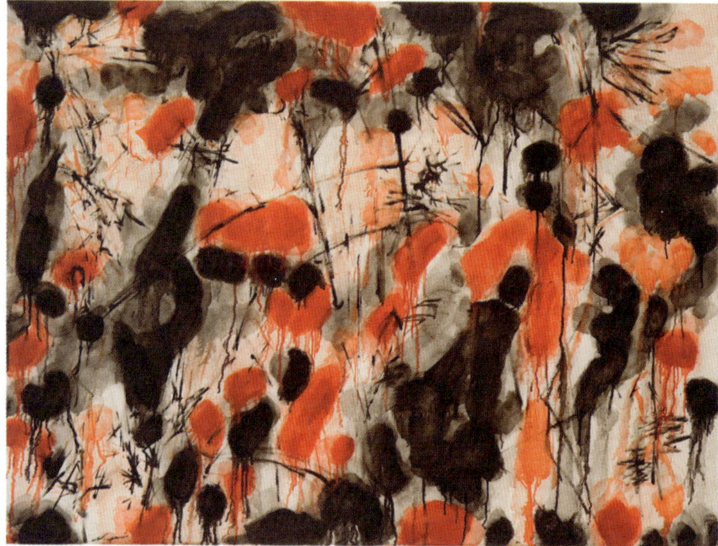

254

Modern Art in America

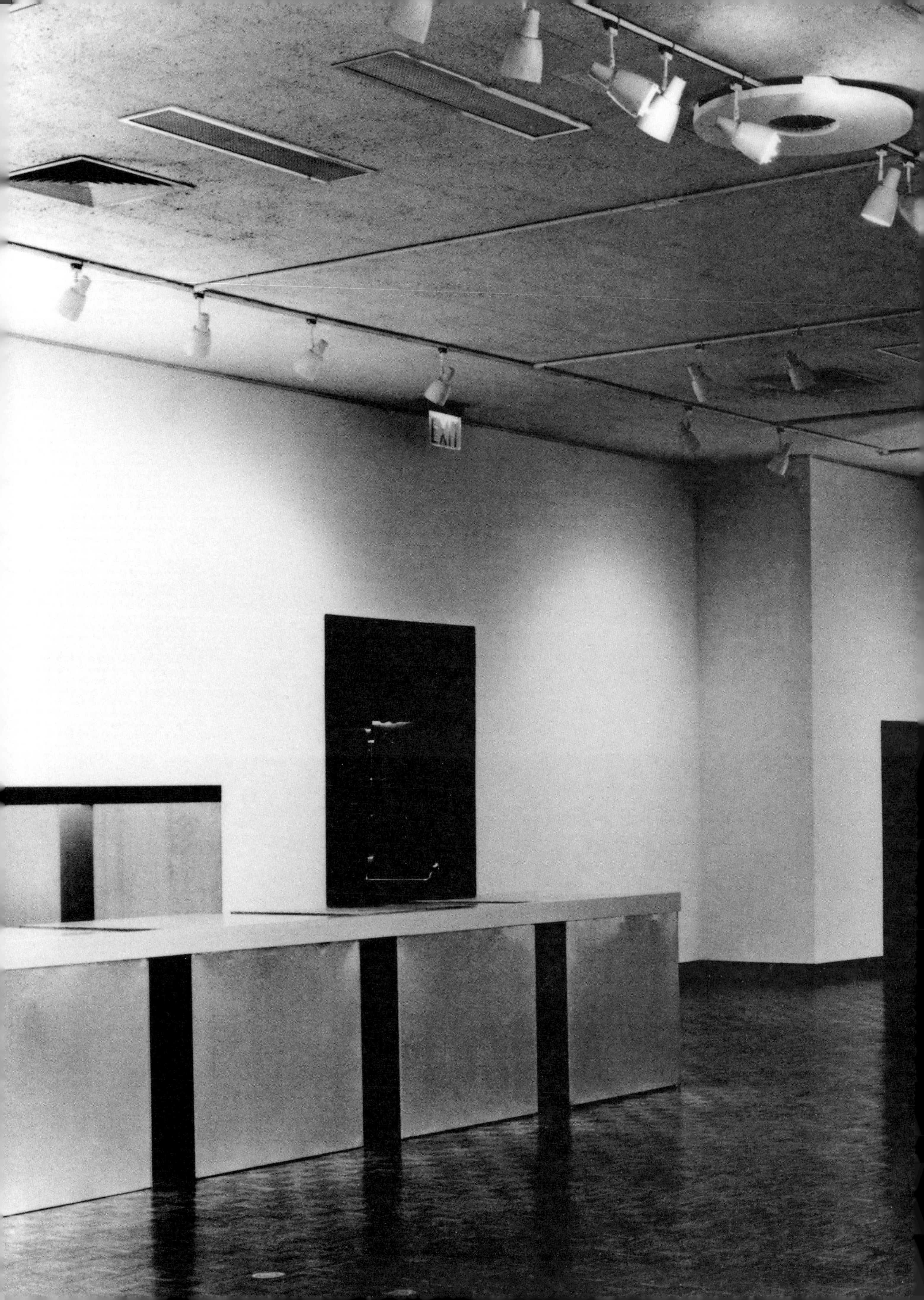

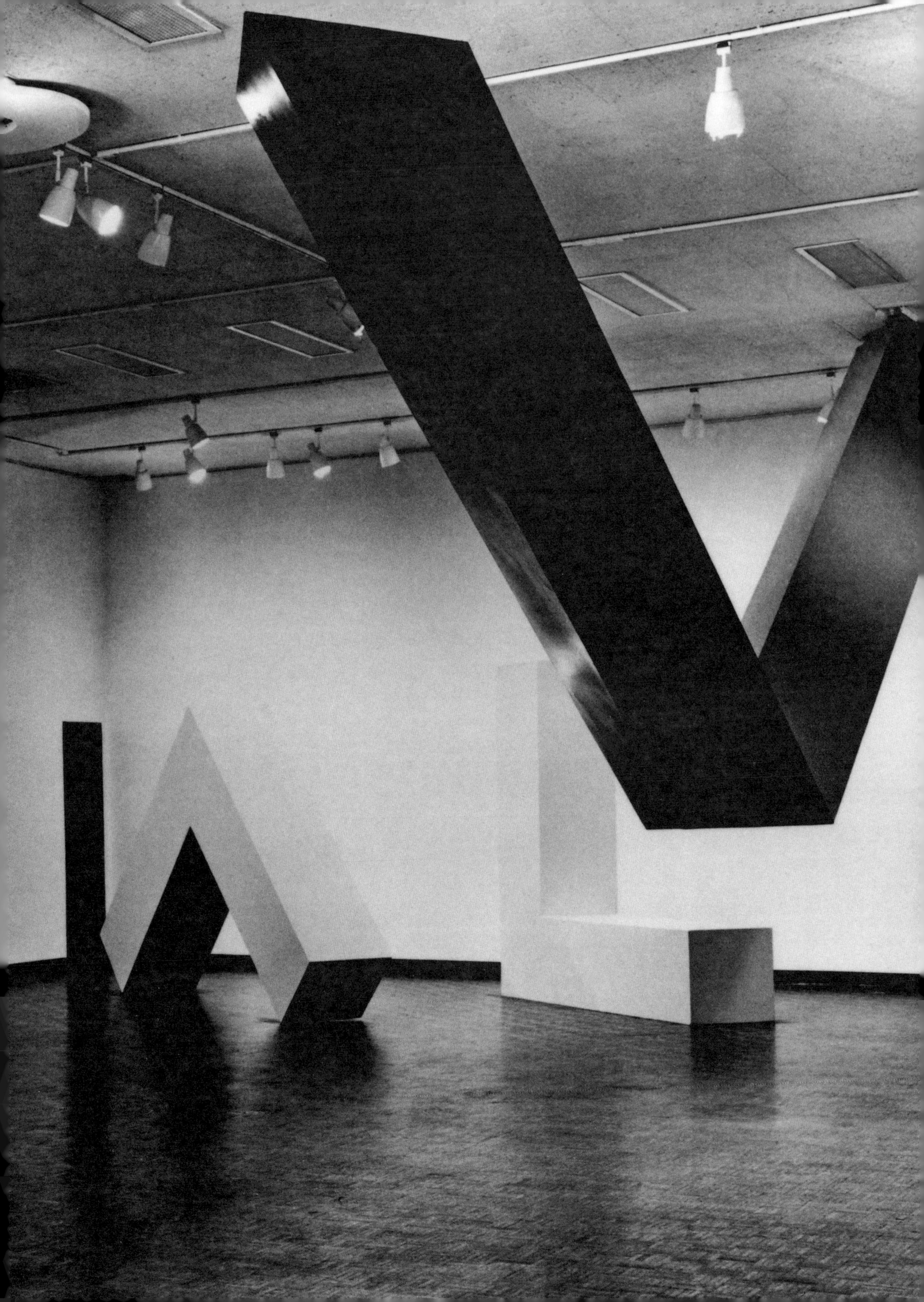

FOR BETTER OR FOR WORSE

THE 1960s

They were the best of times; they were the worst of times. It began with high hopes and promise for art and society, but by 1968 those hopes had been dashed and the country plunged into crisis on many fronts. It can be said that the country has never recovered.

The best art of the 1960s was marked by a new, even more intense use of colour, now in large, unbroken planes. Colour-field art continued apace in the work of Noland, Frankenthaler and, until his death in 1962, Morris Louis, as well as in the art of Ray Parker, Ellsworth Kelly and Josef Albers. Colour made itself felt in Pop art, especially in the work of Andy Warhol and Roy Lichtenstein in the early 1960s. Lichtenstein's colour was as vibrant and sharp as that of any of the colour-field artists, and in his imitation of Ben-Day printing dots that paralleled Seurat's pointillism, he introduced what he called a 'new classicism'.[1] The shapes were stable, clear and centred, especially in his single-image paintings of 1962 – as centred as a Noland circle or a Johns target.

Stuart Davis's Hot Colour

Davis continued his 'hot' colour in the 1960s, and should be included in the body of colour-field work that held such a prominent place in the art of the decade. During these last years, he developed both new images and formats taken from his older work, as he had done since 1940. He began by using a small photo from *The New York Times* of the walled French town of Carcassonne as the source image for the design of several brilliantly coloured paintings. Then, in 1961, in his painting *Standard Brand* and later in *Blips and Ifs* [257] he continued his use of large-scale words. However, he shifted from the sources in the supermarket to entirely personal messages to us, although still couched in commercial language. He zoomed in with increasingly larger type, virtually bellowing: *Complet*, and *Any*, with his signature prominent, as a form itself. He is telling us that any subject (including himself and his feelings) is good for a painting. With

255 Installation view of the 'Primary Structures' exhibition at the Jewish Museum, New York, 27 April–12 June 1966, with works by Donald Judd and Robert Morris on display.

Complet, he announces 'finished', 'full up', referring to the canvas, to his art and to his life, to which he adds the final act of completion – his signature. He has traced his messages for us in these paintings as one would on radar, hence the 'Blips' and 'Ifs' (intermediate frequencies) of the title.

In *Switchski's Syntax* of 1961, Davis repeated the *Champion* motif of 1950, but now with a strip of masking tape placed just above and through the word and running the width of the canvas. For this reason the painting is considered unfinished. But what if he meant to keep the tape? It could easily have been removed, and if it was meant to be temporary, why did he paint it? It is possible that he meant this as one more response to Mondrian, who had fascinated him for years, despite his ostensible down-play of the master in his article of that year, 'Memo on Mondrian'.[2] Mondrian used tape in his last paintings, incorporated for its own purposes. The same, I believe, applies to the tape on Davis's painting.

The photograph of Carcassonne was also the basis for Davis's last painting entitled *Fin* (1962–4) [256]. It is finally over – and he tells us so, with the word 'Fin' in the top left corner, which we know he added the night he died, alone in his studio.[3] He also tells us it hurts: *Owh!* Thus he reveals his final, deepest emotions in his jazzy, hip style, in the brilliant colour of Matisse and the Cubist format of Mondrian. It was as if Matisse were standing by his shoulder right until his death, a vital presence since at least 1917.

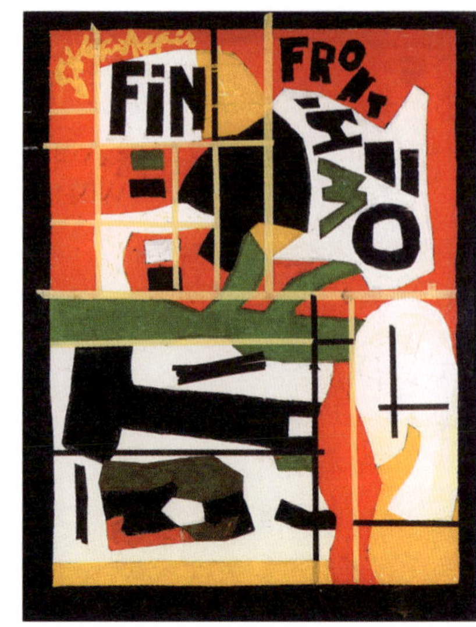
256

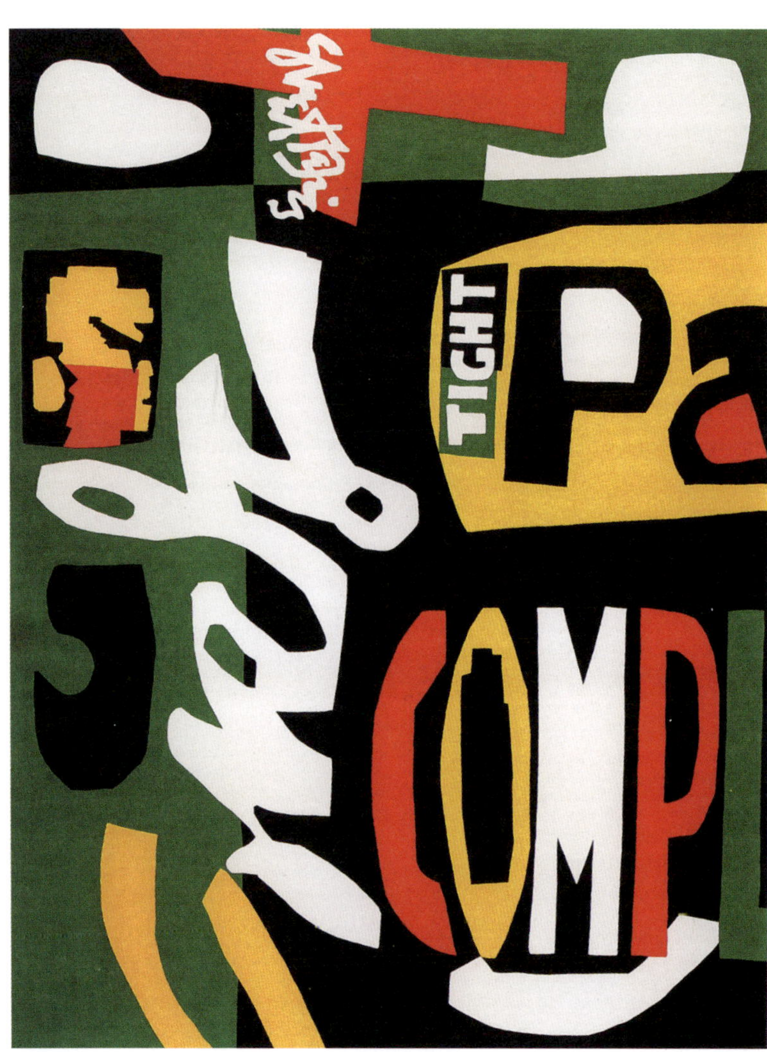
257

256 Stuart Davis, *Fin (Last Painting)*, 1962–4. Oil, casein, wax emulsion and masking tape on canvas, 136.8 × 100.9 cm (53⅞ × 39¾ in). Private collection

257 Stuart Davis, *Blips and Ifs*, 1963–4. Oil on canvas, 180.7 × 134.9 cm (71⅛ × 53⅛ in). Amon Carter Museum of American Art, Fort Worth

258 Helen Frankenthaler, *Flood*, 1967. Acrylic on canvas, 315.6 × 356.9 cm (124¼ × 140½ in). Whitney Museum of American Art, New York

259 Henri Matisse, *The Joy of Life*, 1905–6. Oil on canvas, 176.5 × 240.7 cm (69½ × 94¾ in). The Barnes Foundation, Philadelphia

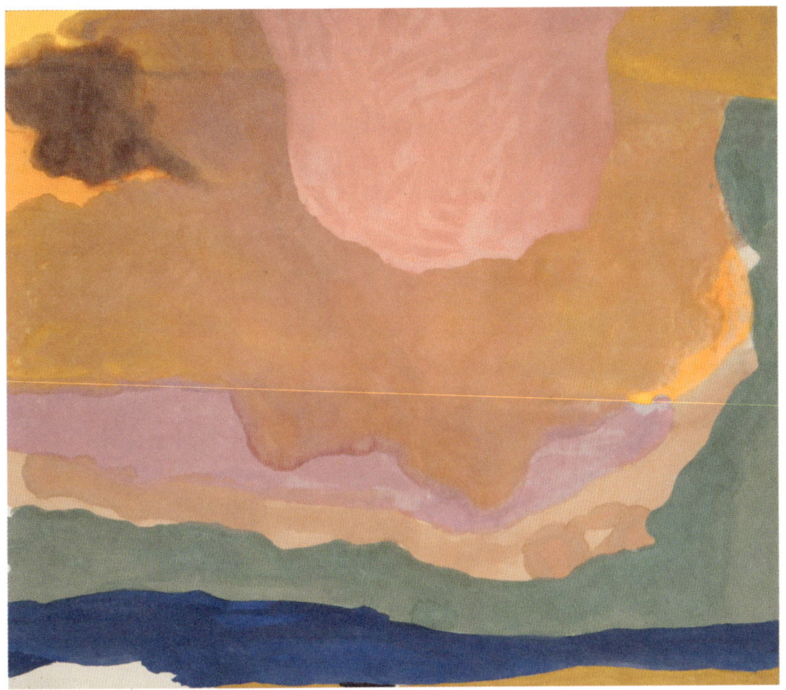

258

Helen Frankenthaler: A Flood of Colour

It is often the case that some of the best painters of a decade are also those of the preceding one. This was true of the 1960s, not only of Davis, but also of Frankenthaler. In that decade she developed her colour and its pouring into larger unbroken areas, and her formats became more focused, more centred, more clarified, often with fewer hues. At points they became quasi-geometric in their outlines, as in *Orange Breaking Through* (1961), in which a roughly formed rectangle identifies and defines the centre of the painting. In *Tangerine* (1964), irregular planes build the base of the painting, a kind of reference to Rothko, leading up to large amorphous shapes that billow and begin to pull away into a larger spatial domain.

Later in the 1960s, Frankenthaler's shapes became even larger and more individual, sometimes to the point of becoming too stiff or rigid. But in 1967, in a glorious painting called *Flood* [258], she fused the larger, layered shapes with a fluid intermixing of rich, deep blues, greens and oranges that completely fill the surface of a 9 × 9-foot canvas, a literal flood of colour that recalls Matisse's *Joy of Life* (1905–6) [259]. Both are keynote paintings of the twentieth century, and suggest a mythic Eden, here emblazoned through a paradise of colour. It is as if this flood – with its biblical reference – had come from above, the result of a cosmic intervention.

Minimalism and Colour:
Judd, Flavin and Chamberlain

Perhaps the most spectacular and consistent use of high and intense colour came from the last place one might have imagined: Minimalism. From the start this style was mischaracterized as plain, austere or reductive, and termed ABC art, or even deliberately boring. As with many movements, the name and descriptions were misleading, far off course from the reality of the art in question. From the start, high colour was an essential mark of Minimalism, exemplified by the work of two Minimalists in particular:

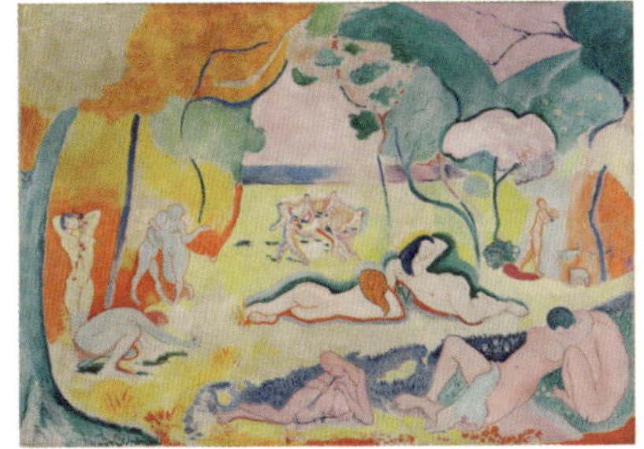

259

Donald Judd and Dan Flavin, as well as John Chamberlain – not really a Minimalist, but an artist whom Judd deeply admired and believed was pursuing similar aims.

The Minimalists continued in the tradition of David Smith by beginning as painters, then, like Smith, moving into relief, and thereafter into full three dimensions. Their art was a fusion of painting and sculpture, making works that Donald Judd (1928–1994) chose to call 'specific objects', to indicate that it combined aspects of both. These three artists were all members of the generation that admired and came on the heels of the Abstract Expressionists. They were not reacting or rebelling against the older artists, but rather sought an art of their own that would continue the qualities, especially the power, scale and size of Pollock, Rothko, Still and Newman. For Judd, Pollock was the benchmark, the artist by whom past achievement and future direction had to be measured. Frank Stella concurred, saying 'Pollock was our Picasso.'[4] Like Kaprow in his article of 1958 on Pollock, Judd saw the future of art as a mandate from Pollock to extend the implications of the physical reality of the painter's work, that is, to extend it into three dimensions. For Judd, as for Morris Louis, Pollock was the step from which all else was possible. But the results achieved by Kaprow and Judd were poles apart. Kaprow's response took the form of happenings; from Judd came a series of reliefs in the early 1960s, then the classic Minimalist box by 1965. From the start, however, Judd incorporated intense colour, primarily a cadmium red light in the reliefs and early objects. He was unequivocal in his beliefs: 'Material, space and colour are the main aspects of visual art.'[5] Thereafter Judd introduced as wide and as inventive a range of colour as had Davis. By 1971, his colour was so intense and original – and so surprising to many – that a leading critic termed him a 'closet hedonist.'[6]

Judd was one of the few artists and critics to recognize the importance of Pollock's colour, terming it the most 'particular' of any artist.[7] But this was part of a deep knowledge of colour that he had amassed over the course of his life and career. He read the colour theorists and had studied and knew well the specific colours in Matisse, Albers, Rothko and Newman. He spoke of the problem of adding colour to an existing surface, remarking that it meant using two separate materials and thus creating separate sets of formal problems to define and resolve. Therefore, early in his career, Judd developed a wide range of materials in which colour was embedded, becoming intrinsic to the material itself. He pioneered the use of Plexiglas, with orange, yellow, amber, green, brown and red tints, as well as the use of cold-rolled and hot-rolled steel, anodized aluminium, iron, nickel, copper and plywood, all with inherent colour and pattern so that material and colour were one and the same. When he applied colour, it was carefully and closely fused with the material, through industrial processes, that made them virtually a single entity. This was a three-dimensional equivalent of direct-stain painting, in which the paint was bound with the weave of the canvas, or at least appeared to be. All these materials and hues could also be profoundly affected by both natural and available light, sometimes causing colours to be misread as other hues. Judd's research into colour continued thoroughly: he gathered a thousand colour samples for his study and consideration. In a sense, he was extending the old sculptural dictum of 'truth to materials' that had been prevalent in the 1920s, espoused by artists such as Brancusi and, in the United States, William Zorach. Indeed, he saw colour as existing in everything, as having endless possibilities, many of which he carried on throughout his work, until his death in 1994.

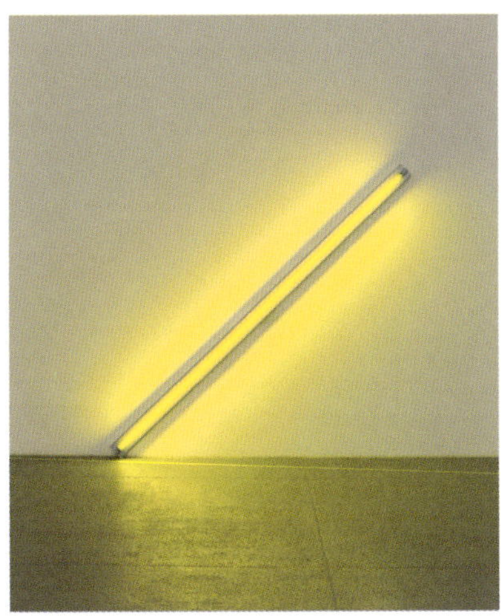

260

Dan Flavin (1933–1996) gradually worked his way into three dimensions at the same time as Judd was engaging real space. Flavin was inspired to use real, albeit artificial, light by Ralph Ellison's book *An Invisible Man* (1952), in which the author envisions himself in a powerfully illuminated environment of multiple light bulbs. Flavin adapted the fluorescent light, first with a single tube set on the wall at a 45-degree angle in his work entitled *The Diagonal of May 25, 1963 (to Constantin Brancusi)* (1963) [260] – an almost singular nod to the erotic in Minimalist art and a piece that Flavin referred to as the *Diagonal of Personal Ecstasy*. The sculpture was dedicated to Brancusi, who had died four years earlier, and was receiving renewed attention from a younger generation for his streamlined art devoid of unnecessary or extraneous parts. In the same year, Flavin constructed the piece entitled *The Nominal Three (To William of Ockham)* from six vertical elements of white fluorescent light that demonstrated the possibilities of simple repetition with built-in order.

Then, in increasingly complex compositions of multiple tubes of single or several hues, Flavin's work became more and more spatial and even architectural. The colour was part of the light and the material, so all three elements – colour, form and space – are one and the same, another parallel to contemporary stain and colour-field painting. Like Judd, as Flavin gained confidence in his work and its possibilities, he could extend his art into ever-closer dialogues with space. In *Untitled* (1969) [261], he extended Smith's use of colour to suggest alternate areas and materiality by using coloured tubes that both face and turn away from the viewer, in a simple square format that also suggested the geometry of Smith's

260 Dan Flavin, *The Diagonal of May 25, 1963 (to Constantin Brancusi)*, 1963. Yellow fluorescent light, length: 243.8 cm (96 in). Dia Art Foundation, New York

261 Dan Flavin, *Untitled*, 1969. Fluorescent lights and metal fixtures, 63.5 × 63.5 × 14.6 cm (25 × 25 × 5¾ in). The Museum of Modern Art, New York

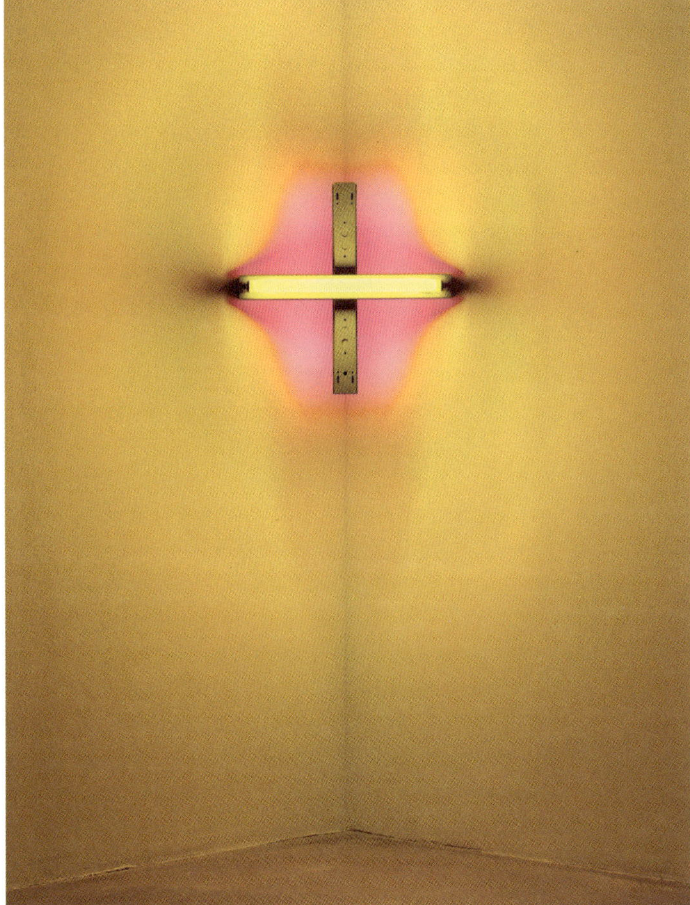

261

Cubi XXVII (1965). *Untitled* illuminated and defined its surroundings in a new way, giving a distinct corporeality to the atmosphere behind, in and in front of the piece and its corner area. Thereafter, Flavin filled entire rooms with progressions of light compositions, the 'barriers' that dramatically altered the nature of the large rooms and made the very air a kind of palpable, coloured light or even atmospheric mist. Judd, too, became more and more interested in identifying a single piece with the space and architecture. Indeed, later one could fairly say that his art *was* architecture.

John Chamberlain and Donald Judd: An Intriguing Relationship

At first glance, no two artists would seem to be more distinct than Judd and John Chamberlain (1927–2011). But they were close in many ways, both personally and in their work, with correspondence and connections that formed a most intriguing relationship. Chamberlain has slipped between the cracks in terms of broad recognition, in great part because we have a hard time getting past his use of junk steel sourced from cars, and our inability to see it as anything more than a comment on the culture of the automobile. In this sense, Chamberlain might be viewed as distantly related to the art of assemblage, to Rauschenberg and his Combines, but his art is very different.

The connections between Judd and Chamberlain begin in the fact that both owed as much to painting as to sculpture, and both worked in the cross-referential mode of 'specific objects'. Chamberlain's reputation suffered at the start because some labelled his work as a literal and too easy translation of de Kooning, without true originality or import.[8] There is some merit in making a connection with de Kooning's broad strokes that fit together on a surface, but there is much more to Chamberlain than this. Judd understood, for example, that the persistent reference to the car enabled his art to transform itself into 'successive states of the same form and material'.[9] He also understood that Chamberlain's work was often referential – pieces could point to Rodin's *Monument to Balzac* (1898) and to a football player dancing after scoring a touchdown. In the fitting process of the auto pieces, Chamberlain produced something akin to poetry: the fitting together of words. 'The assembly was a fit, and the fit is sexual', he said, referring to the squeezing, coupling, compression and massing of the assembled elements.[10] In his later work, as in the 'Kiss' series (1979), he makes reference to both Brancusi and Rodin.[11] Chamberlain's art, it turns out, is highly complex, more so than his use of junk steel might indicate. Judd understood that better than anyone.

What exactly was it that Judd saw in Chamberlain's work? At first, this seems perplexing – one seeking smooth surfaces, the other dealing with beaten-up car parts – but it was an intense commitment that Judd made to Chamberlain, culminating in the magnificent installations at the Chinati Foundation in Marfa [262], where they have their own large, generous space. That in itself is a testament to how deeply Judd felt about Chamberlain's achievement. But it started earlier than that. Chamberlain and Judd were both provincials, from the Midwest, who came to the big city, New York, to make something of themselves, to experience the world in all its intensity, one of the essential leitmotifs of modern American art. They were also close in age; Judd was born in 1927 and Chamberlain in 1928. We know by now that the high achievement of Chamberlain fully measures up to Judd, Flavin, Stella and others of his generation. Judd knew this

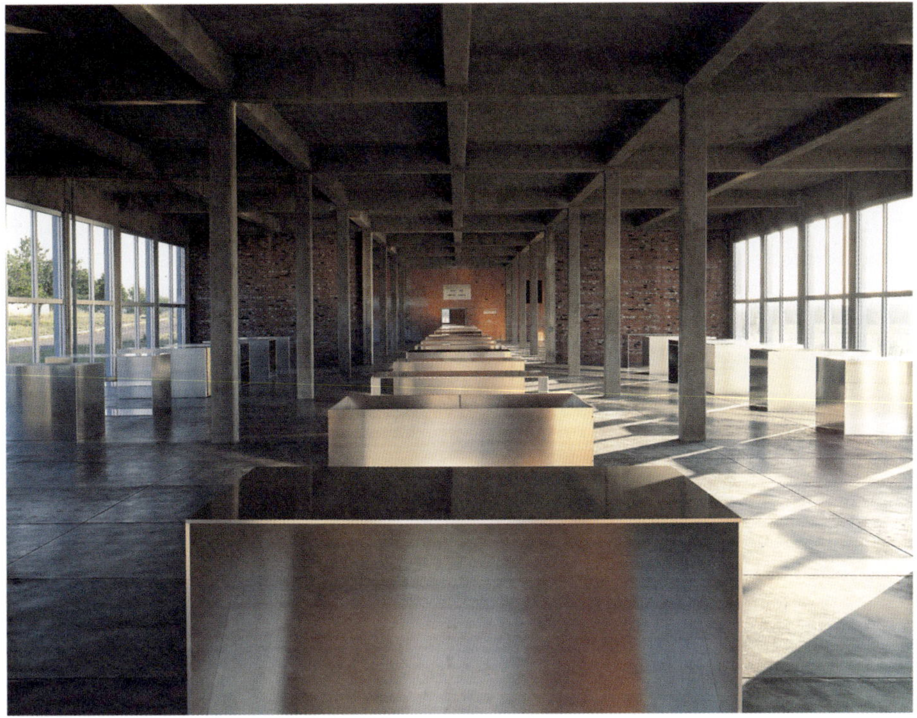

262

then, and I believe he saw Chamberlain as a challenge to be met. Chamberlain recognized the affinity, too; he once told me: 'Part of it was that we were so different, but we both knew that we were on to something of the same thing.'[12] This 'something of the same thing' is well worth exploring, both for their art and in order to explore some larger aspects of art in the late 1950s and 1960s.

Judd's curiosity and interest in Chamberlain dates, at least, to 1960. In 1989, on the occasion of an exhibition of Chamberlain's new work, PaceWildenstein published a catalogue that included all of Judd's writings on Chamberlain. Those writings started in 1962 – but in fact, missed a brief statement of 1960, where the essence of Judd's interest is clear: 'Three aspects are readily apparent in Chamberlain's sculpture: it is redundant; each contains a distinct structure; and it is coloured.'[13] What a typical, get-to-the-point Judd statement! He continues: 'The folded sheet metal from automobile bodies is voluminous, apparently somewhat unmanageable, and constitutes an essential form that is less than its bulk requires.'[14] He closes the two-paragraph review as follows: 'The unique aspect is the colour. The paint is folded into the convolutions of the metal and is unquestionably integral to the work. Coloured sculpture has been discussed and hesitantly attempted for some time, but not with such implications. The colour here is insufficient but the possibilities are exciting, and Chamberlain has a long time and the start to find them.'[15]

This text contains at least three of the crucial aspects to which Judd related – and we must remember, of course, that when he was writing and describing the work of others to whom he felt related, he was really describing his own process of aesthetic maturation. Judd wrote more about Chamberlain, and in greater depth, than about virtually any other artist – even Pollock, for Judd the most important of all. In 1988, in a brief preface to the PaceWildenstein Chamberlain catalogue of 1989, he wrote: 'This, the reviews of Chamberlain's work, the remarks on or by Jackson Pollock on his paintings[which Judd had included], and a few new remarks of mine fit together.'[16] This is fascinating, for there is a three-cornered

262 Donald Judd, *Untitled*
(1982–6), 100 works in milled
aluminium, 104 × 129 × 182 cm
(3ft 5in × 4ft 3in × 6ft) each.
In situ, North Artillery
Shed, Chinati Foundation,
Marfa, Texas

dialogue under way between Judd, Chamberlain and Pollock. We need to remember that in Judd's thinking and in the development of his art, Pollock was always his number one source and influence. For a generation coming of age in the late 1950s, Pollock was, for many artists, the source from where future art might go. For the physicality, the reality, the power of it was such that for Judd, as we have seen, it meant a move into three dimensions if that development was to flourish. Three years later, in December 1963, Judd wrote:

> *Jackson Pollock's paintings are the most recent instance of opposed extremes. The polarity of his work, greater than that of Chamberlain's, is based on corresponding extremes of form. A point of sensation, the immediacy of the dripped paint, is opposed to a volume of structural and imagistic form. Chamberlain's material does not have to be distinctively transformed to appear diversely. The diversity and the unity occur and re-occur; the work explodes and implodes. The proximity of the means is new. In part it is simply unique and in part it is an advance. Chamberlain's work, for example, is more consistent than Pollock's, not because Pollock's great polarity is less consistent, but because the elements which form it are so, especially the shallow space and the descriptive images.* [17]

Judd, it turns out, held Chamberlain in the same high esteem as Pollock; he also talks about the 'redundancy' of Chamberlain's sculpture:

> *There's more metal and space than the structure requires. The voluminousness is a salient aspect of the work. This idea is Chamberlain's alone. The sculpture seems open, which, in the usual sense, it is not, since it is massed. There is not space through the work; there is a lot in it. [...] The metal surrounds space like the eggshell of a sucked egg, instead of defining it with a line, core or plane.* [18]

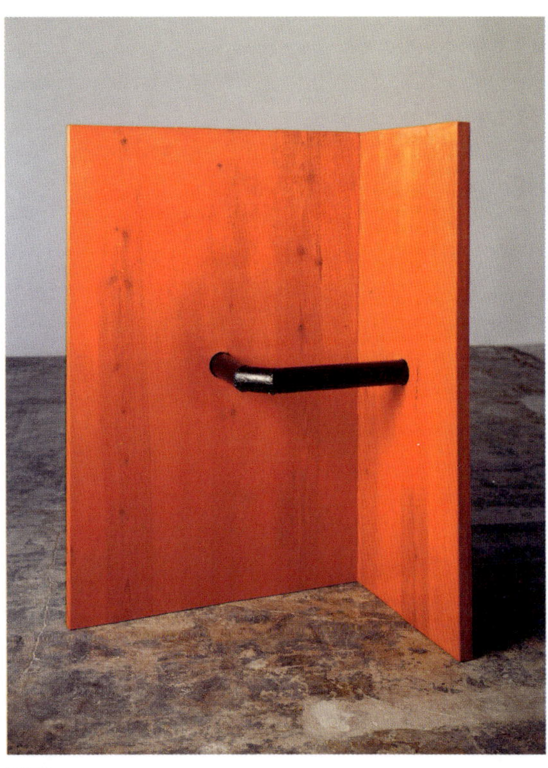

263

263 Donald Judd, *Untitled*, 1962.
Light cadmium red oil on
wood with black enamelled
metal pipe, 122 × 84 × 54.6 cm
(48 × 33⅛ × 21¾ in).
Judd Foundation, Marfa

264 John Chamberlain, *Essex*,
1960. Automobile parts
and other metal,
274.3 × 203.2 × 109.2 cm
(108 × 80 × 43 in).
The Museum of Modern
Art, New York

Modern Art in America

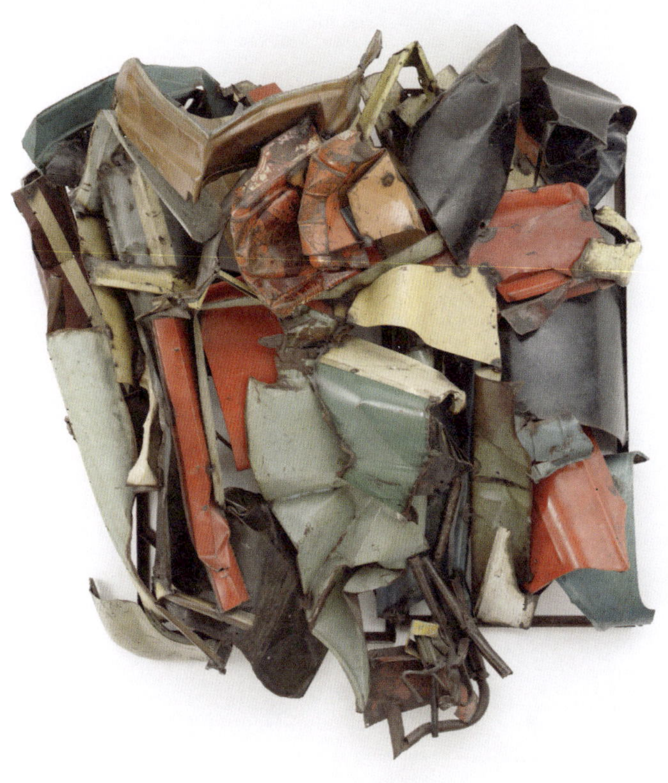

264

These are some of the most salient aspects of Chamberlain's work that Judd perceived, and they helped him to define what direction he himself might take.

The example of Chamberlain's intense colour appeared in Judd's work by 1962. When we talk about colour, we need to remember that we should discuss not just hue, but also the methods of application – the qualities of surface, weight, density, translucence, scale and amount of colour, as well as the nature of the material itself. Consider Judd's first free-standing piece, *Untitled* (1962) [263], made of heavy old wooden doors connected by a stovepipe, which relates to the discarded automobile steel that Chamberlain was using. It seems to have prompted something in Judd, the idea to use material that is non-art – industrial, discarded. In some of Judd's other early works, he used asphalt, pipes, baking tins inserted into wall reliefs, and the kind of discarded junk that he saw in Chamberlain's work. Chamberlain's example helped Judd begin to move from the old illusionism of flat painting into three dimensions. Judd talked about distilling ideas from Pollock and Rothko into three dimensions, but the immediate impetus was in fact Chamberlain, to a greater extent than has perhaps been realized. Judd said a few years later that Chamberlain's reliefs offered the possibility to get rid of the old ideas of the flat surface, to begin to make something three-dimensional to exist in the viewer's space.

Of special note are Chamberlain's lacquer-coated relief paintings [264], lesser known but nonetheless key. Here we see the use of glazes and glistening, reflective flecks in the paint, the build-up of surface that impressed

265

Judd, who takes the idea of car paints and high-gloss colours and built-up surfaces as something integral to the piece itself. His use of Harley-Davidson hi-fi purple in his *Untitled* of 1965 [265] is one of his most effective applications of colour, and clearly comes from the inspiration provided by Chamberlain. In these intense, rich colours of the mid-1960s, we see just how wrong all those early labels about so-called Minimalism were. The colour in Judd and Chamberlain was deep, sensuous, rich and hedonistic, and even sexual, becoming an extraordinary structural and expressive aspect of their art. Car colours from Detroit continued in Judd's use of a '56 Chevrolet 'Baked Regal Turquoise' that derives from Chamberlain, extended by Judd in a continuing study of specific hues throughout his life.

The ways in which Chamberlain's and Judd's work interacts seem infinite, reminding us of the close collaborations between Monet and Renoir in the 1860s, and of Picasso and Braque from 1908 to 1914. It was rich and rewarding for both.

Pop Art's Single Objects

If we think Judd's admiration for Chamberlain is odd, then we should also consider his admiration for Claes Oldenburg. Judd was especially taken by the fact that there were no extraneous parts in Oldenburg's sculptures, that the image was the form, united into a single entity, a goal at which he had aimed himself. They were both intrinsic to the 1960s drive to distil a piece into a single harmonious whole, whether a pristine Judd box or an Oldenburg hamburger or cake [266]. Oldenburg was deeply indebted to Pollock in his early pieces, both in the way they were painted and for their physicality. Abstract art and Pop had similarities beyond Pollock and Oldenburg: compare, for example, a Noland circle with a Lichtenstein object painting such as a ball of yarn or a hot dog. Both images are single, unique, absolutely centred, standing alone in an otherwise empty field; clear, iconic and self-sufficient in their own right, a total shift from the densely filled and worked canvases of painterly abstraction. In fact, Lichtenstein considered these single objects to be part of a 'new classicism',[19] yielding a steady and focused structure after the baroque convolutions of Abstract Expressionism. We might look to the past, to early American Precisionism of c.1916–18, as in the art of Schamberg, in which the single machine is depicted in a similar manner, by itself, tightly drawn, an object isolated and self-sufficient.

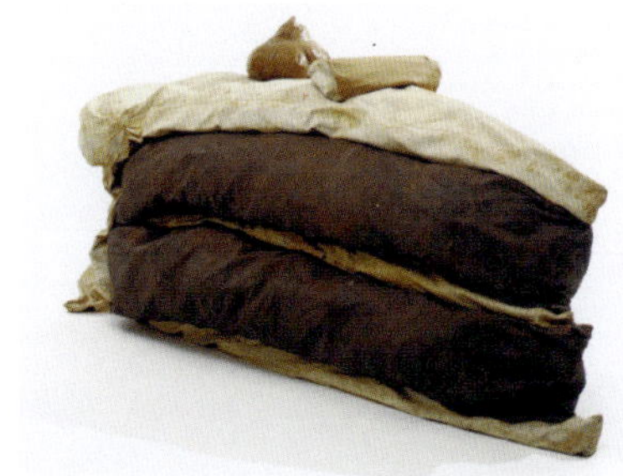

266

Eva Hesse's Eccentric Abstractions

Oldenburg's soft sculptures, so different from the glistening metal and Plexiglas work of Judd, were one of the sources for a now canonical artist of the 1960s, Eva Hesse, born in 1935 and thus a generation younger than Oldenburg, Judd or Noland. Although she attracted attention early on, she was not really a landmark artist in the minds of many until years later, after her early death in 1970 at the age of thirty-four. She had seemed too young to be accorded major status, but as we get to know the totality of her work, it assumes a breathtaking scope that belies the brevity of her career. For many, Hesse's eccentric abstractions, with their wide formal and emotional range and extraordinary nuances and implications, revealed themselves only slowly, over the course of time. They did not have the sheer, immediate power of a Judd or an Oldenburg; they took time, careful looking and steady investigation to be really seen and understood.

While Hesse's work is soft and organic, it also employs the simple, clear-cut shapes used by Judd and others. We see this as early as 1965 in her *Ringaround Arosie* [267], with its circular concentric windings simulating a Noland or Johns target. But it is something very different; it is still a relief, an object in the process of evolving from painting and drawing into three dimensions, the same process through which Judd and the other Minimalists, as well as David Smith, had gone. It is also a highly personal image, clearly referring to the female and male body that indicates a far different approach from Noland or Judd, one closer to Oldenburg, who also referred to the body, both male and female, in works like the *Swedish Light Switch* (1967), *Giant 3-Way Plugs* (1970) and others. For Hesse, the references are usually more subtle. We may also usefully compare her works with the soft, floppy latex-and-rubber pieces done by Bruce Nauman in San Francisco in 1966, that could be held in your arms and cradled like an alien from outer space. They were remarkable sculptures, but were soon abandoned for pieces of conceptual and performance art after 1970.

Oldenburg was not the only realist whom Hesse admired. For her, Andy Warhol was 'the most artist that you could be. His art and statement

265 Donald Judd, *Untitled*, 1965. Aluminium, 21 × 642.6 × 21 cm (8¼ × 253 × 8¼ in). Whitney Museum of American Art, New York

266 Claes Oldenburg, *Floor Cake*, 1962. Synthetic polymer paint and latex on canvas filled with foam rubber and cardboard boxes, 148.2 × 290.2 × 148.2 cm (58⅜ × 114¼ × 58⅜ in). The Museum of Modern Art, New York

267 Eva Hesse, *Ringaround Arosie*, 1965. Pencil, acetone, varnish, enamel paint, ink and cloth-covered electrical wire on papier-mâché and Masonite, 67 × 41.9 × 11.4 cm (26⅜ × 16½ × 4½ in). The Museum of Modern Art, New York

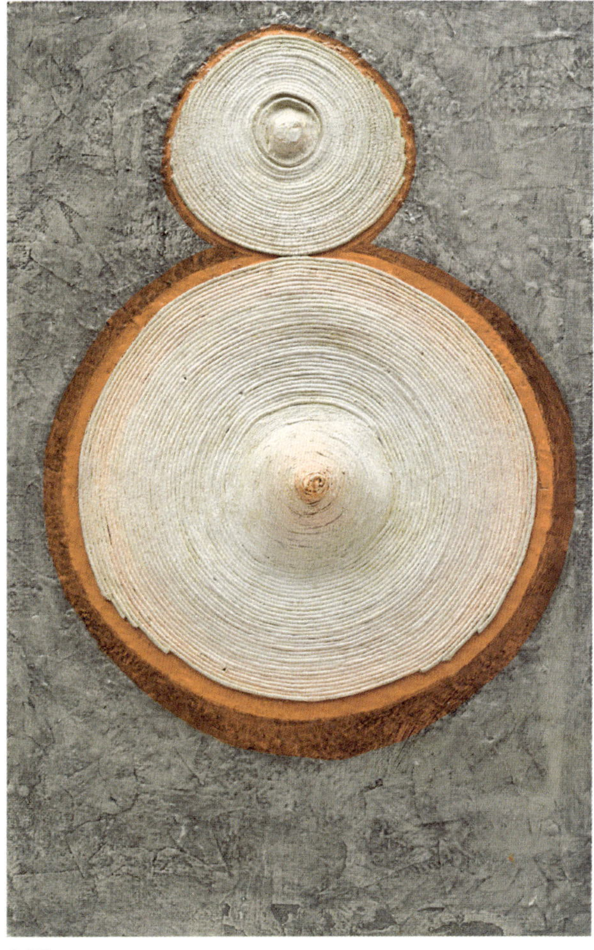
267

and his person are so equivalent. It is what I want to be, the most Eva can be as an artist and as a person.'[20] This, it seems to me, is at the core of what any really good artist is and what they strive for. She sought and found a unity between person and artist, with a fusion of heart, mind and soul, all acting in concert. She had also deeply respected Pollock, as had Oldenburg, making them two more 1960s artists who followed Kaprow's dictum that from Pollock artists could move into three dimensions.

In her *Hang Up* (1966) [268], Hesse refers to the long, painful journey of her life, including the brain tumour that finally killed her in 1970, as well as her tragic past. The piece is a single frame, emulating a picture frame, but with nothing in it. The simple shape points to her studies with Josef Albers while a student at Yale, as do the texture and the gradated shades of grey that colour the compulsive wrapping of tape around the frame, recalling Albers's colour course. The colour is embedded in the materials as it is in the work of Flavin and Judd. For seemingly no reason at all, a long wire is attached at top and bottom and loops out into our space. Why? Maybe it points to a Pollock line; but, more likely, it is simply there because it is so absurd, just as life is, with no rhyme or reason. Hesse said that it had a 'kind of depth to it – a depth and soul and absurdity and life and meaning or feeling or intellect that I want to get'.[21] The work overall is surely a masterpiece of our time, as is her series 'Accession' (1966–9) [269]; the latter relates to Judd's primary box shape, but is sticky and strange to the touch, live and moving under the hand. It is one more example in America of an artist responding to a development of a clear and strong structure but adding to and changing it with a personal, often eccentric modification. We have seen this before, as when numerous painters in the 1940s strove to adapt Mondrian's exacting structure into a personal vocabulary.

In 2011, the American art historian Thomas Crow gave a moving lecture on Hesse and Rothko,[22] drawing an unexpected connection between two artists of different generations, relating intimately to the theme of art and life, or in this case, art and death. In 1968, Rothko suffered a heart attack and collapsed on the streets of New York; he survived, but his doctor gave him no more than three years to live. At the same time, Hesse was diagnosed with a brain tumour that despite two operations doomed her to an early death. Both artists – one sixty-five, the other thirty-two – were facing death, which arrived for both in 1970. Despite their differences in age and styles of art, they had some things in common. Both were Jews, had immigrated from Europe at an early age and both had suffered through a painful life. In his last years, Rothko became morose and depressed, and his art grew darker, marked by heavy strokes. Hesse, in her last years, undertook a piece called *Contingent* (1969) [270], consisting of eight separate sheets of fibreglass and latex, measuring between 9½ and 11 feet in height and 3–4 feet wide, each semi-transparent, rough and gritty. The colours in the materials were ingrained, inherent. The result looked like a series of hanging Rothko paintings. In the face of death, two very different artists, each unknown to the other, had embarked on similar courses of self-discovery, of the ultimate reality of life.

With their deaths, and that of Newman in the same year, America lost three great artists, two older, one just coming to the height of her powers. We can only wonder what might have been had they lived. But this much we know: America was deprived of three exceptional talents that, as it turned out, it could ill afford to lose. With the additional early deaths of Pollock, Gorky and Kline, American art had no older generation to look to, to take courage and guidance from. The absence soon showed in the early 1970s, as more and more postmodernist artists took the easy way out.

268 Eva Hesse, *Hang Up*, 1966. Acrylic on cloth over wood, and acrylic on cord over steel tube, 182.9 × 213.4 × 198.1 cm (72 × 84 × 78 in). Art Institute of Chicago

269 Eva Hesse, *Accession II*, 1968 (1969). Galvanized steel, plastic, 78.1 × 78.1 × 78.1 cm (30¾ × 30¾ × 30¾ in). Detroit Institute of Arts

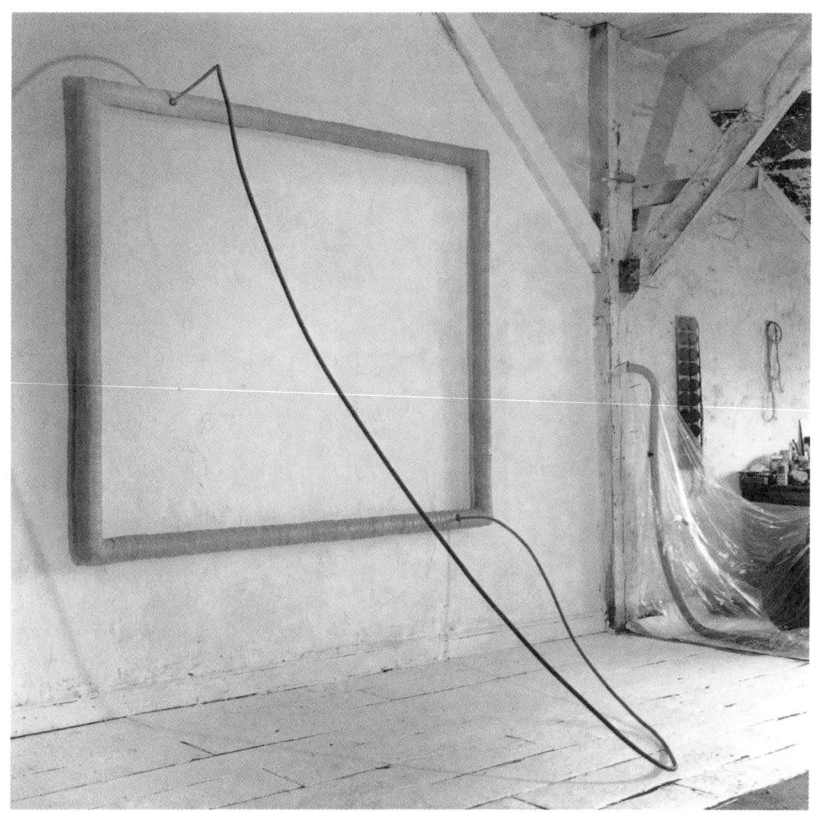

268

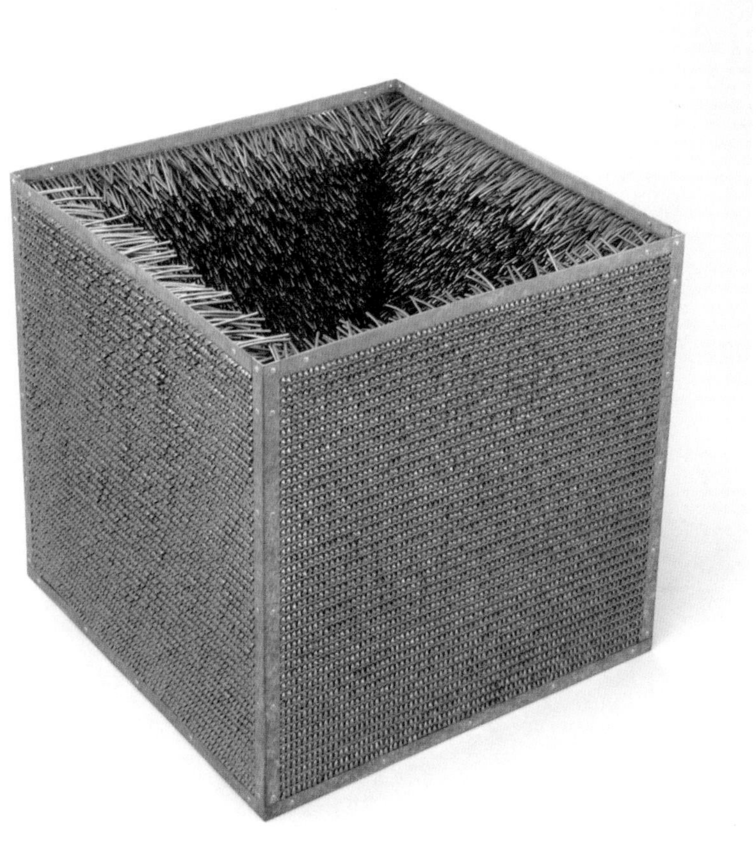

269

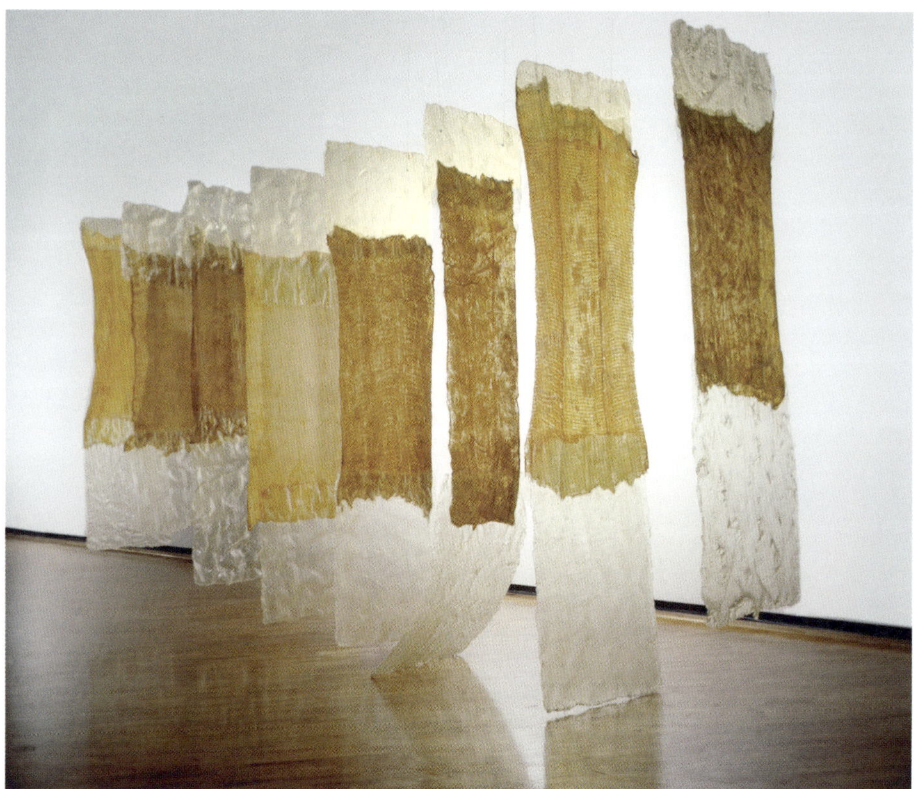

270

Art from Life in the 1960s

Hesse, like Oldenburg and all those considered Pop, was part of the generation that insisted that art comes directly from life, and that depicted their experience of life in immediate and unequivocal terms. This perspective had a long tradition that in this century dates back to the Ashcan school and the urban scenes of Robert Henri, John Sloan and early Stuart Davis. It follows in the wake of the rhetoric of the Abstract Expressionists, who saw art as embarking on a cosmic voyage, going to strange new worlds, or of Newman's fancy that he was the first artist. In the face of this, Warhol painted tomato soup cans because, as he said, that's what he had for lunch every day; not another world, but the one we see and live in every day. Hesse made it even more personal with references – which may only appear over time, but are there, real and true – to her life, to her very soul. Oldenburg best and famously summed up the attitude:

> *I am for an art that is political-erotical-mystical, that does something other than sit on its ass in a museum …*
> *I am for an art that imitates the human, that is comic, if necessary, or violent, or whatever is necessary.*
> *I am for an art that takes its form from the lines of life itself, that twists and extends and accumulates and spits and drips, and is heavy and coarse and blunt and stupid as life itself.* [23]

But abstract art, such as the works of Judd and Stella, has 'meaning' too; it is not empty formalism, as those who see art as theory-based like to say. Judd's art demands the need for specific and clear thinking and working. He insisted on the real and concrete: 'Things that exist, exist.' He was talking about real life, not an abstract construct. He understood the dangers of general, broad statements and ideas; exactitude is required; the nature

270　Eve Hesse, *Contingent*, 1969. Cheesecloth, latex and fibreglass, 350 × 630 × 109 cm (137.8 × 248 × 42.9 in). National Gallery of Australia, Canberra

271　Edward Hopper, *New York Office*, 1962. Oil on canvas, 102.9 × 140 cm (40½ × 55⅛ in). Montgomery Museum of Fine Arts

of materials and ideas must be tested and investigated over and over again in the greatest detail. Any given Judd piece is the story of long and painstaking work and investigation. Making it was not a matter of ordering something on the phone; there were innumerable discussions with the fabricator as to the limits and tolerances of certain materials over given areas. Even before this process, Judd would do countless drawings to get the precise outlines, measurements and scale he wanted. His explorations and experimentations with colour are famous – thousands of colour samples were gathered to test possibilities. He loved colour and its effects, and he loved how pieces could become literally part of the land and light in their setting in the west Texas landscape at the Chinati Foundation.

LIGHT AND SPACE

Hopper and Allan D'Arcangelo

Hopper remained a vital, innovative artist, one who contributed to and took from other sources until his death in 1967. He continued to paint until late in life; in 1962 in *New York Office* [271], a highly distilled painting whose structure points to the soon-to-appear boxes of Minimalism, a solitary blonde woman stands alone, framed by the window, depicted as if she were on a movie screen or in a magazine spread. Hopper pays homage to the late Marilyn Monroe, an American icon who had just committed suicide, in a meditation on fame and its solitude. The architecture is bare, a kind of coffin for her, its starkness overbearing and desolate. This appears in other late paintings too, as a kind of solemn lament for the designs and idiosyncratic structures and roofs of older, turn-of-the-century architecture. The sharp clarity suggests that Hopper was well aware of Minimalist directions and before that of the structural probity of Mondrian's art.

In the 1960s, Hopper was discovered by many of the Pop artists, most famously George Segal and his isolated plaster figures. Less noticed, however, was the art of Allan D'Arcangelo (1930–1998) and its nod to

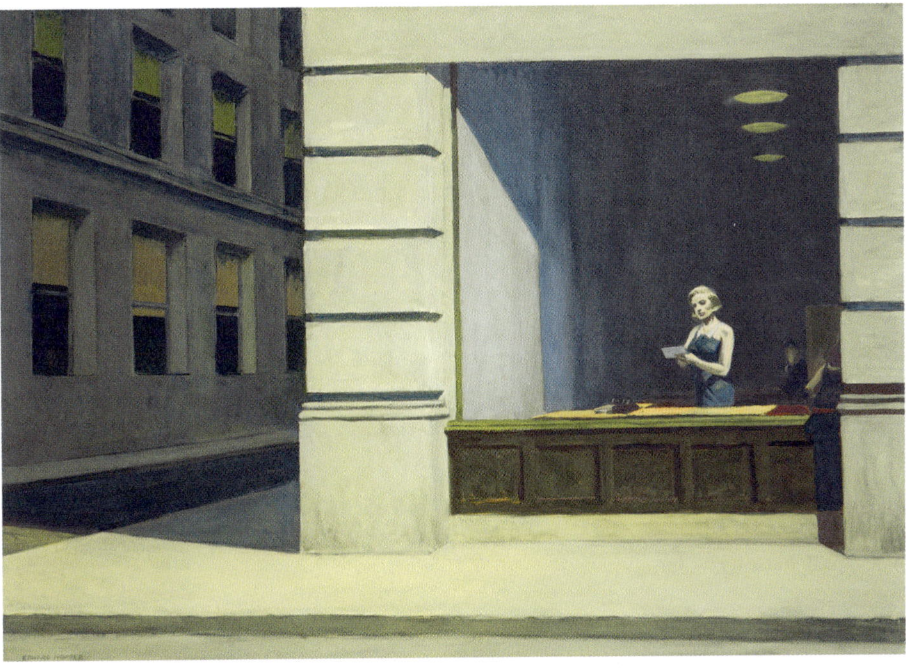

271

Hopper. D'Arcangelo, too, loved the open American road, as depicted by Hopper in *Gas* (page 190) and many other pictures, as can be seen in his *Pegasus* (1963)[272], a contemporary update of the Hopper: a pitch dark road bisected by three verticals indicating the white line into the distance. Overhead, Hopper's Pegasus flies, dominating the picture to comment on the dominance of car culture. Hopper loved driving, travelling over the country and to Mexico, and often sketching from his car. No wonder, then, that so many of his paintings show or imply a car moving away from us, down the road, into an unknown future. Indeed, one of his very last, if not the last, of his paintings, *Road and Trees* (1962), depicts nothing but a road, set against the woods, moving from one edge to the other, moving through the surface and time and our vision. Otherwise it is completely blank.

Californian Light: Turrell, Irwin and Bell

Hopper's light looks down the road even further to James Turrell (b.1943)[273] and Robert Irwin (b.1928) and the other artists who founded the Light and Space movement in Los Angeles in 1967, the very year of Hopper's death. Light as perceived volume marked the work of these two artists from then on, whether in Irwin's apparently rotating discs of light and his later environmental installations defined by sheer scrim and diffused light, or in Turrell's mammoth, enveloping light environments that have been installed in museums the world over. These beguiling demonstrations of the power of light seem to be acknowledging and paying homage to the rooms of luminosity with which Hopper filled his apparently modest canvases, works that spoke of whole worlds of thought and perception. In turn, the rise of Land and Earth art at the same time pointed to whole universes of light, primarily in the wide expanses of the west, but later in urban environments as well.

The fusion of light, colour and material as a single phenomenon developed in California throughout the 1960s. By 1968, objects had all but vanished in favour of pure rooms that constituted a pure environment of light, the source of which was generally hidden and unnoticed. Larry Bell (b.1939) began as a painter, then moved to reliefs, and by 1968 had developed a series of glass boxes in which the colour was embedded, giving off even more light than Judd's boxes did. Bell developed a process of vacuum-coating the glass so that the colour was literally intermixed with the material. This process was later used by the architect Frank Gehry to coat the windows in his IAC Building of 2007 on West 18th Street, creating a beautiful architectural surface that reflected the light from the Hudson River. Irwin used intense floodlights set on the floor and directed on to white discs protruding from the wall to virtually dissolve the discs' materiality into an aura of light. Similar auras were evident in the plastics of Craig Kaufmann, in the glistening high-intensity colour of John McCracken's high-gloss single-element sculptures, and in the soft, even light of Diebenkorn's abstractions of the 1950s and in his post-1968 work, the 'Ocean Park' series [274]. The light of California is special and different – as recorded in Californian Impressionism, which thrived well into the 1940s – so it is no surprise that this school of light had developed by 1968.

The profusion of coloured light in the 1960s, whether in the work of Flavin or Irwin, was new to modern art in one sense, but in another it was the fulfilment of an old prophesy that could be traced to the first American movement dedicated to colour, Synchromism. The brash and unfounded claims made by the young Americans at the time of its appearance were

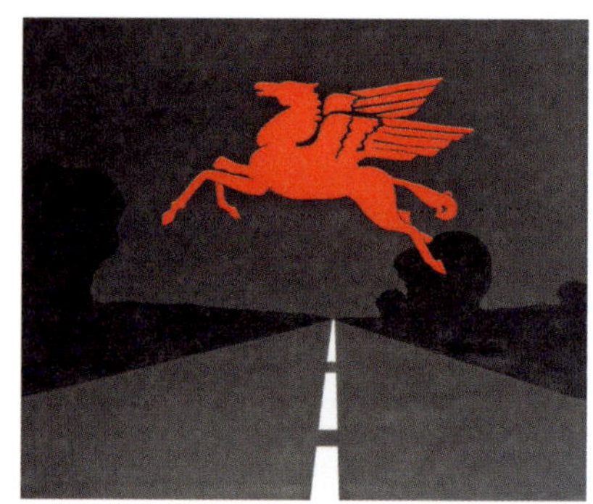

272

272 Allan D'Arcangelo, *Pegasus*, 1963. Acrylic on canvas, 111.7 × 130.2 cm (44 × 51¼ in). Private collection

273 James Turrell, *Afrum (White)*, 1966. Projected light, dimensions variable. Los Angeles County Museum of Art

Modern Art in America

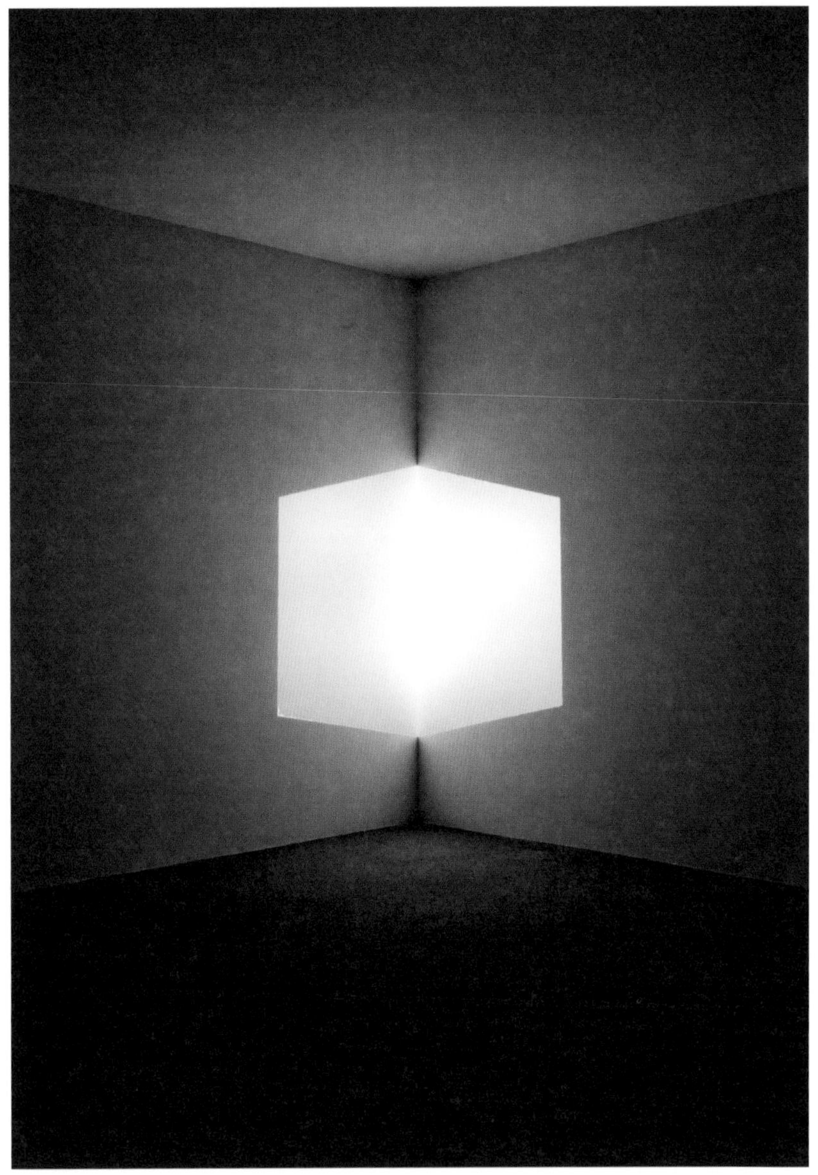

273

exacerbated by the writings of Willard Huntington Wright, Stanton's brother. Willard was a brilliant, early critic and historian of modern art, and his book *Modern Painting, Its Tendency and Meaning*, published in 1915,[24] holds an important place in the literature on the field. Important, that is, except for its wild-eyed claims for Synchromism and its place in the history of art. These claims were repeated and expanded in his book *The Future of Painting*, which appeared in 1923. Here, he dwelled on colour again, but now he predicted that in the future painting would belong exclusively to colour, and most especially to coloured light. Of course, the book did not attract much attention, certainly little serious attention. But fast-forward to the late 1960s and imagine yourself in the midst of the world of intensely coloured light of an installation by Flavin or Irwin, and it is as if Wright's book – his vision – had literally come true. In a way, it had been fulfilled by his brother Stanton, who by 1920 had pioneered a light and colour machine, propelled by music, that gave forth illuminated images. Stanton had worked on the light machine for years, but it was only in the 1960s, living in California, that he had the technology and means to create a fully realized colour organ. Morgan Russell had

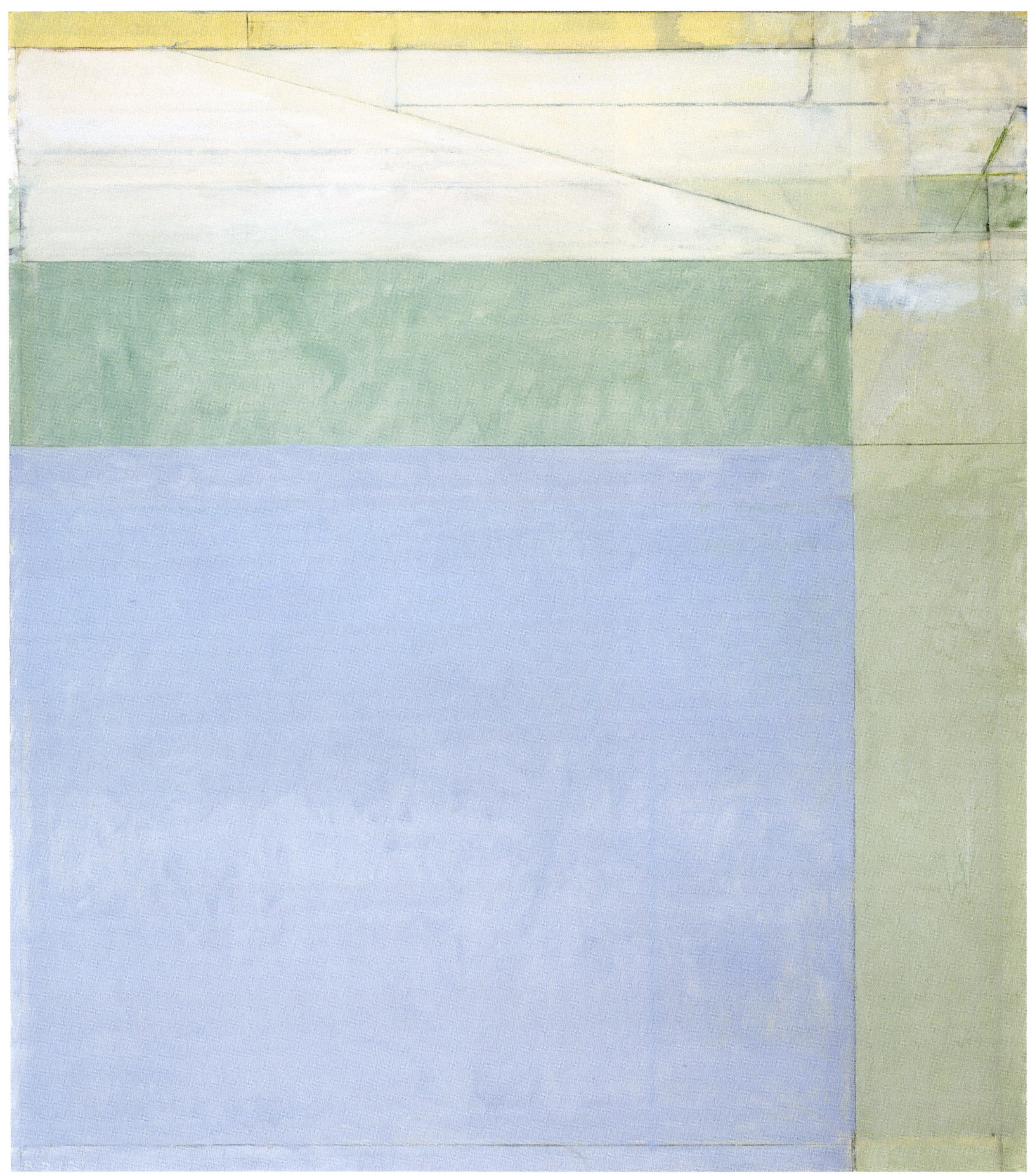

274

also long been interested in a colour-light machine, but had not found the means to complete it.

However, in the early 1920s, Russell did create a small version of what he had in mind: a series of tempera paintings, part of a group of abstract works he called *Eidos*, that were mounted on glass covering the front of a light box and that were illuminated from behind. Thus we can add one more continuity to the many that have informed earlier and later modern art in America.

Andy Warhol: Death and Disaster

At the same time as Hopper was painting Marilyn Monroe, in 1962, another famous artist, of an entirely different order, was also depicting the actress. Andy Warhol made an image of her face on a gold ground, and his subsequent series of multiple Marilyn images show that he understood the course of fame. His Marilyn paintings should be seen as part of his early series of Death and Disaster images based on suicides, plane crashes, car crashes and murders. In these works, Warhol both summed up and forecast the course of the decade.

When I first encountered Warhol's work in the early 1960s, I thought it strong, to be sure, but he seemed so odd that it was hard to take him seriously. More of a partygoer than a serious artist, he was the centre of a social order that (like Vladimir and Estragon in Samuel Beckett's *Waiting for Godot*) was always waiting for Andy. I remember a show of his at Leo Castelli Gallery, featuring the cow wallpaper, which I thought was silly, as were the helium balloons floating around. But no one was in the show itself: twenty people were jammed into the back room, milling about, asking plaintively, 'You seen Andy? No – you seen Leo? Yes I saw Leo an hour ago. OK, where's Andy?', like a desperate Greek chorus. Art had gone social. But as these memories recede and the art becomes better known and can be seen in some perspective, I now understand him to have been a genius who understood and portrayed his time as no one else did, either then or now.

Indeed, Warhol was the complete American artist, a real American from a working-class, immigrant family living in Pittsburgh, with its gritty steelworks. His work and persona, which were identical, touched on virtually every aspect of the country's voyage through modernism, and on virtually all the themes discussed in this book. He identified with the common objects used by everyone: Coca-Cola, Brillo, Campbell's soup, all things from the supermarket, and it was farewell to Rothko's trip into the unknown. This art represents the ultimate joining of art and life, one of the primary themes discussed here. He is the quintessential American realist, who depicted life in America, such as death by car crash or suicide, the culture of glamour (Marilyn and Liz), the electric chair and the sad reality of America as Murder, Inc., in the images of the grieving Jackie Kennedy. Ironically, Warhol too was shot, two days before Robert F. Kennedy, in 1968 (exactly the explosive year at which this book concludes), by the radical feminist writer Valerie Solanas.

Most poignant and telling in their indictment of America are the 'Race Riot' silkscreen paintings, so vivid that even today one cringes at the inhumanity they embody. In these, which are on a level that calls to mind Goya's *Disasters of War* (1810–20), Warhol establishes himself as the most relentless of social realist and social protest artists the country has produced. Less known and understood was the fact that he was a devout Catholic, with a deep-seated spiritual life that seems totally at odds with

274 Richard Diebenkorn, *Ocean Park No. 66*, 1973. Oil on canvas, 236.22 × 205.74 cm (93 × 81 in). Albright Knox Art Gallery, Buffalo, New York

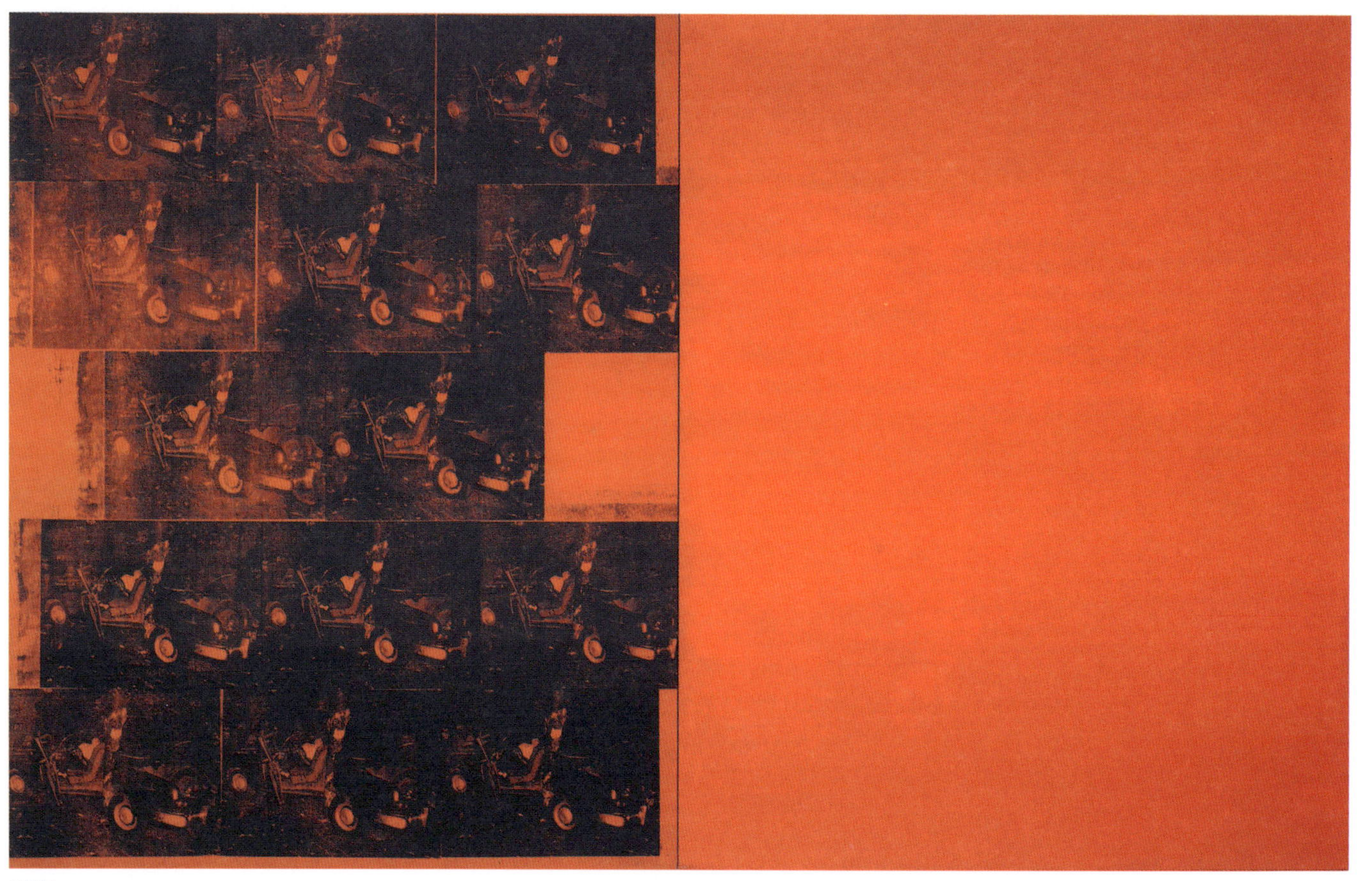

275

his public personality. But there it is, made explicit in his later series of religious paintings, most especially his versions of Leonardo's *Last Supper*. These images are real and heartfelt, not corny ironies. He was the complete American painter, and continued the use of the Cubist grid well into the 1960s.

Warhol was also a far better painter than I had understood. He tried to pass himself off as a machine, working in his studio, which he called the Factory, but there is far more feeling and touch, both formal and emotive, in his silkscreen process. He made constant painterly decisions, moving from dark to light and back again, giving the painting's surface more evidence of the hand and heart than we might ever suppose. 'I always wanted to be Matisse,'[25] he said, and he incorporated the brilliant colour of the French master. In his *Orange Car Crash Fourteen Times* (1963)[275], Warhol's red-orange panel clearly points to *The Red Studio*, then on display at MoMA, which had also inspired Rothko in 1949, and Newman with his *Vir Heroicus Sublimis* (1950–1). The stencilled, repeated black images of the gruesome accident recall Pollock's death in a car crash in 1956, an event that both changed the course of art and anticipated the coming disasters in America. Like Matisse himself, Warhol was often sick as a youth, and while in bed he had begun to draw and collect photos and images.

Warhol, it turns out, was a prophet, seeing what was coming because he was already living it – the car crash of fame and society itself. *Orange Car Crash*, so redolent of Pollock's fatal accident a few years earlier, can stand as a pointed metaphor for the decade, in which the best and the worst existed simultaneously side by side. Perhaps this had always been the history, even the nature, of America, which produced the greatest document of the Western world proclaiming the inalienable rights of man, liberty and justice for all, while slavery flourished as never before, and after wiping out the First Nations; a country of peace that has been fighting wars continuously, for fifty years and counting.

Now that we think of it, we can see that Warhol extended the vivid hues of the Matissean tradition from early in the 1960s, virtually throughout his life. Where else could they come from? Erika Doss has suggested the garish colours of his parish church in Pittsburgh.[26] Did this church serve as his Matisse Chapel of the Rosary in Vence? Did he take inspiration from this as well? By any measure, his colour is more varied and intense than that of any other artist of the 1960s, ranging from the shrill and off-beat to the gold paint recalling Byzantine icons in his depiction of Marilyn.

Frank Stella's New Order

Few artists have affected the course and the character of painting in the second half of this century as decisively and consistently as Frank Stella (b.1936). In December 1959, when still only twenty-three, he showed at MoMA four of his 'Black' paintings, consisting solely of bands in linear, quasi-geometric patterns. The unyielding literalness of these pictures shocked many observers as a seeming abnegation of the very practice of painting. But they clearly announced a seismic shift in the history of art.

In 1959 the 'Black' pictures appeared to some as if born overnight, but they were rooted in Stella's earlier paintings, done at Andover and Princeton. Stella was attracted to the power, openness and directness of Abstract Expressionism, then at the peak of its prestige in New York, and he painted in a manner inspired by de Kooning, Kline and Frankenthaler. By his senior year, in 1958, however, he had begun to question the rhetoric

275 Andy Warhol, *Orange Car Crash Fourteen Times*, 1963. Silkscreen ink on synthetic polymer paint on two canvases, 268.9 × 416.9 cm (105¾ × 164¼ in). The Museum of Modern Art, New York

and the excessive brushwork and paint handling of Abstract Expressionism. In January 1958 he was deeply impressed by Jasper Johns's first New York exhibition. He was especially struck by the idea of repetition inherent in the stripes of Johns's 'Flag' paintings, the way they 'stuck to the motif'[27], their intervals, elements that offered a corrective to the composing and drawing inherent in Abstract Expressionism.

In *East Broadway* (1958)[276], he used an all-over pattern of uneven horizontal bands in alternating yellow and black, with a rectangular box shape set at the lower centre. The stripe pattern is clearly indebted to Johns's flags, but it also relates to certain paintings by Alfred Leslie, as well as Diebenkorn, an artist whom Stella admired; the vertical box shape recalls the floating rectangles of Rothko, at whom Stella also looked. *East Broadway* and its companion works of 1958 retained the painterly look and feel, as well as the scale and directness, of Abstract Expressionism, while attempting to make it more concrete. Certainly, Stella belongs to this tradition rather than to that of geometric painting. In these works he was among the first of his generation to seek – and to find – a new order, a stability, an even more pronounced simplicity and immediacy of a directly given experience. They are harbingers of his 'Black' and 'Aluminium' pictures of 1959–60, which heralded the arrival of a younger generation in American art. Stella's colours in the works from 1958 have the gritty, grimy feel of urban blight, of filtered sunlight pulsing over ageing New York buildings, while the insistence of the bands underlines the unrelenting pace of city life. This same combination of yellow and black was later transformed, reappearing as brilliant, high-keyed hues in paintings of an altogether different mood, his Moroccan series of 1964–5.

In paintings such as *East Broadway*, Stella first realized his ambition to make a completely independent abstract art that severed all roots

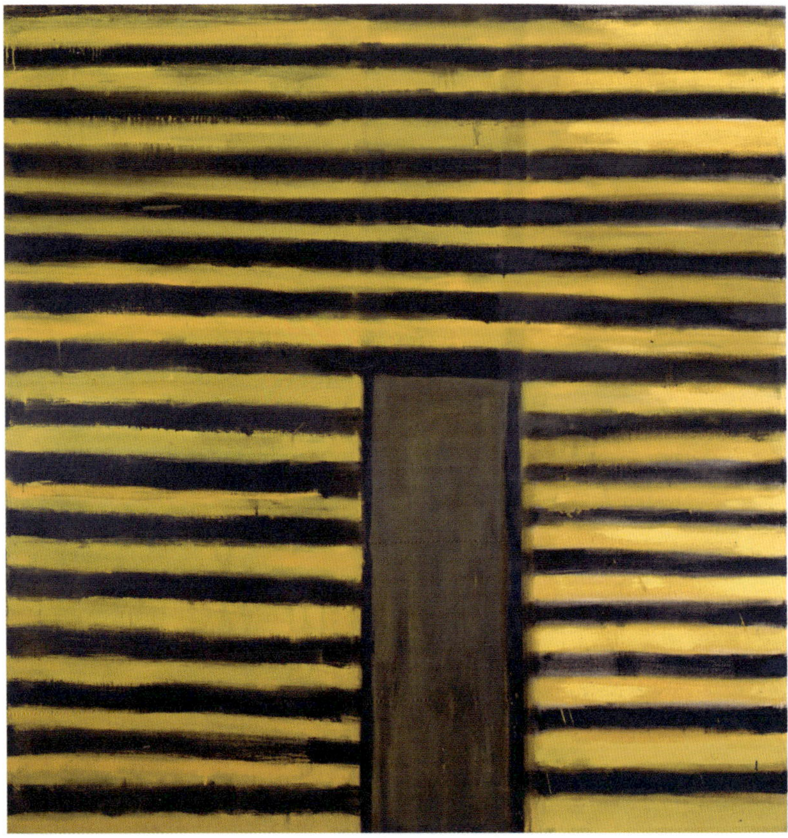

276

in representation, an ambition that has marked his art to the present day. In such early paintings, he established a distinct mood and atmospheric feel, as his 'Black' paintings did, suggesting an eerie, romantic kind of setting. Here is an instance where the art is highly abstract yet still conveys a personal note, as well as the feel of a particular urban setting that recalls the work of Sloan and other Ashcan realists.

Stella moved from the early austere black and aluminium paintings into increasingly complex compositions, as in the irregular polygon *Tuftonburo IV* (1966), and then in an ever-more flamboyant and baroque direction that has recently included monumental architectural constructions of unending complexity. For more than thirty-five years, Stella has offered one surprise after another that has always pointed to new directions and possibilities.

Hunter College Artists: Ray Parker, Sanford Wurmfeld and Robert Swain

By 1968, colour held an important place for several of the young and gifted artists who were teaching at Hunter College, New York, long the seat of a famous art department where Motherwell, Reinhardt and Tony Smith had taught. Eugene Goossen, an inspirational and enormously supportive chair of the department, was in no small part responsible. He had written early and important catalogues on Helen Frankenthaler and Ellsworth Kelly, so he knew full well the importance of colour to modern art. He featured it in his seminal show held in 1968 at MoMA, 'The Art of the Real', whose title inspired one theme in this book.

The earliest and most important colour artist, after Reinhardt, was Ray Parker (1922–1990), who came to Hunter College in 1955 and taught there until his death. Parker's talent had been recognized early on, and his first mature works, which he called the 'stroke paintings', were an original contribution to Abstract Expressionism. They were based on a loose Cubist armature filled with multiple patches of strong colour that from the start showed their debt to Cézanne's colour blocks. By 1955, Parker's colour shapes had become larger, more prominent and had showed signs of asserting their independence.

Parker was then able to place full confidence in colour alone to carry the painting. By 1958 he had begun his 'Simple' paintings [277]. Composed of just a few shapes – sometimes as many as five, sometimes only one – they are simple in name only. They stemmed from isolating and enlarging the colour shapes from his 'stroke' paintings. Monumental, dense, literal, almost human in the presence of their shapes, they recall Rothko's declaration that his forms were like actors in a drama. The canvases, too, echo the reach of a man, like Leonardo's *Vitruvian Man*, measuring no more than six or seven feet in any direction. That is why Parker once said that he felt that 'You could go up and put your arms around one of them.'[28] Indeed, their human qualities would lead Parker later to recall: 'I found shapes that floated, rested heavily, hung, nudged, bumped, touched, hovered in vast voids of separation, were many, were few, single, alone.'[29] He further described them as 'quiescent, bound by gravity that makes bodies in orbit hang in a stillness where the slowest movement marks the space from one to another.'[30]

Parker, along with other younger painters at that time, retained the scale, immediacy and power of Abstract Expressionism, which they held in high esteem. But they now sought to reinvigorate it, feeling it had become too predictable, rhetorical, or in some cases even academic. The 'Simple' paintings have much of the brushing and rough edges of Abstract

277

Expressionism, but the forms are more clearly articulated, defined and focused, pointing the way to the lean geometries of 1960s art. The impetus for the new paintings had been Parker's mastery of colour, the desire 'to cut out everything but pigment on the ground and let colour tell the whole story.'[31] Working out of his material – pigment – Parker could enable the forms to grow and spread, becoming bigger or smaller, rounder or more square, more ragged or more exact and regular, 'all according to the need of the colour surface to make itself dense enough and real.'[32] Thus the 'Simple' paintings both announced and participated in the colour-field painting of the late 1950s and early 1960s.

Parker's working method, steeped in Abstract Expressionist practice, was improvisational and confrontational. He tacked bare canvas to the wall, keeping the ground neutral with only a priming coat to maintain and heighten the clarity of the colour shapes. There was no preconceived plan or preliminary sketch. He often used rags to apply the paint, allowing the colour to spread to its 'fullness of volume,'[33] as he termed it, letting it respond to the pressure of his hand, recording the nuances of touch and feeling, change and movement, like a psychic seismograph. He let the materials dictate his moves, exploring and discovering as he went, working out of the materials and beauty of the picture as you see it, an old practice dating back to 1903 and Alfred Stieglitz in his art.

Parker's colour could be flat and uniform, but often it was, he said, 'mixed up – wet in wet, as though the canvas itself was a palette where things were being mixed.'[34] Or it could be high-keyed, sometimes working within a narrow range of gradated reds and red-oranges, for example. We find abrupt changes of hue and value, as well as rich layering, which are among the constant surprises that we encounter in these paintings. To be convincing and real, his colour depended not only on hue and value, but also on amount, proportion, luminosity, texture and weight. Also important is the internal scale of colour, the relation of shapes to themselves and to the edges of the canvas. Parker's fullness of scale coincides with the fullness of colour volume. To ensure the unity and wholeness of the painting, changes were made only in the process; no additions or corrections could be imposed afterwards. The whole painting might be in error, but never a part of it.

Shapes could be arranged as horizontal or vertical in format. They could be stacked, adjoining or separate. The paintings can be slow and still or floating, off-centre or frontal, or architectural, post-and-lintel style, like a modern Stonehenge. In turn they can be meditative and contemplative, or playful and light-hearted. One work, *For Kate* (1963), a triptych six feet wide [278], consists of single solemn vertical shapes, the forms isolated and immovable, recalling Giacometti's standing figures or the characters in Samuel Beckett's *Waiting for Godot*, both cultural icons of the 1950s. The possibilities were endless. We cannot help but feel in these poetic and moving paintings an urgency, an inner imperative that tells us just how powerfully colour speaks to us.

Sanford Wurmfeld, who has been at Hunter College for over thirty years, came to art in the early 1960s at Dartmouth College, first by studying architecture, then by learning from Hans Hofmann and others who had visited the college. Thereafter, in Europe, he took interest in the ceiling paintings of baroque churches in Rome, and the way they enveloped the observer. Back in New York he began an intensive study of colour, first through close study of Albers and his *Interaction of Color*, and then through looking at the colour usage of Kelly, Noland and Stella. He embarked on a series of enormous canvases of pure colour, with intimations of environmental effects. After seeing the Monet murals in Paris that encircle the

278 Ray Parker, *For Kate (Triptych)*, 1963. Oil on canvas, each panel 188 × 91.4 cm (74 × 36 in). Private collection

278

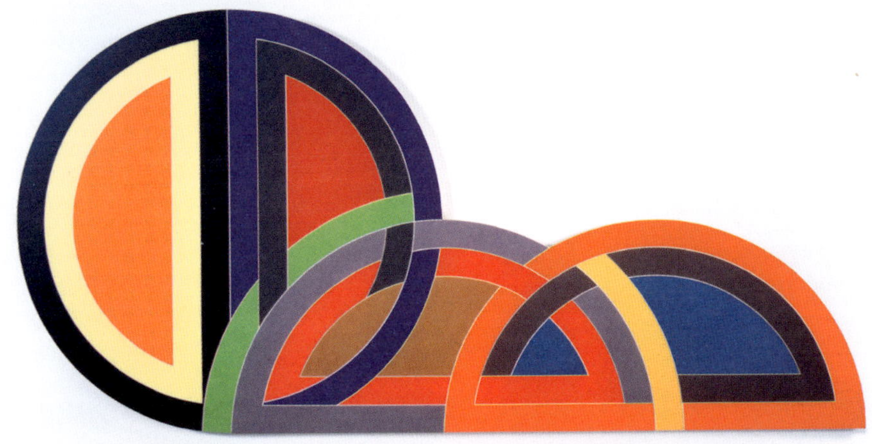

279

viewer, and nineteenth-century Dutch panoramas at Mesdag, Wurmfeld went on to create full 360-degree environments he called *Cycloramas* (1966–2013), one of the most prodigious accomplishments ever with pure colour, now united with his early interest in architecture. We enter the circular platform and as we move so does the colour, extending from the darkest to the lightest extremes of the spectrum, as night follows day, and as the course of life unfolds.[35]

In the mid-1960s, another Hunter artist was developing colour planes of spectral hues that had their source in Cézanne. Robert Swain,[36] working at the Phillips Collection, studied the constructive colour patches of the Cézanne painting *Le Jardin des Lauves* (c.1906). This painting was the ultimate source for his life's work, seen at the place that had inspired so many artists to pursue colour. It was in turn the same type of colour construction that Albers had admired in 1908, in his native Germany. Colour painting took many twists and turns, but could be traced back to the same sources, early in the century.

Colour had become so pervasive by the early 1960s that it could be employed effectively in almost any mode. Matisse, despite critical opinion of the time, remained widely admired by artists, still one of the form-givers for successive generations. By 1968, Stella, for example, had moved beyond the obdurate flatness of his work of the early 1960s into a new type of abstract illusionism of rich plays on depth and intersections of forms and shapes, first in his *Irregular Polygons* and then in his 'Protractor' series, such as *Ctesiphon I* (1968) [279], which were based on a riot of colour. The circular forms of these paintings recalled the Delaunays – and the Synchromists – and their cosmic circles that had defined so much of early colour painting. The hues could be bright and brash, or soft and pastel, and their circular arrangements allowed for a maximum of colour contrasts and interplays. Stella had, in his own words, vowed to engage Matisse at his fullest, to 'make Matisse abstract'.[37]

Hofmann Reappears

Stella once claimed, when writing about the importance of Hofmann to modern art, that colour had trumped Cubism. His connection to Hofmann can be traced back to his days at Phillips Academy, Andover, in Massachusetts, where he had first seen Hofmann's painting *Exaltment* (1947) (page 219) at the Addison Gallery of American Art. It was the painting Stella later told me he had been 'chasing all his life'.[38] He said he revered Hofmann as he did Pollock and Rauschenberg, 'for proving that the straightforward manipulation of pigment can create exalted art'.[39] He saw Hofmann's late work of the 1950s and 1960s as the equivalents of the explosions of a bomb, and related him back in time to Van Gogh, and ahead to Smithson, Serra and Michael Heizer, their surfaces topographical equivalents of Hofmann's dense quasi-reliefs of colour. Stella especially praised Hofmann's painting of 1963, *Gloriamundi*, noting that although Johns and Rauschenberg were more famous at that point, Hofmann had still made the best picture in the world.[40] Once again, an older artist forces his stamp on the art of a decade apparently dominated by younger artists, a story we have seen over and over again in this history.

In the 1960s, Hofmann blossomed as never before, consistently making many of the best pictures he had ever done. In *Summer Over the Land* (1962) and *Fiat Lux* (1963)[280] he demonstrated two of the endless possibilities of colour. The first work is a literal landscape, soft, calm and serene; the other is a painting of turmoil, made shortly after his wife's death in what the artist called a 'negative ecstasy'.[41] The works are but two examples of the moods and structures Hofmann could create through colour. His range could lead observers to think of him as without focus; they are, however, quite the opposite, an indication of his protean energies.

In Hofmann's art there seems always to be references to nature or to the universe beyond us. In *Black Diamond* (1961)[281], there are two circles: one surrounding the black mass, the other a ring of large tabs of colour, recalling Seurat's pointillism. They are brilliant colours, starting with intense yellows, which are then modulated, turning to cadmium reds and oranges as they enclose the centre. Only then do we understand that this circular movement is an abstract depiction of the sun as it rises, reaches

279 Frank Stella, *Ctesiphon I*, 1968. Polymer and fluorescent polymer paint on canvas, 304.8 × 609.6 cm (120 × 240 in). The Museum of Contemporary Art, Los Angeles

280 Hans Hofmann, *Fiat Lux*, 1963. Oil on canvas, 182.9 × 152.4 cm (72 × 60 in). Museum of Fine Arts, Houston

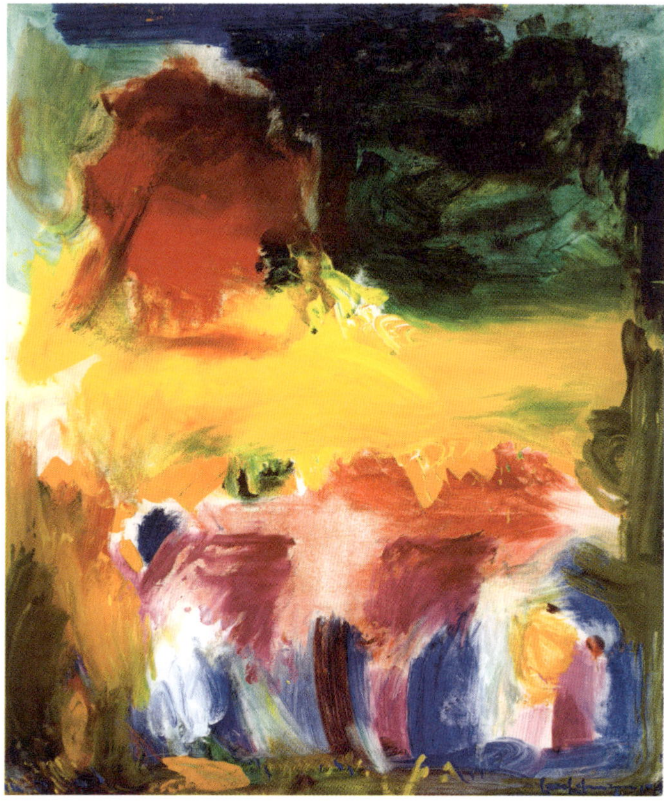

280

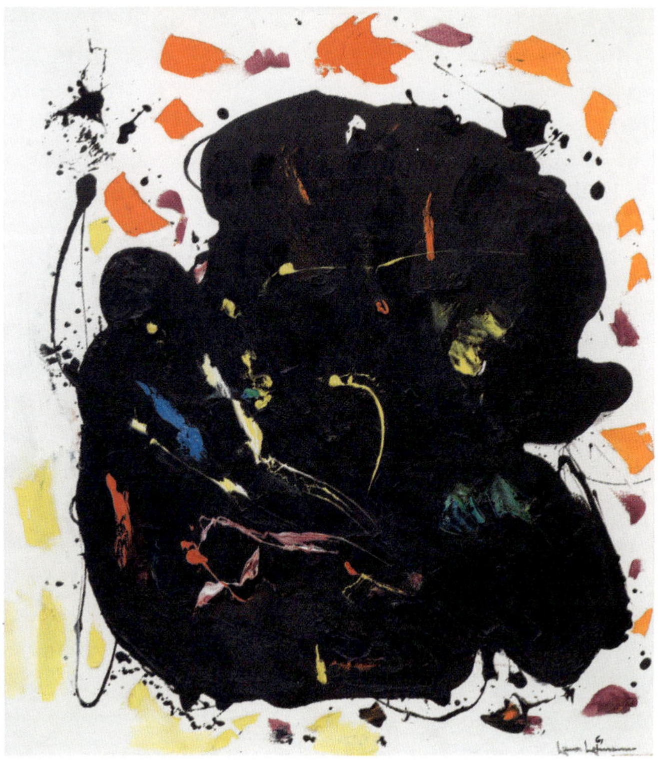

281

high noon, then descends into twilight and evening. Indeed, it is Hofmann's own solar system of colour and paint brought to new life, like another update of Van Gogh's *Starry Night*.

In 1962, at the age of eighty-two, Hofmann was as active as ever. He never let himself settle for a signature style, always pushing himself to go beyond that. His late work joins the exalted ranks of other artists through the ages who underwent a virtual rebirth in their last years: Michelangelo, Rembrandt, Cézanne, Matisse, Davis, Marin and Noland.[42] He was a generous man, and was open in his appreciation and respect for other artists, both earlier and those of the time. This, remember, was in a period when artists such as Newman, Still, Rothko, and Gottlieb all thought they were the best artists in the world, and as Thomas Hess observed, any mention of possible influence was like a trial for an act of high treason. But with all the attention given to the young Abstract Expressionist artists after 1945, as in Pollock's spread in *Life* in August 1949, Hofmann felt that the pioneers of American modernism were overlooked. In 1950, he spoke of them as the forerunners of a 'true and great American tradition that is being carried on by the vanguard of the most advanced modern artists.'[43] He counted among these pioneers Alfred Henry Maurer, John B. Flannagan, Arthur B. Carles, Arshile Gorky and Albert Pinkham Ryder. Hofmann himself should be counted among them, standing tall as a beacon in a long and glorious tradition still being defined today. He had an effect on many artists, and today his art lives on, as in the baroque swirls of Frank Stella's later art, all based on the twists and turns in *Exaltment*.

Jules Olitski: A New Kind of Colour

Hofmann's influence, particularly his dense surfaces, can also be seen in the later work of Darby Bannard (b.1934) and Jules Olitski (1922–2007). Noland had said he wanted to get colour down on the thinnest possible surface, a surface as if sliced in air,[44] but it was Olitski who came closer than anyone to attaining this result. As Seurat and Cézanne had built on Impressionism, giving it new types of structure, so Olitski built on Abstract Expressionism. Starting from Abstract Expressionism's scale, size and all-over surfaces, as in the case of the colour painters, especially Rothko, he then sought to eliminate all signs of the tactile surfaces of the 1950s, to make colour as closely integrated with surface as possible, so that they would be read as one. In the early 1960s, he had started with large eccentric portions of thick circles, but these were still distinct shapes. He wanted colour and colour alone to take on the 'full burden of pictorial structure', as noted by Michael Fried, his greatest champion at that time.[45]

By 1965, Olitski had developed a new kind of colour, applied through a radical new means – a spray gun [282]. Such practices had been investigated by Siqueiros at his workshop in New York in 1936, but Olitski developed it into a full working methodology capable of achieving an entirely new and different range of colour application and effects. In a sense, the spray-gun technique is a development from Pollock, following the hand as it moved across the surface; in Pollock's art it was with a stick, a brush, a turkey baster, whatever worked. For Olitski it was the spray gun, and with it he developed the same dexterity, the same variety of application and touch that Pollock had. When we watch Hans Namuth's film of Pollock painting, we can see and inventory the number and type of strokes that Pollock used. They are numerous, at least thirty, depending on how one counts, showing his sheer skill in applying paint. This parallels Robert L. Herbert's study of the Monets in the Boston Museum of Fine Arts in 1979,[46] in which he disproved the idea of the typical, single Impressionist stroke. Instead he was able to account for twenty-six different types of these.

281 Hans Hofmann, *Black Diamond*, 1961. Oil on canvas, 152.4 × 132 cm (60 × 50 in). Private collection

282 Jules Olitski, *Total Trend*, 1966. Acrylic on canvas, 226 × 165 cm (89 × 65 in). Private collection

282

Olitski developed the same range and repertoire, so that his gestures with the gun became intuitive, free and liberating, thus giving an enormous variation of surface colour and facture. We might say that by atomizing colour particles, he had taken Seurat's pointillism to new extremes. It is on the surface, but the spray paintings give distinct illusions of, if not depth, then certainly infinite space. The primacy of paint and colour was thus given new meaning. For all the complexity of the mix and fusion of multiple tiny droplets of different hues, the proposition was quite direct for Olitski. No fancy theories: 'I think of painting as possessed by a structure … but a structure born of the flow of colour feeling. Colour *in* colour is felt at any and every place of the pictorial organization; in its immediacy – its particularity. Colour must be felt throughout … What is of importance in painting is paint. Paint can be colour … I begin with colour.'[47]

Olitski had studied Matisse carefully, yet he more openly admired the northern masters, especially Rembrandt and his use of light, and Van Gogh, whose sun paintings with their intense light and dense surfaces influenced Olitski's late work, after 2000. He was widely respected and admired by many artists, critics and writers, but like the other colour-field painters of the time he was denigrated because of his close association with Greenberg. We should be clear about what Greenberg, as well as his fellow critic and art historian Michael Fried, did: they gave a new precision and depth to art analysis, a new order to modern art, then a field that was in its formative stage and filled with inexact and wrong-headed ideas. Further, Greenberg insisted on standards for modern art that were as high as those for Old Masters. He brought a discipline that was sorely needed. To achieve that, he could be overly restrictive in his taste, which resulted in hurt feelings and resentment, but that has been corrected. His name is almost universally reviled these days, but he should be honoured, with our gratitude. In turn, Fried gave us brilliant observations on how painting and art are actually made, fulfilling the idea that the best criticism is the best description.

James Daugherty: A True *Alter Stil*

In 1965, James Daugherty, then in his late seventies, newly inspired by the Synchromist show of that year for which he had designed the cover of the catalogue, pursued a series of large and powerful colour abstractions that picked up where he had left off in about 1920. It was as if he had not missed a beat, for his new colour paintings, while looking back, also took colour into new paths. We have mentioned him earlier, but his full story is worth telling for it reveals much about the course of modernism, through the life and work of an artist not well known either then or today. The story shows us the depth of American modernism that we have tended to miss, as well as the enthusiasm and spirit the new art generated in this country.

Writing in 1949, Daugherty declared with his usual optimism that modern art was 'liberating and expansive, rousing and freeing human consciousness from materialism to infinite possibilities of living, creating universal harmony, energy and renewal'.[48] One could easily have assumed that Daugherty, who was then sixty-two, was simply looking back to the early years of the twentieth century and his own beginnings as a pioneering modernist artist. As it turns out, however, this was only part of it, and his statement now has a new and prophetic meaning. Daugherty was looking ahead, as if issuing a personal manifesto for a renewed burst of abstract painting to take place. The results of these almost twenty years of abstract painting, begun in 1953 and ending only with his death in 1974 at the age of eighty-four, were clear in his posthumous exhibition held in

2005 in fact – a revelation. The late paintings are startling, revealing, even astonishing in their clarity and brilliant colour. Their power and resolution strike us as the work of a man half his age. They form a true *alter Stil*, a distinctive old-age style that extended further into the century than that of any other first-generation American modernist.

Daugherty saw no break or barrier between earlier and later modernism. He embraced the continuity between the two generations of modern art, understanding that Rothko and others were building on what he had been instrumental in establishing. *Abstraction with Red Sun* (c.1960) retained a heavily textured surface, but two subsequent works, *The Day the Sun Stood Still* (1961) [283] and *Yellow Sun* (1961) [284], show a lighter, more refined painterly touch. Their layered, almost transparent colour surely recalls the colour veils of Rothko's art that he admired. As the titles tell us, the subject is the generating source of life itself, the sun. Thus the paintings refer to the cosmos, the vast universe in which we live, a subject that had long run deep in modern art. The brilliance of light and colour in *Yellow Sun* (1961) and its aura call to mind a tradition dating back to the American Luminists, the sun paintings of Van Gogh, and the variations of Orphic circles of light found in the works of the Delaunays, Bruce, Frost and in Daugherty's own early abstractions. In turn, Daugherty's painting points to and reflects the new clarity and luminous colour of art in the late 1950s and 1960s, as can be found in the burst paintings of Adolph Gottlieb,

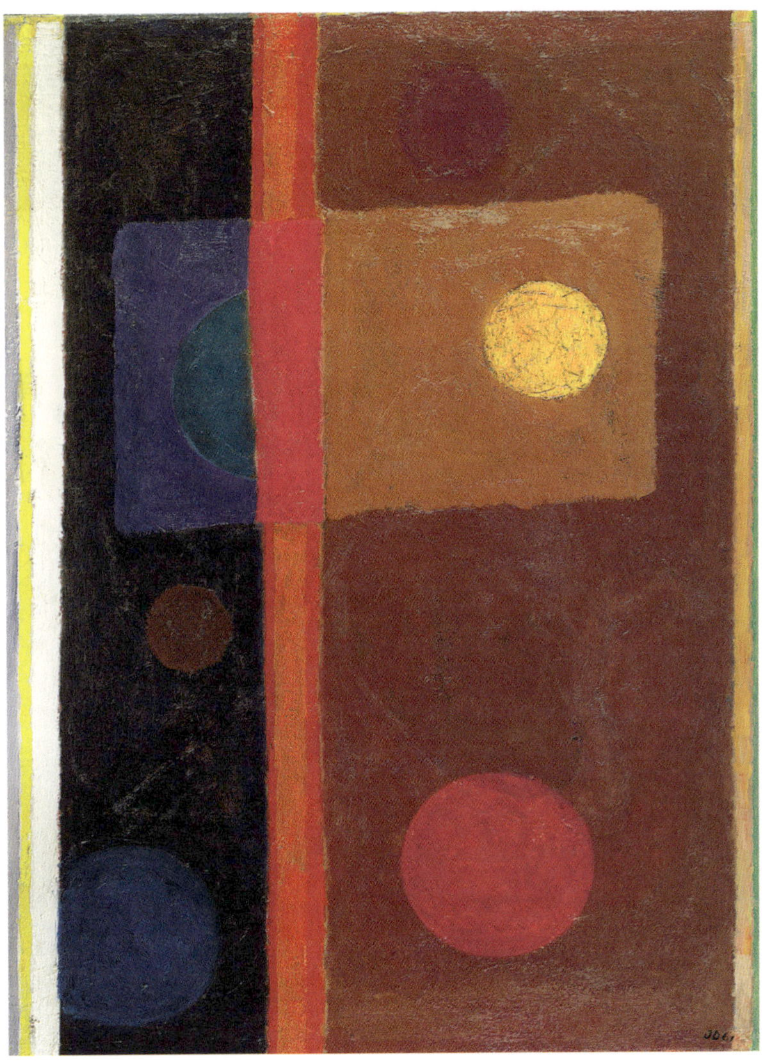

283 James Daugherty, *The Day the Sun Stood Still*, 1961. Oil on canvas, 104.1 × 76.2 cm (41 × 30 in). Private collection

283

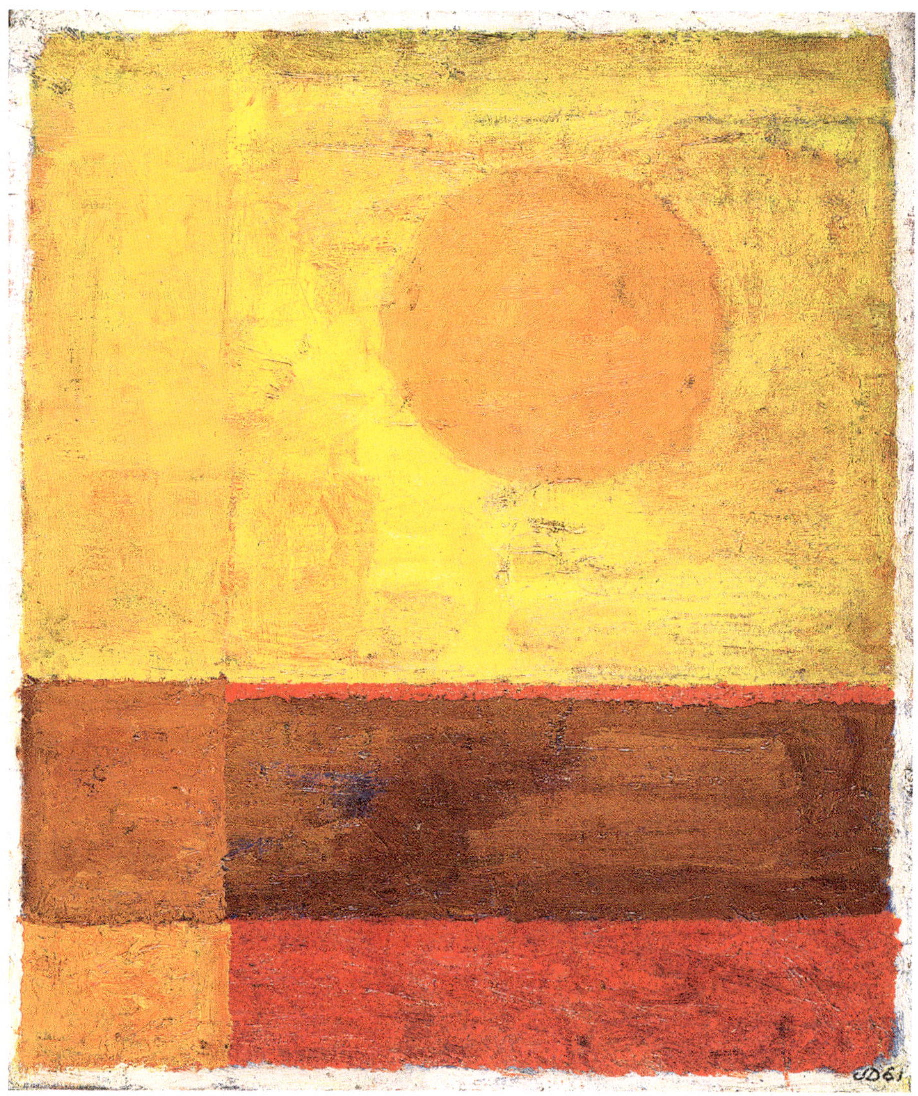

284

the concentric circles of Kenneth Noland, and in much of the newer colour-field painting of the time. In this way, Daugherty both affected and in turn was affected by newer developments, an age-old process of art. He was a deeply spiritual man of profound faith who believed in the power of prayer. His art was nothing less than an expression of his beliefs. We only need to think of the thunderous *Moses* (1922), or the series of works based on biblical themes dating from the 1940s, to understand how open his spirituality had always been.

The Red Studio: A Summary

The Red Studio deserves a sub-chapter to itself in the art of the twentieth century.[49] There it is: colour itself as the painting and its structure, as clear a statement as any of the equality of colour with Cubism as the two funda-mental systems of modern painting. It was the source for Davis's *Studio Interior* of 1917 (page 67); Schamberg adapted the envelope of colour to many of his paintings done right after the Armory Show. There, Sheeler was impressed by it, not for the colour but for the line, which was one of the sources for his and Schamberg's first precisionist paintings from 1916 onwards. Thereafter the painting was lost to public view in a London club until 1942, when it reappeared at the Bignou Gallery in New York, and

284 James Daugherty, *Yellow Sun*,
1961. Oil on canvas,
61 × 50.8 cm (24 × 20 in).
Private collection

　　　　Modern Art in America

seven years later the painting was acquired by and installed at MoMA in 1949. Rothko looked at it every day for six weeks, and found in it the means to an overall unity of colour, the floating rectangles of his mature style. The painting clearly set the example for de Kooning's *Gansevoort Street* (c.1949), Richard Diebenkorn's *Untitled* (1949), Newman's *Vir Heroicus Sublimis* (1950–1), Anthony Caro's *Early One Morning* (1962), Judd's early floor boxes, and it still appears today in works such as Sarah McEneaney's *Every Day* of 2013. We can say that *The Red Studio* was the first painting to depend entirely on colour.

The Development of Land Art

Late in his life, in about 1990, I asked Donald Judd what his next project might be. He thought for a while then said he wanted to do something with and on the land. Like Jefferson at Monticello, Judd was imagining the ideal in the wilderness, only now in the vast spaces of the West Texas desert. He sketched out a rough diagram of a large enclosed structure, of about what he said would be a hundred yards on each side. Then he said that with this he wanted to do something on the land to 'challenge the Greeks'.[50] In another interview, also done late in his life, I asked Judd if there was anything that he loved as much as his art, and his work. Judd paused, and said, 'Yes, the land.'[51]

Therein lies a summary of a long and rich chapter in American art and life, one that we can trace from early explorers right down to the present day: our dilemma in the face of the vast American space and land, how to confront it and how to work with it.[52] One of the last manifestations of a deep love of the land within the boundaries of this book was of course the development of Land art in 1968 and thereafter. The most famous work is Robert Smithson' *Spiral Jetty* of 1970 [285]. Think of it: the spiral, a signature form of modern art, from Van Gogh's *Starry Night* and Brancusi's sketch of Joyce's ear, to Arthur Dove's spiral works of the early 1940s, Pollock's spirals in the mid-1940s, then the *Spiral Jetty* itself. Working with the land, discovered by artists as the early explorers – only after a long and arduous search – seems a natural continuation of the nineteenth-century artists who depicted the glories of the American land. Listen to Smithson speak as he traced the shape of his work:

> *Following the spiral steps we return to our origins, back to some pulpy protoplasm, a floating eye adrift in an antediluvian ocean … All was enveloped in a flaming chromosphere; I thought of Jackson Pollock's* Eyes in the Heat [1946] … *The dizzying spiral yearns for the assurance of geometry. One wants to retreat into the cool rooms of reason. But no, there was Van Gogh with his easel on some sun-baked lagoon painting ferns of the Carboniferous Period. The mirage faded into the burning atmosphere.*[53]

For Smithson, art had the power to transcribe the history of the earth, from its protoplasmic beginnings to its most intense experiences of the infinite cosmos. Yet the land where he built was also covered with the detritus of modern technology and industry, reminding us that the country welcomed, indeed was addicted to, the technology and growth that have now brought the earth and its environment close to breaking point. And while we look with awe and nostalgia at the glories of landscape and the painting it has inspired, we do nothing to prevent the planet as we know it from its doom.

But let us take one last look at the jetty. Smithson was originally attracted to the area because of the colour of the water, affected by the algae.

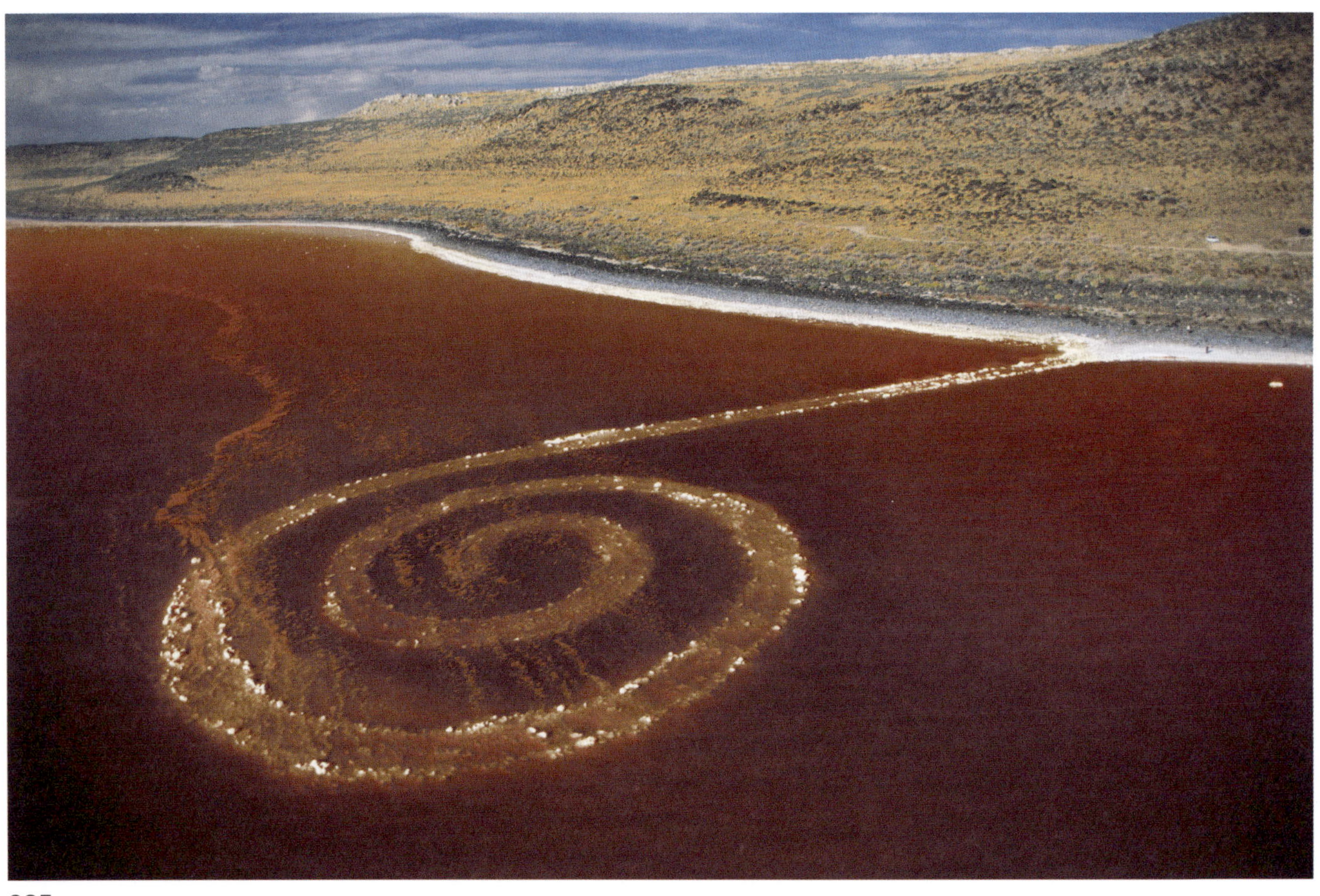

285

And what was the colour? Red, of course: 'the most joyful and dreadful thing … the fiercest … it burns through', as Smithson himself described it, quoting G.K. Chesterton's famous remark.[54] The jetty seen from above, in a distant aerial view, with red spreading and surrounding us, reminds us of nothing less than *The Red Studio*. Indeed, colour trumps Cubism. Thus the book ends where it began, in a spiral recalling T.S. Eliot:

> *We shall not cease from exploration*
> *and the end of all our exploring*
> *Will be to arrive where we started*
> *And know the place for the first time.*[55]

In the Aftermath of 1968

By 1968, the divisions in the nation were as deep as they had been in the 1860s – indeed, Americans were in the midst of a virtual civil war, as they had been 100 years before.

The decade had begun with the election of a young president who brought a fresh vision to government and the country. He launched the last great adventure undertaken by America – a campaign to reach the moon by the end of the decade. It was successful, but by the end of the decade no such grand achievement could have been proposed, let alone achieved. The optimism of the early 1960s was first undermined by southern racism and violence that greeted the freedom riders, the Civil Rights activists who rode interstate buses into the segregated south, as early as 1960. In 1962, troops had to be sent to the University of Mississippi to protect the African-American student James Meredith as he entered the university there. By then, the country was once again at war with itself. It ended with the murder of John F. Kennedy in Dallas, launching a seemingly unending succession of assassinations and untrammelled violence: another Kennedy, Martin Luther King, Malcolm X, Medgar Evers, murders in Philadelphia – on it went. This continued and expanded in Vietnam, a useless and treasonable war since officials such as Robert McNamara knew full well it could not be won, but nevertheless continued to send thousands of soldiers to their deaths. We will never know how many civilians were killed – the count is still rising as the effects of America's chemical warfare, Agent Orange, continue to exact their toll on the country. That the United States of America was defeated by a small, under-armed people in a tiny country in which the US had no interest, started the decline and fall of the country as a superpower, and even as a decent society. The war was the latest extension of Theodore Roosevelt's declaration in 1908 by means of the world tour of the Great White Fleet that America would use military power to secure market positions it deemed to be in the nation's best interests, those of oil and the big corporations. The war exhausted the country, and cost it its soul. It also cost it its position as the sole leader of world art.

In 1968, the Chicago police rioted at the Democratic convention, injuring thousands while the nation and world looked on in disbelief. By 1970, the United States government was murdering its own citizens – four dead at Kent State University for exercising their right of freedom of assembly. The photo of a woman kneeling over the body of a fallen student, shrieking in pain and distress, echoes the weeping woman in Picasso's *Guernica*. By 1972, the Nixon administration was well on its way to subverting the constitution and creating a secret government within the government, to establish an imperial presidency that was accountable to no one. The corruption of government and society was complete.

285 Robert Smithson, *Spiral Jetty*, 1970. Mud, precipitated salt crystals, rocks, water, coil, 457.2 m (1500 ft) long and 4.6 m (15 ft) wide. Rozel Point, Great Salt Lake, Utah

When the authority of old conventions and institutions was lost forever, it is little wonder that the authority of established traditions of art came into doubt, most especially the arts of painting and sculpture. The civil discord had sown its poison into the world of art, undercutting the run of consistently first-rate art that America had produced over the past sixty years. The run ended with the institutionalization and celebration of anti-art, or rather what I would call 'non-art'. The old ideas of skill, craft, intelligence and feeling were widely questioned. Off-hand Duchampian derivations were much easier. Thus postmodernism was born, based on the idea that one thing was as good as another, and to make distinctions of quality became known as 'privileging'. People bought into it as a fast way to fame and fortune. Any gesture, any spectacle, anything to make money began to replace the meditative and contemplative, the thoughtful and intelligent. Art became highly political, and protest was accepted as an art form in itself. The art of the 1940s to the 1960s that had been celebrated as a national treasure was largely marginalized in favour of art promoting race, gender and sexual orientation, often putting political correctness above artistic ambition. The 1960s marked the end of the glorious unbroken tradition of four generations of artists in America, from Marin and Dove to Davis, to Pollock and Rothko, then to Frankenthaler, and to Stella and Judd.

There has been good art after 1968. The one good thing to come out of Conceptualism was the work of Sol LeWitt, because he was a real artist; his wall drawings – first delicate, quiet markings, then, thirty years later, glorious and monumental walls of the most intense, vibrant colour – continued and expanded the tradition of colour painting to new horizons. The colour of Matisse continued in ever-richer ways, as in the constructed paintings, then sculptures, of Frank Stella, still America's greatest living artist as his work continues to find new and more baroque forms. The art of Richard Diebenkorn grew better after 1968, as he continued to use both the colour and the architecture of Matisse as his model. Kelly, Judd, Noland, Serra and others continued apace. Sanford Wurmfeld and Robert Swain went on to become even stronger painters of colour fields, thus continuing the tradition of colour as a formal and emotive language.

Thus new and good artists appeared after 1968. But the older artists who had matured before that year were still the best. None of the newer artists reached the level of achievement that the three generations before them had. The best art continued to flourish, even if overshadowed by glossy-type art shown at Salons at the Whitney and the Carnegie museums, and now in the ubiquitous international art fairs. How it has managed to flourish under present social and political conditions tells us that art is a matter of personal experience translated into convincing forms. The best art is still not necessarily spectacular, but is quiet and meditative, as Matisse pointed out as early as 1908 in his *Notes of a Painter*. Working out of the materials, handling the paint, forms and colours taken to their fullest possibilities of thought and feeling – these paintings are exalted. They tell us that good art wins. Always. That is the power of art.

NOTES

On Art in America

1. Emilio de Antonio, 'Interview with Barnett Newman' (1970), reprinted in John Philip O'Neill (ed.), *Barnett Newman: Selected Writings and Interviews*, University of California Press, Berkeley, 1990, pp.302–8.

2. The idea of continuity was introduced to the author by John McCoubrey in his excellent book *The American Tradition in Painting* (1963); and by Robert Rosenblum in *The Abstraction of Landscape: From Northern Romanticism to Abstract Expressionism* (2007); also by Barbara Novak in her seminal work on nineteenth-century American art, *American Painting of the Nineteenth Century: Realism, Idealism, and the American Experience* (1969). Rosenblum and Novak also made important contributions to the exhibition catalogue *The Natural Paradise: Painting in America, 1800–1950* (1976). To them the author owes a profound debt of gratitude.

3. Alfred H. Barr, Jr., 'Report on the Permanent Collection', 1933, typescript, Alfred H. Barr, Jr., Papers, 9a 7A, MoMA Archives.

4. See William C. Agee, 'John Marin's Greatness: The Late Oils & Post-1945 Art', in *John Marin: The Late Oils*, exh. cat., Adelson Galleries, New York, 2008, pp.7–21.

5. Clement Greenberg, 'Review of Exhibition of John Marin', *The Nation*, 25 December 1948, p.675, reprinted in John O'Brian (ed.), *Arrogant Purpose, 1945–1949*, University of Chicago Press, Chicago, 1988, p.268.

6. Clement Greenberg, 'Review of Jackson Pollock', *The Nation* (24 January 1948), p.108.

7. Clement Greenberg, 'The Decline of Cubism', *Partisan Review* 3 (March 1948), reprinted in John O'Brian (ed.), *Clement Greenberg: The Collected Essays and Criticism: Volume 2*, University of Chicago Press, Chicago, 1986, p.212.

8. See William C. Agee, 'New Directions: The Late Work: 1938–1946', in Agee, Debra Bricker Balken and Elizabeth Hutton Turner, *Arthur Dove: A Retrospective*, exh. cat., Addison Gallery of American Art, Andover, MA, 1997, pp.133–53.

9. Donald Judd, 'In the Galleries: Stuart Davis', *Arts Magazine* 36:10 (September 1962), reprinted in *Donald Judd: Complete Writings 1959–1975: Gallery Reviews, Book Reviews, Articles, Letters to the Editor, Reports, Statements, Complaints*, Nova Scotia College of Art and Design, Halifax, 1975, pp.55–6.

10. 'Questions to Students', typescript c.1953–4, David Smith Papers, Archives of American Art, Smithsonian Institution, Washington, DC.

11. Quoted in ibid.

12. Donald Judd, 'Kansas City Report', *Arts Magazine*, December 1963, reprinted in *Donald Judd: Complete Writings*, op. cit., p.103.

13. Walt Whitman, 'Book II: Starting from Paumanok', in *Leaves of Grass* (1892), The Modern Library, New York, 1921, p.13.

14. Ibid., 'Book III: Song of Myself', p.69.

15. For the best description of this process, as well as the best history of modernism in Europe, see George Heard Hamilton, *Painting and Sculpture in Europe*, Yale University Press, New Haven, 1993.

16. Henri Matisse, 'Exactitude is Not Truth', in Jack Flam, *Matisse on Art*, University of California Press, Berkeley and Los Angeles, 1995, pp.179–81.

17. William Rubin, *Frank Stella*, The Museum of Modern Art, New York, 1970, p.149.

18. Quoted in ibid.

19. Quoted in Carol Salus, 'Behind the Celestial Enchantment: The Private Self and Early Movie Star Portraits of Andy Warhol', in Anna-Teresa Tymieniecka (ed.), *The Poetry of Life in Literature*, Kluwer Academic Publishers, Dordrecht, 2000, pp.195, 205 (n.1); Patrick Smith, *Andy Warhol's Art and Films*, UMI Press, Ann Arbor, 1986, p.367.

20. See Barbara Novak's several books on nineteenth-century American art: *Cole and Durand, Criticism and Patronage: A Study of American Taste in Landscape, 1825–65*, Ph.D. dissertation, Radcliffe College, Cambridge, MA, 1957; *American Painting of the Nineteenth Century: Realism, Idealism, and the American Experience*, Praeger, New York, 1969; *Nature and Culture: American Landscape and Painting 1825–1875*, Oxford University Press, New York, 1980; *Next to Nature: Landscape Paintings from the National Academy of Design*, National Academy of Design, New York, 1980.

21. See Gail Stavitsky and Katherine Rothkopf, *Cézanne and American Modernism*, exh. cat., Montclair Art Museum and Baltimore Museum of Art, Montclair and New Haven, 2009.

22. F. Scott Fitzgerald, *The Great Gatsby* [1925], Scribner, New York, 2004, p.180.

23. Philip Roth, *Portnoy's Complaint* [1969], Vintage Books, New York, 1994, p.69.

24. Herman Melville, *Moby-Dick*, C.H. Simonds Company, Boston, p.116.

25. Marius de Zayas, 'Picasso Speaks', *The Arts* III/5 (May 1923), pp.12–14.

26. See Rackstraw Downes (ed.), *Art in its Own Terms/Selected Criticism 1953–1975*, Zoland, Cambridge, MA, 1993, p.259. See also Fairfield Porter, Ted Leigh and Justin Spring, *Material Witness: The Selected Letters of Fairfield Porter*, University of Michigan Press, Ann Arbor, 2005, and Agee, *Porter Pairings: A Selection of Works by Fairfield Porter from the Parrish Art Museum, Southampton, New York*, exh. cat., Bertha and Karl Leubsdorf Art Gallery, New York, 1992; *Fairfield Porter, An American Painter*, exh. cat., Parrish Art Museum, Southampton, NY, 1993; *Fairfield Porter: A Catalogue Raisonné of the Paintings, Watercolors, and Pastels*, Hudson Hills Press, New York, 2001; *Fairfield Porter: March 8–April 15, 2006*, exh. cat., Betty Cunningham Gallery, New York, 2006.

27. See Agee catalogues, ibid. See also the Fairfield Porter quotations in *Porter Pairings*, op. cit.

28. John Cage, 'On Robert Rauschenberg, Artist, and his Work' (1961), in *Silence: Lectures and Writings by John Cage*, University Press of New England, Hanover, NH, 1961, p.108.

29. See Donald Judd, 'Specific Objects', *Arts Yearbook*, 8 (1965), reprinted in *Donald Judd: Complete Writings*, op. cit., pp.181–9.

30. Lawrence Gowing, 'Paint in America', *New Statesman* (24 May 1958), pp.669–70, reprinted in John McCoubrey, *The American Tradition in Painting*, G. Braziller, New York, 1963, p.1.

31. *Charles Baudelaire: Selected Writings on Art and Literature*, trans. P.E. Charvet, Penguin, Harmondsworth, 1972, p.403.

32. Charles Baudelaire, *The Mirror of Art: Critical Studies*, trans. J. Mayne, Anchor, New York, 1956, pp.43–4.

33. Allan Kaprow, 'The Legacy of Jackson Pollock', *Art News* 57:6 (October 1958), pp.24–6, 55–7.

34. See Jim Rasenberger, *America, 1908: The Dawn of Flight, the Race to the Pole, the Invention of the Model T, and the Making of a Modern Nation*, Scribner, New York, 2007.

35. Mark Dorrian and Frédéric Pousin, *Seeing from Above: The Aerial View in Visual Culture*, Palgrave Macmillan, New York, 2013.

36. See Mark Kurlansky, *1968: The Year that Rocked the World*, Ballantine, New York, 2004.

37. Sylvan Barnet, *A Short Guide to Writing About Art*, Pearson, Upper Saddle River, 2008, p.8.

Towards a New and Modern American Art 1908–10

1. Henri Matisse, 'Notes of a Painter', *La Grande Revue* (25 December 1908), reprinted in Flam, *Matisse on Art*, op. cit., pp.30–42.

2. Rémy de Gourmont, Juan Diego Martín and Odilon Redon, *Colores*, Sevilla Barataria, La Puebla de Cazalla, 2008. See also, Alicia Cooper, 'Odilon Redon in America',

M.A. Thesis, Hunter College, City University of New York, 2014.

3 Charles Caffin, 'Henri-Matisse', *Camera Work*, January 1909, pp.17–18.

4 For a full history, see William Innes Homer, *Stieglitz and the Photo-Secession, 1902*, Viking Studio, New York, 2002.

5 See unpublished letter from Marius de Zayas to Alfred Stieglitz, 11 June 1914, Alfred Stieglitz Archives, Yale University, New Haven.

6 The photograph has perhaps received more attention and scrutiny than virtually any other work of art in America in the twentieth century, as has Stieglitz himself. He has been resented and mocked because he was such a towering figure, a founding father not just of photography but of modern art itself in America. We have viewed him (erroneously) as a Moses-like giant, descending as from above with the commandments of modernism. He himself did nothing to dispel the idea, but he was in fact a working artist who struggled to understand modernism in both his own work and the art of others, including the masters of Europe and his young painter colleagues. Thus while we have seen him as a father figure – and he was to many, including Dove – he was also a novice modernist working side by side with younger colleagues. See also for a revised account, Jason Francisco and Elizabeth Anne McCauley, *The Steerage and Alfred Stieglitz*, University of California Press, Berkeley, 2012.

7 See William Innes Homer, *Robert Henri and his Circle*, Cornell University Press, Ithaca, 1969.

8 Stuart Davis, 'Autobiography', American Artists Group Monographs, 6, New York, 1945, reprinted in Diane Kelder (ed.), *Stuart Davis, Documentary Monographs in Modern Art*, Praeger, New York, 1971, p.24.

9 Winslow Homer in a telegram to Knoedler on 14 January 1902, reprinted in Stuart P. Feld et al., *American Paintings: A Catalogue of the Collection of the Metropolitan Museum*, New York Graphic Society, Greenwich, 1965, p.491.

10 Matisse, 'Notes of a Painter', op. cit., p.35.

11 See ibid., p.40.

12 The first was actually Stieglitz, in 1903, who spoke of this same process.

13 This was first pointed out to the author by Jules Prown in conversation, c.1976.

14 Homer's colour was described as 'cheap' in the review 'Fine Arts. Society of American Artists', *Brooklyn Daily Eagle*, 31 March 1901. For the full review, see Marc Simpson (ed.), *Winslow Homer: The Clark Collection*, Sterling and Francine Clark Art Institute, Williamstown, 2013, p.114.

15 In conversation with the author, c.1990.

16 Nancy Mathews, *The Art of Leisure: Maurice Prendergast in the Williams College Museum of Art*, Williams College Museum of Art, Williamstown, 1999, p.43. See also Richard Wattenmaker, *Maurice Prendergast*, Harry N. Abrams, Inc., New York, 1994.

17 Maurice Denis, 'Cézanne', in *Théories, 1890–1910*, Paris, 1912, p.242.

18 Picasso as quoted in John Richardson, *A Life of Picasso, vol.1, 1881–1906*, Random House, New York, 1991, p.469.

19 Reprinted in *Sheldon Reich, Alfred H. Maurer, 1868–1932*, Smithsonian Institution Press, Washington, DC, 1973, pp.117–18. See also Agee, 'The Tommy and Gill LiPuma Collection: Exploring American Art, 1906–1946', in Agee, Tommy LiPuma and Bruce Weber, *High Notes of American Modernism: Selections from the Tommy and Gill LiPuma Collection*, exh. cat., Berry-Hill Galleries, New York, 2002, pp.23–43.

20 For the full and only account, see Agee and Barbara Rose, *Patrick Henry Bruce, American Modernist: A Catalogue Raisonné*, The Museum of Modern Art, New York, 1979.

21 Matisse as quoted by Sarah Stein, 'Sarah Stein's Notes' (1908), in Flam, *Matisse on Art*, op. cit., p.50.

22 Ibid., p.45.

23 See Matisse, 'Notes of a Painter', op. cit., pp.37–42.

24 See Agee entry on Dove in Stavitsky and Rothkopf, *Cézanne and American Modernism*, op. cit., pp.206–7.

25 Dove apparently stayed primarily outside Paris, although it is hard to believe that he did not make purposeful trips into the city. New research (Barry King Collection, Santa Fe) has discovered that he exhibited a painting entitled *Pont Croix*, a town in Brittany, in the Salon d'Automne in 1908, with his name misspelled as Arthur E. Door, with a Paris address, 68, boulevard Edgar-Quintet, in Montparnasse. In the 1909 Salon he showed a still life, with his name correctly spelled and with the address in Paris as Chez M.L. Lefebvre-Point at 19, rue Vavin. This would indicate that he travelled more widely than was previously thought.

26 See Agee, 'Nineteenth-Century Eccentrics and the American Tradition', in *The Great Eccentrics, Art News Annual*, October 1968, pp.131–48.

27 See Agee entries on Bruce and Dove in Stavitsky and Rothkopf, *Cézanne and American Modernism*, op. cit., pp.180–1, 206–7.

28 Philip Roth, as quoted in Charles McGrath, 'Goodbye Newark, The Place Roth Never Left', *The New York Times* (21 March 2013), p.C1.

29 D.H. Lawrence, *Studies in Classic American Literature*, Penguin, Harmondsworth, 1971, p.29.

30 Alexis de Tocqueville quoted from *Journey to America* as referenced by Barbara Novak in 'On Divers Themes from Nature: A Selection of Texts', in Kynaston McShine (ed.), *The Natural Paradise: Painting in America, 1800–1950*, exh. cat., The Museum of Modern Art, New York, 1976, p.62.

31 Leo Marx, *The Machine in the Garden: Technology and the Pastoral Ideal in America*, Oxford University Press, New York, 1964.

32 Frumkin & Struve Gallery, *Frank Lloyd Wright: Wasmuth Portfolio*, Frumkin & Struve Gallery, Chicago, 1980.

33 Roberta Smith, 'Out of Berlin, the Heart of an Artist: Marsden Hartley Gets his Due in Berlin', *The New York Times* (12 June 2014), p.AR20.

34 Gail Scott's *Marsden Hartley*, Abbeville Press, New York, 1988, is the best overview of the artist and his work.

35 Ibid., p.26.

36 Ibid., p.31. See plate 19.

37 Melville, *Moby-Dick*, op. cit., p.16.

38 Marsden Hartley, *Adventures in the Arts: Informal Chapters on Painters, Vaudeville and Poets*, Boni and Liveright, New York, 1921, p.40.

39 See Agee, 'Hans Hofmann: Art Like Life Is Real', in *Hans Hofmann: Art Like Life Is Real*, Ameringer McEnery Yohe, New York, 2012; and 'Spirit, Spirituality, and the Cosmos', in *Hans Hofmann: Magnum Opus*, exh. cat., Museum Pfalzgalerie Kaiserslautern, Hatje Cantz, Ostfildern, 2013.

40 Pollock, in an answer to a questionnaire published in *Arts and Architecture* LXI (February 1944), wrote that 'the only American master who interests me is Ryder.' Reprinted in Bryan Robertson, *Jackson Pollock*, Abrams, New York, 1961, p.193. I think he was exaggerating.

41 Roger E. Fry, 'The Art of Albert P. Ryder', *The Burlington Magazine for Connoisseurs* 13:61 (April 1908), pp.55, 59, 62–4.

42 Ibid., p.63.

43 Ibid., p.64.

The Advance to the New 1910–14

1 Henri-Frédéric Amiel, journal entry, 25 November 1861. Reprinted in *Journal: The Journal Intime, Volume 1*, Macmillan, New York, 1895, p.184.

2 We must also give credit to Arthur Wesley Dow (1857–1922), one of the most influential teachers in the development of modern art in America. His ideas regarding simple yet rich harmonies, gradually built up through flat areas of colour and form, defined by sure line, had an impact on many artists including O'Keeffe and Dove, and even

perhaps Milton Avery. Dow had in turn been influenced by Ernest Fenollosa, an expert on Asian art at the Boston Museum of Fine Arts, who believed that harmonies in painting paralleled and indeed embodied the rhythms of music, an idea that extended deeply into American art over the ensuing decades. This also alerts us to the importance of Eastern thinking on American art in the coming years.

3   Matisse, 'Notes of a Painter', op. cit., pp.30–42.

4   See Sarah Greenough, 'Alfred Stieglitz's Photographs of Clouds', Ph.D. Dissertation, University of New Mexico, 1984, as well as her numerous writings on Stieglitz, including her magisterial catalogue raisonné *Alfred Stieglitz, The Key Set: The Alfred Stieglitz Collection of Photographs*, National Gallery of Art, Washington, DC, 2002.

5   See Agee, 'Manuscript Notes' on Raymond Duchamp-Villon, in Agee and Heard Hamilton, *Raymond Duchamp-Villon, 1876–1918*, exh. cat., M. Knoedler & Co., New York, 1967, for a description of these ideas c.1910–14.

6   See Agee in Boyajian, Rutkoski, Agee and Wilkin, *Stuart Davis: A Catalogue Raisonné*, Yale University Art Gallery, New Haven, in association with Yale University Press, 2007.

7   Untitled statement, reprinted in *Mark Rothko 1903–1970*, exh. cat., Tate Gallery, London, 1987.

8   Elaine de Kooning, 'Stuart Davis: True to Life', *Art News* 56 (April 1957), reprinted in Elaine de Kooning, *The Spirit of Abstract Expressionism: Selected Writings*, George Braziller, New York, 1994, pp.156–7.

9   Quoted in Agee, '1909–February 1913', in Boyajian et al., *Stuart Davis: A Catalogue Raisonné*, op. cit., vol.1, p.46.

10 Caffin, 'Henri-Matisse', op. cit., pp.17–18.

11 See Robert Hunter, 'The Rewards and Disappointments of the Ashcan School: The Early Career of Stuart Davis', in Lowery Stokes Sims, *Stuart Davis: American Painter*, exh. cat., The Metropolitan Museum of Art, New York, 1991, p.31.

12 See Agee, essay on early Davis, '1920–1926', in Boyajian et al., *Stuart Davis: A Catalogue Raisonné*, op. cit., vol.1, pp.57–66.

13 Quoted in Agee, 'Stuart Davis in the 1960s: "The Amazing Continuity"', in Sims, *Stuart Davis: American Painter*, op. cit., p.20.

14 Quoted in Harlan B. Phillips, *Stuart Davis Reminisces: As Recorded in Talks with Dr. Harlan B. Phillips* (unpublished transcription of interviews with the artist, original bound typescript in the Estate of Stuart Davis archives), Archives of American Art, Brandeis University, New York, 1962, pp.6–7.

15 See Agee and Karen Wilkin, *Stuart Davis: Black and White*, exh. cat., Salander-O'Reilly Galleries, New York, 1985.

16 For more on John Sloan, see Hunter, 'The Rewards and Disappointments of the Ashcan School', op. cit., pp.31–44.

17 John Sloan and Helen Farr Sloan, *Gist of Art: Principles and Practice Expounded in the Classroom and Studio*, American Artists Group, New York, 1944, p.209.

18 Edward Hopper, 'John Sloan and the Philadelphians', *The Arts* 11:4 (April 1927), pp.169–78. Many thanks to Francis M Naumann for his expertise on the subject.

19 See Agee, Irving Sandler and Karen Wilkin, *American Vanguards: Graham, Davis, Gorky, De Kooning, and Their Circle, 1927–1942*, exh. cat., Addison Gallery of American Art, Phillips Academy, Andover, MA, 2011.

20 The Armory Show opened first in New York from 17 February 1913 to 15 March 1914 at the 69th Regiment Armory; then at the Art Institute of Chicago from 24 March 1913 to 16 April 1913; and finally at the Copley Society in Boston from 28 April 1913 to 19 May 1913.

21 See Francis M. Naumann, '"An Explosion in a Shingle Factory": Marcel Duchamp's *Nude Descending a Staircase (No. 2)*', in Marilyn Kushner, Kimberly Orcutt and Casey Nelson Blake (eds), *The Armory Show at 100: Modernism and Revolution*, exh. cat., New-York Historical Society, New York, 2013, pp.203–9.

22 See Melissa Renn, 'Beyond the "Shingle Factory": The Armory Show in the Popular Press after 1913', *Journal of Curatorial Studies* 2:3 (October 2013), pp.384–404.

23 See Agee, 'Henri Matisse at the Armory Show – And Beyond', in Kushner et al., *The Armory Show at 100*, op. cit., pp.219–25.

24 For full accounts see Agee, *Morton Livingston Schamberg (1881–1918)*, exh. cat., Salander-O'Reilly Galleries, New York, 1982, and *Morton Livingston Schamberg (1881–1918): The Machine Pastels*, exh. cat., Salander-O'Reilly Galleries, New York, 1986.

25 See Agee, essays in *Sam Francis: Paintings, 1947–1990*, Museum of Contemporary Art, Los Angeles, 1999, and *Sam Francis: Catalogue Raisonné of Canvas and Panel Paintings, 1946–1994*, University of California Press, Berkeley, 2011.

26 William Rubin noted this to the author, c.1970.

27 See Agee, *Synchromism and Color Principles in American Painting 1910 –1930*, M. Knoedler & Co., New York, 1965, which first researched and presented these ideas, and in which I laid the groundwork of my present views on colour as the binding agent in American art for the last 100 years. See also Gail Levin, *Synchromism and American Color Abstraction, 1910–1925*, exh. cat., Whitney Museum of American Art, New York, 1977.

28 See Agee, *Synchromism and Color Principles*, op. cit., and essay in *Masterpieces of American Modernism: From the Vilcek Collection*, Merrell, London and New York, 2013, pp.15–35.

29 Andrew Dasburg, 'Cubism – Its Rise and Influence', *The Arts* 4:5 (November 1923), pp.279–84.

30 Rachael Z. DeLue, 'With Color', in *Inventing Abstraction 1910–1925: How a Radical Idea Changed Modern Art*, exh. cat., The Museum of Modern Art, New York, 2012, p.101.

31 Agee, *Synchromism and Color Principles*, op. cit.

32 See Agee, 'Manuscript Notes', op. cit., f.n. 139.

33 See Wassily Kandinsky, *On the Spiritual in Art*, Solomon R. Guggenheim Foundation, New York, 1946.

34 See William James, *The Varieties of Religious Experience: A Study in Human Nature*, Floating Press, Waiheke Island, 2008.

35 Scott, *Marsden Hartley*, op. cit., p.39.

The World Changed Forever 1914–18

1   Picasso, as quoted in Richardson, *A Life of Picasso*, op. cit., vol.2, p.345.

2   Kenneth Silver, *Esprit de corps: The Art of the Parisian Avant-Garde and the First World War, 1914–1925*, Princeton University Press, Princeton, 1989.

3   Jean Cocteau, 'Return to Order', published in 1926.

4   The last two paintings of the series are titled *Composition I* and *Composition II*. The numerical designations of the Compositions were not Bruce's but were assigned in the order in which they were purchased by Katherine Dreier. Based on stylistic analysis, we can postulate with some certainly the order of execution of the six paintings as follows: first, *Composition III*, then *VI*, *V*, and *IV*, and lastly *I* and *II*. See Agee, 'The Recovery of a Forgotten Modern Master', in Agee and Rose, *Patrick Henry Bruce, American Modernist*, op. cit., p.22.

5   See Agee essays in *James Henry Daugherty*, exh. cat., Robert Schoelkopf Gallery, New York, 1971; *James H. Daugherty: An Exhibition of Work from Seven Decades*, exh. cat., Westport-Western Arts Council Gallery, Westport, 1983; *James Daugherty: Works from the Estate of the Artist*, exh. cat., Salander-O'Reilly Galleries, New York, 1988; and *James Daugherty: Late Abstractions*, exh. cat., Spanierman Gallery, New York, 2002; *In his Image: 60 Biblical Paintings by James H. Daugherty (1887–1974)*, exh. cat., First Presbyterian Church at Caldwell, Caldwell, 2003. See also William A. Camfield et al., *Francis Picabia Catalogue Raisonné: Volume 1*, Mercatorfonds, Brussels, 2014.

6   James Daugherty Papers, Archives of American Art, Smithsonian Institution, Washington, DC.

7   See Will South, *Color, Myth, and Music: Stanton MacDonald-Wright and Synchromism*, exh. cat., North Carolina Museum of Art, Raleigh, 2001, for an excellent and full discussion of the artist.

8 Stanton Macdonald-Wright, 'Influence of Aviation on Art: The Accentuation of Individuality', *Ace: The Aviation Magazine of the West* 1:2 (September 1919), pp.11–12.

9 See Agee, 'Willard Huntington Wright and the Synchromists: Notes on the Forum Exhibition', *Archives of American Art Journal* 30:1–4 (1990), pp.88–93.

10 See Agee and Rose, *Patrick Henry Bruce, American Modernist*, op. cit., and Silver, *Esprit de corps*, op. cit.

11 Tristan Tzara, 'Dada vs. Art', in *Dada 1916–1923*, Sidney Janis, New York, 1953.

12 See Agee, 'New York Dada, 1910–1930', *Art News Annual* 34 (1968), pp.105–13.

13 Benjamin de Casseres, 'The Ironical in Art', *Camera Work* (April 1912), pp.17–19.

14 Agee, 'New York Dada', op. cit.

15 For full Picabia coverage, see the monumental monograph by William A. Camfield, *Francis Picabia: His Art, Life, and Times*, Princeton University Press, Princeton, 1979.

16 See Agee, 'New York Dada', op. cit., and Francis Naumann, *Walter Conrad Arensberg: Poet, Patron and Participant in the New York Avant-garde, 1915–1920*, Philadelphia Museum of Art, Philadelphia, 1980.

17 Sarah Archino, 'Reframing the Narrative of Dada in New York, 1910–1926', Ph.D. Dissertation, The Graduate Center, City University of New York, 2012.

18 Agee, 'New York Dada', op. cit., p.108.

19 For the only correct accounts, see ibid. and Gail Stavitsky, *Precisionism in America, 1915–1941: Reordering Reality*, exh. cat., Abrams in association with the Montclair Art Museum, New York, 1994.

20 Morton Livingston Schamberg, statement in 'Post-Impression Exhibit Awaited', *Philadelphia Inquirer* (19 January 1913), sec. 2, p.3.

21 Museum of Art, Rhode Island School of Design, 'Selection V', Museum of Art, Rhode Island School of Design, Providence, 1975.

22 Max Weber, Foreword, *Cézanne Exhibition: Through January Nineteen Sixteen: Catalogue*, exh. cat., Montross Gallery, New York, 1915.

No Retreat: Advances in Modern American Art: 1919–29

1 Gertrude Stein, as quoted by John Hightower in *Four Americans in Paris*, The Museum of Modern Art, New York, 1970, p.8.

2 Marcel Duchamp, interview with the author, 29 November 1963.

3 Barbara Haskell, *Charles Demuth*, Whitney Museum of American Art in association with Harry N. Abrams, New York, 1987.

4 See Diane Kelder (ed.), *Stuart Davis, Documentary Monographs in Modern Art*, Praeger, New York, 1971, p.24 for this and other writings in full.

5 See Agee, 'Gerald Murphy, Painter: Recent Discoveries.

New Observations', *Arts Magazine* 59 (May 1985), pp.81–9.

6 See Wanda Corn's essay on Gerald Murphy's *Villa America*, in William Agee and Elizabeth Armstrong, *Villa America*, exh. cat., Orange County Museum of Art, Newport Beach, 2005, pp.59–60.

7 Marsden Hartley's 'The Importance of Being Dada' was first published in *International Studio*, 74 (November 1921) and again in *Adventures in the Arts* in the same year. See Hartley, 'The Importance of Being Dada', in *Adventures in the Arts: Informal Chapters on Painters, Vaudeville and Poets*, Boni and Liveright, New York, 1921.

8 Hans Hofmann, 'Search for the Real', in Sara T. Weeks and Bartlett H. Hayes (eds), *Search for the Real, and Other Essays*, Addison Gallery of American Art, Andover, MA, 1948 (reprinted MIT Press, Cambridge, MA, 1967).

9 Stieglitz to Dove, Lake George, 28 August 1920, reprinted in Ann Lee Morgan (ed.), *Dear Stieglitz, Dear Dove*, University of Delaware, Newark, 1988, p.72.

10 Dove to Stieglitz, probably August 1921, reprinted in ibid., p.75.

11 Dove, diary entries on 1, 7 and 8 October 1924, microfilm roll N70-52, frame 41, Archives of American Art, Smithsonian Institution, Washington, DC.

12 Helen Torr diaries, 30 January 1926, microfilm roll N70-52, frame 130, Archives of American Art, Smithsonian Insitution, Washington, DC. Stieglitz, on 4 December 1924, frames 56–7, same source, told Dove he couldn't wait to show Dove's collage of himself to Duchamp.

13 See Étienne-Jules Marey, *Movement*, D. Appleton and Company, New York, 1895, pp.57, 61, 136, 144, 181 and 209. Confirmed by Duchamp in interviews with the author, March 1963.

14 I am grateful to the art historians Linda Dalrymple Henderson and Francis M. Naumann who have generously offered their insight and expertise. See Linda Dalrymple Henderson, 'X Rays and the Quest for Invisible Reality in the Art of Kupka, Duchamp and the Cubists', in *Art Journal* 47:4 (Winter 1988), pp.323–40; 'Duchamp's First Quest for the Invisible: X-Rays, Transparency, and Internal Views of the Figure, 1911–1912', in *Duchamp in Context: Science and Technology in the 'Large Glass' and Related Works*, Princeton University Press, Princeton, 1998, pp.3–15; 'Vibratory Modernism: Boccioni, Kupka, and the Ether of Space', in *From Energy to Information: Representation in Science and Technology, Art, and Literature*, Stanford University Press, Stanford, 2002, pp.126–49. See also Francis M. Naumann, 'Nude Descending a Staircase', in *The Recurrent, Haunting Ghost: Essays on the Art, Life and Legacy of Marcel Duchamp*, Readymade Press, New York, 2012, pp.13–29.

15 Katherine Dreier referred to Dove as 'the only American Dadaist' after seeing his assemblages in 1926. See Francis M. Naumann with Beth Venn, *Making Mischief: Dada Invades New York*, exh. cat. Whitney Museum of American Art, New York, 1996, p.207.

16 See Agee, essay on Dove's *Moon and Sea II*, in Agee and Armstrong, *Villa America*, op. cit., pp.55–6.

17 Quoted in Rudi Blesh, *Stuart Davis*, Grove, New York, 1960, p.17.

18 Ibid.

19 Ibid., p.16.

20 See Agee, '1950–55', in Boyajian et al., *Stuart Davis: A Catalogue Raisonné*, op. cit., vol. I, p.102.

21 The comment was made in 1918 on the back of a Gloucester landscape. Stuart Davis Papers, 1918, Harvard University Art Museums, Fogg Art Museum, Cambridge, MA.

22 Davis's writings are partly published in *Stuart Davis*, American Artists Group, New York, 1945.

23 Stuart Davis, *Journal, 1920–22*, n.p., Pierpont Morgan Library, New York. See also Agee, *Stuart Davis: The Breakthrough Years, 1922–1924*, exh. cat., Salander-O'Reilly Galleries, New York, 1967, n.p.

24 Blesh, *Stuart Davis*, op. cit., p.58.

25 See Davis, *Journal, 1920–22*, op. cit.

26 Quoted in Agee, '1920–26', in Boyajian et al., *Stuart Davis: A Catalogue Raisonné, Volume 1*, op. cit., p.64.

27 Ibid., pp.57–66; for another view, see the order proposed by Ani Boyajian and Mark Rutkoski in ibid.

28 'Picasso Speaks', *The Arts* (May 1923), pp.315–26, reprinted in Alfred H. Barr, Jr., *Picasso*, Rizzoli, New York, 1946, pp.270–1.

29 See Davis, *Journal, 1920–22*, op. cit.

30 See Agee, *Stuart Davis (1892–1964)*, op. cit.

31 Ibid., and Agee, '1920–26', in Boyajian et al., *Stuart Davis: A Catalogue Raisonné, Volume 2*, op. cit., pp.57–66.

32 Ibid.

33 See Agee, '1950–55', in ibid., pp.98–103.

34 Clement Greenberg, 'Review of Exhibitions of the Pyramid Group and Alfred Maurer', *The Nation* (14 December 1947), reprinted in O'Brian (ed.), *Clement Greenberg: The Collected Essays and Criticism, Volume 2*, op. cit., p.190. See also Agee, 'The Tommy and Gill LiPuma Collection', op. cit.

35 See Meyer Schapiro, 'The Apples of Cézanne: an Essay on the Meaning of Still-life', *Art News Annual* XXXIV (1968), pp.35–53.

36 Quoted in Michael Doran, *Conversations with Cézanne*, University of California Press, Berkeley, 2001, p.39.

37 Joshua Taylor, 'Preface', in *Alfred A. Maurer, 1868–1932*, exh. cat., Smithsonian Institution Press, Washington, DC, 1973, p.12.

38 Hans Hofmann, 'Homage to A.H. Maurer', Berthe Schaeffer Gallery, New York, 12 October 1950.

Modern Art Marches On:
The 1930s

1 This is still the dominant approach of much art history, even today. That it was certainly the approach in 1968 is evidenced by the response to the exhibition 'The 1930s: Painting & Sculpture in America', organized that year by the author at the Whitney Museum of American Art. The show covered all phases of painting and sculpture of the 1930s – probably too ambitious a goal, and to be sure it had its flaws, but largely it went against the grain with its inclusion of so much abstracting art. The flow of anger, outrage even, from artists, critics and museum personnel that quickly descended upon it came as a surprise. The Whitney's directors swiftly organized a symposium to give vent to the almost universal condemnation of the show. One speaker after another trooped to the microphone to complain that this was not a true picture of the 1930s. The 1930s were hard times of the Depression, unemployment, poverty, and social unrest. The assumption was that art always automatically followed the dominant social and political currents of the day. Harold Rosenberg claimed that the failed socialist agenda of the period deserved only failed art, and wrote: 'The 1930s is a good show – much better, indeed, than the 1930s deserve (except that the first thing anything deserves is itself)', perhaps the last polemic of the American cultural inferiority complex to be manifested by a well-known critic. See Harold Rosenberg, 'The Art World: The Thirties', *The New Yorker* (30 November 1968), p.206.

2 Quoted in Irving Sandler, *From Avant-Garde to Pluralism: An On-the-Spot History,* Hard Press Editions, Lenox, 2006, p.35.

3 See Constance Rourke, *Charles Sheeler, Artist in the American Tradition*, Kennedy Galleries, New York, 1969.

4 For more see Agee, Sandler and Wilkin, *American Vanguards*, op. cit.

5 John Graham, *Systems and Dialectics of Art*, Johns Hopkins Press, Baltimore, 1971.

6 Ibid., pp.75–6.

7 See Agee, *American Vanguards*, op. cit., for more on this.

8 See William Seitz (ed.), *Arshile Gorky: Paintings, Drawings, Studies*, exh. cat., The Museum of Modern Art, New York, 1962, p.7.

9 Quoted by Selden Rodman in *Conversations with Artists*, Devin Adair, New York, 1957, p.82.

10 See John Elderfield, *De Kooning: A Retrospective*, exh. cat., The Museum of Modern Art, New York, 2011; and Willem de Kooning and George Scrivani, *The Collected Writings of Willem de Kooning*, Hanuman Books, Madras and New York, 1988.

11 Quoted in Dore Ashton (ed.), 'Two Statements by Picasso', in *Picasso on Art: A Selection of Views*, Da Capo Press, New York, p.5, first published as 'Picasso Speaks', in *The Arts* (May 1923).

12 John Graham, New York, to Duncan Phillips, Washington, DC, 28 December 1930, The Phillips Collection Archives, Washington, DC.

13 See David Anfam and Matthew Spender, *Arshile Gorky: Portraits*, exh. cat., Gagosian Gallery, New York, 2002.

14 Harold Rosenberg, *Arshile Gorky: The Man, The Time, The Idea*, Horizon Press, New York, 1962, p.25.

15 Willem de Kooning, 'The Renaissance and Order', lecture delivered at Studio 35, autumn 1949, reprinted in Thomas B. Hess, *Willem de Kooning*, The Museum of Modern Art, New York, 1968, pp.141–3.

16 Quoted in Irving Sandler, *The New York School: The Painters and Sculptors of the Fifties*, Harper and Row, New York, 1978, p.9.

17 Willem de Kooning, 'The Renaissance and Order', in Hess, *Willem de Kooning*, op. cit., p.142.

18 Sally Yard, *Willem de Kooning: The First Twenty-Six Years in New York, 1927–1952*, Garland, New York, 1986.

19 Willem de Kooning, 'Content Is a Glimpse', *Location 1*, no.1 (Spring 1963). Excerpts reprinted in *American Artists on Art*, p.21.

20 Interview with Paul Cummings, 6 June 1968, Archives of American Art, Smithsonian Institution, Washington, DC, reprinted in Kenworth Moffett, *Fairfield Porter: Realist Painter in an Age of Abstraction*, Museum of Fine Arts, Boston, 1982, pp.49–60.

21 See Barbara Haskell, 'Swing Time: Reginald Marsh and the Exuberant Chaos of Modern Life', in *Swing Time: Reginald Marsh and Thirties New York*, exh. cat., New-York Historical Society, New York, in association with D. Giles Ltd, London, 2012, pp.10–57; Thomas H. Garver, 'Reginald Marsh and the City that Never Was', in *Reginald Marsh: A Retrospective Exhibition*, exh. cat., Newport Harbor Art Museum, Newport Beach, 1972.

22 Haskell, 'Swing Time', op. cit., p.37.

23 Clement Greenberg, *Artnews* 56:4 (June 1957), reprinted in John O'Brian (ed.), *Clement Greenberg: The Collected Essays and Criticism, Volume 4: Modernism with a Vengeance 1957–1969*, University of Chicago Press, Chicago and London, 1993, p.21.

24 Hofmann, Weeks and Hayes (eds), *Search for the Real*, op. cit., p.7.

25 Frederick Wight, *Hans Hofmann*, University of California Press, Berkeley and Los Angeles, 1957, p.14. See also Agee, *Hans Hofmann: Art Like Life is Real*, op. cit.

26 Ibid.

27 Wight, *Hans Hofmann*, op. cit., p.15.

28 See Agee, *Hans Hofmann: Art Like Life is Real*, op. cit., p.8.

29 Quoted in ibid., p.9.

30 For Dove, see Agee, 'New Directions', op. cit., p.133, and Debra Bricker Balken, 'Continuities and Digressions in the Work of Arthur Dove from 1907 to 1933', in Agee, Balken and Turner, *Arthur Dove: A Retrospective*, op. cit., p.17.

31 See Agee, 'John Marin's Greatness', op. cit., pp.7–21.

32 The Greenberg essay of 1947 and the Kramer essay of 1983 are both reprinted in full in *Arnold Friedman: The Last Years,* Salander-O'Reilly Galleries, New York, 1989, n.p.

33 Guy Eglington, *Art News* (December 1925), otherwise unidentified clipping, Friedman family archives.

34 Clement Greenberg, *Arnold Friedman, 1874–1946, A Memorial*, George Walter Vincent Smith Art Museum, Springfield, MA, 1947.

35 Quoted in Thomas B. Hess, 'Friedman's Tragedy and Triumph', in *Arnold Friedman: The Last Years*, op. cit., n.p. See also Agee, 'Arnold Friedman', in *Arnold Friedman: The Language of Paint*, Hollis Taggart Galleries, New York, 2006.

36 *Still Life with Yellow Flowers and Plaid Tablecloth,* reproduced in Hilton Kramer, *Arnold Friedman (1874–1946), an Exhibition: Paintings, Drawings and Watercolors*, exh. cat., Salander-O'Reilly Galleries, New York, 1986, cat. no.77, pl.20.

37 Clement Greenberg, 'Art', *The Nation*, 15 April 1944.

38 Ibid.

39 Clement Greenberg, 'Art', *The Nation*, 17 March 1945.

40 Ibid.

41 Mark Rothko, 'Memorial Address', New York Ethical Culture Society, 7 January 1965, excerpts reprinted in Burt Chernow, *Milton Avery: A Singular Vision*, The Center for Fine Arts, Miami, 1987, pp.11, 13.

42 Quoted in Stuart Davis calendars, 5 January 1938, Estate of the Artist Archives.

43 Alfred Appel Jr., *The Art of Celebration: Twentieth Century Painting, Literature, Sculpture, Photography, and Jazz*, Alfred A. Knopf, New York, 1992 and 1993, pp.157–59, 162, 164, 165, 166, 178, 228.

44 Quoted in Stuart Davis calendars, 8 June 1938, Estate of the Artist Archives.

45 Gustaf Almenberg, *Notes on Participatory Art: Toward a Manifesto Differentiating it from Open Work, Interactive Art and Relational Art*, AuthorHouse, Milton Keynes, 2010, p.57.

A New World Order:
The 1940s

1 See Pamela Koob, 'Edward Hopper's New York Movie', in *Edward Hopper's New York Movie*, exh. cat., The Bertha and Karl Leubsdorf Art Gallery, Hunter College of the City of New York, New York, 1998, pp.4–18.

2 See Barbara Novak, 'On Divers Themes from Nature', in *The Natural Paradise*, op. cit., pp.60–102.

3 Clement Greenberg, 'Review of the Whitney Annual', *The Nation* (28 December 1946), reprinted in O'Brian (ed.), *Clement Greenberg:*

The Collected Essays and Criticism: Volume 2, op. cit., p.118.

4 See Pamela N. Koob, 'States of Being: Edward Hopper and Symbolist Aesthetics', *American Art* 18:3 (Autumn 2004), pp.52–77.

5 David Anfam, 'Rothko's Hopper: A Strange Wholeness', in Sheena Wagstaff (ed.), *Edward Hopper*, exh. cat., Tate Modern, London, 2004, p.39.

6 McCoubrey, *The American Tradition in Painting*, op. cit., 1963, p.123. This small but extraordinary book gave me my first exposure to the idea of continuity in American art. I am deeply indebted to it.

7 Edward Hopper to Guy Pène du Bois, 11 August 1940, Archives of American Art, New York.

8 Katherine Kuh, *The Artist's Voice: Talks with Seventeen Artists*, Harper & Row, New York, 1962, p.134.

9 Alfred H. Barr, Jr., *Edward Hopper Retrospective Exhibition*, exh. cat., The Museum of Modern Art, New York, 1933, p.15.

10 See David Katz, *The World of Colour*, K. Paul, Trench, Trubner, London, 1935.

11 See Agee, *Charmion Von Wiegand: Improvisations*, exh. cat., Michael Rosenfeld Gallery, New York, 2003.

12 'Are These Men the Best Painters in America Today?', *Look* (3 February 1948), pp.44ff.

13 Clement Greenberg, 'Review of an Exhibition by John Marin', *The Nation* (25 December 1945).

14 See Agee, *John Marin: Between Realism and Abstraction*, exh. cat., Kennedy Galleries, New York, 1997.

15 Quoted in Cleve Gray (ed.), *John Marin by John Marin*, Holt, Reinhardt and Winston, New York, 1977.

16 Ibid.

17 Paul Strand, 'John Marin', *Art Review* (22 January 1922), pp.22–3.

18 Clement Greenberg, 'The Decline of Cubism', *Partisan Review*, 3 (March 1948), reprinted in O'Brian (ed.), *Clement Greenberg: The Collected Essays and Criticism: Volume 2*, op. cit., p.212.

19 Robert Goldwater, 'Arthur Dove', *Perspectives USA*, no.2 (Winter 1953), pp.78–88.

20 Helen Harrison, 'Arthur G. Dove and the Origins of Abstract Expressionism', *American Art* 12:1 (Spring 1998), pp.66–83.

21 See Frederick Wight, *Arthur G. Dove*, University of California Press, Berkeley, 1958; Alan Solomon, *Arthur G. Dove*, Cornell University Press, Ithaca, 1954; Barbara Haskell, *Arthur Dove*, New York Graphic Society, Boston, 1974; Elizabeth Hutton Turner, 'Going Home: Geneva, 1933–1938', in Agee, Bricker Balken and Hutton Turner, *Arthur Dove: A Retrospective*, op. cit., p.10.

22 James W. Lane, 'Dove: Abstract Poet of Color', *Art News* 41 (15–31 May 1942), p.21.

23 Arthur and Helen Torr Dove papers, 1905–75, Archives of American Art, Smithsonian Institution, Washington, DC, reel 40 (1938,1939), 17 December 1942.

24 Renilde Hammacher and Abraham Marie Hammacher, *Van Gogh: A Documentary Biography*, Macmillan, New York, 1982, p.163.

25 Quoted in Avis Berman, 'Artist's Dialogue: A Conversation with Frank Stella', *Architectural Digest* 40:9 (September 1985), p.74.

26 Paul Rosenfeld, 'Arthur G. Dove', in *Port of New York: Essays on Fourteen American Moderns*, Harcourt, Brace, New York, 1924, p.174.

27 Reprinted in Sheldon Reich, *Alfred Maurer*, exh. cat., National Collection of Fine Arts, Washington, DC, 1973, pp.117–18.

28 Clement Greenberg, 'Review of Exhibitions of van Gogh and Alfred Maurer', *Partisan Review* (February 1950), reprinted in John O'Brian (ed.), *Clement Greenberg: The Collected Essays and Criticism, Volume 3*, University of Chicago Press, Chicago, 1993, p.17.

29 See Robert Rosenblum, 'Resurrecting Augustus Vincent Tack', in *The Abstractions of Augustus Vincent Tack (1870–1949)*, M. Knoedler & Co., New York, 1986, p.4.

30 In conversation with William Rubin, Chief Curator of the Museum of Modern Art, c.1970, passed on to the author.

31 See Katy Siegel, *Since '45: America and the Making of Contemporary Art*, Reaktion, London, 2011.

32 See Irving Sandler, *The Triumph of American Painting: A History of Abstract Expressionism*, Harper & Row, New York, 1982.

33 Clement Greenberg, 'Review of an Exhibition of Georgia O'Keeffe', *The Nation* (15 June 1946), reprinted in O'Brian (ed.), *Clement Greenberg: The Collected Essays and Criticism, Volume 2*, op. cit., p.85.

34 Dorothy C. Miller, *Fourteen Americans*, exh. cat., The Museum of Modern Art, New York, 1946, p.8.

35 Robert Motherwell, in ibid., p.36.

36 Ibid., pp.35–6.

37 Ibid.

38 Robert M. Coates, 'The Art Galleries', *The New Yorker* XXII:7 (30 March 1946), p.83.

39 Thomas B. Hess, *Barnett Newman*, Walker and Company, New York, 1969, pp.56–7.

40 See David Anfam, *Jackson Pollock's Mural: Energy Made Visible*, Thames & Hudson, London, 2015, for an excellent in-depth analysis of the painting.

41 Donald Judd, 'Back to Clarity: Interview with Donald Judd', in *Donald Judd*, exh. cat., Ed. Cantz, Stuttgart-Bad Cannstatt, 1989.

42 Francis V. O'Connor, 'Jackson Pollock's Phosphorescence', in *Addison Gallery of American Art: 65 Years*, exh. cat., Addison Gallery of American Art, Phillips Academy, Andover, MA, 1996, pp.448–9.

43 See chapter A New Depth in American Art, for the difference between colour-field and field-of-colour painting.

44 Clement Greenberg, 'Review of Exhibitions of Worden Day, Carl Holty, and Jackson Pollock', *The Nation*, 24 January 1948, reprinted in O'Brian (ed.), *Clement Greenberg: The Collected Essays and Criticism, Volume 2*, op. cit., p.202.

45 Quoyted in Lee Krasner, interview with Dorothy Seckler, 14 December 1964, in the Lee Krasner Papers (LKP), Archives of American Art, Smithsonian Institution, Washington, DC.

46 Conversation with the author, in front of the painting.

47 Hofmann, Weeks and Hayes, *Search for the Real*, op. cit., p.67.

48 David Anfam, 'Still's Journey', in Anfam and Sobel, *Clyfford Still: The Artist's Museum*, Skira Rizzoli, New York, 2012, pp.57–8.

49 Quoted in Sam Hunter, *Masters of the Fifties: American Abstract Painting from Pollock to Stella*, exh. cat., Marisa del Re Gallery, New York, 1985, n.p.

50 See Anfam, *Jackson Pollock's Mural*, op. cit., for a moving account of Still and his relationship with Pollock.

51 George L.K. Morris, 'A Brief Encounter with Matisse', *Life* 69 (28 August 1970), pp.44–6.

52 Dore Ashton, *About Rothko*, Da Capo Press, Cambridge, MA, 2003, p.187.

53 Adolph Gottlieb and Mark Rothko with the assistance of Barnett Newman, letter to Edward Alden Jewell, Art Editor, *The New York Times* (7 June 1943), reprinted in *Adolph Gottlieb: A Retrospective*, Arts Publisher in association with the Adolph and Esther Gottlieb Foundation, New York, 1981, p.169.

54 Statement to Edwin A. Jewell, often referred to as a manifesto, written 7 June 1943; published 13 June 1943.

55 See Agee, essay in *Sam Francis, Paintings 1947–1990*, Museum of Contemporary Art, Los Angeles, 1999.

56 Judd, 'In the Galleries: Stuart Davis', op. cit., pp.55–6.

57 See Rosalind Krauss, 'Grids', *October* 9 (Summer 1979), p.31.

58 Statement in Russell Lynes, *Ralston Crawford*, exh. cat., Middendorf/ Lane Gallery, Washington, DC, 1977.

59 Hans Hofmann, introduction to *Exhibition of Paintings by Burgoyne Diller*, exh. brochure, Contemporary Arts, New York, 28 February– 18 March 1933.

60 Michael Plante, '"Things to Cover Walls": Ellsworth Kelly's Paris Paintings and the Tradition of Mural Decoration', *American Art* 9:1 (Spring 1995), pp.37–53.

61 Quoted by Diane Dewey in Raymond W. Merritt (ed.), *Shared Space: The Joseph M. Cohen Collection*, Cygnet Foundation, New York, 2009, p.302.

62 See *Henri Matisse: The Cut-Outs*, exh. cat., The Museum of Modern Art, New York, 2014.

63 James Johnson Sweeney, *Sam Francis*, exh. cat., The Museum of Fine Arts, Houston, and University Art Museum, Berkeley, 1967, p.21.

A New Depth in American Art: The 1950s

1. Philip Roth, *Reading Myself and Others*, Vintage International, New York, 2001, *passim*.
2. See Hofmann, Weeks and Hayes (ed.), *Search for the Real, and Other Essays*, op. cit.
3. *The Ice Man Cometh* (1946), *A Streetcar Named Desire* (1947), *Mister Roberts* (1948), *Death of a Salesman* (1949).
4. *Carousel* (1945), *Annie Get Your Gun* (1946), *South Pacific* (1949), *Guys and Dolls* (1950), *My Fair Lady* (1956), *The Sound of Music* (1959).
5. Stuart Davis calendar, 24 February and 3 March 1951, Yale University Archives, New Haven.
6. Stuart Davis, 'What Abstract Art Means to Me: Statements by Six American Artists: Stuart Davis', *Museum of Modern Art Bulletin* 18:3 (Spring 1951), reprinted in Kelder (ed.), *Stuart Davis, Documentary Monographs in Modern Art*, op. cit., pp.142–3.
7. Stuart Davis calendar, 6 January 1954, Collection of Earl Davis.
8. Elaine de Kooning, 'Stuart Davis: True to Life', op. cit., p.155.
9. See Boyajian et al., *Stuart Davis: A Catalogue Raisonné*, op. cit., vol.III, pp.402–5.
10. David Anfam, 'Who's In, Who's Out: Stamos, Simonds, Stella', lecture, 'Reclaiming American Art: 18th Annual American Art Conference', The Graduate Center, City University of New York, 18 May 2013.
11. John Elderfield, in conversation with the author while viewing the exhibition.
12. Willem de Kooning, 'Content Is a Glimpse', op. cit., p.21.
13. Quoted in Gene Baro, 'The Achievement of Helen Frankenthaler', *Art International* 2:7 (September 1967), p.36. See also John Elderfield, *Frankenthaler*, Abrams, New York, 1989.
14. 'A Conversation: Helen Frankenthaler with Julia Brown', 1997, Connecticut and New York City, reprinted in *After Mountains and Sea: Frankenthaler 1956–1959*, exh. cat., Guggenheim Museum, New York, 1998, p.39.
15. Quoted in Cindy Nemser, 'Interview with Helen Frankenthaler', *Arts Magazine* (November 1971), reprinted in Johnson (ed.), *American Artists on Art*, op. cit., p.55.
16. Quoted in John Elderfield, *Morris Louis*, exh. cat., The Museum of Modern Art, New York, 1986, p.13.
17. See Agee, *Kenneth Noland: The Circle Paintings, 1956–1963*, exh. cat., The Museum of Fine Arts, Houston, 1993.
18. This quotation comes from my own lengthy discussions with Noland from 1990 to 1993. See Agee, 'Kenneth Noland: The Circle Paintings 1956–1963', in ibid., pp.12–45.
19. *Master Paintings from the Phillips Collection, Created for Penshurst Books and the Phillips Collection*, Shorewood Fine Art Books, New York, 1981.
20. Peter Plagens, 'Overwhelmed', *Art in America* 3 (March 2010), pp.41–2.
21. Ibid., p.42.
22. Robert Rauschenberg, in Dorothy C. Miller, *Fourteen Americans*, op. cit., p.58.
23. Henri Matisse, 'Témoignages de peintres: Le noir est une couleur', *Derrière le miroir*, December 1946, pp.2, 6, 7, reprinted in Flam, *Matisse on Art*, op. cit., pp.165–6.
24. See Emily Lembo, 'Primitivism and Mannerism in Henri Matisse's Chapelle du Rosaire', M.A. Thesis, Hunter College, City University of New York, 2014, pp.89–90.
25. See David Anfam, *Abstract Expressionism: A World Elsewhere*, exh. cat., Haunch of Venison, New York, 2008.
26. Kaprow, 'The Legacy of Jackson Pollock', op. cit., pp.24–6, 55–7.
27. Carol Troyen, '"From the Eyes Inward": Paintings and Drawings by Charles Sheeler', in *Charles Sheeler: Paintings and Drawings*, Museum of Fine Arts, Boston, 1987, p.6.
28. Fairfield Porter, 'Art and Knowledge', 1966, reprinted in Rackstraw Downes, *Fairfield Porter: Art in its Own Terms. Selected Criticism, 1935–1975*, Taplinger Press, New York, 1979, p.259.
29. Porter, unpublished letter to Allen C. DuBois, 8 April 1963, Archives of American Art, Smithsonian Institution, Washington, DC, roll D-176, frame 444.
30. Fairfield Porter, 'Willem de Kooning', 1959, reprinted in Downes, *Fairfield Porter*, op. cit., p.37.
31. Daniel Catton Rich, 'Seurat's Paintings', in *Seurat: Paintings and Drawings*, exh. cat., The Museum of Modern Art, New York, 1958, pp.20–1.
32. David Smith, 'Second Thoughts on Sculpture', *College Art Journal* 13 (Spring 1954), p.205.
33. See Robert Rosenblum, *Modern Painting and the Northern Romantic Tradition: Friedrich to Rothko*, Harper & Row, New York, 1975; McShine (ed.), *The Natural Paradise: Painting in America, 1800–1950*, op. cit.
34. Donald Judd, 'In the Galleries: Al Jensen', *Arts Magazine* 37 (April 1963), p.52.
35. Ibid.
36. Allan Kaprow, 'The World View of Alfred Jensen', *Art News* 62 (December 1963), pp.28–31, 64–6.
37. Donald Judd, 'Specific Objects', *Arts Yearbook* 8, (1965), reprinted in *Donald Judd: Complete Writings*, op. cit., pp.181–9.
38. Donald Judd, 'Black, White, and Gray' (1964), in ibid., p.117.
39. Lawrence Gowing, 'Paint in America', *New Statesman*, 24 May 1958, reprinted in McCoubrey, *The American Tradition in Painting*, op. cit., p.1.
40. Donald Judd, 'Nationwide Reports: Kansas City Report', *Arts* 37 (December 1963), p.25, reprinted in *Donald Judd: Complete Writings*, op. cit., p.103. See Agee, 'Judd and the Endless Possibilities of Color', in Marianne Stockebrand (ed.), *Donald Judd: The Multicolored Works*, Yale University Press, New Haven, 2014; 'Judd and Chamberlain: A Working Dialogue, a "Kind of Sympathy"', in *It's All in the Fit: The Work of John Chamberlain*, The Chinati Foundation, Marfa, 2006, pp.213–31; 'Judd and the Endless Possibilities of Color', in Dietmar Elger (ed.), *Donald Judd, Colorist*, Hatje Cantz Publishers, Bonn, 2000, pp.33–51; 'Donald Judd in Retrospect: An Appreciation', in *Donald Judd: Sculpture*, exh. cat., Pace Wildenstein Gallery, New York, 1994, pp.5–17; 'Some Notes on Early Judd', in *Donald Judd: Early Works*, Blum Helman, New York, 1983, n.p.; *The Sculpture of Donald Judd*, Art Museum of South Texas, Corpus Christi, 1977, pp.5–20; 'Unit–Series–Site: A Judd Lexicon', *Art in America*, 63, 3 (May–June 1975), pp.40–9; 'Don Judd', in *Don Judd*, exh. cat., Whitney Museum of American Art, New York, 1968, n.p.
41. See Kaprow, 'The Legacy of Jackson Pollock', op. cit.
42. 'Questions to Stella and Judd (Interview by Bruce Glaser)', first broadcast on WBAI-FM, New York, February 1964, as 'New Nihilism or New Art?' and edited by Lucy Lippard for *Art News*, September 1966, reprinted in Johnson (ed.), *American Artists on Art*, op. cit.
43. Donald Judd, *Some Aspects of Color in General and Red and Black in Particular*, Sikkens Foundation, Sassenheim, Netherlands, 1993, published in cooperation with the Stedelijk Museum, Amsterdam.
44. After Smith's death, his executor, Clement Greenberg, had the paint stripped from some of the sculptures, claiming colour was antithetical to sculpture. It was a brazen and wanton act, ignoring the fact that traditionally in classical ages sculpture was always painted, and that Smith had cherished its use.
45. Edward F. Fry, entry for *Bec-Dida Day* in *David Smith*, Solomon R. Guggenheim Foundation, New York, 1969, p.130.
46. Ibid.
47. E.A. Carmean, Jr., 'Forged in the Classical Tradition', *Wall Street Journal* (15 October 2011), p.C19.
48. Ibid.
49. Dorothy Seckler, unpublished interview with Conrad Marca-Relli, 10 June 1965, Archives of American Art, Detroit.
50. Ibid.

For Better or for Worse: The 1960s

1. Quoted in Michael Lobel, *Image Duplicator: Roy Lichtenstein and the Emergence of Pop Art*, Yale University Press, New Haven, 2002, p.155.
2. Stuart Davis, 'Memo on Mondrian', *Arts Yearbook* 4 (1961), pp.66–8.
3. William Innes Homer, 'Stuart Davis, 1894–1964: Last Interview', *Art News* 63 (5 September 1964), pp.43, 56.
4. In conversation with the author, c.2004.

5   Judd, *Some Aspects of Color in General*, op. cit., p.5.
6   Hilton Kramer, 'Display of Judd Art Defines an Attitude', *The New York Times* (14 May 1971), p.48.
7   See Agee, 'Judd and the Endless Possibilities of Color', in Marianne Stockebrand (ed.), *Donald Judd*, op. cit., pp.33–51.
8   William Rubin, 'The International Style: Notes on the Pittsburgh Triennial', *Art International* (20 November 1961), pp.26–34.
9   Donald Judd, 'Local History[1964]', in *Donald Judd, Complete Writings*, op. cit., pp.152–3.
10 From an unpublished interview with Michael Auping from 1 October 1981, quoted in Michael Auping, *John Chamberlain Reliefs, 1960–1892, John and Mable Ringling Museum of Art Foundation, Sarasota, 1982, p.12*.
11 David J. Getsy, 'Immoderate Couplings', in *It's All in the Fit*, op. cit., p.197.
12 In conversation with the author, c.2006.
13 Donald Judd, 'In the Galleries: John Chamberlain', *Arts*, February 1960, reprinted in *Donald Judd, Complete Writings*, op. cit., p.10.
14 Ibid.
15 Ibid.
16 Donald Judd, *John Chamberlain: New Sculpture*, exh. cat., The Pace Gallery, New York, 1989.
17 Donald Judd, 'Chamberlain: Another View', *Art International* (Christmas–New Year 1963–4), reprinted in *Donald Judd, Complete Writings*, op. cit., pp.108–10.
18 Ibid.
19 Quoted in Lobel, *Image Duplicator*, op. cit., p.155.
20 Cindy Nemser, 'A Conversation with Eva Hesse (1970)', reprinted in Mignon Nixon (ed.), *Eva Hesse*, MIT Press, Cambridge, MA, 2002, p.24.
21 Ibid., p.7.
22 Thomas Crow, 'Rothko and Hesse between Painting and Sculpture', lecture delivered at the 2011 Symposium 'Challenging 1945 – Exploring Continuities in American Art, 1890s to the Present', Santa Fe, New Mexico. See also Thomas Crow's article, 'Unknowing Parallels: The Last Artistic Thoughts of Mark Rothko and Eva Hesse', in *Late Thoughts: Reflections on Artists and Composers at Work*, Getty Research Institute, Los Angeles, 2006, pp.55–61.
23 Claes Oldenburg, 'I am for an art…', in Claes Oldenburg and Emmett Williams, *Store Days, Documents from the Store (1961) and Ray Gun Theater (1962)*, Something Else Press, New York, 1967, reprinted in Johnson (ed.), *American Artists on Art*, opus. cit., p.98.
24 Willard Huntington Wright, *Modern Painting, its Tendency and Meaning*, John Lane, New York, 1915.
25 Quoted in Carol Salus, 'Behind the Celestial Enchantment: The Private Self and Early Movie Star Portraits of Andy Warhol', in Anna-Teresa Tymieniecka (ed.), *The Poetry of Life in Literature*, Kluwer Academic Publishers, Dordrecht, 2000, pp.195, 205 (n.1); Patrick Smith, *Andy Warhol's Art and Films*, UMI Press, Ann Arbor, 1986, p.367.
26 See Erika Doss, 'In Conversation: Disputation Over Sacred Space in Contemporary America', *Material Religion: The Journal of Objects, Art, and Belief* 7:2 (July 2011), pp.269–71.
27 *MoMA Highlights*, The Museum of Modern Art, New York, 2004, p.233.
28 Statement by Ray Parker in *Catalogue of the American Collection*, Tate Gallery, London, 1978, p.5.
29 Ibid.
30 Ibid.
31 Ibid.
32 Letter to Gerald Nordland, quoted in Gerald Nordland, 'A Few Thoughts on Ray Parker and his Work', in Agee et al., *Ray Parker 1922–1990*, exh. cat., The Bertha and Karl Leubsdorf Art Gallery, Hunter College, New York, 1990, p.17.
33 Statement by Ray Parker in *Catalogue of the American Collection*, Tate Gallery, London, 1978, p.5.
34 Ibid.
35 See Agee and Michael Fehr, *Sanford Wurmfeld Cyclorama 2000*, Karl Ernst Osthaus-Museum, Hagen, Germany, 2000.
36 See Agee, essay in *Visual Sensations: The Paintings of Robert Swain, 1967–2010*, exh. cat., Hunter College/Times Square Gallery, New York, 2010.
37 William Rubin, *Frank Stella*, The Museum of Modern Art, New York, 1970, p.149.
38 In conversation with the author, 2006.
39 Frank Stella, 'The Artist of the Century', *American Heritage* 50:7 (November 1999), pp.14–17.
40 Ibid.
41 See Agee, 'Hans Hofmann: Art Like Life Is Real', op. cit.; and 'Spirit, Spirituality, and the Cosmos', in *Hans Hofmann: Magnum Opus*, op. cit.
42 See William C Agee, 'Kenneth Noland: The Last Paintings', in *Kenneth Noland: Into the Cool* (New York: Pace Gallery, 2017).
43 Hans Hofmann, 'Homage to A.H. Maurer', Berthe Schaeffer Gallery, New York, 12 October 1950.
44 Kenneth Noland, statement quoted by Philip Leider, 'The Thing in Painting Is Color', *The New York Times* (25 August 1968), reprinted in Johnson (ed.), *American Artists on Art*, opus. cit., p.50.
45 Michael Fried, 'Jules Olitski's New Paintings', *Artforum* 4 (November 1965), p.38.
46 Robert L. Herbert, 'Method and Meaning in Monet', *Art in America* 67 (September 1979), p.90.
47 Jules Olitski, 'Painting in Color', *Artforum* (January 1967), reprinted in Johnson (ed.), *American Artists on Art*, op. cit. p.50.
48 Statement, *Catalogue of the Collection of the Société Anonyme*, Yale University Art Gallery, New Haven, 1949, p.182.
49 See William C Agee, 'How *The Red Studio* Shaped American Art', in Gail Stravitsky et al., *Matisse and American Art* (Montclair: Montclair Art Museum, 2017). 58-69.
50 In conversation with the author.
51 See Agee, 'Donald Judd in Retrospect: An Appreciation', op. cit., p.7.
52 See Edward F. Fry, *David Smith*, op. cit.
53 Robert Smithson, 'The Spiral Jetty', in Gyorgy Kepes (ed.), *Arts of the Environment*, G. Braziller, New York, 1972, reprinted in Johnson (ed.), *American Artists on Art*, op. cit., p.175. See also Jennifer Roberts, *Mirror-travels: Robert Smithson and History*, Yale University Press, New Haven, 2004.
54 Smithson, 'The Spiral Jetty', op. cit. p.169.
55 T.S. Eliot, 'Little Gidding', from *Four Quartets* (1944).

Books

William C. Agee and Debra Burchett-Lere, *Sam Francis: Catalogue Raisonné of Canvas and Panel Paintings, 1946–1994*, Berkeley, 2011.

William C. Agee, Lewis Kachur, Rick Kinsel and Emily Schuchardt Navratil, *Masterpieces of American Modernism: From the Vilcek Collection*, London and New York, 2013.

William C. Agee, Richard Shiff and Marianne Stockebrand, *Donald Judd: The Multicolored Works*, New Haven, 2014.

David Anfam, *Abstract Expressionsim*, New York, 1990.

—, *Jackson Pollock's Mural: Energy Made Visible*, London, 2015.

David Anfam and Dean Sobel, *Clyfford Still: The Artist's Museum*, New York, 2012.

Sylvan Barnet, *A Short Guide to Writing About Art*, Upper Saddle River, 2008.

Ani Boyajian, Mark Rutkoski, William C. Agee and Karen Wilkin, *Stuart Davis: A Catalogue Raisonné*, New Haven, 2007.

William A. Camfield, *Francis Picabia: His Art, Life, and Times*, Princeton, 1979.

Wanda Corn, *The Great American Thing: Modern Art and National Identity, 1915–1935*, Berkeley, 1999.

Erika Doss, *Twentieth-Century American Art*, Oxford, 2002.

Jack Flam, *Matisse on Art*, Berkeley and Los Angeles, 1995.

Bartlett H. Hayes and Sara T. Weeks (eds), *Search for the Real, and Other Essays*, Cambridge, 1967.

Linda Dalrymple Henderson, *From Energy to Information: Representation in Science and Technology, Art, and Literature*, Stanford, 2002.

William Innes Homer, *Stieglitz and the Photo-Secession, 1902*, New York, 2002.

—, *Robert Henri and his Circle*, Ithaca, 1969.

Robert Hughes, *American Visions: The Epic History of Art in America*, New York, 1997.

Donald Judd, *Donald Judd: Complete Writings 1959–1975: Gallery Reviews, Book Reviews, Articles, Letters to the Editor, Reports, Statements, Complaints*, Halifax, 1975.

Lewis Kachur and Karen Wilkin, *The Drawings of Stuart Davis: The Amazing Continuity*, New York, 1982.

John McCoubrey, *The American Tradition in Painting*, New York, 1963.

Leo Marx, *The Machine in the Garden: Technology and the Pastoral Ideal in America*, New York, 1964.

Francis M. Naumann, *New York Dada, 1915–23*, New York, 1994.

—, *The Recurrent, Haunting Ghost: Essays on the Art, Life and Legacy of Marcel Duchamp*, New York, 2012.

Barbara Novak, *American Painting of the Nineteenth Century: Realism, Idealism, and the American Experience*, New York, 1969.

John O'Brian (ed.), *Clement Greenberg: The Collected Essays and Criticism, Volumes 1–4*, University of Chicago Press, Chicago, 1986–93.

Jim Rasenberger, *America, 1908: The Dawn of Flight, the Race to the Pole, the Invention of the Model T, and the Making of a Modern Nation*, New York, 2007.

Jennifer Roberts, *Mirror-travels: Robert Smithson and History*, New Haven, 2004.

Robert Rosenblum, *Modern Painting in the Northern Romantic Tradition: Friedrich to Rothko*, New York, 1975.

Irving Sandler, *From Avant-Garde to Pluralism: An On-the-Spot History*, Lenox, 2006.

—, *The Triumph of American Painting: A History of Abstract Expressionism*, New York, 1982.

Gail Scott, *Marsden Hartley*, New York, 1988.

Kenneth Silver, *Esprit de corps: The Art of the Parisian Avant-Garde and the First World War, 1914–1925*, Princeton, 1989.

Judy Sund, *Van Gogh*, London and New York, 2002.

—, *True to Temperament: Van Gogh and French Naturalist Literature*, Cambridge and New York, 1992.

Gail Stavitsky et al., *Matisse and American Art*, Montclair, 2017.

Karen Wilkin, *David Smith*, New York, 1984.

—, *David Smith: Two Into Three Dimensions*, Miami, 2000.

—, *Stuart Davis*, New York, 1987.

Willard Huntington Wright, *Modern Painting, Its Tendency and Meaning*, New York, 1915.

Exhibition Catalogues

William C. Agee, *Arnold Friedman: The Language of Paint*, Hollis Taggart Galleries, New York, 2006.

—, *Charmion Von Wiegand: Improvisations*, Michael Rosenfeld Gallery, New York, 2003.

—, *Don Judd*, Whitney Museum of American Art, New York, 1968.

—, *Donald Judd: Sculpture*, Pace Wildenstein Gallery, New York, 1994.

—, *Hans Hofmann: Art Like Life Is Real*, Ameringer, McEnery and Yohe Gallery, New York, 2012.

—, *John Marin: Between Realism and Abstraction*, Kennedy Galleries, New York, 1997.

—, *John Marin: The Late Oils*, Adelson Galleries, New York, 2008.

—, *Kenneth Noland: The Circle Paintings, 1956–1963*, The Museum of Fine Arts, Houston, 1993.

—, *Morton Livingston Schamberg (1881–1918): The Machine Pastels*, Salander-O'Reilly Galleries, New York, 1986.

—, *Sam Francis: Paintings, 1947–1990*, Museum of Contemporary Art, Los Angeles, 1999.

—, *Sam Francis: Paintings & Works on Paper from the 1950s*, Lawrence Rubin Greenberg Van Doren Fine Art, New York, 1999.

—, *Sam Francis: The Edge*, Richard Gray Gallery, New York and Chicago, 2000.

—, *Stuart Davis: The Breakthrough Years, 1922–1924*, Salander-O'Reilly Galleries, New York, 1987.

—, *Synchromism and Color Principles in American Painting 1910–1930*, M. Knoedler Gallery, New York, 1965.

William C. Agee and Elizabeth Armstrong, *Villa America*, Orange County Museum of Art, Newport Beach, 2005.

William C. Agee, Debra Bricker Balken and Elizabeth Hutton Turner, *Arthur Dove: A Retrospective*, Addison Gallery of American Art, Andover, MA, 1997.

William C. Agee, Dietmar Elger and Martin Engler, *Don Judd, Colorist*, Sprengel Museum Hannover, Bonn, 2000.

William C. Agee and George Heard Hamilton, *Raymond Duchamp-Villon, 1876–1918*, M. Knoedler & Co., New York, 1967.

William C. Agee, Tommy LiPuma and Bruce Weber, *High Notes of American Modernism: Selections from the Tommy and Gill LiPuma Collection*, Berry-Hill Galleries, New York, 2002.

William C. Agee and Robert Pincus-Witten, *Sam Francis: 1953–1959*, L&M Arts, New York, 2009.

William C. Agee and Barbara Rose, *Patrick Henry Bruce, American Modernist: A Catalogue Raisonné*, The Museum of Fine Arts, Houston; Museum of Modern Art, New York; Virginia Museum of Fine Arts, 1979.

William C. Agee, Irving Sandler and Karen Wilkin, *American Vanguards: Graham, Davis, Gorky, De Kooning, and Their Circle, 1927–1942*, Addison Gallery of American Art, Andover, MA, 2011.

William C. Agee and Karen Wilkin, *Stuart Davis: Black and White*, Salander-O'Reilly Galleries, New York, 1985.

David Anfam, *Abstract Expressionism: A World Elsewhere*, Haunch of Venison, New York, 2008.

Stacey Epstein, *Alfred Maurer: At the Vanguard of Modernism*, Addison Gallery of American Art, Andover, MA, 2015.

Marilyn Kushner, Kimberly Orcutt and Casey Nelson Blake (eds), *The Armory Show at 100: Modernism and Revolution*, New-York Historical Society, New York, 2013.

Gail Levin, *Synchromism and American Color Abstraction, 1910–1925*, Whitney Museum of American Art, New York, 1977.

Kynaston McShine (ed.), *The Natural Paradise: Painting in America, 1800–1950*, The Museum of Modern Art, New York, 1976.

Francis M. Naumann with Beth Venn, *Making Mischief: Dada Invades New York*, Whitney Museum of American Art, New York, 1996.

Lowery Stokes Sims, *Stuart Davis: American Painter*, The Metropolitan Museum of Art, New York, 1991.

Will South, *Color, Myth, and Music: Stanton MacDonald-Wright and Synchromism*, North Carolina Museum of Art, Raleigh, 2001.

Gail Stavitsky, *Precisionism in America, 1915–1941: Reordering Reality*, Abrams in association with the Montclair Art Museum, New York, 1994.

Gail Stavitsky and Katherine Rothkopf (eds), *Cézanne and American Modernism*, Montclair Art Museum and Baltimore Museum of Art, Montclair and New Haven, 2009.

James Johnson Sweeney, *Sam Francis*, The Museum of Fine Arts, Houston, and University Art Museum, Berkeley, 1967.

Sheena Wagstaff (ed.), *Edward Hopper*, Tate Modern, London, 2004.

Journal Articles/ Chapters of Books

William C. Agee, 'New York Dada, 1910–1930', *Art News Annual* 34 (1968), pp.105–13.

Linda Dalrymple Henderson, 'Duchamp's First Quest for the Invisible: X-Rays, Transparency, and Internal Views of the Figure, 1911–1912', in *Duchamp in Context: Science and Technology in the 'Large Glass' and Related Works*, Princeton, 1998, pp.3–15.

—, 'X Rays and the Quest for Invisible Reality in the Art of Kupka, Duchamp and the Cubists', *Art Journal* 47:4 (Winter 1988), pp.323–40.

Erika Doss, 'In Conversation: Disputation Over Sacred Space in Contemporary America', *Material Religion: The Journal of Objects, Art, and Belief* 7:2 (July 2011), pp.269–71.

Michael Fried, 'Jules Olitski's New Paintings', *Artforum* 4 (November 1965).

Robert Smithson, 'The Spiral Jetty', in Gyorgy Kepes (ed.), *Arts of the Environment*, New York, 1972, pp.222–32.

Dissertations/Theses

Sarah Archino, 'Reframing the Narrative of Dada in New York, 1910–1926', Ph.D. Dissertation, The Graduate Center, City University of New York, 2012.

Alicia Cooper, 'Odilon Redon in America', M.A. Thesis, Hunter College, City University of New York, 2014.

Films

'The Polio Crusade,' PBS documentary. A Sarah Colt Productions film for AMERICANEXPERIENCE. ©2009 WGBH Educational Foundation.

INDEX

          Modern Art in America

       Modern Art in America

CREDITS

©1998 Kate Rothko Prizel & Christopher Rothko ARS, NY and DACS, London: 252, (photo ©2014 The Museum of Modern Art, New York/Scala, Florence: 227), (Bridgeman Images: 199 top). ©2014 Albright Knox Art Gallery/Art Resource, NY/Scala, Florence: 80, 82. ©2014 DeAgostini Picture Library/Scala, Florence: 103. ©2014 Digital Image Museum Associates/LACMA/Art Resource NY/Scala, Florence: 206, 313. ©2014 Image copyright The Metropolitan Museum of Art/Art Resource/Scala, Florence: 52, 53, 54 bottom, 75, 95, 125, 126, 290. ©2014 Museum of Fine Arts, Boston. All rights reserved/Scala, Florence: 273. ©2014 Photo Art Resource/Scala, Florence: 232. ©2014 Photo Fine Art Images/Heritage Images/Scala, Florence: 30. ©2014 Photo Scala, Florence: 100 bottom. ©2014 Photo Smithsonian American Art Museum/Art Resource/Scala, Florence: 70. ©2014 Photo The Philadelphia Museum of Art/Art Resource/Scala, Florence: 40 bottom, 87–8. ©2014 White Images/Scala, Florence: 236. ©2015 Photo Smithsonian American Art Museum/Art Resource/Scala, Florence: 284 top. ©2016 Helen Frankenthaler Foundation, Inc./ARS, NY and DACS, London: 257, Photography by Sheldan C. Collins: 299 top. ©2016 Milton Avery Trust/Artists Rights Society (ARS), New York and DACS, London, Courtesy Rose Art Museum, Brandeis University, MA; Gift of Mr. Roy R. Neuberger, New York: 175. ©2016 Stephen Flavin/Artists Rights Society (ARS), New York ©2014: (Digital image, The Museum of Modern Art, New York/Scala, Florence: 301 bottom), (Photo: Billy Jim, New York. Courtesy Dia Art Foundation, New York: 301 top). ©2016 The Andy Warhol Foundation for the Visual Arts, Inc./Artists Rights Society (ARS), New York and DACS, London/©2014. Digital image, The Museum of Modern Art, New York/Scala, Florence: 316. ©2016 The Barnett Newman Foundation, New York/DACS, London: 201 bottom, (©2014 Image copyright The Metropolitan Museum of Art/Art Resource/Scala, Florence: 201 top). ©2016 The Estate of Edward Steichen/ARS, NY and DACS, London Image copyright The Metropolitan Museum of Art/Art Resource/Scala, Florence: 25 top. ©2016 The Willem de Kooning Foundation/Artists Rights Society (ARS), New York and DACS, London: 160, 254, 255, (Bridgeman Images: 278), (Collection of Harry W. and Mary Margaret Anderson: 212), (Frederick R. Weisman Art Foundation, Los Angeles, CA, USA/Bridgeman Images: 213). ©2016 Sam Francis Foundation, California/DACS, ©2014 Digital image, The Museum of Modern Art, New York/Scala, Florence: 228. ©Ad Reinhardt/ARS, NY and DACS, London 2016/©2014 Albright Knox Art Gallery/Art Resource, NY/Scala, Florence: 229. ©Adolph and Esther Gottlieb Foundation/VAGA, NY/DACS, London 2016. The Art Archive/The Solomon R. Guggenheim Foundation/Art Resource, NY/Solomon R. Guggenheim Museum, New York. Gift, Susan Morse Hilles, 1978: 261. ©Alfred Jensen/ARS, NY and DACS, London 2016 Photograph by Ellen Page Wilson, courtesy Pace Gallery: 280. ©Arshile Gorky/ARS, New York/DACS, London 2016: 155, 157, (Albright Knox Art Gallery/Art Resource, NY/Scala, Florence: 209), (DeAgostini Picture Library/Scala, Florence: 156), (Digital image, The Museum of Modern Art, New York/Scala, Florence: 215), (Image copyright The Metropolitan Museum of Art/Art Resource/Scala, Florence: 214). ©Benton Testamentary Trusts/UMB Bank Trustee/VAGA, NY/DACS, London 2013/©Burstein Collection/CORBIS: 101 top. ©Calder Foundation, New York/DACS London, 2016/©2015 Digital image, The Museum of Modern Art, New York/Scala, Florence: 182. ©Christie's Images/Bridgeman Images: 96 top. ©City & County of Denver, Courtesy Clyfford Still Museum/DACS 2016: (©City and County of Denver: 221, 222 top), (Museum of Fine Arts, Houston, Texas, USA/Museum purchase funded by The Brown Foundation, Inc./Bridgeman Images: 222 bottom). ©Corbis: 65. ©Digital image, The Museum of Modern Art, New York/Scala, Florence: 42 bottom, 47–8, 64, 73, 124, 145–6, 180 top, 190, 191, 195 top, 235, 24, 282, 283 top, 307, 314, 306 bottom, 117, 239–40. ©Estate of Allan D'Arcangelo, DACS, London/VAGA, New York 2016, Image coutesy of Hollis Taggart Galleries, Photographer: Joshua Nefsky: 312. ©Estate of Arthur G. Dove courtesy Terry Dintenfass, Inc.: 178, 223, (Bridgeman Images: 135, 218 top), Collection of Barney A. Ebsworth: 238 top, (©2014 Digital image The Museum of Modern Art, New York/Scala, Florence: 133), (©2014 Museum of Fine Arts, Boston, all rights reserved/Scala, Florence: 203 top, 203 bottom), (Courtesy Alexandre Gallery, New York: 136), (Courtesy of Amon Carter Museum of American Art: 134 top, 202), (Myron Kunin Collection of American Art: 34 top), (Collection of Michael Scharf: 200), (Terra Foundation for American Art, Chicago/Art Resource, NY: 36), Yale University Art Gallery: 168. ©Estate of Burgoyne Diller/DACS, London/VAGA, NY 2016. ©2015 Image copyright The Metropolitan Museum of Art/Art Resource/Scala, Florence: 234. ©Estate of David Smith/DACS, London/VAGA, New York 2016: 287 top, 288, (Photograph by the artist. Courtesy The Estate of David Smith, New York: 287 bottom), (Jerry L. Thompson, courtesy The Estate of David Smith, New York: 286). ©Estate of Gerald Murphy/DACS, London/VAGA, New York 2016: (courtesy Alexandre Gallery, New York: 129), (Myron Kunin Collection of American Art: 128), (Bridgeman Images: 127). ©Estate of John Sloan, ARS, NY/DACS, London, 2016: (©2014 Digital image, The Museum of Modern Art, New York/Scala, Florence: 72 bottom), (Addison Gallery of American Art, Phillips Academy, Andover, Massachusetts, museum purchase,1938.67: 63), (Bridgeman Images: 60), (Courtesy of the Pennsylvania Academy of the Fine Arts, Philadelphia. Henry D. Gilpin Fund: 61), (The Art Archive/DeA Picture Library: 62 top). ©Estate of Jules Olitski/DACS, London/VAGA, New York 2016/©2014 Photo ©Christie's Images/Bridgeman Images: 325. ©Estate of Kenneth Noland. DACS, London/VAGA, New York 2014: 260, 262 top and bottom. ©Estate of Mark Tobey, ARS, NY/DACS, London, 2016. ©2015 Image copyright The Metropolitan Museum of Art/Art Resource/Scala, Florence: 205. ©Estate of Raphael Soyer, courtesy of Forum Gallery, New York/Collection of the New Jersey State Museum, Museum Purchase, FA1986.15, reproduced with permission: 163 top. ©Estate of Robert Smithson/DACS, London/VAGA, New York 2016/©George Steinmetz/Corbis: 330. ©Estate of Stuart Davis/DACS, London/VAGA, New York 2016: 57, 67 top, 67 bottom, 137, 140 bottom,142, 143, 197, 246, 247, 249, 251, 298 top, 298 bottom, (Digital Image ©Whitney Museum, NY: 250), (London/Scala, Florence: 62), (©2014 Image copyright The Metropolitan Museum of Art/Art Resource/Scala, Florence: 189), (©2014 Museum of Fine Arts, Boston. All rights reserved/Scala, Florence: 140 top), (Collection of Jan T. and Marica Vilcek, Promised gift to the Vilcek Foundation: 139), (Indiana University Art Museum, 42.1, Photograph by: Michael Cavanagh and Kevin Montague: 176–7), (©2014 Munson Williams Proctor Arts Institute/Art Resource, NY/Scala, Florence: 63). ©Fairfield Porter/ARS, NY and DACS, London 2016: 274. ©Francis Picabia/ADAGP, Paris and DACS, London 2016/©2014 Photo Nat. Portrait Gall. Smithsonian/Art Resource/Scala, Florence: 106. ©Frank Stella, ARS, NY and DACS, London 2016: (Digital image, The Museum of Modern Art, New York/Scala, Florence: 269 bottom), (Addison Gallery of American Art, Phillips Academy, Andover, Massachusetts, gift of the artist (PA 1954), 1980.14: 318), (The Museum of Contemporary Art, Los Angeles, Gift of Jacqueline and Irving Blum in memory of Sayde Moss: 322). ©Frantíšek Kupka/ADAGP, Paris and DACS, London 2016: 134 bottom. ©Franz Kline/ARS, NY and DACS, London 2016, Agnes Cullen Arnold Endowment Fund/Bridgeman Images: 269 top. ©Genevieve Naylor/Corbis: 184. ©Georgia O'Keeffe Museum/DACS, 2016: (Bridgeman Images: 122), (©2014 Digital image, The Museum of Modern Art, New York/Scala, Florence: 96 bottom), (©2014 Photo Georgia O'Keeffe Museum, Santa Fe/Art Resource, NY/Scala, Florence: 265 top), (Collection of Jan T. and Marica Vilcek, Promised gift to the Vilcek Foundation: 265 bottom). ©Hans Hofmann/ARS, NY/DACS, London 2016: 245, 324, (Bridgeman Images: 272 top, 323), (courtesy of Ameringer/McEnery/Yohe: 218 bottom), (Addison Gallery of American Art, Phillips Academy, Andover, Massachusetts, museum purchase, 1960.6: 219), (Courtesy of University of California, Berkeley, CA, USA: 167, 209), (With permission of the Renate, Hans & Maria Hofmann Trust and the University of California, Berkeley Art Museum and Pacific Film Archive: 167, 209 bottom, 323). ©Heirs of Josephine N. Hopper, Licensed by Whitney Museum of American Art, Digital Image ©Whitney Museum, NY: 56. ©Jasper Johns/VAGA, New York/DACS, London 2016: (©2014 Digital image, The Museum of Modern Art, New York/Scala, Florence: 266), (©2014 Image copyright The Metropolitan Museum of Art/Art Resource/Scala, Florence: 268). ©John Chamberlain/ARS, New York/DACS, London 2016, ©2015. Digital image, The Museum of Modern Art, New York/Scala, Florence: 305. ©John Marin/ARS, NY and DACS, London 2016: 198 top, bottom,199, (Collection Cordelia Nicholas LLC, courtesy Alexandre Gallery, New York: 170 bottom), (courtesy Alexandre Gallery, New York: 170 top), (photo by Joshua Nefsky, Karen and Kevin Kennedy Collection: 101 bottom). ©Jose Clemente/DACS, London, 2016: 179, Corbis: 180 bottom. ©Judd Foundation/VAGA, New York/DACS, London 2016: 303, (Photography by Sheldan C. Collins: 306 top), (Courtesy Judd Foundation Archives: 304). ©Kurt Schwitters/DACS, London, 2016/Bridgeman Images: 131 top. ©Louise Nevelson/ARS, NY and DACS, London 2016 ©2014 Digital image, The Museum of Modern Art, New York/scala, Florence: 270. ©Morris Louis/2016 Maryland College Institute of Art (MICA), Rights Administered by ARS, NY and DACS, London, All Rights Reserved: ©2014. Christie's Images, London/Scala, Florence: 263 top, 264), (Photo The Jewish Museum/Art Resource/Scala, Florence: 263 bottom). ©Peter Horree/Alamy: 120. ©Peter Titmuss/Alamy: 291. ©R. Hamilton, All Rights Reserved, DACS 2016. Kunsthalle, Tubingen, Germany/Bridgeman Images: 277. ©Reginald Marsh/ARS, NY and DACS, London 2016: (akg-images: 162), (Art Students League, New York/Artists/Corbis Artists: 163 bottom). ©Richard Poussette-Dart/ARS, NY and DACS, London 2016/©2014 Digital image, The Museum of Modern Art, New York/ Scala, Florence: 276. ©Robert Motherwell/Dedalus Foundation, Inc./VAGA, NY/DACS, London 2016: (2014 Digital image, The Museum of Modern Art, New York/Scala, Florence: 208), (©2014 Digital image, The Museum of Modern Art, New York/Scala, Florence: 196 bottom). ©Robert Rauschenberg Foundation/DACS, London/VAGA, New York 2016: 267 top, 267 bottom. Artwork: ©Succession H. Matisse/DACS 2016: (Photo: Bridgeman Images: 35, 42 top, 225, 299 bottom), (Digital image, The Museum of Modern Art, New York/Scala, Florence: 66 bottom and 226). ©Succession Marcel Duchamp/ADAGP, Paris and DACS, London 2016: (©2015 Photo The Philadelphia Museum of Art/Art Resource/Scala, Florence: 108), (The Philadelphia Museum of Art/Art Resource/Scala, Florence: 66 top). ©Succession Picasso/DACS, London 2016, Image copyright The Metropolitan Museum of Art/Art Resource/Scala, Florence: 58. ©SuperStock/Alamy: 192. ©The Easton Foundation/VAGA, New York/DACS, London 2016/©2014 Digital image, The Museum of Modern Art, New York/Scala, Florence: 284 bottom. ©The Estate of Eva Hesse: (courtesy Hauser & Wirth, 309 top), (courtesy the Estate of Eva Hesse, Galerie Hauser & Wirth, Zürich/Bridgeman Images: 310), (Detroit Institute of Arts, USA/Bridgeman Images: 309 bottom). ©The Josef and Anni Albers Foundation/VG Bild-Kunst, Bonn and DACS, London 2016: (Addison Gallery of American Art, Phillips Academy, 1944.11: 230), (James Goodman Gallery, New York, USA/Bridgeman Images: 231). ©The Pollock-Krasner Foundation ARS, NY and DACS, London 2016: 210–11, (Addison Gallery of American Art, Phillips Academy, Andover, Massachusetts, gift of Peggy Guggenheim, 1950.3: 216 bottom), (Bridgeman Images: 217), (©2014 Digital image, The Museum of Modern Art, New York/Scala, Florence: 196 top, 216 top, 244). ©Underwood & Underwood/Corbis: 149. Addison Gallery of American Art, Phillips Academy, Andover, Massachusetts: (gift of anonymous donor, 1928.24: 29 top), (gift of Mr. and Mrs. William H. Lane, 1958.38: 116). akg-images: 54 top, 311. Allentown Art Museum, The Grippe Collection, 2009 (2009.21.20): 283 bottom. Apic/GettyImages: 22. Cincinnati Art Museum, The Edwin and Virginia Irwin Memorial: 74. Collection of Barney A. Ebsworth: 151, 253 bottom. Collection of Jan T. and Marica Vilcek, Promised gift to the Vilcek Foundation: 77, 78. Collection of Lucy Beck, Vermont, USA: 171 bottom. Collection of Martin Stogniew, Photography Courtesy of Sotheby's, Inc (2015): 165. Collection of Stillwell House Fine Art & Antiques, Red Bank, New Jersey: 71. Courtesy of Hollis Taggart Galleries: 171 top. Courtesy of Kenneth Snelson: 285. Courtesy of Mrs. Henry M. Reed: 79. Courtesy of the LiPuma Collection: 144. Currier Museum of Art, Manchester, New Hampshire, Gift of Paul and Hazel Strand in Memory of Elizabeth McCausland, 1965.4: 84. Fred W. McDarrah/Getty Images: 271. George Heyer/Getty Images: 289. Gift of Peggy Davis Winston on memory of Thomas B. Winston/Bridgeman Images: 237. Haags Gemeentemuseum, The Hague, Netherlands/Bridgeman Images: 195 bottom. Hirshhorn Museum and Sculpture Garden, Smithsonian Institution, Gift of the Joseph H. Hirshhorn Foundation, 1972, Photography by Mysti Scott: 166. Hirshhorn Museum and Sculpture Garden, Smithsonian Institution, The Joseph H. Hirshhorn Bequest, 1981, Photography by Cathy Carver: 37. Image copyright The Metropolitan Museum of Art/Art Resource/Scala, Florence: 41, 97 bottom, 104. Image courtesy of Stanley Whitney and Team (gallery, inc.): 272 bottom. Image courtesy the National Gallery of Art, Washington: 85. John Solum: 94. Museum of Fine Arts, Houston, Texas, USA/Gift of Mr. and Mrs. Ralph O'Connor in honor of Mr. and Mrs. George R. Brown/Bridgeman Images: 83. Museum of Fine Arts, Houston, Texas, USA/Museum purchase/Bridgeman Images: 100 top. Museum purchase funded by Mr. and Mrs. George R. Brown and George S. Heyer, Jr./Bridgeman Images: 154 top. Museum purchase with funds from the Dillard Paper Company for the Dillard Collection, 1969: 131 bottom. Myron Kunin Collection of American Art: 33, 68, 159. Courtesy of Hollis Taggart Galleries: 43. Photo by George Karger, courtesy Solomon R. Guggenheim Foundation and The Pollock-Krasner House and Study Center: 183. Photo by Jacques Faubour for the Conseil Général de l'Yonne, 2001: 154 bottom. Photo courtesy of Spanierman Gallery, LLC, New York: 72 top, 327, 328. Photo courtesy Walker Art Center: 40 top, 233. Photo Smithsonian American Art Museum/Art Resource/Scala, Florence: 45. Photo The Jewish Museum/Art Resource/Scala, Florence: 293–4. Photograph by Joshua Nefsky/Courtesy of Michael Rosenfeld Gallery LLC, New York, NY: 292. Photograph Courtesy of Sotheby's, Inc. ©(2015): 97 top, 99. Photography by David M. Thum: 118. Photography by Erik Gould, courtesy of the Museum of Art, Rhode Island School of Design, Providence: 38, 109. Sterling and Francine Clark Art Institute, Williamstown, Massachusetts, USA/Bridgeman Images: 27. The Art Archive/The Solomon R. Guggenheim Foundation: 238 bottom. The Barnes Foundation, Philadelphia, Pennsylvania, USA/Bridgeman Images: 31. The Estate of Ray Parker: 319, 321. The Phillips Collection, Washington, DC: 204.

Acknowledgements

I want to thank my teachers Barbara Morgan, Patrick Morgan, James Holderbaum, Robert Rosenblum, Robert L. Herbert, John McCoubrey, George Heard Hamilton, Vincent Scully and Barbara Novak for the inspiration they have provided me. In particular, my ideas of continuities and connections owe their inception to the work of Professors McCoubrey, Rosenblum and Novak.

I am grateful to David Anfam of Phaidon for commissioning this book and for his acute editing and encouragement along the way. My editors at Phaidon, Rebecca Morrill and Kim Scott, have shaped this book into its present form and have made it a better book. I am deeply grateful to them both.

I have been fortunate to have the assistance of three remarkable graduate students of mine from Hunter College who have provided untold assistance in many ways: Emily S. Navratil, Bridget McCarthy and lastly, Emily Lembo, who saw this book home with me in its last stages.

Phaidon Press Limited
Regent's Wharf
All Saints Street
London N1 9PA

Phaidon Press Inc.
65 Bleecker Street
New York, NY 10012

phaidon.com

First published 2016
©2016 Phaidon Press Limited
Reprinted in paperback 2017

ISBN 978 0 7148 7524 8

A CIP catalogue record for this book is available from the British Library and the Library of Congress.

Project Editors: Rebecca Morrill and Kim Scott
Production Controller: Leonie Kellman
Design: A Practice for Everyday Life

Printed in China